BRITISH DOCUMENTS ON THE END OF EMPIRE

General Editor S R Ashton
Project Chairman D A Low

Series B Volume 3

Malaya

Editor
A J STOCKWELL

Part II
THE COMMUNIST INSURRECTION
1948–1953

Published for the Institute of Commonwealth Studies
in the University of London

LONDON : HMSO

ISBN 0 11 290541 2

British Library Cataloguing in Publication Data

A CIP catalogue record for this book
is available from the British Library

Write to PC11C, Standing Order Service, HMSO Books, PO Box 276,
LONDON SW8 5DT quoting classification reference 040 30 017 to
order future volumes from the British Documents on the End of
Empire project.

Published by HMSO and available from:

HMSO Publications Centre
(Mail, fax and telephone orders only)
PO Box 276, London, SW8 5DT
Telephone orders 0171 873 9090
General enquiries 0171 873 0011
(queuing system in operation for both numbers)
Fax orders 0171 873 8200

HMSO Bookshops
49 High Holborn, London, WC1V 6HB
(counter service only)
0171 873 0011   Fax 0171 831 1326
68–69 Bull Street, Birmingham, B4 6AD
0121 236 9696   Fax 0121 236 9699
33 Wine Street, Bristol, BS1 2BQ
0117 9264306   Fax 0117 9294515
9–21 Princess Street, Manchester, M60 8AS
0161 834 7201   Fax 0161 833 0634
16 Arthur Street, Belfast, BT1 4GD
01232 238451   Fax 01232 235401
71 Lothian Road, Edinburgh, EH3 9AZ
0131 228 4181   Fax 0131 229 2734
The HMSO Oriel Bookshop
The Friary, Cardiff CF1 4AA
01222 395548   Fax 01222 384347

HMSO's Accredited Agents
(see Yellow Pages)

and through good booksellers

Printed in the United Kingdom by HMSO
Dd299902   C7   7/95

Contents

	page
Malaya: Schedule of contents: parts I–III	ix
Abbreviations: part II	xi
Principal holders of offices 1948–1953: part II	xv
Summary of documents: part II	xix
Documents: part II	1
Index: parts I–III	471
MAPS	
The Malayan Peninsula	vi
South-East Asia and the Far East	vii

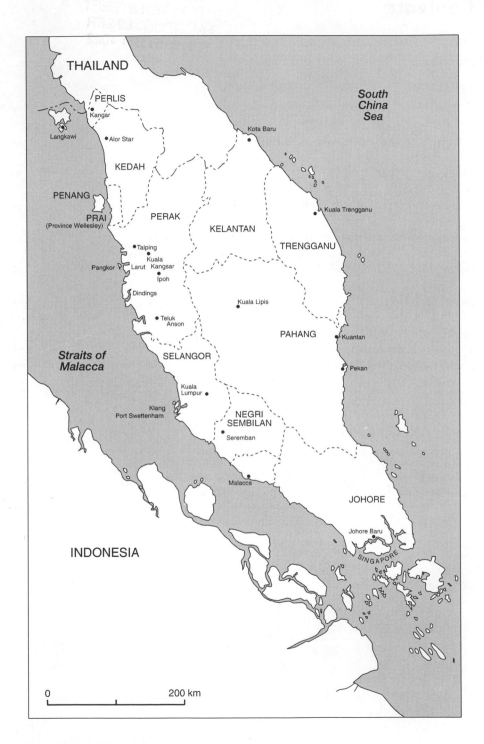

The Malayan Peninsula

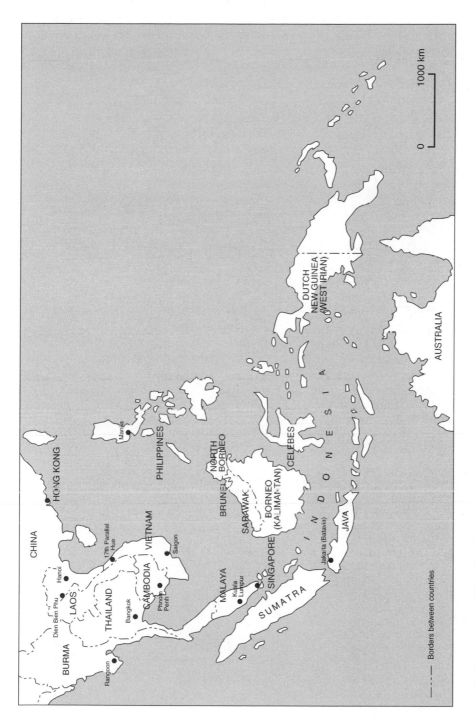

South-East Asia and the Far East

Malaya

Schedule of Contents: Parts I–III

PART I   THE MALAYAN UNION EXPERIMENT 1942–1948

Chapter 1   Wartime planning, Mar 1942 – Aug 1945
               Document numbers 1–42

Chapter 2   British Military Administration, Aug 1945 – Mar 1946
               Document numbers 43–81

Chapter 3   Constitutional conflict: from Malayan Union to Federation, Apr 1946–
               Feb 1948
               Document numbers 82–138

PART II   THE COMMUNIST INSURRECTION 1948–1953

Chapter 4   The origins of the emergency, Feb–Sept 1948
               Document numbers 139–167

Chapter 5   Combating communism and communalism: diagnoses and
               prescriptions, Oct 1948 – Dec 1950
               Document numbers 168–205

Chapter 6   Combating communism and communalism: progress and frustration,
               Mar 1950   Oct 1951
               Document numbers 206–247

Chapter 7   Changes at the top, Oct 1951 – Feb 1952
               Document numbers 248–268

Chapter 8   Fulfilling the directive: Templer's regime to the declaration of the first
               'white area', Feb 1952 – Aug 1953
               Document numbers 269–303

PART III   THE ALLIANCE ROUTE TO INDEPENDENCE 1953–1957

Chapter 9   Planning federal elections, Sept 1953 – July 1954
               Document numbers 304–334

Chapter 10   Taking stock: regional security, Malayanisation and the first MCP peace
               offer, July 1954 – July 1955
               Document numbers 335–355

Chapter 11   Alliance ascendancy: electoral vicory and Baling talks July–Dec 1955
             Document numbers 356–391

Chapter 12   The London conference and the Reid Commission, Jan 1956 – Feb 1957
             Document numbers 392–443

Chapter 13   Achievement of independence within the Commonwealth, Feb–Aug
             1957
             Document numbers 444–467

Abbreviations: Part II

ABM	Association of British Malaya
ADO	assistant district officer
AMCJA	All Malayan Council of Joint Action
AOC	air officer commanding
AP	auxiliary police
APC	armoured personnel carrier
API	Angktan Pemuda Insaf (youth movement for justice)
BBC	British Broadcasting Corporation
BDCC(FE)	British Defence Co-ordinating Committee (Far East)
BDEEP	British Documents on the End of Empire Project
BMA	British Military Administration
CAB	Cabinet
CCP	China Communist Party
CDC	Colonial Development Corporation
CD(&)W	Colonial Development and Welfare
C-in-C	commander-in-chief
CID	Criminal Investigation Department
CIGS	chief of the imperial general staff
CLC	Communities Liaison Committee
CO	Colonial Office
comm-gen	commissioner-general
COS	Chiefs of Staff
COSSEA	Chiefs of Staff South-East Asia
DDO	deputy director of operations
Dept	Department
D of O	director of operations
DWEC(S)	district war executive committee(s)

ECA	Economic Commission for Asia
ECAFE	Economic Commission for Asia and the Far East
ER	Emergency Regulations
EXCO	Executive Council
FAO	Food and Agriculture Organisation
FARELF	Far East Land Forces
FMS	Federated Malay States
FO	Foreign Office
FOA	French Overseas and Associated Territories
FRWLU	Federation of Rubber Workers Labour Unions
GHQ	general headquarters
GMC	General Motors Company
GOC	general officer commanding
GOC-in-C	general officer commanding in chief
HC	high commissioner
HH	His Highness
HM	His/Her Majesty
HMG	His/Her Majesty's Government
HMS	His/Her Majesty's Ship
H of C Debs	House of Commons Debates
H of L Debs	House of Lords Debates
HQ	headquarters
IBRD	International Bank for Reconstruction and Development
ICI	Imperial Chemical Industries
ICFTU	International Confederation of Free Trades Unions
IF	Imperial and Foreign (Division, Treasury)
IMP	Independence of Malaya Party
INDYL	Indian New Democratic Youth League
JPS	Joint Planning Staff (Ministry of Defence)
KAR	King's African Rifles
KL	Kuala Lumpur
KMT	Kuomintang

LMG	light machine gun
MBDC	Malaya and Borneo Defence Committee
MCA	Malayan Chinese Association
MCP	Malayan Communist Party
MCS	Malayan Civil Service
MDU	Malayan Democratic Union
memo	memorandum
MIC	Malayan Indian Congress
MNP	Malay Nationalist Party
MPAJA	Malayan Peoples' Anti-Japanese Army
MRLA	Malayan Races' Liberation Army
MTUC	Malayan Trades Union Congress
NCO	non-commissioned officer
NDYL	New Democratic Youth League
OAG	officer administering the government
OC	officer commanding
OCPD	officer commanding police district
OCTU	officer cadet training unit
OSPC	officer superintending police circle
PEA	People's Education Association
PETA	Ikatan Pembela Tanah Ayer (patriotic league; Communist Party's Malay front)
PIJ	Political Intelligence Journal
P/Lt	police lieutenant
PMFTU	Pan-Malayan Federation of Trades Unions
PMR	Pan Malayan Review (of intelligence)
PRC	People's Republic of China
PUTERA	Pusat Tenaga Raayat (lit. centre of people's strength: Malay movement for justice)
PWD	Public Works Department
RAAF	Royal Australian Air Force
RAF	Royal Air Force
RGA	Rubber Growers' Association

RI	rigorous imprisonment
RIDA	Rural and Industrial Development Authority
RM	Royal Marines
RN	Royal Navy
RNVR	Royal Naval Volunteer Reserve
RWAFF	Royal West African Frontier Force
SCA	secretary for Chinese affairs
SEA	South-East Asia
SEACOS	South-East Asia Chiefs of Staff
SHLU	Singapore Harbour Labour Union
S of S	secretary of state
SWEC(S)	state war executive committee(s)
TUC	Trades Union Congress
UK	United Kingdom
UMNO	United Malays National Organisation
UNO	United Nations Organisation
UPAM	United Planters' Association of Malaya
US(A)	United States (of America)
VCIGS	vice-chief of the imperial general staff
VHF	very high frequency
WO	warrant officer
WRAF	Women's Royal Air Force

Principal Holders of Offices 1948–1953: Part II

UNITED KINGDOM

1. *Ministers*

(a) *Labour governments (26 July 1945 – 26 Oct 1951): prime minister Mr C R Attlee*[1]

S of S colonies	Mr A Creech Jones (4 Oct 1946) Mr J Griffiths (28 Feb 1950)
Chancellor of Exchequer	Sir Stafford Cripps (13 Nov 1947) Mr H T N Gaitskell (19 Oct 1950)
S of S foreign affairs	Mr E Bevin (27 July 1945) Mr H S Morrison (9 Mar 1951)
S of S defence	Mr A V Alexander (20 Dec 1946) Mr E Shinwell (28 Feb 1950)
S of S war (office not in Cabinet)	Mr E Shinwell (7 Oct 1947) Mr J Strachey (28 Feb 1950)
Minister of state, CO (junior minister)	Earl of Listowel (4 Jan 1948) Mr J Dugdale (28 Feb 1950)
Parliamentary under-secretary of state, CO (junior minister)	Mr D R Rees-Williams (7 Oct 1947) Mr T F Cook (2 Mar 1950)

(b) *Labour government Cabinet Committees*

Cabinet Malaya Committee

The Committee sat between Apr 1950 and July 1951. S of S defence (chairman), S of S colonies, S of S war, S of S Commonwealth relations (Mr P C Gordon Walker), FO minister of state (Mr K Younger).

(c) *Conservative government (from 26 Oct 1951): prime minister Mr W L S Churchill (KG 24 Apr 1953)*[2]

S of S colonies	Mr O Lyttelton (28 Oct 1951)

---

[1] Details from Mar 1948.　　　　　　　　　　　　　　　　[2] Details to Aug 1953.

Chancellor of Exchequer	Mr R A Butler (28 Oct 1951)
S of S foreign affairs	Mr R A Eden (28 Oct 1951)
Minister of defence	Mr W L S Churchill (28 Oct 1951) Earl Alexander (1 Mar 1952)
Minister of state, CO (junior minister)	Mr A T Lennox-Boyd (2 Nov 1951) Mr H L D'A Hopkinson (7 May 1952)

(d) *Conservative government Cabinet Committees*

Cabinet Malaya Committee

The Committee met only once in Jan 1952 to consider the recommendations made by Mr Lyttelton in his report on Malaya (see documents 257 & 266). Lord privy seal (Lord Salisbury, chairman), S of S colonies, home secretary (Sir David Maxwell Fyfe), minister of housing and local government (Mr M H Macmillan), chancellor of the Duchy of Lancaster (Viscount Swinton).

2. *Civil servants*

(a) *Secretary to the Cabinet*   Sir Norman Brook (1947–1962)

(b) *Colonial Office*

Permanent under-secretary of state	Sir Thomas Lloyd (1947–1956)

Deputy under-secretary of state	Sir Sydney Caine (1947–1948) Sir Charles Jeffries (1947–1956) Sir Hilton Poynton (1948–1959)	joint joint

Assistant under-secretary of state, with superintending responsibility for Eastern Department, South-East Asian Department from 1950	J J Paskin (1948–1954)
Assistant secretary, head of Eastern Department, South-East Asian Department from 1950	H T Bourdillon (1947–1948) J D Higham (1948–1953)

SOUTH-EAST ASIA

British territories in South-East Asia

Commissioner-general   Mr M J MacDonald (1948–1955)

MALAYA

(a) *Federation of Malaya*

High commissioner	Sir Edward Gent (Feb–June 1948) (died in plane crash, 4 July 1948)
	Sir Henry Gurney (6 Oct 1948) (assassinated, 6 Oct 1951)
	Sir Gerald Templer (7 Feb 1952)
Deputy high commissioner	Sir David MacGillivray (7 Feb 1952)
Chief secretary and officer administering the government	(Sir) Alexander Newboult (1948–1950) (Sir) M V Del Tufo (1950–1952) (Sir) David Watherston (1952–1957)

(b) *Rulers of Malay States*[3]

Johore	HH Ibrahim (1873–1959) Accession 7 Sept 1895
Pahang	HH Abu Bakar (1904–1974) Accession 23 June 1932
Negri Sembilan	HH Abdul Rahman (1895–1959) Accession 3 Aug 1933
Selangor	HH Alam Shah (1898–1960) Accession 4 Apr 1938
Perak	HH Abdul Aziz (1886–1948) Accession 1938
	HH Yussuf (1890–1963) Accession 31 Mar 1948
Kedah	HH Badlishah (1894–1958) Accession 15 May 1943 (position confirmed by British in 1945)
Perlis	HH Syed Putra (b 1920) Accession 4 Dec 1945

---

[3] Rulers are listed in order of seniority, not with their full titles but with the name by which they are normally referred to.

Kelantan

HH Ibrahim (1897–1960)
Accession 21 June 1944 (position
confirmed by British in 1945)

Trengganu

HH Ismail (b 1907)
Accession 16 Dec 1945

SINGAPORE

Governor

Sir Franklin Gimson (3 Apr 1946)
(Sir) John Nicoll (21 Apr 1952)

Colonial secretary

P A B McKerron (1946–1950)
W L Blythe (1950–1953)

Summary of Documents: Part II

Chapter 4
The origins of the emergency, Feb–Sept 1948

NUMBER		SUBJECT	PAGE
		1948	
139	W Linehan (Kuala Lumpur)	2 Mar — Note on prospects of emergence of strong independence movement; Malay dimension	1
140	W L Blythe (Singapore)	[Mar] — Note on prospects of emergence of strong independence movement; Chinese dimension	2
141	CO	Apr — Record of meeting with Mr M J MacDonald on closer association of Federation of Malaya & Singapore	4
142	Sir H Shawcross (attorney-general) & Sir F Soskice (solicitor-general)	4 May — Joint memo, 'Malay states: opinion of the law officers of the crown', on His Majesty's jurisdiction in Malay states	6
143	Comm-gen's conference Singapore, 2nd meeting	10 May — Minutes (item 1) on preliminary discussion of closer constitutional association between Singapore & Federation of Malaya	9
144	Mr M J MacDonald (Singapore) to Mr Creech Jones (CO)	19 May — Letter on Dato Onn & Sir E Gent	13
145	Mr Rees-Williams to J B Williams (CO)	27 May — Minute on future policy in Malaya	15
146	J B Williams & G F Seel (CO)	28–31 May — Minutes on internal security	15
147	Mr Creech Jones to Mr M J MacDonald	12 June — Tel on use of deportation & detention to combat lawlessness	17
148	Sir E Gent (Kuala Lumpur) to Mr Creech Jones	17 June — Tel on declaration of emergency	19
149	W J Sullivan (secretary, Rubber Growers' Association)	22 June — Notes of meeting between CO & delegation representing European business interests on Malayan lawlessness & Sir E Gent's countermeasures	20

NUMBER SUBJECT PAGE

1948

150	Mr Creech Jones	22 June	Tel on demands made by businessmen in 149 and government's assurances	33
151	Mr M J MacDonald to Mr Creech Jones	29 June	Tel on replacement of Sir E Gent	34
152	Mr Creech Jones to Mr M J MacDonald	30 June	Tel (reply to 151) [Extract]	36
153	Mr Creech Jones	1 July	Cabinet memo, 'The situation in Malaya'	37
154	Mr M J MacDonald to Mr Creech Jones	2 July	Tel (reply to 152) [Extract]	42
155	Sir A Newboult (OAG, Kuala Lumpur) to Mr Creech Jones	4 July	Tel transmitting text of message from Tan Cheng Lock protesting against recall of Sir E Gent	44
156	Mr M J MacDonald to Mr Creech Jones	6 July	Tel on appointment of new high commissioner	45
157	Mr Creech Jones to Mr M J MacDonald	7 July	Tel on appointment of new high commissioner (reply to 154 & 156)	46
158	Cabinet meeting CM 50(48)3	13 July	Conclusions on British response to Malayan disorders	47
159	Mr Creech Jones	19 July	Cabinet memo, 'The situation in Malaya'	47
160	Cabinet meeting CM 52(48)5	19 July	Conclusions on proscription of Malayan Communist Party (MCP)	50
161	Cabinet Defence Committee meeting	13 Aug	Minutes on military reinforcements for Malaya	51
162	Malayan Security Service	15 Aug	Political Intelligence Journal no 15/48 (supplement no 11) on effects of action by governments in Malaya to counteract plans of MCP	53
163	Sir T Lloyd (CO) to Sir F Gimson (Singapore) & Sir A Newboult (OAG, Kuala Lumpur)	23 Aug	Letter on disorders & ways of enlisting Chinese support	65
164	Mr M J MacDonald to Mr Creech Jones	24 Aug	Letter on Dato Onn's mistrust of the late Sir E Gent & his threatened resignation [Extract]	67
165	Mr M J MacDonald to Mr Creech Jones	31 Aug	Tel on appointment of Sir H Gurney as high commissioner; Malay criticisms	68
166	Mr M J MacDonald to Mr Creech Jones	1 Sept	Tel on timing of Gurney's arrival	70

NUMBER		SUBJECT		PAGE
		1948		
167	CO Eastern Dept	[Sept]	Note on future political & economic developments in Malaya	71

Chapter 5
Combating communism and communalism:
diagnoses and prescriptions, Oct 1948 – Dec 1950

		1948		
168	Sir H Gurney (Kuala Lumpur) to Sir T Lloyd (CO)	8 Oct	Letter (reply to 163), + *Enclosure*: note on groups in Chinese community in Malaya	73
169	Sir H Gurney to Mr Creech Jones	25 Oct	Tel on measures to deal with alien Chinese squatters	77
170	Sir F Gimson (Singapore) to Sir T Lloyd (CO)	8 Dec	Letter (reply to 163), + *Annex*: memo by T P F McNeice, G C S Adkins & G W Webb (Singapore government)	79
171	Sir H Gurney to Mr Creech Jones	19 Dec	Tel on enlisting Chinese support & plans for a Malayan Chinese Association (MCA)	88
172	Sir H Gurney to Sir T Lloyd (CO)	20 Dec	Letter on problems & methods of winning Chinese support [Extract]	89
173	J J Paskin (CO) to Sir H Gurney	22 Dec	Letter on discussions with Dato Onn at CO	91
		1949		
174	Sir T Lloyd (CO) to Sir H Gurney	Jan	Draft letter on future policy with special reference to Malays, + *Minute* by Mr Rees-Williams	97
175	Sir H Gurney to Mr Creech Jones	8 Jan	Secret despatch no 1 on expenditure on security measures [Extract] + *Minute* by J I C Crombie (Treasury)	102
176	Sir H Gurney to J D Higham (CO)	10 Feb	Letter on objects & rules of MCA	112
177	Sir H Gurney to Sir T Lloyd (CO)	24 Feb	Letter requesting a statement by HMG on British intentions in Malaya to restore confidence	113
178	Sir H Gurney to Mr Creech Jones	28 Feb	Letter on internal security & Chinese; measures to avoid stalemate	114
179	Sir H Gurney to J J Paskin	1 Mar	Tel on public launch of MCA	116
180	Mr Creech Jones	5 Mar	Cabinet memo, 'Situation in Malaya and Hong Kong' [Extract]	117

NUMBER		SUBJECT	PAGE

1949

181	Sir T Lloyd (CO) to Sir H Gurney	11 Mar	Letter (reply to 177)	120
182	Sir H Gurney to J D Higham (CO)	17 Mar	Letter on Dato Onn's changes of mood	120
183	Sir H Gurney to Sir T Lloyd	18 Mar	Tel reporting a conversation with Mr Eden on British intentions in Malaya, + *Minutes* by N D Watson, J D Higham, Mr Creech Jones & Mr Rees-Williams (CO)	123
184	Sir T Lloyd (CO) to Sir H Gurney	2 Apr	Letter (reply to 183)	125
185	Mr Attlee	2 Apr	Minute of prime minister's meeting with Mr Creech Jones, Mr Alexander (Defence) & Mr Shinwell (War) on British intentions in Malaya	127
186	Mr Creech Jones to Mr M J MacDonald	4 Apr	Tel requesting an appreciation of security situation [Extract]	127
187	Sir H Gurney to J J Paskin (CO)	4 Apr	Letter on Tan Cheng Lock	128
188	Sir H Gurney to Mr Creech Jones	11 Apr	Despatch no 4 (reply to 186), + *Enclosure*: paper by Lt-Col Gray & Maj-Gen Boucher on security situation in Federation of Malaya [Extract]	129
189	Sir H Gurney to Mr Creech Jones	30 May	Despatch no 5 on insurgency and counter-insurgency	133
190	Sir H Gurney to J J Paskin (CO)	2 June	Letter on slow progress of counter-insurgency; measures to speed action with particular attention to communist propaganda from China & squatter problem	144
191	Sir H Gurney to Mr Creech Jones	5 July	Despatch no 7 on policy towards Chinese	145
192	Sir H Gurney to J J Paskin (CO)	25 Aug	Letter on communalism & nation-building, assessing likelihood of political integration of Malays & Chinese [Extract]	147
193	Mr Rees-Williams (CO)	12 Sept	Minute on local government	149
194	Col W R Edmunds (Treasury)	23 Sept	Minute of inter-departmental meeting with CO & Ministry of Supply on repercussions of devaluation of tin prices	150

NUMBER　　　　　　　　　　　　SUBJECT　　　　　　　　　　PAGE

1949

195	CO for Mr Rees-Williams (during tour of Hong Kong, Singapore & Malaya, Oct–Nov 1949)	[Oct]	Departmental brief, 'Political developments in Malaya'; communalism and nation-building	152
196	Permanent Under-Secretary of State's Committee, FO	[Oct]	Memo for Cabinet, 'The United Kingdom in South-East Asia and the Far East'	158
197	Cabinet meeting CM 62(49)7	27 Oct	Conclusions on recognition of Chinese communist government; basis of UK policy in region	171
198	Cabinet meeting CM 62(49)8	27 Oct	Conclusions on general policy in S E Asia & Far East (see 196)	172
199	Field Marshal Sir W Slim (CIGS)	[Nov]	Report on tour of S E Asia, Oct 1949; importance of civil action in counter-insurgency [Extract] + *Minutes* by O H Morris (CO) & W C Johnson (colonial police)	173
200	J I C Crombie (Treasury)	16 Nov	Minute on financial assistance to Malaya for security measures	177
201	Far East (Official) Committee	[Nov]	Report, 'Economic and social development in South and South-East Asia and the Far East', + *Appendix* A [Extract]	177
202	CO & FO	Dec	Joint note on attitude to be adopted in publicity towards communism in Malaya & China	186
203	Sir H Gurney to J J Paskin (CO)	? Dec	Letter on recent developments in Malayan politics	187
204	Mr Creech Jones to Sir H Gurney	5 Dec	Letter on policy towards Chinese	189
205	Sir H Gurney to J J Paskin (CO)	31 Dec	Letter suggesting moves towards a member system for federal government	192

Chapter 6
Combating communism and communalism:
progress and frustration, Mar 1950 – Oct 1951

1950

| 206 | Mr Shinwell (Defence) to Mr Attlee | 7 Mar | Minute recommending appointment of Gen Briggs as director of operations | 194 |

NUMBER		SUBJECT	PAGE

1950

207	Mr Griffiths (CO) to Mr Attlee	8 Mar	Minute on Malayan operations & policies	195
208	CO for Treasury	[Mar]	Note on economic & social policy in Malaya	195
209	Mr Shinwell (Defence) to Attlee	27 Mar	Minute proposing a ministerial committee on Malaya	200
210	Mr Attlee to Mr Shinwell	1 Apr	Minute (reply to 209)	200
211	Mr Griffiths to Mr M J MacDonald	7 Apr	Tel on Colombo proposals for economic development of S E Asia; line to be taken by UK at Commonwealth Conference in May	201
212	Sir H Gurney to Mr Griffiths	9 Apr	Despatch no 6 proposing a member system for federal government	202
213	Mr Griffiths & Mr Younger (minister of state, FO)	21 Apr	Joint Cabinet memo, 'Chinese consuls in Malaya'	206
214	A Emanuel to Sir H Poynton (CO)	26 Apr	Minute on arguments in favour of Malaya's membership of sterling area	211
215	Mr Strachey (War) for Cabinet Malaya Committee	12 May	Note, 'The present day situation and duties of the Malayan Communist Party', on a captured MCP document	213
216	COS for Cabinet Malaya Committee	24 May	Report, 'Federation plan for the elimination of the communist organisation and armed forces in Malaya' (Briggs plan)	216
217	Sir T Lloyd (CO) to Sir H Gurney	31 May	Tel (reply to 212)	222
218	Comm-gen's conference Bukit Serene	7 June	Minutes (item 1) on constitutional development	223
219	Mr Griffiths	13 June	Cabinet memo, 'Preliminary report on a visit to Malaya and Singapore'	230
220	Mr Strachey (War) for Cabinet Malaya Committee	17 June	Memo, 'The military situation in Malaya'	234
221	Cabinet meeting CM 37(50)1	19 June	Conclusions on reports by Griffiths & Strachey following their visits to Malaya	239
222	Cabinet Malaya Committee meeting	19 June	Minutes on civil situation in Malaya	242

NUMBER   SUBJECT   PAGE

1950

223   Mr Griffiths   18 Sept   Letter on UK financial assistance for   246
       to Sir S Cripps   emergency, proposing a fixed percen-
       (Exchequer)   tage

224   Mr Gaitskell   29 Sept   Letter (reply to 223)   252
       (Exchequer)
       to Mr Griffiths

225   Mr Griffiths   24 Oct   Letter (reply to 224)   253
       to Mr Gaitskell

226   Mr Shinwell (Defence)   24 Oct   Joint memo on present situation in   258
       & Mr Strachey (War)   Malaya
       for Cabinet Defence
       Committee

227   Mr Griffiths   15 Nov   Memo, 'Political and economic back-   259
       for Cabinet Defence   ground to the situation in Malaya'
       Committee

228   Mr Gaitskell   15 Nov   Letter (reply to 225)   270
       (Exchequer)
       to Mr Griffiths

229   A H Clough (Treasury)   28 Nov   Minute of meeting between Mr Gaits-   271
                                          kell & Mr Griffiths on UK aid to Malaya

230   Mr Strachey (War)   11 Dec   Minute on Malayan situation & Far   272
       to Mr Attlee   East, urging appointment of a regional
                                          supremo

1951

231   COS   23 Feb   Note, 'Preparations for the defence of   276
       for Cabinet Defence   Malaya', on the plan to occupy Song-
       Committee   khla in event of Thailand falling to
                                          communists

232   Cabinet Office   27 Feb   Summary of meeting called by Attlee   277
                                          to consider slow progress of Briggs
                                          plan

233   Cabinet Office   9 Mar   Summary of further meeting called by   279
                                          Attlee to consider slow progress of
                                          Briggs plan

234   Cabinet Office   13 Mar   Summary of resumed meeting to con-   283
                                          sider progress of Briggs plan

235   Sir H Gurney   19 Mar   Letter offering his resignation   286
       to Sir T Lloyd (CO)

236   Sir T Lloyd   5 Apr   Letter (reply to 235)   287
       to Sir H Gurney

NUMBER		SUBJECT	PAGE

1951

237	Sir H Gurney to J D Higham (CO)	28 Apr	Letter on Executive & Legislative Councils, and recent constitutional innovations [Extract]	289
238	Mr Shinwell (Defence) to Mr Attlee	22 May	Minute on emergency situation	290
239	Sir H Gurney & Lt-Gen Sir H Briggs (director) (of operations)	4 June	Joint memo, 'Federation of Malaya – combined appreciation of the emergency situation'	291
240	Sir H Gurney to J D Higham (CO)	13 June	Letter on Dato Onn and Independence of Malaya Party (IMP), discussing Onn's intentions	293
241	Sir H Gurney to Mr Griffiths	22 June	Tel on Dato Onn & IMP	295
242	Mr Griffiths	6 July	Memo commenting on 239	296
243	CO	Aug	Note of inter-departmental meeting with FO on future of office of comm-gen, S E Asia	297
244	Sir H Gurney to J D Higham (CO)	29 Aug	Letter on Tunku Abdul Rahman & leadership of UMNO	299
245	Sir H Gurney	[Oct]	Note expressing his frustration with Chinese community (Gurney's 'political will')	300
246	M V del Tufo (chief secretary, Kuala Lumpur) to Mr Griffiths	6 Oct	Tel on assassination of Gurney	301
247	M V del Tufo (OAG, Kuala Lumpur) to Mr Lyttelton	30 Oct	Savingram on meetings with rulers, *mentris besar* & Chinese leaders; political stalemate	302

Chapter 7
Changes at the top, Oct 1951 – Feb 1952

1951

248	Mr Lyttelton (CO) to Mr Churchill	30 Oct	Minute on his visit to Malaya	304
249	R H Scott to Mr Eden (FO)	31 Oct	Minute on FO interests in & views on Malaya	304
250	Mr M J MacDonald to Sir T Lloyd (CO)	5 Nov	Tel opposing appointment of soldier as new high commissioner [Extract]	306

NUMBER   SUBJECT   PAGE

1951

251 CO   15 Nov Record of meeting on the emergency   307
                                         between Lyttelton and delegation rep-
                                         resenting UK business interests

252 Mr Lyttelton   20 Nov Cabinet memo, 'The situation in   310
                                         Malaya', + *Annexes* I–III

253 Cabinet meeting   22 Nov Conclusions on 252, current situation   315
     CC 10(51)2   & Lyttelton's forthcoming visit

254 J D Higham (CO)   3 Dec Tel requesting clarification of Lyttel- 316
     to A M MacKintosh   ton's statement to Malayan press
     (Kuala Lumpur)   [Extract]

255 A M MacKintosh   4 Dec Tel (reply to 254)   316
     to J D Higham

256 Mr Lyttelton   8 Dec Tel on reorganisation of Malayan gov   317
     (Kuala Lumpur)   ernment
     to Mr Churchill

257 Mr Lyttelton   21 Dec Cabinet memo, 'Malaya', report & re-   318
                                         commendations, + *Appendices* I–XV

258 Field Marshal   27 Dec Letter on colonial secretary's plan for 353
     Lord Montgomery   Malaya
     to Mr Lyttelton

1952

259 Mr Lyttelton   4 Jan Tel on appointment of Sir C Templer   356
     to Mr Churchill
     (New York)

260 Field Marshal   4 Jan Letter on appointment of Sir G Tem-   356
     Lord Montgomery   pler, + *Enclosure*: note by Montgom-
     to Mr Churchill   ery, 'Success in Malaya'
     (New York)

261 Mr Fraser   9 Jan Tel on reorganisation of Malayan gov- 359
     (Kuala Lumpur)   ernment
     to Mr Lyttelton

262 Sir G Templer   12 Jan Minute on the task in Malaya   361
     to Mr Churchill
     (Ottawa)

263 Sir G Templer   14 Jan Minute on first meeting of Cabinet   362
     to Mr Churchill   Malaya Committee
     (Ottawa)

264 Mr M J MacDonald   14 Jan Tel on reorganisation of government   363
     to Mr Lyttelton

265 Mr Fraser (CO)   16 Jan Memo on reorganisation of govern-   364
     to Mr Lyttelton   ment   [Extract]

NUMBER   SUBJECT   PAGE

1952

266   Lord Salisbury   26 Jan   Cabinet note, 'Report by the Commit-   366
       (lord privy seal)   tee on Malaya'

267   Mr M J MacDonald   29 Jan   Savingram on closer association of   369
       to CO   British territories, + *Minutes* by J D
                                            Higham & J J Paskin (CO)

268   Mr Lyttelton   1 Feb   Directive issued on behalf of HMG   372
       to Sir G Templer

Chapter 8
Fulfilling the directive: Templer's regime to the declaration of the first 'white area', Feb 1952 – Aug 1953

1952

269   Sir G Templer   28 Feb   Tel on reorganisation of government;   373
       (Kuala Lumpur)   new measures
       to Mr Lyttelton

270   Sir G Templer   12 Mar   Tel indicating line on elections he   376
       to Mr Lyttelton   proposes to take in speech to Legisla-
                                          tive Council

271   Pan-Malayan Review   Apr   Report no 4/52 on UMNO general   379
       of Intelligence   assembly, 29–30 Mar   [Extract]

272   J D Higham (CO)   10 Apr   Letter on visit of Dr Purcell & Mr   380
       to D C MacGillivray   Carnell to Malaya, + *Enclosure*
       (Kuala Lumpur)

273   O A Spencer (Treasury,   6 May   Letter on rural development; proposals 384
       Kuala Lumpur)   for land & development banks
       to H T Bourdillon (CO)

274   O A Spencer   9 May   Letter suggesting a World Bank mis-   386
       to J D Higham (CO)   sion to Malaya, + *Enclosure*: memo by
                                          Spencer on revision of Malaya's de-
                                          velopment plan

275   J D Higham   26 May   Letter (reply to 274)   390
       to O A Spencer

276   Mr M J MacDonald   10 June Savingram on closer association of   391
       to CO   British territories, + *Minutes* by J D
                                          Higham & Sir T Lloyd (CO)

277   Sir G Templer   27 July Tel on pace of constitutional advance 393
       to Mr Lyttelton   and talks with Onn, + *Minutes* by T C
                                          Jerrom, J D Higham & Sir T Lloyd
                                          (CO)

NUMBER			SUBJECT	PAGE

1952

278	R J Vile (CO) to O A Spencer (Treasury, Kuala Lumpur)	14 Aug	Letter (reply to 273)	397
279	Pan-Malayan Review of Intelligence	Oct	Report no 10/52 on UMNO general assembly, 12–15 Sept & central executive committee, 9 Oct [Extract]	399
280	D C MacGillivray to J D Higham (CO)	18 Oct	Letter on current plans for elections, + *Minutes* by A S Gann, T C Jerrom & J D Higham (CO)	402
281	Sir G Templer to Mr Lyttelton	17 Nov	Despatch no 2311/52 on expansion of Malaya's land forces	413
282	O A Spencer (Treasury, Kuala Lumpur) to J D Higham (CO)	26 Nov	Letter (reply to 275)	418
283	CO	3 Dec	Minute of departmental discussion with Sir G Templer on political advance	421
284	Mr M J MacDonald to FO	8 Dec	Tel on communist tactics in S E Asia, reporting discussions at comm-gen's conference	422
285	Mr Lyttelton to Mr Grimond MP	10 Dec	Letter in support of Sir G Templer's methods of collective punishment	424
286	J J Paskin to Sir T Lloyd (CO)	10 Dec	Minute on discussions with Sir G Templer & COS on closer association of British territories [Extract]	425

1953

287	Sir D MacGillivray to Mr Lyttelton	3 Jan	Despatch no 5/53 on reform of Malayan Civil Service (MCS); agreement of rulers to admission of non-Malays	427
288	J D Higham (CO) to J J Paskin (CO)	20 Jan	Minute on closer association of British territories [Extract]	428
289	T C Jerrom (CO)	22 Jan	Minute on economic position of Malays	430
290	J J Paskin (CO) to Sir D MacGillivray	23 Jan	Letter (reply to 280), + *Minutes* by A S Gann, T C Jerrom & A M MacKintosh (CO)	433
291	Sir G Templer	Feb	Monthly administrative report (Appendix 'A'); general priorities of a district officer, + *Minute* by T C Jerrom (CO)	436
292	J J Paskin to Sir T Lloyd (CO)	5 Mar	Minute on closer association of British territories	437

NUMBER		SUBJECT	PAGE

1953

293	CO for Joint Planning Staff, Ministry of Defence	10 Mar	Memo on political objectives in British territories of S E Asia	441
294	Sir D MacGillivray to Sir T Lloyd (CO)	14 Mar	Letter suggesting extension of member system & appointment of working committee to examine question of federal elections	447
295	Sir D MacGillivray for CO	6 Apr	Note on national conference	451
296	J D Higham (Singapore) to J J Paskin (CO)	14 Apr	Letter giving his impressions of Alliance leaders [Extract]	455
297	Sir D MacGillivray to Mr M J MacDonald	17 Apr	Letter on Alliance constitutional plans, + *Enclosure* "A": 'MCA–UMNO blueprint'	456
298	Sir G Templer to Mr Lyttelton	1 May	Tel proposing early announcement of intention to appoint working party on federal elections	460
299	CO	18 May	Note of departmental meeting with Sir G Templer on constitutional advance	462
300	CO	18 May	Note of departmental meeting with Sir G Templer & Sir J Nicoll (Singapore) on closer association between Federation of Malaya & Singapore	463
301	CO for Far East (Official) Committee	13 June	Memo, 'Political effects that a deterioration of the situation in Indo-China might have in British colonial and protected territories' [Extract]	465
302	Mr Lyttelton to Mr Butler (Exchequer)	30 July	Letter seeking an assurance of UK financial assistance to Malaya	467
303	Sir G Templer to Mr Lyttelton	28 Aug	Savingram on proposal to declare part of Malaccca a 'white area' for relaxation of emergency regulations	469

139   CO 537/3746, no 9, enclosure   2 Mar 1948

[Prospects of the emergence of a strong independence movement]:
note by W Linehan[1] on the Malay dimension

[On 7 Apr 1948 Gent supplied the CO with two notes (139 and 140) to counter the recent
assertion made by P J H Stent of the FO, in a recent paper on the 'British Commonwealth
and Asia', that 'the pressure of nationalism and the example of its neighbours will
certainly hasten and strengthen the demand for Malayan independence'.]

1. The prospects of the rise of a strong independence movement in Malaya, at any
rate within the next generation or so, appears to be exceedingly remote. Such a
movement would be impossible unless it received very substantial support from the
Malays. In the present political state of affairs and in the state of affairs likely to
develop in the future (so far as one can reasonably look ahead) the Malays may be
expected to withhold that support. The reasons for the Malay attitude may be gauged
as follows:

(1) They fear above all Chinese political domination, and they realise that in their
present weak position the withdrawal of the Protecting Power would immeasur-
ably increase that danger.
    They appreciate that they are not yet ripe for independence and that their
political, economic and social progress will be advanced by British help. They
know that for a long time to come they cannot afford to dispense with that help.
The policy of U.M.N.O. as repeatedly voiced by Dato Onn, is to put a strong curb on
any Malay urge that there may be for immediate independence so that the Malays
may learn to walk before they attempt to run.
(2) The propoganda [sic] for an independent Malaya comes almost altogether from
the mouths of Communist or Communist-inspired orators, and any doctrine
tainted with communism (one of whose aims is the destruction of religion) is
utterly repellent to the Muslim Malays.
(3) Peninsular Malay interest in the Indonesian independence movement (whatever the reason therefor) appears to have waned considerably within the past year
or so (Indonesia gets much less notice in the Malay papers nowadays than
formerly).
(4) The disturbances in India on the withdrawal of the British has opened the eyes
of thinking people of the Malay race as to the dangers inherent in a British
withdrawal from Asian territories.
(5) The local manifestations of extreme Indian nationalism originating with some
members of the M.I.C., coupled with the anti-Federation attitude of that body,
makes the Malays extremely suspicious of any advocacy of Malayan independence
coming from such a source.
(6) The return of settled conditions and of prosperity to Malaya will go far to
obviate unrest, the existence of which would be a predisposing factor towards an
agitation for independence. Added to this there is little prospect of agrarian unrest

---

[1] Dr William Linehan, entered the service of the FMS, 1916; director of education, Straits Settlements,
and adviser on education, FMS, 1939; interned 1942–1945; constitutional adviser, Malayan Union,
1946–1948.

making its appearance in Malaya as there is an abundance of land for everybody and there exists a very satisfactory system of land tenure in Malaya whereby the Government deals direct with the peasant proprietor and is thus readily in a position to intervene to alleviate his lot in various ways when the occasion arises.

2. As mentioned above, an independence movement not based on strong Malay support would be impossible. The local advocate of immediate independence, the A.M.C.J.A.—P.U.T.E.R.A. combination, has been fatally weakened by the formation of the Federation and by the failure to attract right-wing Chinese support. That combination now appears to be dissolving into its constituent parts though no doubt the P.M.F.T.U., M.N.P. and M.D.U. with of course the predominant partner, the M.C.P. will still continue to use the name. They may be expected to continue their policy of exploiting nationalism to gain their ends.

Tan Cheng Lock's new Malayan Chinese League may here be left out of consideration as one of the planks of its platform is the maintenance of the British connection.

140 CO 537/3746, no 9, enclosure [Mar 1948]
'On the prospects of the emergence of a strong independence movement in Malaya in the near future': note by W L Blythe[1] on the Chinese dimension

The Chinese community in Malaya has never been subject to Malay rule to any significant extent. Until about the beginning of the nineteenth century the Malay occupation of the Malay Peninsula was, with few exceptions, confined to riverine villages, starting at the river mouths and spreading up-river. The rivers were the obvious channels of entry to a country completely covered with jungle.

2. Consequent upon the establishment of the British at Penang (1786), Singapore (1819), and Malacca (1824), and the rapid development of these places by swarms of Chinese immigrants, there began—about 1850—a rapid inthrust of Chinese to the mainland of the peninsula intent upon the wealth to be obtained from tin-mining and the possession of agricultural land. The result of this was that the main centres of population today—Kuala Lumpur, Ipoh, Taiping, Seremban,—began as Chinese mining camps, ruled by the leaders of the Chinese Triad Societies, and not by the Malay Chiefs of these areas.

3. So rapidly did the Chinese communities in the mining areas spread that, in 1901, the Chinese formed 65% of the total population of Selangor, and were more than twice as numerous as the Malays. In Perak, they formed about 46% of the total population—about equal to the Malays.

4. It was because of the inability of the Malays to govern or control the Chinese communities in their States that the British entry to the Malay States began. The question immediately arises

---

[1] W L Blythe entered the MCS in 1921; secretary for Chinese affairs, Malaya, 1946; president, municipal commissioners, Singapore, 1948; colonial secretary, Singapore, 1950–1953; author of *The impact of Chinese secret societies in Malaya: a historical study* (London, 1969).

"What did the British have that the Malays did not have which enabled them to control the Chinese?"

Doubtless the British had superior qualities of administrative ability and compromise, but these would probably have been ineffective were it not for two factors— Pickering and guns. Pickering[2] was a Chinese-speaking officer who through his knowledge of Chinese was not only able to secure the confidence of the Chinese but was also to probe to the roots of the trouble. Guns were lethal weapons, and the originators, though not the entire content, of British prestige.

5. And so it is that the system of "indirect rule" beloved of Lord Lugard[3] and hated by modern native democratic intellectuals in Africa had no place in the history of the government of the Chinese in Malaya. They passed from the direct rule of their Triad leaders to the direct rule of the British. Added to this is the fact that three large aggregations of Chinese in Singapore, Penang and Malacca were never even nominally under Malay rule.

6. So much for history. What is the position now? The British prestige founded on force has been strengthened by over half a century (and in Singapore, Penang and Malacca over a century) of reasonable administration in Malaya. The Chinese, like many other races, are firmly convinced of their racial superiority. The man in the street still refers normally to Europeans as "Red-haired Devils" and to Malays as "Native Devils". But he has had evidence here of European capabilities in commerce, the professions and government. He knows that in the fields of Commerce, Banking, Engineering, Medecine, [sic] Law, Public Finance and Public Administration we have something which is worth learning and which he can learn from us. He is quite convinced that the Malays can never learn these things, and so he has no respect for them, and they have no prestige in his eyes. It should, however, be said, to complete the picture, that European prestige has suffered considerably, partly through the retrogression of Western civilization leading to two World Wars, partly through the universal diffusion of news and the spread of Western education, and partly through the emergence of China to the semblance of a World Power, and the stage had been reached at the time of our re-occupation of Malaya when Chinese Leftist leaders walked into Government offices and greeted British administrative officers with "You First Class Power—me too". But there has, i think, been some retreat from this position since China has fallen once more into chaos. It still remains true that the Chinese will accept government by the British in Malaya but regard government by the Malays with contempt. Apart from the greater esteem with which they regard the British, they know that they have greater chances of advancement in the political and administrative fields under the British than under the Malays, who rightly fear the greater capacity and industry of the Chinese. The Chinese regard the institution of the new Malay hierarchy as a retrograde step and the conducting of the first Selangor State Council in the Malay language as deplorable.

7. It seems clear that no such thing as an independent Malaya, standing on its

---

[2] W A Pickering (1840–1907) worked as a merchant sailor, as an official in the China Maritime Customs and later as a trader in Formosa before becoming Chinese interpreter to the government of the Straits Settlements in 1871; he was the first protector of Chinese in the Straits Settlements, 1877–1889.
[3] F J D Lugard (1858–1945) created Baron Lugard, 1928; high commissioner, Northern Nigeria, 1899–1906; governor, Hong Kong, 1907–1912; governor, North and South Nigeria, 1912; and governor-general, Nigeria, 1913–1919.

own feet without British support, can emerge in the near future. Either it would form part of a greater Siam, or of a greater Indonesia or of a greater China. The first of these possibilities would be resisted by Malays and Chinese alike. The second would be vigorously resisted by the Chinese, who are well aware of what has happened to Chinese communities in Free Indonesia. But the Chinese in Indonesia are a small minority of the total population, and even the possession by the Malays of a greatly enlarged military force would not avail to keep the large Chinese population of Malaya in subjection to a hated and despised government. What the attitude of the Malays would be to the possibility of becoming part of a greater Indonesia is not clear. U.M.N.O., presumably, would resist it. But it is unlikely that U.M.N.O. is the last word in Malay politics. It is highly probable that the rising tide of democracy will, before long, swamp the Sultans, and the Malays may then regard Indonesia with greater favour. Much of course depends upon the progress of events in Indonesia. As to the third possibility, this would obviously be vigorously resisted by the Malays, and would give them good grounds for linking up with Indonesia.

8. Any Malayan independence movement, to be successful, must comprise both Malays and Chinese in partnership. There are already organisations which see this and aim to awaken a Malayan consciousness, but they are in their infancy. The Malayan Communist Party, the A.M.C.J.A.—P.U.T.E.R.A. combination, the Malayan Democratic Union and the proposed Malayan Chinese League all have this aim, though the Malayan Chinese League stipulates that the self-governing Malaya shall be an integral part of the British Commonwealth and Empire. These organisations are bound to be regarded with suspicion by the bulk of the Malays lest here, too, the Chinese should dominate. The opposition of the Malay Press to the proposed establishment of a Malayan University is an indication of this attitude.

9. I reach the conclusion, then, that in Malaya, where the two principal races are numerically so evenly balanced but culturally so far apart, there is no prospect, for a long time to come, of the emergence of a strong independence movement, and that it will be the lot of the British, if we retain the power and the will to do so, to keep the ring until a closer fusion of the two races is produced. This will only be achieved by a rapid advance of the Malays, intellectually, politically and administratively, so that they can compete on equal terms with the Chinese. It remains to be seen whether the stimulus of their new constitutional position will produce this advance within measurable time. If not, they may well find that they are engulfed by the rapidly rising tide of local-born Chinese eligible for Malayan citizenship and becoming ever more irresistible in their demands for equality of representation.

141   CO 537/3669, no 3   Apr 1948
[Closer association of Federation of Malaya and Singapore]: CO record of a meeting with Mr M J MacDonald on 16 Apr[1]

[This note was drafted by O H Morris on 20 Apr; G F Seel then added paragraph 5, expanding the reference to the East African High Commission, which A Cohen amended. The final version was enclosed in a letter to MacDonald on 18 May.]

---

[1] The CO representatives were Lord Listowel (minister of state), Sir T Lloyd, Sir S Caine, G F Seel, H T Bourdillon and O H Morris.

1. The *Governor General*, after saying that circumstances might have changed in some particulars during his 3 months absence from Singapore, explained that he, Sir E. Gent and Sir F. Gimson were agreed in principle that Singapore should come into the Federation as early as possible. The High Commissioner for the Federation of Malaya though agreeing in principle might ask for less advantageous terms than the Governor of Singapore would like. Sir E. Gent had a great deal of pressing work in connection with the bringing in of the Federation of Malaya, and had the difficulty that the Malays were firmly opposed to a Chinese majority in the Councils of any Federation which might include Singapore.

2. The *Governor-General* continued that it would be fatal to get things going before we were sure that Dato Onn was ready to suport the proposals or the people of Singapore ready to accept them. As a first step he thought that private talks should be held with the Malays and the Chinese of the Federation separately, and concurrently private informal talks should be held with Singapore representatives. He hoped that machinery could be brought into being before the end of the year.

3. In the discussion which followed Lord Listowel emphasised the need for getting the right machinery and Sir Thomas Lloyd mentioned the difficulty of getting anyone to take the initiative. There were three possibilities; one, to get either the Federation or Singapore to raise the matter with the other, (and neither party would want a possible rebuff), two, for joint talks among unofficials, three, for Sir E. Gent and Sir F. Gimson to discuss the question with Mr. MacDonald. Of these three alternatives the second was generally commended.

4. Mr. Seel enquired whether some form of a super-Federation with the Federation and Singapore as equal parties might be possible. Mr. MacDonald said that the suggestion would be unacceptable to Sir E. Gent, while the counter-suggestion that Singapore should become the 12th member of the Federation would not commend itself to Singapore. Sir E. Gent was in favour of a compromise which would allow Singapore certain powers in addition to those enjoyed by the other Settlements as parts of the Federation.

5. Mr. Seel also enquired whether any consideration had been given in Malaya to the possibility of some arrangement on the lines of the new East African High Commission.[2] In discussion it was observed that under the East African arrangement the territories concerned retained their full legislative and political authority, but had delegated certain functions in respect of common services to a separate authority with a legislative body on which they were represented. Except in the case of self-contained services, i.e. railways and ports and posts & telegraphs, the East Africa High Commission was dependent for funds upon votes of the territorial Legislatures, who thus retained ultimate control. A feature which might be of interest in Malaya was that the scheme was an experimental one which could be abandoned if at the end of a few years it had not proved its usefulness. A scheme on these lines would not deal with the political questions involved in the relationship of Singapore to the Federation of Malaya; it might, however, provide machinery for some action in joint economic and allied matters, and it might ultimately prove that if satisfactory

---

[2] The East African High Commission, embracing Kenya, Tanganyika and Uganda, was established on 1 Jan 1948 to replace the East African Governors' Conference. It was charged with the administration of certain common services.

provision could be made for these, the necessity for political integration would be lessened.

It was agreed that there was no question of endeavouring to impose any such arrangement in Malaya, but that there was no harm in furnishing the local authorities with material about the East African High Commission. The question whether anything of this kind should be brought into discussion was one which could only be decided by those on the spot; as was also the further question whether, if it were put forward, this should be done (a) as a possible means of paving the way for political federation later on (if there should be no immediate desire for that), or (b) as a pis aller[3] after an attempt to get agreement on political closer union had failed, and no other means of securing economic co-ordination was in sight.

6. Further points made in discussion were that the possible inclusion of Singapore might have a good effect on the loyalty of Singapore Chinese by bringing them in contact with the traditionally loyal Straits Chinese of Penang and Malacca. Singapore, a predominantly Chinese city, might be a danger in time of war if it were a unit on its own. There was the fear that Singapore might have to support the Federation financially. Finally, the *Governor-General* mentioned that if a joint Committee representing the Federation and Singapore were established to consider the question of amalgamation it might ask for an independent Chairman to be sent from this country.

---

[3] *Pis aller*: a last resort. Seel and Cohen expressed reservations about the East African High Commission on the ground that it lacked a strong central authority.

---

142   CO 537/3679, no 13   4 May 1948

'Malay states: opinion of the law officers of the crown': joint memorandum by Sir H Shawcross[1] and Sir F Soskice[2] on His Majesty's jurisdiction in the Malay states

[The question of the rulers' sovereignty and the extent of the crown's jurisdiction in their states had not been wholly resolved in the new agreements setting up the federation. As already noted (see part I of this volume, 136; also CO 537/3665), one issue on which Anglo-Malay accord had snagged during the closing stage of negotiations was control over defence and external affairs. Though a crucial British interest, it was not one over which the CO were prepared to risk renewed confrontation with the Malays. The CO legal adviser, Sir K Roberts-Wray later argued, however, that such concessions that had been made did not in effect remove essential British jurisdiction in these matters, and it was in order to seek confirmation of this interpretation that he approached the attorney-general and solicitor-general. Their opinion was requested on two specific questions: (1) whether the terms of the Federation Agreement gave His Majesty jurisdiction in matters of defence and external affairs of the federation so as to enable laws to be made on these subjects by acts of parliament or by order in council; and (2) whether, if His Majesty did have such jurisdiction, legislation for one or more individual states in the federation, as opposed to legislation for the federation as a whole, could be enacted in the exercise of that jurisdiction. The CO felt that the law officers' opinion was 'not very conclusive' and decided not to pass it on to Malaya, although Roberts-Wray did inform E P Bell, acting attorney-general in the federation, that 'if it were contended that His Majesty has no jurisdiction, we should not agree.']

---

[1] Sir Hartley Shawcross, attorney-general, 1945–1951; president, Board of Trade, Apr–Oct 1951.
[2] Sir Frank Soskice, solicitor-general, 1945–1951; attorney-general, Apr–Oct 1951.

This is a matter of some difficulty.

Prior to the MacMichael Agreements which were concluded in December, 1945, His Majesty had no jurisdiction over the Malay States and His Majesty's relations with the States were governed by various treaties under which His Majesty exercised control over foreign relations and the several rulers undertook to accept advice in all matters except Malay custom and the Mohammedan religion. The States were, therefore, in the position of protectorates.

Under the MacMichael Agreements the several rulers granted to His Majesty "full power and jurisdiction" within their respective States; and in virtue of this and under the Foreign Jurisdiction Act, 1890, the Malayan Union Order-in-Council 1946 was enacted. This Order-in-Council was, however, revoked in January 1948 by the Federation of Malaya Order 1948, subject to Clause 54 thereof, which provided that:—

> "Nothing in this Order shall affect the power of His Majesty to make laws . . . relating to the defence or external affairs of the Federation."

This saving Clause did not, however, purport to, nor could it create any power to make such laws. For such a power, if any there be, it is necessary to look elsewhere.

Scheduled to the Federation of Malay [sic] Order 1948 were, however, a number of Treaties respectively described as State Agreements and the Federation Agreement. These had been entered into shortly prior to the date of the Federation of Malay [sic] Order 1948 and the State Agreements all expressly revoked the MacMichael Agreements. Unless, therefore, the State or Federation Agreements themselves preserved or created some jurisdiction in His Majesty there was no power to make laws which could be saved by Clause 54 of the Order.

The Federation Agreement by Clause 154 purports in the following terms expressly to preserve such a power:

> "Nothing in this Agreement shall affect the powers of His Majesty to make laws . . . relating to the defence or external affairs of the Federation. . . ."

But whilst this Clause appears to assume the existence of such powers it gives no indication as to their source and can hardly have been intended to preserve the powers conferred by the MacMichael Agreements since those agreements were revoked by the State Agreements and were not in any way affected by the Federation Agreement. The Federation Agreement, however, also contained an express provision in Clause 4 that:—

> "His Majesty should have complete control of the Defence and of all external affairs of the Federation and undertakes to protect the Malay States from external hostile attacks and for this and similar purposes His Majesty's forces and persons authorised by or on behalf of His Majesty shall at all times be allowed free access to the Malay States. . . ."

Clauses in substantially identical terms are contained in the State Agreements. It is, however, possible to exercise control over the defence and external relations of foreign territory without having legislative powers within such territory. That indeed is not infrequently the position in the case of Protectorates and was in fact the position in the Malay States before the MacMichael Agreements. We hardly think that this Clause, or its counterpart in the State Agreements, taken alone, can be said to confer jurisdiction.

It is to be observed, moreover, that express powers of legislation in connection with matters affecting external relations or defence are given by Clause 48 of the Federation Agreement to the Federal legislature and the High Commissioner appointed by His Majesty has, under Clause 52, power to act without the concurrence of the legislative council. Whether he can make laws as to such matters without the concurrence of the Conference of Rulers is less clear. The proviso to Clause 51 seems to suggest that he can, but Clauses 54 and 76 lead to a contrary conclusion. As, however, the Rulers act on his advice the point may not be very significant. What is, however, perhaps material, is that since the powers of legislation in regard to external affairs and defence are in fact very much subject to the control of His Majesty the preservation of separate and independent powers in His Majesty-in-Council or in the Imperial Parliament is the less necessary to the constitutional scheme apparently envisaged by the Agreements.

On the other hand, it is to be observed that each of the State Agreements contains a clause providing that:—

"The prerogative powers and jurisdiction of (The Ruler) within the State . . . shall be those which (the Ruler) possessed on the 1st day of December, 1941, subject nevertheless to the provisions of the Federation Agreement and of this Agreement."

So far as concerns powers and jurisdiction, therefore, we think that it is arguable that the Federation Agreement and the State Agreements are to be read together (they were in fact part of one transaction) and that in view of the wide and general terms of the Clause 4 of the Federal Agreement relating to defence and external affairs and the analogous Clauses of the State Agreements and to the fact that, up to the time of the signature of the State Agreements there were undoubted powers under the MacMichael Agreements, Clause 154 of the Federation Agreement may be read either as preserving those powers so far as defence and external relations are concerned, or when read in conjunction with Clause 4, by implication granting them. We feel bound to say, however, that the matter is one of much doubt.

1. Our answer to the first question put to us, therefore, is that whilst we hardly think the clauses relating to external affairs and defence in themselves confer jurisdiction, we are inclined to the view that Clause 154 of the Federation Agreement should be construed as in effect involving a regrant, for the purposes of the Federation, of the jurisdiction hitherto existing in respect of the several States.

2. Assuming that the position be as we have indicated in our answer to the first question, we think that the second question presents less difficulty and that His Majesty, by virtue of his power to legislate for the Federation, may by Order-in-Council enact laws relating either to the whole Federation or to one or more of the States within it or to all the States but with variations appropriate to each one. We think that the power to legislate for the Federation in these matters includes a power to legislate for the States.

143   CO 537/3669, no 13   10 May 1948

'Preliminary discussion on closer constitutional association of Singapore with the Federation of Malaya': minute 1 of the 2nd commissioner-general's conference in Singapore

The *Commissioner-General* stated that he had had discussions with the Secretary of State and Lord Listowel on this subject.[1] It was agreed in London that, on the merits of the case, the policy should be to create a closer political association of Singapore with the Federation of Malaya as soon as practicable. The Secretary of State was anxious that the Commissioner-General should consider this without delay. Unless the matter moved reasonably quickly the opportunity might be lost for some years and the opinion in favour of the present arrangements might crystallise both in the Federation and in Singapore. Generally, unofficial opinion in the Federation does not appear strongly in favour of fusion with Singapore, while in the Island the urge for inclusion in the Federation seemed to be waning as a result of the recent acquisition of more power by the unofficials in the Government of Singapore. The Secretary of State felt that the possibility of giving serious examination to the problem should, therefore, be explored at once. He recognises the difficulties involved. One fundamental issue would be the attitude of the Malays; the firm support of the Malays and of the population of Singapore is necessary. The Secretary of State is not approaching the problem with any preconceived ideas; all matters should be open for exploration and consideration and no set conditions ought to be laid down in advance. The Colonial Office recognises that local interest should be mainly responsible for discussing and resolving the difficulties. Therefore, local machinery representative of the two territories should be devised and there would be no question of sending out a Royal Commission with instructions from H.M.G. The Secretary of State would, however, be prepared to consider the advisability, if it were desired locally, to select and send out an independent person of high standing from the United Kingdom to preside over whatever local body was set up for the purposes of the discussions between the two territories.

The *High Commissioner* said that in the approach to this problem it must be appreciated that the inclusion of Singapore in the Federation would require the Rulers' consent and consequent amendments to the Federation Agreement which would also require their consent. Nothing can be achieved unless the Rulers agree, and UMNO would doubtless be consulted by the Rulers and would largely determine the Rulers' attitude. The first step, therefore, must be to get the Rulers' agreement that the time had come to consider the problem. In seeking their concurrence to investigate the matter it would be necessary to assure them that no commitments, especially with Non-Officials would be made in any discussions which ensued, and that the Rulers would be consulted again as soon as the best line or lines for working out detailed proposals could be suggested. Assuming that His Majesty and The Rulers agreed to this course, the next step would be for the matter to be considered confidentially by selected officials of both territories who would be instructed to frame one or more possible schemes in general outline for the achievement of the end in view. The Rulers would then be asked to agree to the more detailed

---

[1] See 141.

elaboration of those proposals by means of a Joint Committee between the Federation and Singapore with Official and Non-Official representation. At all stages it would be necessary to keep the Rulers fully informed and to retain their support and confidence.

The *Commissioner-General* said he appreciated the High Commissioner's point in regard to the position of the Rulers, but enquired whether in fact it was not UMNO rather than the Rulers which had to be so seriously considered.

The *High Commissioner* said this was true to a very large extent.

The *Commissioner-General*, therefore, suggested that the first informal approach might best be made to the leaders of UMNO rather than to the Rulers themselves.

The *High Commissioner* said that in his view, the approach should be to the Rulers who would certainly then approach UMNO, but it was the Rulers who have the Constitutional position. If the British authority were to make the preliminary approval [approach] to one political party such as UMNO it would seem to the High Commissioner that there would be very reasonable grounds of criticism by other political groups, both Malay and non-Malay.

The *Commissioner-General* said he would not be entirely happy to let the Rulers refer the matter to UMNO since they might put an entirely wrong complexion on the matter and create suspicion and hostility in the minds of Dato Onn and his supporters. In his view, it would be better to talk privately to Dato Onn in the first instance.

The *High Commissioner* said he was referring to official approaches; there would be no objection to an entirely informal confidential, and personal approach to Dato Onn himself, but in all official moves the correct procedure should be observed with the greatest care.

The *Commissioner-General* enquired what were the High Commissioner's views as to the correct line of approach.

The *High Commissioner* said the crucial matters in any discussions from the point of view of the Malays would be the questions of citizenship, immigration, and representation on the Federal Legislative Council; to these problems there were various possible methods of approach.

The *Commissioner-General* enquired whether the High Commissioner thought that the Rulers would be receptive of the general idea of exploring the problem within a comparatively short time.

The *High Commissioner* said he thought the Rulers would.

The *Chief Secretary, Federation* aid he was not so sure that at the present time the Rulers and UMNO would be receptive of the idea.

The *High Commissioner* said much would depend on the way in which the matter was presented to them. If the possible advantages of fusion with Singapore could be stressed, he felt that there would be no objection in principle to a detailed examination of the problem. For example, it could be urged that considerable advantage would accrue to the present Federation if Singapore conformed to the Federation's policy on immigration.

The *Chief Secretary, Federation* agreed with this but anticipated that there would be considerable suspicion on the question of the representation of the Malays; this was a problem which had proved excessively delicate on the previous Working Committee.

The *Commissioner-General* said that he agreed that the legal position of the

Rulers must be recognised but said that the Singapore authorities also had rights to be considered. It might be fatal if it became known in Singapore that an approach had been made to the Rulers when no approach had been made to Singapore.

The *Governor of Singapore* said it would be very difficult to keep any approach to the Sultans confidential, and if the matter leaked out in Singapore he agreed with the Commissioner-General in thinking that a very serious reaction might be expected in the Colony, particularly among the Chinese. The fact was that Singapore was constitutionally in advance of the Federation and the present tendency seemed to be that the Unofficials wished to retain and indeed increase the power which they had recently acquired, and for this reason were less favourable to a policy of fusion with the Federation. They were not yet fully alive to the tremendous importance of complete co-ordination as between Singapore and the Mainland on all major questions of policy, which, under the present arrangement of two separate Governments, would become increasingly difficult. He felt that if any move was to be made to explore the problem of fusion, it would be essential for him to take his responsible Non-officials into his confidence as was his practice on every major question.

The *Commissioner-General* said that the only proposal at the moment, was to ask the Sultans to agree that a body of officials should explore the matter, and enquired whether the Governor of Singapore would, himself, consent to this or whether he would feel bound to consult his Unofficials.

The *Governor of Singapore* said he would feel it necessary to consult his Unofficials.

The *Commissioner-General* then enquired whether the exploration of the problem could not be conducted informally in secret by Officials without the necessity of first mentioning the matter to the Rulers. Many confidential talks go on among officials about all sorts of subjects before any formal representations are made to bodies and authorities, which, under the Constitution, have to deal with them.

The *Chief Secretary, Federation* said that when discussing the matter in Kuala Lumpur with the High Commissioner, he thought it had been agreed that non-committal and exploratory talks among officials would be necessary in order to ascertain whether there was any common ground between the Governments upon which negotiation could usefully proceed. If there was no common ground, any further steps would be useless at present.

The *Commissioner-General* said he was inclined to agree that the first step might be confidential exploratory talks behind closed doors by selected officials; they should not even been appointed as a formal Committee.

The *High Commissioner* considered it would be most unwise to take this step; there would be most unfortunate reactions in Malay circles if it were discovered that a group of British officials was engaged in making plans for a highly important amendment of the Federation Agreement without any prior consultation with the Signatories of the Agreement.

The *Commissioner-General* agreed but thought it quite unnecessary that such talks should become known.

The *High-Commissioner* said that he thought the risk was too great to take, and it was most important to keep the confidence of the Rulers.

The *Chief Secretary, Federation* agreed with this view and said further that he did not think that the approval of the Rulers to initiate discussions would be forthcoming unless they were given some idea as to the conditions upon which Singapore would be admitted to the Federation. If no such intimation were given they might take fright and refuse to agree, or merely say that the time was not ripe.

The *High Commissioner* said he thought it would depend on how the matter was put to the Rulers. It would be preferable to stress that we wished to have their confidence and co-operation and to say frankly that we had not yet considered the matter but wished them to agree, that we should now have the various factors involved brought under confidential consideration.

The *Commissioner-General* said that the present point of the discussions seemed to turn upon the danger of a leakage; neither Government would be involved if the Commissioner-General himself started thinking with his advisers. The Deputy Commissioner-General (Colonial Affairs) might consult certain officials of both Governments secretly and informally and this would not implicate either of the governments.

The *Deputy Commissioner-General* said that he had hoped that it might be possible that the question of fusion would come into prominence as a result of unofficial opinion expressed in both territories in the Press and in public speeches. Some time ago, the matter had been quite freely ventilated in Singapore. If the urge to discuss this question were a matter of popular opinion, the Rulers, UMNO and everyone else concerned would recognise it as a political issue which was ripe for discussion; no one would be taken by surprise, and the need for secrecy would disappear.

The *Governor of Singapore* said that so far as Dato Onn was concerned, Mr. Thio Chan Bee[2] had already informally discussed the matter with Dato Onn who had apparently indicated that UMNO would not object to discussing the matter. Indeed it seemed that he regarded some linking up with Singapore as a right policy.

The *Chief Secretary, Federation* expressed the view that Dato Onn would only regard it as the right policy if Singapore came into the Federation on his (Dato Onn's) own terms. The fact was that the Malays were frightened of being swamped by the Chinese and the inclusion of Singapore would greatly increase their apprehensions.

The *Commissioner-General* pointed out that on an elective basis in the Federation, the Malays would secure a straight majority.

The *Chief Secretary, Federation* agreed, if the qualification of franchise were based on Malayan citizenship.

The *Commissioner-General* said that if the initial difficulties were overcome and a Working Party set up to consider the matter in detail, he would like to know whether the Malays would expect the Working Party to be composed, in the first instance, at any rate, entirely of Malays as was the case when the Federation Agreement was negotiated.

The *High Commissioner* said that he thought that they would not adopt this attitude, though they would make it quite clear that the final right of consent to an amendment of the Agreement would rest with the Rulers.

The *Commissioner-General* remarked that it was interesting to see how the Malays were beginning to rely in various matters upon the qualification of Malayan citizenship a conception which they had at first strenuously opposed.

The *Chief Secretary, Federation* said there was no doubt they had accepted

---

[2] Member of the Straits Chinese Association and the Singapore Progressive Party.

citizenship because, on the opening of the negotiations, the Secretary of State had stipulated that some form of common citizenship must be devised as one of the conditions precedent to H.M.G.'s acceptance of any plan evolved.

The *Commissioner-General* said he did not think the discussion should be pursued much further, and suggested that the question of procedure should be examined by the Chief Secretary of the Federation, the Colonial Secretary, Singapore and the Deputy Commissioner-General. The Conference could consider the matter further when they had received the views of these officials.

The *Chief Secretary, Federation* enquired whether it would be advisable to stimulate the Press to raise the issue as an immediate practical problem to be solved.

The *Governor of Singapore* said that he might raise the question at one of his off the record Press Conferences, by remarking that the matter had not recently been ventilated in the Press and enquiring from the Press correspondents why it had apparently been dropped for the time being.

The *Commissioner-General* thought this move would be inadvisable; any such statement by the Governor of Singapore might very well be misrepresented or miscontrued.

The *High Commissioner* said that there might be no harm in "flying a kite" on the subject but not from an official stand. Dato Braddell had always taken a great interest in the matter; he represented a section of opinion in Singapore and had also the Malay point of view well in mind. One or more thoughtful and objective articles by Braddell in the Press might very conveniently raise the problem in a practical form.

The *Chief Secretary, Federation* agreed that Dato Braddell had important views on the problem but any "kite flying" by him might be strongly prejudiced by his own personal views and have a strong Singapore bias, which might antagonise opinion in the Federation.

The *Commissioner-General* thought that Dato Braddell might be extremely helpful; he was not sure, however, to what extent Dato Braddell represented Chinese opinion in Singapore.

The *Governor of Singapore* said he thought Dato Braddell had the support of much responsible Chinese opinion in the Colony.

After further discussion *it was agreed* that the question of initial procedure should be examined without delay by the Chief Secretary of the Federation, the Colonial Secretary, Singapore, and the Deputy Commissioner-General.[3]

---

[3] ie Newboult (chief secretary), McKerron (colonial secretary) and Hone (deputy commissioner). Not only differences between Malaya and Singapore but also problems of internal security meant that, while closer association remained a principle of policy, practical considerations were regularly cited as reasons for delaying advance towards it (see CO 537/2155 for 1947, CO 537/3669 for 1948, CO 537/4743 for 1949, CO 537/5962 for 1950 and CO 537/7151 for 1951).

144   CO 537/3686, no 1A   19 May 1948
[Dato Onn and Sir E Gent]: letter from Mr M J MacDonald to Mr Creech Jones

[The inauguration of the federation did not expunge Malay animosity towards Gent. On the contrary, MacDonald's concern about continuing Malay ill-will, at a time of considerable labour unrest, prompted Creech Jones to prepare for Gent's transfer and provoked Rees-Williams to call for a progressive long-term policy (see 145 and 146). During a visit to London in Jan 1948 MacDonald had discussed with the CO plans for Gent's replacement and a decision on this was taken in mid-April. MacDonald notified Gent of his impending move on 3 or 4 May, giving as the reason his failure to win the confidence of Asians (but see 155) and Creech Jones informed the prime minister 'some weeks' before 30 June (see PREM 8/1406/1, minute from Creech Jones to Attlee, 30 June 1948). The security crisis in June, however, precipitated a collapse of business confidence in the high commissioner (see 149 and 150), led to Gent's immediate recall (see 151 and 153 para 15(viii)), delayed Onn's visit to London until late Oct (see 173) and postponed further thinking on the longer-term future.]

Dato Onn is anxious to come to London some time this year. Gent may already have indicated this in a letter to Lloyd or someone else in the Colonial Office. Gent thinks the plan a good one, and so do I.

Dato Onn spoke to me about this suggestion the other day and said that he would like to come to London in June or July. I encouraged the plan in principle, but said that I was not sure that June or July would be the best date. What I had in mind (of course, I did not give any hint of this to the Dato) was that undoubtedly one of his purposes in coming to London will be to urge you to remove Gent from the High Commissionership. It would be unfortunate if he came to London prior to the announcement that Gent is in fact to receive another appointment, as the impression would spread in Malaya that Dato Onn had insisted upon his removal and secured it. On the assumption that the announcement about Gent may not be made until towards the end of June or some time in July, I therefore resisted Dato Onn's proposal to visit London during those months.

I told him that June and July are likely to be extremely busy months for you and your Ministerial colleagues and principal advisers, since the Parliamentary session is then drawing to a close and all Ministers and government departments are overwhelmed with work. I suggested that September or October might be a more suitable time. He accepted this suggestion. I told him that it was personal and tentative, and that I would write to London to see what your programme of engagements might be during the remainder of the year. I told him that I knew you were contemplating a possible visit overseas some time this year.

If Dato Onn comes, it is of course important that you should be free to see him and to give him a little of your time, as well as that other Ministers and officials should pay him a certain amount of attention. In that case the visit could do a lot of good from many points of view.

I wonder whether you could give me some indication of what would be likely to suit you best about this. In the meantime I have asked Dato Onn to regard all his plans as provisional.

Naturally I have not felt able to tell Gent the whole of the above, but he and I have discussed the visit in principle and he is in favour of it.

Incidentally, Dato Onn in his talks with me since I returned has shown strong hostility to Gent. The sooner an announcement can be made about Gent's future, the better it will be here. I keep impressing on Dato Onn the immense services which Gent has performed to Malaya and the Malays. He says that he fully recognises these, but that Gent has performed them in such a way that the Malays dislike and distrust him intensely, and that there will be constant friction between them.

145   CO 537/3746, no 11   27 May 1948
[Future policy in Malaya]: minute by Mr Rees-Williams to J B
Williams[1]

I think it is very important that we should have a clear line of policy to pursue in
Malaya, and in my view these three factors should be taken into consideration.

(1) The people should be brought to an ever increasing extent into the work of
Government by their elected representatives. There is a tendency at the moment,
especially in the States, for the Ruler to select the representatives and the people
to have little say in the matter. This, I think, will never satisfy the aspirations of
the Malays, and there will tend to be friction between them and the Rulers who
will inevitably be regarded as tools of the occupying power.
(2) We must press the whole time the need for the Government of Malaya to
encourage a more diversified economy than it had before the war. While not
neglecting rubber and tin, they should proceed with the cultivation of rice up to
the target figure of 700,000 additional acres and the introduction of new crops and
products, such as cocoa, and possibly small factories to produce consumer goods.
(3) It is essential that the Malays themselves should be encouraged to take up
business and positions as artisans. Anything the Government can do in the way of
training schools and the like in this regard should be fostered. At the present
moment the Malay sits back and grouses about the Chinese and the Indian, but is
not himself making any great effort to do the jobs or to learn to do the jobs which
the Chinese and the Indians perform. In other words, we have got to industrialize
a portion of the Malay community. If we do not do this, should a very strong
Pan-Malay movement arise, they will find themselves in the ludicrous position
which the Burmese are now in, without the very strong asset which the Burmese
have got, namely their exportable surplus of rice.
    Please take the necessary action.

With reference to rice, I should be glad to know how it is that, in spite of the fact that
some 150,000 acres are now under production more than in 1938/9, there is some
40,000 tons a year less produced. Perhaps you can explain this phenomenon.

---

[1] Assistant secretary, CO.

146   CO 537/3755   28–31 May 1948
[Internal security]: minutes by J B Williams and G F Seel[1]

... I would finally like to say one word on the general picture presented by the
present report.[2] Reading a report such as this inevitably gives an impression of
drama; almost of melodrama. It conjures up pictures of hordes of people burrowing
mole-like in the interstices of Malayan society or scurrying hither and thither on

---

[1] Assistant under-secretary of state, CO.
[2] Williams is referring to 'Malaya—Political Intelligence Summary for May 1948', notes by D J Kirkness,
who had entered the CO as an assistant principal in 1947.

their mischievous errands, so that one may almost wonder whether that society is not about to rock to its fall. I think it is inevitable that a report of this kind which is devoted to the activities of the more subversive elements must give such an impression, read by itself. In fact, however, I do not think that any information which has reached the Eastern Department during the last month would lead us to suppose that any serious trouble is brewing in Malaya. There was, it is true, a strike of Singapore Harbour Board workers last month accompanied by intimidation and violence but the strike ended without any really serious incidents occuring [sic] and a procession which the organisers of the strike proposed to call for May Day was prohibited by the Government with no more adverse repercussions than when the Government here prohibited the march which Sir Oswald Mosley[3] proposed to hold through the East End of London on the same day.

The above, of course, is not intended to suggest that there is no danger from Communist activities in Malaya. The greatest immediate danger undoubtedly arises from Communist attempts to gain control of the trade unions and the High Commissioner for the Federation has proposed vigorous action to counter these attempts in the shape of amending trades union legislation which at this moment of writing is about to be considered by the Secretary of State.

In the general field of public order in Malaya all is not yet entirely settled but such threat to public order as there is seems to come much more from mere bandits than from members of left-wing organisations. By far the most serious threat revealed in recent months, namely, a body of well-disciplined men with a fortified training camp which was destroyed by Police operations in Northern Perak was, in fact, associated with the right wing, Kuomintang, but here also the persons concerned seem to have been much more mere bandits than representatives of a serious movement against the Malayan administration.

A real threat to Malayan internal security seems unlikely to arise unless the Communists succeed in gaining control of China. In that event a Communist movement among the Malayan Chinese would no doubt become a very serious menace and for that reason it is obviously necessary, as the Malayan Governments are already doing, to watch Communist activities very carefully, even though their immediate threat is but slight.

J.B.W.
28.5.48

. . . It is true that there is apparent quiet at the moment, but the situation is not free from anxiety. The best antidote will be to make the Malayan peoples interested in running their own affairs, local, state and ultimately national. . . .

G.F.S.
31.5.48

---

[3] Sir Oswald Mosley, founded British Union of Fascists, 1932; detained 1940–1943; leader of the Union Movement, 1948–1966.

147   CO 717/167/52849/2/1948, ff 314–317   12 June 1948
[Action against lawlessness]: outward telegram no 70 from Mr Creech
Jones to Mr M J MacDonald on the use of deportation and detention

Your telegram No. 60.

High Commissioner's telegram No. 570.

Governor, Singapore's telegrams ending with No. 398.

2. House of Commons statement 11th June[1] will have made it clear that I fully appreciate seriousness of position, and endorse firm action already taken by High Commissioner and Governor, Singapore to meet it. After full consideration I have reached the following conclusions which I hope will give you all a clear line of action. You are, of course, at liberty to comment but obviously speedy action is now a prime consideration.

3. *Deportation.*[2] I will deal first with the Federation, and with those who cannot (repeat cannot) be regarded as belonging to the Federation. In the situation which has arisen I have decided to give High Commissioner forthwith authority to use the Banishment Ordinance without prior reference to me, against any persons who are not Federal Citizens and who are implicated in acts of violence, or in organising or inciting persons to take part in strikes, disturbances or demonstrations in which violence or threat of violence is used. I should be prepared to consider any additional categories of malefactors against whom High Commissioner would wish to use Ordinance. In my view it is essential, however, to restrict the use of this arbitrary power to certain defined classes of ill-doers who cannot be reached by normal processes of law.

4. Limitation of this extended use of Banishment Enactments to those who are not Federal Citizens (although I appreciate that Enactments themselves are not so limited) might help us in avoiding complications with other Governments, especially India. As you know from my confidential despatch No. 122 of the 7th April to the High Commissioner, it is His Majesty's Government's policy to discourage Government of India from taking up the cause of Indians who "belong" to a colonial territory. We could not with consistency expel Indians who "belong" to Malaya and still resist the interference of the Government of India in matters concerning similarly situated Indians (as we want to) on the ground that they belong to Malaya.

5. As regards procedure where Banishment Enactment is used, I consider that subject to what is said in paragraph 6 below, the examination of a person arrested under the Enactment should be before a Supreme Court judge, although final decision would and must rest with High Commissioner. I attach great importance to examination by judge which might go far in my view to discredit charges of police state methods and arbitrary rule. It will be necessary to consult the Acting Chief Justice as to the employment of judges in this capacity, and it may possibly be necessary to provide for it by an amendment of the Banishment Enactment. This would remove any ground for allegations that judges were acting in compliance with administrative directions. Intention that examination will be before a Supreme Court

---

[1] Rees-Williams made a parliamentary statement on 'Malaya (crimes of violence)' on 11 June 1948 (*H of C Debs*, vol 451, cols 2669–2772).

[2] For previous correspondence on banishment, see part I of this volume, 129 and 130.

judge should, I think, be announced and High Commissioner may also feel that it would be advisable to say quite frankly and publicly that law is only being applied to cases which fall into the categories mentioned in paragraph 3 above. (This might forestall or at any rate counter the obvious objections to the indiscriminate use of legislation conferring powers on Executive without the normal safeguard of the Courts.)

6. I do not suggest that this procedure of examination by a judge should be applied in the case of gangsters and violent criminals against whom High Commissioner has been authorised to use banishment powers in the past.

7. I shall be glad to learn as soon as possible whether it is proposed that the above arrangements regarding deportation should be extended by legislation to the Settlements, in addition to provision for detention (see next following paragraph).

8. *Detention.* It is clear that something further is needed to deal with persons of the kind mentioned in paragraph 3 above who are Federal Citizens, especially in view of evidence that British subjects and others to whom Banishment Enactment has hitherto been applied as stooges. Although I have naturally great reluctance in considering anything resembling the wartime provision for detention I am driven to conclude that deportation alone will not be effective.

9. Accordingly I suggest that High Commissioner should consider enacting an Emergency Powers Bill, which would empower him to proclaim a state of emergency, and thereafter to detain persons falling into the categories set out in paragraph 3. Such legislation should, of course, lay down that each case should be considered by a Supreme Court judge, as suggested in paragraph 5 above. There should be provision also:—

(a) that the state of emergency should lapse (without prejudice to any acts done by virtue of the proclamation) after 30 days, if the proclamation is not adopted by Resolution of the Legislative Council within that time;
(b) that the period of detention should be for a maximum of two years;
(c) that the period of detention of individuals should not be terminated merely by reasons of the ending of the state of emergency;
(d) that there should be provision for periodic review of the case of each individual under detention;
(e) detention should be without prejudice to criminal proceedings being taken against the detained person during or after the period of detention.

10. *Singapore*

(a) Deportation. The Governor is authorised to proceed under the existing law against any non-British subjects in the categories listed in paragraph 3 above, subject to the procedure described in paragraph 5. I note from paragraph 6 of your telegram No. 60 that Governor does not favour amendment of Straits Settlements Banishment Ordinance to provide for deportation of British subjects and I agree.
(b) Detention. I should on the other hand raise no objection to the enactment in Singapore of an Emergency Powers Ordinance on the lines suggested for the Federation in paragraph 9 above. This would cover the compulsory detention referred to in paragraph 3 of Singapore telegram 398, and indeed would seem necessary unless Singapore is to become a harbour of refuge from the Federation. It will clearly be desirable if practicable (and unless there is some strong local

objection) that the emergency powers legislation in each territory should provide for detention of persons implicated in violence etc. in the other territory.

11. Legislation of this type would, I hope, go far to meet the situation described in paragraphs 1 and 2 of Singapore telegram no. 398. I do not find myself able, however, to agree to the proscribing of persons because they are Communists, or to the banning of the M.C.P. as such. Apart from the objections on prinicple to the banning of political parties as such, or prosecution of persons merely for being members of them, I cannot believe that it would not be possible for the Communists and those behind them to continue their activities underground or evade the legal proscriptions by infiltrating into innocent organisations which might make matters worse. Furthermore I have noted that the banning of the M.C.P. was not recommended by your Special Committee.

12. I have given careful consideration also to ways in which I can support the other measures described in paragraph 4 of High Commissioner's telegram No. 570.

(1) I have considered again proposed subsection 26 (3) of Trade Union Amendment Bill. While I am most anxious to avoid the charge of forcing Unions now in the formative stage into models devised by Government and of restricting the well-established right of workers to choose their own leaders, I would be agreeable to replacement of the present s. 26 (2) of the Trade Union Enactment 1940 on the following lines:—

"The High Commissioner may, by special or general order published in the Gazette,
(a) declare that the provisions of this section shall not apply to any registered trade union or class of registered trade unions specified in the order, or
(b) grant exemption from the provision of this section in respect of such officers or such proportion of the officers of any registered trade union or class of registered trade unions as may be specified in the order."

Subject to an amendment substantially in accordance with the above I would be prepared to agree to reinstatement of your proposed clause 26 (3).
I must ask, however, that in introducing a Bill to effect this amendment the Government spokesman would undertake that the new provision would be subject to review in two years' time.
(2) We are doing what we can to expedite supply of material on indent for police. I am telegraphing separately on the question of the adequacy of the police for task in hand.
(3) I have noted with appreciation the co-operation Army is affording.

148   CO 717/167/52849/2/1948, f 302   17 June 1948

[Declaration of emergency]: inward telegram no 641 from Sir E Gent to Mr Creech Jones

[On 16 June three European planters in the Sungei Siput district of northern Perak were murdered by members of the Malayan Peoples' Anti-British Army. They were Arthur Walker, manager of Ephil Estate, and John A Allison and I D Christian, manager and assistant manager of the Sungei Siput Estate. On the same day two Chinese were also murdered: one on an estate near Johore Bahru and the other on a Taiping estate (Perak). Although these incidents did not mark the start of Malayan violence, they did trigger the state of emergency which was declared in three stages: over parts of Perak and Johore on 16 June, over the rest of Perak and Johore on 17 June, and over the whole of the Federation on 18 June.]

Repeated to the Commissioner General and Governor of Singapore.

My telegram No. 630.

Police have not yet made any arrests in triple assassination cases and information from Security Service points to imminence of organised campaign of murder by Communist organisation(s) on the lines of paragraphs 8 and 9 of enclosure to your savingram to the Commissioner General No. 32. Two Chinese overseers on estates in Perak and Johore, where stikes had just ended, were shot yesterday by Chinese gunmen. Emergency Regulations have today been extended throughout the state of Perak.

2. On unanimous advice of the G.O.C. and all other Officials and Unofficial members of my Executive Council, I have decided that it is essential to extend Emergency Regulations mentioned in my telegram No. 630 so as to make them applicable to the whole of the Federation.

3. Certain provisions of these regulations will apply throughout Federation, including particularly liability to death penalty for unlawful possession of arms, power of detention of any persons, search of persons and premises without warrant, and power to occupy properties. Whereas other provisions will only be applied as and when conditions in any locality require e.g. curfew, closure of roads etc.

4. Regulations will be so extended as from tomorrow, Friday.

5. Powers to detain any person provide for the setting up of one or more Advisory Committees on the lines of Regulations 21 (1), (2), (3) & (4) of Straits Settlements Defence Regulations 1939.

149   CO 717/172/52849/9/1948, no 15   22 June 1948

[European business interests in Malaya]: notes by W G Sullivan of a meeting between the CO and a delegation representing European business interests on Malayan lawlessness and Sir E Gent's counter-measures

[Sullivan, secretary of the Rubber Growers' Association, forwarded these notes to the CO in a letter to O H Morris on 9 July. The following attended the meeting: Creech Jones, Rees-Williams, O H Morris, G F Seel and J B Williams (CO); Charles Mann, A H Doherty, H B Egmont Hake and Sullivan (RGA); S B Palmer and H H Facer (UPAM); D Stewart, S A Gray, E W Paton and Sir Evan Meredith Jenkins (Eastern Exchange Banks Association); A R Malcolm and H S Russell (British Association of Straits Merchants); R C Savory and H D Kiddle (mining interests); E N Bradley and J C Bennett (Rubber Trade Association of London); A J Makins (British Insurance Association); C E Wurtzburg (ABM); Lt-Commander C Powell (Incorporated Society of Planters); and E D Shearn (Malayan Association). On the same day that this delegation met the secretary of state in London, MacDonald, conferring in Kuala Lumpur with Gent, Gimson, the GOC Malaya and the heads of the Police and Intelligence services, apparently reached the conclusion that the high commissioner should be recalled immediately.]

Mr. Creech Jones. I should like to express my pleasure at meeting you although the business is a melancholy one. I hope that you will not expect too much from me because I am very anxious to hear what you have to say to me, and any suggestions or proposals you care to make I shall be very happy to listen to them, and I can assure you that we will give them in the Colonial Office, and in the government, our very close attention.

Mr. Mann. I want to say how much we thank you for having agreed to receive us at such short notice. From your remarks we assume you are as persuaded as we are as to the need to restore order. We have set out our suggestions on the paper which we shall leave with you. Meanwhile, Mr. Facer, who has just arrived by air from Malaya for this meeting, will be our chief spokesman.

Mr. Facer. I have been sent from Malaya not to talk to you about rubber or tin industries—we have got past that stage—we are concerned about the safety and the future of Malaya.

The forces of disorder which have used the labour trade unions as covers are now adopting other methods. I think you probably realise with us, that they are threatening established Government in Malaya. We feel the country's future is at stake.

Pamphlets to labour have been issued to our knowledge in parts of Northern Malaya telling them not to worry about the police or military—"they will be looked after". Only a few days before I left, the O.S.P.C. of the district in Johore addressed a meeting of the local District Planters' Association at which he said in the course of his talk "I have definite information to the effect that the 'body' behind the present trouble in Johore are going to make a move to eliminate all Europeans and for this reason these security measures must be followed." That has been borne out by what subsequently happened in Perak.

You probably know, Sir, that in the days between the first and second wars we had in Malaya a number of very bad types of individual who got in by various underground methods. They did not trouble us very much because we had a splendid police force, with an excellent intelligence section. This section dealt with them and many were caught and banished, and in that way the trouble was kept down. Now Sir, I ask you to imagine the situation we met after the war, there having been no British rule at all for three and a half years. The rule of the gun and knife had held sway and there were many more bad hats than there had been in those pre-war days. During those three and a half years I have no doubt they would have drawn up their scheme for a form of Government in Malaya to suit their own ends. We have had trouble from these people from the start of re-occupation and they have been very well supplied with arms.

His Excellency has been advised that the situation was dangerous—not only just recently, but as long ago as February 1947, and later on about September 1947.[1]

Now in pre-war days the banishment order undoubtedly saved the situation to a very great extent. It certainly acted as a deterrent to many who would otherwise have taken up a criminal career and it did get rid of those guilty people who were caught by the police. There is no doubt that the banishment order was the means of preventing a great deal of lawlessness and bloodshed in Malaya. Since the war we have still had the banishment order, but it was very sparingly administered and in no case was it enforced, as far as British subjects were concerned.

---

[1] For the situations in Feb and Sept 1947 see part I of this volume, 117, 122, 129 and 130.

Now we do know out there that the subversive elements—call them Communists or what you will—are mainly of Chinese nationality, but they have been wise enough to use as their dupes Indians who may be classed as British nationals. We are quite convinced in our own minds that the use of these dupes is part of their planned procedure, for they know that those British nationals will not be banished. They give the orders, the stooges carry them out.

Having enjoyed immunity for so long, the criminal elements are coming out into the open. There are reports in the press of armed gangs appearing in the streets of small towns armed and unmasked. In Rengam village[2] several murders were committed in sight of the police station. This will give you an idea of how bold they are getting. The police have advised planters to go about armed, and on a number of estates protection is given. This action is necessary even on estates where there is no dispute with labour at all. It bears out the statement of the O.S.P.C. which I read to you that the body responsible for the trouble does propose to make a move to eliminate Europeans. I can say that when I left Malaya, although there was no panic amongst planters they were definitely apprehensive as to the future. If you consider their situation living practically alone miles away from their neighbours, and many of them with no telephones, you will appreciate that they just haven't a chance if gangsters come along. There is no warning that the gangsters will be at a certain house at a certain time. You will understand the apprehension of the planters who do not know whether they are next on the list. In the case of the murders which were committed on the day I left, the subordinate staff in the office were told "we are out for Europeans" and they were not molested, in fact they were told to go away.[3]

Now, representations have been made to the High Commissioner that this would happen if stronger measures were not taken.[4] I do not propose to enlarge on that point as Mr. Palmer and Mr. Shearn were among those who conveyed the warnings and they will no doubt inform you on that. I would like to say that not only are Europeans threatened. I have here a letter which was sent to the British Advisor, Johore Bahru by a union of contractors:—

"We most respectfully beg to bring the following facts for your urgent consideration and assistance.

Our Union represents about 60 Contractors who control over 6,000 rubber estate workers within the District of Johore Bahru.

Since the middle of the last month a lot of unrest has been caused in many estates in the Johore Bahru district and especially since the beginning of this month several cases of murder and criminal intimidations have also come to our knowledge. It is believed that Communist agitators are responsible for fatal attacks on some unarmed Contractors.

---

[2] Rengam in central Johore where European planters formed a 'mutual protection corps'.

[3] It would seem that Facer is referring here to the murders at Sungei Siput (see 148, note) when, according to the *Straits Times* journalist, Harry Miller, a 'Malay-speaking gangster said . . .: "We are out only for Europeans . . .; we will shoot all Europeans' (*Menace in Malaya*, p 83).

[4] Representations had been made both in London and Kuala Lumpur since at least February 1947. Facer may be referring here to the warnings conveyed by businessmen at the time of the Kedah disturbances in February 1947 or to the meeting between Gent and Europeans at King's House on 8 June 1948 when S B Palmer 'asked, point blank, exactly what the government was doing to restore the situation.' Anthony Short, *The communist insurrection in Malaya 1948–1960* (London, 1975) p 73.

Our work has been mainly to assist the rubber producing Companies to keep peace and order in estates within our control. Since all these murders and criminal intimidations are the handiwork of the Communist agitators, we Contractors have had no peace of mind. We are in constant fear of being attacked while we supervise work during the day or while we are asleep at home. Most of the Communists pose as labourers and it is not possible for us to ascertain those who possess firearms.

In view of the above mentioned circumstances and in view of the fact that most of us are unarmed, we shall be very much obliged if you will be good enough to consider the matter sympathetically and see your way to give us adequate protection against similar dastardly attacks. If this is not practicable at an early date, we shall have no alternative but to abandon our contract work which may seriously affect the financial stability of the country."

I have referred to the danger to Europeans—now the Chinese contractors are threatened, the men who provide the labour for the estates. Another class and a very much bigger class that needs protection is that of our labour who are members of the trades unions, and who are having to do things that they do not want to do for fear of assault or even death. The labourers do not want to strike. I would be prepared to guarantee that not one in a hundred labourers wish to go on strike at all. They have very little to complain about and they have admitted that they are being forced by subversive elements to go on strike. So we have all classes, the Europeans, the native employers of labour, and the labourers themselves, threatened by these disruptive elements.

Now, Sir, one of the things that I have been asked to bring to your notice is that we feel that the case has not been represented to you sufficiently strongly. We feel that you may not have realised, that you may not have had the information to realise, the very serious position in Malaya to-day. We have had a number of interviews on these matters with His Excellency and at last it did appear that he appreciated the full seriousness of the situation. At the same time we had the wireless address by the Commissioner-General in which he stated quite definitely that the trouble was due to Communist influence working through the trade unions, and in which he said that this influence must be eliminated. We had an interview with His Excellency at the end of last month at which were present the Presidents of the M.P.I.E.A., the U.P.A.M., the Chamber of Commerce, and the Chamber of Mines. After that meeting we received a letter from His Excellency signed by his Private Secretary, and if I may, I would like to read one paragraph from that letter:—

". . . The government shares the belief of your Association that in many instances of unrest on estates the workers are being subjected to exploitation by subversive political elements which have no interest except to disturb good relations in industry to the detriment of both workers and employers. . . ."

Now that is a direct indictment of the subversive elements. That letter is dated 25th May. A week ago to-day His Excellency called a Conference in Kuala Lumpur. I was not invited to the Conference because I am not a member of the Federal Council, but I was told about it by His Excellency who asked me to brief representatives of our organisation on the matter. I was unable to do that because I did not know the exact terms of reference for the Conference, but I received afterwards a copy of the memorandum which accompanied the invitation to that Conference:—

"*Memorandum.* The present disturbed labour conditions in certain parts of Malaya have been interpreted as indicating a serious loss of confidence between employers and workers in the industries concerned. Further, present expressions of feeling in certain sections of public opinion and the Press inevitably give the impression, which is not in fact held amongst responsible associations either of employers or workers, that Trade Unions, as at present constituted in Malaya, are being commonly abused as instruments by subversive criminal gangs for their own financial profit or for spreading the doctrines of communism by violence and intimidation.

I consider that in order to defeat insidious and dangerous misbeliefs it would be helpful to convene a conference of Members of the Legislative Council who are leaders of employers' Associations and of registered Trade Unions, together with members of the Labour Advisory Board. The purpose of the Conference would be to discuss the best means (1) of exploding these misconceptions (2) of ensuring that mutual confidence between employers and workers is demonstrably established, (3) of establishing consultative machinery and procedure in each important industry to ensure the maintenance of such confidence."

Now, Sir, when we saw this complete change of front from the terms of the letter of 25th May we could think only of one reason for a conference to discuss a memorandum of that sort. It was that if this memorandum could be generally accepted, a despatch might be sent to you of a reassuring nature to create the impression that this unrest is a trade dispute only. It is nothing of the sort. I am very glad to be able to tell you that the first people to refuse to accept the terms of the memorandum were the union leaders on the Legislative Council, who told His Excellency that it was not a labour dispute, but something else. That is what I mean when I say that we feel you have not had as realistic a picture painted as you should have had.

The only other thing I have to say is about the police. The police have done a magnificent job of work, everybody agrees, but they are working under very difficult conditions. They are not in sufficient strength to tackle the situation which has arisen. They have not the equipment they should have. We understand that certain wireless equipment has now been on order for two years, and is not yet delivered. How much has arrived we do not know, but His Excellency admitted it had not arrived. I heard that possibly 10% had been received.

In Johore on Sunday 13th May a police corporal armed with a shot gun attacked a gang of three, one with a tommy-gun, one with a Sten gun and the other with a revolver. He shot one of them. That will give you some indication of how the police are armed. We hear of the police tracking criminals in the jungle. They have had to go long distances with no ground sheets, and no water bottles. We do suggest that at any rate some endeavour should be made to bring their equipment up to what it should be.

That is all I have to say. I have told you about the representations which have been made to His Excellency, and Mr. Shearn and Mr. Palmer will be able to bear out my statement on that.

Mr. Shearn. . . .[5] In this connection I would like to support what Mr. Facer indicated. As long ago as February 1947, Mr. Palmer and I saw the High Commissioner and we pointed out to him that in our view, from the information we had, the trades unions were getting into the hands of the Communists, and we asked him to take such steps as available. We pressed for sentences of flogging and banishment. As regards banishment, you will know the figures, how early in 1947 there were a few, but later they were more numerous, and we feel if the Banishment Ordinance had been applied earlier it might have been more effective, and when the banishment orders were made, if we knew they could be made against British subjects. Then there was the question of reprieves when people [were] sentenced to death; in too many cases they have been reprieved. There was the case of 57 Malays done to death by Chinese, and not a single sentence of death was carried out. If you talk to police officers they will tell you of case after case of the greatest difficulty of getting their men tried and sentenced to death, and, although his death sentence has been confirmed on appeal, yet he has been reprieved. The police officers say it is very discouraging to them. Lastly, at this meeting in February 1947 we strongly stressed the question of counter-propaganda, but although we had a very polite reception, so far as we can say, nothing has been done in counter-propaganda in Malaya. I am sure it is no new argument to you that on the question of banishment, the reason that we stress it is not only because you get rid of the offender, but because under the banishment proceedings the witnesses are in much less danger, and our experience is that they will not come into open court. To every person who likes freedom, banishment is horrible, but we think it is necessary.

Mr. Palmer. I can confirm that Mr. Shearn and myself and one or two others, saw His Excellency in February last year, and we pressed all the points of which Mr. Shearn has told you. I have seen His Excellency probably on 10 occasions on the same subject since then and I feel that although His Excellency had the powers of banishment he was rather afraid to use them. I think the Governor of Singapore who had some trouble and realised the difficulty he was up against used his powers long before they were used in the Union—it was not until October 1947 that the Governor as he was then, started to use the banishment powers although I know the police and the Attorney-General, who have been with me at meetings, did their utmost to persuade him that banishment and flogging were two of the greatest deterrents of this crime-wave then sweeping Malaya. I would like also to emphasise, Sir, that I travel from estate to estate throughout the peninsula, and I can assure you that the relations between employer and employee are really good. The average labourer trusts his employer, he goes to him with his troubles, but the labourers are not in a position to stand up against the criminal element which goes on to the estate and says "If you work to-morrow your mother's head will be cut off". That is a frequent occurrence. The result is labourers go out on strike, not because they are dissatisfied, but because they are intimidated by Communist-paid agitators.

Mr. Facer. The present wave of lawlessness is very much worse and of quite a different character from anything we had before. It is a very curious thing that this wave occurred after we had come to an arrangement with the unions for a new scale of wages which was very generous, and which in some parts of the country had never

---

[5] In this section, which has not been printed, Shearn makes a number of cryptic references to a number of points agreed at an earlier meeting that day.

been asked for at all. The unions expressed themselves as very well satisfied. That leads us to conclude that the Communist element, who were at the back of this labour trouble, realised that the labour had nothing to grumble about, and wanted nothing further, and they then had to start a new campaign altogether which was a campaign of intimidation of labourers to leave their work on all sorts of ridiculous pretexts, threatening them with violence if they did not do so.

Mr. Creech Jones. I do not know if any of the other gentlemen would like to add to what has been said or whether there are any other points you would like to make. I do not want necessarily to close the discussion on your side, and if there are suggestions or proposals which you feel ought to receive the consideration of Government, I welcome them being put forward. But I would like to make perfectly clear that the Government in Malaya is fully seized with the seriousness of the situation there, and it is clear from telegrams we have received and the action they have taken, and the powers they have asked for that they are very alive to the importance of action and of rooting out the lawlessness which exists at the present time. And they are aware that unless energetic action is taken now, the situation can deteriorate with very grave consequences to all. And in the proposals which have been submitted to us, and the proposals which we ourselves have made, we have I think been fully conscious of the gravity of the situation which exists, and we are determined to do all in our power to meet that situation and get a return to normal conditions and sound and effective order in the peninsula. We at this end, as I have said, have received very urgent and very comprehensive telegrams setting out the situation as it is known, and I think our response in practically all or in most directions has been generous and fairly complete. It is not always possible, for a variety of reasons, to concede every proposal which is made to us, sometimes a situation can be met in another way, but we have not been withholding the necessary powers to the Local Authorities to cope with the situation which has developed. Now I think that it would be unfair to assume that the High Commissioner or Mr. Malcolm MacDonald had any misapprehension in regard to the deteriorating conditions, and in various directions they have taken steps in anticipation of what might arise, or in order to prevent certain tendencies creating new evils. It has been for us, as it has been for them, a very troubled background. The violence and the practices which occurred during the war and followed on the war, coupled with the economic instability which followed when the war was over, the difficulties of food supplies and in various other ways, the whole background of Malaya has been one of very considerable difficulty for Government, and I am very glad to know and I congratulate the employers groups concerned, whether rubber or tin, on the way in which a complicated situation has been coped with, and after all these difficulties, reasonable order was secured, but it was a very very difficult background. We appreciate your contribution to it and we to some extent did fear that because of what had happened only a few years back the reactions and repercussions would be felt in the life of Malaya for some time to come, and I think the administration had prepared to meet that situation.

Now we abhor the violence which is occurring, we will do everything in our power to check it and we will do all we possibly can to root out the causes of it. I don't want any ambiguity. We will clothe the local authority with all the necessary powers so far as they have not got them, but I understand that for all practical purposes they have the powers to cope with the situation. I will indicate in a few minutes the additional powers which have been given to the local Government and which should prove efficacious under this head.

Now we are conscious that most of this trouble is not of the ordinary industrial dispute kind. We appreciate that a great deal of this trouble is brought about by various subversive propaganda and it does not spring from the combinations of workers who normally would seek to maintain fair industrial relations and would seek to get their grievances removed by normal negotiations. We are conscious that this is something more than a struggle as an industrial dispute sometimes is for progress or standards, but elements exploiting the workers' organisations for certain purposes, and consequently we have no doubt that the functions of established authority are being challenged. Certain people think they can destroy authority in Malaya and that the means of so doing is to create chaos by violence in order that confusion shall be established, and that as has been said, Europeans and others eliminated. That means of course that Government must have full powers to cope with that situation, and emergency powers have been proclaimed, and the Government will, and has been, acting. Now let me therefore take some of the proposals which have been advanced this afternoon.

First of all in regard to the workers' organisations themselves which it is alleged are being used by certain subversive elements in order that certain new type of leaders are foisted on to these organisations and certain consequences are followed. I say without hesitation that to the Colonial Office, trade unions regulations are matters of great difficulty where trades unions are operating in other than industrial countries and where the workers to some extent are merging in comparatively new economic conditions. But we have taken it as axiomatic that the structure of the trades unions must be determined by the workers themselves and that it is not for Government to shape the form of organisations, nor is it for Government to determine the leadership of organisations. But we will do what we can to enable working-class organisations to produce their own leaders, to make them less exploitable by the external interests, and in other respects to safeguard them against the very real dangers which we are witnessing in Malaya at the present time. And while we maintain that view we have now given the authority to the Governor to amend the Trades Unions Regulations in such a way that unless persons belong to the trade and industry and have been in it for a period of years, such persons cannot function inside these trades union organisations. I think that the legislature will have the right to lay it down that the organisations within a limited period of a few weeks must put their house in order, that they must appoint officials or re-appoint officials only from the trade and industry to which they belong, and such persons must have been in the employ of that industry or trade for a period of three years. Now that should go some way to protect the trades union machine, and this measure I think is being brought in, probably to-day, certainly immediately, and we hope that some of the difficulties which have been pointed out to-day will thereby be avoided. There are other aspects of the trade union law which we have given attention to, regulations in many respects have been tightened up, a form of federation has been disallowed and we insist that only bona fide industrial trade unions should receive the protection of law, and in any case we must try to create conditions whereby unions cannot be exploited by subversive elements.

It has also been said that some measures should be adopted against the Communist Party. It is very difficult to define what are Communists and even more difficult to suppress or destroy an existing political organisation. It usually rears its head under another name or another form, or is driven underground, and its iniquitous work can go on by other means or forms. What we have done is to give powers to the local Government for effectively dealing with every and any type of subversive organisation. There is no reason why the Communist Party should be singled out. Every organisation of whatever name or type must be dealt with and the officers dealt with and the activities brought under control, and that should meet the position in regard to the Communist Party because in view of all the allegations made in respect of the Communists and organisations [?they] will receive closer attention of Government and certain actions will undoubtedly follow.[6]

In regard to the proposal about the Police Forces, we have been in touch with the administration and obviously have been rather concerned at some of the statements that have been made to us that the forces are undermanned and not sufficiently equipped. We have taken steps to improve the organisation of the police force and give it immediate support in various ways. We have discussed the problem of new recruitment and the various sources from where recruits can be drawn, and we have taken what steps are possible to hurry up outstanding equipment so that the police can act effectively in the territory. I do not think you need have any undue apprehension as to the Police Force, certainly we have given all possible support at this end and will continue to meet any demands that are made on us to supplement existing resources to the best of our ability. The obtaining of some types of equipment, as we all know, is not easy, but where possible we have hurried up some deliveries, and I hope some of the difficulties which have been expressed here will be overcome.

The problem of the Forces has not been overlooked—that obviously is a matter of some difficulty, but I think that you can take it that so far as troops are concerned that position has been studied and we have discussed it with the territory, and what action is required has been, or will be, taken, but I cannot be more precise in regard to that. I can only say it has obviously received the careful attention of the Office.

Now the major demand as I understand it, is that we should take further steps to consider the law in regard to the Banishment Ordinance and to increase the penalties for offences, and generally make it possible for these subversive elements that function in Malaya to attempt it, or do it, under pain of the banishment penalty. The alterations of the law and any alterations which may exist in regard to detention or deportation have been looked at very carefully, and I think that your representations on these points have already been met. There will probably be at once, in fact I think legislation is being pushed through now, amendments to the Banishment Ordinance covering the difficulties expressed in regard to the exclusion of British subjects—that has been covered—and there will be reasonable uniformity of law for the whole of the peninsula so that with this method of clearing out or rooting out those who are instigating crime or encouraging violence, I doubt whether there is more in the way

---

[6] Preparing a brief for Creech Jones's use when he met the delegation, O H Morris had minuted on 21 June, 'while organisations like the Federation of Trade Unions which are Communist controlled are behind the present troubles, no direct evidence connecting the Malayan Communist Party as such with any outrage has been received by us. In any case, it is difficult to tell when a crime is the work of gang robbers, or of gangsters employed by political groups'. The difficulty identifying the perpetrators of violence lay behind the government's reluctance to banish the MCP until 19 July, see 160.

of powers that can be conceded, but other legislation has also received our attention—the Bill to amend the Restricted Residence Law to make more rigorous detention permitted—Seditious Publications Enactment. There are other proposals as well which are being dealt with by the Government.

Now I think you will see that along the lines of your suggestions there is little more that can be suggested, that is to say that the amending Trades Unions Bill has been attended to, an extension of the Banishment Order is under way, and that will include British subjects that transgress. The problem in relation to the Police, increasing weapons and numbers, questions arising out of the support on the military side, that has been studied, various penalties are being considered, banning of organisations which are found conspiring and engaging in subversive activity, the granting of full powers to the High Commissioner to cope with the situation, all those matters are very much in hand and now being actually brought into force in the territory.

One further point was made for propaganda against Communism. As I have said we have considered the Seditious Publications Enactment and the Printing Press Enactment. We are trying to alter the whole of our Public Relations set-up, and the information services, and I would add to that that this problem of agitation from subversive elements in South East Asia is one Government has given quite a lot of thought to because we are not blind to what is happening in the World. We had anticipated for a period that once the path of the Communists was blocked in Europe in reaching fulfilment, there would be a very concerted effort in the East in the areas in which European powers have some responsibility, and we have been building up and engaging in a great number of anti-Communist arrangements in order that that situation should be coped with. A very geat deal more has been done than known. We are very very alive to the importance of meeting this challenge and every means that we can employ for defeating it, and ourselves taking the aggression and becoming more aggressive, those means will be used. Now I don't know on the suggestions put forward I can say very much more. I do want to reassure you that we are fully alive to the problem. We have not sat down under it, or the local Government.

There has been some criticism of the High Commissioner. I want to say that we have the completest confidence in him, he is a man of considerable integrity and energy, a person who has enormous drive.[7] I think he has done a very good job in Malaya and we should be behind him in all steps he takes to meet this situation, and I do not think in practice he will be found to be wanting. The suggestion has been made that warnings have been issued before and they have not been met as fully and as comprehensively as you on the spot would have liked. I do not seek at this moment to defend the High Commissioner, but I do regard Gent as a person of liveliness and very great energy, and I feel that whatever his other qualities may be, he is not lacking in the quality of energy and an apprehension of the danger of this kind of political nature in the territory for which he is responsible. I do want, therefore, to say that we are anxious to meet this situation as fully as possible and you can depend upon it that we will act with energy and give what powers are necessary in order that this situation shall not only be held in check but also that a much more positive constructive policy shall be possible once this danger is over. I do not know whether I can say any more, but perhaps there are some points further which you would like to

---

[7] Plans were, in fact, afoot for Gent's recall, see 144, note.

make. I do not know whether Mr. Rees Williams would like to say a few words, but he knows the Malayan background and has taken steps with the situation.

Mr. Rees-Williams. I do not think there is much I want to say. I think the Secretary of State has covered the ground, and in fact I do not know what other powers can be given to any Government than the ones we have given. We will be in for a great deal of criticism for giving as many powers from some quarters and that we will have to face, but certainly we have given more powers to Malaya than we actually used in this country during the worst time of the war. As regards Police and Military, we are entirely at the service of Government. Any possible help of the Police they can have. We have got a certain number of police available to go there if necessary, but I do want to point this out, that with regard to all these matters it is very difficult for Government here, especially in these days, to take more than a certain amount of action without carrying the Government of the territory with it. We can very often see certain things are necessary and we suggest those things, but with increasing evolution it is very difficult, if not impossible, to order them. If any of these gentlemen present are on the Legislative Council, they will substantiate that. There have been times when we have suggested to various Colonies that certain Information Officers were very desirable to combat this sort of thing we have been getting, in order to develop the anti-propaganda we have heard. We are then told that they do not think it is necessary and they are not prepared to spend money on them. This is the sort of thing we get. As regards police, we have warned the Colonies that it is desirable to increase the police establishment and even to take an over-plus for the time being. We are often told by the various Colonies that this is desirable but the Unofficial Members would not agree to the cost. They can't have it both ways, and that is our difficulty as I see it, and it is going to increase with the years. It is very necessary we think, but it is very difficult to persuade Unofficials on the spot that they are necessary, particularly when it comes to paying, and income tax is necessary to pay for them. To cope with this you have got to have certain services always at a pretty keyed-up level, and a great deal of expense is involved to keep them up to the level, and the people of the territory must be prepared to put their hands in their pockets and pay for them, otherwise it is no use coming along when things flare up and grumbling that you haven't modern police services. This is an issue we shall all have to face.

I lived for some years in Malaya and I objected to paying income tax and it is a very long history of Malayan's [sic] objections to paying for services. We lived in Malaya for years on the payments from Opium and Chinese Brandy. That is not possible now, and if you have got to run a modern service you have got to pay for a modern service.

Mr. Creech Jones. I might add that the delegation is fully alive to certain things done in the last week or two, the protection of managers on their estates, and where managers asked for a licence to possess weapons it was granted, and where there has been difficulty of getting a weapon, the manager was assisted by the police. Very extreme powers have been given to the police in regard to search both of persons and premises without warrant. Very drastic emergency powers have been conceded to the authorities there to cope with the difficulties which we are facing, and as Mr. Rees-Williams has said some of these powers exceed in many ways the powers which were exercised in this country during our own war period.

Are the any other observations you would wish to make, because I do want to press on you that our minds are open and we are anxious to cope with this situation. We are as desperately anxious as you for the safety of the people and maintenance of authority that we should root out those who are causing the trouble in Malaya.

Mr. Facer. I think I must go back to your remarks about His Excellency the High Commissioner. You assure us that you are fully alive to the position in Malaya, you are fully alive to the fact of subversive elements. To me that sounds very extraordinary when only a short time ago, a week ago, His Excellency said "we must explode this myth" if he knew it was not a myth. Quite frankly we are very glad to hear this afternoon your proposals and promises, but we are still apprehensive that even given these powers His Excellency won't use them.

Mr. Creech Jones. Extraordinary powers are being exercised at the present time. The ordinary newspaper reports do show clearly that very extraordinary things are being done, and certain powers are being exercised by the Police. The Government possessed with extraordinary powers has faced up to a situation which could not be faced up to in that particular way unless there was war.

Mr. Facer. Agreed Sir, but in February 1947, a year ago, His Excellency was warned. We had trouble in Kedah, action was taken, and the thing died down. What we are afraid of is not that action will not be taken but that action may not be continued.

Mr. Creech Jones. Every effort will be made to stamp out the causes of the trouble and to deal with a repetition of the trouble, but there must be some time limit to these extraordinary powers. We do seriously hope this tragic position will pass and the regulations will only be modified when the situation warrants, but you dare not repose these extraordinary powers in the executive without the protection of the public. We have a constant agitation in this country for the removal of all controls and all regulations and so on—the fact that danger is past, even though the Government do not feel the danger is past, and we are pressed that controls should go. The same sort of thing will arise there. The local government will use all the powers within its possession so long as conditions require it. I think very firm energetic effort will be made to get at the cause of these groups to break them up and eliminate them, and have them brought to justice.

Mr. Facer. I should like to emphasise that there is no personal animus against His Excellency, but we just feel that he has not treated the situation realistically.[8]

Mr. Creech Jones. I thought that perhaps one of his faults might be impetuosity.

Mr. Shearn. One reason that I believe the public has little confidence is that we feel that there has been a time-lag. Energetic steps have been taken now, but something ought to have been done to prevent the situation arising. We feel that a great number of people of bad character should have been rooted out a long time ago—it must have been known but it was dealt with too late—that is the feeling of many responsible people.

Mr. Creech Jones. That would be a view which would require a great deal of evidence to substantiate it. These powers could not be conceded in normal conditions. We were all conscious in the very troubled and unstable background that there was a fair amount of disorder and difficulty until we could get the flow of foodstuffs and the economic background much more settled. That has always been

---

[8] Similarly, the stinging headline of the *Straits Times* editorial on 17 June, 'Govern or Get Out', was followed by the disclaimer, 'Our heading . . . is not aimed personally at the High Commissioner of the Federation'.

understood by the local Government. How can we guarantee food supplies and a more economic background, and it took quite a period after the war to get reasonable security and reasonable stability, and obviously we have not got it yet, and as we approach a more stable and satisfying background the Communists and thugs come in and create that situation. I agree with what has been said that this does not spring from the usual economic causes which are associated with an industrial struggle, it is something wider than that, and it is that situation we have got to energetically meet. I do not want to hold an inquest on the past, and I do not think it would be profitable at this point when we are faced with a very grave danger and we must try somehow to meet it.

Mr. Rees-Williams. What does the Malay think about it, the ordinary kampong Malay?

Mr. Shearn. To some extent he is becoming an estate labourer, he is also being terrorised with other labourers.

Mr. Creech Jones. On the question of deportation I do not doubt that a very large number of people of liberal sympathies, particularly in the legal profession, will have sympathy with a point of view that it is drastic action. The critics are not always found where we expect to find them. We find them coming both from the Right and Left and from the Middle, people who imagine the World is such that liberal feelings can be expressed.

Mr. Russell. Will these things apply to Singapore as well?

Mr. Creech Jones. Singapore has a different Government, but I can assure you there is the completest collaboration between Malaya and Singapore. To a great extent there will be uniformity.

Mr. Russell. Only these people have a great habit of slipping over the border.

Mr. Creech Jones. We have been mindful of that possibility and I think you can be sure that what were known as the Straits Settlements will be properly brought into the general picture.

Some of the extraordinary powers must be reviewed from time to time, some will have to be allowed to lapse. One has to have some regard to the rights of individuals against the powes of the executive, but while you have a state of emergency, for some time after the situation, obviously those powers must be imposed in the executive, but you cannot keep them there for ever, you must modify the powers of the executive and always be ready and have the means should the situation deteriorate again.

All I am trying to say is that where you have granted to the executive of a territory very exceptional powers, there must be a period only in which those powers can be exercised. You cannot, when an emergency is through and you get normal life restored, you cannot continue those extraordinary powers. You cannot have the police searching and arresting without warrants and taking action against individuals. It doesn't make human life tolerable. You can justify these powers while the situation warrants it, but when the situation has improved, obviously you must modify the powers which the executive can exercise.

Mr. Hake. They would remain on the Statute Book?

Mr. Creech. Jones. Yes.

Mr. Mann. Before we go, Sir, I would again thank you for the pains you have taken to explain to us the situation in Malaya, and the steps being taken to counteract it. What you have told us is very encouraging.

This is the paper[9] we wish to leave with you setting out our detailed suggestions.

9 Not printed.

150   CO 717/172/52849/9/1948, no 10/12   22 June 1948
[Delegation of European businessmen]: outward telegram 750 from
Mr Creech Jones to Sir E Gent about the businessmen's demands and
the government's assurances made at the meeting

I report following to you for information.

2. I received today deputation representing planting, mining, commercial and other interests in Malaya, who represented to me urgent need for dealing effectively with present dangerous wave of murder, arson and intimidation. Text of agreed communique issued after the meeting has already been telegraphed to you separately.

3. Following are names of members of delegation and bodies they represented:—.
  [1]
...

4. Members of delegation said that present wave of lawlessness was much worse than anything before and was in no way due to dissatisfaction by labour with conditions of employment. On contrary it represented an organised attack on established Government through the use of violence and intimidation. The delegation had come because they were not sure that I realised sufficiently the gravity of the situation. To meet this situation the delegation said that sterner measures were required. Their own view was that if unofficial warnings given in the past of pending trouble had been heeded and sterner measures applied, then present, troubles might not have arisen.

5. The delegation urged me to agree to the following specific measures:—

(i)   the immediate application to British subjects of the provisions of Banishment Ordinance;
(ii)   Enactment of Clause 7(3) of the Trade Unions bill, 1948;
(iii) Army in Malaya to be reinforced by half a division of fully trained troops;
(iv)   immediate despatch by air to Malaya of wireless and other equipment required by police;
(v)   recruitment of additional European policemen. The delegation urged recruitment of Police from Palestine should not be overlooked;
(vi)   increased penalties, including flogging;
(vii) banning of the Communist Party;
(viii) active propaganda to be undertaken by Government against Communism;
(ix)   the authorities in Malaya should be given full powers needed for the maintenance of law and order.

6. In reply I told the delegation that His Majesty's Government agreed that the present trouble was political in origin and not due to dissatisfaction with working conditions. I assured them that I fully appreciated seriousness of the situation and

1 The names of those who attended are listed at 149, note.

that His Majesty's Government were determined to do all in their power to meet the situation and restore peaceful conditions and that I had the fullest confidence that you would achieve this. I explained that I had received from you urgent and comprehensive telegrams fully informing me of the situation and of the measures needed to meet it, and that while it was not always possible to accept every individual suggestion, no powers needed by you for controlling the situation would be withheld.

7.   I explained briefly the position with regard to the suggestions by the delegation listed at (i) and (ix) above. On point (i) I left delegation in no doubt that banishment action would be taken if necessary against British subjects and the law extended to the Settlements. I said that I could not discuss (iii) as this was a matter for the War Office and said that I was opposed to (vii) as this would merely drive the party underground. I said, however, that the Government were fully prepared to take action against any body engaged in subversive activities or intimidation.

151   CO 537/3686, no 6   29 June 1948

[Replacement of Sir E Gent]: unnumbered telegram from Mr M J MacDonald to Mr Creech Jones

[The collapse of confidence in Gent expressed by European businessmen and evinced in high-level meetings of officials in Malaya, occasioned a series of telegrams from the commissioner-general between 22 and 25 June asking the secretary of state to recall Gent without further delay. On 26 June Gent received a telegram from Creech Jones asking him to come home at the earliest opportunity. It was stated that he was returning 'for consultations' but it was confidentially understood that he would resign on arrival in London. Gent left Singapore at midnight 28 June. Delayed a day at Colombo, he transferred to a York freighter which collided with another aircraft as it approached Northolt airport on the morning of 4 July, killing the high commissioner.]

As I say in my telegraph No. 101 of yesterday, it is important that our friend's resignation and name of his successor should be announced as soon as possible after his arrival in London.

2.   I have been thinking about succession and venture to put the following points to you.

3.   Two alternatives are possible. Firstly, we can appoint a successor who has the qualities required not only for dealing with the immediate emergency, which (barring accidents or a serious deterioration) should not last more than 6 months, but also for leading the Federation through the next 5 years. Secondly, we can appoint a man with the first lot of qualities but not necessarily the second. In the latter case the appointment can be made as an emergency appointment not (repeat not) intended to last anything like the normal full term.

4.   If a candidate is also available and free to come to Malaya in the near future who answers to the first description, that is of course the best solution. If such a (? candidate omitted) is not immediately available, then I think we should look for the second type. I am not sufficiently familiar with the senior colonial governors and other possible candidates who may be immediately available to suggest with (?confidence) any name which carries the qualifications for 5 year term. He should preferably be a man with an already established reputation, which will from the beginning restore confidence in the Government in Kuala Lumpur. In addition he should have experience of colonial government, or a government of a similar type

elsewhere. One of the reasons for our friend's (? omission), not only in recent weeks but during much of the two years, was his inexperience in practical administration. The public here will feel no (repeat no) confidence in a High Commissioner whose record seems to foreshadow a repetition of this serious defect. In addition, what are needed are qualities of ability, drive and capacity to win the people's confidence and friendship. Some knowledge of Asiatic peoples and problems is highly desirable. A long term High Commissioner should also be a man who will take a sympathetic view of constitutional trades union development and democratic social and political reform. Our policy of repression against extremists must be combined with consistent and steady encouragement of these movements.

5.   The name of Lord MILVERTON (Sir Arthur Richards)[1] springs to my mind. He has a reputation for possessing these qualities, and in addition is known and remembered with high respect and regard in Malaya. If he were younger he would be an obvious candidate to serve as High Commissioner for a five year period. I fear that his age and other circumstances rule him out for an appointment of this nature, but I wonder whether you would consider him for appointment on other basis, i.e. for a temporary period of, say, a year to deal with the emergency. I realise that in normal circumstances this appointment would be regarded as less responsible than his governorship of Nigeria. But in present circumstances the responsibility of the High Commissioner in the Federation of Malaya is of very high importance. I realise also that he wishes to get on with his new career in the House of Lords. If his appointment here were temporary, (? need omitted) not be long interrupted and I have no doubt that he would return to the Lords with fresh laurels ENTWINED in his CORONET.

6.   A man of a different type whose name comes to mind is that of General Sir Archibald (? Nye).[2] I have no personal acquaintance with him and my knowledge of him is therefore secondhand. I am not sure whether he has the experience necessary to enable him to fulfil successfully the long-term, but he may have and this could be decided during an appointment made in the first place for a shorter period. He does seem to have the experience and qualities desirable for dealing with the immediate situation in Malaya.

7.   I have been much impressed by GRANTHAM[3] during my two visits to Hong Kong. He strikes me as a man who might be a fine High Commissioner in the Federation. Unfortunately there is a factor connected with him which, I think, rules him out. His brother-in-law, Scott, was I believe killed by the Japanese whilst he was interned in Hong Kong. I happen to know that Grantham and his wife, as well as his

---

[1] Arthur F Richards (1885–1978); 1st Baron Milverton 1947; entered the MCS in 1908; served as governor of North Borneo in 1930–1933, the Gambia in 1933–1936, the Western Pacific in 1936–1938, Jamaica in 1938–1943, and Nigeria in 1943–1947. At one time it had been expected that he would return to Malaya as governor of the Malayan Union but in 1945 he could not be moved from Nigeria and was reaching retirement age by then anyway. In the House of Lords he sat on the Labour benches until June 1949 when he joined the Liberals, shifting his allegiance to the Conservatives eighteen months later.
[2] Sir Archibald E Nye (1895–1967); lt-general and vice-chief of the Imperial General Staff under Sir Alan Brooke, Nye retired from the army to become governor of Madras in 1946, staying on after Indian independence as governor of Madras until 1948 and British high commissioner in New Delhi until 1952. He was high commissioner to Canada, 1952–1956.
[3] Sir Alexander Grantham (1899–1978); entered Hong Kong government service in 1922; served also in Bermuda, Jamaica, and Nigeria; governor of Fiji and high commissioner of the Western Pacific, 1945–1947; governor of Hong Kong, 1947–1957.

sister-in-law, are inclined to blame Gimson for Scott's death on the grounds that Gimson was not firm enough in his dealings with the Japanese. This would inevitably militate to some extent against completely friendly cooperation between Grantham in Kuala Lumpur and Gimson in Singapore. Probably you do not in any case wish to move Grantham so early from Hong Kong, but I suggest this in case Grantham's (? name omitted) may be (as it deserves to be) on your list.

8. I have considered the possibility of Gimson going to Kuala Lumpur, but he is not a strong and firm enough administrator for this. He is doing admirably in the smaller governorship at Singapore, and is the right man in the right place there.

9. I dare say that GUERNEY [sic] will be a name on your list. I do not know him, and I feel sure that he is an excellent man. But I do not think enough prestige attaches to his name to make it one which would quickly restore confidence in administration in Kuala Lumpur. Perhaps he could fill the governorship of another territory whose present governor is qualified to come here. If the new High Commissioner is to be a colonial or Indian service man—and barring a really considerable (? omission) from outside, this is desirable—he should be one who has already established a reputation as a governor.

10. The above are some thoughts. No doubt you and your advisers are already preparing a better short list of candidates composed with greater knowledge and wisdom from a more comprehensive field. But the above reflections may be of some use to you.

152 CO 537/3686, no 8 30 June 1948
[Appointment of new high commissioner]: outward telegram (reply) no 127 from Mr Creech Jones to Mr M J MacDonald [Extract]

. . . 5. The last name you mention is one which I had myself picked out after surveying the Colonial field.[1] Gurney would certainly have achieved a senior Governorship by now had he not agreed from a sense of public duty to serve as Chief Secretary Palestine. His record in both East and West Africa and in Palestine (where his name came into some prominence) is such as to ensure that he would very quickly overcome any initial handicaps which might arise from his not actually having held a Governorship before. I doubt whether we are likely to improve on his clear mind and calm temperament, his administrative qualities and his capacity to delegate and to gain the confidence and respect both of his staff and of unofficials. Moreover as Chief Secretary to the East African Governors Conference during the war he was markedly successful in cooperating with Service Leaders. These qualities to my mind are sufficient to outweigh the fact that he has not before served in an Asiatic country other than Palestine.

6. I was in fact proposing to invite your comments on his candidature. Upon further reflection in the light of your telegram I am now disposed to fix on him as my first choice but will await your further observations. There is no serving Governor who would really fill the bill apart from Macpherson[2] who as you will realise could not in any case be moved from Nigeria so soon. . . .

---

[1] See 151.
[2] Sir John Macpherson, governor of Nigeria, 1948–1954.

153   CAB 129/28, CP(48)171   1 July 1948

'The situation in Malaya': Cabinet memorandum by Mr Creech Jones

[A draft of this memorandum was sent to the prime minister on 30 June in advance of its circulation for the information of Cabinet which did not discuss Malayan disorders until 13 July (see 158 and also PREM 8/1406/1).]

My colleagues will wish to have a summary of the present situation in Malaya and of the measures which are being taken to meet it.

Background to recent events

2. Malaya is about the size of England without Wales, it has a population (including Singapore) of approximately 5,800,000 people, of whom 2,200,000 are Malays, 2,600,000 Chinese, and 600,000 Indians.[1] It is at present divided into two administrations, namely the Federation of Malaya comprising the whole peninsula with the exception of Singapore Island, and the Colony of Singapore. The Federation of Malaya (apart from two small areas, Penang and Malacca, which were formerly part of the old Colony of the Straits Settlements) is a Federation of nine States, each under a Malay ruler. Executive authority is, however, exercised in most matters not by the State Governments but by the Federation Government under the High Commissioner. Executive authority in Singapore is exercised by the Governor.

3. The Commissioner-General for the United Kingdom in South-East Asia, Mr. Malcolm MacDonald, has his headquarters in Singapore. He has taken over the functions of the former office of Governor-General, Malaya, but has no direct executive authority. In regard to the British territories within his jurisdiction he has a general responsibility for co-ordinating policy and administration.

4. Since the war the whole of South-East Asia has been a disturbed area. The Japanese occupation which overthrew European and Colonial Governments and deeply upset the whole social structure of the occupied countries released a surge of nationalist movements whose force is by no means spent to-day. Furthermore, during the time of occupation it was, of course, greatly to our own interests that subversive movements against the Japanese occupation should be encouraged and supplied with arms. It is no wonder that some of the resistance groups which sprang up at that time should—as happened also in Europe—prove after liberation an embarrassment to their own Governments.

5. Until the outbreak of the present wave of crime Malaya was, in fact, the most peaceful country in South-East Asia and had taken long strides towards the re-establishment of stable, prosperous conditions. During 1947 the total value of the exports of Singapore and the Federation together was £151 million, of which dollar exports accounted for £56 million. It is by far the most important source of dollars in the Colonial Empire and it would gravely worsen the whole dollar balance of the sterling area if there were serious interference with Malayan exports.

6. Most of the present trouble in Malaya is due to Chinese groups opposed to the régime of the Chinese National Government. The trouble is almost certainly Communist-instigated, though direct connection between the gangsters and the

---

[1] The first census since 1931 was taken in 1947, see M V del Tufo, *Malaya: report on the 1947 census of population* (London, 1949).

Communist Party cannot always be traced. Secret Societies have always been a prominent feature of Chinese life and were a thorn in the flesh of Government in Malaya right through the 19th century. At various times during that century they led to outbreaks of armed violence, principally between opposing factions of Chinese.

7. On the reoccupation after the recent war, the Chinese Communist guerillas (the Malayan Peoples' Anti-Japanese Army) were in control of large areas, particularly in Johore and Perak. Their excesses were the cause of bloody Sino-Malay clashes in the month following the reoccupation.

8. Although the present trouble is largely instigated by the Chinese, a word must be said about the other two main communities in Malaya, the Malays and the Indians. The *Malays* have been largely preoccupied with the constitutional negotiations which led to the modification of the Malayan Union proposals and the shaping of the present constitution. The Malays are satisfied with this and have so far been very little concerned in the present disturbances. There are nevertheless a number of Malays in the Malayan Communist Party and there are Malay organisations thoroughly permeated with Communist influences. The *Indians* now provide many of the overt leaders of the Communist Party and its satellite organisations, because, being British subjects, they have not been treated since the reoccupation as liable to deportation under the law in force in the Malay States. The Indian leaders are, however, suspected to be mainly men of straw, and the real organisers are Chinese who have gone underground. Indian community is largely employed as estate labour, and is traditionally passive and unaggressive, but easy prey for agitators.

9. It is also necessary to mention the position of the trade unions in Malaya. The trade unions are still young and poorly organised owing to the fact that the majority of workers are unsophisticated and illiterate. Encouragement has been given to the growth of trade unions but unfortunately a large number of the existing unions have been infiltrated by what may be called professional "organisers," whose main object is to turn the trade unions into a profitable source of income and political advantage for themselves. As in some other countries, these "organisers" are influenced and often controlled by the Communist Party. The evils have not stopped short at mere unscrupulous use of union organisation for ends other than the workers' advantage. There has been physical intimidation of workers on a large scale. Indian estate labour in some areas has been organised into disciplined bands, sometimes uniformed, armed with lathis and knives. In Singapore an illegal strong arm force (the "Workers' Protection Corps") has been organised by the Singapore Federation of Trade Unions (a Communist-dominated body) for purposes of intimidation and extortion.

10. We have had several experienced British trade union officials working to guide and help the trade unions and my Labour Adviser has also examined and discussed problems on the spot and suitable action taken. In addition, early this year at the request of the local authorities in Malaya I arranged for Mr. S Awbery, M.P., of the Transport and General Workers' Union, and Mr. F.W. Dalley, of the Railway Clerks' Union, to visit Singapore and Malaya to report on the state of trade unionism. I have just received their report (which has not yet been published.)[2] It draws attention to the difficulties of developing healthy trade unionism where the workers

---

[2] S Awbery and F W Dalley, *Labour and Trade Union Organization in the Federation of Malaya and Singapore* (Kuala Lumpur, 1948).

have still a low standard of education and have been exploited by unscrupulous so-called organisers; and makes recommendations which I shall follow up.

Present situation

11. In the last few weeks violent crimes have again broken out in the Federation, and labour unrest has become more marked. On 1st June a strong force of police had to be used to clear 200 Chinese labourers from an estate in Johore where they had taken control. After a police charge seven Chinese were found dead. On 4th June the High Commissioner reported that in recent weeks there had been twelve serious attacks, all save one attributable to organised politically-inspired violence. In the week ending 12th June there were five murders and two attempted murders, all, save one attempted murder, political in origin. On 16th June three European planters in Perak were attacked and murdered in their bungalows by a gang of Chinese armed with Sten guns, while elsewhere in Perak and on an estate in Johore, where strikes had just ended, a Chinese foreman and a Chinese labour contractor were killed.[3] On 17th June twelve armed Chinese raided the police station at a small village twelve miles from Johore Bahru, and made off with a police rifle, after wounding a passer-by. From the 18th to 29th June inclusive, fifteen murders and fifteen attempted murders have been reported to me. It is noteworthy that a number of these attacks conform to a pattern. They are directed against:—

(a) The managerial staff, European and Asian, of outlying estates.
(b) Leaders of local Kuo Min Tang parties.
(c) Persons who have given evidence in intimidation cases.

The attacks are carried out by bands of well-armed Chinese, either as ambushes or by sudden descents (sometimes by bicycle) on isolated buildings. There have been no large-scale disturbances by labour, and the strike situation which was at no time really serious is now very good: there are now only eight small strikes in progress involving less than 900 workers in all.   ˜

12. In Singapore there was a wave of unrest among waterfront labour and among workers in rubber milling factories during April. There were a few incidents, but Government remained in control of the situation, and attempts at one-day general strikes were failures. Since 5th June no cases of violence or intimidation of a political nature have been reported from Singapore. Agitators have continued to make inflammatory speeches, and it is reported that in spite of arrests of ringleaders the "Workers Protection Corps" is being expanded.

13. Although there is less violence in Singapore, the basic situation in both the Federation and the Colony is the same. There is no concrete evidence that the Malayan Communist Party is directly responsible for the present lawlessness but extreme political factions and certain trade unions have been infiltrated by communism. The same methods of attack are used—intimidation and the wrecking of normal industrial conciliation machinery. Asian born Chinese, who until recently were active in organisations associated with lawlessness, now seem to use Indian or British nationality for their purpose.

14. The Commissioner-General has represented that the first objective of the Communist gangs has been and is still by terrorist campaign to produce the

---

[3] See 148, note.

maximum industrial unrest and disruption of economic life of the country, with a view amongst other things to destroying the Government's authority. Evidence is that the tactics of the Communist gangs are changing from fomenting labour disputes to a policy of picking off the managerial staff of installations and mines. Cash is also being obtained by hold-ups on pay day, particularly in isolated areas. It may be reasonably expected that attempts will be made to sabotage communications, industrial plants and factories, power stations and other vital points. In addition to terrorist acts by individuals or small gangs there are many persons who do not engage in violence themselves but who foster and direct these activities by various methods. Such persons are distributed throughout the Federation and Singapore, and most are overt or covert members of the Malayan Communist Party and kindred organisations. Further, there is information that mobilisation and training of bands of guerillas in jungle hide-outs is now coming into force and they will be well organised and armed and their activities will include attacks on villages and small towns to commit murders and robberies and to dislocate transport systems with ultimate objective of controlling certain areas. As police and military operations succeed in restoring law and order in the more settled areas, such malefactors who escape will tend to join the guerilla bands in the jungle. Guerilla bands may attack Malay kempongs [sic] (or homesteads of scattered buildings) in particular, partly in order to obtain food, &c., for their maintenance, but also as part of a preconceived plan to stir up gradual Malay enmity such as occurred during the Japanese occupation and immediately after. This may result in outbursts of violence by Malays against innocent Chinese and adds to the general state of unrest.

Measures to meet the situation

15.   In this situation of violence and murderous outrages in various States, with labour troubles and lawlessness, the following steps have become necessary:—

(i)   Temporary amendment of trade union legislation to limit trade union officers to persons associated with the trade or industry concerned and to confine federations of trade unions to *bona fide* industrial organisations in the particular trades or callings.

(ii)   A state of emergency was proclaimed on 16th June in certain areas of Perak and Johore, and extended on 17th June to the whole of the State of Perak and on 18th June to the remainder of the Federation.[4] Emergency Regulations have been made which include the reimposition of the death penalty for the offence of carrying arms, and the authorities have been empowered to detain any person without trial, to search persons and buildings without warrant and to occupy properties. Where local conditions require, the authorities have power to impose a curfew and to control the movement of persons and vehicles.

(iii)   The use of the powers of deportation conferred by existing legislation in Malaya was, prior to the present disturbances, confined by my direction to aliens. In response to strong representations from the authorities in Malaya that British subjects (mainly Indians) were in consequence being used as stooges by organisers of seditious movements I have agreed to deportation powers being exercised

---

[4] See 148.

throughout the Federation against any person who is not identified with the country as a Federal citizen.

(iv)   The emergency legislation referred to at (ii) above will, upon the declaration of a stage [sic] of emergency, enable the High Commissioner to make regulations providing *inter alia* for the detention of any person for a period not in excess of two years. I have given directions that these powers of detention are only to be exercised against persons who are implicated in acts of violence or in organising or inciting persons to take part in strikes, disturbances or demonstrations in which violence or threat of violence is used. I have also given directions that papers relating to each case in which detention is recommended must be reviewed by a Supreme Court Judge. The above powers of detention will enable action to be taken against Federal citizens who will, as indicated in (iii) above, not be regarded as liable to deportation.

(v)   Very active measures are being taken to strengthen the police in both the Federation and Singapore. These measures include the organisation of a force of special constabulary; the increase of the regular police force by further recruitment and training of local personnel; the formation of a frontier force or gendarmerie to patrol the northern frontier where undesirable persons and arms can enter Malaya; the diversion of civil officers from ordinary duties to assist in the administrative work of the police, and in organising and directing the special constabulary; special measures to expedite the supply of equipment on existing orders, and to obtain new equipment, such as scout cars, armoured cars, mobile wireless sets, and additional supplies of arms and ammunition.

(vi)   In addition to the other measures for strengthening the police force, I have sent out to Malaya Mr. W.N. Gray, late Inspector-General of the Palestine Police, who has special experience in combating terrorism. His mission will be to discuss all measures likely to increase the efficiency of existing police action against terrorism, including the possibility of strengthening the police with recruits from the Palestine Police. I am expecting to get, within the next few days, estimates from Malaya of the number of men from the Palestine Police who could usefully be employed. In any case I have been asked to recruit 60 additional assistant superintendents of police.[5]

(vii) The Army and R.A.F. are giving the fullest support to the Police and close co-operation between the military and the civil authorities is provided by the British Defence Co-ordination Committee, Far East, over which the Commissioner-General presides, and the local Defence Committees in Singapore and the Federation of Malaya.

(viii) In the last few days the Commissioner-General, Mr. Malcolm MacDonald, has represented to me that the High Commissioner for the Federation of Malaya, Sir Edward Gent, has lost the confidence of the public in the Federation and the heads of other Services. He reported that in consequence it was essential, in his

---

[5] Gent had turned down the offer of a contingent of Palestine police on the grounds that the reintroduction of non-commissioned European ranks into the police force would be unacceptable to public opinion, as well as on the general ground that the present force was sufficient. Colonel W N Gray, former commissioner of police in Palestine, was at this time invited out as an adviser; on the strength of the report, which he submitted in July, he was appointed in Aug to fill the post of commissioner of Malayan police vacated by Langworthy soon after the start of the emergency.

view, to recall Sir Edward Gent to England at once, and that he should not return to Malaya. His recommendation was made in such terms that I had no alternative but to agree to it at once, and Sir Edward Gent is now flying home.[6] He is due in England on 3rd July. The Chief Secretary of the Federation of Malaya, Sir Alexander Newboult, is now acting as High Commissioner pending another appointment.

Plan of future operations

16. The Commissioner-General has sent me the following summary of the operations proposed as a result of inter-Service discussions in Malaya. Operations are planned in two phases:—

17. In phase 1 the objective is to restore law and order in settled areas of the territory and to maintain the economic life of the country and restore morale. This will be carried out through two distinct types of operations: (a) by offensive operations to round up gangsters, including the establishment of road blocks and traffic control, periodical sweeps where murders or robberies have been committed, and widespread searches for arms and other incriminating evidence; (b) protective measures, through provision of armed guards for police stations, power stations, prisons, warehouses, factories, docks and other vital points. In order to maintain the economic life of the country and restore confidence in outlying districts it is also necessary to provide static guards for the larger rubber estates, mines, transport system and Malay villages.

18. Phase 2 will comprise the operations necessary to liquidate the guerilla bands whose headquarters are in the jungle. This will involve the destruction of their camps, cutting off of food supplies, and uncovering dumps of arms and equipment. These operations will be primarily of a military nature in which, however, the police will participate. The operations may take a considerable time owing to the nature of the country involved. Phase 2 cannot be extensively undertaken until sufficient success has been achieved in phase 1.

19. The Civil and Service authorities in Malaya are, of course, in consultation as to whether the existing forces in Malaya are adequate to meet all foreseeable calls upon them arising from the present disturbances.

---

[6] See 151, note.

154   CO 537/3686, no 20   2 July 1948
[Appointment of new high commissioner]: inward telegram (reply) no 112 from Mr M J MacDonald to Mr Creech Jones   [Extract]

Following top secret and personal for the Secretary of State from MacDonald. *Begins.*
    Your telegram No. 127[1]
    I agree that if possible we should go for a man who has both the qualities required for short-term emergency and those needed for long-term policy in Malaya. If this is impossible and we have a fall back on someone primarily suited to deal with the

---

[1] See 152.

emergency, I strongly support your aversion to the appointment of someone obviously chosen on account of his suitability to carry out a militant policy. This is not a Palestine, either actually or potentially, and it will be a serious mistake to give any impression that the Government think it so.

2.   I am very sorry that you say that Lord Milverton is not available even on a temporary basis. The more I think about the problem of a candidate, the more I think that he is by far the most suitable man. He has all the qualities, including immense prestige. I know from conversations with various Malay leaders during the last year that he would be a very popular choice with them. Do you think that there would be any chance at all of persuading him to come for, say, a year. He and I are old friends and I know how keen and close is his interest in Malaya. I would gladly send him a personal message through you telling him

(a) that there is a real man's job to be done, and
(b) that we Malayans all very greatly hope that he will (? come omitted) and do it, if you think that it will help.

3.   Incidentally, when Newboult was staying with me last night, I tried out on him a number of names, including Milverton's. He thought this an absolutely first-class suggestion and said that if appointment were possible it would immediately have a great effect. Failing Milverton, he liked the idea of Nye. Incidentally Newboult said that he is definitely in favour of making a short-term emergency appointment if you are impressed with the gravity of the emergency.

4.   I like very much what you say about Gurney. It looks as if he may (repeat may) have the qualities required for both the short-term and long-term situations. I still however, feel that there are two disadvantages about him. Firstly, whatever his merits may be, his name would undoubtedly initially be a disappointment to the public here. He is unknown, whereas local people are looking for someone with a big reputation whose outstanding qualities are beyond question. There is no doubt that, if he were appointed, we should have to face this disappointment. It need not necessarily be very serious, and we could do something to counteract it, for example, try to get the press to write him up well, telling them some of the things which you say in your telegram under reference. The point that he would before this have had a senior Governorship but for his agreement from a sense of public duty to take the difficult Palestine job would certainly go down rather well. Moreover, the very fact that he has recent experience of high responsibility in Palestine could to some extent be judiciously played up.

5.   The other snag is that to some extent he is an unknown quantity. Will he really succeed in achieving the big personal success which is necessary in the Federation at the present time? Has he for example the gift for politics which is highly desirable? It would be an awful pity if for some reason or other he did not (? hit omitted) it off with Malays and Chinese here and repeated Gent's failure on the personal side. That would definitely shorten the period during which we British can expect to maintain our influence in this important corner of the earth. I do not know Gurney's standing. In any case your experience and judgment is more valuable than mine. I shall be more than happy to accept your verdict on him.

6.   To see what would be Newboult's reactions I asked Hone to bring Gurney into a conversation which he was holding with Newboult today, mentioning him as a possible who had come into Hone's own mind. Newboult was not (repeat not)

impressed. He thought that the people would be very disappointed. I do not attach any decisive importance to this because I think that the people in Malaya are assuming too easily that they will now get as High Commissioner a great public figure with a high and mighty reputation. But I mention Newboult's reaction so that you are fully aware, to begin with at any rate, that Gurney's appointment would not (repeat not) be regarded here as a good one.[2]

7. I repeat that I like what you say about him. I would not mind the initial impression about him being unsatisfactory if he really did remove that initial impression soon after getting here. If you think his potentialities are big enough, and if someone of Milverton's stamp is not (repeat not) available, then I expect that Gurney is as good as we are likely to get. . . .[3]

---

[2] When MacDonald and Newboult discussed Gurney's appointment with the rulers and *mentris besar* on 31 Aug the attitude of the Malays was 'definitely unfriendly', see 165.

[3] In paragraph 8 MacDonald added that Newboult's tiredness (TB was suspected) made 'it important that the new High Commissioner should be appointed and arrives here fairly soon'. On Gent's death Newboult became officer administering the government, July–Oct 1948.

155 CO 537/3686, no 23   4 July 1948

[Recall of Sir E Gent]: inward telegram no 733 from Sir A Newboult (OAG) to Mr Creech Jones giving the text of a message from Tan Cheng Lock in protest against Gent's recall

My telegram No. 732, following is text of the message from Mr. Tan Cheng Lock addressed to the S. of S. for the Colonies. *Begins.*

I wish to respectfully point out to your Government Prime Minister the Right Honourable Clement Attlee and H.M. Government that, in my humble opinion and in that of many people here who share my views, the decision of the Colonial Office in recalling Sir Edward Gent from his post of High Commissioner for the Federation of Malaya without consulting the local Asian feelings and interests but wholly prompted by the strong pressure from European unofficial quarters and direct representations made to the Colonial Office by European vested interests and big business connected with Malaya, on alleged grounds that Sir Edward is to be blamed for the state of emergency prevailing in Malaya has dumbfounded this country and is not only an act of gross injustice to him in being made scapegoat for ill consequence of an inherent unhealthy situation arising out of war, but also may well turn out to be a major blunder with far reaching and serious consequence for this country.

2. It was humanly impossible for Sir Edward, or any one else in this land, to foresee with such perfect accuracy precise course of events leading to the present state of affairs in this country, for which Sir Edward has been wrongly held responsible, as to warrant him in resorting to more extensive and stronger repressive measures than those which he has been taking during the last year or so to deal with the violent crimes here.

3. To say that he should have done more than what he has accomplished to the best of his ability and judgment under the peculiar circumstances obtaining here to

nip the trouble in the bud is nothing short of making a false show of wisdom after the event.

4. Sir Edward has endeared himself to many Asians of all classes by keeping in constant personal touch with them, by his habit of seeing things, by his invariable courtesy and democratic demeanour when moving amongst them, and by the utmost consideration he has shown for the social welfare of the people here through several administrative measures effected during his regime.

5. I earnestly pleased with H.M. Government to reinstate Sir Edward in his office as High Commissioner for the Federation of Malaya on the ground that any abrupt break in the continuity of the administration by the appointment of a new High Commissioner in the place of one who has abundantly manifested his high capacity, brilliancy, infinite painstaking, and popularity would be disastrous in existing difficult and critical state of the country, especially should his successor prove to be an official of essentially bureaucratic and autocratic type with lack of political sense, of spirit of democracy and constructive statesmanship, and only intent on repressive and negative action.

6. It is a matter of supreme importance and significance to this country in these troubled days of political ferment and social unrest in South East Asia that the Government of Malaya must strive to win the confidence and take root in life of the people. *Ends.*

156   CO 537/3686, no 27   6 July 1948
[Appointment of new high commissioner]: inward telegram no 121 from Mr M J MacDonald to Mr Creech Jones

Following personal for the Secretary of State from MacDonald. *Begins.*

My telegram No. 118.

At the risk of appearing intolerably persistent, I should like to put the following suggestion into your mind as a possibility in connection with succession.

(1) You yourself, if necessary with supporting message from the Prime Minister, should ask Milverton to come here as High Commissioner for, say, nine months.

(2) Gurney should in the meantime be posted in the Colonial Office or elsewhere whence he could be extracted at the end of Milverton's short period of office.

(3) Gurney should then be appointed High Commissioner.

2. In the course of discussion on the general situation today with some of the leading and most knowledgeable European journalists in Malaya, they asked when the new High Commissioner would be appointed. I answered that it would be soon. In subsequent conversation they expressed strongly the view that he must be a man with an established reputation as a Colonial Governor or a considerable public figure.

3. As you know, I shall think that whatever decision you (with your ripe judgment of men and sympathy with our Malayan problems) reach on this matter is the wisest decision, and shall support it whole-heartedly. *Ends.*

157 CO 537/3686, no 28   7 July 1948

[Appointment of new high commissioner]: outward telegram (reply) no 148 from Mr Creech Jones to Mr M J MacDonald

Following personal for MacDonald from Secretary of State. *Begins.*

1. Most grateful for your telegrams Nos. 112[1] and 118, and 121.[2] I had not answered the earlier ones before in view of Gent's tragic death, which seems to me to have altered the situation in that the need for a decision, though still urgent, is not now so pressing that we must announce something this week. You will I hope, agree that we should avoid any action such as an immediate appointment, which would strengthen the belief that the selection of Gent's successor was already in hand when he was killed. I realise that doubts of Newboult's health[3] do not admit of any long delay but, if I judge the situation rightly, we can afford to wait up to say the middle of the month and I propose, therefore, to take a day or two further to consider the possibilities.

2. I shall, of course, telegraph further as soon as possible. Meanwhile, however, I see little chance of the appointment of Lord Milverton. Quite apart from the fact that he has entered into many commitments here, you may not be aware that it was considered inadvisable last year to give him a further extension (which would have been acceptable to him) of his appointment in Nigeria; also from what I have heard about his present state of health, I seriously doubt whether it would be fair at his age to expect him to stand the strain of the High Commissionership, even for a short period.

3. Indeed, now that the complications arising from Gent's position have been disposed of in this unforeseen way I am more than ever inclined to go for a permanent appointment rather than a stopgap one whether civil or military. I have carefully thought over all you say about Gurney, and I do not doubt that he has the qualities required. I believe that his achievements could be built up satisfactorily before he arrived, if it should be decided to appoint him. However, I shall be seeing Cunningham[4] tomorrow and I shall put your points to him very closely and satisfy myself thoroughly before going further.

4. My strong inclination to a regular rather than a temporary appointment has been reinforced by a message from Tan Cheng Lock (and especially paragraph 5 of that message) which has just been conveyed to me in Newboult's telegram No. 733 Confidential.[5] If you have not seen that telegram, also Newboult's telegram No. 732, please obtain copies. Although the immediate purpose of Tan Cheng Lock in protesting against recall of Gent has passed it will be necessary in due course to make some reply and I shall be grateful for your advice. I am sure that you will agree that it will not (repeat not) be necessary in the new circumstances to make any public reference in this or any other connection to the fact that had Gent survived it was contemplated that he would be relieved of his appointment. *Ends.*

---

[1] See 154.   [2] See 156.   [3] See 154, note 3.
[4] General Sir Alan Cunningham (1887–1983) had been Britain's last high commissioner in Palestine and Transjordan, Nov 1945–May 1948, and Gurney's immediate superior.
[5] See 155.

158   CAB 128/13, CM 50(48)3   13 July 1948
'Malaya': Cabinet conclusions on British response to Malayan disorders

The Secretary of State for the Colonies gave the Cabinet a brief report on the
disorders in Malaya. All the requests for military assistance which had been made by
the authorities on the spot had been, or were being, met and there was close
collaboration between the civil and military authorities under the supervision of the
British Defence Co-ordinating Committee. The local governments had been authorised to introduce emergency powers; and there was reason to believe that the
situation was now being brought under control.

In discussion it was suggested that a comprehensive review should be made of the
organisation of the Colonial police services, with a view particularly to improving
their intelligence work. There was little doubt that the situation in Malaya had been
exploited by Communists, and similar attempts to foment disorder must be expected
in other parts of the Colonial Empire. While we should not be deterred by this threat
from continuing to pursue a progressive Colonial policy, Colonial Governments
must be prepared to deal effectively and promptly with any such outbreaks.

The Cabinet:—

(1) Took note of the position;
(2) Invited the Secretary of State for the Colonies to confer with the Minister of
Defence regarding the need for a review of the organisation of the Colonial police
services.[1]

---

[1] On 5 Aug 1948 Creech Jones sent a secret circular despatch to the governors on the subject of colonial
police forces, in which he requested reviews of internal security (in the light of unrest in the Gold Coast
and Malaya) and stressed the need to develop intelligence and special branches. He followed this up on 20
Aug with a demi-official letter enjoining colonial governments to be alive to dangers arising from the
spread of political ideologies. The despatch of 5 Aug is probably at CO 537/2768 [14882] for 1948, which is
continued at CO 537/4401 [14882] for 1949, but both files have been 'retained', as has CO 537/2793
[14882/24] which would appear to contain related papers with respect to Malaya. A copy of the despatch as
sent to Uganda is, however, at CO 537/4426. Papers on organisation for research into political intelligence
in the colonies should be at CO 537/2676 [14355/5] for 1948, but this file has also been 'retained'. One
policing scheme, which was considered towards the end of 1948 but in the end dismissed on practical
grounds, was the creation of a colonial gendarmerie of locally recruited forces associated with London
though partly supported from colonial finance (see CO 537/4402, note by Creech Jones [Oct 1948], and
CAB 130/44, GEN 264/1st meeting, 10 Dec 1948).

159   PREM 8/1406, CP(48)190   19 July 1948
'The situation in Malaya': Cabinet memorandum by Mr Creech Jones

I circulate for the information of my colleagues an account of further steps taken
since 1st July, when I circulated a paper (C.P.(48) 171)[1] describing the main features
of the situation in Malaya up to the end of June.

2. During the first eleven days of July there was no great improvement or
deterioration in the situation. During that period, bandits were responsible for 26
murders, all but one of them non-European, in country districts mainly in the

---

[1] See 153.

estates of Perak and Johore. There was no large-scale operation by the bandits until 12th July, when there occurred the incident at Batu Arang, the site of the only coal mine in Malaya, in which a band attacked the village and murdered four people. No important incident has occurred in the few days since the Batu Arang raid, though there were three murders on the following day, 13th July.

Measures to meet the situation

3. The authorities in Malaya and Singapore have continued their action to improve the means of protection and counter-attack against terriorists. The following additional measures have now been taken.

Federation of Malaya:—

(i) The regular police force is to be expanded by 3,000 local other ranks and 85 officers, most of whom will be looked for from the Palestine Police.[2]

(ii) A considerable additional force of Special Constabulary is being raised consisting of voluntary part-time constables, and paid full-time constables. The present strength of the Special Constabulary is between two and three thousand: the ultimate target will be in the region of six thousand. This plan will require up to 500 Palestine constables for training, inspection, etc.

(iii) A scheme has been drawn up by G.O.C., Malaya District,[3] for the formation of jungle units for offensive operations against guerillas in the jungle. Four units are to be raised initially. Each unit will be officered by ex-officers of Force 136, where available, and both Malays and Chinese will be recruited. The force, which is being given the code name "Ferret",[4] is to be raised under Emergency Regulations, but will be administered by the Malay Regiment and trained at the Malay Regiment H.Q. at Port Dickson. No publicity is being given to the raising of this force.

(iv) A scheme has also been drawn up by the G.O.C., Malaya District, for the formation of a mixed force to operate in the Northern Frontier to prevent illegal immigration and gun running. This will probably make necessary the raising of a third Battalion of the Malay Regiment;[5] this question is still being studied by the Acting High Commissioner and his advisers.

(As these additional police and other locally recruited forces become operational, two Battalions of the Malay Regiment and one Squadron of the R.A.F. Regiment (Malaya) now employed on static guard duties, can be released for operational roles. In addition some 4,000 Gurkha troops now used as guards at strategic points could be returned for further training.)

---

[2] Colonel W N Gray, formerly commissioner of Palestinian police, took over as commissioner of Malayan police in Aug, see 153, note 5.

[3] Major-General C H Boucher was GOC, Malaya, 1948–1950.

[4] 'Ferret Force', devised by Force 136 veterans J L H Davis, R N Broome and R C K Thompson and consisting of small operational units of troops, police and hand-picked local Asians, has been called the first group of real jungle fighters of the emergency. The force was, however, soon disbanded because of administrative reasons and the services' dislike of 'private armies'.

[5] The frontier with Thailand had been dominated by guerrillas, usually from the KMT, since the end of the war. Various schemes for a special frontier force had been considered. The proposal to raise an additional battalion of the Malay Regiment (which had been founded in 1933 to replace the Indian garrison in the FMS and consisted of two battalions in 1948) was not implemented, and in 1949 a frontier force was set up under police control.

Singapore:—

(v) The situation in Singapore has up to now been a good deal less difficult than in the Federation, though there is evidence that we must be prepared for the possibility of trouble. The Governor is recruiting twenty-five additional commissioned police officers, of whom one will be a Gurkhali-speaking officer, four will be locally promoted Asiatic inspectors, and twenty officers selected from this country. I am endeavouring to obtain as many as possible from among the ranks of the former Palestine Police.

(vi) In addition 600 special constables and a considerable number of unpaid part-time volunteers are being raised in Singapore.

Equipment of the police

4. Measures are being taken here to expedite the despatch of all the equipment required by the police. The authorities in Malaya have telegraphed statements of outstanding orders and new orders which they wish met quickly, and already a substantial part of their requirements has been despatched by air and by fast passenger vessel. Three items are causing a little difficulty which will, I hope, be quickly overcome. The Malayan authorities asked me for 10,000 carbines. These are not obtainable in this quantity: I have asked them to accept Stens or Lanchesters instead and am awaiting their reply. They have just asked me for 200 mobile wireless sets and supply possibilities are under urgent investigation. (The need for these, to enable forces to be summoned urgently to points of attack, is obvious.) They also require five armoured reconnaissance cars and 70 armoured cars. The War Office have offered instead 100 Lynx armoured cars and a reply from Malaya is awaited. The Lynx cars can be shipped quickly.

Strength of the garrison

5. My colleagues will wish to have a statement on this subject. In paragraphs 16 to 19 of C.P.(48) 171 I gave a brief summary of the plan of operations proposed by the Commissioner-General after consultation with the civil and military authorities. The plan of operations was drawn up in two phases, phase 1 consisting of the measures required to restore law and order in the settled areas of the territory, to maintain the economic life of the country, and restore morale, and phase 2—the further measures necessary to liquidate the guerilla bands whose headquarters are in the jungle. In submitting this plan of operations to me the Commissioner-General said that the C.-in-C. Far East Land Forces,[6] considered that the military forces available to him were, for the time being, sufficient, with some additional assistance from the Royal Air Force. The 1st Inniskillings are being moved from Hong Kong to Singapore, and the additional air assistance required, which consisted of sufficient O.P. Flights to bring the total up to five Flights, is being provided. The Commissioner-General and the civil and military authorities have recently assured me that they have sufficient forces to ensure that phase 1 is successful.

6. I have now received a telegram dated 14th July from the Acting High Commissioner, Kuala Lumpur, reporting representations by the leading Malayan rubber and tin interests, who assert that unless the situation is cleared up in a few

---

[6] General Sir Neil Ritchie was commander-in-chief, Far East Land Forces, 1947–1949.

months they cannot guarantee to continue production, a demand as an immediate reinforcement two further brigades. The Acting High Commissioner, Sir Alec Newboult, is discussing this matter with the British Defence Co-ordination Committee.

7. The number of troops required for phase 2 depends, as already indicated, upon the success of phase 1, and I was warned by the Commissioner-General that if phase 1 went badly an additional Division of troops would be required for phase 2. I have since seen Ministry of Defence telegram to G.H.Q. FARELF (COSSEA 653) of 14th July warning FARELF that there will be great difficulty in sending reinforcements on a large scale for phase 2, and that there is no prospect of sending a division; one brigade is being earmarked for reinforcement should this be essential, and the possibility of sending another brigade is being considered.

160 CAB 128/13, CM 52(48)5   19 July 1948
[Proscription of the Malayan Communist Party]: Cabinet conclusions

> [The government had been reluctant to ban the MCP for a number of reasons: lack of proof that the party itself was instigating violence, belief that a ban would merely drive marked men underground, desire to maintain a progressive approach and concern about the political repercussions of proscription. On 17 July, however, largely on account of 'urgent representation' from MacDonald, Creech Jones and Bevin accepted the need to ban the MCP and other related organizations. Attlee was notified the same day and Creech Jones raised the question in Cabinet on 19 July (see PREM 8/1406/2).]

The Secretary of State for the Colonies informed the Cabinet that there had been no marked change in the situation in Malaya in July. Terrorist activities had continued, and over thirty persons had been murdered by bandits during the month. The Commissioner-General, South-East Asia, had now reported that he had conclusive evidence that the Malayan Communist Party was actively responsible for planning and directing this campaign of violence and terrorism. This was now well-known in Malaya and the local Government were being criticised for failing to take action against the Party. The Commissioner-General therefore proposed that the Party, together with certain other political parties with Communist connections or sympathies, should be proscribed on the ground of their subversive activities. He had made it clear that there was no question of imposing restrictions on political opinions or discussion.

The general view of the Cabinet was that, in the light of the information received from the Commissioner-General, the Malayan Communist Party should be declared an illegal organisation. The House of Commons should be informed of the decision in advance of the debate on Colonial Affairs on 22nd July. The Commissioner-General should be asked to provide fuller information regarding the nature of the evidence implicating the Malayan Communist Party in the present wave of terrorist activities.

The Cabinet:—

(1) Agreed that the Commissioner-General, South-East Asia, should be authorised to declare the Malayan Communist Party, and certain connected parties, to be illegal organisations.[1]

---

[1] In addition to the MCP, government also banned the Malayan People's Anti-Japanese Army Ex-

(2) Invited the Secretary of State for the Colonies to ask the Com General for fuller information regarding the evidence implicating these p the present campaign of violence.[2]

(3) Invited the Secretary of State for the Colonies to consult with the Pr Le Minister regarding the terms in which the decision noted in Conclusion (1) above should be announced in Parliament.[3]

Servicemen's Association, New Democratic Youth League, Ikatan Pemuda Tanah Ayer (or PETA, a Malay youth movement which succeeded API after the latter was banned in July 1947), and the Indian New Democratic Youth League.

[2] Watertight proof of MCP involvement was still lacking months later (but see 162). According to a CO assessment in early Oct, although in 'Malaya the evidence of direct connection between the Cominform and the present outbreak of lawlessness as organized by the Malayan Communist Party is accepted by the local Government as proof of such connection', it was 'a connection which is only by chance susceptible of absolute proof'. Nonetheless, a wide range of circumstantial evidence provided 'substantial grounds for regarding the Malayan outbreak as stimulated from Moscow' (CO 537/2638, Fortnightly review of communism in the colonies, to 8 Oct 1948). In May 1950 an MCP pamphlet, whose title translated as *Present day situation and duties*, reached the attention of ministers. Produced in June 1949, captured some time later and transmitted to London in Nov, this document satisfied the Cabinet Malaya Committee that there had been a 'communist plot' to topple the Malayan government (see 215; cf PREM 8/1406/2, MAL C (50)12, 12 May 1950 and DO (50)42, 1 June 1950, and also CAB 21/1682 and CAB 134/497).

[3] Creech Jones made the parliamentary announcement on 23 July as follows: 'The Commissioner-General in Malaya has reported to me that *he is satisfied on the evidence* [emphasis added] that the Malayan Communist Party has been mainly responsible for planning and arranging for the carrying out of the present violent attack on established government *and the campaign of murder of peaceful citizens* [emphasis added]; and is the mainspring in the present disturbances and the directing and nerve centre of the whole subversive movement.' The two emphasized passages indicate Attlee's amendments to Creech Jones's draft: the first replaced the phrase 'substantial evidence exists' and may suggest an attempt to distance the government from the commissioner-general's assessment; the second was inserted probably to draw attention to the plight of ordinary people in addition to the difficulties being experienced by the colonial authorities (see *H of C Debs*, vol 454, vol 787 ff, and also PREM 8/1406/1).

161 PREM 8/1406/1, DO 16(48)3   13 Aug 1948

'Malaya—present situation': Cabinet Defence Committee minutes on military reinforcements

The Committee had before them:—

(a) A telegram from the British Defence Co-ordination Committee, Far East, re-examining the need for further reinforcements from [sic] Malaya and recommending that a brigade with certain ancilliary [sic] troops be despatched as reinforcements.

(b) Two telegrams from the Commissioner General, South East Easia [sic] and from the acting High Commissioner, Malaya, urging support for the despatch of additional reinforcements.

After the Chief of the Air Staff[1] had drawn the attention of the Committee to the need for bearing in mind the assistance that might be given by the Dominions in this situation, the Chief of the Imperial General Staff then gave his considered appreciation.[2]

---

[1] Lord Tedder was chief of the air staff, 1946–1949.

[2] Lord Montgomery was chief of the imperial general staff, 1946–Oct 1948.

despatch of reinforcements at the present time to any part of the world needed
al thought. The policy governing the size and shape of the army had been to
its essential structure in the course of a rapid run-down from its war-time size.
same time they had to meet operational commitments throughout the world
.id to continue with the training of recruits. This policy had been decided on the
assumption that there would be peace and our immediate post-war commitments
reduced. Many of these commitments had not been reduced and the extra effort
required of the army had so far been managed. Now that further reinforcements were
required His Majesty's Government would need to face a big risk.

The world was now very far from peaceful and the army was getting very stretched.
If the training machine and the essential structure of the army was affected, they
would be unable to handle any big emergency. Part of the army intention in the
move towards its peace-time shape was to have three infantry brigade groups
available for reinforcement to any part of the world in support of our foreign policy.
The formation of these brigade groups had been delayed because of present
commitments, but the first brigade was nearly ready.

The three main trouble areas were Western Europe, Middle East and Far East. To
which area was this first brigade to be sent?

As he saw it, the situation in Western Europe was not such that it could be said to
be "alight". In any case, if there was trouble in this area one brigade would be of little
use. Therefore, we could take a risk in the west.

In the Middle East the commitments were so heavy that the army was under severe
strain to meet them. The size of the army in the Middle East was nearly down to its
peace-time garrison of one division and one brigade. At the present time there was
one brigade in Greece, one in Egypt, one in Tripoli, two battalions in Eritrea and one
battalion each in Mogadishu and Somaliland. The Middle East was not *at the
moment* alight, but there was very serious trouble brewing. There was no doubt that
any reinforcements we had would be needed there very soon.

The situation in the Far East was "alight" now. In Burma, one-third of the
Burmese army had defected to Communist forces. In Malaya the trouble was not only
local but was instigated by Chinese Communists and kept going by Communist
reinforcements from across the Siamese border. The situation had not been firmly
handled in the first place—the police force had been weak—but the fact was that
Malaya was the only place in all three areas where we were actively fighting against
Communism and it was British Empire territory. Moreover, our own nationalists
[nationals] were being killed. We could not stand this nor could we afford to lose
Malaya to Communism.

His conclusion was that we should take the risk in the West and in the Middle East,
and his recommendation was that immediate help should be sent to the Far East
because it was needed now.

There must be no delusion, however, that by sending one brigade to the Far East
the situation there would be solved. The arrival of the brigade would help stabilize
the position and improve morale but it was not the long term solution. This would
require a thorough re-organisation of the internal security forces of the Colonies in
the Far East, including such measures as the establishment of a Home Guard,
reinforcements and re-organisation of the police, and in addition it would probably
require three or four divisions to clear up the whole situation. The latter reinforcement was clearly out of the question.

The Chief of the Imperial General Staff said he had been asked the previous evening by the Australian High Commissioner what was to be done to meet the Malayan situation, and after receiving his reply the Australian High Commissioner had been emphatic in his recommendation that His Majesty's Government should ask the Australian Government if any assistance could be provided.

In sum, his recommendation was that immediate help should be sent to the Far East and that Australia should be asked to provide assistance. Provided the Ministry of Transport could make the ships available, the brigade group could be got ready to leave by about the end of August.

In the discussion which followed the Ministers were agreed that preparations should be put in hand at once to send the brigade to Malaya by the end of August. The discussion then turned on what approach could be made to the Dominions. On the advice of the Chancellor of the Exchequer[3] and the Secretary of State for Commonwealth Affairs[4] it was thought inappropriate to approach either Pakistan or India. They were unlikely to accede to the request because of the commitments in which they were involved. On the other hand, the change of outlook on the part of Australia held out some hope that assistance would at least be considered, if not forthcoming. The approach would need to be made on a Prime Minister to Prime Minister basis.

After the Secretary of State for the Colonies had endorsed the Chief of the Imperial Staff's appreciation and his recommendation that it was necessary to send reinforcements now, he explained that all measures possible were being taken to reinforce the Malayan police and to create jungle fighting units.

The Committee:—

(a) Invited the War Office in consultation with the Ministry of Transport to proceed as urgently as possible with the preparations for the despatch of a brigade to Malaya by the end of August.[5]

(b) Invited the Secretary of State for Commonwealth Affairs, in consultation with the Minister of Defence, to prepare a draft telegram for the Prime Minister to send to the Prime Minister of Australia[6] enquiring what assistance could be given to meet the situation in Malaya.

---

[3] Sir Stafford Cripps was chancellor of the exchequer, 1947–1950.

[4] Philip Noel-Baker was secretary of state for Commonwealth relations, 1947–1950.

[5] Three days later Cabinet approved a press release on the despatch of an additional brigade to Malaya (CAB 128/13, CM 56(48)6, 16 Aug 1948).

[6] John Curtin, leader of the Australian Labor Party, was prime minister of Australia, 1941–1949.

162   CO 537/3753, no 35   15 Aug 1948
'Effect of action by the governments in Malaya to counteract Malayan Communist Party plans': supplement no 11 of 1948 issued with Malayan Security Service Political Intelligence Journal no 15/48 of 15 Aug 1948

[Controversy as regards the aims and objects of the MCP and the extent to which the federal government ignored warnings of imminent insurrection raged at the time and since (see 160, note 2). The Malayan Security Service, the quality of whose intelligence was hotly discussed, presented its account two months after the Emergency was declared and in such a way that, as J D Higham minuted, the 'moral the reader is obviously intended to draw is that Singapore acted in accordance with M.S.S. advice and retained control of the situation, while the Federation did not'. He then went on to give his view that, while 'there is some justification for saying that the authorities were not given full warning of the scale and manner of the attack . . . my own belief is that armed insurrection was intended all along once the country had been "softened up" by economic dislocation' (CO 537/3753, Higham to Paskin, 30 Sept 1948).]

The following is a brief outline of events leading up to the armed insurrection of the Malayan Communist Party including action taken by the Governments of the Federation of Malaya and Singapore and the effect of that action.

During the months of February and March 1947 there was considerable labour unrest throughout Malaya particularly in Singapore. It appeared at that time as if the Malayan Communist Party was preparing for a trial of strength and about to instigate a general strike throughout the whole of Malaya. Towards the end of February the situation was very critical and the Singapore Government proceeded to make administrative arrangements whereby they could arrest and banish some of the leading Communist instigators of these strikes. Before these administrative arrangements could be made, however, the strikes ceased and the psychological moment for action was lost. From then on, the Malayan Communist Party proceeded to consolidate their position through their policy of "rightist opportunism". They extended their control over organised labour, they infiltrated into Nationalist Parties and gained a large measure of control over pseudo-political parties. They took a leading part in opposing Government's constitutional programme. They were behind, through their secret agents, the formation of the PUTRA/A.M.C.J.A. They organised the Malayan-wide Hartal which took place on the 20th November 1947. In addition to their activities among labour and political parties they intensified their propaganda activities among Malays, particularly among the peasants in the more remote areas. They endeavoured to obtain control over the Malay peasants through the Peasants Party, the KAUM TANI, and they obtained control of the Youth Movement, A.P.I., which was the Youth Movement of the Malay Nationalist Party. This Youth Movement, A.P.I. was subsequently banned by the Malayan Union government, but shortly afterwards its place was taken by another Youth Party, PETA, which came under direct Communist control.

During the whole of this time there was ample evidence to show that the Malayan Communist Party kept in being the Malayan People's Anti-Japanese Army. They recruited youths through the New Democratic Youth League. Military training continued throughout the year, not only among the Chinese but also among members of A.P.I. and PETA. It was known that the Malayan Communist Party possessed a large number of arms and ammunition hidden in the jungle throughout the country. Some of these were uncovered by the Police and gave an indication of the large number of arms available to the Communist Party.

The strikes instigated in South Kedah by the Communist Party among Indian labour during the early part of 1947 were of particular significance. It showed that they could incite Indian labour to violence and it is significant that the Communist BALAN[1] was particularly active in Perak during most of the year among Indian

---

[1] R G Balan, a communist and promoter of strikes in Perak, was arrested in May 1948 and detained for ten years.

labour and that by May 1948 he had obtained a large measure of control over Indian labour in North Malaya. The activities of the Malayan Communist Party were not confined to any particular area. They were particularly active, however, in the States bordering Siam. This may have some significance which will be seen in the future. There was evidence, both documentary and otherwise that their objective was revolution and the control of the Government of Malaya and there was definite indication that their ultimate objective was the Communist Republic of South East Asia.

During 1947 it was possible to bring a number of criminal charges against some of these labour agitators, but their arrest and conviction had little or no effect on the Communist organisation, and their plans proceeded apace. The end of 1947 found the Malayan Communist Party in a stronger position than they were at the beginning of 1947. They had a larger measure of control and influence among organised labour. They had infiltrated and obtained a large measure of control of Nationalist Movements both Malay and Indonesian, and they controlled Youth Movements throughout the country. They had made a further approach to the Malays under the religious cloak of the Supreme Islamic Council and later through the pseudo-political party Hazbul Muslimin.

1948 began with comparative calm in Singapore, but in the Malayan Union, particularly in the North, there was considerable labour agitation among the Indians. Leading Indian agitators, particularly BALAN, were active throughout Malaya. APPADURAI was arrested and convicted on 10th January for criminal intimidation. His place, however, was quickly taken and the labour agitation proceeded without a break. In Negri Sembilan the struggle for power between the Negri Sembilan Rubber Workers Union and the pro-M.I.C. Indian Labour Union was intensified. In February labour agitation in the Malayan Union, which had now become the Federation of Malaya, shifted farther South. The Singapore Federation of Trade Unions sent GURUDEVAN to Seremban to direct the activities of the Communist controlled N.S.R.W.U. in an attempt to break the influence of the Indian Labour Union among Indian labour on rubber estates in Negri Sembilan. BALAN continued his activities in Perak and turned his attention particularly to Cameron Highlands. A new Farmers and Cultivators Union at Cameron Highlands applied for registration, the president being an ex M.P.A.J.A. officer with headquarters in the premises of the New Democratic Youth League at Ringlet. Strikes started on Lima Blas Estate in South Perak which were later to have some significance. Agitation among labour in Kedah continued, while Selangor also had its troubles. The Pan-Malayan Federation of Trade Unions held its second anniversary meeting on 11th February in Singapore at which attempts were made to disassociate it completely from the Malayan Communist Party, but at the same time tribute was paid to the guidance of the World Federation of Trade Unions. The P.M.F.T.U. at that time called on the Singapore Federation of Trade Unions to provide seasoned workers for special organisational duties in the Federation of Malaya. An analysis of Trade Unions under Communist control at the end of 1947 by the Pan-Malayan Federation of Trade Unions discloses that in Kedah the Communist Party controlled 90% of organised labour, in Penang they controlled 85% and in Johore 69%. Action taken by the Government of the Federation of Malaya included an order by the Registrar of Trade Unions for the dissolution of the All-Malayan Rubber Workers Council and on 18th February prohibited all registered Unions from contributing to the funds of the unregistered

Pan-Malayan Federation of Trade Unions and to the unregistered State Federations of Trade Unions. MANIVELLU, the general secretary of the Kedah F.R.W.L.U. was convicted of criminal intimidation and was sentenced to 18 months R.I. In Selangor the Transport Services went on strike and the Road Transport Department arranged with private bus companies to take over the more important routes. In Singapore signs of labour unrest began to show themselves and it was disclosed that the Malayan Communist Party controlled 70% of the Labour Unions in Singapore and that they were ready for a trial of strength with the Government. BALAN had by this time succeeded in planting his agents in all large labour forces on rubber estates throughout Perak and in spite of his obvious Communist Party connections he was permitted to register a new union, the Planting Labourers Union of Perak State. The Kinta Rubber Factory Workers Union was also registered. This too was under Balan's influence and as soon as the union was registered it presented demands to the managements of the various rubber factories throughout Kinta. In Selangor the Government set up a Board of Arbitration in an attempt to settle the strike of the General Transport Company. The Communists attempted to bolster up the strikers' morale and threatened "black-legs" and talked of sabotaging the company's buses. The strikers returned to work, however, on the 23rd March, while the final decision on all disputed points was left to the Arbitration Board. There was unrest among the Harbour Workers Trade Union at Port Swettenham and intimidation took place on a number of estates where strikes were either in progress or threatened throughout the country. In Johore further strikes broke out.

In addition to the brief details of the Communist Party activities during 1947 mention should have been made of the formation of the Singapore Workers Protection Corps. This was a "strong-arm" corps organised by the Malayan Communist Party for the purpose of intimidating workers and forcing them to strike. The strongest units of the Protection Corps were in the Singapore Harbour Board and in the rubber factories, and in addition to the Singapore Workers Protection Corps, the Indian Section of the Communist Party formed the THONDAR PADAI, also a "strong-arm" corps, used for the purpose of intimidation. This THONAR PADAI even made arrests and held summary trials of members of Trade Unions who failed to obey the orders of their leaders. The THONDAR PADAI was not confined to Singapore alone. There were units of it throughout the whole of Malaya, wherever the Communist Party had any influence or control. In March there was an increase in labour agitation throughout Malaya, including Singapore.

On the 5th April, the Pan-Malayan Federation of Trade Unions began its ten day Third General Assembly in Singapore. The Singapore Malayan Communist Party representative gave an address of welcome, while LAM SWEE,[2] the Chairman, claimed—"The Third General Assembly to be full of fighting significance to end all hallucinations and to decide on a new policy." The Pan-Malayan Federation of Trade Unions also took an interest in Ceylonese labour which had been imported into the country and it was obvious that they considered the possibility of this labour force being used as strike breakers, if and when they attempted to organise a general strike throughout the country. Of the 27 members of the Central Council of P.M.F.T.U., 18 were known Communists and 13 Central Executive Committee members were also Communists.

---

[2] In June 1950 Lam Swee would be the first major defector from the senior ranks of the MCP.

Communist agitators were particularly active in Penang and on the 18th April the Secretary of the Penang Federation of Trade Unions stated that it was decided at the P.M.F.T.U. Congress in Singapore, "that the time had come for all Trade Unions to take the offensive. It was necessary that labour should be prepared to sacrifice their lives in the cause of labour." BALAN and his newly-registered trade union was active. His agents began to instigate strikes throughout Perak. His Union claimed membership of 13,700 covering 133 estates and BALAN on a visit to Sungei Karuda Estate stated that his Union is "now strong enough to fight it out with anyone." At the same time it was noted that BALAN was extending the membership of the I.N.D.Y.L. which was under direct Communist Party control. New Branches of the THONDAR PADAI were being organised throughout the country. In Singapore tension began to increase. The approach of Labour Day, May 1st, was to be the opportunity for the Communist Party to show its strength and convince any waverers that the Communist Party was powerful enough to defy the Government.

On 1st April 1948 information was received of pending changes in the Party Plans and that there was likely to be conflict with Government within one or two months. On the 2nd April the Singapore Federation of Trade Unions held its first Labour Day Meeting where it was decided to stage a mass assembly and procession through the streets of Singapore. On 9th April the Singapore Harbour Labour Union issued pamphlets and posters inciting labourers to violence and strikes. Meanwhile at a secret meeting of the Committee of the S.H.L.U. the date for the strike was fixed for April 15th. On the 12th April the Singapore Federation of Trade Unions issued a pamphlet entitled "Outlines of Propaganda. The Commemoration of May 1st Labour Day 1948." All this preparatory propaganda for May 1st was inflammatory and more intensive than during any previous year.

The pattern now became clearer. Additional information from secret sources showed that the Singapore Harbour Board was to be the principal target of the Communist Party. The Party had complete control of the Union and the Protection Corps could be used to enforce its orders. A strike of Wharf Labourers would be called on 15th April which would spread to all other branches of the Singapore Harbour Board workers.

On May 1st the Malayan Communist Party intended to stage a mass assembly and procession of 100,000 labourers through the streets of Singapore, controlled and directed by the Malayan Communist Party marshals and the Singapore Workers Protection Corps. It was their intention that the whole of the centre of Singapore would be under the control of the Communists and that any interference by the Police would be met by violence. The experience of the funeral procession of the notorious Communist LIM AH LIANG in August 1947 gave the Party every reason to be confident of their success. The result of the show of force would intimidate the population of Singapore and would be followed by sympathy strikes of the Habour workers which would spread to all centres of labour in Singapore, culminating in the complete stoppage of all essential services, shipping, transport etc. This was intended to coincide with further incitement to violence in the Federation of Malaya. Efforts had also been made to coordinate the activities of the Habour Labour Unions of Penang and Port Swettenham to ensure united action with the Harbour Workers in Singapore. On the 12th April 1948 the position in Singapore was extremely critical, although on the surface there was apparent calm. On the 13th April 1948 the Government of Singapore, as a result of information made available to them, decided that despite the apparent calm a serious situation existed and that immediate action must be taken. It was decided that banishment warrants should be issued against the leaders of the Chinese Section of the Singapore Harbour Labour Union who had issued a pamphlet which was regarded as seditious and a[n] incitement to violence and bloodshed. At the same time it was decided that the proposed Labour Day procession should be banned. On the 14th April 1948 the Police raided the premises of the Singapore Harbour Labour Union and arrested four of the leaders. Documents were found with the names and descriptions of many of the active members of the Singapore Workers Protection Corps, Singapore Harbour Board Section. The premises of the Singapore Federation of Trade Unions were raided on the same day and also the premises of the Indian Section of the Singapore Harbour Labour Union. Efforts were made on the 15th April 1948 by the Singapore Federation of Trade Unions to rally the Unions to demand the release of the leaders of the Singapore Harbour Labour Union but the issue of further warrants of arrest on the 16th April 1948 for other leaders of the Singapore Harbour Labour Union resulted in the disintegration of the Union and the remaining leaders went into hiding. Thus began what became known as "Operation Bull-dog". It was the policy of the Singapore Government to arrest on banishment warrants those labour agitators and Communist Party members who were in any way implicated in strikes in which intimidation or other criminal acts had taken place or were threatened. The operation was to be continuous and not spasmodic. As new leaders came forward so they too would be arrested until the power of the Communist Party over the Trade Unions was broken and intimidation of the workers ceased. The Indian Section of the Singapore Harbour Labour Union, however, under the President, VEERASENAN, continued to make every effort to continue the Malayan Communist Party strike policy and assaults and intimidation of Chinese workers by Indians took place, culminating in two incidents where handgrenades were thrown. On the 26th and 27th April prompt Police action resulted in the immediate arrest of one of the perpetrators and information obtained from this man resulted in another raid on the Singapore Federation of Trade Union premises in search of an accomplice. Between the 16th and 20th April five more Singapore Harbour Board workers were arrested for being members of the Protection Corps and were charged in Court. The four leaders of the Singapore Harbour Labour Union were also charged in Court and the production of the Protection Corps documents and the list of members had the immediate effect of causing the disintegration of the Corps. Some leaders fled from Singapore and members destroyed all documents in their possession and went into hiding. VEERASENAN himself went into hiding when subpoenaed by the Criminal District Court to give evidence in the case against the four leaders of the Singapore Harbour Labour Union. It was most fortunate that the Singapore Government had retained the full powers given to it by the pre-war Societies Ordinance. If this Ordinance had been amended as it has been in the Federation of Malaya this prompt and salutory action could not have been taken against the Singapore Workers Protection Corps.

On the 22nd April 1948 the Singapore Federation of Trade Unions received a letter from the Police refusing a permit for a procession in Singapore on May 1st, although an assembly at Farrer Park was permitted. On the 26th April at a meeting held at the Singapore Federation of Trade Unions it was decided that the Police ban on the procession should be defied and on the 28th April 1948 A.V. RAJAGOPAL, Assistant Secretary of the Singapore Federation of Trade Unions wrote a provocative letter to the Colonial Secretary containing the ultimatum that unless the ban was lifted Government would be solely responsible for any outbreak of violence as the Singapore Federation of Trade Unions proposed to hold the procession regardless of the Government ban. The Government replied to the Chairman on the same day by banning the assembly at Farrer Park as well as the procession and a Government Gazette notification was issued banning assemblies of five or more persons as and from the 1st May 1948 until further notice. Full Police and Military precautions were taken to ensure that the Government ban should be effective. On 29th April 1948 convictions were obtained in the Criminal District Court against the leaders of the Singapore Harbour Labour Union who were all sentenced to varying terms of imprisonment. Between the 20th and 29th April the Police had not only arrested two more members of the Protection Corps but had arrested the Indian responsible for the throwing of a handgrenade into a coffee shop near the Singapore Habour Board on the 26th April. A gang of Indians responsible for this incident and another grenade throwing incident on the previous day, were also arrested.

The Singapore Federation of Trade Unions met on the evening of the 29th April in very different circumstances to those of the meeting of the first Labour Day Preparatory Committee on the 2nd April.

The strike in the Singapore Harbour Board had failed owing to the arrest of the Communist leaders. Documents obtained by the Police had revealed that the proposed strike had been dictated and was not the will of the workers. The Protection Corps in the Singapore Harbour Board had disintegrated following the Police arrests and convictions and the publication of names and lists of members. The Singapore Federation of Trade Unions itself had been raided and implicated in violence in the Harbour Board. The challenge to Government and the demands for the release of the Union leaders had been met with firmness and the open threat to Government had resulted in the complete banning of all May Day assemblies and processions. Government had taken the initiative at the psychological moment and had maintained it. The Singapore Federation of Trade Unions found no other course than to abandon its proposed show of force and workers were instructed to accept the Government's rulings. "Operation Bull-dog" had succeeded in its first phase. May Day passed off without incident.

Although the Singapore Harbour Board has been, and still is, the most important centre of Malayan Communist Party activities the Singapore Rubber Workers Union was one of the main targets for Communist propaganda and a powerful weapon in the hands of the Malayan Communist Party. The continual strife between the owners and workers made the Rubber Factories in Singapore Communist strongholds. With the loss of the Singapore Harbour Board the Malayan Communist Party turned its attention to the Rubber Workers Union and on the 29th April the first issue of a publication was issued of the "Voice of the Workers" and was distributed in Singapore mainly among Rubber Factory workers. The first issue of this anonymous publication contained direct incitement to violence and the three articles were entitled:

(1) "Welcoming the New Struggle."
(2) "The Steadfast Struggle of the Wharf Workers Smashed the Plot of Government and the Employers."
(3) "The Bloody Incident in the Bin Seng Factory Awaits Vengeance. Abandon the Idea of Lawful Struggle."

On the 10th May and Bin Seng Rubber Factory was burnt down and the damage was estimated at $1,750,000 and there was clear evidence of arson. On the 14th May 1948 the third issue of the "Voice of the Workers" was published in which the burning of the Bin Seng Factory was described as retribution of evil for evil. Information was received that the "Voice of the Workers" was being printed at the Singapore Fisheries Workers Union which is a Malayan Communist Party-controlled organisation. On the 22nd/23rd May this Union was raided and although no evidence was found to prove that this publication was printed in those premises, it is noteworthy that since that date there has been no further issue of the "Voice of the Workers." "Operation Bull-dog" continued, banishment warrants were issued for the arrest of the Communist leaders of the Rubber Factory Workers, and the arrest on 3rd June 1948 of KHO SUI GOAN, president of the Singapore Rubber Workers Union had an immediate effect. Protests against his arrest were ignored and once again it was proved that the arrest of one so-called leader had the desired effect of removing a source of intimidation which was appreciated by the community as a whole.

The Malayan Communist Party returned to the attack at the end of May with the object of regaining complete control of the Singapore Waterfront by the end of August. Members of the Malayan Communist Party and Protection Corps (now known as the Liberating Army) infiltrated into the Harbour Board to organise the workers. By this time "Operation Bull-dog" was making itself felt and the continual Police action and arrest of leaders was making the workers chary of joining secret organisations which advocated violence. The first Malayan Communist Party representative sent to the Singapore Harbour Board in May 1948, WONG EE SENG, was elected president of a newly-formed Singapore Harbour Labour Union. His responsibility was to organise a strike in three months' time and not to enter into any negotiations. There would be arson and sabotage at the same time. He was arrested and his arrest resulted in the dispersal of his assistants. During July 1948 two other leading members of the Malayan Communist Party and of the former Protection Corps returned secretly to the Singapore Harbour Board to carry out the same plans. Both have been arrested and in their statements confirmed the information already in our possession. It is noteworthy that by the end of July the Singapore Harbour Board had successfully selected and re-registered a permanent directly-employed labour force of 952 stevedores and 840 wharf labourers and that there has been no stoppage of work in sympathy with the Communist terrorists in the Federation. Continual Police pressure by raids in town areas, as well as in outlying districts, has had a marked effect on the morale of the population and "Operation Bull-dog" has succeeded in maintaining a grip on a situation which could have easily become completely out of control. This grip must not be released. Banishment has once again shown itself itself to be the most powerful weapon against the revolutionists and the Government's action in using the banishment weapon against so-called leaders has been thoroughly justified by the proof which has emerged that these men hold their power through intimidation and not through the spontaneous support of the workers.

Short details of events in the Federation of Malaya during April have already been given. May 1st passed off comparatively quietly in the Federation, probably as a result of the firm action taken by the Singapore Government in Singapore. May, however, showed further signs of labour unrest and resort to violence by labour, especially in Johore. In Penang the Communist Party made efforts to stir up trouble among the

Harbour labourers, and labourers were urged to assault any new labour employed and to assault their employers, to loot their shops and to assault the Police, if any members of the Harbour Association should be arrested. Arrangements were made to organise a Special Service Corps to intimidate "obstinate" merchants. The situation in Penang in the Oil Mills was similar to that in the Rubber Factories in Singapore. Discharged workers refused to leave and the Police were called in to evict them. The Indian merchant who gave evidence against APPADURAI, who was convicted of intimidation, was shot and killed. This had a bad effect on the morale of the merchants who then secretly began to pay the Harbour Labourers Association the difference between charges they demanded and those laid down by the Employers Association.

BALAN and his agents in Perak continued their activities. On the 3rd May 2,000 Indian and Chinese workers on Lima Blas Estate in South Perak went on strike without awaiting a reply to their demands from the management. Other estates in the area were told to strike in sympathy by BALAN and his agents. Inflammatory leaflets in Jawi and Tamil were distributed by BALAN's agents. BALAN was particularly active visiting all branches of his newly registered Labour Union. Intimidation became wide-spread. Chinese Labour Contractors were threatened and a number of assaults took place. Propaganda throughout the Federation was intensified and labour leaders exhorted their followers to fight to the death to achieve their demands. On the 17th May ONG SWEE LIONG, the manager of a rubber factory near Ipoh was shot dead. He had recently dealt firmly with labour agitators. On the following day a smoke-house belonging to the same rubber company was burnt down. Communist agitation among workers in Saw-mills in other areas was intensified. The Communist Press both in Chinese and English urged the peasants to unite to struggle against British Imperialism. Violence and threats of violence by striking labourers continued. The Police were forced to send parties to guard both personnel and property on estates to protect them against striking labourers. The strikes spread to Selangor and Communist agitators at Port Swettenham joined in the negotiations between the striking Harbour workers and the employers. The dispute was settled finally by direct negotiations in spite of the fact that Government set up a Court of Enquiry. The setting up of this Court of Enquiry had a salutory [sic] effect on the strikers and this led to the publication of a paper by the president of the Pan-Malayan Federation of Trade Unions denouncing Government's action in setting up this Court of Enquiry. After the strike ended, however, there were two cases of arson and a European, employed by one of the labour contractors was assaulted. On a rubber estate where Indian labour was prepared to return to work they were prevented from doing so by the Chinese labourers. The Chinese labourers slashed 1,400 trees. Offensive posters in Tamil appeared on estates throughout Selangor. A European manager of another estate was attacked by labourers while evicting a dismissed kepala [ie headman]. Negri Sembilan Rubber Workers Union instigated strikes in Negri Sembilan. On another estate the police were called in and when they attempted to take seven of the strikers away for interrogation they were prevented from doing so. On an estate in North Johore all the labourers observed May Day as a holiday except the Malay labourers. Those who were under Communist Party control chased the Malay labourers away and then assaulted the British Assistant manager who was taken to hospital. A Police party of 60 went to the estate and were met with violence from the strikers. Order was restored but on the 11th May the entire labour force stopped work. A Police patrol detained two Chinese and three Indian suspects but they were attacked by the labourers and forced to retreat leaving the arrested men behind. Later a Police party found a young Tamil who had been giving information to the Police locked in a Hindu Temple, having been taken there to be tortured. When they were questioning him labourers surrounded them. Police reinforcements were called and four persons were arrested after the Police had charged with batons. The arrest of the leading Chinese agitator in this area lessened the tension. He was found to be in possession of documents which were obviously of Communist origin. They included printed propaganda and one document was the agenda of the Communist Party Branch meeting. They also included instructions to resort to violence, sabotage, seizure of cash and goods and contained orders that Commissioners of Labour should be ignored if called on to arbitrate unless the employers showed willingness to compromise. On another estate a European was prevented from inspecting his estate by the workers who adopted a menacing attitude, and threatened to tap the trees themselves if they did not get full satisfaction. Force had to be used to effect entry to the estate. Rubber Factories were burnt down on a number of estates. Chinese armed with sten guns held up an estate staff and took goods and money. On other estates Police were called in, often arriving in insufficient strength to be effective.

We have seen how the fight for the control of Rubber Unions in the Federation has gone on over a long period and that Indian Communists led by BALAN endeavoured to gain control of rubber estates throughout the Country. We have seen how in February 1948 the Communist Party began to instigate strikes in the Federation and in March the Communist Party propaganda amongst labour throughout the Federation was considerably intensified. The Penang Federation of Trade Unions issued a booklet entitled: "Malayan Trade Union Movement and the Chinese Revolutionary Strife", calling upon workers to intensify the political struggle and to support the war of liberation in China. One article concluded: "Upon the successful consummation of China's Democratic Revolution the day of realization of Malaya's Democratic Government will not be far distant." These were not the only symptoms of impending unrest in the Federation. Information was received from many sources of intensified Communist activities among the Malays. Reports were received of drilling and military training and reports that the Communists and their satellite organisations were preparing for some important event. We have seen how the Communist Party activities amongst labour was [sic] synchronised throughout Malaya. Orders were given to Labour Unions to defy the ruling of the Registrar of Trade Unions in the Federation, particularly over payment of money to the Federation of Trade Unions. A recruiting drive for the N.D.Y.L. was made and intimidation was used in this recruiting drive which led to the arrest of seven members of the League. Labour in many areas became more truculent and in many instances, violent. Arson and sabotage took place. May Day passed without any major incidents, mainly due to the action taken by the Singapore Government, but May Day propaganda inspired by the Malayan Communist Party was issued on a wider scale than usual throughout Malaya. Support for the Malayan Communist Party was one of the key-notes, but the campaign of non-cooperation and hate against the authorities was the most prominent feature of the propaganda. All the propaganda was inflammatory and much could be interpreted as incitement to violence, some of which was bordering on sedition. The number of strikes increased as time went on and in the majority of them intimidation took place. Assaults on managerial staff on rubber estates increased in number and in a number of cases the Police were called upon to supply guards on estates to protect not only managerial staff, but also property. In some cases the Police were attacked and labour forces on estates were being encouraged by their leaders to resort to violence. The attack upon a Police patrol at Bukit Serempang, their retreat and the loss of their prisoners gave the strikers an exaggerated sense of their own strength. As was happening in Singapore acts of violence and intimidation were increasing. Full details of labour unrest throughout the Federation are recorded in the Political Intelligence Journals. But this labour unrest was not all—information was received and there was considerable confirmation of this information that the Malayan Communist Party was mobilising its armed forces under the name of the Special Service Corps. These in the Federation were organised much on the same lines as the Singapore Workers Protection Corps. It was ascertained that leading Malayan Communist Party members had disappeared from their usual haunts and information was received that they had gone into the jungle for a course of Military training. Another report from a usually reliable source stated that the Malayan Communist Party Mobile Corps was formed in Perak with selected ex-M.P.A.J.A. members, led by YONG LAM, the president of the Perak M.P.A.J.A.. Information was also received that the M.P.A.J.A. ex-Service Mens Association, Trade Unions and other organisations affiliated to the Malayan Communist Party were instructed on May 29th to remove all photographs, list of names and other documents which might be of use to the Police and be ready for the closing down of open operations as from June 5th, when terrorists [sic] action against all hostile to the Malayan Communist Party would commence. Information received from a separate source confirmed the formation of this Corps and stated that it would be armed and be ready to move into town areas by June 5th. Information was received from Johore that the populace had been warned to grow local produce, with which to feed guerilla bands. This was similar to a separate report in which the objective was "Preparedness for the World War." From secret sources, late but reliable, it was known that on April 15th the M.P.A.J.A. Central Association in Kuala Lumpur had issued instructions to State Standing Committees to spare no efforts to safeguard the identity and whereabouts of members of this Association. Information on registration forms concerning specific duties, present address and permanent addresses of members should be left blank or if already filled in should be obliterated. Another late report graded A.1 stated that a Kota Bahru member of the M.P.A.J.A. returned to Kota Bahru on April 30th with 500–3 star badges which were distributed in Kota Bahru, Kuala Krai, Pasir Mas and Tanah Merah. Further evidence of a Communist Party uprising was supplied by the discovery of hand-grenades and ammunition in a raid upon a camp in South Kedah. Several arrests were made and documents were found indicating that this camp was being run by the Malayan Communist Party. A recently opened arms and ammunition dump was found by the Police. It was also noted that CHANG MING CHING, the open representative of the Malayan Communist Party was preparing to go undergound.

During May in the Federation there were eight murders, two attempted murders and five cases of arson. The Malayan Communist Party campaign of terrorism had begun.

There was one outstanding event in May and that was the arrest of BALAN in Ipoh under the Restricted Residence Enactment. He had, however, provided for his arrest by planting trained agents in all areas in the North of Malaya. Protests by Communists and Labour Unions were made against his arrest, but beyond making these protests they took no further action, but continued their campaign among the labour forces.

Mention has already been made of the intensified Malayan Communist Party propaganda throughout Malaya. On the 1st June 1948 the Ming Sheng Pau, published in Kuala Lumpur, became the official organ of the Malayan Communist Party with Liew Yit Fun[3] as its editor. This newspaper became more and more inflammatory and on the 9th June the editor, Liew Yit Fun, was arrested on a charge of sedition. The newspaper, however, did not cease publication as the result of this arrest and it was not until June 17th that the Police raided the Ming Sheng Pau Press, and other buildings in and around Kuala Lumpur where property of the Press was to be found. A total of 63 persons were detained on these premises and of these five were identified as persons of major importance. The Press was closed down and the closing of the Press meant the closing of the "Combatants Friend," the organ of the M.P.A.J.A. and "The Vanguard" and the "Munani" the Chinese and Indian organs of the Pan-Malayan Federation of Trade Unions. These were the first important arrests to be made in June.

During the first two weeks in June there were 19 cases of murder and attempted murder and 3 cases of arson. At the beginning of June plans were made for the arrest of those persons who were known to have taken a leading part in strikes in which criminal intimidation or acts of violence had taken place, but these plans were never put into effect. From the 8th June onwards plans were ready for concerted raids on branches of the Malayan Communist Party and its satellite organisations, the M.P.A.J.A., N.D.Y.L., PETA and KAUM TANI, in spite of the fact that it was already known that most of the important leaders had already gone underground and that instructions had been issued by the Communist Party for the destruction of important and incriminating documents. On the 18th June Emergency Regulations were published in the Federation. On the 20th June a signal was sent to the Police in all States in the Federation ordering them to carry out an operation to which the Federation Police gave the code word "Frustration". On the 21st June Operation "Frustration" was the searching of the premises planned early in the month and the arrest of the leaders of the Communist Party and its satellite organisations under the Emergency Regulations. Many arrests were made, but as might have been expected, few important leaders were arrested and few important documents were found in open premises. Operation "Frustration" did little to upset the Malayan Communist Party's plans which are summarized on pages 409 and 410 in the P.I.J. published on the 15th June 1948.

There had been another event of some importance early in June and that was the revision of the Trade Union Enactment in the Federation of Malaya which enabled the Registrar of Trade Unions to order the closure of all State Federations of Trade Unions and the Pan-Malayan Federation of Trade Unions. This act deprived the Malayan Communist Party of powerful weapons and a prolific source of income.

By the end of June the Malayan Communist Party terrorists [sic] campaign was in full swing. While during the first half of June there were 19 cases of murder and

---

[3] Liew Yit Fun, a Eurasian, had formerly been political secretary of the second regiment of the Anti-Japanese Army and in mid-1947 had been 'open' representative of the MCP.

attempted murder in the second half there were 26 murders, 22 attempted murders and 2 cases of arson. The stage had been reached when attacks on Police Stations and isolated villages were being made, and the cold-blooded murder of three European rubber planters left no doubt as to the anti-white nature of the Malayan Communist Party's campaign. Finally on July 23rd when there could be no doubt of the responsibility of the Malayan Communist Party for this campaign of terrorism the Malayan Communist Party and its satellite organisations, the M.P.A.J.A., N.D.Y.L. and PETA were proscribed by both the Federation of Malaya Government and the Government of Singapore.

163   CO 537/3758, nos 16/18   23 Aug 1948
[Disorders and ways of enlisting Chinese support]: letter from Sir T Lloyd to Sir F Gimson and Sir A Newboult

[Two months into the emergency, CO officials were becoming perturbed that the necessary military campaign against Chinese insurgents would alienate the bulk of the Chinese community whose support was essential in order to push ahead with what J B Williams called 'all those plans of social progress and development which are normally a feature of British Colonial Administration' (Williams to Seel, 19 Aug 1948, CO 537/3746). During the weeks spent preparing for his Malayan assignment, Gurney worked on the problem of how to enlist Chinese support and formally responded to Lloyd's letter soon after his installation as high commissioner (see 168).]

The daily reports about the struggle to get the upper hand of the terrorist campaign continue to present a fluctuating record of success and disappointment, and there is still no definite indication of that lessening, for which you must be looking anxiously, of the heavy strain under which all of you in the Malayan area, especially the Federation, have been working. At the moment it seems as if at last the counter measures are beginning to bear some fruit. Of course, it is far too early to say, and doubtless there will be many disappointments, but we have noticed with great satisfaction a new aggressive note in the daily police reports from the Federation. These read as if the terrorists now by no means have it all their own way.

In spite of that, it is clearly going to be a long business before terrorism is altogether liquidated, and in that prospect of a long pull there clearly lurks danger. The danger we fear is that, by the very fact of their continuing resistance against authority, men who were at the start no more than a band of thugs preying on the law-abiding members of the community may attract to themselves some of the glamour of national heroes. It is already a prime aim of Russian and other Communist propaganda to bring about precisely this result—i.e. to get the terrorists recognised as fighters for liberation. Unfortunately, too, past history shows that this danger can be real. The dividing line between the terrorist and the fighter for freedom is not always so clear in the minds of the outside world or the people of the terrorists' own country as it seems to us.

The moral of this is, of course, not for a moment that we should relax our campaign against the terrorists—indeed the exact contrary, for it is the long drawn out struggle which mobilises popular support for such people. But it does point to the need for seeing that Government has a programme which commands not merely acquiescence of the people of the country but their enthusiastic support, and that we are not gradually, and against our will, being forced into the position of Europeans fighting the Chinese, or at least of Europeans and Malays together fighting the Chinese.

We should be glad to know whether you and Newboult,[1] to whom I am also writing, feel that this danger is real in Malaya. If it is are there any further measures which we could take to mobilise Chinese support behind us more effectively than hitherto? Reports which we have seen from Malaya have spoken of the Chinese community as sitting on the fence. We realise that the main reasons for this attitude—if it exists—are doubt about our ability to protect the law-abiding Chinese and eventually to liquidate the terrorists, and also the uncertainty which many Chinese feel about the eventual outcome of the struggle between the K.M.T. and the Communists in China itself. As the efficiency of our counter measures increases we may hope that these doubts may be overcome as far as concerns our position in Malaya itself. But even so there may be room for more active efforts to enlist the enthusiasm of these people. Men will suffer far greater risks if their heart is really in a cause than if they are merely indifferent to it. Indeed, the history of Sun Yat Sen's crusade is very clear evidence that the Chinese are prepared to suffer a great deal once their enthusiasm is really roused. If there are any new lines of policy which might secure more active support from the people against the terrorists we will gladly do all we can to help in furthering them.

It seems particularly difficult, at least for us here in London, to know what the ordinary Chinese man or woman is thinking. The explanation may be that there is a gap in our knowledge in London. But there are some indications that the Malayan Administrations themselves may be less closely in touch with Chinese opinion than they are with Malay. Far fewer officers in the Malayan Civil Service speak Chinese than Malay, and in spite of the various official reports which we get, covering Chinese affairs, we seem to have a far less clear impression of what the Chinese want than what the Malays want. This was certainly the case, for example, at the time of the discussions leading up to the establishment of the Federation. (We are, of course, thinking here not of intelligence in the police sense,—not of information about criminals and subversive movements—but of a general picture of what the ordinary law-abiding person in the different communities is thinking and feeling, what are the motives for his actions, and what is likely to arouse his interest and enthusiasm.)

We recognise that the Chinese community is traditionally, almost notoriously difficult to get in among, but this very difficulty seems an additional reason why we ought to make a specially intense effort now to do it. Another reason why this question seems to have special importance just now is the unpredictable course of future events in China itself. If Communist successes there increase and the Kuomintang Government is finally reduced to powerlessness, it will become more than ever important that we should know the minds of the Chinese domiciled in our own territory and be able to appeal to their interest and enthusiasm. It may, of course, be that the latter task would become impossible, but we should clearly do all we can to maintain our influence with them.

We can, of course, point to a good deal that we have done. Apart from the restoration of settled Government and the opportunity to resume trading in conditions of security, we have given the Chinese the means of acquiring citizenship

---

[1] 'Gimson' was substituted for 'Newboult' in the otherwise identical letter to Newboult.

and of participating in the Government. We have also launched the University project. All these things one would assume in ordinary circumstances would make a particular appeal to the Chinese, even if in some respects, such as the present constitution in the Federation, they do not go quite so far as some of them would like. The questions which we would like you to turn over in your mind, in such leisure as you are likely to obtain in present circumstances, are whether there are any other things which could be mooted as likely to make an active appeal to the well-disposed section of the Chinese, without arousing hostility in other quarters; and also how far you think we have taken adequate means to understand their thoughts and aspirations, or could do more to this end.

These questions scarcely admit of an early or easy answer, but I am sure you will agree that we ought to be searching for one.

I am sending a copy of this letter to MacDonald.

164 CO 537/3756, no 1   24 Aug 1948
[Dato Onn, Sir Edward Gent and the workings of the federal government]: personal letter from Mr M J MacDonald to Mr Creech Jones about Onn's mistrust of the late Sir Edward Gent and his threatened resignation   [Extract]

[MacDonald became a staunch believer in Onn's potential as leader of the Malayan nation but Onn's mistrust of the British and swings in his mood, which CO officials would experience at first hand during his visit to London towards the end of 1948 (see 173), tried the patience of other administrators.]

This is a brief warning that we may in the near future be faced with Dato Onn's resignation from the Federal Executive Council and from all other Federal bodies. I hope that we can prevent him from taking this step, but he may insist on it. The origins of this trouble go back to Gent's administration. As you know, Dato Onn and Gent disliked each other intensely, and neither Dato Onn nor many of his Malay colleagues trusted Gent. They never forgave him for being one of the authors of the Malayan Union, and after the inauguration of the Federation I am afraid that he did many things which made them feel that he was trying to make the Federation into the Union under another guise. I have reported to you earlier, partly in writing and partly orally during our talks in London, some cases where Gent, not only in the opinion of the Malays but also in the opinion of his Chief Secretary, Attorney-General and other principal officials, broke or tried to break the spirit, and sometimes the letter, of the Federal Agreement in order to concentrate power in Kuala Lumpur and take it away from the States. There were many cases of this, but after my return from London in May I did not trouble too much about them for I knew that Gent would be leaving in August and that a new High Commissioner would have an opportunity to tidy up the matter. One trouble with Gent was that he did a lot of things without telling anybody, and his officials in Kuala Lumpur and I here only heard about them when the Malays complained bitterly weeks afterwards.

2.   Sir Alec Newboult largely agreed with the criticisms of Gent's policy, but felt helpless to correct his mistakes in more than a few cases. In their loyalty to the High Commissioner, he and his colleagues kept a lot of their misgivings and disagree-

ments with him to themselves, and therefore the Malay leaders gained the impression that they all agreed with Gent, and that the Kuala Lumpur administration as a whole were resolved to work the Federal Agreement in an improper way to the prejudice of State rights and responsibilities. Over and over again Dato Onn's temper reached boiling point, when he used to come to me and I had to calm him down and tell him to be patient. I could not, of course, tell him a solution was at hand in the impending departure of Gent, but managed to persuade him to carry on as a duty to the Malays and Malaya.

3. When Newboult became Acting High Commissioner I hoped that early action could be taken to correct the administration of the Federal Agreement, and bring it into conformity with the letter and spirit of the Agreement. Unfortunately, but inevitably, Newboult got so involved in the hectic work of dealing with the emergency that consideration of this larger problem got postponed. I told Dato Onn, shortly after Newboult's accession, that Newboult agreed with many of his criticisms of past practice in Kuala Lumpur, and that changes would soon be inaugurated. However, this did not happen immediately. Without Newboult's realising it, the machine of government in Kuala Lumpur went on working as Gent had ordered it to work, and the invasion of State rights and liberties continued. Dato Onn's patience gave out again. . . .

165   CO 537/3687, no 51   31 Aug 1948
[Appointment of Sir H Gurney as high commissioner]: inward telegram no 1067 from Mr M J MacDonald to Mr Creech Jones about Malay criticisms

[Since the Cabinet had refused the rulers' request for the right of concurrence in the appointment of the high commissioner (see part I of this volume, 128, note 3), their views were not taken into account at the time of Gurney's selction. Both the method of his appointment and the new high commissioner himself (in particular Gurney's lack of Malayan experience) aroused opposition from the rulers and their *mentris besar*. Although the British government refused to compromise the authority of the Crown in this respect, MacDonald pressed for some concession, and at the end of the year he was assured that 'His Majesty has accepted the principle of prior informal consultation subject to the definite understanding that no legal limitation is thereby placed on his prerogative and that the discretion of his Ministers in submitting to him the name of the person most suitable for the appointment is not thus infringed' (Lloyd to MacDonald, CO 537/5760, 24 Dec 1948). MacDonald later became a great admirer of Gurney, privately describing him as 'the outstanding Colonial Governor within the whole of his experience' (CO 537/5962, T Lloyd to J Paskin, 5 Oct 1950). As regards procedure, after Gurney's assassination and during the secretary of state's visit to Malaya in Dec 1951, Lyttelton was punctilious in keeping the rulers abreast of prospective changes at the top of the administration.]

Following from Commissioner General.

My unnumbered telegram of 25th August.

Newboult and I had informal discussion with the Rulers and Mentris Besar this morning on appointment of new High Commissioner. It was a very difficult discussion and attitude of Malays was definitely unfriendly.

2. They raised two points. The first was person of new High Commissioner. They urged strongly that either someone who had previously served in Malaya like Milverton or Macpherson should have been appointed, or Sir Alec Newboult. In reply

to reminder that previous High Commissioners had frequently been appointed without any previous experience of Malaya, they answered that in those days High Commissioners[,] advisers and officers from Chief Secretary downwards had been men with long experience and knowledge of Malaya and its problems but that this condition now only partially existed. They are extremely apprehensive lest a High Commissioner from outside will not (repeat not) appreciate importance of protecting special position of Malays. They feel there is a particular danger of this in the case of Gurney whose Palestine experience may make him inclined to think that, like Arabs and Jews, the Malays and Chinese in Malaya should be treated as races with equal rights.

3. Regarding the method of appointment, they concurred it has been in accordance with terms of Federal Agreement. But they strongly expressed view unsatisfactory result of method in this case showed that they were right in urging that during negotiations Rulers should be consulted before an appointment was made. They revived arguments that Federation agreement set up a partnership between the King and (corrupt group) [ie words garbled in transmission] Malay Rulers and that the High Commissioner not only represents the King but also in many important matters has powers delegated to him by Rulers. They said that is was contrary to spirit of the Agreement that no consultation whatever with Rulers should be held prior to a new High Commissioner's appointment.

4. Regarding their plea that an ex-Malayan official or Sir Alec Newboult should be appointed, I explained: —

(a) Candidates like Milverton and Macpherson had been considered only to be rejected on grounds of health in the first case and Nigerian appointment in the second and
(b) Sir Alec Newboult's physical strength was unlikely to enable him to carry on in top post for an indefinite period. I praised Gurney's qualifications and countered suggestion that he would arrive imbued with the idea that Malaya is a second Palestine. I pointed out that in any case only $1\frac{1}{2}$ out of his $26\frac{1}{2}$ years of service had been spent in Palestine.

5. With regard to method of appointment, we insisted that it was wholly in accordance with Agreement which they and we had recently (group omitted) and that therefore they could not reprove His Majesty's Government for their action. We reiterated that their original proposal for prior concurrence by Rulers would have involved an invasion of His Majesty's prerogative.

6. The discussion developed along very difficult lines, it being reiterated by several speakers that this was an illustration that His Majesty's Government did not intend to observe the spirit of partnership which inspired the Federal Agreement. Interspersed with this general argument were constant suggestions that Gurney's appointment should somehow be undone. They were especially insistent that he should not arrive in Malaya until the present emergency is over, but this argument was presented as of minor importance to their main contention that the High Commissioner should be a man with previous knowledge and understanding of Malayan affairs.

7. Newboult and I stuck firmly to line that they could not question the method of appointment employed and that Gurney has excellent qualifications for the post.

8. At the end of nearly three hours talk, the Malays showed no sign of yielding.

They now propose to give us further deliberations in a letter tomorrow morning, and it may be that when they come to compose it, they will decide to make their protest in moderate terms.

9. We recommended that announcement of Gurney's appointment should be published at six (repeat six) o'clock G.M.T. on Thursday, which means that it will appear in Friday morning's papers in Malaya. We shall have to wait and see what the reaction is. There can be no wavering in the decision to make appointment and to publish it, but we cannot pretend that Malays are at all happy about it or that they have been appeased by any of our arguments.

10. Regarding text of communiqué proposed in paragraph 1 of your telegram No. 293, we strongly urge that phrase "formerly Chief Secretary, Government of Palestine" should be omitted. Any special reference to Palestine will aggravate criticism. The balanced account of Gurney's career contained in biographical note which we shall issue with communiqué puts Palestine episode in its proper perspective and shows Gurney's experience is much wider.

11. We will telegraph to you contents of Rulers' letter referred to in paragraph 8 above.[1]

---

[1] A copy of this letter, dated 1 Sept 1948 and signed by the Sultan of Selangor as president of the Conference of Rulers, is at CO 537/3760.

166   CO 537/3687, no 52   1 Sept 1948

[Appointment of Sir H Gurney]: inward telegram no 214 from Mr M J MacDonald to Mr Creech Jones about the timing of Gurney's arrival

Following personal for the Secretary of State from MacDonald. *Begins.*
Paragraph 1 of your unnumbered telegram 14th August.
We all look forward to welcoming Gurney, but I am glad that your proposal is that he should not (repeat not) arrive here until about the end of September.

2. Newboult continues to do well and his physical fitness is holding admirably, though he has to take some care of himself. I still consider it of very great importance that he should remain in top command at Kuala Lumpur until the worst and most hectic period of the emergency is passed. Newboult and his colleagues would have to spend much time teaching new man about the situation, which would be an unfortunate addition to their heavy labours.

3. As you know, some leakage about Gurney's appointment appeared in local newspapers several days ago. We are seeking to trace the origin of this. In the meantime it is significant that as a consequence there has been a good deal of press and other comment to the effect that Newboult should be left in charge until the emergency is over, and that no new High Commissioner should be introduced in the meantime. Apart from other considerations, I think it would be wise from the point of view of Gurney's getting a friendly and good start here that we should take note of this point.

4. I am happy to know that Gurney's reactions to your original proposal of High Commissionership to him shows that he himself appreciates and sympathises with this point.

5. We hope that the worst of the emergency may be definitely behind us by the

end of September. We cannot, however, yet be sure of this. During the last few days there has been a definite falling off in terrorist activities. At the same time our own offensive strength increases steadily and actions by the police and military are gaining more success. But it is too early to say with confidence that this double tendency will continue. It may be that the enemy (?are) organising fresh dispositions or plans with a view to a new all-out effort to cause trouble in September. We know that they themselves hope to complete what they call their mobilisation early in the month. We think that we have probably damaged this plan seriously and that their striking power is permanently badly crippled. But we are keeping our fingers crossed. The guerillas are still elusive and appear to retain a good deal of freedom and power to murder and burn in some places, e.g. central Johore.

6. If the present improvement does continue, about the end of September would be a wholly suitable time for Gurney to arrive. If on the other hand our difficulties increase in the early part of September, we may still be grappling with intensely grave troubles in the latter part of the month. In that case I would hope that Gurney's arrival might be postponed for, say, a couple of weeks. Perhaps we may leave this question of date open for a while. We should know during the next fortnight which way the situation is going to develop. *Ends.*

167 CO 537/3746, no 19   [Sept 1948]

'Future political and economic developments in Malaya': note by CO Eastern Department

1. Attached is a letter from the late Sir Edward Gent,[1] enclosing notes by Dr. Linehan,[2] a senior M.C.S. officer who had been seconded to the Secretariat for special service in connection with the constitutional negotiations last year, and Mr. Blythe,[3] then Secretary for Chinese Affairs, on the possibility of a strong independence movement arising in Malaya.

2. Ministers have urged the need for a plan, or at least a clear line of policy, for the political evolution of Malaya.[4] The moment may seem unpropitious for thinking about Malaya's political future (though a crisis often forces an administration to take stock), but it is clear that we cannot afford to lag behind events. The aim of "eventual self-government" has been made so much of in official statements and in the constitutional instruments themselves that we should have the next steps clear in our minds. We must, in fact, keep the initiative, and it is the purpose of this note to set down our first thoughts on the subject.

3. In the first place, we should like to have an early forecast of the dates by which elections, in some form or other, to State and Settlement Councils, and to the Legislative Council, can be introduced. We have no illusions about the length of time which it may take before electoral laws can be worked out and the machinery created. The example of Singapore shows that even with a wide measure of general agreement, or indifference, the actual mechanics of registration and the like can be expected to take the better part of a year. The danger is that our hand may be forced (as it is being forced elsewhere in the Empire). It is better for us to run risks of our own choosing than those which the mere pressure of events, or the growth of a heady

---

[1] Not printed.   [2] See 139.   [3] See 140.   [4] See eg 145.

political consciousness hurry us into. Ministers attach the greatest importance to the introduction of elected representation at the earliest possible moment, and it is very necessary that we should have an early expression of the views of the Federation Government on the subject.

4.   It seems to the department that the development of local government can play an important part in the political evolution of Malaya. In many colonial countries it is a training ground for the native administrator and an introduction to the ways of responsible government. It is a medium for stimulating a sense of responsibility for the conduct of public affairs. The Colonial Office and Colonial Governments have been much concerned in Africa, in particular, to lay the foundations for a sound system of responsible government at the centre by encouraging the effective participation of the people in local government, and by stimulating in the Africans themselves an interest in the processes, obligations and responsibilities of good administration. We find that our information in the Office on local government in Malaya is extremely scanty. With a few exceptions it seems to have escaped the notice of students, and the Office has not given it the same attention as local government in Africa, for example. We are familiar, of course, with the Sanitary Boards Enactment and the Straits Settlements Municipal Ordinance, and have some knowledge of the organisation of the mukim.[5] We noted (from the press) the erection of Kuala Lumpur into a Municipality in April. We have no evidence, however, about the *working* of these bodies, their efficiency, or the degree of public acceptance of, and participation in, their processes. In particular we have no idea of what part they can play in building up a system of responsible local government. The deduction from this is that these very important matters may not have had (as far as our records show) as much attention in Malaya in the past as they deserve.

5.   As a first step, we should be glad to receive any information which there may be readily available on the organisation, and problems, of local government in Malaya. We do not want to call, at this moment, for a detailed study for which the men or the time could ill be spared. It occurs to us that officers (not necessarily the most senior) with a good knowledge of the subject might be asked to call and talk to the Eastern Department about it. After learning the present situation, we should be ready for the views of the Federation Government on the future. An African Studies Branch has been organised in the Office for the study, *inter alia*, of the problems of local government in Africa. A summer school on local government was held last year at Cambridge, and its Report was adopted by the Conference of African Governors held last autumn.

6.   Now a different but not unrelated point. We have been looking into the measures which have already been taken to diversify the economy of Malaya, and in particular those designed to bring on the Malays in the fields of industry and commerce. An account of these measures is at Appendix A.[6] It is clearly impolitic, if no more, that the Malays should continue to be, in their own country, strangers to the enterprises that make it wealthy. This can only lead, in the long run, to frustration and resentment, however much the Malays are to blame for their complacent and lazy lack of interest in industry and commerce. Here too we should be grateful for the views of the Federation Government, both on the general question

---

[5] A *mukim* was the administrative sub-division of a district and supervised by a Malay *penghulu*.
[6] Not printed.

of diversifying Malayan economy and on the measures which should be taken to bring Malays into effective *economic* control of a significant part of the capital invested in the country's principal undertakings. At the moment the Malays, as a result of the Federation settlement are well on the way to *political* control—if only of a negative kind. The dangers of full political control by a community without a substantial economic interest in the major enterprises which outside capital has financed in their country is shown, for example, by the expropriations in Burma and by the crippling requirement so often demanded by countries such as Egypt that a fixed proportion of directorships, or of invested capital, shall be held by natives of the country. If we must look forward to the day when British political control will end in Malaya, we should not be resigned to the end of British investment and enterprise there; let Ceylon rather than Burma be our exemplar. We can build up the Malays' *economic* interest in the extractive industries (we suggest) in two ways. Some Malays can be brought on as individual capitalists, either operating themselves or investing in foreign-owned undertakings. On the other hand might it not be possible to build up some form of really large-scale cooperative enterprise? Tiny cooperatives are no good; it must be something so large that its production is a major factor in Malayan economy and the capital invested in it a significant portion of the total capital investment in the country. There need not be elaborate communal or cooperative planning. The enormous groundnut and cocoa crops in West Africa are the products of peasant enterprise fostered and directed, and perhaps point the way in Malaya. (In this connection will the development of liquid latex export stimulate small holding production?)

7. Ministers have remarked that the Malay is often conveniently forgetful of the state of the country before we came in during the last century. In particular, they tend to attribute the presence of the Chinese community in Malaya to the sinister machinations of the British, whereas we all know that our early intervention in the affairs of the Malay States was in many cases prompted by the inability of the Malays to control the Chinese who were already there. An occasional reminder, at some suitable time, might in the long run strengthen our position with the Malays. It would be a pity for a dangerous untruth to go on gaining credence.

168   CO 537/3758, no 19   8 Oct 1948
[Disorders and ways of enlisting Chinese support]: letter (reply) from Sir H Gurney to Sir T Lloyd. *Enclosure*: note on 'Groups in the Chinese community in Malaya'

[This letter was drafted before Gurney arrived in Malaya and was followed up by what O H Morris called 'a much more stimulating letter' at the end of Dec (see 172).]

The questions which you raise in your letter of the 23rd August[1] to Newboult on the subject of ways and means of enlisting greater support from the Chinese are not easy ones, as you realise, and in this letter I will do no more than set out certain aspects of the general problem, many of which will no doubt already be familiar to you. A

---

[1] See 163.

solution of the problem, in its long-term aspect, seems at the moment to be as far off as ever, but we fully recognise that it is essential that we should continually strive to find one and that, unless we do, the future outlook is black indeed.

In the first place I can say that I do not think that there is any serious danger of the bandits acquiring, in Malaya at least, the glamour of national heroes. They have of course already been so represented outside Malaya, but it is universally agreed here that the support which they get is almost wholly through intimidation and cannot by any stretch of the imagination be described as 'popular'. It is impossible to overstress the extent to which intimidation and extortion is practised. You will have seen evidence of this in recent intelligence reports which mention cases of Asiatic estates and mines who actually refuse offers of protection from the security forces, the reason being that they prefer to buy peace and quiet by paying a regular contribution to terrorist funds. The truth is that the Chinese are accustomed to acquiesce to pressure. It does not occur to them to do anything about it and a very few can intimidate a great many. Last year, for instance, a gang collected $10,000 a month from the inhabitants of Serdang, a village a few miles from Kuala Lumpur. This went on for some months until the Police finally broke up the gang. This sort of thing is going on all over the country to a greater or lesser extent according to whether any particular place is near to or some distance from a group of bandits. Squatters in bandit areas are under continual pressure.

Our first task is then to create confidence in Government's ability to exterminate the bandits, and I think we can say that steady, if slow, progress is being achieved. The arrival of the Police and Army reinforcements has undoubtedly helped to raise morale. As time goes on we can hope to secure more active co-operation from the Chinese, particularly in such an important matter as the supply of information to the Police, and also in the recruitment of part-time Police Auxiliaries. As to this, the Chinese general attitude is adequately expressed in the following extract from the Chung Shing Jit Pao (Singapore)[2] of July 24th:—

> "The auxiliary police, the special constabulary and other similar measures being taken by the Government are but passive defence measures. They contribute little, we are afraid, towards the wiping out of the terrorist menace. What is required to this end is to despatch troops to comb the jungles while static guards remain at their posts so that the terrorists have nowhere either to hide themselves or to create mischief. Once the people feel secure and have confidence in the ability of the authorities to wipe out gangsterism they will no longer hesitate to come forward and join the auxiliary police".

But when it comes to arousing enthusiasm, it has to be remembered that the great majority of Chinese who have had any education look at the situation against a much wider background than Malaya alone. However successful we may be here in stamping out Communism in the immediate future, they see the Communists in China in occupation of great tracts of the country and threatening to extend their control to the South, and Communist risings in Burma, Indo-China and Indonesia. They have seen the British pushed out of Malaya by the Japanese and they see the

---

[2] *Chung Shing Jit Pao* (1947–1957) was the organ of the KMT in Singapore and had a daily circulation of 4,500.

possible makings of another war between the great powers, which might again result in Britain being unable to defend Malaya either against an internal or an external enemy. There is therefore always the fear with them that at some later date if the Communists regained the upper hand, the families of those now taking an active part in resisting them might be victimised.

Another most important point is that, partly no doubt on account of Government's tolerant attitude towards dangerous and subversive left-wing movements since the reoccupation in 1945, many local Chinese who might have been prepared to give a lead to moderate Chinese opinion along peaceful and progressive lines compatible with Malay interest, have moved towards the K.M.T. as being the only party which can give them the protection which they feel they need. And the K.M.T. can never, as you will realise, be a Malayan Chinese party.

I enclose with this letter a short note on the four main groups which make up the Chinese community in Malaya. What we need to do is to encourage local-born and locally settled Chinese of intelligence and initiative who belong to one of the first two groups and who have no previous political affiliations, to come forward as leaders in local Chinese society, reconciling differences of opinion, encouraging their more timid compatriots, and promoting good relations between the Chinese and the Malays. They would have strongest motives for doing this as their personal interests are vitally connected with the defeat of Communism. It is in the highest degree unfortunate that Dr. Ong,[3] the most outstanding, if not the only, Chinese of this category who had shown real qualities of leadership, has been murdered.

Enclosure to 168

Group I. Local-born Chinese of at least two generations of residence in Malaya: their fathers are local-born
Products of English schools (which are inter-communal with active Old Boys Associations); English-speaking is their natural habit, and their knowledge of the Chinese written language is slight or nil. In Penang and Malacca some even cannot speak Chinese. Their feeling for China is only a sentiment, and they would be helpless if they returned there. They have married into families with a similar background and have relatives in different parts of Malaya. They seek careers in the local professions and with European business firms. With some exceptions they are not among the extremely rich Chinese in Malaya. Many of them are clerks.

Their natural loyalty is obviously to Malaya, the only country where their children can grow up in the same social and cultural atmosphere to which they themselves have been accustomed. This group certainly deserves an assured position in Malaya.

Group II. Local-born and English-speaking Chinese of the first generation: their fathers are immigrants
It is unlikely that the fathers of this group ever spoke English, and Chinese traditions are strong in the homes. Their families are apparently settling down in Malaya, with the children entering the family businesses or becoming clerks. Knowledge of

---

[3] Dr. Ong Chong Keng of Penang was a member of the legislative council; his murder in 1948 was not established as the work of the MCP.

English gives them an opportunity of extending their business interests and is an asset rather than a habit.

From the point of view of the possibility of a growth in Malayan consciousness, the future behaviour of this group is more important than that of any other group in local Chinese society. Recently established, they are more opportunist than those who have come to regard Malaya as their only home.

Political parties based on China such as the K.M.T. (or C.D.L.)[4] may appear to be the only appropriate organisations for protecting their class interests in Malaya from left-wing movements. In some parts of the country members of this group have already tried to control labourers through K.M.T. contractors. English-speaking Chinese of the first generation are found in varying degrees of sympathy with the K.M.T., a tendency which necessarily hinders the growth of a genuine Malayan conscious among this group.

Further, a Malayan Government policy which seemed to threaten the interests of this group would increase their affiliations with China-based parties because they would look towards China for the protection of their communal as well as their class interests in Malaya. They are therefore potential Chinese nationalists.

The extent to which this group sways between loyalty towards Malaya and loyalty towards China may be taken as an indication of the degree of confidence which the first-generation Chinese have that their position in Malaya is secure. If all goes well, they will in time become assimilated with the older group of local Chinese. Otherwise they may become the frontier force of a Chinese expansionist movement if the Nationalist Government of China survives the threat facing all non-communist Governments.

Group III. Local-born and non-English speaking Chinese of the first generation whose fathers were immigrants.

Group III can only be regarded as a menace, and its outlook presents a double threat to peace in Malaya; for this group must be divided into two sub-groups:—

(i)   Business men of varying degrees of wealth. What has been said of the latent sympathies of Group II can be said with much more emphasis of the members of this sub-group. Their outlook is entirely capitalist and Chinese which means that their affinities are with the KMT—the only party for Chinese business men in Malaya. They value Malaya as a place for making money and as a safe place to live in. If the local Government were unable or unwilling to maintain either of these conditions of their present political neutrality, they would certainly look to China for help. The difference in outlook between this sub-group and newcomers from China is slight.

(ii)   Members of the second sub-group constitute an even greater menace which cannot be stressed too frequently or too urgently. They are the labourer-sons of labourer-immigrants who still have as little in common with other Malayan communities as their fathers have. Their numbers are expanding in labour forces and squatter settlements and they can fairly be described as Chinese colonists in Malaya. They are hardy and prolific, and nothing can be done to convert them into Malayan citizens. Their outlook is entirely Chinese, and it must be remembered

---

[4] China Democratic League: a China-oriented radical party.

that an effect of the Japanese occupation has been to settle many of them on the land from which it is difficult to dislodge them. These squatter areas are Chinese colonies in Malaya, equipped with Chinese schools which intensify their Chinese outlook and riddled with Chinese secret societies.

Among this sub-group are found most of the left-wing leaders and guerillas.

IV. Newcomers born in China who are similar to (ii) of Group III only more so.

It may be possible, slowly, to achieve our object by giving some guidance as to the lines on which a genuinely Malayan Chinese Party might develop. The ideas on which it would be based would be:—

(a) a revulsion against Communism;
(b) an appreciation of the principles of British rule and policy;
(c) a recognition of the connection between the morale of local Chinese society and internal security.

This line of approach has the advantage too that it would not necessarily arouse hostility with the Malays as the Party would have as its nucleus those Chinese who are already Federal Citizens or are qualified to apply for citizenship; as you know, it would be politically impossible at present to make any attempt to widen the clauses of the Federation Agreement which lay down the qualifications for citizenship. These ideas have yet to be worked out in detail and, in doing so, the maximum use will have to be made of existing organisations whose members are either local-born Chinese or Chinese with established local interests.

The above, which had been drafted before my arrival, covers the various points in your letter. You will appreciate that it may be possible to say more on this subject a little later on.

169   CO 717/167/52849/2/1948, ff 108–110   25 Oct 1948
[Squatters]: inward telegram no 1326 from Sir H Gurney to Mr Creech Jones on measures to deal with alien Chinese squatters

[Before Gurney's arrival, the commissioner-general's conference at Bukit Serene, 12 Sept 1948, had identified squatters as the insurgents' source of food, had considered measures (including banishment) to control them and had agreed that an investigative committee should be set up (see CO 717/167/52849/2/1948, ff 119–122). This committee reported in Jan 1949. It recommended the resettlement of squatters largely on the land they currently occupied and the more intensive administration of squatter areas.]

Since my arrival, I have been giving most careful consideration to question whether measures being taken to meet terrorist situation are adequate. By what we have done we have to some extent restored confidence, increased the flow of information and killed or captured a number of bandits. It is true that their destruction is only a matter of time but it is time that matters. It is vitally important that we should prevent situation dragging on which we cannot afford financially or in any other way. Estates and mines are now fairly well protected but whole fields of operation lie wide open to the bandits, e.g. roads and railways, power lines and water pipelines and kidnapping. Attacks of this kind have already started. During the past week, there have been seventy-three attacks of all kinds, which is thirty more than the preceding

(?week omitted) and only three short of the highest recorded. In some ways we are on top of the problem; in others I feel that our troubles from terrorism have scarcely yet begun.

2. All my advisers are in unanimous agreement that we must make an immediate and serious attempt to deal with alien Chinese squatters who are providing bases from which bandits operate and are helping them, in some cases under duress and in many others willingly with food, arms, money and other means of resistance to our Forces. These people are a positive and formidable menace to security and a fundamental obstacle to the re-establishment of settled conditions. In many cases, they are illegally occupying land (which is an added reason for assisting bandits) and living in remote areas where Government writ does not run. They warn bandits of movements of Security Forces.

3. I went to Ipoh last week, partly to get first-hand impressions of removal by the Army of some 450 squatters from Sungei Siput area, which has been infested with bandits, and of their resettlement by the Government in Dindings area. Most of them were glad to go and the Chinese Consul himself expressed appreciation of arrangements made. Resettlement in other appropriate cases can and will be done but in several areas it will be impracticable and undesirable because it will merely disperse bad elements. I and my advisers are satisfied that the only answer to this problem is to require dangerous alien elements to leave the Federation.

4. This cannot be regarded as "banishment". It will merely involve sending back to their own country alien elements who have illegally entered the Federation and who are illegally occupying land here. They are disrupting the life of the country and there is no doubt that large numbers of them are actively assisting Communist bandits and unless their repatriation is effected, the position here is never likely to be cleaned up. Such repatriation is the action which would be taken by any other country in similar circumstances and we would, in the view of my advisers and myself, be failing in our duty to the people of this country if we permit these disruptive elements to continue to impede the restoration of law and order.

5. We have now some 3,800 persons detained but their term of detention is limited to one year by present Emergency Regulations. By Regulation 17, any detainee who objects has his case reviewed by an Advisory Committee under the Chairmanship of a person holding judicial office. Detentions on scale which is likely to increase place an unduly heavy strain on our Security Forces, who could be more usefully employed in re-establishing law and order.

6. A great deal of information is now coming in about what is going on in these squatter areas. Generalisations about squatters are dangerous and nearly all areas present different problems. They cannot be recited in a telegram and I must content myself with saying that an essential preliminary to tackling them is to possess power to repatriate rapidly.

7. My immediately following telegram contains draft of an Emergency Regulation empowering the High Commissioner in Council to order a detained person to (corrupt group ?leave) the Federation and remain therefrom. This would not apply to any Federal citizen or any British subject born in the Federation or in Singapore. I appreciate that when the Regulation ceases to have effect, such orders would also die.

8. Cases of banishment will continue to be dealt with under the Banishment Ordinance in accordance with procedure approved by you. I should repeat that what I am proposing is not banishment but repatriation of undesirable aliens to their own

country. It is a measure which will have the whole support of the law-abiding community here; one which will have a (group omitted ?salutary) effect on waverers and more especially on those aliens whose desire is to live under the protection of the Federal Government but who are now terrified by bandits into neutrality or worse; and one which I am convinced will do more to damage the course of bandits than any other step which can be taken at this stage.

9. Extent to which rich Chinese are contributing to bandit funds owing to extortion was brought home to me recently in Perak when several Chinese mine owners admitted to me openly that they were contributing up to $10,000 a month each. One of their number who had refused had been kidnapped and had not been seen since.

10. I do not wish to appear to be overstressing the financial effect of our failing to clear up the present situation but we are already in serious financial difficulties and I have learnt lately how much terrorism costs if it is allowed to go on.

11. I propose to place Draft Regulation before the Executive Council early in November and I trust that action I propose will receive your full support. I have considered all possible objections to this that occurred to me and am convinced that action on these lines is in future essential.

12. I am repeating this telegram by bag to Governor Singapore and suggest that in view of the urgency of the matter, he should telegraph his comments to you. I should be most grateful for a very early reply.

170   CO 537/3758, no 23   8 Dec 1948

[Disorder and ways of enlisting Chinese support]: letter (reply) from Sir F Gimson to Sir T Lloyd. Annex: memorandum by T P F McNeice, G C S Adkins and G W Webb[1]

I was glad to receive your letter of the 23rd August, 1948, on the subject of the attitude taken by the Chinese community in Malaya.[2]

This question has caused me considerable anxiety as I fear that there is a danger of injustice being done to the Chinese of these two territories. I am, therefore, looking at this problem possibly with a bias in favour of the Chinese whose activities on behalf of the internees during the Japanese occupation will always evoke in me a sense of gratitude for the bravery and courage they displayed in giving such assistance as they could. If any further apology is needed it can be found in the fact that the Malay angle has been stressed on many occasions so that it might be regarded as imperative that the Chinese angle should be viewed in its most favourable light.

I attach herewith a report which has been compiled by three Senior Officers who are closely in touch with the Chinese community. In fact one of them is married to a Chinese lady of a family of high standing in Malaya and one of the other two to a Eurasian who is partly of Chinese extraction. Their comments may be tinged by this

---

[1] T P F McNeice (secretary for social welfare), G C S Adkins (secretary for Chinese affairs) and G W Webb (secretary for internal affairs) in the government of Singapore.

[2] See 163 (for Gurney's reply to the same letter, see 168).

relationship and if they speak with more emphasis than is usual in official reports I am sure that you will appreciate their attitude.

Their remarks call for considerable attention but I should first like to explain one point which is not perhaps, universally appreciated. There is a tendency to talk as if the Chinese in Malaya were one homogeneous community and which for the most part, has no permanent loyalty to Malaya and no ties with this country.

This appreciation is scarcely correct as there is a considerable body of Chinese who are deeply loyal to Britain. They are to be found in Singapore, Penang and Malacca where they have been established ever since the British occupation, one hundred and fifty years ago. They are extremely proud of their British nationality and are a valuable asset to the British influence in South East Asia.

As indicated in the Report, this community, at any rate in Singapore, is very perturbed by the fact that their compatriots in Penang and Malacca are now subject to the legislative authority of the High Commissioner and to Their Highnesses the Sultans in Malaya. This is a matter of considerable concern to them and possibly, when the Federation was established their status as British subjects was not properly appreciated. In the Malayan Union, the formation of which was welcomed by the Chinese, there was no provision for the enactment of legislation except by the authority of the Governor.

I do not know if you have read the recent report of the Social Survey in Singapore[3] but this Survey attempts to show that a large number of the immigrant Chinese in Singapore have ceased to have much connection with their mother country and have come to Singapore to stay.

This Survey is the first of its kind to be made and disposes of many wide generalisations with regard to the Chinese community in this Colony.

In approaching this subject the Survey indicates that there is a possibility that Chinese have ceased to be a migrant population and have established themselves definitely in this country. This conclusion must be regarded with some caution but there is no doubt that once a family comes to Malaya its interests in Chinese politics tends to become a secondary matter provided they are given a chance to take some part in Malayan politics.

As a whole the Chinese recognise that their interests at the present time may best be served by the continuance of the British rule, provided the British protect their interests. This is the class of people who will form the majority in the future, if immigration is restricted and it is the policy of this Government that they should be taught to look to Malaya rather than to China. At present they are at the cross roads, undecided which way to take.

The attached report refers to the difficulties which many Chinese would experience in applying for British naturalisation, in that they have an insufficient knowledge of the English language. The necessity for this knowledge prevents a very large number of the members of the Chinese Chamber of Commerce from applying for naturalisation and so deters them from participating in the civil life of the Colony.

On the other hand the Legislative Council, in prescribing the qualifications for the franchise for election to that Council, were emphatic that it should be restricted to

---

[3] Department of Social Welfare, *A social survey of Singapore, a preliminary study of some aspects of social conditions in the municipal area of Singapore, December 1947.*

British subjects and to those born in Malaya. They went further and said that if any elector indicated that he had allegiances other than those to the British Crown, he would be automatically disqualified from voting.

The intention was that if a Chinese who had been registered as an elector, applied for a Chinese Passport, his name would be struck off the electoral roll.

This view was held most emphatically and in deference to the opinion of the Chinese who are British subjects I feel it must be supported, though I am aware that there is a contrary view that civic rights should be granted to citizens of other nationalities who have resided for some considerable period in British territory.

If any alteration could be made to facilitate the grant of naturalisation, such as non-insistence of the requirement of a knowledge of English, it is possible that many rich Chinese would acquire British nationality.

The Report again refers to the question of the members of the Malayan Civil Service who have acquired a knowledge of Chinese. I have already raised this matter with Gurney and a paper is being written on the subject for discussion at a forthcoming Governor's Conference.

There is also a reference in the Report to the re-establishment of the Chinese Protectorate. I regret that I have no personal experience of this Department but I feel that a step was made in the right direction when it was abolished and when other Departments undertook the duties previously performed by the Protectorate. The creation of a Social Welfare Department and the extension of the responsibilities of the Labour Department to Chinese workers are developments which are more in keeping with the modern trends of policy.

Incidentally, these Departments in Singapore are manned chiefly by officers who possess a knowledge of the Chinese language and customs.

Again, the policy which has been pursued in this Colony in the last few years in the matter of education has shown the interest of this Government in the provision of education for the Chinese and the educational plan provides, at the special insistence of Chinese unofficial members of the Legislative Council, for the extension of the teaching of English. This is a very satisfactory development as it lessens the tendency to spread K.M.T. and Communist propaganda through the schools.

The Report makes no reference to the necessity for the early establishment of a University of Malaya. I cannot over-estimate the importance of this, especially in the promotion of higher education for the people of this Colony so that they can take an increasing part in public affairs as well as secure additional appointments in the Government Service. The social atmosphere created in a residential university will obviously do much to develop a Malayan as opposed to a Malay atmosphere.

Carr Saunders[4] was impressed, when he visited this country, with the development of a political consciousness amongst the Chinese and thought that our attitude in the next few years would decide as to whether they would look towards Britain or China. The establishment of a University was, Carr Saunders considered, a vital factor in effecting this development.

Incidentally, it would enable the local population to achieve promotion to the

---

[4] Sir Alexander Carr-Saunders, director of the London School of Economics, 1937–1956, chaired the Commission on University Education in Malaya, 1947. The ceremonial founding of the University of Malaya took place at Raffles College, Singapore, on 8 Oct 1949 when Malcolm MacDonald was installed as its first chancellor.

higher ranks of Government Service and so remove what is regarded at the present moment as a failure on the part of the local Government to implement their promises for the further employment of Asians.

However, I have just heard that opinion has been expressed by the Chinese in Singapore that they see little use for the establishment of a University if the Chinese are not to be permitted to serve in the Federation. If they are deprived of this opportunity of employment the graduates of the future University will find difficulty in obtaining employment suited to their qualifications.

Dato Onn is reported to have intimated to the Secretary of State that the Chinese could be so employed and I have suggested to unofficial members that Dato Onn should himself give them that assurance.

I fear, however, that the present financial predicament of the Federation will not permit the establishment of the University on any large scale for some considerable time. This postponement would be most unfortunate but I think that a start could be made at an early date by the amalgamation of the Medical and Raffles Colleges.

As far as Singapore is concerned I consider that the grant of the franchise both in central and local government administration has done much to assure the Chinese of the intention of the British Government that they should participate in the administration of the Colony but from conversations I have had with them I find they are still very apprehensive of their position in the Federation.

I understand the Chinese community are quite satisified with the Malayan Union Plan and felt that they could take a part in Malaya which they had not taken hitherto. The present constitution of the Federation, however, was planned largely in conjunction with the Malay leaders and the Chinese community resented the small part they took in its formation.

My own opinion is that though they played but little part in its planning the final results give them a fair share in the administration of that territory.

However, the recent visit of Dato Onn to London and the reports of his conversations in the press have aroused their apprehension again that there will be a further constitutional development in favour of the Malays at the expense of the Chinese. This is most unfortunate as it will tend to widen the gulf between Singapore and the Federation so that all hopes of fusion will disappear.

I have advised the local Chinese leaders to approach Dato Onn as I am certain that he is a big enough statesman to appreciate that the cause of the Federation can be best served by the alliance between Malays and those Chinese who are loyal British subjects.

In addition the Chinese appear to feel that there is a lack of sympathy with their failure to assist the efforts in suppression of the present disturbances.

I will try to picture what might be their point of view though I cannot guarantee that I have formed a correct impression of it.

During the fighting of 1941/42 the Chinese played a considerable part in the defence of Malaya, and again during the occupation the resistance movement was largely manned by the Chinese. Of this movement the Chinese are proud and I have seen references in books to the exploits of members of the movement, the importance of which, as is usual in such cases, has been largely exaggerated.

The Chinese population possibly do not feel that sufficient justice has been done to the part they played and that they have not been given their fair share in the modern political developments, whereas the Malays, whose conduct during the occupation was not too praiseworthy, have been preferred to the Chinese.

They display, perhaps naturally, reluctance to assist the form of administration which has not done justice to the loyalty and support which they gave to the Allied cause.

I do not say definitely that this picture is correct but I have had some indication that there are their feelings. They are unfortunate, in that again they tend to widen the gulf between the Federation and Singapore with the result that fusion, unless handled extremely tactfully, is likely never to take place.

This fusion[5] between the two territories has, I fear, been widened owing to the lack of sympathy which, it is considered, Kuala Lumpur shows towards Singapore. I regard it as imperative that every effort should be made to assure the Chinese that their legitimate political aspirations will not be overlooked, and that the British Government has no intention of not according them their full place in the administration of the territories.

I deem any announcement will require to be carefully worded, so as not to offend the susceptibilities of the Malays.

Generally, I should say the policy of this Government in problems of health, social welfare, education and housing is regarded as being directed just as much to the betterment of the Chinese as to the Malays, and I do not consider that, as far as Singapore is concerned, there is any doubt in this respect. The doubts which are entertained are that the British Government should subordinate the interests of the Chinese to those of the Malays, and every effort should be made to ensure that this will not take place.

I am sorry to have written at such length on this subject but it is one on which much more could be written and I hope I have done something to put the Chinese in the picture as far as the future of Malaya is concerned, so that justice will be done to the part they have played in the past and will play in the future.

Annex to 170

In connection with Sir Thomas Lloyd's letter of August 23rd, it is perfectly true that the ordinary Chinese population of Singapore is to a very large extent out of touch with Government, and vice versa. It is a fact that this is a potentially dangerous position. The main reason for this is mentioned in paragraph 6 below.

2. The situation postulated in the letter of Europeans fighting the Chinese, or at least of Europeans and Malays together fighting the Chinese, is also a most dangerous one, but it is felt that this danger is not so great in Singapore as in the Federation, as we certainly have the support of the Chinese British subjects here. If however, we are to keep this and strengthen it further, as it must be strengthened, much more must be done to make them—and others too—feel that British nationality is something of great value, carrying with it privileges which those who are not British subjects have not and cannot obtain. We experience at the moment extreme difficulty in satisfying the local-born Chinese on their status. The problem of the dual nationality of the Chinese born in the Colony has always been a very thorny one for us. Dual nationality exists of course in other countries, but the problem is

---

[5] Gimson more likely means 'fissure' than 'fusion' in the context of this sentence.

greater here than in those other countries because of the numbers involved here. A far more precise agreement with the Chinese Government about the jurisdiction and powers of Chinese Consular officers in Malaya must be arrived at, and it must be made absolutely clear to the latter, through the proper diplomatic channels, that they have no jurisdiction over and no concern whatsoever with local-born Chinese while they are on British soil, and that the latter are not Chinese nationals until they set foot on Chinese soil. Frequent and emphatic statements to this effect should be made on all appropriate occasions and in the places where they will carry the most weight. This should go far towards clearing up the position and making local-born Chinese feel that they are valued by us and are incontrovertibly part of the Commonwealth.

3. There is considerable perturbation in the minds of some of the British-born Chinese leaders in Singapore over recent developments in the Federation and the purpose of Dato Onn's visit to London.[6] Recent Press reports of the latter's utterances in London have not discounted this perturbation,—on the contrary, the reported hardening of his "Malaya for the Malays" policy, (particularly his request for all Malay battalions of the Malay Regiment officered by Malays only) has made some of the Chinese leaders in Penang and Malacca, and consequently in Singapore too, fear that the policy of goodwill, trust and co-operation among the various communities in Malaya, which has hitherto progressed fairly smoothly, may become discredited and jeopardised. This feeling has been by no means allayed by Mr. MacDonald's assurance that there is no need for anxiety on that score, and many Chinese are beginning to wonder if they should not have supported Mr. Tan Cheng Lock more whole-heartedly in his opposition to the Federal proposals near the end of last year. Chinese Leaders are thinking now on the lines of:—

(a) appealing to the British Government to stand firm on the policy of a secure and proper place in Malaya for every community willing to co-operate for the good of the whole country.

(b) sending one of their number to England to present the Malayan Chinese point of view and so counterbalance the effects of Dato Onn's visit.

(c) asking for the restoration of the Straits Settlements so that there can be at least one place where all communities can live and work happily and peacefully together. (c) arises from a conviction that at the present moment British Nationality in the two Settlements of the Federation has little value. (Examples: possibility of banishment from the Federation of British subjects born in Penang and Malacca and the new Courts Bill 1948 in the Federation.) It is quite clear that the majority of Malayan Chinese favour the retention of British sovereignty in Malaya, as they realise that a Government composed only of Malayans without the British cannot preserve a proper balance among the various communities. The Malays also favour the retention for the moment of British sovereignty, but for a different and almost opposite reason! The most careful consideration should be given to measures which will eradicate this feeling of perturbation. This is primarily a matter for the Federation and the High Commissioner, but it has its repercussions in the Colony too.

4. On the question of British naturalisation, while relaxation in qualifications for

---

[6] See 173.

granting it is by no means suggested, it is felt that spoken and written English should not be insisted upon in cases where it is clear that the applicants have identified themselves completely with the country.

5. There is no doubt whatsoever about the difficulty of knowing what the ordinary Chinese man or woman is thinking. This is due in very large measure to the fact that there is an insufficient number of Chinese speaking officers in the administration. At present, a totally disproportionate number of M.C.S. officers are learning Malay and far too few learning Chinese. Out of 83 M.C.S. officers at present learning a first language, only 17 are learning Chinese. Of the 7 new Cadets to come to Malaya next year only 2 are to learn Chinese. 100% of all other officers engaged in administrative work speak no Chinese at all—a preposterous position in Singapore especially, where about 75% of the population is Chinese. That close day-to-day contact, particularly with the humbler section of the Chinese community, which is indispensable if we are to know what the ordinary man and woman is thinking is therefore lacking. The vast majority of the Chinese population, being non-English speaking, is very ignorant of the precise situation. They are affected mainly by gossip and word of mouth propaganda and such statements as we issue never reach them. They are bewildered, and because the British have failed once, they are afraid that they may fail again. They are out of touch with the Government; they do not understand it; and they regard it as something inevitable functioning on high without reference to their well-being. Arising out of this ignorance, we get the corruption which may be said to prevail throughout Singapore life. The non-English speaking individual who has to do anything which involves contact with a Government office has only one method of procedure owing to the fact that he cannot himself read the forms and regulations. He approaches some English-speaking clerk and proffers what he considers to be the correct sum of money. When he does this, he has no sense of injustice, no idea that he is doing wrong. To him it is the system. The fact that he has the right to demand certain things and to receive service in offices is quite outside his understanding. In other words, the Government does not represent to him a helpful force but merely a disagreeable necessity. Added to this is what might be called the "Secret Society complex" in the life of the ordinary Chinese, more particularly the China-born section of the population, which makes intimidation and extortion such a simple matter. "Secret Societies" have been the real makers of Chinese history. Many of the present leaders of the Communist Party in China served their apprenticeship with the Elder Brothers' Society in North China, while the Kuomintang has frequently had support of Triad groups. Any political or socio-political Party based on China must inevitably have these secret society characteristics, i.e. undergound pressure, intimidation, the impalpable influence which no-one dares to defy.

6. We are worse off now than we were in pre-war days. The difficulty was realised quite early and the Chinese Protectorate was set up to meet it. Ordinary day-to-day contact existed there, and the information so collected was collated and sifted and a balanced assessment of it presented to Government through the Secretary for Chinese Affairs. The Protectorate grew to be an extremely efficient organisation, respected and appreciated by law-abiding Chinese and feared by wrong doers. It was well known to all Chinese, from the highest to the lowest. They knew that they could be sure of a patient hearing there in their own language by European officers who understood them, and help in all their troubles, both great and small. Since the War

this Department has been abolished and its duties have not been handed over to any one organization; the S.C.A. who is the adviser to Government on Chinese matters is thus left "high and dry," a "head without a tail" as the Chinese so aptly put it. It is impossible to know the precise reason for such an important decision. It would, however, appear that the planners of the new Malaya felt that the existence of a specifically Chinese Department was inconsistent with the ideal of Malayan citizenship as it would perpetuate communal division. Administrative officers in these days are so occupied with problems of various kinds which did not exist in pre-war days that they have not the time to maintain that intimate contact with the people which we regard as absolutely essential not only for the acquisition of knowledge of what the ordinary man and woman is thinking, and why he is thinking on those lines, but also for the setting of that knowledge in its proper perspective. The new Civil Servant is expected to be an expert on various aspects of government and to pass on his knowledge to local officers who will eventually take over the Government. Any policy which does not lay full stress on the possession by administrative officers (and others as well) of intimate knowledge of the colonial people and territories is in our opinion bound to fail at the present juncture, however ideal it may appear to be for the future. The time has not yet come for the complete discarding of the old quasi-parental relationship between administrative officers and the local population. This relationship should be changed gradually, not completely overnight. The introduction into Malaya at a high level of officers with expert knowledge but no local or colonial experience is dangerous and can only lead to loss of public confidence. The real solution is that all administrative officers, and as large a proportion as possible of other officers should learn some colloquial Chinese (which is not as difficult as is sometimes made out). Only in this way can they inspire confidence and understand the local people and their outlook properly. Officers in the highest positions in the administration should have Chinese experience where possible, (pending the acquisition by all Chinese in the Colony of an education in English side by side with children of all other races.)

7. Free universal education in English is considered essential. Our ten-year educational plan is a start in the right direction, but not more than a start. Children of all races, if there is to be any attempt at Malayanisation, must start at the same level, with the same teaching, and the obvious language in which to carry this out is English. Educationists say that children must commence their education in their own vernacular. While we accept this dictum we have in Malaya considerations which reduce its force. In China the educational system in schools was started in the early 1920's with, as one of its main objects, the arousing of nationalistic feelings in the notoriously apathetic Chinese population and of anti-foreign feeling. All the textbooks are written with this object in view, and all the teachers are educated under this system. The failure of the Governments in Malaya to provide education for their Chinese populations has meant that this deliberately anti-foreign education has been stimulated and has flourished in this country. Secondly, it is not generally realised that children in Chinese schools in Malaya do *not* learn in their own vernacular. Mandarin (called in Chinese the "national language") is as much a foreign language to them as French is to an Italian. The most that can be said for it is that it is nearer to their own vernacular than is English. Thirdly, the original ten-year educational plan in Singapore has been modified to include "regional schools" which children of all races can attend. The parents in the areas to be served

by these schools are being asked whether they prefer English or vernacular schools. So far English schools are favoured without exception. In these schools the parent's language can be taught as a separate subject like any foreign language in a school in England. It is most significant that the majority of Chinese parents would prefer to send their children to a Government English school if there were sufficient accommodation for them. The Chinese schools are so full at present because there is not sufficient accommodation, and education in a Chinese school is considered better than none at all.

8.   It is obvious that any policy which has as its aim the welding into one of the various racial groups in Malaya within any reasonable period of time pre-supposes severe restriction of immigration. Such a measure is indicated on economic and educational grounds alone, if no others, in view of the current rate of increase in the local populations (approximately $2\frac{1}{2}$% per annum) and our difficulties in housing and feeding our present population. Immigration has for some months past been severely restricted and the most careful consideration is being given to the problem at present.

9.   To sum up, it is recommended that:—

(1) Every possible step be taken immediately to enhance, in the eyes of all communities, and particularly of those who possess it as a birthright, the value of British nationality and make its possessors feel that they are the backbone of the country. The first step is a more precise agreement with the Chinese Government over the jurisdiction of its Consular officers *vis-à-vis* Chinese British subjects. Precise and repeated statements regarding the facts of Chinese-British nationality and its rights should be made in order to clear up the persistent doubts in the minds of the local Chinese.

(2) Immediate steps be taken for all European administrative officers to learn some dialect of colloquial Chinese as a first language in order to effect closer contact with the ordinary people. As many other officers as possible in the public service should also learn some Chinese as the first step towards attacking corruption in the public service. The present system whereby Chinese trained officers do not hold the most senior posts in the administration would appear to be at the root of the trouble and should be altered.

(3) Every possible effort be made to expedite the establishment of more English schools in which children of all races can be given the same teaching side by side, and so eliminate slowly any feeling of communal division. It is realised that this must be a slow process, and that the speed at which additional schools can be established is limited by many factors largely beyond our control, but it is felt the process must be pushed on relentlessly if results are to be produced.

(4) Immigration be restricted to the utmost possible limit. Considerable progress has been made on this question during the last few months and it is still under active consideration. It is obviously useless to implement (3) above as long as the door is left open for even more raw material to come in.

171   CO 537/4242, no 1   19 Dec 1948

[Enlisting Chinese support and plans for a Malayan Chinese Association]: inward telegram no 1636 from Sir H Gurney to Mr Creech Jones

[Recalling the concern felt in the Eastern Department over 'what seemed to be the negative attitude of the Govt. of the Federation towards the Chinese community, the key to a solution of our present difficulties', O H Morris of the CO welcomed this telegram as 'one of the most encouraging developments' since the inauguration of the Federation (CO 537/3758, minute by Morris, 22 Dec 1948). Amongst the encouraging initiatives emanating from Malaya at this time were: the firm stand taken against payment of protection money, attempts to foster the Malayan Chinese Association and the formation of the Communities Liaison Committee.]

I have recently had long and frank talks with the Chinese members of the Legislative Council and representatives of mining and rubber interests with a view to obtaining more active help from the Chinese against the terrorists.

2.   Steps are now being taken by leading Chinese to form a Malayan Chinese association open to all who have made their home in the Federation with the object of co-operating with the Government and with other communities in restoring peace and good order in this country. Rules are now being drafted and will be discussed with me in draft before further action is taken, and Chinese members of the Legislative Council have undertaken to start to enlist support actively for this move in their districts at once. I have mentioned this development to Dato Onn and am satisfied that it will be helping in forthcoming Malay-Chinese conversations on long term problems.[1]

3.   Perak Chinese Miners Association will meet Tuesday to call upon all their members to stop paying protection money. I hope that this will be followed by similar action by the Selangor and Negri Sembilan Associations. A deputation of Malay Estate Owners Association yesterday agreed to call a meeting for the same purpose, and representatives of the Chinese bus companies and road transport interests (who are all paying protection money) are being convened with a view to making similar declaration. My purpose is to get cessation of these payments already demanded by public opinion and not merely by the Government. Chinese public opinion has hitherto been silent on this point but now that both extortion and police pressure have increased there is a natural revulsion of which full advantage can be taken.

4.   I intend to pursue these developments strongly since, without active help of the Chinese, 90 per cent of whom only want peace but have so far preferred to leave the job of restoring it to somebody else whenever possible, we cannot succeed. They are as you know notoriously inclined to lean towards whichever side frightens them more and at the moment this seems to be the Government.

---

[1] On the initiative of Malcolm MacDonald, prominent Malay and Chinese leaders met in Penang in Jan 1949 to consider ways of alleviating Sino-Malay tension. Known first as the Malay-Chinese Goodwill Committee, its membership expanded to include other community leaders and its name changed to the Communities Liaison Committee.

172 CO 537/3758, no 25   20 Dec 1948
[Enlisting Chinese support]: letter from Sir H Gurney to Sir T Lloyd
on the problems and methods of winning Chinese support   [Extract]

It is quite true that the Federation and State Governments are out of touch with their Chinese communities. The decision to abolish the Chinese Protectorate[1] as such was no doubt perfectly right (a Protectorate for half the population would be inconsistent with our policy of Malayanisation and as inappropriate as, say, a Department of Native Affairs in Uganda), but in splitting the administration of Chinese between various specialised Departments, especially Labour and Social Welfare, we have gone too far in the other direction, with the result that we have lost touch with the day to day affairs of the ordinary Chinese, who themselves greatly miss the paternal interest of the Protectorate officers and the contact previously afforded by the Chinese Advisory Boards.

Moreover, the present troubles have tended to make all Chinese suspect in the eyes of State administrations, most of which have a strong Malay bias at the higher levels. For example, the Perak State Security Committee has no Chinese member, though it is dealing with little else than Chinese affairs; because, I am told, no Chinese could be found who could be trusted with the Committee's secrets. Naturally enough the Chinese resent this exclusion not only as a loss of face but as a deliberate deprivation of opportunity to help. Chinese from Perak have complained to me that they never see any Government officer, except a policeman or detective, of whom they have a deep-rooted fear.

Although this is an exaggerated account, it represents a serious weakness of a nature that is familiar enough to any administrator. If we had in the Federation a straight British administration it would be easy enough to remedy. I have now talked about it in all the States (except Johore) and find a general agreement that our Deputy Commissioners for Labour, who are our best Chinese-speaking M.C.S. officers, should subordinate their labour duties (particularly now that the labour front is quiet) to their duties as Advisers or Assistant Secretaries for Chinese Affairs, with Chinese Advisory Boards on the old model whenever practicable, with the main purpose of restoring the confidence of the Chinese in the local administration. They must be made to feel that they "belong" and are not just unwanted children, and that there is someone in authority taking an interest in them.

Parallel with development along these lines, I hope that the Malayan Chinese Association whose projected formation I have reported separately[2] will also provide a focus for loyal Chinese aspirations and a means of contact with the Federal Government to the corresponding disadvantage of Chinese consular influence. I do not deny that such a development has possible dangers, but with wise guidance and

---

[1] The Chinese Protectorate, which had dealt with all aspects of Chinese affairs from the late 1870s to 1942, had been abolished by wartime planners because it was deemed to be incompatible with a common Malayan citizenship. However, the postwar substitute, the Secretariat for Chinese Affairs, was hamstrung by a lack of staff with knowledge of Chinese languages and customs. The worries expressed by Gurney on this issue were echoed in Britain where the Scarborough Report had recently revealed the paucity of the resources devoted to the study of the Far East (see CO 537/3758, minute by O H Morris, 21 Jan 1949).
[2] See 171.

proper presentation to the Malays, as an anti-lawlessness movement, it can be made a powerful force for good. It is certainly better than nothing.

An interesting example of Malay statesmanship (or perhaps political acumen) was recently provided in the Legislative Council debate on the Courts Bill. The Government motion to include a clause to give, in effect, the Public Prosecutor the right of appeal against acquittal, was known to be hotly opposed by the Settlement members, who had told me that they regarded it as a test case to show how far the Federal Legislature was going to override them on a motion that would deprive Penang and Malacca of rights held there for a long time and greatly prized. The clause had the backing of the Malay members, but Dato Onn, aware of the fact that the Penang secession movement was not unconnected with his visit to London, got up and spoke for the Settlements, with the result that, much to the wrath of the Attorney General, the motion was lost and the Penang members highly gratified. This is a small instance of political sense, but I quote it as illustrating that the Malays and not only Dato Onn are ready to show it.

To revert to the problem of instilling confidence into the Chinese, I feel that nothing would have greater long-term effect than two statements by H.M. Government; first, that their policy is that the Federation should be constitutionally linked with Singapore by means which would have the agreement of both territories and would involve the minimum loss of rights at present possessed by the people of both of them; and, secondly, that the British have no intention of leaving Malaya within the foreseeable future. I think both of these pronouncements need to be made, and much unnecessary controversy and political nervousness could be saved if they were to be made firmly and at an early date.

It is quite clear that responsible Malays recognise the existence of a body of Chinese who are loyal to Malaya, but they find it difficult to distinguish those whose only loyalty is to Malaya from those who keep a foot in both camps. This is the reason why the qualifications for citizenship by operation of law were made so restricted. It is by no means certain that birth in Malaya necessarily implies either permanent residence in or loyalty to Malaya. The answer lies largely in a more open profession by the Chinese of their single minded interest here and no where else.

We must also be careful not to overestimate the part which the Chinese played during the campaign and during the occupation. In the fighting of 1941–2 this part was played merely as anti-Japanese. The help which they gave to the British in internment camps was beyond praise but as the large majority of internees were in Singapore people up country heard little about it. The latter had the exploits of the guerillas nearer home and these did not tend to endear them to the majority of the population. One of the tragedies of the occupation was that British help to the resistance movement was almost wholly given to the Chinese and the possibilities of encouraging a resistance movement amongst Malays were overlooked until the last few months.

It seems to me over-optimistic to suppose that the Chinese will become loyal citizens of Malaya out of any wish to do anything of the sort. What will count with them is whether in fact they have to become loyal citizens as the only means of being allowed to continue their industry and occupations with the minimum of interference and the maximum of profit. This motive of self-interest will have to be reinforced during the coming months by a strong Government pressure which may often seem to observers even as near as Singapore to be almost anti-Chinese in character. We are now aiming at banishing and repatriating Chinese at a total rate of two thousand a month including dependants. The only estimate I have given officially for this is five thousand over the next six months and I should prefer not to depart from this official forecast at present. We are hoping, however, at least to double this figure.

The Committee on the squatter problem has begun its work and there is an accumulating body of knowledge on the size of this problem and of what the long-term answers are likely to be. I myself doubt whether it is feasible to find any short-term answer to the general problem and feel sure that on both practical and humanitarian grounds it is wrong to concentrate all the blame and military operations on these small people when the big men who are paying thousands of dollars a month to the bandit movement are allowed to go free. Action against the big men will, of course, cause more of a howl and one of my objects in writing you this letter is to show you that if in the course of our efforts to defeat the bandits quickly we are accused of being harsh to the Chinese we are also trying to help forward any movement among the Chinese themselves which would hold promise of any reasonable alternative to Communism and attach them more closely to the Government and the Malays.

I am sending copies of this letter to MacDonald and Gimson

173 CO 537/3759, no 17   22 Dec 1948
[Dato Onn]: letter from J J Paskin to Sir H Gurney on discussions in London in late Oct and early Nov between Mr Creech Jones, Dato Onn and CO officials

[Informed of his mercurial temperament, his obsession with Johore rights and his still smouldering resentment over the Malayan Union, CO officials did not share MacDonald's enthusiasm for Onn (see 164), whose visit to London was delayed by the Emergency until late Oct. Since he lacked the constitutional status of a 'senior Colonial Minister', such as that enjoyed by Bustamente of Jamaica at that time, CO officials rejected any notion of Onn having an audience with the King or even lunching with anyone grander than the secretary of state for the colonies (see also CO 537/4251 and 4790).]

I am sorry that it has taken so long to let you have a fuller account than that given in our telegram No. 1419 of the discussions which Dato Onn had with the Secretary of State, and subsequently with various members of the Eastern and other Departments in the Colonial Office. I have covered a little of the ground in my letter about his proposal that there should be a Malay Deputy High Commissioner. In this letter I will try to give you a more general impression of the atmosphere of these various conversations.

2. There were only two formal meetings with the Secretary of State, at which members of the Department were present, on the 27th October, and 2nd November. But Dato Onn had lunch with the Secretary of State and Mr. MacDonald on Monday 25th October (the day after his arrival here) and thereafter, met the Secretary of State and other Ministers informally on a number of occasions. There was an official (Government Hospitality) luncheon in his honour on 29th October and Ministers arranged a number of informal parties. He himself gave a large dinner party on 10th

November. On the day before his return he saw the Prime Minister. There is no record of the matters discussed at these informal meetings.

3. He also had a number of talks, both individual and collective, with a variety of unofficial (mainly, I gather, rubber) interests, but we do not, of course, know what passed there.

4. So far as the Colonial Office talks were concerned, I do not think that any of us were quite prepared either for the degree of bitterness, under which he still labours, at what was done in 1945/46, or for (and especially this) the strength of his assertion (constantly repeated—or suggested—in a wide variety of connections) that H.M.G. has not yet regained the confidence of the Malays, and that—by the actions of the Federation Government—we are not going the right way about doing so. Why is it, he asked the Secretary of State, that when this or that proposal is put forward, our first though is "What will the Chinese think about it?" whereas it ought to be "What will the Malays think about it?". In his talks with both Ministers he showed misgivings in regard to the Colonial Office as such.

5. In the first formal meeting with the Secretary of State, Dato Onn was clearly trying, (not always successfully) to keep this bitterness under restraint and it may be for this very reason that he did not develop some of his ideas (e.g. as to the functions that might be performed by a Malay Deputy High Commissioner)[1] as fully as he might have done.

6. Rather to our surprise (and perhaps also for the same reason) he did not embark upon such controversial issues as consultation with the Rulers on the appointment of a new High Commissioner (though this matter was, I understand, touched upon at one of his meetings with the Secretary of State), or (at our formal meetings) on the relations between the Federal and State Governments. (On this issue, he very sensibly and moderately expressed satisfaction at the setting up of your Committee,[2] which he recognised as the proper body at which to ventilate this issue).

7. Nor did he, at our formal meetings, press unduly his proposal that H.M.G. should make a grant of £10 million for the benefit of the Malays (as distinct from Malaya). But he reverted to this matter—at some length—and with some bitterness—at his final meeting with Higham and me, on the afternoon before his departure. I shall be dealing more fully with that meeting later on in this letter (paragraphs 13–23), so will not say more about it at this point, except to remark that we were surprised that he seemed to be so much in the dark about development plans, that he had a feeling that these were being worked out in the Federal Departments without the Councils having any say, and that he appeared unaware of the extent of the C.D. & W. allocation to Malaya.

8. As a set off to this rather gloomy picture, I should however make it clear that, (though always against the background conception that Malaya is primarily a Malay

---

[1] The proposal to establish the post of deputy high commissioner, to be filled by a Malay, aggravated the distrust between Onn and the Malay rulers. Expecting Onn to be appointed to the position and fearing his vaulting ambition, the Sultans would eventually veto the creation of this appointment.

[2] The federal constitution had devolved considerable power to Malay-dominated state governments and Gurney was frustrated by the lack of co-operation from state authorities and administrative bottle-necks at the centre. On 14 Oct 1948 Gurney and Newboult convened a meeting of Malays, which Newboult chaired, to discuss relations between the federal and state governments (see CO 537/3756, Gurney to Paskin, 21 Oct 1948).

country) Dato Onn was quite reasonably responsive to the Secretary of State's suggestion that members of other races who (in the stock phrase) have made Malaya their home and the object of their loyalty, should be accorded the rights of citizenship, including a fair share of appointments in the public services. Indeed, in a variety of connections, we gathered the impression that some of the present anxieties of Dato Onn and his friends may be due to their uncertainty as to how many Chinese are likely to become Federal citizens. If, when the roll is reasonably complete, they find that the Malays are in a substantial preponderance, their attitude on a number of issues on which they at present feel obliged to take a rather uncompromising line, may well change.

9. On a number of matters, it seemed to us that Dato Onn established at any rate a good case for enquiry—e.g. as to the small proportion of British Council, and C.D. and W. training, scholarships awarded to Malays, increasing the number of Malay battalions and giving them territorial titles, opportunities for advancement to higher ranks in the Police and the Malay Regiment, King's Commissions for Malay officers, the possibility of facilitating both the entry of greater numbers of local candidates into the Public Services and their promotion to positions of greater responsibility and in particular the appointment of Malays as Heads of Departments—even at the sacrifice of some degree of efficiency. As regards scholarships, we gathered that steps had already been taken to meet his point, and that his purpose in mentioning it was by way of illustrating the kind of mistakes which would not be made if the Federal authorities always (as he maintained they should) keep in mind their special responsibilities towards the Malays.

10. As regards the students in this country, he not only criticised the allocation of too small a proportion of scholarships to Malays, but also took Mr. MacDonald to task for having, during his earlier visit to England, addressed a gathering of students (preponderately Chinese) as those in whose hands the future of the country will rest.

11. I should also make it clear that, while he asked (and was assured) that all the points which he raised would receive due consideration, his requests were by no means expressed as "ultimatums". Indeed, throughout these discussions, he professed himself as wholeheartedly in favour of the British connection. It was not that he spoke "more in sorrow than anger"—indeed at times his anger was apparent—but he constantly reverted to the theme that if H.M.G. would only demonstrate (by the actions of the Federal Government) that (while dealing fairly with the other communities) they still recognise their special responsibilities towards the Malays, and so win back their confidence, we can be assured of their loyalty and cooperation for as far ahead as we can foresee. But we have reached the stage when only deeds, and not merely assurances, will tell. Moreover, the sands are running out, and unless the Malays are able *soon* to see some appreciable indications of a recognition by H.M.G. of what is due to them in their own country, Dato Onn fears what the consequences may be. Such was his general theme.

12. At the second formal meeting with the Secretary of State, and at a variety of social functions thereafter, Dato Onn was progressively more at his ease and was prepared to discuss affairs in a much more objective frame of mind. We were particularly gratified that he not only consented to come to a students tea party but that he brought himself to say a few well chosen words to the students about the desirability of all races co-operating for the common good of Malaya. About half way through Dato Onn's stay in London, Mr. MacDonald asked me what kind of

impression he had made on the Department. I was glad to be able to say that our impression was quite favourable—surprisingly so in view of the rather "tense" opening meeting. We heard from a variety of outside sources, who had had contacts with him either individually or at meetings (e.g. with the rubber growers) that he was returning to Malaya in a very much better frame of mind than when he came.

13.   This being so I was not at all prepared for the renewal of his bitter comments in the course of the last talk which Higham and I had with him and Che Abdullah[3] on the last afternoon before he left England. As I have explained in the letter which I have written in connection with Dato Onn's submission that a Malay Deputy High Commissioner should be appointed, the purpose of this meeting was to show him the draft of our despatch which had been prepared on that subject and to run over with him again the list of other matters on which despatches had been promised, but not yet drafted. We had therefore expected that the meeting would be informal and friendly and rather in the nature of a farewell party than a business meeting.

14.   I have told you in my earlier letter of his reactions to the draft despatch and the remarks which it gave rise to. Whether or not it was because of that bad start it is difficult to say, but thereafter almost every topic that we touched upon produced some acid comment or other.

It was the British who have been mainly responsible for the present troubles by bringing hordes of Chinese into the country in the past.

In 1945 we came back to the country not as friends but as alien conquerors—or at any rate that was how the B.M.A. behaved.

In the events leading up to the creation of the Malayan Union we had torn up all our Treaties and gone back on all our pledges to the Malays. It was tantamount to annexation in the worst tradition of British Imperialism.

Not content with that, we had put the cat among the pigeons (he did not use that phrase, but it conveys the sense of his remarks) by producing the Citizenship proposals which, as drafted would have led to the Malays being swamped by the Chinese. (I demurred to this as being quite contrary to our estimate of the effect even of the original proposals, but he stuck to his view). If we had not produced these proposals, it would never have occurred to the Chinese to demand political rights. We had wantonly put the idea into their heads.

The Federal Government functions as an out and out Crown Colony Government. It is as much an instrument of an unsympathetic British Government as the Malayan Union Government which preceded it.

15.   These comments about the Federal Government were provoked by what I thought was a quite innocent suggestion on my part that we couldn't usefully carry much further in London some point which we were discussing (I cannot now recall what it was, but I think it was the inadequate pay of Malay Officers of the Malay Regiment) and that it would be better for him to pursue it on his return to Malaya. In justification of his remarks he said that it was quite useless to pursue in Kuala Lumpur any matter to which the Malays attached importance. Either they were told that the matter could not be discussed owing to some ruling or other of the Secretary of State, or that it would have to be referred to the Secretary of State, or (as in the

---

[3] Abdullah bin Mohamed was a Johore Malay who had been educated at Cambridge and London and had worked for the BBC during the Second World War. He later became state secretary of Johore.

case of the Malay Deputy High Commissioner) the matter was just pigeon holed and not even reported to the Secretary of State.

16. Another topic which provoked some bitter remarks was his suggestion that H.M.G. should now make a grant of £10,000,000 for expenditure on objects of benefit to the *Malays*. At the first meeting with the Secretary of State Dato Onn put forward this proposal on two grounds:—

(a) As a means of improving the competitive position of the Malays *vis-à-vis* the Chinese (by providing in the rural areas social services comparable with those provided in the towns, by establishing a land bank with a view to reducing rural indebtedness, etc., etc.): and thereby

(b) as a gesture to reassure the Malays that H.M.G. is mindful of their special position in their own country. He said that a gesture of this kind would do more than almost anything else to restore the shaken confidence of the Malays in the bona fides of the British Government.

17. As I have said in paragraph 7 above, he did not press this proposal at the opening meeting with the Secretary of State. He mentioned it in his interview with the "Daily Telegraph", but (so far as I am aware) it was not discussed again in the Colonial Office until the last meeting on the afternoon before his departure.

18. At that meeting, I explained that, on this topic, it would inevitably be some little time before the Secretary of State could be in a position to address a despatch to you. His proposal would have to be examined in the Colonial Office against the background of all the discussions which had already taken place with the Treasury on the subject of the finances of Malaya. As he was aware, the financial position of this country was precarious, and in considering any proposal which the Secretary of State might feel able to put to them, the Treasury would be bound to take into account the general financial position of Malaya and the financial assistance which had already been made available (i.e. the £10 million free grant, the offer of £35 million interest free loan, the £12½ million loan to be raised on the London Market, the £5 million allocation from C.D. and W. funds plus £1 million for the University).

19. At this exposition, Dato Onn clearly lost patience. Dato Onn seemed to be under the impression that the "justice" of his proposal was so self-evident that it had only to be mentioned by the Secretary of State to the Chancellor of the Exchequer for the money to be forthcoming, almost without question. This £10 million would be chicken feed to the Treasury, whereas it would make all the difference in the world to the attitude of the Malays to the British Government. Moreover it would be no more than a gesture of restitution of the reserve balances of the States which H.M.G. had virtually "stolen" when it handed these balances over to the Government of the Malayan Union, by which they had been "dissipated" before the Federation had come into existence. The result was that these balances were no longer available to be expended by the State Governments on matters of concern to the Malays. Indeed his attitude seemed to be that the period of the Union should be regarded as a nightmare gap in the progress of time, that as much as possible of what was done during that period should be expunged from the records and that by some wave of a magician's wand the Federal and State Governments (at any rate as regards the old State balances) should be put into the position in which they would have been if the Union had never existed. I am afraid that I was incapable of doing a rapid mental calculation to see how the sum of £10 million would fit into this picture. But Dato Onn left no

doubt on our minds that he regarded this proposal as affording the British Government an opportunity to make a gesture of restitution. From his point of view, no grant to "Malaya" could be regarded as an adequate substitute for a grant for the benefit of the *Malays*.

20. For the reason that it is clear that this request must necessarily be considered against the general background of the financial arrangements as between H.M.G. and Malaya (as to which separate correspondence is proceeding) the Secretary of State's official despatch will probably do no more than to ask for your observations on Dato Onn's request. We should be grateful for a full expression of your views on this issue as soon as possible in the light of the considerations adduced by Dato Onn.

21. The question of the relationship between the Federal and State Governments came up incidentally in a variety of connections in the course of this last meeting and eventually Che Abdullah chipped in with a remark that as a member of the Johore State Secretariat he was in a good position to see how the machine actually works. It was, he represented, a painful experience by comparison with the time when Johore managed its own affairs. This gave me the opening for which I had been looking.

22. At an earlier stage of the discussion I had taken Dato Onn up on his assumption that, in the steps leading up to the creation of the Union, H.M.G. had been actuated by such despicable motives as he was suggesting. I asked him to believe that however unwise, or injudicious, the action by H.M.G. might appear to those who did not agree with the action taken, the fundamental thought present in the minds of those who were concerned in that action was the ultimate long range benefit of Malaya itself. This action did not spring from any outmoded "Imperialistic" desire to turn Malaya into a Colony which could be exploited for the benefit of Great Britain. The fundamental conception was that, especially in the turmoil and ferment which was to be expected in the post war world, there could be no possibility whatever of a political future for Malaya as a country unless some means could be found to weld it into a country instead of allowing it to remain as a jumble of small states each concerned with its own local affairs. It was for this reason (i.e. in the future political interests of Malaya itself) that, in the negotiations which led up to the formation of the Federation such emphasis was laid on the necessity for the retention of a strong central Government.

23. When therefore Che Abdullah gave me the opening mentioned in paragraph 21, I reverted to this theme and obtained an admission from Dato Onn that he also still recognized the importance of maintaining a strong central Government in the Federation. I then pointed out that it was very natural that, in a State like Johore, which had been accustomed in the past very much to manage its own affairs, in the process of adjusting itself to the situation in which it has surrendered many of the more important functions of government to a central authority at Kuala Lumpur there must be many quite painful readjustments to be made. But these readjustments are only part of the growing pains through which they must expect to pass in the process of developing Malaya into a great country. Moreover this process is bound to take a considerable time, before the new political arrangements can be expected to work smoothly. I therefore appealed to Dato Onn to continue to exercise patience. To this he replied that he was perfectly prepared to be patient, provided that there could be, without too long a delay, some visible signs that the new Federal authorities themselves recognise the necessity for making adjustments to meet the natural aspirations of the constituent States and in particular of the Malays who form

the basic part of the population of those States. In particular he appealed for some action to be taken soon to meet the various requests that he had put forward in his talks with the Secretary of State. It was by such means that the Malays could again be brought to a feeling of confidence in the British Government, which they had before the war, but which has been completely destroyed by all that has happened since 1945.

24.   All this gives rise, of course, to a string of question marks as to the policy to be followed in dealing with Dato Onn and his friends. I had hoped to include a few notes on that in this letter. But I have kept you waiting so long for this account of our impressions arising from our conversations with Dato Onn that I have come to the conclusion that I had better now let this letter issue as it stands. I hope to let you have a further one very shortly.

25.   I am sending a copy of this letter to Mr. MacDonald.

174   CO 537/3746   Jan 1949

[Future policy with special reference to the Malays]: draft letter from Sir T Lloyd to Sir H Gurney. *Minute* by Mr Rees-Williams

[This draft letter for Lloyd's signature was not sent to Gurney. It is significant, however, in indicating CO thinking after Onn's visit to London and six months into the emergency.]

In his letter 55400/12 of the 22nd September [sic][1] reporting the conversations which we had with Dato Onn, Paskin promised a further letter on "the string of question marks" with [which] Dato Onn's visit left in our minds. This letter is an attempt to put into writing some of these, and other thoughts on future policy for Malaya which we have been turning over in our minds in the past few months.

2.   The first question is not, I think, how far the views expressed by Dato Onn are shared by the Malay leaders and people in general. You answered that question in the negative in your telegram No. 1277. We should be glad to know whether your longer experience of the country has led you to modify that view.

3.   Nor does there seem to be any doubt as to the answer to the more important question as to the effectiveness of the influence which Dato Onn still wields or is capable of wielding. In your telegram No. 1277 you said that his leadership is unchallenged. This was in accordance with what we were told by MacDonald, in whose view Dato Onn should be regarded as the accepted leader of the Malays, in a position to make his views prevail with them. He was to be taken as a man who, with proper handling, was capable of a statesmanlike approach to the problems of Malaya and who, if himself satisfied with our treatment of the Malays, could ensure their loyalty to the British connection. Conversely, we have assumed that even if the uneasiness and bitterness voiced by Dato Onn were not widely felt by the Malays, they could be readily instilled by him, if he himself remains dissatisfied.

4.   On the whole, in spite of some disconcerting quirks, Dato Onn left us with the impression that he has the makings of a statesman. We were left with the feeling that in spite of his rancour, his unnecessary and unjustified suspicions and the narrow

---

[1] The letter was actually dated 22 Dec, see 173.

parochialism which he sometimes evinced, Onn was capable of a broader vision, and was a man with whom (except on the subject of our "misdeeds" of 1945/46) one could reason. It is on the assumptions in this and the preceding paragraph that we have drafted what follows.

5. Proceeding from this point, our questions seem to branch out along three separate paths:—

(a) Leaving aside the history of 1945/46 (as interpreted by Dato Onn), have the Malays any legitimate grievances which should and can be remedied? We here feel (and I am sure that you will agree) that everything possible should be done *quickly* both to find the answer to the question and to apply any remedies that may be found to be necessary. Your Committee on the working of the administrative machinery of the Federation will no doubt cover a great part of the ground and we were glad to get the encouraging account in your letter of the 21st October of the start of its labours. I do not know whether this Committee is likely to deal with such matters as excessive "authoritarianism" at Departmental headquarters without due regard to the susceptibilities of local authorities and personalities. But this is such an obviously fruitful source of irritation (especially on the part of technical departments) that I have no doubt that you have it well in mind and that you will have made adequate arrangements for any signs of it to be brought to your notice.

(b) It seems to us that Dato Onn is also looking for something in the nature of a gesture of atonement not only for our sins of 1945/46 but also for what he seems to regard as our continuing sinful disregard of the paramount interests of the Malays. We should be glad to have your comments on this.

(c) Does Dato Onn really believe in the fundamentals of H.M.G.'s policy in Malaya—the strong central government and a form of common citizenship with all that that implies—and is it possible for the action necessary to secure the wholehearted (or at any rate reasonable) co-operation of the Malays to be taken within the limits of this accepted policy?

The succeeding paragraphs of this letter deal with this last question.

6. In the first place, does Dato Onn believe so wholeheartedly in the need for a strong central government in Malaya that he will be really co-operative in achieving and maintaining it? Having played so large a part in winning acceptance for the Federal constitution, he would hardly be likely to go back overtly on the first principle enunciated by the Working Committee in its December 1946 Report (paragraph 17) and reiterated, with the agreement of the Malays, in Cmd.7171, "that there should be a strong central government so as to ensure economical and effective administration of all matters of importance to the welfare and progress of the country as a whole". Some of his remarks in London encouraged us in the belief that he was still convinced that a strong central government was needed, and was right.

7. Nevertheless from some of his remarks a natural deduction would be that Dato Onn was concerned again to build up the States at the expense of the Federal Government. What is the explanation of this apparent inconsistency? Our impressions for what they are worth, are as follows. The first is, as you yourself have remarked, that the State authorities, at any rate in Johore which so largely ran its affairs, are finding it a painful process to adjust themselves to a situation in which they have surrendered such a large part of their authority to a central government at

Kuala Lumpur. Secondly—for whatever reasons—Dato Onn has come to regard that Government (especially perhaps its departmental manifestations) as alien, unfriendly and unmindful of the interests of the Malays which he regards as paramount, whereas the States, with their predominantly Malay Administrations—the Malay Mentri Besar, State Secretaries and District Officers—are still strongholds of Malay influence. It may be that when his suspicions of the good faith of that administration are greatest, so his concern for State rights becomes more assertive. We feel, therefore, that what the Dato really wants is not to weaken the Federal Government but to secure the position of the Malays. But if their position can only be secured by favouring the State administrations at the expense of the Federal Government and Federal institutions then, naturally enough, then [sic] Dato Onn's aims would be to see that Malay interests are entrenched behind State rights.

8.   Even if we are right in assuming that the Dato is not at bottom opposed to a strong central government, provided it is compatible with the safeguarding of Malay interests, we are left with the impression that at present he sees the future Malaya as a predominantly *Malay* country in which Chinese and others are on sufferance, whether Federal citizens or not, rather than a *Malayan* country in which non-Malay Federal citizens share equally with Malays in civic rights and duties. However, the question is largely one of degree—how far will non-Malay Federal citizens be accepted into the public life of this Malay country? We were encouraged by some of his remarks, and especially by MacDonald's account of Dato Onn's policy in Johore itself, where, it appears, he has favoured the admission of non-Malays to the State Administrative Service, and, on the whole, we feel fairly confident that Onn is prepared to give Federal citizenship a fair trial. This perhaps gives us some reason to hope that, by positive policy on our part, he may be brought to accept with conviction the policy of H.M.G. which, while recognising the special interests of the Malays, requires that non-Malay Federal citizens should enjoy the privileges of citizenship as their right. We think we begin to see three essential components of such a positive policy.

9.   The first is that some means should be found to stimulate the Malays to take such interest in the work of the central government and its departments that they will feel that the Federal Government is as much their own Government as the State Governments were. Is the *political* power which the Malays could wield through their strength in the Federal Executive and Legislative Councils, matched by effective participation in the processes of Goverment? The Malays, if Dato Onn expresses their views aright, clearly feel out of touch with the administrative machine. Another aspect of the same problem is that of the position of Malays in the public service. Another is the request put forward by Dato Onn for the appointment of a Malay as Deputy High Commissioner. As Paskin has pointed out, Dato Onn did not develop the idea and we do not know what functions he has in mind for such a post; perhaps he has no clear picture in his own mind. But it is that he sees in this idea a means of associating the Malays more closely with the work of the central government. As you know, the African colonies are experimenting with the "Member system" whereby unofficial members of Excutive Council are appointed to answer for departments in Legislative Council and there are also interesting experiments in the Sudan. Both the Sudanese and the East African experiments may be of help to you in devising ways of associating the Malays more closely with the central government and its agencies, and in associating the Legislative Council with the work of

Government; and I will have accounts of these experiments prepared and sent to you if you think they would be useful.

10. The second point is the need for building up the economic position of the Malays, so that they can compete on fair terms with the Chinese and the Indians. At the moment the Malays by virtue of their strong position in the Federal Executive and Legislative Councils, their entrenched position in the State administrations and the rights assured to them by Treaty and Statute (e.g. Malay Land Reservations) are well placed for eventual *political* dominance, even if non-Malay Federal Citizens participate fully in public life. But it is clearly not in the Malays' interest, and certainly not in ours, that they should continue to be, in their own country, strangers to the enterprises that make it wealthy. Even from the narrow point of view of British commercial interests, if we must look forward to the day when British political control will end in Malaya, we should now be working for the closer association of local people with U.K. commercial enterprises in the hope of this guarding against the expropriation of these enterprises when that control ends. The process by which the economic position of the Malays might be built up of course demands much further study. We realise, of course, that much thought has already been given to the problem of diversifying Malayan economy and to improving the position of the Malay smallholder. However, it seems to us that emphasis should be laid in the future on making the volume of Malay economic activity commensurate with their potential political power. We are thinking further about ways and means of achieving this, and will let you know if any ideas occur to us. In any case we should welcome your views and suggestions.

11. It seems to us that the third element of our policy should be to build up an effective system of democratic local Government in which all races can participate fully. (Incidentally this might well be the most effective counter to the undue re-development of the States as political entities). We were very concerned at the description, in a paper prepared for MacDonald's forthcoming conference, of predominantly Chinese areas being administered (if administered at all) by a Malay Penghulu or so and a few Malay police. We have no doubt that you will be giving urgent attention to the problems of local government, and I will do no more than mention that in recent years the Colonial Office has acquired a considerable fund of knowledge of the theory and practice of local government which we will gladly place at your disposal.

12. Another matter on which we may be able to assist you is mass education, the theory and practice of which has been much studied in the past few years.

13. Most of this letter has been concerned with the Malays, since Dato Onn's visit has concentrated attention upon them. As a corollary to any such positive policy, designed to influence the Malays, as that suggested in the preceding paragraphs, positive measures will also be needed to assure the non-Malay Federal Citizens of their position, and to distinguish them from the mass of aliens into which they might only too easily relapse. I do not feel I need say more about this since it is clear from your letters of the 8th October and 20th December,[2] that the problem is near to your mind.

14. I hope you will not feel that I have sought to attempt more than to pose (on

---

[2] See 168 and 172.

certain assumptions, which may not be wholly justified) a series of questions about the future of Malaya which must be as obvious to you as they are to us; but we think it is most important that we should have as clear as possible in our minds the objects we wish to achieve and the means of achieving them. We would like you to let us know how you and your advisers see the position, and whether you endorse the provisional conclusions outlined in this letter.

15. I am sending a copy of this letter to MacDonald.

Minute on 174

1. If the Department had consulted me on this matter I could have told them what the feelings of the Malays were and saved them 3 pages of ruminations in the despatch.

2. What is needed above all, and to my mind this despatch fails because it does not bring this point out, is that we here realise the need for and promulgate a bold, imaginative, and constructive policy on the economic, political, social, educative, labour and health fronts and a statement that to the limit of the available resources we mean to carry such a policy out.

3. The Malays are intensely suspicious of the Colonial Office. They regard it as entirely ignorant of Malay ways and aspirations and desirous of supporting the Chinese against them.

4. The Malays are a friendly and kindly people, however, and will respond eagerly to a gesture of friendliness.

5. As I said in the House of Commons when I was a private member, what to the Occidental is a shadow is often to the Oriental the substance.

6. If my suggestion of a broad plan for Malaya,[3] recognizing the rightful place of the Malays, had been carried out, we should now be in a position to give the High Commissioner a broad picture of our policy which would have been much better than a series of despatches dealing with isolated topics.

7. There are some good points of detail in the despatch and the suggestions in §9 and §10 are excellent.

8. As to paragraph 11 I am at variance with the Department on this. I believe in associating other races, eventually by democratic means, with the work of the State Councils. It is desirable to have municipalities in the towns and this aspect of local government should be developed within the framework of the State.

9. Why is not the question of King's Commissions raised and also that of child welfare among the Malays in the rural areas?

10. If we want to avoid another Indonesia I beg the Department to realise that I know the Malays well, I believe I am trusted by them, and that in my view they are not getting that clear and stimulating lead which the situation demands and in some respects, e.g. in local government,[4] proposals are being made which will accentuate the animosity of the Malays which is now beginning to die down.

D.R.W.

7.1.48[sic][5]

---

[3] See, eg, 145.   [4] See 193.   [5] The year was actually 1949.

175 T 220/86   8 Jan 1949

[Expenditure on security measures]: despatch no 1 from Sir H Gurney to Mr Creech Jones on UK financial assistance   [Extract]
Minute by J I C Crombie[1]

[Gurney's appreciation of the internal security forces, which was printed for secret circulation, had been requested by the secretary of state, following a meeting of the Cabinet Defence Committee on 3 Nov 1948, and was prepared in consultation with the commissioner general and the British Defence Coordination Committee, Far East. Given the urgency of Malayan security, proposals for expanding the armed forces were immediately followed up in discussions with the Chiefs of Staff, Ministry of Defence and Treasury.]

I have the honour to acknowledge the receipt of your telegram No. 1518 of the 2nd December, in which you ask to be furnished with my plans for the building up of the police and local forces in the Federation of Malaya, with an indication of the extent to which the necessary expansion can be financed by this Government.

2.   In accordance with your request, the requirements set out in this despatch are related to two phases:

PHASE A.—From the beginning of 1949 until the final defeat of the militant communists as an effective force;

PHASE B.—The period following Phase A in which the internal security situation has been restored to the extent that it is no longer necessary for Imperial troops to be permanently deployed on operations in aid of the civil power.

Phase A is taken as lasting for the whole of the year 1949. There are no factors at present visible in the internal security situation that would indicate either a shorter or a longer period for this phase, although developments may occur at any time which would affect this estimate. For the purpose of planning it is the best that can be given. Phase B has been extended from the beginning of 1950 to the end of 1951.

The Commander-in-Chief, Far East Land Forces, has expressed the hope that all the present troops will not be needed until the end of 1949 and that from mid-1949, when the expanded Police Force has completed training and is deployed on the ground, it will be possible to start reducing the number of regular military units engaged in operations in the Federation.

3.   The principal instrument which it is desired to develop for the maintenance of internal security is the Police Force. It is also the principal means of defence against external attack, when that attack takes the form of subversion, sabotage and the "cold war". The day is past in which a clear dividing line could be drawn between the responsibilities of the police for maintaining law and order and the role of local military forces in defence against external attack. When this attack comes from within, aimed at the destruction of economic resources, the organisation of strikes and the paralysis of the civil power, and accompanied by all the ruthless and bitter phenomena of organised political revolution (as in the circumstances of this country

---

[1] J I C Crombie, third secretary, Treasury, 1946–1955; appointed chairman, Board of Customs and Excise, 1955.

is its most probable form), the Police Force is the first and vital means of defence. It is the only Force which has the information and intelligence necessary for the conduct of an underground war, and can only succeed if it is built up well in advance with long and thorough training. The formation of an effective trained Police Force takes a longer time than the formation, say, of a battalion of infantry and is not something that can be left to a late stage. It must be done, as it is being done—now.

4. I have noticed that your request for an indication as to the extent to which this Government can finance expansion is limited to the "expansion of local forces". Since, for the above reasons, the Police Force is by far the most effective "local force" in the circumstances for which we have to provide, I have assumed in this despatch that it was not intended that this indication should exclude the Police. To exclude the Police for any purpose from the forces necessary to conduct war in Malaya in its new form would be anachronistic and unreal.

5. The requirements are set out in the following paragraphs under six heads:—

  (i)   Police.
  (ii) Local Naval Forces.
  (iii) Local Land Forces.
  (iv) Local Air Forces.
  (v)   Civil Defence.
  (vi) Summary.

Items (ii), (iii) and (iv) include Forces required not only for the maintenance of internal security but also for defence against external attack in the early stages of a war, on the assumption that South East Asia would be a minor theatre of operations.

(i)—*Police*

6. For a number of years before the war the Federated and Unfederated States and the Straits Settlements of Penang and Malacca, which now comprise the Federation, were comparatively peaceful and law-abiding. There was, therefore, no necessity for large Police forces, nor was there any urgent need for modern methods of communication and transport as public order could be maintained without these aids.

In 1941 the country was over-run by the Japanese. These war years brought about a serious deterioration in Police morale, training and equipment. The task of reorganising the Force after the reoccupation was difficult, if only because of:

  (a) shortage of experienced officers fit to undertake duty;
  (b) loss of majority of personnel and other records;
  (c) difficulties in obtaining supplies of essentials such as uniforms.

In addition to these administrative problems there was a volume of post-war lawlessness and unrest with which to contend.

Thus even before the present emergency the Police Force was at a grave disadvantage. What was in fact an adequate pre-war Police Force cannot in any way be considered sufficient to meet present or future security requirements. The population has increased, jungle areas have been opened up, often illegally, and, apart from the deterioration in public security which inevitably follows a major war, subversive influences are rampant, both in the Federation and many of the neighbouring countries.

7.   The short-term policy is to take every possible measure to bring about rapidly the final defeat of the militant communists as an effective force and to deal with their supporters, passive and active. This policy is a clear priority at present but must not be allowed to obscure the long-term policy of building up a strong regular Police Force on modern lines capable of maintaining internal security without the assistance of the Armed Forces.

8.   The present authorised strength of the regular Police Force is: officers—245; Inspectors—237; British Sergeants—500; rank and file—14,291. These figures will be reached by June, 1949. The overall strength is thought to be satisfactory for both Phase A and Phase B until the end of 1951, with the exception of officers who need to be strengthened by a further 25 European cadets and 25 Asian officers bringing the total officer strength to 295. This increase is necessary because many officers are badly in need of leave and if this is not allowed in 1949 cases of breakdown will be more frequent than at present; officers must be available for duty throughout the 24 hours; reorganisation and re-distribution of police areas is necessary and new officer commands will be created; there must be sufficient officers to enable some to attend higher training courses in modern police methods and equipment even during the emergency. The increase in Asian officers is needed for the additional reason that provision must be made for a training reserve and to enable experienced officers to be released for Special Branch work.

9.   It is urgently necessary to develop the Special Branch and the Criminal Branch of the Criminal Intelligence Department, taking in as many qualified Chinese as possible. An increase of 200 on this account can be found from within the overall increase in strength approved for 1949 but if the right material is to be obtained the present rates of pay for detectives will have to be considerably increased.

10.   In regard to the frontier force, this will be an integral part of the regular Police Force and will come under existing Police organisation to ensure the most efficient flow of information and to obtain complete co-operation and unity of command. Provision has been made for a Force of 600 men who will be stationed at suitable places on the Siamese frontier and in depth. In some cases they will be based on existing Police stations and in others new stations will have to be erected. Small reserves will be held at suitable points. Operating from posts which are tactically sited, they will be capable of dealing with either the individual law-breaker or armed bands. The governing principle will be that each detachment should be capable of patrolling its area adequately and if necessary of defending itself against superior forces until assistance can arrive. The equipment for this force will include wireless and, in many cases, rivercraft with outboard motors. The integration of this force of armed constabulary in the Police Force is an illustration of the impossibility of disentangling functionally the local forces from the Police.

11.   It is essential that the Police should operate and maintain their own signals equipment with uniformed and disciplined members of the force. They must be able to operate in both the English and Malay languages in order to work closely with the armed forces during the emergency and with Commonwealth forces at any time. In order to achieve this object the conditions of service of those policemen who will be trained and employed on signals duties will have to be revised. New terms are being considered which include better pay and chances of promotion within the signals branch as specialists. If this is not done the Police Force will merely become a training school for operators who will resign after a short period for better paid work

elsewhere. The immediate necessity is to equip every Police station with wireless and to recruit and train operators for this equipment.

12. In regard to transport, there are 1,400 vehicles on the strength at present. During 1949 approximately 100 of these will have to be written off as unserviceable and approximately 180 which have been requisitioned during the emergency for Police use but are now uneconomical to run or mechanically unsound will have to be de-requisitioned. These 280 vehicles must be replaced. It is also proposed to develop the police transport organisation, particularly facilities for maintenance and repair work, including the provision of a number of mobile workshops.

13. The great majority of the arms at present on issue to the regular police, and to the Special Constabulary, are on loan from the Army and it is essential that the Police should have sufficient stocks of their own to arm at least all the regular police and the Volunteer Auxiliary Police proposed in paragraph 18 below, plus a reserve. In addition a substantial number more automatic weapons and pistols will be required. In all, it is estimated that a total of 27,000 weapons will have to be purchased in 1949 at a cost of approximately $2,800,000. This will be no more than sufficient, together with the 30,000 rifles and other weapons on loan from the Army, to meet police requirements during the emergency while the Special Constabulary, Extra Police and Auxiliaries are at full strength. So long as the emergency continues it will be impossible for any of the weapons on loan to be returned to the Army.

14. Accommodation, on which the operation and efficiency of the force largely depends, is now in a parlous state in respect of both capacity and suitability. Existing accommodation is inadequate for the number of men already on duty and much of the accommodation now occupied, e.g., rented shop-houses, is unsuitable and insecure. Headquarters of Police establishments down to and including districts are severely handicapped by a lack of accommodation which prejudices the security of information and documents. The accommodation problems confronting the force are:

(a) Provision of accommodation for 3,600 men who will be posted from training depôts to duty by June, 1949.

(b) Provision of suitable accommodation for 600 men comprising the frontier police.

(c) Provision of officers' and inspectors' quarters to meet the increased establishment.

(d) The re-housing of unsatisfactory and insecure police stations.

(e) Provision of office accommodation for increased staffs, including intelligence.

15. Basic recruit training has been reduced to a minimum in order to get the greatest number of men on duty as soon as possible. No higher training is in fact taking place, nor is it possible to provide any at the present time. On a small scale tactical training in anti-bandit methods is in progress. This tactical training will be increased after June, 1949, when basic recruit training commitments will have been reduced.

Specialist training for the Signals Branch is taking place.

Before the end of 1949 a minimum amount of training in transport maintenance will have to be undertaken if police vehicles are to be kept fully operational.

16. The regular Police Force is augmented by Extra Police, Special Constabulary, Auxiliary Police and kampong guards. The authorised establishment of Extra

Police who are paid and are mostly ex-regular policemen or drivers is fixed at 3,904. These men will be required until the emergency is over. The ceiling at present fixed for Special Constables is 32,000 and it is now apparent that the majority of these men will be required until the end of the emergency period. They are in the main, employed on static defence duties as vital points, important installations, rubber estates and mines. No provision has been made in the 1949 Estimates for their cost, estimated at $27 million. The employment of Auxiliary Police, who are volunteers and part-time, is naturally limited by the requirements of their normal occupation. They do, however, give considerable help in certain areas and efforts must be made to retain their services during the emergency. Kampong guards are selected Malay villagers who contribute to the maintenance of morale in the kampongs. Their needs are confined to shotguns and an adequate supply of ammunition. They will be essential until the emergency ends.

17. The requirements of the Marine Police, who are concerned with the prevention of illegal immigration, smuggling and the enforcement of Federation laws within the territorial waters, are:

(a) six sea-going launches capable of remaining on patrol for three to four days;
(b) two power-driven locally built craft to act as "plain clothes vessels"; and
(c) adequate maintenace facilities.

The short-term requirements of sea-going craft are the two power-driven locally built craft and the placing of the orders for the six sea-going launches. It is not thought that more than two of the latter would be available before the end of 1949, but these should be in commission in time to prevent a breakdown in existing patrols due to lack of replacements and wear and tear on the three sea-going craft at present in police hands.

To maintain internal security by patrols and to supply a number of outlying police establishments a considerable number of river craft is also required. Owing to seasonal fluctuation of water levels and currents it is thought that the most practical craft is the local boat fitted with an outboard engine.

It is estimated that the requirement is not less than 50 of such craft and 75 engines.

18. The preceding paragraphs have dealt with Phase A. It is now necessary to consider what reductions are likely to be possible at the end of that Phase. Having regard to the necessity to make up leeway on training at all levels as soon as possible after the emergency is over, I do not consider that any reduction in the regular Police Force will be advisable. At the end of Phase A, however, the Extra Police and Auxiliary Police can be disbanded and the Special Constabulary demobilised as fast as is compatible with efficiency, reabsorption into civilian life, and the collection of arms, ammunition and stores, but the value of the training which these men will then have had should not be lost and I am considering the possibility of retaining them as Volunteer Auxiliary Police who would be required to do a short attachment to the force each year for training, on full pay. One officer would be required at each contingent Headquarters to perform the functions of an Adjutant of a Volunteer Unit. He would be a regular Malay police officer. The figure tentatively contemplated for Volunteer Police is 11,000.

19. It is most important that at the end of Phase A attention should be paid to higher forms of training in the regular Force. No facilities exist for this in the Force

at present and it will be necessary to send officers for instruction elsewhere. Funds will be required for this.

20. There is one other matter which should be mentioned as it closely concerns both Police and the Army. This is the construction of the following roads which are urgently required for strategical reasons and the lack of which is a serious handicap during the operations now proceeding:

(a) Temerloh-Maran in Pahang;
(b) Kroh-Grik in Perak;
(c) Kaki Bukit-Padang Besar in Perlis;

together with a few other roads of lesser importance in Perak. The total expenditure involved will run into several million dollars, but I have not included any figure in the summary in paragraph 35 below. . . .[2]

(vi)—*Summary*

35. 1949—

		$
Police	... ...	94,030,323
Malay Regiment	... ...	15,436,565
R.N.V.R.	... ...	120,000
Volunteer Land Forces	... ...	20,000
Volunteer Air Forces	... ...	50,000
		109,656,888

1950—

		$
Police	... ...	44,572,743
Malay Regiment	... ...	21,391,669
R.N.V.R.	... ...	77,000
Volunteer Land Forces	... ...	2,000,000
Volunteer Air Forces	... ...	250,000
		68,291,412

1951

		$
Police	... ...	44,572,743
Malay Regiment	... ...	19,962,000
R.N.V.R.	... ...	77,000
Volunteer Land Forces	... ...	3,000,000
Volunteer Air Forces	... ...	250,000
		67,861,743

36. I come now to the question as to how far this necessary programme can be financed by this Government. In my despatch of the 17th December on the Estimates for the year 1949, which provide for a deficit of $24 million, I have referred to the facts that the Federation cannot fairly be expected to shoulder this burden of security expenditure unaided; that the people of this country, from which the United

---

[2] Paragraphs 21–34, which are not printed here, contain details of estimated costs in 1949 and 1950 of the following: police, local naval forces, local land forces, Malay Regiment volunteers units, and local air forces. All these items are summarised in paragraph 35. Gurney did not include proposals for expenditure on civil defence.

Kingdom has drawn and continues to draw very considerable wealth by methods inconsistent with His Majesty's Government's declarations on Colonial policy, would amply repay in renewed loyalty and service to the British connection some offer of financial help to them in their hour of need. Their public funds, accumulated over many prosperous years, have now been wholly expended on rehabilitating their country and repairing war damage without any contribution from the United Kingdom other than an offer of £10 million towards the cost of the War Damage Compensation Scheme, which will itself involve the Federation in further heavy expenditure. In listening to statements made in England as to the cost of British forces in Malaya, for whose presence here they are grateful, they are not persuaded that if, for example, the Brigade of Guards were not in Malaya, its cost would be saved. They have not, however, yet learnt that even the *additional* cost of British troops serving here is being chalked up against them with a view to ultimate recovery, which I have reason to think cannot be seriously intended.

37.   I might mention here a point which has given rise to no little feeling locally and which has caused a loss of wealth to this country and of revenue to the Government. This is the forced sale of Malayan products to His Majesty's Government in 1946 and 1947 at prices far less than the world price. While it is true that Malaya benefited from other similar controls applied elsewhere, e.g., on rice and flour, it has not gone unnoticed that controls at the the same level were not applied to territories such as Ceylon which were further on the road to self-Government and which had no big rehabilitation bill to pay.

38.   It would not be out of place too to recall that Malaya, in her years of prosperity, contributed generously to Empire Defence. During the 1914/1918 war she gave the Battle Cruiser H.M.S. "Malaya" and, in the years between the wars and during 1940–41, until she was occupied, the various Governments now comprised in the Federation made very substantial contributions. These gifts were freely made to the common cause and now that this country is in straitened circumstances it would be natural for the United Kingdom to come to her assistance.

39.   Before leaving London I mentioned to you personally that on the information then available to me we would be running into a serious financial crisis about the middle of 1949, and this forecast is now fully confirmed.

40.   At the same time I must make it plain that I regard the programme outlined in this despatch as necessary to restore and maintain internal security. The problem of how to find $109 million in 1949, $68 million in 1950 and $67 million in 1951 for security services from within a total revenue of about $306 million is insoluble, and I have therefore approached it from the standpoint of what percentage of revenue can properly be allocated to these purposes, having regard to the political necessity of avoiding such curtailment of administrative and social services as would itself tend to create insecurity and to the undoubted need for developments in education and other social fields with which His Majesty's Government so often publicly express their agreement.

41.   It is interesting to note that during the years 1933 to 1941 Federated Malay States expenditure on Police and defence forces declined from 10.63 per cent. to 6.61 per cent. of the total revenue, police expenditure remaining actually constant in amount against increasing revenue. The proportion in the Straits Settlements was much higher, but still did not approach Palestine's 1947 figure of 35 per cent. I note that the percentages in other territories, on the information available to me, are:

Trinidad and Tobago (1947)	...	...	...	8.94 per cent.
Nigeria (1946–47)	... ...	...	...	6.43 "
Tanganyika (1947)	... ...	...	...	5.16 "
Jamaica (1947) ...	... ...	...	...	7.72 "
Mauritius (1947–48)	... ...	...	...	7.97 "
British Guiana (1946)	... ...	...	...	7.04 "

In the present circumstances in which Malaya finds herself as a country on whose shores the Communist tide in South East Asia is already breaking I do not suggest that the percentage which the Federation should expect to have to allocate to police and defence services during the coming three years should be less than 15 per cent. of revenue. On the assumption that there will be no drop in revenue on account of rubber prices, dislocation of tin mines or other causes we could provide on this basis $45 million per annum against $109 million, $68 million and $67 million required for the three years in question, leaving a balance of $64 million, $23 million and $22 million respectively for these years to be contributed by His Majesty's Government.

42. I should mentioned that after discussion of this problem with the Governor of Singapore, whom I have found very ready to be helpful in this matter, this Government has now approached the Singapore Government with a request for financial assistance, which I hope may be forthcoming, in spite of the fact that Singapore already has claims against the Federation amounting to more than $50 million.

The Federation has recently taken various steps to increase its revenue by the imposition of measures which the Singapore Government has not agreed to introduce in the Colony. I see no method of appreciably further increasing rates of taxation in the Federation without similar action in Singapore, and it would in my opinion be unwise, at this early stage of income tax collection, to consider increasing the present initial rates before 1950.

43. I have repeatedly emphasised since my arrival that speed in dealing with the menace of communist terrorism is vital and all-important. We are by no means yet on top of it and everything depends upon what we are able to achieve during 1949. If by the end of 1949 we have not restored peace and security to this country, we shall have failed, and perhaps, if my appeal in this despatch is unsuccessful, for the lack of a comparatively small sum of money.

44. I have not referred in this despatch to the additional demands made on the revenue by the maintenance of several thousands of persons in detention and by the banishment and repatriation at public expense of similar numbers to China: to the no less necessary positive measures of resettlement of squatters, necessitating the provision of transport, food and housing in most cases: to the cost of defence works on rubber estates, tin mines, power houses and other places that have to be protected: to the cost of repairing damaged bridges, burnt post offices and railway stations and sabotaged railway tracks: nor to the cost of pensions and compensation for death or injury suffered by civilians during the present emergency. All these will amount to many millions of dollars in the coming year, but as the amounts are impossible to estimate I have included no figures for them. They must, however, be taken into account as a heavy liability.

45. To summarise, the police force is our most important local force in the conditions that exist here to-day and will have to be faced during the next few years:

this force has been expanded but cannot be maintained by the Federation unaided. If no assistance is forthcoming, I can see no alternative to steps being taken in a few months' time to reduce it, which would be deplorable and might have most serious consequences. The financial assistance required by this Government is of the order of £7½ million in 1949, £2½ million in 1950 and £2½ million in 1951, so far as can be foreseen. I earnestly trust that these contentions can be accepted. They are of some urgency.

46. The Commissioner-General and his colleagues on the British Defence Co-ordination Committee have seen and reviewed the draft of this despatch, copies of which are being sent to the Commissioner-General and to the Governor of Singapore for their information.

Minute on 175

1. A decision is urgently necessary on the extent of the financial assistance which the U.K. should give to Malaya in connection with her expenditure on internal security. The question is fully examined in Mr. Pitblado's minute of 24th February below.[3]

2. Briefly, the position is that Malaya estimates that the cost of internal security measures in 1949 will be £13.5 millions and in 1950 and 1951 £8.5 millions each, and she asks for U.K. help to the extent of £7.5 millions in 1949 and £2.5 millions in each of the two succeeding years. It is to be noted that these expenditures are for internal security measures only, and include nothing in respect of the cost for Imperial defence purposes in Malaya. The internal security forces are mainly the Police and the Malayan Regiment, of which it is proposed to raise a Fourth Battalion immediately.

3. Internal security measures are normally a responsibility of the local Government. A recent decision of Ministers reaffirmed this principle in the following terms:—

"Agreed that Colonial Governments should be expected to bear the cost of maintaining internal security; and that in so far as assistance from U.K. funds might be required in individual cases, the necessary provision should be made in the Colonial and Middle Eastern Services estimate."

The question of financial assistance from H.M.G. should, therefore, be determined in the light of a Colony's general financial position and its ability to pay its way from its own resources. It should be noted, however, that the distinction between internal and external security has become somewhat blurred in the case of Malaya (and it can be argued, in the case of the Colonies generally) by the fact that internal troubles are to a considerable extent Communist-inspired; not unnaturally, it is argued that a particular Colony which has become a focal point for Communist anti-imperial influence cannot be expected to bear by itself the full cost of counteracting it.

4. The question of financial assistance for internal security in Malaya must, therefore, be considered against the background of the Malayan Federation's own financial position, and it must be recognised that, quite apart from the present

---

[3] Not printed.

special problems, Malaya would have been in some financial difficulty anyway. She has been compelled to use up her pre-war balances in rehabilitation measures and to meet various claims outstanding as the result of the war. She hopes, however, to raise a loan of £12 millions in the London market. Except for the remission of U.K. claims in respect of war-time administration, she has had no direct help from H.M.G. apart from the promise of a £10 millions grant for war damage and a £35 millions interest-free loan for the same purpose. This offer by H.M.G. has not yet been accepted by Malaya, where there is a great deal of opposition to the idea of Malaya herself bearing any of the cost of a war damage scheme. In all our financial relations with Malaya, and particularly in connection with this question of her internal security expenditure, we have to bear in mind that she is our biggest dollar-earner and knows it, and, therefore, considers she has a strong claim on H.M.G.'s assistance in restoring and maintaining peaceful conditions.

5. Malaya's Estimates for 1949 have been carefully examined here and, though we feel that in general they have been framed on a reasonable basis, we consider (and the Colonial Office agree) that estimated expenditure might be somewhat reduced and revenue somewhat increased. The net result of our examination is that we think that Malaya's claim for help in 1949 might be reasonably reduced from £7.5 millions to £4.5 millions, (this to include a War Office bill of £1,625 millions which Malaya has not taken into account).

6. Strictly speaking, before we assist a Colony financially we should impose strict Treasury control over its finances. In the case of Malaya, however, there is already an informal control which is working satisfactorily, and we should be reluctant to impose a strict formal control as a result of any financial assistance towards internal security. There is no doubt that any such strict control would be strongly resented in Malaya, partly because of her recognised economic value to us and partly because, as mentioned above, Malaya feels that the full cost of internal security should not be charged up against her. In any case, as we are now proposing financial help for the first year only, and as it is certain that further help will be required in succeeding years, there will be an opportunity of making any necessary adjustments later if we find that Malaya had not been prudent in managing her financial resources.

7. Our recommendation, therefore, is that we should be authorised to tell Malaya that we will give her a grant-in-aid of £4.5 millions towards internal security measures in 1949, without commitment for future years. The Governor will no doubt press for more than this (apart from other grounds there is a possibility that a Fifth Battalion of the Malayan Regiment will be required) and it may be that he will convince us that we must promise more forthwith, but the assurance of £4.5 millions will, at any rate, enable him to deal with the initial steps towards building up internal security. The provision of £4.5 millions, or any other sum, will, of course, involve a Supplementary Estimate, as was foreshadowed when the original Estimates for 1949 were submitted.

8. In summary, the grounds on which we think that a subvention of this magnitude from H.M.G. is justified are:—

(a) Malaya is highly important to us strategically and economically.

(b) She has had to run down her financial resources and had no direct help from H.M.G. since the war, though we had expected that we should have to provide some.

(c) She is unfortunate in having become the focal point of a Communist-inspired drive which has involved her in heavy internal security expenditure for what are partly Imperial reasons.

(d) As financial help will almost certainly be necessary in subsequent years, we are taking no great risk in promising £4.5 millions for 1949 without strict Treasury control.

(e) Reasonably generous treatment in the matter of security expenditure may help somewhat in achieving a settlement of the other outstanding financial issues, e.g. war damage.[4]

J.I.C.C.
28.2.49

---

[4] On 1 Mar 1949 the chancellor of the Exchequer approved a grant in aid of £4.5 million ($38 million), but, after further correspondence with Gurney and discussions with the CO, the Treasury agreed in mid-March to raise the level of UK assistance to a maximum of £6 million ($51 million), though only £5 million of this was taken up in the end.

176 CO 537/4242, no 3   10 Feb 1949
[Malayan Chinese Association]: letter from Sir H Gurney to J D Higham on the objects and rules of the MCA

You may like to have the latest draft of the rules[1] of the Malayan Chinese Association which is to be launched at a meeting in Kuala Lumpur on the 27th February.

You will notice that the objects in Rule 2 include:

"(c) To promote and assist in the maintenance of peace and good order for the attainment of peaceful and orderly progress in Malaya."

As this had naturally been the principal purpose in my mind in discussing the formation of this Association with the Chinese, I was a little surprised to find that the first draft, which the promoters had circulated about the 20th January, did not include this object at all. We therefore had to get hold of the promoters and point out that an Association without such an object at the present time would only lead to criticism of half-heartedness and so paragraph (c) is now in. This was, however, an interesting illustration of the art of fence sitting.

You will also see from Rule 4 that the Association will not be confined to Federal citizens but to any Chinese who has lived here for five years and intends to have his permanent home in Malaya. There is reason to think that there will be no Malay objection to this.

You will see from Rule 12 that Chinese members of Federal Executive Council and Federal Legislative Council are to be *ex-officio* officers of the Association. Rule 16(xii) which empowers the Association to collect or receive donations and contributions envisages that the Association may appeal for funds to assist in the settlement of squatters. I think that they could get very large sums for this purpose, particularly from Singapore, and this would be all to the good. The Association is not

---

[1] Not printed.

to be open to Singapore Chinese at the outset but the idea is that they should be brought in later. This seems to me wise.

Malays generally have welcomed this Association of which it seems likely that Yong Shook Lin will become President.[2]

Apart from this Association, I propose to constitute a Chinese Advisory Board to advise the Government on matters directly connected with the present emergency. The Secretary for Chinese Affairs will be Chairman and a Secretariat officer from the Defence Branch will also be a member. I have made it clear to the Chinese leaders that the purpose of such a Board will be to give a direct channel for communicating constructive proposals from the Chinese community and not a medium for complaints and petitions.

The Association is likely to be widely supported by the Chinese and may become a powerful body in the future. It will be interesting to see how far it will be prepared to declare itself openly against Communism but we have not reached that stage yet and must concentrate more on the short-term problem of getting co-operation for the purposes of the emergency.

---

[2] As it happened (see 179) Tan Cheng Lock was appointed chairman of the protem committee and later became the MCA's first president, 1949–1958. Yong Shook Lin and Leung Cheung Ling were appointed joint secretaries, and Khoo Teik Ee was made treasurer. Yong Shook Lin, a prominent member of the Selangor Chinese Chamber of Commerce, would later resign from MCA to work closely with Dato Onn and the IMP.

177   CO 537/4741, no 16   24 Feb 1949

[British intentions in Malaya]: letter from Sir H Gurney to Sir T Lloyd requesting a government statement to restore confidence

I have been meaning for some time to write to you about one aspect of our task of rebuilding confidence among the people of this country in the value of British protection. Recent events in India and Burma, coupled with ministerial promises of self-government for Malaya, have certainly contributed to the local feeling of insecurity: among the Malays, because they know in their hearts that by themselves they could not compete with the Chinese, particularly an expansionist Communist China; among the Chinese, who would be contented with any stable and peaceful regime and have misgivings about the power of the Malay States; among the people of the Settlements, who want to remain British subjects; among British Government officers who are anxious about their future in the Colonial Service; among British troops and police who wonder whether their efforts may have the same results as in Burma; among rubber planters and tin miners who are facing continued heavy strain and danger in maintaining dollar-earning production. This feeling of insecurity, coming on top of the destructive effects of the Japanese occupation and reflecting itself in doubts as to whether the British will suddenly decide to withdraw from Malaya at short notice, helps to keep alive mutual suspicions between the Malays and Chinese and to encourage a general jockeying for position in preparation for the state of independence which they apprehend might be thrust upon them at any time.

While it is no doubt desirable to emphasise for external consumption that our aim in Malaya is self-government, the first object in Malaya itself must be the restoration of confidence. We have said enough to dispose of any international or local questioning of our motives, but we have not said enough to convince the people of Malaya that we intend to stay in this country at least until they are able to stand on their own feet and maintain their independence among the various disruptive forces emerging in South East Asia.

Success in the present emergency will depend primarily upon recognition by the people that the Government is strong and is not thinking of leaving them in a year or two to the mercies of Chinese Communist forces who might take vengeance for collaboration with the present Government. Such recognition is not assisted by declarations giving the impression that the British intend to abandon their share in the government of the country as soon as they can.

It is pertinent to remember that there is not at present one single elected member of any public body in the country. Nor can we have one, until we have our federal citizens registered, which will take some time.

On the long-term and the short-term view it seems desirable that H.M. Government should take an early opportunity of stating that they have no intention of relinquishing their responsibilities in Malaya until their task there is completed. There is no desire on the part of the people of either the Federation or Singapore that they should do so. Self-government is the goal to which their policy is directed, but it is not desired that this should be achieved at the expense of security or of the liberty of the peoples for whom H.M. Government are responsible.

I find that both the Commissioner General and the Governor of Singapore are in general agreement with this proposition. I am sending them copies of this letter and the Commissioner General has agreed to send you his own suggestions as to the form of words that such a statement might take. They have agreed that I should write to you myself in the first instance, because I feel that such a statement would contribute considerably to the restoration of peace and good order and the ending of our Emergency. If the situation in Burma strengthens public criticism of premature withdrawals, a statement on these lines in regard to Malaya might perhaps also be desirable from H.M. Government's own standpoint.

178 CO 537/4750, no 35 28 Feb 1949
[Internal security and the Chinese]: letter from Sir H Gurney to Mr Creech Jones on measures to avoid a stalemate

I am very grateful for your letter of the 14th February,[1] in which you raise the question whether, if there is no immediate and spectacular result of the intensified efforts we have made during the past two months, there might be a sort of stalemate.

It is a question that I have naturally raised myself here from time to time, since a cessation of bandit incidents might well lead to a general slacking off and make it more difficult for public opinion to accept rather severe measures of the kind we have been taking, particularly against Chinese squatters. My statements emphasising the seriousness of the situation have been made for the purpose of avoiding any

---

[1] In this letter, which is not printed here, Creech Jones, though heartened by Gurney's recent successes in winning the confidence of the Chinese and the energetic action in support of the security forces, asked whether stalemate had set in (see CO 537/4750 no 15).

questioning that these measures are necessary (as indeed they are), and the position is to my mind very much better than I have indicated publicly. One sign is that incidents last week dropped to 22, the lowest since September, but there are other more reliable signs. We have in fact attained our first objective of driving the hard core fairly deep into the jungle, where they are now on the defensive and trying to reorganise. Both the Police and the Army are fully alive to the importance of allowing them no breathing-space at this juncture, but there are killer squads left behind in the populated areas. We are getting information about these squads and are picking up some of their members every day.

The Police and military plans, and here I may say that Gray[2] is fully accepted by all concerned as in charge of operational planning, thus provide for:

(a) mopping up the killer squads and the gradual turning over of "clear" areas to normal but intensified police work;

(b) increased probing of the jungle areas, on a basis of complete and centralised knowledge of all jungle tracks, with a view to surprise air strikes on enemy concentrations and ambushing of their communications. They must get food and supplies.

For this work it is not more troops but police that are required. Incidentally, I do not remember expressing the view attributed to me by Lord Listowel in the House of Lords that more troops are not required. It certainly is my view, but I thought that I had kept it to myself, in spite of frequent interrogation on the point here. In this sort of thing troops are useless without police, and the police are overstrained as it is.

We have reached a point where maintenance of the pressure coupled with some new measures may be expected to bring about disintegration of the Communist forces. What are these new measures to be?

I have wondered for some time how far it is right to treat as separate problems the payment of what we call protection money and the whole vast racket of black-marketing, smuggling and commercial corruption that go to make up Chinese business methods. In the countries round us where Communist or nationalist banditry is rampant, the Chinese flourish. They finance it, because on the short-term it pays and the short-term profits appeal to Chinese philosophy. The rubber smuggling from Sumatra into Malaya and the profits taken off it here are probably all linked up with the black market rubber dealers who get rubber from the estates and pay part of the proceeds to the bandits. To these people banditry pays, because the police tend to go off looking for the bandits and have not so much time for the supervision of rubber dealers or, as Lord Mancroft puts it, issuing dog licences. We are now going in for a drive on the rubber dealers, as a result of which perhaps some Malays might find an opportunity of entering the field of commerce.

I do not think we yet know enough about how Chinese millionaires in Singapore and the Federation really get their money or how they spend it. The evidence against "big" Chinese of paying protection money is not such as to warrant prosecution in any court, but on evidence of that degree we recently arrested and detained a number of Chettiars (including a millionaire) who have all confessed to the Police, though Mr. Thivy, the Indian Government representative, has since persuaded them to

---

[2] Commissioner of police, 1948–1952; see 153, note 5.

retract their admissions. The Police have also had Tan Siew Sin up for interrogation in this connection. He is Tan Cheng Lock's son and a member of Legislative Council and though he appears shaken we have not yet enough evidence to pick him up.

The big Chinese we are after are in Singapore and I am in consultation with Gimson about this, because so far the Singapore police have felt themselves unable to act on the information Gray has given them. I am sending Gray down to see Gimson about this, since I am convinced that nothing would have a greater effect than to detain (and, of course, if possible prosecute) one or two really big Chinese towkays. It would have been wrong to do this before the Chinese here were equipped with an organisation, representing all the leading Chinese, in support of the Government, namely, the Malayan Chinese Association. Such action might well have scattered them into all sorts of camps and broken the last remaining contacts with the Government. I am afraid that, die-hard though it may sound, the treatment of the Chinese in this problem must be such as to give them a much more healthy respect for authority than for anybody else and for the power of that authority to affect their business and profits if the respect does not take a practical form. I say "I am afraid", because it is impossible not to sympathise with Chinese industry, enterprise and skill, as compared with Malay inertia.

Another measure that is being examined with planters is tighter control over the composition of Chinese labour forces on estates. I was surprised to find that the system of employing Chinese contractors gives the estate manager no control over the important matter of whom the contractor employs. Many of these murders are "inside jobs" and obviously the estate manager ought to have some system of registration whereby he knows the individuals working on his estate.

It should not be overlooked that we are killing bandits at an average rate of 3 or 4 a day, and arresting about 50 a day. There is a steady flow of surrendered arms, for which we pay.

We shall therefore be doing everything we can to avoid a stalemate, the dangers of which we fully appreciate. Personally, I do not expect it.

I am grateful for your invitation to mention any particular needs, including equipment. I shall be telegraphing separately in regard to equipment, but there are two items I should like to mention here, as really urgent. First, the recruitment and despatch of the twelve police cadets for whom we asked recently: we shall probably be asking for more soon.

Secondly, financial help as asked for in my despatch No.1 of the 8th January.[3] This is my greatest worry.

It is quite true that the present stage of the campaign is the critical one.

---

[3] See 175.

179   CO 537/4242, no 5   1 Mar 1949
[Malayan Chinese Association]: inward telegram no 282 from Sir H Gurney to J J Paskin on the public launch of the MCA

Following for Paskin.

Malayan Chinese Association was successfully launched at public meeting here on

27th February. Speakers were inclined to dwell rather on racial harmony than on ending the emergency but following extracts from speeches are encouraging.

2.   Tan Cheng Lock who was elected temporary Chairman for three months said "The first duty of the Association will be to co-operate with other communities and to find ways and means of helping the Government to solve its problems and restore law and order". H.S. Lee said "Sino-Malay relations have improved since the liberation but chances of further improvement are obstructed by an unlawful element who created terrorism in June last year. All law abiding people want peace and order to be restored early". Ce Yew Kim [sic][1] who presided at the meeting, exhorted all Chinese to take concerted action in co-operation with the Government and other communities. Other speakers urged formation of Association on the ground that without it there could be no co-operation with the Government.

3.   After the meeting Yong Shook Lity [sic][2] as Secretary issued a statement to the press which included the following *Begins*.

> "The principal object of the Malayan Chinese Association is to assist and maintain peace and order in the whole of Malaya and to strive for advancement under this policy. All law abiding Chinese should have this as their object. All lovers of peace and orderly progress must naturally stand on side of law and order. Therefore it is incumbent to every Malayan Chinese to join this Association". *Ends*.

4.   As was to be expected communism seems not to have been mentioned. I fully appreciate that this Association is quite capable of going wrong and will want careful handling but at present this Movement is genuine.

---

[1] Actually Ee Yew Kim, a leading member of the Chinese Chambers of Commerce and a member of the Federal Legislative Council.
[2] Actually Yong Shook Lin, see 176, note 2.

180   CAB 129/33/1, CP(49)52   5 Mar 1949
'Situation in Malaya and Hong Kong': Cabinet memorandum by Mr Creech Jones   [Extract]

. . .

Malaya
8.   (a) *Security forces*
There are now over 14,000 Regular Police (an increase of over 3,000 since June, 1948) and the force will have reached its planned permanent strength of over 15,000 by June, 1949. In addition there are some 3,600 Extra Constables (mostly ex-regular policemen); 30,000 Special Constabulary (a paid full-time force, mainly Malay, employed chiefly on static defence duties) and 19,000 part-time unpaid Auxiliary Police and village guards.

The total number of British, Gurkha and Malay fighting troops stationed in the Federation of Malaya and Singapore is 14,600. Administrative troops total 26,800. One Battalion of Gurkhas had to be returned to Hong Kong in December. A Third Battalion of the Malay Regiment has now completed its training and the recruitment of a Fourth Battalion is to be started almost at once.

(b) *Internal security situation*

The High Commissioner estimates that the bandit forces now consist of some hundreds of "hard-core Communists" aided by some thousands (probably not exceeding 5,000) of armed auxiliaries of various kinds. Some 500 bandits have been killed (all but 10 of them Chinese).

The bandits have undoubtedly been forced to change their tactics owing to the operations of the Security Forces and have in the main now transferred their attentions from well defended targets to more vulnerable objectives. Their present campaign appears to be almost purely one of murder and the larger bands have withdrawn more deeply into the jungle, leaving behind small killer squads and spies. This disengagement may be only temporary and, in future, other fields of operation, such as the sabotage of power-lines, water supplies and bridges and attacks on Government targets may be more vigorously exploited.

While the situation in certain districts continues difficult and dangerous, the local authorities assure us that, taking the situation as a whole, there has been an overall improvement. The peak of bandit activity appears to have been reached in November when there were 278 attacks. The figure fell to 232 in December and to 198 in January and the decrease continued during February. The monthly civilian fatal casualty rate was 31 in January as opposed to a monthly average of 48 in June/December. Total civilian fatal casualties were 387 up to 24th February, of whom 269 were Chinese and 30 European.

(c) *Siamese frontier*

One of the most difficult problems has been the ease with which bandits could retire across the frontier into Siam and subsquently recross into Malaya. The Siamese Government have all along expressed their willingness to co-operate and steps have been taken to translate this willingness into effective action. Two conferences between Siamese and Malayan officials have recently been held and a jointly planned operation was carried out early in February. Although this achieved no spectacular results, it is hoped that it marks an important step towards establishing a regular and direct liaison between the Security Forces on both sides of the frontier.

(d) *Government action against bandits*

The main difficulty is that the mass of the Chinese population, and in particular their "squatters"—for the most part illegal settlers in areas bordering on the jungle—has been unwilling or unable to co-operate actively with Government. This is not because the Chinese are in sympathy with Communism or the bandits, but because they are so easily intimidated into providing shelter, supplies and money and withholding information about bandit movements.

The squatter problem is being vigorously tackled. Some squatters are being resettled in areas where they will be under close police supervision. Four of the worst areas have been dealt with under a new Emergency Regulation which enables the High Commissioner to deport the inhabitants of certain areas who have persistently declined to co-operate with the

Security Forces against the bandits. These repatriations are being carried out with humanity but with thoroughness. During the first two months of this year, over 1,600 persons have been repatriated. Compensation is paid for animals that cannot be removed and the most careful investigation is made to see that relatives are given the opportunity of accompanying repatriates if they so wish. This action has led to more co-operation between the squatters and the authorities. The Government also has under urgent consideration constructive proposals recently submitted by a Federal Committee for the settlement of squatters on land and bringing the areas under proper administration and this holds out a real prospect for these people of an alternative to Communism.

The payment of "protection money" by all sections of the Chinese community is still a disturbing feature of the situation. Resolute action is being taken against persons known to persist in paying this blackmail; some 300 detentions have already been made. The Government has also introduced National Registration and this is almost completed. Powers have also been taken to declare "closed areas". The declaration of the first "closed area" produced immediate results in the form of volunteered information. I should also add that the High Commissioner is trying to awaken among the Chinese a determination to resist the impositions of the bandits; various Chinese associations have now come forward openly to denounce the payment of protection money and, still more important, a Malayan Chinese Association has been formed on his initiative which has among its objects co-operation with the Government in restoring peace and in providing money and men to help in settling the squatters as peaceful citizens.

9. Nevertheless, the European community, on whose efforts the maintenance of the whole rubber and tin economy of the country depends, is feeling the effects of the strain and danger. There are constant demands for more troops to be sent. The situation would be helped by a few spectacular successes and more active collaboration of the Chinese community; otherwise it looks as if we are faced with a long struggle of attrition. All the help possible is being given to the planters and miners but it is difficult to see what additional assistance could relieve the strain to which they are constantly subjected.

10. A paper on the internal security and local defence forces required in Malaya is now before the Chiefs of Staff and will form the basis of a report by the Minister of Defence and myself to the Defence Committee. The High Commissioner has strongly represented that financial assistance from His Majesty's Government will be necessary if the present scale of police forces in Malaya is to be maintained and if the planned expansion of the Malay Regiment and other local defence forces is to go ahead; and the Chancellor of the Exchequer has agreed that substantial help must be forthcoming. It is hoped that this expansion will in due course release part of the strategic reserve in the Far East for service in Hong Kong, if necessary, but it is unlikely that this could take place before the end of the year, at the earliest.

11. I am confident that the High Commissioner will represent urgently to me any further powers he may need or assistance in men and materials as he may require. I do not think there are any further measures which can be taken in London to strengthen our position.

181   CO 537/4741, no 17   11 Mar 1949
[British intentions in Malaya]: letter (reply) from Sir T Lloyd to Sir H Gurney on the question of a government statement

I was very interested to read your letter of the 24th February[1] in which you state your view that it is important that His Majesty's Government should take an early opportunity of making a statement to the effect that they have no intention of relinquishing their responsibilities in Malaya until their task there is completed. I note that MacDonald is giving thought to the question and has agreed to send his suggestions as to the form of words such a statement might take.

We are, of course, fully aware of the importance of not giving any impression of a withdrawal in anything that may be said here about Malaya, and we have taken particular note of the emphasis you place on the contribution a statement such as you propose would make to the restoration of order, the ending of the Emergency, and communal stability. In fact there is no question of our abandonment of Malaya to chaos and anarchy. Our policy here, as elsewhere, has been laid down in general terms by the Secretary of State, it is "to guide the colonial territories to responsible self-government within the Commonwealth in conditions that ensure to the people concerned both a fair standard of living and freedom from oppression from any quarter." This of course means, in the particular circumstances of Malaya, that our trust must be operated for the benefit of the inhabitants for many years to come. There is, of course, no reason why that, which has been said before, should not be said again and you can be assured that Ministers will consider sympathetically any suggestions that MacDonald may make as to how that can best be done.

---

[1] See 177.

182   CO 537/4785, no 4   17 Mar 1949
[Dato Onn]: letter from Sir H Gurney to J D Higham commenting on Onn's changes of mood

This is not a full reply to your letter No.14349/12 of the 10th March[1] to which I should like to send a more considered answer in due time but some interim information may help to prevent some unnecessary scratching of heads in the Colonial Office about Dato Onn.

The paragraph in the Pan-Malayan Review for the first half of February[2] was based on the report of a Special Branch officer who had gone to see Onn and was treated to a specially virulent exposé of Onn's views in general as they happened to be at that apparently unfavourable moment. He was, no doubt[,] aware that the interview would be reported to myself and others and I took the opportunity of showing it to MacDonald at the time.

---

[1] This was an enquiry about Onn's activities (see CO 537/4790).
[2] The Pan-Malayan Review, no 4, 16 Feb 1949 (see CO 537/4790, no 10) reported that Onn was considering resigning as *mentri besar* of Johore in order to devote himself entirely to UMNO and that the *mentris* of Perak and Kelantan were of like mind.

Shortly before the interview Onn had told me of his intention to resign from his Johore post in order to have "a free hand to fight the Federation" and said that the Sultan of Johore was the only man who would prevent him from doing so. I asked him to think twice before taking such an irrevocable step not because Newboult and I and others do not think that it might really be a good thing if he did resign but because the present moment, at which we are trying to restore confidence all round, would not be the time to take this move which may well have to be taken sooner or later. He has not mentioned it to me since and in the various talks we have had has always been cordial and apparently co-operative.

But the fact is that there is a great difference between Onn met socially and by himself and the Onn sitting as a member of Council or Committee. As a result of his irresponsible behaviour on almost any body on which he sits, he is undoubtedly losing a great deal of the support of the better Malay elements. In my letter to Paskin of the 26th February I enclosed a copy of a letter which I had had sent to all the Mentris Besar saying that I proposed to raise, at the Conference of Rulers on the 2nd March, the question of the competence of State members of Legislative Council to oppose Government measures in the Council without previously letting the official members know that they intended to do so. We had quite a friendly Conference with the Rulers until we came to this point when I explained that I was not seeking in any way to bind the State members to vote in any way other than as they liked, as indeed they are entitled to do under paragraph 38(2) of the Federation Agreement, and all that I was asking for was that we should recognise a practice whereby prior notice will be given to the Federation Government members of any intention on the part of the State members to oppose a Government measure so that we could avoid the awkward situation which arose over the Loan Bill. It was clear to me from nods and looks from the Rulers and other Mentris present that they fully agreed with my proposition, but Onn got up and contended that I was trying to coerce the State members and finished up by saying "I challenge the authority of Your Highnesses to deal with this point". There was then an awkward pause after which I said that I was asking not for any authority to be exercised but for an expression of agreement with the principle in regard to the working of the Federal Legislature. After a few more rude remarks from Onn we all adjourned for lunch when Dr Jekyll reappeared[3] and he became quite reasonable and pleasant over a discussion on education. I then left and Their Highnesses were occupied with the problem I had put to them until 6 o'clock when, after Onn had threatened to resign from Legislative Council and take all the Malay members with him, the Conference agreed to refer the point to State Councils.

This may prove quite good tactics but it was disappointing to see Their Highnesses so spineless in the face of insults to them (not to me) from Onn, for which, before the war, he would have been thrown out of the room. Had it not been for him, the point would have been readily agreed in five minutes.

At the last meeting of Executive Council I made it clear to the members that I expected them to let me know if, having approved a measure in Executive Council, any of them wished to oppose it in Legislative Council. Onn accepted this and said that he hoped to meet my point about Legislative Council procedure by having a small Committee of his State Council to advise him how to act in the Legislative

---

[3] ie Onn resumed his other self.

Council. There is such a Committee in Perak and the State members sit as President of the State Council and not as Mentri Besar; this may well be part of the solution. I do not propose to let this matter slide as it is clearly most important.

Both MacDonald and Palmer[4] have told me that Onn is losing a good deal of ground in the Communities Liaison Committee[5] by his occasional outbursts against the British and the Federation and, indeed, the world in general, which nobody now pays any attention to and this rather annoys him. Like all players to the gallery he does not like it when the gallery fail to respond.

On my recent visit to Kedah and Perlis I heard a good deal of criticism of Onn and his irresponsibility and the mention of his name in those parts usually provokes a smile. As regards Penang, the secession[6] barometer rises or falls exactly according to Malay pronouncements generally by Onn and if the Pronouncements can be kept moderate, the secession movement will fade away.

Palmer told me that at Ipoh two days ago, after a meeting of the Communities Liaison Committee, he walked out with Onn to the British Adviser's car which was flying, as usual, the Union Jack and State flags. Onn made some rude comment about there being no reason for the Union Jack to be flown adding that he was thinking of abolishing the custom in Johore. Palmer gave him a suitable rebuke. But this is a small though illuminating incident.

Mr. Anthony Eden[7] has taken a pretty poor view of him.

Neither Onn nor the politically minded Malays in general have expressed any opposition to the Malayan Chinese Association. In fact, the Mentri of Perak[8] is strongly supporting it and has, I am told, included a Chinese squatter among the representatives of the various communities in the State to the installation of the Sultan on the 16th April. But I know that Onn is personally unhappy about my support for the M.C.A., though he has never mentioned it to me. As may be apparent to you, one of our difficulties in dealing with Onn is his proximity to the Commissioner General whose office, I believe, issued the P.M.R. which was the occasion of your letter. Unfortunately it is not always possible to give these reports a proper slant; hence your questions.

My own feeling about Onn is that he is so irresponsible and unreliable that the support which he has built up for himself on the discontent connected with the Malayan Union will detach itself noticeably quite soon if he does not change his attitude and if, in the meantime, he is firmly handled.

---

[4] Sir Sydney Palmer (1890–1954) came out to Perak as a rubber planter in 1909; he was president of the United Planting Association in Malaya, 1935–1936, 1938, 1940–1942, 1946–1948; member of the Advisory Council of the Malayan Union, 1946–1947, Federal Legislative Council, 1948–1949, Communities Liaison Committee, 1949; retired from Malaya to assume directorships of rubber companies in London, c 1950.

[5] Acting as 'liaison officer' MacDonald was instrumental in convening a meeting of Malay and Chinese leaders in Jan 1949 with the object of resolving communal differences. Known at first as the Malay-Chinese Goodwill Committee, it was renamed the Communities Liaison Committee when representatives of other communities joined the group, see 195 paras 4 & 5.

[6] ie opposition in Penang to its incorporation within the Federation.

[7] Eden, deputy leader of the Conservative opposition, was visiting Malaya at the time, see 183.

[8] ie the Dato Panglima Bukit Gantang who was secretary general of UMNO and a close ally of Onn.

183   CO 825/76/2, no 7   18 Mar 1949

[British intentions in Malaya]: inward telegram no 337 from Sir H
Gurney to Sir T Lloyd on a conversation with Mr Eden. *Minutes* by
N D Watson,[1] J D Higham, Mr Creech Jones, Mr Rees-Williams

Following personal for Lloyd from Gurney.

You may like to have the following notes on Mr. Anthony Eden's visit.

He left here this morning for Singapore after a day in Johore seeing Dato Onn,
planters and troops, a day in Penang where he met the Secession Committee, a day in
Ipoh with miners, planters, troops and many hundreds of all communities and two
days here including a visit to Police Headquarters, a large Malay party and talks with
commercial people.

2. Visit has been a great success. He told me he was much impressed with the
progress being made in restoring peaceful conditions and entirely agreed that more
troops was not the answer. He was greatly interested in our police work, for which he
expressed admiration. He said most planters and miners had told him that they
thought there was a considerable improvement in the situation, though some feared
trouble might become chronic. He took a poor view of Dato Onn, and appeared to
accept my view, which I expressed to him frankly, that no greater contribution to
restoring confidence here could be made at the moment than an assurance by
H.M.G. that they have no intention of relinquishing their responsibilities in Malaya
until their task is completed. On this point, Macdonald [sic] and I have not yet been
able to agree on the draft.

Minutes on 183

Mr. Higham
The Secretary of State had already commented, on seeing his own copy of the
telegram at 7, that he was not clear about the meaning of Sir H. Gurney's statement
to Mr. Eden recorded at Y.[2] Does it mean that we have in some way been negligent at
this end in refusing to make a statement by H.M.G. such as Sir H. Gurney suggests,
and has the latter in fact asked for such declaration and it has been refused? The
Secretary of State is sorry that the matter should have been discussed with the
Deputy Leader of the Opposition before it was raised with himself. As it is, Sir H.
Gurney's conversation with Mr. Eden appears to convey the impression that H.M.G.
have been withholding something that Malaya wanted, and that we are uncertain in
policy and unable to give them a clear lead—whereas in fact we have already taken up
the point of drafting a declaration of this kind.

I therefore return this paper to you before submitting it to the Secretary of State.
Perhaps you can clarify the points on which the Secretary of State is doubtful and
recirculate with any advice for further action.

N.D.W.
23.3.49

---

[1] Principal, CO, 1948–1950; private secretary to Creech Jones.
[2] ie the sentence in para 2 of the telegram under discussion starting 'He took a poor view of Dato Onn . . .'

Mr. Watson

I attach 52243[3] on which discussion has been proceeding in this matter of a possible statement by H.M.G. regarding our intention not to quit Malaya before our task is completed in an orderly fashion. The letters to which I would especially draw your attention are Sir H. Gurney's of the 24th February to Sir T. Lloyd (16)[4] and the latter's reply (which was agreed by Mr. Rees Williams) at (17).[5] As you will see there has at no time been any question of H.M.G. having refused to make a statement; we have noted the High Commissioner's view that such a statement is desirable and are now awaiting Malaya's suggestions as to the terms in which it should be made.

2. In view of the terms of the correspondence I do not think that Sir H. Gurney could possibly have conveyed to Mr. Eden the impression that H.M.G. had exhibited any reluctance in this matter. I should not be at all surprised if Mr. Eden had gathered from conversations with various people in Malaya that there was considerable anxiety in the country regarding H.M.G.'s intentions; many letters from planters, etc., are couched in this strain and you will see from (15) on 52243 that this feeling is abroad among the soldiers as well. As far as the department is concerned no further action is necessary on this personal telegram from Sir H. Gurney.

3. Incidentally I do not read the telegram as meaning that Sir H. Gurney conveyed to Mr. Eden the sense of the final sentence, i.e. that Mr. MacDonald and he had not yet been able to agree on a draft.

4. I should like 52243 back as soon as possible for further action on (18) as indicated in the minutes.

J.D.H.
23.3.49

Yes but I regret the matter was discussed at all with Mr. Anthony Eden. I certainly had not been informed until I saw this telegram No 337 that any declaration was thought desirable. The matter of a declaration seems to have got into the newspapers, the *Daily Mail* on 24/3/49 through its correspondent Lachie McDonald writing a great deal of nonsense with the usual idiocy about the Labour Govt. & Colonial Office. He proclaims to the British public "what is most needed in Malaya . . . is something only Westminster can provide—a firm clear statement that British intend to remain in Malaya for 20 or 30 years at least." So far as I know there has been no shadow of a suggestion here or in Malaya or any where else by any responsible person that such a thought had ever crossed anyone's mind—indeed, it never has. Who then is putting this nonsense round & why? Surely Gurney, quite apart from consideration of any public statement, ought to know my views immediately as the point seems to worry him.

A.C.J.
25/3/49

Secretary of State

1. There is undoubtedly some disquiet in Malaya, Hong Kong and East Africa owing to their fear that there may be an abandonment of these Territories by His Majesty's Government. I think the fear has arisen from two sources: first, owing to a misunderstanding of the Government's policy in the circumstances by which

---

[3] Not printed; the reference is to CO 537/4741.   [4] See 177.   [5] See 181.

independence was granted to India, Pakistan and Burma, and secondly, owing to the constant campaign by the Tory Party and their supporters in the Press that Britain is "liquidating" the Colonies and "scuttling" out of the Empire. This latter reason makes it so unfortunate in my opinion that the subject should have been raised by the High Commissioner in Malaya with the Deputy Leader of the Opposition.

2. I personally get a large number of letters and interviews from unofficials in these Territories who all express the same fear. I try to reassure them.

3. You will remember that Sir Philip Mitchell[6] referred to this question in a speech he made in East Africa, a copy of which he sent to us.

4. The High Commissioner, Malaya, has been in communication with us for some time on this question desiring that a statement should be made. The matter was also discussed so far as I remember with Mr. Macdonald [sic] when he was home, and so far as we are concerned we have, while keeping in touch with the Governor of Singapore, asked that an agreed statement should be submitted for your consideration. That has not yet been done.

5. When it is done, then I take it that it will be considered by you with your Cabinet colleagues as to whether they agree:—

(a) that the statement should be made, and
(b) that it should be made in the form desired.

6. I was hoping that we would have got out by this time a statement of all declarations of Government policy relating to the Colonies, the draft of which you have seen and which I believe is now in course of production. This will go round to all the Public Relations Officers in the Colonies, and then for the first time people will have in short compass authoritative statements made by Ministers in Parliament on these various matters.

7. I do think that an approach should be made to the High Commissioner on his conversation with the Deputy Leader of the Opposition in order that similar occurrences may be avoided in future. I think that an approach to him on the lines indicated in Mr. Watson's minute[7] and in the light of what has transpired will be salutary.

D.R.W.
25.3.49

---

[6] Sir Philip Mitchell, governor of Kenya, 1944–1952.
[7] This minute of 25 Mar, following up Creech Jones's of same date, is not printed. For the CO's reply to Gurney, see 184.

184   CO 537/4741, no 27   2 Apr 1949
[British intentions in Malaya]: letter (reply) from Sir T Lloyd to Sir H Gurney

[Lloyd toned down the wording of this letter to avoid any hint of rebuke that might unsettle Gurney who, Lloyd informed Rees-Williams, was 'particularly sensitive, almost touchy'.]

Ministers were much interested in your telegram No.337[1] (which arrived while I was on leave) reporting on Mr. Eden's visit to Malaya.

2. In connection with the last two sentences of that telegram you may know that the Press here has recently carried quite a crop of suggestions that uncertainty about the British Government's intention to stay in Malaya for many years to come is having an unsettling effect. Walter Fletcher[2] is reported by Reuter from Singapore on March 26th to have said that "Britain should state clearly she intends to stay in Malaya for many more decades: such a declaration should quell some unhealthy political ambitions . . . Britain was obliged to remain in the country until political stability had been reached". The *Daily Mail* correspondent in Malaya, Lachie McDonald, wrote from Kuala Lumpur on the 23rd March that: 'What is most needed in Malaya to-day isn't more soldiers and policemen, but something only Westminster can provide—a firm, clear statement that the British intend to remain in Malaya for 20 or 30 years at least. For a week now I have talked to planters, miners, soldiers, policemen, and civil servants. The majority of these men on the spot are sick and tired of semi-official hints that "soon Malaya will be left to itself".'

3. There have also been articles in the same strain emanating from business interests in London.

4. Before the Secretary of State left for Central Africa[3] he asked me to let you know that he is disturbed at the way in which this insidious campaign of rumour appears to be gathering momentum, particularly as, so far as he is aware, there has been no shadow of suggestion here or in Malaya by any responsible person that there can be any question of Britain leaving Malaya for many years to come or of any abdication of our responsibility until our task has been faithfully discharged. Mr. Creech Jones has noticed that underlying some of these reports there is the suggestion that the present Government are showing a reluctance to state their attitude in this matter and that indeed the Government have doubts about what their policy should be. From that point of view the Secretary of State was a little concerned that the matter came up in the course of your talks with Mr. Eden but he is sure that you would be careful not to convey any impression that the Government are being in any way laggard in this matter.

There is in fact no ground for such an impression since as you will know from a personal telegram I sent to-day to MacDonald (and repeated to you) the view at this end is that a statement should be made and that soon.

---

[1] See 183.

[2] Walter Fletcher, Conservative MP for Bury 1945–1955, was a businessman with a particular interest in Malayan rubber.

[3] Creech Jones's visit to Central Africa took place after delegates of Southern Rhodesia and unofficial representatives of Northern Rhodesia and Nyasaland had met at the Victoria Falls in Feb and agreed on the desirability of forming a Central African federation.

185   CO 537/4751, no 68   2 Apr 1949
[British intentions in Malaya]: minute by Mr Attlee of his meeting
with Mr Creech Jones, Mr Alexander and Mr Shinwell[1] on 1 Apr 1949

It was agreed:—

(a) that a Statement emphasising that we had no intention of leaving Malaya
should be made by the Prime Minister soon on a convenient occasion.[2] Colonial
Office to provide a draft.

(b) Mr. MacDonald to be asked if he would agree to a suggestion by the Secretary
of State for War that a small hand-picked party of Journalists should visit Malaya;

(c) Mr. MacDonald to be asked for an appreciation of the situation by the Defence
Committee over which he presides.[3]

---

[1] Alexander was minister of defence, 1946–1950; Shinwell was secretary of state for war, 1947–1950.
[2] On 13 Apr 1949 Attlee made the following statement in the House of Commons: 'His Majesty's
Government have no intention of relinquishing their responsibilities in Malaya until their task is
completed. The purpose of our policy is simple. We are working, in co-operation with the citizens of the
Federation of Malaya and Singapore, to guide them to responsible self-government within the
Commonwealth. We have no intention of jeopardising the security, well-being and liberty of these peoples,
for whom Britain has responsibilities, by a premature withdrawal' (*H of C Debs*, vol 463, col 2815; see also
PREM 8/1406/1).   [3] See 186 and 188.

186   CO 537/4751, no 71/2   4 Apr 1949
[Security situation]: outward telegram secret no 196 from Mr Creech
Jones to Mr M J MacDonald requesting an appreciation[1]   [Extract]

Before the Secretary of State left for Africa the Prime Minister discussed situation in
Malaya with him, the Minister of Defence, and the Secretary of State for War.
Ministers expressed great appreciation of the efforts which have been and are
continuing to be made by the civil and military authorities and of the results so far
achieved. They fully appreciate the reasons why it has not yet been possible to
achieve any decisive success against the bandits. They nevertheless are greatly
concerned at the probable consequences, both in Malaya and here, if (as they realise
may well be the case) the struggle drags on for very much longer without any
obvious turning point being reached. They are conscious that, in certain circles in
this country, especially

(a) those with business interests in Malaya involving the employment of Europeans who have already been subject to such a prolonged period of nerve-racking
strain, and,

(b) relatives and friends of members of the security forces, both military and civil,
there is a growing sense of anxiety, which will inevitably be aggravated if an
intensification of bandit activity foreshadowed in recent reports leads to increased
casualties both among European civilians and security forces in the next few
weeks.

---

[1] This telegram was repeated to Gurney who sent a despatch in reply, see 188.

2. Ministers accordingly wish to have available the most comprehensive picture possible of the situation so that they may be in a position not only to reassure as necessary public opinion here but also to deal with the greatest promptitude with any requests for assistance in any form that either the civil or military authorities might find it necessary to make. . . .

187   CO 537/4761, no 14   4 Apr 1949
[Tan Cheng Lock]: letter from Sir H Gurney to J J Paskin

[Surprised to hear that Tan Cheng Lock had been elected chairman of the MCA (see 179) and somewhat dubious about his dependability, Paskin had asked Gurney for 'an up to date appreciation both of Tan Cheng Lock's attitudes to Government and of the probable value of his influence with moderate Chinese opinion in Malaya' (see CO 537/4242, no 6).]

You asked in your letter No.52849/48/49 of the 8th March for an appreciation of Tan Cheng Lock.

I think it may be said that Tan Cheng Lock was disgruntled at being left out of Government's circle and Councils on reoccupation. This was a blow to his pride and he wandered off into other camps, which he now regrets.

He has always been regarded as a sincere man by the Chinese; his aim has been the political unification of all the races of Malaya. In 1946 and 1947 he was surrounded by members of the Malayan Democratic Union and other exponents of left-wing politics, and he supported their policies as Chairman of the Pan-Malayan Council of Joint Action. When the emergency began, however, he was left alone except in Malacca and in a somewhat dubious position. It is possible that he regrets his earlier association with these promoters of violence. Nevertheless, it should be remembered that he was connected with the Council of Joint Action, and there were many moderate Chinese who shared his view on the constitutional issue. Nor did his former political activities lead to a severance of his ties with or to a weakening of his position on the Malacca Chinese Chamber of Commerce. Thus one should not infer from his post-war record that he was a very eccentric figure in the Chinese world.

The Chinese have retained a high regard for his sincerity and when the time came to elect a temporary chairman of the Malayan Chinese Association, only two men were considered; these were H.S. Lee and Tan Cheng Lock. Perak (with the exception of Lau Pak Kluan [Khuan]), Negri Sembilan and Johore would not have H.S. Lee, and Tan Cheng Lock remained for the post. It should be noted that neither at the meeting which gave him the post nor subsequently in the Chinese press has there been any mention of his earlier activities and there is general recognition that he is one of the few men here who may be able to hold the Chinese together. To find a man who can bring and keep together several personal followings amongst Chinese is always an important and difficult matter.

Since my telegram of 1st March, Tan Cheng Lock has agreed to sit on the Chinese Emergency Advisory Committee to which I referred towards the end of my letter to Higham of the 10th February. The terms of reference of this Committee are to advise on all matters in which the Chinese community are concerned in the present emergency; the first meeting is on 5th April. The former Chinese Advisory Board at Malacca is about to be revived and Tan Cheng Lock will also be invited to serve on it.

The position at present is, I think, that he commands considerable respect amongst the Chinese. He is 66 years old; he has had experience in Malayan politics, he is sincere; and he is able to rise above the arguments of the different dialect groups in Chinese society. He is sincere in his efforts to do the best for the Chinese in Malaya and to encourage co-operation with the Malays. He has, therefore, a strong influence with moderate Chinese opinion here. He is still independent and will support Government if he is convinced that Government desires to treat the Chinese fairly. I do not think that he is very different from other Chinese in his attitude towards the pressure aspects of my emergency policy. This does not imply his or their fundamental opposition to Government but rather their wish that Government should have confidence in them and listen to their views concerning the emergency, which is exactly the object I had in mind in setting up the Emergency Advisory Committee and in lending my support to the Malayan Chinese Association.

I enclose a copy of a letter[1] from MacDonald of the 21st March giving his opinion of Tan Cheng Lock. The description which I gave, and to which he refers in his second paragraph was "gaga". This was based on a limited knowledge and is, no doubt, an overstatement, but I cannot myself see Tan Cheng Lock as capable of any great things. On his last visit to me, he took some time to represent that the squatters of Kajang[2] were good and blameless people. At the end of the meeting, I asked him whether he was returning to Malacca that evening and he said, no, he thought that it was too late in view of possible dangers on the road. I asked him where the dangers lay and he said "Kajang". Let it be to his credit that he also laughed.

---

[1] Not printed.   [2] Hotbed of guerrilla activity in Selangor.

---

188 CO 537/4751, no 80   11 Apr 1949
[Security situation]: despatch (reply)[1] no 4 from Sir H Gurney to Mr Creech Jones. Enclosure: paper by Lieutenant-Colonel Gray and Major-General Boucher[2]   [Extract]

. . . 3. As you are aware, the "operational" features of an anti-terrorist campaign of the type now being fought in the Federation are not more than half of the plan. In this campaign the Malays have been and still are solidly behind the Government and the trend of Malay opinion is towards stronger action and more impatience with the Chinese. The Malayan Chinese Association, which has come out openly with appeals to all Chinese to co-operate with the Government, to give information and to stop giving any help to the bandits, is receiving widespread support and so long as it keeps on this platform will disarm Malay criticism, which the Chinese themselves are equally anxious to avoid. On the one hand the Association must be allowed to make enough "face" to enable it to attract adherents and on the other it must be

---

[1] This despatch was sent in reply to 186.
[2] Gray was commissioner of police, Malaya, 1948–1952; Boucher was GOC, Malaya, 1948–1949.

continually pushed into taking action and its instinct to pursue purely Chinese interests guided into the Malayan channel. Without these civil and political measures of organising an object of affiliation for the Chinese, evacuation and repatriation of squatter areas, national registration, detention of collaborators and protection money payers, careful nursing of trade unions and greatly intensified police work, the operations carried out by the military forces could have achieved little. In fact, they have achieved a great deal and the plans made six months ago have been generally proved to be right.

4. It is now proposed that the military forces should maintain a continuous and heavy pressure on the main bandit bodies in the remoter jungle areas to which they have retired or are retiring. This is a most difficult and arduous task for any troops. It must be accompanied by vigilance on the part of all police and local authorities to spot bandits who break back and attempt to settle down in villages and squatter areas as ordinary civilians. This means a live and efficient administration and good police work. The reluctance of many Malay District officers and penghulus to do any more than is strictly necessary where Chinese are concerned puts more of the burden on the police. Good police work, as is well known, demands an intimate knowledge of individuals and of everything that goes on, and at the present time must not be sacrificed to operational work. The expansion of the Malay ranks of the Regular Force enables it to do both, provided that the officers for whom I have asked urgently are forthcoming. The Force is badly under-officered for what it now has to face, and we are in danger of putting too long and heavy a strain on the good officers. Troops rely on the Police for practically all their information and on operations are accompanied by Police. New Police cadets have to be trained. I asked for twelve in January and have now asked for fifty-five more. None has so far arrived, though I appreciate that efforts are being made. The full weight of the Police can be applied only through strengthening control and leadership in the Force.

5. I recognise that in saying this I am repeating what I have said many times already. But the lesson has not apparently yet been generally learnt that the answer to Communist terrorism equipped with modern arms is not the soldier but the policeman. In the Federation of Malaya the policeman is fully armed, jungle-trained, knows his people and country and is doing his life's job. It is of immense political advantage in restoring confidence if the inhabitants of this country can be organised and led to put their own security house in order, rather than have the impression that it is being done for them by troops on whose inevitable departure there will be no guarantee of peace. This guarantee they are anxious to create, so far as they are able, and it seems to me to be our duty to assist them to do so and to exploit fully their sense of pride in doing so.

6. It remains to be said that the States and Settlements of Johore, Negri Sembilan, Malacca, Penang, Kedah and Perlis are now comparatively clear of active bandits. The main operations of the next stage of the campaign will be in Pahang, Perak and Selangor and to a lesser extent in Kelantan and Trengganu.

7. Your telegram under reference mentions an "obvious turning point".[3] There is no obvious turning point in any conflict with terrorism until the stage of surrender. A murder can be committed by one terrorist as easily as by fifty. It is not yet possible

---

[3] See 186, para 1.

to predict the manner in which the present campaign will end. If the terrorists bury their arms and reappear as ordinary citizens, there is a danger of a false end. In fact, the main turning point occurred about two months ago, but it was not obvious at the time. . . .

Enclosure to 188: 'A paper on the security situation in the Federation of Malaya, 1st April,[4] 1949'

Introduction

1. This paper is primarily intended to deal with the security situation in the Federation of Malaya but it cannot be in any way complete or give a true picture unless it touches briefly on certain political aspects of the problems which have a direct bearing on the internal security situation. Also, the situation is now fluid and changing rapidly.

2. The political aspects are of vital importance. If public opinion, and in particular Chinese opinion, could be influenced or swung sufficiently far in an anti-communist and anti-bandit direction the militant communists would be unable to carry on their campaign.

Political

3. It is abundantly evident that communist successes in China and elsewhere have had a very considerable effect on the political, and indeed the security problem in Malaya. The majority of the Chinese are still undoubtedly sitting on the fence. Few of them have a Malayan outlook or feel that they owe allegiance to this country, and they are therefore reluctant to commit themselves to a pro-Government policy. They feel that a complete communist victory in China is not far distant and are unwilling to compromise their future and connections with that country. Moreover, they fear that whatever the outcome of the present emergency, His Majesty's Government would shortly give Malaya self-government, and the conviction that the communists would then gain control of Malaya has been a very powerful reason in the minds of the Chinese for sitting on the fence.

4. Many efforts have been made by the Government to induce the Chinese in Malaya to adopt a more helpful and forthright attitude. Some progress has been made. The Malayan Chinese Association which is now showing some signs of actively committing itself on the side of law and order can fairly be described as a Government inspired and sponsored movement. A meeting of representatives of all Branches of the Association held on the 4th April decided to start a publicity campaign calling upon all Chinese to co-operate with the Government. The Chinese controlled or owned sections of the press have in general adopted a more moderate and helpful attitude towards the Government.

5. It is noticeable, however, that very little progress was made until the Government and the security forces legislated for and carried out far more drastic security measures than had previously been applied. It also remains to be seen whether the Malayan Chinese Association or similar bodies who are undoubtedly in a position to do so, e.g., Chinese Chambers of Commerce, will in fact produce concrete

---

[4] The date, '1st April', in this printed version has been altered in manuscript to '5th April'.

assistance which will have any direct bearing on the security situation.

6. It may be argued that it takes time to gain confidence and to swing public opinion sufficiently far to obtain practical assistance, particularly with the present Chinese political background, and that early results cannot be expected. As against this it is thought that the strong measures taken in the security field have been the means of forcing the Chinese into making some gestures at least, although they are unlikely to commit themselves any more than they can help.

7. On balance it is considered that the security measures and activities have been the real cause of the political progress made. It is therefore essential that these measures be kept up and intensified, until the Chinese are forced into giving practical assistance, whether by fear of consequences if such co-operation is not forthcoming or by the more wholesale conviction that the Government will win before the situation in China can influence Malaya effectively, and that it is better to be on the winning side. Eventually, and there is evidence to support the contention, the scales will be tipped, and information leading to the destruction or capture of the bandits will be forthcoming in generous measure. Then and not before, care must be taken to ensure that the Chinese population is not alienated by the unnecessary prolonging of the more drastic measures. In other words the stage has not yet been reached when political opinion is leading and ensuring internal security. At present security measures are the chief factor affecting and influencing public opinion.

8. Security measures should be supported by the removal of doubts about the future. A clear statement should be made to dispel apprehensions that His Majesty's Government contemplate an early termination of their responsibilities for the people of this country. . . .[5]

Conclusions

90. The following main points emerge:—

(a) For political reasons and to help the Government to swing Chinese opinion further towards a positive pro-Government and pro-law and order attitude, it is essential that the security forces continue and intensify their activities. Their efforts will not produce a quick decision unless the Government's measures to swing Chinese opinion in our favour are quickly successful.

(b) The time factor is still all-important and the longer disorders continue the more difficult will they be to stamp out owing to influences outside the control of the Government of the Federation.

(c) It is evident that the initiative has largely passed to the security forces and that the bandits are in considerable difficulties. This is an added reason for making even greater efforts.

(d) The basic difficulty of large tracts of the country being still not policed or administered and therefore exposed to communist activities remains and must be remedied.

(e) As the bandits withdraw into remote or unpopulated areas they must be pursued by the security forces.

(f) Measures under Emergency Regulation 17D[6] must be undertaken in more of the areas which are being used by the bandits as bases.

---

[5] Paras 9–89, containing details of security measures, are not printed here.

[6] Introduced on 10 Jan 1949, Emergency Regulation 17D gave the high commissioner the right of

(g) Purely police measures, backed up by the necessary legislation, must be intensified to prevent a reinfiltration into normal civilian life by bandits or active communist sympathizers in addition to routing out those who still exist under cover.

(h) Adequate control of entry to Malaya by legal means must be instituted if the full benefit of National Registration is to be obtained.

(i) It is still most important to prevent illegal immigration, arms running and other means of assistance to communists.

(j) No amnesty can be considered for a period of at least three months.

(k) No reduction in military forces can yet be considered. Even if the militant communist campaign collapsed—and there are no signs yet of that stage being reached—the present strength would be essential to back up the police in showing the flag and generally bringing the country under an adequate measure of control.

(l) The police force, its development and efficiency, are likely to remain the decisive factors in the drive to smash the bandits and eventually to ensure that there is no recurrence of the disorders.

---

ordering collective detention and of banishing any person so detained (other than a Federal citizen or British subject). It was intended to supplement 17D with measures recommended by Gurney's Squatter Committee but it also turned many Chinese against the authorities. Repatriation of Chinese ended with the victory of the communists in China when attention shifted to detention and resettlement in Malaya.

189   CO 537/4773, no 3   30 May 1949

[Insurgency and counter-insurgency]: despatch no 5 from Sir H Gurney to Mr Creech Jones

[Creech Jones's despatch of 4 Jan 1949 and the original of Gurney's reply are probably still retained at CO 537/6403-6406. Gurney's despatch was subsequently printed and was given restricted circulation on a top secret basis. Sir Charles Arden-Clarke, governor of the Gold Coast 1949–1956, referred to Gurney's despatch as he handled Nkrumah's Positive Action, see BDEEP series B, vol 1, R Rathbone, ed, *Ghana*, part I, App, note and para 38. Some years later R L Baxter of the CO called it 'the nearest approach' to a post-mortem on the outbreak of insurrection though admitted that it 'deals more with the grand lessons of the Emergency' (CO 1030/16, minute by Baxter, 8 Feb 1955).]

In your Top Secret Despatch No. 1 of the 4th January you asked me to arrange for the preparation of a paper setting out the experience gained in the present operations in Malaya which the Oversea Defence Committee could consider with a view to its use as a basis for general guidance to Colonial Governments.

2. I have sent you in my Secret Despatch No. 4 of the 11th April a paper on the security situation in the Federation[1] which describes the effect of the various counter-measures taken against the Communists' plans. I propose to exclude from the present despatch any account of those measures which might be regarded as peculiar to Malayan conditions and having little relevance elsewhere. These condi-

---

[1] See 188.

133

articular, the existence of large stocks of arms and ammunition
ᵢe country by our forces during the war and not subsequently
resence of the Malayan People's Anti-Japanese Army, recruited and
...ᵤu as underground fighters during the war and afterwards left high and dry; and
the Chinese mind. It is not, fortunately, in many Colonial territories that these
phenomena occur, and it may therefore be more helpful to confine the suggestions
in this despatch to considerations of fairly general application and to read the lessons
of Malaya in the light of my own limited experience of East Africa, Jamaica, the Gold
Coast and Palestine.

3. *The Communist Plan.*—Communist infiltration of trade unions and the labour
front resulting in complete domination of these workers' organisations, was the
prelude to "military" operations in Malaya and may well be the same elsewhere. The
wholesale arrest of these Communist leaders and the proscription of the parties to
which they belonged came just in time to be welcomed with relief by the vast
majority of trade union members, but these measures came too late to prevent the
escape of many of the leaders, who disappeared and went underground on the
declaration of the Emergency. Had the Communists continued to confine themselves
to dominating and controlling trade unions, organising strikes and obtaining by
intimidation and incitement a firm grip of the whole labour front, they would have
been very difficult to deal with. But their plans in Malaya, as elsewhere, laid down
that the next stage was to be a campaign of terrorism, developing into guerrilla
warfare, with a view to the establishment of "liberated areas" to serve as bases from
which the final attack to overthrow the Government would be launched. This second
stage was embarked upon not because the "infiltration" campaign was proving
unsuccessful (on the other hand it was succeeding very well) but as part of the
standard Communist plan.

Communist control of trade unions may therefore be regarded as the first step in
the process in which terrorism is the next. It is wise to bear this in mind in
considering the difficult question of the precise time at which the Government
should take action to prevent the next step occurring, but the fact of such control
should indicate that the time has come to proscribe the local Communist Party and
arrest its leading members. The choice of the moment to act is difficult because too
early action may involve a lack of public support and delay may create an infinitely
more difficult and prolonged problem. It is probably better to be too soon than too
late.

4. *Terrorism.*—Terrorism equipped with modern automatic weapons and political aspirations is a new development in the British Commonwealth. It is a method of
warfare to which the training and traditions of our police and military forces have
not yet been adapted. Since, however, it is a part of the Communist plan and is
provided for in the Communist "cell" organisation, some of the characteristics of
terrorism need to be recognized. In the first place, the terrorist tends always to have
the initiative. It is impracticable to defend against assassination all the individuals
who may be attacked, or to defend against sabotage all the railway tracks, telephone
and electric power lines, factories, Government offices and other installations that
are vulnerable. Nevertheless, the ease with which successful attacks on these targets
can be made, their effect on public morale and the help obtainable by the terrorists
from an uneducated and intimidated community as a result of a few spectacular
successes require the immediate protection of the more important targets. Little

result can be expected from such static defence, beyond satisfying public opinion and strengthening public confidence. Determined terrorists can defeat any plan of static defence by attacking elsewhere, leading to public outcry (which must be resisted) for the diversion of more security forces to the defence task. The first point, therefore, is that against terrorism static defence is largely useless but has to be provided. How it should be provided is dealt with below.

Secondly, Communist terrorism is completely ruthless and uses the technique of sheer intimidation. Its exponents rely upon dominating, by murder and abduction, the inhabitants of an area who can supply them with food, money and shelter. They exploit for this purpose any secret societies and native superstitions that will give them a hold over the local inhabitants, and operate an intelligence system that enables them to dispose of potential informers. They extort money and food with threats which they are prepared to carry out. The longer they are allowed to remain, the firmer their hold becomes. The area then becomes a "liberated area".

The ruthless character of terrorism, the ineffectiveness of any defence against it and the suddenness with which it may be launched demand that the Government (if it has been unable to forestall the outbreak) should be ready to take the initiative with its full-scale measures at the very outset. In Palestine the Emergency Regulations were continually being added to and tightened up, so that at the end it might almost have been said that the whole book of Regulations could have been expressed in a single provision empowering the High Commissioner to take any action he wished. If all these powers had been taken and exercised immediately at the beginning, perhaps the outcome might have been different. Similarly, in Malaya, the same process has developed and powers for the more drastic and indeed ruthless measures were not provided or exercised until six months after the outbreak.

5. *Maintenance of civil authority.*—There is an obvious reluctance on the part of any civil authority, particularly one nurtured in the British tradition, to administer drastic remedies. It has indeed been the practice in the past to hand to the military authorities the unpleasant job of restoring law and order in a situation demanding treatment to which the civil authorities felt unable to lend themselves. Martial law was proclaimed or introduced in effect by Regulations giving wide powers to military commanders, and it is worth while pausing to consider what martial law means.

The effect of proclaimed martial law is to hand over all power, in the area to which it is applied, to a military commander, to close the civil courts and so to deprive the public of the right of redress in the courts. The orders of the military commander are not open to challenge by any legal process, so long as there are no courts open having jurisdiction in the area. But in the case of application of martial law to a part of a territory, there will be courts which will remain open and will have such jurisdiction, e.g., to hear habeas corpus applications. The closing of all civil courts is a serious step that only arises for consideration if and when their continued operation is obstructive.

The proclamation of martial law places upon the military commander, under present-day conditions, the responsibility for a military administration, with all its complexities. This responsibility the Army are naturally reluctant to assume.

Moreover the withdrawal of the civil power and the substitution of military control represent the first victory for the terrorists. The civil administration appears in the light of being too weak to carry on. Unfriendly propagandists paint the picture of political failure and of resort to force and repression. This picture is to-day more easily presented by the mere fact of military control than by strong civil action taken by the Government itself, action which some years ago would have been regarded as appropriate only to military orders and operations.

6. But there is another and stronger reason for the maintenance and exercise of the full authority of the civil power. The Government's principal instrument in this matter is the Police Force. The combating of subversive propaganda, intimidation, extortion, sabotage and armed terrorism is primarily a police task and this needs to be clearly understood by both the police and the armed forces. The day is past in which a clear dividing line could be drawn between the responsibilities of the police for maintaining law and order and the role of local military forces in internal security or in defence against external attack. When this attack comes from within, aimed at the destruction of economic resources, the organisation of strikes and the paralysis of the civil power, and accompanied by all the ruthless and bitter phenomena of Communist revolution, the Police Force is the first and vital means of defence. The old concept that police must do the policing and the armed forces the fighting is both dangerous and dead (or should be). A very cursory study of the Maquis movement in France and of similar movements elsewhere during and since the last war clearly indicates that these movements have a greater fear of police than of soldiers, and with good reason.

An interesting article* on the situation in Greece, showing the development of brigandage into guerilla war and then into civil rebellion points out that to eliminate brigandage is not a military operation at all. "It is a civil and political task, for which the primary responsibility rests with the police and the Ministry of the Interior, not with soldiers and the War Office; and the secondary responsibility rests in the long run on those charged with the reconstruction of the country, with particular emphasis perhaps on the building of roads and schools to eliminate the physical conditions and moral incentives to brigandage. In 1945 this point was missed. Generals were put into the Ministry of the Interior to do civilians' jobs; soldiers instead of policemen organised the hybrid forces designed to restore order; and reconstruction never had a chance to begin."

The Police are the only force possessing the information and intelligence necessary for the conduct of an underground "war" and this force can only succeed if it is built up well in advance with long and thorough training. The formation of an effective trained Police Force takes a longer time than the formation, say, of a battalion of infantry and is not something that can be left to a late stage. The most important lessons that can be learnt from my experience of internal disturbances is that the whole structure of Government and the activities of all departments within that structure may depend for their adequate functioning, and even for their existence, upon the efficiency and strength of the Police.

7. *Relationship of the police and armed forces.*—The military forces available to aid the civil power should be at the disposal of the Commissioner of Police and operate under his general directions. This has been recognized and carried out in Malaya. The manner in which troops are employed is, of course, a matter for the military commander, but there should be no difference of opinion that the general power of direction of the operations in which police and troops are engaged belongs to the Commissioner of Police. This relationship extends to Superintendents of

* *Spectator*, September 3rd, 1948.

Police vis-à-vis subordinate military commanders operating in their districts. It is of great importance that police and military officers, down to the lowest levels, should work in the closest touch.

The ordinary Colonial Police Headquarters organisation makes no provision for staff officers on the operations side (on a 24 hours basis) as distinct from the Criminal Intelligence Department and Special Branch, administrative, quartermaster's and financial branches.

The Federation Police Force now has a strength approaching that of two Army Corps (including Special and Auxiliary Police it has a strength of over 72,000) and if these men were troops there would be an elaborate and extensive headquarters staff. The pressure on Police Headquarters from above and below and from all sides, including the armed forces, is very heavy. If in the exercise of his responsibility for the general direction of the operations of both police and troops the Commissioner is to retain the confidence of the Army, he must be given adequate senior staff to assist in the planning and execution of operations.

8. *Co-ordination.*—It may be of interest to set out shortly the procedure which appears to me to be the most effective and economical and which is adopted here. Once a week I hold a conference attended by the General Officer Commanding, the Air Officer Commanding, the Chief Secretary, the Commissioner of Police, the Secretary for Defence and, when necessary, the Naval Liaison Officer. At this conference any question can be brought up without notice; no record is kept, but each member notes the action required of him. (A great deal of time can be wasted in making and correcting records of conferences.)

The Secretary for Defence presides over an Internal Security Committee with Police, Service and unofficial representation. This serves as a channel through which the views and demands of planters, miners and others can be brought forward at the centre, in addition to the State and Settlement Security Committees which have similar representation.

The Commissioner of Police has a weekly meeting with Secretariat Heads with a view to speeding up civil action on police problems, and there is a fortnightly conference on public works including buildings for the police and military forces, detention camps, strategic roads and airfields.

The Secretary for Chinese Affairs presides over his own Emergency Chinese Advisory Committee, on which the Defence Branch and the Police are also represented.

It may be said that the Federal constitution, comprising twelve separate governments, adds to the work involved in achieving full co-ordination, but to all intents and purposes does not prejudice speed and efficiency. A "strong central government" in this country depends upon the confidence that the other eleven governments have in it rather than upon any written constitution, and this confidence can best be fostered by the central government showing its confidence in them.

9. *Information and intelligence.*—Under modern conditions and trends the police must be sufficiently well-informed to forestall where possible and meet if necessary any threat to internal security. They require detailed and precise information regarding political movements, trends and personalities. Politics and crime can quickly become integrated and almost inseparable. The Police must therefore know and understand political movements and trends and their interrelation. In other words, the Police must have an efficient Special Branch which will

in fact be the eyes and ears both of the Government and the Police themselves. They must work in the closest co-operation with other intelligence organisations and the intelligence branches of the armed forces in the territory. There has been in the past a tendency for some sources of intelligence to use their own watertight channels or to use no channels at all. Police intelligence, for example, often obtained through agents, has not been checked at a sufficiently early stage against information possessed by political officers, who may be reporting to a Secretariat where their reports are filed and put away. Similarly, the Labour Department often possesses valuable and reliable information which may be held up for inclusion in a monthly report, or its immediate value to the Special Branch may be overlooked or not be apparent.

The answer to this problem is that sources of civil intelligence should report to or send copies of their reports to the Special Branch.

I have heard it said elsewhere that very few Colonial Special Branches are equipped to appraise political intelligence or can be relied upon to draw the right deductions from it. I agree that the task now demanded of the Special Branch demands a very high standard and a great deal of research and study, but it must be attempted.

Without information the large sums spent on the police and troops will be useless. Information generally may not flow in until there has been success and there is unlikely to be success without information. It is wise, therefore, to pay for information (i.e., adequate staff and agents) at the beginning.

10. The Joint Intelligence Committee system has produced the proposal that each Colonial territory in the area of a Joint Intelligence Committee should set up a Local Intelligence Committee. I have resisted this proposal both in Palestine and in this country for the following reasons. The Joint Intelligence Committee is primarily an inter-services body and in this Command contains no representative of the Governments or Police Forces of the Colonial territories in its area. Secondly, the appreciation or collation of intelligence is not a matter for a Committee with fixed membership, but for the officer best qualified to judge it after conference with experts or specialists in the particular subject. For instance, intelligence relating to Chinese affairs requires quite a different set of minds from those qualified to deal with a particular Malay problem. The importance of the Labour Officer in this matter is often overlooked. A fixed Committee may appeal to the tidy mind, but is not so useful in practice as a flexible system of conferences and the appointment of a correspondent whom the Joint Intelligence Committee can approach when they need a paper or information.

Thirdly, a Local Intelligence Committee here would naturally be subordinate to the Local Defence Committee, which may include unofficial representation.

I mention this point in passing, as it seems to me that the arrangements for the collation of political intelligence from Colonial territories are in some danger of becoming confused with Joint Intelligence Committee functions.

11. *Registration.*—The natural complement to efficient information coverage is registration of the population. It is a comparatively simple matter for a political malcontent to disappear underground and to continue to work and to exert influence from a hidden base or bases when people go about their business with no ready means of identification and move from place to place at will. But it is not so easy, in fact it is difficult to remain out of sight of the police if a comprehensive and efficient system of national registration exists.

The Communists in Malaya have shown a particular dislike for national registration. This was started here last July and finished in eight months. The system provides every adult with an identity card bearing his photograph, and each card is issued against a thumb-print record. Photographers' charges had to be controlled and photographers became targets for the bandits. Registration is not only of great help to the police in dealing with immigration and movements of individuals, but it can also, if properly put across, be made to give an added sense of security to those who have nothing to fear from the police.

Registration is made more effective if it is linked with the various contacts an individual may have with the authorities, e.g., he should be required to produce his identity card when applying for trade licences, vehicle licences, passports, ration cards, etc.

An adequate staff is necessary and sufficient supplies of photographic material.

If registration of employment can be included, so much the better.

12. *Immigration and frontier control.*—When means have thus been provided whereby the police are equipped to watch political trends, identify and keep track of political personalities and, which is equally important, obtain adequate information and knowledge of the criminal elements upon which subversive political movements inevitably draw when the time is considered ripe for armed action, it becomes necessary to secure the frontiers and adequate control of travellers.

The work of passport control is normally part of the functions of the Immigration Department. Experience of terrorism in Palestine and Malaya, however, has shown clearly that it is in the interests of security and good order generally that the police should take a large part in these duties since they are in possession of information regarding political and criminal suspects both in their own and in neighbouring territories. It is an established fact that the Home Office Special List, a very bulky work, is of little or no use to the security forces as a check on the movements of political undesirables, yet it constitutes the only check normally used by an Immigration Department, other than the names of individuals which may be supplied by the police from time to time with requests for reports of arrival or departure, passport particulars, etc., or those individuals for whom the police have requested, and obtained, orders of exclusion under the immigration laws. The police, on the other hand, are well equipped to compile and maintain an adequate "Black List" of those political and criminal personalities whose movements it is necessary to check or limit and the possession of which, for security reasons, cannot be permitted to pass outside police hands.

In Palestine, the system of frontier control by police enabled instructions and information to be transmitted rapidly from Police Headquarters to gazetted points of entry and proved practical and efficient.

13. *Arms and explosives.*—The first move by militant Communists in any Colonial territory, apart from infiltration of the labour movement, is likely to be towards equipping themselves with arms, ammunition and explosives. It is well worth while ensuring that customs examination at ports of entry is really tight enough to ensure that arms and ammunition are not being smuggled in. Attempts may be expected to steal explosives issued to mines, quarries and other users of explosives, and the conditions under which these are kept need periodical inspection. In Malaya one of the principal objects of attacks on police and troops has been the capture of their arms and ammunition. (For this reason alone it is wise to reduce to a

minimum the number of rounds carried by a man. Operating against terrorists he will generally need far fewer rounds than the scale lays down.) In Malaya, the bandits, having lost some 800,000 rounds captured since the Emergency began, have become so short of ammunition as to resort, it appears, to matches for their phosphorus. But it was still possible for them quite recently to use the Railway for transport of boxes of ammunition disguised as ordinary goods traffic.

In arming village guards in outlying areas with shotguns, in order to provide protection and confidence for the village, one of the considerations that has had constantly to be borne in mind is the danger of their being stolen and so augmenting the enemy's stock of arms.

14. *Police preparations.*—The preceding paragraphs have referred to the importance of maintaining an efficient Special Branch capable of producing and dealing with all required intelligence, political and criminal; and of setting up and maintaining the closest and most friendly relations between the police and the armed forces in their territory at all levels. In normal times and before any cause for anxiety as to internal security arises the Police Force should be organised and equipped to

(a) operate on a twenty-four hours basis with adequate officer control. (This, coupled with (b) below and Special Branch requirements, implies a far higher proportion of officers to lower ranks than is usual in Colonial and similar forces);
(b) be capable of rapid expansion and of the enrolling, training, equipping and controlling large numbers of Special and Auxiliary Police; and
(c) operate and maintain their own wireless communications and transport, independent as far as possible of purely civil departments such as Post Office or Transport Departments.

In regard to (b) Special and Auxiliary Police, Malaya had none of these at the outbreak of the Emergency and much time and loss of confidence could have been saved if they had been available. No Government can afford to maintain as a regular force in normal times the numbers of police required for duty in a serious Emergency. The problem is therefore one of rapidly augmenting the Force by the employment of Auxiliary and Special Police, primarily for the static defence tasks referred to in paragraph 4. In Malaya a force of 31,000 special constables had to be recruited, armed, clothed and given elementary training over a few months. Planters and other suitably qualified members of the public were given powers as auxiliary police officers.

The defence tasks that can be entrusted to special constables do not require more than the simplest basic and weapon training, and it is wasteful to employ regular police or troops on them at the expense of the initiative against the terrorists. A fortnight's training a year on full pay should be available for an auxiliary force of special constables enrolled on a purely local or district basis. Ex-policemen will naturally be included. The police can be provided in this way with a kind of territorial force at immediate call. Moreover, the creation of such a force spreads among the community a sense of sharing in the responsibility for maintaining law and order, which otherwise may come to be looked upon as only the function of the police and disseminates knowledge of and contacts with the Regular Force.

Arms and ammunition and simple uniforms for special constables should be available for training and to be held in reserve. Uniforms are better than armlets, which are easily imitated and are less satisfying to the ordinary special constable.

The rapid mobilisation of this force of special and auxiliary police can be greatly helped, if the administrative problems are thought out beforehand, e.g., rates of pay and allowances, accommodation and feeding.

15. In regard to (c), wireless communications and transport, it is obvious (but not always recognized) that telephone lines are liable to be cut and telephone conversations are in any event insecure. Telegraph lines are also easily disrupted. In a serious emergency the police wireless net may be called upon to carry all civil official traffic and should be built up and equipped with this in view. This system of communication is of importance not only to the police themselves but to other services such as the Observer Corps and Coastguards who can more economically use the police net than operate their own. In Palestine telegraph and telephone circuits were destroyed with such frequency that the police wireless service came to be used by all Departments as the only means of communication. It is wise to foresee that in an Emergency this situation is likely.

Moreover, a comprehensive W/T network means that Police Headquarters are always in possession of more up to date and reliable information than any other service. This is soon recognized by the Press, whose confidence in the police is influenced by the efficiency of the "news service" that the police can provide in the form of daily bulletins. It is desirable that this reliance on the police as the source of news should be encouraged as against the use of local press correspondents for this purpose, since it facilitates the security control of published information. Press censorship, which was necessary in Palestine to prevent the publication of inflamma tory abuse of one side by the other and to protect personnel against being advertised as targets for the terrorists, has not been introduced in Malaya nor should it be necessary, provided that powers are taken to suspend any newspaper which in any way supports the insurgents.

It is desirable that the police themselves should appear at Press Conferences.

Police Headquarters require both a Chief Signals Officer and a Press and Public Relations Officer for the purposes outlined in this paragraph.

In regard to transport, in time of internal disorder or during trade disputes amounting to strikes, civil departments are often unable to function. These are the very times when police are most needed and they should therefore be equipped to carry on independently.

It is an added advantage to have all clerical work in the police department performed by disciplined members of the Force. In addition, actual plans should be produced and continually reviewed, to meet varying degrees of threats to security, e.g., plans and orders for the calling up of Auxiliary Police for the protection of vital points or essential public services. Clear-cut policy instructions and detailed orders should at all times exist to cover likely eventualities such as attacks on Government offices, officials, prison establishments, mailbags and other communications. Unless these exist a great deal of very precious time will be lost in the initial stages of an Emergency.

16. *Insurance.*—In the event of prolonged terrorism and heavy damage to property, the insurance companies may consider withdrawing cover under the "riot and civil commotion" clause of their policies. In Palestine no cover was available, and in Malaya the London Insurance Committee have shown signs from time to time of reluctance to continue it. The importance of the withdrawal of commercial cover lies in its effect on bank loans and credits, which become no longer obtainable, and it is

therefore advisable to avoid the use of terms in official statements which might serve as a handle to the insurance companies. These terms include "enemy", "war", "insurrection", "insurgents", "rebellion", etc., and these considerations lie behind the preference for such names as "bandits", "thugs" and "terrorists" which have not the same significance for insurance companies.

17. *Emergency legislation.*—The Emergency Powers Ordinance and the Regulations made thereunder, of which copies are being sent separately, make provision for the seizure and destruction of property in certain circumstances without compensation, for the payment of compensation to civilians in respect of death or injury, and *inter alia* for the detention of persons by order of the Chief Secretary. The Advisory Committees (now called Committees of Review) appointed to hear objections to detention are not a part of the judiciary, though their chairmen are persons holding judicial office. Advocates may appear before these Committees, who sit in camera, but in order to reduce the strain on the police the Committees only require oral evidence from the police in cases where the written dossier appears to them to afford insufficient ground for continued detention.

It is important that the Government should be ready to issue at the outset of the Emergency the full set of Regulations, and that the police and armed forces should know beforehand what the Regulations will contain and should be in a position to act under them and take full advantage of them at once.

Emergencies are extremely expensive and unless they can be ended quickly are bound to become more so. It is better to be too drastic at the start than to take risks of the situation dragging on.

18. A point of psychology in connection with official statements in an Emergency is perhaps worth mentioning. If a situation requires drastic measures (as are expected in an "Emergency"), it is better to present it as serious and requiring all the co-operation and help that the civilian population can give than to create the impression that the Government has the situation well in hand, needs no help from anybody and is confident to the point of complacency. Most people respond to being told the truth and to a call for their assistance, even on the lines of "blood, sweat and tears". Severe measures can then be made acceptable, progress can be demonstrated and confidence built up. But optimism followed by reverses destroys confidence and tends to deprive any success of its value to morale.

19. *Miscellaneous.*—There are some minor points that may usefully be noted:—

(a) The general experience of road ambushes is that they are impossible to prevent. But their effect can be greatly lessened and the consequent loss of arms and ammunition reduced, if vehicles travel in pairs and never singly. The clearing of roadside bush and jungle at likely spots has been done in Malaya to satisfy public demand, but is probably not worth the cost.

(b) Language is an important factor in an efficient police force. British officers, particularly those in the Special Branch or C.I.D., should know the language or languages of the territory. Information is best collected in direct conversation. Translations of documents must in many cases be done by British officers for security reasons. Training in languages takes time and provision should be made for it in planning higher training.

(c) If roads are unsafe, air-drops of money for the payment of wages, etc., in outlying areas can easily be arranged and avoid the risk of providing the enemy with large sums of money lost in road ambushes.

(d) There should be a police fund from which, in the event of casualties, immediate payments can be made to dependants for funeral expenses, etc., without waiting for the computation of pensions or gratuities, which take some time. It may be of interest that the Earl Haig (Poppy Day) Fund has agreed to allocate a portion of the Malayan collection to the police for this purpose, which is an extension of the objects of the Fund not hitherto recognised.

20. I appreciate that this despatch may be thought to place undue emphasis on the functions of the police. In normal circumstances it is, of course, good administration that is the best guardian of internal security. But militant communism, exploiting legitimate political movements and putting modern arms into their hands, is really something new and cannot be combated by good administration alone. It is so ruthless and may flare up so suddenly, that it must be matched with a police weapon prepared to act with greater strength than commends itself to many administrators who have rightly taken in the past a more limited view of the role of the police.

It appears still to be held in some quarters that a Communist threat to internal security is the sort of situation that calls for the despatch of a brigade of troops. It is, I suggest, very important to review the soundness of this opinion in the light of recent experience, and I have therefore set out at length and at some risk of distortion the considerations which appear to me to bring into the foreground the vital functions of the police arm. The equipment of the police to meet this threat need in no way prejudice their character as friends of the people and guardians of their institutions.

The desiderata which have been sketched in the preceding paragraphs need to be set out in greater detail if other Police Forces are to be given the full benefit of experience in actually giving effect to them. What may be required is a new police manual of measures that should be taken by the police to meet the Communist threat to internal security. If your Police Adviser agrees with this suggestion and desires to develop the lessons of our experience in greater detail for the guidance of others, I should welcome a visit by him at any time.

21. I am also conscious of the shortcomings of this despatch, which has been prepared under pressure. It makes strange reading in comparison with other correspondence descriptive of our aspirations in the fields of political development and social welfare, but I venture to think that it reflects some experience of human nature and is not over-realistic.

22. Since the Commissioner-General and the Commander-in-Chief, Far East Land Forces, are absent in London I am not holding up this despatch for consultation with them. Copies are being sent to the Commissioner-General's office for such comments as he and his colleagues on the British Defence Co-ordination Committee may wish to offer in due course, and to the Governors of Hong Kong and Singapore for their information.

190   CO 537/4751, no 122   2 June 1949
[Slow progress of counter-insurgency]: letter from Sir H Gurney to J J
Paskin on measures to speed up action with particular attention to
communist propaganda from China and the squatter problem

The two main reasons why we are not making quicker progress with the Emergency
are the Communist drive in China, which has given a boost to bandit morale and a
check to willing co-operation from some Chinese, and the slowness of State
Governments in getting down to the constructive side of the squatter problem.

I have been wanting for some time to issue a strong anti-Communist statement,
such as that put out on the 31st May, but felt that I must first make quite sure that
we were going to be able to give confidence to the Chinese and the squatters that we
would act quickly on the Squatter Committee's Report. I therefore had a conference
on the 17th May with all the Mentris Besar, Resident Commissioners and British
Advisers at which it was clear that they were all (except Kedah, which does not
matter) ready to act and we agreed on the ways in which the Malayan Chinese
Association could help. Perak are already doing a great deal, Negri Sembilan has
allocated land and so have Selangor and Johore. Powers to evict and resettle are now
given by new Emergency Regulations published last week, which enable the Ruler in
Council to make the necessary orders. These have been widely welcomed and the
question now is one of maintaining pressure on all the States to use these powers, in
addition to providing the sites for the new police stations and posts now to be built in
the areas in which the squatters will remain.

I have therefore sent all the State and Settlement Governments a minute,[1] which I
have asked should be communicated to their Executive Councils, drawing attention
to the importance of exercising these powers. I have told the Police that we cannot
for the moment have any more E.R. 17D[2] operations outside Pahang and that they
must put pressure on State Governments when they want the inhabitants of an area
shifted and so help to strengthen the impression that this is an administrative and
social problem as well as a security one. The Malayan Chinese Association, who now
have 15,000 members and will have another big meeting at Ipoh on the 12th June,
have been advised behind the scenes that the time is now ripe for them to
demonstrate what they can do.

In thus adjusting the balance between the constructive remedies and the more
unpleasant medicine required for treatment of the squatter problem, a statement
regarding our attitude towards outside Chinese interference was an important
ingredient and the opportunity was provided by the Peiping broadcasts. I wonder
whether anyone in the Colonial Office thought that my wish to make the statement
on the 31st May was somehow connected with a perverse desire to give as little notice
as possible. It was not really feasible to explain all the factors that lay behind the
timing, nor shall I bother you with them now; I know that it is appreciated that the
successful admixture of the various types of cure for our troubles depends greatly on
timing.

---

[1] 'Minute by HE the high commissioner', S.214/H/49, 31 May 1949, not enclosed with this letter but there
is a copy at CO 537/4761.
[2] See 188, note 6.

We hope to repatriate about 2,000 people to China this month. With Rothery[3] at Swatow, this channel seems to be going well at present, but we are still uncertain as to how we are going to get our Cantonese through. Priority is given to the 17C[4] repatriates and their families; 17D families without their males are not being sent at present and these will in due course be one of the residual problems.

You will have seen that the U.M.N.O. Assembly in Perlis revised the constitution of the organization so as to admit non-Malays as associate members.[5] Dato Onn stuck to business and did not use the opportunity for any attack on the Federation. The extension of U.M.N.O. membership is a far-sighted move, designed, I think, to undermine the M.C.A. as a political force, but I can see little real platform for it other than independence and it may well become a movement (at which Dato Onn will place himself at the head) for "self government" in the Federation. I imagine that is the form, but I do not see many Malays supporting it enthusiastically if non-Malays have any power in it nor the non-Malays being particularly keen on it if they haven't.

It has been impossible for us recently to keep you properly posted as to what is going on and I appreciate your forbearance in not asking for more information. (I wish the same forbearance extended to other branches of the Colonial Office, e.g. is it really necessary for us at the moment to spend much time on banking problems ?)

But Watherston will be home early in July and, though I hope that his holiday will not be interfered with, nobody is better qualified to tell you about our emergency situation here.

---

[3] G W Rothery had been appointed vice-consul at Swatow in May 1949.
[4] Emergency Regulation 17C permitted repatriation of individuals.
[5] At its general assembly in May 1949 UMNO agreed to accept non-Malays as associate members. This was the first of several steps taken by Onn in an attempt to convert UMNO into a 'Malayan' movement, culminating in his break with UMNO in 1951 over the proposal to open the party fully to non-Malays.

191   CO 717/157, 52294/31/1949   5 July 1949
[Policy towards the Chinese]: despatch no 7 from Sir H Gurney to Mr Creech Jones

I have the honour to enclose copies of the secret Annual Report for 1948[1] of the Department of Chinese Affairs. You have been kept informed through monthly political reports and special reports of the efforts which are being made to free the Chinese from the grip of the terrorists and to persuade them that they have a future in Malaya if they choose to accept the Federal Constitution. I do not therefore propose to comment in detail on the report but will confine myself to a few general observations which I regard as particularly important to bear in mind in evolving our policy towards the Chinese.

2. The first point is that it is necessary to have a special policy regarding the Chinese. Their customs, habits and beliefs are different from those of the Malays and Indians and so is their attitude towards the Administration. It is premature to treat the people of Malaya as so many individuals all sharing a similar upbringing and similar aims. The Malayanisation of the Chinese will be a long and difficult process in

---

[1] Not printed.

which wise guidance and help will be required at every step. This help and guidance must be based on intimate knowledge and understanding of the Chinese and there was never a time in the history of Malaya when expert advice about the Chinese and special attention to the problems they present was more necessary. On these grounds Government intends to send a greater proportion of Administrative Service and Police cadets to China to study Chinese; the proposal, which State and Settlement Governments have accepted, has been made to establish or re-establish Chinese Advisory Boards; and to deal with our immediate problems, there has been established an Emergency Chinese Advisory Committee.

3. The second point emerging from the enclosed report, with which I wish to deal briefly in this despatch, is the comparative lack amongst the Chinese of the kind of public spirit which is the essential basis of true democracy. It is this lack which has so far vitiated our well-intentioned attempts to lay the foundations of Malayan democratic Government. The chief consequences of the liberal policy introduced in Malaya by H.M. Government at the end of the war were, on the one hand, an enormous expansion of the Kuomintang, whose interests and outlook were completely bound up with Nationalist China, and on the other hand, the attempted regimentation of Malayan labour by the Malayan Communist Party, who were undoubtedly acting under orders from Moscow. The final result was the emergency, which has compelled the Malayan Governments to interfere with the freedom of the individual in a way unknown in Malaya since the British have been associated with its Government.

4. Dr. Ong Chong Keng, the only Chinese who had sufficient courage and faith in the future of the Chinese in Malaya to defy the Communists in the early stages of the emergency, is dead,[2] and it is only now, when Government has begun to get the upper hand in its struggle against the Communists, that other Chinese leaders have begun to emerge to take his place, though even now they have not displayed his courage and leadership. We must recognise that the growth of democratic spirit among the Chinese will be a slow process and it may be that no significant progress will be showed until a new generation, born and brought up in Malaya, has produced new leaders. The establishment of the University of Malaya, the expansion of English education and plans which are now under consideration for loosening the grip of China on the Chinese schools, will assist the process.

5. The enclosed reports refer to dissatisfaction among the Chinese with the Federal Constitution, but Chinese generally are now disposed to suspend agitation against the Constitution for the time being and to accept such benefits as it offers them. This attitude will be encouraged if the Malays adopt an accommodating attitude in the forthcoming discussions of political matters in the Communities Liaison Committee.

6. Since the end of last year, the Communist rising in Malaya has begun to be overshadowed by the danger from China itself and, until the impetus of the southward sweep of the China Communists has exhausted itself, it is difficult to predict how the new situation in China will affect our plans for Malayanising the Chinese. So far thay have betrayed few signs of excitement about the news from China and their attitude towards the Government and other communities in Malaya has not been noticeably affected. It is clearly in the interests of the Chinese to cut

---

[2] See 168, note 3.

themselves adrift from China especially now that the Communists seem likely to secure control of the whole country, but their attachment to their ancestral homes is strong. If possible, the prospect of becoming Malayans must be made more attractive to them. It is less than half the truth to say that this can be done by giving them more political privileges. In the past they found Malaya preferable to China because they found Malaya free from political strife. What would make the majority of Chinese most contented would be a stable bureaucracy on the pre-war model, but since this is impracticable we must give them the next best thing, a firm Government under which they will be able to cast off the tradition of corruption and extortion which they brought with them from China and to learn, in association with other communities, the art of self-government.

192   CO 967/84, no 70   25 Aug 1949

[Communalism and nation-building]: letter from Sir H Gurney to J J Paskin assessing the likelihood of the political integration of Malays and Chinese   [Extract]

[This extract was attached to the departmental brief 'Political developments in Malaya' (an extract from which is reproduced as 195 in this collection) prepared for Rees-Williams who made a short tour of Hong Kong, Singapore and the Federation of Malaya in Oct and Nov 1949 (see CO 537/4870 and also CO 537/4741, no 74). The prime purpose of his visit was to attend a conference on the likely regional impact of Britain's impending recognition of communist China. This conference was chaired by MacDonald and was held at Bukit Serene, Johore Bahru, 2–4 Nov (see 197).]

. . . Any forecast of the political future of the Federation must start from some hypothesis as to the likelihood of the Chinese and Malays forgetting their differences to the extent of political integration of the two races. I am bound to say that I find it difficult to discern any common objective capable of actually achieving this miracle, unless it is, conceivably, the pursuit of independence on an anti-British platform, where there is plenty of attractive material. The inter-racial harmony existing in Malaya up to the war was remarkable and is still a tradition of the country. The Malay hierarchy was preserved under a paternal British Administration blessed with much prosperity, and the Chinese were content to live under a stable regime, in which they took little part, and to pursue their remunerative business enterprises. To-day all this is changed. There are political claims from the Chinese, promises of self-government, financial stringency and a Malay awakening. There is at present very little clear idea of the shares to be allotted to the respective communities in an ultimately self-governing Malaya.

The Malay leaders are well aware that the chief hope of effective survival of the Malays lies in co-operation with the British, whose departure would leave them at the mercy of a Chinese population already numerically almost equal and increasing rapidly. They mean by self-government political power for the Malays, but the experiences of the past year have shown them how truly, without economic control, this is a shadow. They are not blind to the true meaning of Chinese support for any Malay independence movement, and recognize that the Chinese will use them for so long as Chinese interests are served and will then drop them at any convenient time.

I am not speaking here of Dato Onn's own ideas. Malay confidence in British good faith, so badly shaken in 1942 and again in 1946, is beginning to be built up again. The Emergency has given the Malays an outlet for the expression of national enthusiasm for the defence of their country against a threat inevitably associated with China and the Chinese. Movement towards self-government in the Federation may well entail, unless we are very careful, a widening rather than a closing of the gap between the races, which will be jockeying for position and losing the sense of security which each still associates with British Administration. The worst error that H.M. Government could make in this situation would be to appear in the role of an impartial arbitrator and so attract to themselves the suspicions and latent apprehension that each community feels towards the other. We have had experience in Palestine of how easy such deflection of antipathy can be.

In the Malay States H.M. Government have no commitment to the Chinese community. They are partners with the Malay Rulers, and the maintenance of the British share in the government of this country appears to me to depend upon the support and co-operation of the Malays. It is better that the British and the Malays should work to a common policy, even at the expense of legitimate Chinese interests, than that we should appear to support any Chinese political claims other than those which non-Malays will be entitled to make as Federal citizens. This is what we should mean by the "special position" of the Malays. In the Malay States it is the Malays, not the Chinese, who wish to find and work to a common policy with the British.

What then have we to offer to the Chinese, including the Straits-born British subjects, apart from federal citizenship? It may be expected [that] within the next two or three years there will be strong Chinese pressure for increased Chinese representation on the Legislative Council. There is room for some concession here without weakening the Malay unofficial majority, which it will be important to retain, but this will not satisfy the Chinese. It is not, however, to the Federal centre that the Chinese must look for political advance, but to the Settlement Governments, their Nominated and Settlement Councils, and to Municipalities and the field of urban local government. In this sphere there [are] very wide opportunities for meeting Chinese democratic aspirations for participation in the conduct of their own affairs, without encroaching on Malay interests. About 70% of the population of Kuala Lumpur and of the population of Penang Island is Chinese. Steps are being taken to prepare for municipal elections in both places. Elections to the Settlement Councils will follow in due course.

Nevertheless, it is a mistake to suppose that such advances will have any notable effect upon the Chinese political leaders. Municipal elections were discarded in Penang in 1913 because there was no popular support for them, the buying and selling of votes was rampant and the most capable and trustworthy people, while prepared to accept nomination, would not submit themselves to election. There is today in Penang very little real public demand for municipal elections and when it is known that the Government is preparing for them, there may be less still.

Such measures will have to be complementary to a strong and stable central administration which will be acceptable to the Chinese, by contrast with a regime characteristic of conditions in China, not for the share which the Chinese will have in it but for its protection and tolerance of their money-making pursuits.

If any further argument were needed in support of the preceding paragraphs, it lies in the fact that in the battle with Communism, already joined, the Malays are on our side and while our Chinese may also be today they may not be tomorrow. This is where Newboult's memorandum[1] comes in. The threat from China is political rather than physical, and it is felt as such by our neighbours in South-East Asia. They all have problems of their own to solve before they can be sure of resisting it successfully. In the Federation we have already admitted the Chinese to a share in the government, and the national movements amongst our neighbours which we wish to support and stabilise might feel some apprehension if any further opportunity for political power were offered to Chinese here.

These conclusions follow from the hypothesis in that the conversion of the Chinese into Malayans is an unlikely development. That hypothesis, because it is of fundamental importance, deserves some analysis. A Malayan consciousness can be built up only on a community of interests and loyalties, mutual trust and acceptance, or a common language, script, heritage and culture. The Chinese and Malays have none of these things in common. There is moreover the difference of religion. Chinese thought and culture turn to China with the same traditional persistence that characterizes the refusal of the Zionist to forget Zion. A Malayan consciousness has to grow and needs roots to live. If it has no roots, no amount of watering will keep it alive. There is no longer time for such growth to take place, in a normal and healthy way, if a stage of maturity is to be reached sufficiently quickly that will have the strength to stand up to the dangers that threaten to overwhelm it. It would not, I think, be helped by any legalistic fertilisers such as the substitution of nationality for citizenship, even if that were feasible. The most powerful agency will be education, but time is not on our side and the breaking-down of the present Chinese vernacular system will be a long process with a very long-term effect. . . .

---

[1] Not traced.

193   CO 537/4790   12 Sept 1949
[Local government]: minute by Mr Rees-Williams

If we are not careful we shall make the same mistakes in Malaya as we did in India & Burma.[1] In my view every C.O. officer should study the history of these two countries & I have offered to give a lecture on lessons to be drawn from Burma but nothing has yet been arranged.

2.   One obvious mistake is that no one seems to be bothering about local Govt. Onn & all these fellows have their heads in the clouds on the subject of cabinet Govt but what about local govt? What for example is the situation regarding the Penang (Georgetown) Municipal Commission? (We have been in Penang since 1789 [sic] or so).[2] How many of the Commissioners are elected by popular vote? How many local authorities are there in Kedah or Johore? Are there any local councillors in these States? I know the answer [sic] to these questions & they are illuminating. The Malayan system is top heavy. I am in favour of constitutional advance in Malaya & I believe that the Dept. & Onn, who think more or less alike, are on sound lines so far

---

[1] Rees-Williams had chaired the Burma Frontier Areas Committee of Enquiry in 1947.
[2] Francis Light had occupied Penang for the East India Company in July 1786, and, in June 1800, the coastal strip on the mainland opposite was acquired and named Province Wellesley.

as the central govt is concerned but all will be built on sand unless local government is built up far more rapidly than it is at present.

3. As to language, what is required is that every child in school shall learn the language of the country, Malay, & the Commonwealth language, English. I would definitely discourage other oriental languages being taught in school at public expense.

194   T 220/134, no 74   23 Sept 1949
'Malaya: tin': minute by Colonel W R Edmunds[1] recording an inter-departmental meeting on 20 Sept to discuss the repercussions of devaluation on tin prices

1. I accompanied Mr. France to a meeting in Mr. Bowyer's room, Ministry of Supply, on 20th September to discuss the new prices for tin arising out of the change in the sterling-dollar rate.[2] Sir Hilton Poynton and Sir Gerrard [sic] Clauson from the Colonial Office were present. The problem was a complex one with its wide and difficult ramnifications [sic]; but on the I.F. side the question whether Malayan tin should or should not be paid for at a higher price than the £550 per ton, the pre-change rate, was of chief interest. There was a similar problem in respect of Nigeria.

2. The Chancellor had firmly ruled that the price paid by the Ministry of Supply for Malayan tin should not be more than the old dollar-sterling rate of £550 per ton; and that Malaya should be straightaway free to sell her tin at the best price she could wherever she found this possible. In equity, the Chancellor's ruling was proper; there should be no excess profit derived by producers purely on a fortuitous impingement of a policy, the Ministry of Supply had given Malayan producers a very beneficial deal, they had taken the whole output and given a firm price while carrying the risk of loss on market prices for tin. Malayan producers had been well treated. The practicability of the Chancellor's point about freedom to sell where they liked was somewhat doubtful as an immediate opportunity to obtain the best deal they could in an open market. Some time must elapse before this could be done. Varying estimates as to the time factor were given as ranging between a fortnight to three months. The problem of stock availability, delivery dates of supplies sold, brought out the question of future and forward selling; the machinery for making such sales, i.e. the London Metal Exchange and Singapore Exchange opening; the termination of the Ministry of Supply agreement with its three months notice.

3. The Colonial Office trumpeted loudly on the nefarious designs of H.M.G. which denied Colonial Governments benefits which they thought were their due (the new sterling-dollar rate projected a sterling price for tin of £760 per ton). Sir Hilton

---

[1] Col W Russell Edmunds, temporary administrative officer, Treasury; principal from 1955. At the meeting the Treasury was also represented by A W France, assistant secretary, 1948–1952; the Ministry of Supply was represented by E B Bowyer, and the CO by Sir Hilton Poynton, Sir Gerard Clauson and A G T Chaplin, assistant secretary.

[2] On 18 Sept 1949 Sir Stafford Cripps announced the devaluation of the pound sterling from US$4.03 to US$2.80.

Poynton was rather petulant about H.M.G.'s action to keep the price at £550 per ton as this, he thought, was taking the child's jam, not for the first time. A compromise was hammered out, subject to the Chancellor's agreement, which fixed the price for Ministry of Supply purchases at £550 per ton, the opening of London and Singapore Metal Exchanges simultaneously as soon as possible and, on termination of the three months notice or on an earlier mutually agreed date turning on the opening of the Metal Exchanges, a profit and loss examination would be conducted on the Ministry of Supply operations and consideration given to the apportionment of profits which might be made, as from say 21st September, against losses suffered by Ministry of Supply, or paid over to the Malayan Government. The Colonial Office while agreeing to the profit and loss examination would certainly expect any profit to go to the Malayan Government. As to the Nigerian producers, they might "thumb their noses" at Ministry of Supply and seek to sell their concentrates—there is no smelter integration in Nigeria—to any buyer at the new figure of 95 cents a pound (£760 per ton). This portended some difficulty for H.M.G. from the point of view of U.K. smelter activities. Nigeria, it was agreed, should be on the same footing as Malaya, i.e. a price of £550 per ton with an examination of the profit and loss position at a later date.

4. I have recorded the foregoing with some trepidation as an I.F. impression of a complicated and little known subject. Mr. France would no doubt be good enough to correct my shortcomings. My main point, however, is to record certain statements made by Sir Hilton Poynton and Mr. Chaplin which indicated the Colonial Office policy in the matter of excess profits which would accrue in Colonies through the change in the sterling-dollar rate. Sir Hilton Poynton intimated that he had been discussing this question of policy on the evening of 19th September and the Colonial Office had reached the conclusion that (a) there was an imperative need to prevent inflationary repercussions in Colonial territories through sudden and unexpected excess profits and (b) to this end, where it was feasible, profits should go direct to the revenues of a Colony; where the producer received the benefits, taxation should take it back from him. Sir Hilton Poynton mentioned cocoa as well as rubber as likely beneficiaries. This outline of policy was a welcome contribution to I.F. problems and could not have been more suitably conceived for dealing with the situation if it had been our own work. In the case of Malaya, this means that the benefit derived by that territory from the new sterling-dollar rate would be taken to revenue and should be used to meet the cost of internal security, thus reducing the amount of H.M.G.'s financial assistance. Mr. Chaplin gave support to such an appreciation as to the use to be made of such windfalls to the Malayan revenue by arguing that if H.M.G. paid out of one pocket, i.e. the profits which may be accrued on the Ministry of Supply activities as from, say, 21st September, it would mean that the amount paid out of the other pocket—grant for internal security—would be this much less.

5. The foregoing policy of the Colonial Office is one we should wholeheartedly support. Towards the end of a long meeting, Sir Hilton Poynton appeared to have second thoughts and attempted to recede somewhat from the forthright declaration he had made earlier. He attempted to add a refinement by saying it would, of course, be up to the Colonial Government to do what it liked with such windfalls to revenue; it might decide to pass the benefit in degree to the producers, it might decide to use the money for other purposes. I made the rejoinder that any Colonial Government could not make such a decision in the light of its financial position, and this was not

countered. The implication being that a deficit would be the first call on such a windfall and needs for financial assistance for specific purposes reduced.

6. I have recorded the policy declarations of the Colonial Office for the express purpose of seizing on them and using them as a basis for the I.F. approach to the way many problems which the change in the sterling-dollar rate throws up. The carrying out of such a policy would appear to have the following implications:—

(i) A strong check to inflationary tendencies in the Colonial territory concerned;
(ii) A reduction in grants-in-aid or, the removal of, or reduction in, calls for financial assistance for specific purposes; there would be the obverse of the coin, that net dollar spenders would need more financial assistance and what we may lose on the "swings" we certainly should get back on the "roundabouts";
(iii) An improved financial position in non-Treasury controlled colonies which should not be lost sight of in arriving at contributions to be made towards the cost of Colonial Forces and/or the contribution towards the cost of Imperial defence;
(iv) A possible acceleration of development projects with its relation to C.D. and W. expenditure and/or loan finance.

7. It might be helpful to members of the Division to know of the Colonial Office policy as indicated above so that they may see if there are other fields which I have not mentioned as well as being able to weigh up the implications as to their particular interests.

195 CO 967/84, no 70   [Oct 1949]
'Political developments in Malaya': CO brief for Mr Rees-Williams for his tour of Hong Kong, Singapore and Malaya, Oct–Nov 1949; communalism and nation-building

1. *The Chinese and the emergency*
(a) *The formation of the Malayan Chinese Association*
It is unnecessary to describe the general attitude of the Chinese community to the Emergency, with which Ministers are already familiar. In the last few months of 1948 the High Commissioner laid much store by the formation of a Malayan Chinese Association (M.C.A.) with Government backing (behind the scenes) which would serve as a rallying point for the Chinese community. Unfortunately the Association has fallen far short of the High Commissioner's hopes. Its leadership inspires little confidence, though it is as good as one could hope. Its achievements have been small, and it has become a buffer between Government and the Chinese community rather than an active agent on the side of Government in the campaign against the Malayan Communist Party (M.C.P.)

(b) *The new administrative approach*
At the same time as the M.C.A. was brought into being steps were taken to bring Government closer to the Chinese people. An important move was the establishment (late in 1948) of a strong Committee to investigate the Squatter problem, and its subsequent Report (January 1949) which recommended the resettlement of squatters, in the main on the land they at present occupy, and the opening-up and more

intensive administration of the squatter areas. The formation of an Emergency Chinese Advisory Committee in Kuala Lumpur, and of Chinese Advisory Boards in the several States and Settlements, together with the appointment of Chinese-speaking officers as Advisers for Chinese Affairs to the State and Settlement Governments have helped to bridge the gap between the Administration and the Chinese community. The Chinese Affairs Secretariat have commented as follows:—

> "Government officers are now paying more and more attention to the direct administrative approach to the Chinese in the small towns and countryside where it is strongly felt that the Chinese must be helped to realise that there is a civil government as well as Security Forces and that the civil government is well disposed to them, wishes to understand their difficulties, and is willing to give them opportunities for self-organisation in order to increase their ties with the administration of the country. . . . It is not imagined that this civilian approach will quickly end the emergency, though wherever it is followed up—as is happening in some places—by the formation of Committees and auxiliary police units composed of volunteers the sense of security and common interest leading to better morale and confidence in Government is bound to improve. But the importance of such ventures is that they are enabling Government to compete with Communist influence in a political as well as a military sense, giving these remote lying areas a more obvious place in the administration of the country and enabling their inhabitants to undertake more responsibility on behalf of Government. . . .
>
> "It is by now apparent that there are limitations to the usefulness of the approach to the Chinese community through the Malayan Chinese Association. Experience has shown that the good services of the M.C.A. are valuable in a number of ways, including the breaking down of Chinese prejudice and the steadying of morale but it is unlikely that the M.C.A. can be so manipulated as to make the Chinese people do everything Government wants it to do and in particular to encourage the growth of law-abiding habits in remote areas. Experience has shown that the most co-operative members of the Chinese community are always several paces ahead of the M.C.A. Anyhow it would be unfair to expect the M.C.A. to work miracles in the squatter areas if Government itself were not disposed to try."

(c) *The appeal of new China*

The seizure of Nanking and Shanghai, the advance on Canton, involving the occupation of Kiangsi and part of Fukien, and the establishment of a Communist Government have had a profound effect on the situation in Malaya.[1] From the operational point of view the end of repatriation to China has deprived the Administration of one of its most potent weapons, and the High Commissioner has commented; "If the door to China had remained open, my estimate[2] that we might see the end at the end of 1949 might have been realised; but in present

---

[1] Chinese communist forces took Beijing in Jan 1949, Nanjing in Apr and Shanghai in May. The nationalists fell back to Canton and finally withdrew to Taiwan. Mao Zedong proclaimed the People's Republic of China in Beijing on 1 Oct 1949.

[2] In Jan 1949, see 175, para 43.

circumstances I consider it unlikely that a successful conclusion can be achieved before June next year." While Government has taken steps to prevent newspapers etc. from publishing comment in support of propaganda from Communist China, developments there, particularly the proceedings of the People's Consultative Conference and the activities of Malayan Chinese such as Tan Kah Kee[3] who are at present in the Liberated Areas are watched with attention. Chinese Communist Party (C.C.P.) propaganda is directed at winning the support of the Overseas Chinese communities—including the bourgeoisie— for the building up of the New China, and this is undoubtedly having some effect in Malaya. In particular students are excited by the appeal of the New China and business men are concerned to maintain trade links. It can hardly be doubted that the Chinese community will be drawn in an ever increasing degree to look for support, inspiration and leadership from the Communist Government in China. This will present Government with a new problem different in kind from that of defeating the militant M.C.P., which at the moment seems to derive virtually no support from the C.C.P.

(d) Sir Henry Gurney's views

In July Sir Henry Gurney sent a despatch[4] enclosing the report of the Chinese Affairs Secretariat for 1948 from which the following extracts are taken.

> "It is necessary to have a special policy regarding the Chinese. . . . It is premature to treat the people of Malaya as so many individuals all sharing a similar upbringing and similar aims. The Malayanisation of the Chinese will be a long and difficult process in which wise guidance and help will be required at every step. . . .
>
> "(The comparative lack amongst the Chinese of the kind of public spirit which is the essential basis of true democracy). It is this lack which has so far vitiated our well-intentioned attempts to lay the foundations of Malayan democratic government. The chief consequences of the liberal policy introduced in Malaya by H.M.G. at the end of the war were, on the one hand, an enormous expansion of the Kuomintang, whose interests and outlook were completely bound up with Nationalist China, and on the other hand, the attempted regimentation of Malayan labour by the Malayan Communist Party. . . . We must recognise that the growth of democratic spirit among the Chinese will be a slow process and it may be that no significant progress will be observed until a new generation, born and brought up in Malaya, has produced new leaders."

After referring to the effect on the Chinese in Malaya of the Communist advances in China, the High Commissioner adds:—

> "It is clearly in the interests of the Chinese to cut themselves adrift from China especially now that the Communists seem likely to secure control of the whole country, but their attachment to their ancestral home is strong. If possible, the prospect of becoming Malayans must be made more attractive to

---

[3] Tan Kah Kee, a leading Chinese industrialist in Singapore, had called upon Malayan Chinese to do their best to end lawlessness on the somewhat ambiguous ground that disorder would lead to unemployment and consequently reduce remittances to kith and kin in China.

[4] See 191.

them. It is less than half the truth to say that this can be done by giving them more political privileges. In the past they found Malaya preferable to China because they found Malaya free from political strife. What would make the majority of Chinese most contented would be a stable bureaucracy on the pre-war model, but since this is impracticable we must give them the next best thing, a firm Government under which they will be able to cast off the tradition of corruption and extortion which they brought with them from China and to learn, in association with other communities, the art of self-government".

It will thus be seen that while the High Commissioner does not rule out the possibility of Chinese becoming "Malayans" with the passage of years, he does not regard it as immediately practical. His analysis is developed in a semi-official letter written at the end of August, the relevant extracts from which are attached.[5] This, while outlining ways in which the aspirations of the Chinese community towards a greater say in the Government of the country might be met says quite bluntly that in the High Commissioner's view the conversion of the Chinese into Malayans is an unlikely development. The despatch (with its enclosure) and the letter show clearly the practical difficulties which face an administrator in dealing with the Chinese community in Malaya.

2. Dato' Onn and U.M.N.O

After its anti-Malayan Union policy was crowned with success by the inauguration of the Federation on the 1st February 1948, U.M.N.O. remained lethargic for nearly 18 months. The emergency which supervened at the beginning of June 1948 distracted everyone's attention from politics, and in any case exposed one of the weaknesses of the party—its leaders are men who hold important public appointments, who had to direct all their energies to the pressing needs of the moment. Dato' Onn showed during his visit to London last autumn[6] that he had wide projects half formed in his mind, and some of these have since been aired. At the U.M.N.O. congresses at Arau in May and Bukit Mertajam in August a new party constitution was settled which recognised, by the innovation of "associate membership" for non-Malays, the interests of the immigrant communities domiciled in Malaya in their country's future government, and Onn outlined to the Bukit Mertajam Congress a broad plan for the advance of the country to self-government. There are still many uncertainties and obscurities in Onn's policy, and it is by no means certain yet that he will win support from U.M.N.O. (which is, in any case, only a tiny fraction of the Malay public) for his more controversial points, such as a Malayan nationality embracing Malays and domiciled non-Malays alike. The important thing is that Onn's policy is not an extreme intolerant nationalism nor is it unrealistic.

3. Dr. Purcell's proposals for a Royal Commission

In March and April Dr. Purcell, with some support from Professor Silcock[7] of Raffles College, urged in correspondence to the Times that a Royal Commission should be appointed to revise the constitution of 1948. The proposal, which is not a new one,

---

[5] See 192.   [6] See 173.
[7] T H Silcock was the author of, amongst other things, *Dilemma in Malaya*, London, 1949, and 'Policy for Malaya, 1952', *International Affairs*, vol XXVIII (Oct 1952) pp 445–451.

was given some prominence by Tan Cheng Lock in an address to a M.C.P. [?MCA] meeting. The proposal has won no support from any other quarter, official or unofficial, and there are many signs that the initiative or [?for] a revision of the constitution can safely be left to come from Malaya itself.

4. The Communities Liaison Committee

When Sir Henry Gurney was tackling the immediate problem of the emergency by calling into being the Malayan Chinese Association and by his new administrative approach to the Chinese, Mr. MacDonald had brought together (with the High Commissioner's approval) a group of influential men, at first Malays and Chinese only, joined later by representatives of other communities, to tackle the long-term political problems of Malaya. After making a slow start with a survey of the economic relations of the Malays and the Chinese, the Communities Liaison Committee tackled a series of major political issues at its meetings on the 14th/15th August and 14th/15th September. Mr. MacDonald was able to report in a personal letter to the Secretary of State. "They look like overcoming many of the difficulties which have beset us here, on inter-communal questions, during the last four years. I feel greatly encouraged by the last two meetings of the Committee, and believe that we are coming in sight of complete agreements between the Malay, Chinese and other leaders."[8]

The Communities Liaison Committee after its meetings in September published a statement of "Agreed Views", which are not in themselves as important as the memorandum of the Committee's unanimous opinions on a number of issues which accompanied the statement. It should be said that the general principles enunciated—the attainment of self-government, the introduction of elections, loyalty to Malaya—find their place already in the Federation Agreement or in Cmd.7171. The significant thing is that they are now expressed by prominent members of *all* communities, including Dato' Tan Cheng Lock. The memorandum concludes: "it would seem that a great change of thought has arisen since the negotiations for the Federal Agreement, that all races are now more liberal in their views, and that working in the Federal Council they have discovered how closely linked in reality they are to each other." The statement and the memorandum both notably adopt the "Malayan" ideal. The memorandum envisages reconsideration of the citizenship qualifications of the Federation Agreement and the Committee reached a tentative conclusion, which was not published, that anyone born in the Federation should qualify for Federal citizenship. Dato' Onn gave this proposal his support provided that Federal citizenship became a nationality. There is a risk that this rather impracticable notion may lead the Committee into technicalities, or at worst, provide Onn with an excuse for procrastination.

It should be added that the press has given a warm welcome to the statement of agreed views published by the Communities Liaison Committee, and has not failed to draw attention to the changed climate of politics in Malaya since 1946/1947.

---

[8] See CO 717/183, 52928/17/49, no 47, MacDonald to Creech Jones, 16 Sept 1949. In his reply of 24 Oct 1949, Creech Jones wrote: 'I am struck by the fact that the agreed views of the Committee as published on the 18th September are so closely in line with the fundamental aims of the policy which has been pursued by His Majesty's Government in relation to Malaya ever since the liberation (not excluding the Malayan Union phase).'

5. *Conclusions*

The Communities Liaison Committee does not envisage a self-governing Malaya for 15 years at least. Mr. MacDonald is optimistic at the progress made in the Committee, and feels that it is on the way to solving the fundamental political problems of Malaya. He has found that the men whose names count most in Malaya have been able to agree on matters where two years ago they would have disagreed, even if they had been prepared to sit around the same table for discussion. Sir Henry Gurney's approach has been diferent. He has had regard to the hard realities of administration of the Malay and Chinese masses.

Some of the conclusions reached by the Communities Liaison Committee and by the High Commissioner are the same—for example, that some concession should be made to the Chinese in the matter of qualification for taking part in the public life of the community, with the corollary that there should be more scope (by the introduction of municipal and Settlement Council elections etc.) for them to do so. The main differences is that Mr. MacDonald is optimistic, Sir Henry Gurney doubtful, perhaps pessimistic. It seems to us that this difference should not be allowed to cloud the realities of the situation. Onn controls Malay public opinion at the moment. The Chinese whom Mr. MacDonald has collected control the Chinese, in so far as that community is susceptible to control at all. (This may not amount to much). Without agreement between these leaders there could be no agreement of any sort between the communities. If their understanding is belied by the stubborn reluctance of the masses of the Malay and Chinese peoples to turn themselves into Malayans (at best) or to live together in peace (at worst) so much the worse. We must of course keep clearly before our eyes the difficulties which Sir Henry Gurney has described. But Burma, India, the Netherlands East Indies and Indo China have all shown us that similar difficulties are momentarily swept away in the excitement of liberation, and it would be unrealistic to suppose that these difficulties in Malaya, vast as they are, would delay for generations the removal of British tutelage. It may be, of course, that the Communities Liaison Committee has really solved nothing, and that no *practical* steps will be agreed upon by the same people who drafted the Agreed Views and the Memorandum. That would make the problem a little more straight forward, since we should simply have to grapple, unaided by the support of popular leaders, with the difficulties which Sir Henry Gurney has propounded. But we think that we are justified in taking as the object of our study in the next few months the much more complex problem, where the only men of influence in the country have agreed on the prime objects of policy but where the communities as a whole maintain the attitude described by the High Commissioner. In these circumstances it seems to us that all the experience of dynamic nationalist movements in South East Asia during and since the war teaches us that we should not tie the hands of the leaders, though we should spare no pains to bring home to them the hard realities of the situation which they are tackling. It is perhaps encouraging that in Malaya the leaders so far have not shown themselves insensible to hard facts.

196 CO 967/84, no 69 [Oct 1949]
'The United Kingdom in South-East Asia and the Far East': memorandum prepared for Cabinet by the Permanent Under-Secretary of State's Committee in the Foreign Office [Extract]

[This paper was a combination of two memoranda that had emerged from exhaustive studies conducted over the course of the previous year by the Permanent Under-Secretary of State's Committee in the FO which had the task of thinking about long-term policy. CO officials had been consulted by the FO during the preparation of this paper and were not surprised by its two main conclusions, ie: (i) the UK should aim at building up some sort of regional association, and (ii) for the present a greater measure of regional co-operation was practicable only in the economic field. CO officials did hope, however, that any regional association would not be modelled upon either the Caribbean or South Pacific Commissions and they felt that the paper was unrealistic in handling the question of US involvement in the area. Although the version printed here does not carry a reference number, it seems certain that it is in fact the foreign secretary's memorandum CP(49)207 of 18 Oct 1949 which Cabinet discussed on 27 Oct (see 198) but which is currently withheld from CAB 129/37/1 at the PRO (see CP 967/84, no 69, minute by O H Morris, 22 Oct 1949, and also PREM 8/1407/1).]

In considering our policy in South-East Asia and the Far East, it is first of all necessary to decide whether the political and economic influence of the United Kingdom in that part of the world is:—

(a) an important factor in the preservation of world peace; and
(b) of direct benefit to the United Kingdom.

2. The United Kingdom has a particular position in Asia which is not enjoyed by other Western Powers; unless this position of advantage is used to bring about closer collaboration between East and West, there is a very real danger that the whole of Asia will become the servant of the Kremlin. The influence of the United Kingdom in South-East Asia and the Far East is therefore an important factor in the preservation of world peace.

3. The benefit to the United Kingdom of its relationship with South-East Asia and the Far East has not yet been measured in terms. Economically we are dependent upon the area for items such as rubber, tea and jute. The dollar pool of the sterling area derives very substantial earnings from Malaya. It is probable that, if the standard of living of the peoples of Asia can be improved, trading potentialities will vastly increase. More than half the population of the world lives in the area; its resources are by no means fully developed, and in the short term it will probably produce a dividend more quickly than the continent of Africa. What Asia has in labour it lacks in skill; a combination of Western technology and Eastern man-power might be welded into a formidable partnership.

The new Asia
4. Nationalism is rampant to-day from Afghanistan to the China Sea; only in Japan is it dormant under American occupation. In Asia, which has lingered behind Europe in the development of nationhood, it is not surprising that nationalism is regarded as something to be fostered and encouraged. But, whereas intense nationalism is considered by Asiatic races to be both necessary and desirable to achieve national solidarity in newly created States, it is liable to lead to friction in

international relationships. South-East Asia and the Far East are new in the sense that nationhood has only recently impinged upon the local consciousness. We are faced, therefore, with an intense nationalism which is prickly in its international relationships. Though the idea of pan-Asia, sponsored originally by the Japanese, creates the danger of a cleavage between East and West, there is, in fact, little or no cohesion between Asiatic countries, and it is probably true to say that there is greater fear, distrust and even dislike between Asiatic neighbours than there is between Asiatic and Western nations. Nevertheless, Asiatic nationalism is abnormally sensitive to anything which savours of Western domination or dictation. Since domination came from the West, there is still a tendency to regard the West with suspicion. Domination by Russia, on the other hand, is something of which South Asia is unconscious; it has yet little meaning or reality. To this extent Russia enjoys a certain advantage over the Western Powers.

5. It is unfortunate that the countries of South-East Asia and the Far East should be passing through this stage of their development at a time when the Soviet Union is seeking to obtain domination over the whole Eurasian continent. The political immaturity of these countries and their economic distress render them particularly susceptible to Communist tactics: of this China presents an almost classic example. It is doubtful whether even Communist China will be able or will attempt to extend direct political control over the area. The existence of large Chinese communities in the countries of South-East Asia, however, presents dangerous possibilities for disruption from within, since all these Chinese must be regarded as potential agents of their Government whatever its political complexion. On the other hand, the unpopularity of the Chinese settlers with the local inhabitants may be considered to be a factor which will encourage resistance to the spread of Communist doctrines propagated from China. Again, India may one day seek to dominate the area politically, but there are few signs at present of the South-East Asian countries willingly accepting a lead from the Indians, who are unpopular and whose expansionist aims are feared. It is, therefore, fair to say that from the Persian Gulf to the China Sea there is no single Power capable of dominating the region nor any combination of Powers which by its united strength could successfully resist Russian expansion. Nor is there at present any one Asiatic Power capable of bringing about unity and co-operation throughout the region. The dangers of the situation are thus manifest and manifold.

United Kingdom influence
(a) *Political*
6. The United Kingdom cannot dominate the region, but we can and should use our political and economic influence to weld the area into some degree of regional co-operation. Politically, the chief advantage to our position is that we have been the most successful of the Western Powers in coming to terms with the new Nationalist spirit in Asia. Of our former possessions, India, Pakistan and Ceylon are now independent members of the Commonwealth, and Burma, though outside the Commonwealth, is friendly. The political systems of all these countries are built upon a British foundation. The Dutch and French, on the other hand, are still in conflict with the Nationalist movements in Indonesia and Indo-China. Moreover, the United Kingdom enjoys the prestige of victory in the Second World War, moderated, it must be admitted, by the memory of our defeats at the hands of the Japanese;

whereas the French and Dutch are regarded by Eastern opinion merely as liberated nations.

(b) *Economic*

7. Our economic influence is also considerable. Up-to-date figures are lacking, but before the war we were the largest foreign investors in Asia and our holdings are still very substantial. The value of our trade with South-East Asia and the Far East is second only to that of the United States, our main supplies to the area being manufactured goods. We have a particularly close relationship with those parts of South-East Asia which fall within the sterling area; Malaya is of particular importance, not only as a source of vital raw materials, rubber and tin, but as a major dollar earner. The oil-fields of Borneo and Sarawak, whose output is growing rapidly and is now the largest in British or Commonwealth territory, may well become a major dollar saver. The jute supplies of India and Pakistan are vital not only to our own jute industries but to the supplying of agricultural commodities within the sterling area. Manganese supplies from India are an important alternative to those from the Gold Coast, and wolfram and chrome from Burma are important elements in the manufacture of steel alloys. The United Kingdom has bought the whole copra supply of Ceylon for the current period, and virtually all the tea in the world comes from Asia.

The position of the United States

8. The other great Western Power, the United States, has the greatest volume of trade with the Far East and South-East Asia, but does not enjoy the same degree of prestige as the United Kingdom, partly because it lacks the historical connections which we enjoy with the area, partly because of the failure of its policy in China, and partly because of its reluctance to play a leading part in South-East Asia. The Americans are concentrating at present on the creation of a friendly and democratic Japan, in which country they enjoy a dominant position. But, although the United States Government is in general sympathetic with Nationalist movements in Asia as long as they are free from Communist domination, the *laissez-faire* American economic philosophy has little appeal in Asia, where practically all progressive thought is Socialist. It is not a great exaggeration to say that, when Asiatic Nationalists consider the future political and economic structure of their independent countries, they contemplate only the alternatives of democratic Socialism and Communism, which they sometimes simplify into a choice between the British and Russian ways of life.

The future development of South-East Asia and the Far East

9. There is a general desire, much handicapped by lack of expert knowledge, among the Nationalist Governments of the new Asia to push through as soon as possible programmes of economic development with the main emphasis on industrialisation. At present many of the essential capital goods are available only in the United States, but as our production expands we should be able to assist increasingly in meeting these needs, particularly since most Asiatic countries have more sterling than dollars at their disposal. Our exports of capital goods to the area are already substantial. These facts place the United Kingdom in a favourable position for helping to plan and co-ordinate economic development in South-East Asia. But,

before much progress can be made, it will be necessary to establish more clearly than has hitherto been done the development requirements and potentialities of the countries concerned. At present development programmes of countries like Burma are quite unrealistic through lack of experience and technical knowledge. It is clear that the full development of the area can only be brought about with United States assistance, but at present there is an obvious reluctance on the part of the Americans to risk a further loss after their experience in China. It is, therefore, all the more important that we should give a lead and, by proving the fitness of South-East Asia and the Far East for consideration as an area capable of profitable development, encourage the Americans to supplement our efforts.

10.   The economic influence which we derive from our capital investments in the area is, of course, a mixed blessing, since it is associated with our former imperialist position and arouses the suspicion of Nationalists, who see in it a method of indirect British control. The leaders of some of the new Asiatic States are not blind to the advantages to be derived from foreign capital if it is properly controlled, and the Premiers of India and Burma have both made encouraging statements on this point. There is, however, much doubt and suspicion in the press and public opinion of the new Asia as to the legitimate rôle, if any, of foreign enterprise in an independent Socialist State, which it is very important that we should strive to dispel.

The rôle of the United Kingdom

11.   Our interests and commitments in Asia, as can be seen from the above, are greater and more varied than those of any other Western Power. The question arises whether they are not in excess of our post-war strength. We have, however, already substantially reduced our political and military commitments in the Indian sub-continent and Burma since the war, and our economic ties are too valuable to us to be severed without serious consequences. In war we could not afford military commitments of a size which would enable us to offer effective resistance against a full-scale attack. Such military commitments as we can afford in peace should be for the purpose of maintaining internal security within our own territories, encouraging confidence in the adolescent nations of the region, and supporting local efforts to place defence establishments on a sound footing. In the long run it will be for the Asian countries themselves to preserve their national integrity and, given guidance on the right lines, there is no reason why, in the event of a world conflict, they should not be able to offer effective resistance to any possible aggression from Russia, whose major commitments will most probably lie in the West and the Middle East.

12.   We must accept the fact that there are also positive disadvantages in the United Kingdom position in Asia. Our imperialist past is by no means forgotten; the suspicion lurks all too frequently that we are seeking by more subtle means to re-establish our domination, and this suspicion is exploited by our enemies. In the areas overrun by the Japanese in the war, the recollection has not yet faded of our early and ignominious defeat. The fact that we were on the winning side in the end does not obliterate the thought that an Asiatic Power was demonstrably able to inflict crushing defeats upon us. As a result our actions to-day are regarded more critically and with less confidence than before the war.

13.   Certainly the advantages which the United Kingdom enjoys outweigh the disadvantages. Equally there is no other Power capable of undertaking the formid-able task of trying to link South-East Asia with the West and to create some kind of

regional association which will be capable of effective resistance against communism and Russian expansion. If we fail, the threat to Western preponderance will be serious; if we succeed, there will be undoubted benefit to the United Kingdom and to the association of Western Powers.

Conclusion

14. The conclusion is that the influence of the United Kingdom in South-East Asia and the Far East is an important factor in the preservation of world peace and of direct benefit to the United Kingdom itself. We are led to the further conclusions that the aim of the United Kingdom should be to build up some sort of regional association in South-East Asia in partnership with the association of the Atlantic Powers. Not only are we in the best position to interest the United States in active participation in maintaining the stability of the area, but our relation with the Commonwealth provides a means of influencing and co-ordinating the policies not only of the Asiatic Dominions, but of Australia and New Zealand, whose strategic interest in the area is, in fact, equal to our own. The immediate object of a wider association of the West, including the Pacific members of the Commonwealth and the South-East Asian countries, would be to prevent the spread of communism and to resist Russian expansion: its long-term object would be to create a system of friendly partnership between East and West and to improve economic and social conditions in South-East Asia and the Far East. The difficulties to be overcome, the methods whereby these objects may be attained and the particular problems of individual countries, whether in the area or with interests involved, will be discussed in the second part of this paper.

II *Regional co-operation in South-East Asia and the Far East**

South-East Asia

General considerations
(a) *Asian nationalism*

15. The whole relationship between the Asian countries and the West has been bedevilled by the historical legacy from the struggle between emerging nationalism and the European colonial Powers. At the end of the war Britain was faced with three possible courses of action: to maintain her political domination of countries in South-East Asia by force; to abandon her entire position in the area; or to come to an amicable settlement whereby both national aspirations and British interests and influence were safeguarded. We chose the last of these courses, and our policy in India, Pakistan, Ceylon and Burma has, in the event, proved to have been one of the

---

* Japan, Korea and China are, for the purpose of this section, taken to be the countries comprising the Far East. The first two remain for the present primarily an American commitment, while the third must be regarded not as a potential candidate for inclusion in any regional arrangement, but as a potentially hostile Power whose existence makes greater regional solidarity necessary. The Far Eastern area, therefore, is of subsidiary importance in any examination of the problem of how United Kingdom policies may best bring about greater unity in Asia. South-East Asia, on the other hand, is an area in which the United Kingdom is already vitally involved and where her influence can best be brought to bear both directly and through the Commonwealth connections. It is therefore in South-East Asia that the United Kingdom must begin with any attempt to promote great regional collaboration, and only later can the Far East become attached to any system which may emerge.

major factors in ensuring that the countries of South-East Asia, if not yet actual allies in the struggle against Soviet Communism, are at least looking to the West for support rather than to Russia.

16. The French and the Dutch have been slower to appreciate the inevitable march of events in Asia, and for a time there was a danger that, not only would they drive the nationalist elements in the areas they controlled into the arms of the Communists, but that they might discredit the West with all Asian national movements—a discredit in which Great Britain, despite her own more generous policy, would share. Fortunately, the signs are now more hopeful that a friendly settlement in Indonesia and Indo-China is in sight. When amicable relations have been established, the invidious choice that Britain had to make between her Western allies on the one hand and her potential Asian friends on the other will have been removed, and our own standing and that of the West as a whole, with India in particular, greatly improved. Suspicion of the West and of imperialism, however, dies hard and only time and the most careful handling of Asian susceptibilities will bring about a fully satisfactory relationship between East and West. With the Asian nations much can be done (or undone) through personal relationships at all levels. It is therefore of vital importance that the right personnel should be employed for our dealings in Asia and particularly in India and Pakistan.

(b) *Inter-Asian relations*

17. The new-found freedom of the Asian countries and the danger that this freedom may yet be lost to Moscow's dictatorship have not, however, served to abolish conflict between the countries themselves. The Afghan-Pakistan dispute, Indo-Pakistan bitterness arising from partition and the question of Kashmir, the chaotic state of Burma and the fears which this arouses in her neighbours, the comparative isolationism of Siam and the disturbed state of Indo-China and Indonesia are all factors contributing to the general lack of co-operation in the area. Again, India is (apart from Communist China) the only country physically capable of acting as a leader to South-East Asia, but the Asian countries appear to fear and mistrust domination by one of their own number as much as they disliked European domination. Any direct attempt by India to act as the sole co-ordinator in any regional system would therefore not prove welcome to the other countries involved, and in particular to Pakistan who still fears that India's aim is to bring about the re-union of the sub-continent by force or threat of force. It is therefore clear that conditions do not at present exist in which the Asian countries are likely to combine of their own accord, without a lead from elsewhere.

(c) *The United States*

18. No final regional system of collaboration can, in the long run, hope to exist without American participation. Unfortunately the Americans appear to be holding aloof from South-East Asia problems at the present time. It appears that after their failure in China they are content to let us develop plans for regional co-operation and will wait to see if they work in practice before offering to assist or participate in them. Whereas in the Middle East the Americans have told us they are prepared to help us to maintain our position, provided we ourselves are determined to do our utmost to maintain it, in South-East Asia only the success of our efforts is likely to encouage the Americans to come in with us at some later stage. In Japan and South Korea the

United States already have a commitment, and they will certainly maintain some line of strategic defence in the Pacific.

Particular factors
(a) India

19. India is the key to the whole problem of South-East Asian regional co-operation. Without India we can achieve little, but India is at present in no mood to co-operate in any joint move to establish an anti-Communist front in South-East Asia and the Far East. Her attitude can be summed up as:—

(1) A mistrust of the West based on the legacy of imperialism.

(2) A fear that she may be embroiled by the West in a struggle with Russia, and hence an avowed desire to remain clear of entanglements with either of the Great Power *blocs*. Subsidiary to this is the fear that we may exploit the Commonwealth relationship to draw her imperceptibly into our own policies.

(3) A belief, based on a failure to realise that the Soviet Communist threat is world wide and not directed solely against the West, that it is, in fact, possible to sit on the fence. This leads to a disinclination to believe that the Chinese Communists are willing to follow direction from Moscow, or that a Communist China may threaten Asian National Governments.

(4) A belief in India's destiny as the leader of the Asian peoples.

20. The Indian attitude in (1) to (3) above can be said to be representative to a greater or less degree of the attitude of all South-East Asian countries. Therefore, taking these factors into account it must be assumed that any general policy towards South-East Asia and the Far East must:—

(1) strive to dissolve the suspicions directed against our colonial policy;

(2) convince all the nations of South-East Asia that any position between the two Great Power *blocs* is illusory and persuade them that the front against Communism, which the West is building up, is as much in their interest as in that of Europe, and that they are not merely regarded as auxiliaries to be used in any conflict that may come about;

(3) in regard to India, induce a realisation that while we view her aspirations with sympathy, time is short and unless she is prepared to play a more positive rôle, there may be no Asia left for her to lead.

While something can be done on these lines in the political field, concrete help of a technical, financial and economic nature is likely to be of the greatest influence in achieving the first two points of policy mentioned above. This aspect will be examined later in the paper. Further there are signs that Communist expansion, just as it served to bring about the greater cohesion of the West, is bringing the leaders of the countries of Asia to a more realistic frame of mind with regard to regional co-operation in the face of the common danger. Unless the Communists are very much more skilful than in the past, their future actions and successes are likely to accelerate this process.

(b) The Commonwealth and South-East Asia

21. The defence of South-East Asia is of vital concern to Australia and New Zealand. In addition, three other fully independent members of the Commonwealth

(India, Pakistan and Ceylon), the economically important colonies of Malaya and Hong Kong, and Burma in special treaty relationship with ourselves, all lie in the area under consideration. Thus seven out of the nine fully independent Commonwealth countries are directly interested in safeguarding against Communist inroads the defence of a line stretching from Afghanistan to the China Sea, while Burma has recently looked to the Commonwealth for help in her military and financial crisis. There is therefore a nucleus upon which to build any system of regional co-operation. Two immediate obstacles must, however, first be overcome before any practical steps are taken to build on this nucleus—the Kashmir dispute and India's fear that the regional strength of South-East Asia is to be exploited for the sake of a war in the West between the Western Powers and Russia. Other dangers are the racial policies of South Africa and Australia. The present South African Government's attitude is provocative of anti-European sentiment, and her membership of the Commonwealth tends to involve us in an accusation of "Colonialism." Despite Australia's professions of sympathy for the struggle nationalisms in Asia there has been evidence recently that the execution of the "White Australia" policy has begun to cause resentment in Asiatic countries, and there is a danger that this policy may ultimately embitter relations between Australia and Asia.

22. Having agreed that it is for Great Britain to play a major (if unobtrusive) part in organising South-East Asia for regional political, economic and military co-operation, there is much to be said for using a Commonwealth rather than a purely United Kingdom approach to achieve our aims. Not only will India be less suspicious that she is being used as a pawn in a European-Moscow chess match, but her aspirations to be a leading member of the team can largely be satisfied without:—

(a) causing undue offence to Pakistan and Ceylon (since the United Kingdom, Australia and New Zealand will all be playing too);

(b) frightening other countries in the area that Asian Regional Collaboration is not another name for Greater India or Mahabharat.

23. The suggestion to hold a Commonwealth Conference in Ceylon in 1950 remains at the moment in abeyance. If such a Conference can be held it should provide a suitable occasion for a discussion on South-East Asian affairs. Though the presence of South Africa at the Conference may encourage India to expound her views on racial questions, it is unlikely that South Africa will wish to intervene on questions which are concerned only with South-East Asia. There is therefore no reason why a satisfactory understanding should not be reached on the latter. Further Communist success in China, increasing Communist disturbances in India and a successful launching of independent régimes in Indonesia and Indo-China, may do much in the meantime to bring India to the Conference table in a realistic frame of mind. . . .[1]

(h) *Malaya*

31. Malaya is of the utmost importance strategically and economically to the United Kingdom, and is the major dollar earner of the sterling area. There is a growing Malay nationalist movement which, but for the promulgation of the new

---

[1] Sub-sections (c)–(g) (ie paras 24–30), on Pakistan, Afghanistan, Burma, Siam, Indo-China and Indonesia, have not been printed.

constitution, might have become anti-British. But owing to the Malay fear of the Chinese, coupled with an appreciation of our liberal policy, this movement is not directed against the British connection. The campaign against the Communists is proceeding satisfactorily, although the danger of the large Chinese community acting for a Communist China will remain a constant threat to be watched. On the other hand nothing succeeds like success in the Orient, and the final liquidation of the Communists in Malaya and the assurance that we are not prepared to abandon the area and are taking effective steps to safeguard it from external aggression may do much to encourage the local Chinese to believe that reinsurance with a Communist China is not an absolute necessity. There are indications that if we pursue our present course in Malaya the Indian Government would prefer us to retain a stake in the country rather than push their views on "colonialism" to the lengths of condemning our presence. . . .[2]

General conclusions on political collaboration on a regional basis

39. From all the above it is clear that the situation in South-East Asia would not allow of any attempt being made in the immediate future to bring about a greater degree of political co-operation on the lines that have been followed in Western Europe. The United States are not prepared to play the same part or to produce the same material incentives to greater unity. A system which excluded Great Britain, France and Holland would be weak and would lack community of purpose with the West. For the time being, however, France and Holland, and to a lesser extent Britain, are suspect. There are further many local jealousies and rivalries to be overcome (as in the Middle East) before the countries concerned can be expected to work in harmony. Any thought of a South-East Asia Pact can therefore be ruled out for the time being.

40. At the same time, our policy can follow certain definite lines in the political field which will prepare the ground for greater future regional co-operation in the political sphere. These lines are:—

(1) The removal of East-West discord by developments that will prove that imperialism and racial superiority are dead.

(2) The use of our influence in bringing about the settlement of national rivalries in the area.

(3) The discreet promotion of greater solidarity between the Commonwealth countries of the area (including Australia and New Zealand).

(4) Keeping the United States informed of our positive programme and, as occasion arises, getting them to afford such assistance as they can.

(5) Emphasis in propaganda on the menace that Soviet Communism presents to nationalism. The countries of South-East Asia have not emerged from dependence merely to fall under the new Russian (or Chinese) Imperialism.

41. In pursuing this policy, we shall have to face the difficulty of being unable to satisfy Asian demands for large amounts of material assistance. The Asian countries will constantly subject us and the United States to threats that unless more help is forthcoming they may have to make the best terms they can with Communism and

---

[2] Sub-sections (i) and (j) (ie paras 32–38), on the Philippines and Hong Kong, have not be printed.

Russia. Further, we cannot expect democracy to develop necessarily on our pattern, or that corruption and inefficiency will vanish overnight. We must take a realistic view of the East as it is and rest content that if we can get it on our side that is the most we can hope for. It will for a great many years be the fact that the masses of the peoples of Asia will have little voice in government and universal suffrage is only likely to be exploited by the governing classes who, on the whole, are few and venal and in many cases inexperienced in the art of government. . . .[3]

Military co-operation

The danger of Chinese aggression

50.   China is so weakened by years of war, maladministration and economic chaos that it is unlikely that the Chinese Communists will embark on any military adventures against their neighbours for some years to come, unless in the course of a general world conflict between Russia and the West. This does not, however, mean that territorial claims, accompanied by threats may not be put forward against China's southern neighbours. Any weakness or wavering among these neighbours will also be exploited.

51.   Far more obvious dangers are:—

(1) Active support of the Communists in Burma and Indo-China and the "Freedom Movement" in Siam, thus producing a situation similar to that in Greece in all three countries; and

(2) The use of large local Chinese communities in South-East Asia as a powerful Communist Fifth Column, corroding from within and ultimately, if circumstances are favourable, seizing power.

These dangers may become imminent in the near future and will affect the whole security of South-East Asia.

Security considerations

52.   The countries most open to direct aggression by the Chinese Communists are Burma, Siam and Indo-China, while all the other countries in South-East Asia are extremely vulnerable to Communist disruption and subversion from within.

53.   It is therefore vital that the countries south of China should be not only politically stable, but capable of dealing militarily with insurrectionist bands either operating from China or from within as in Malaya and India.

54.   The vastness of the area to be covered and the slenderness of Britain's military resources mean that we could not undertake to provide military support on any appreciable scale in the face of widespread Communist guerrilla activities over the whole area or in the event of a world war. Nor, in view of the lack of political cohesion in South-East [Asia], it is likely that other countries in the area would wish to become involved in helping a neighbour, even if they felt capable of doing so, which in their present state of unpreparedness would be extremely unlikely. Ultimately the responsibility for the defence of South-East Asia must rest on the countries concerned themselves. For the time being, however, there is little hope of any wide strategic co-operation between all the countries concerned. The most that

---

[3] Paragraphs 42–49, on China, Japan and Korea, have not been printed.

can be aimed at therefore is that each country individually should put its armed forces in the best possible shape to prove effective in the event of internal disorder or infiltration from without.

The United Kingdom's rôle in the military field

55. The security problem, unlike the political or economic one, is of some urgency since the Communists may well soon control all China. It is primarily a problem of security against internal unrest stimulated from outside. It is in United Kingdom interests that some priority should be given to the security of the area, without which political and economic co-operation are unlikely to advance at all. Much can be done politically to encourage the will to resist, but in the purely military field, despite our lack of real forces, we shall again have to play a positive rôle if the area is not to fall piece-meal into Communist hands. To this end the most hopeful couse seems to be to:—

(1) Persuade the countries of South-East Asia that their ultimate military salvation lies in their own hands.

(2) Encourage them by our continued strategic interests in the area, by readiness to help with technical advice and military missions if welcome, and by supplying arms to the greatest extent possible. In supplying armaments American help would be of the utmost value, and despite American reluctance to provide assistance for South-East Asia, it may be necessary to try and convince them of the need for arms now, if the programme we should like to follow in the economic and political fields is to have any chance of success from its inception.

(3) Finally, as in the political field, to attempt to obtain a nucleus of strategic co-operation between the Commonwealth countries of Asia, ourselves and the Australians and New Zealanders, before any wider regional defence system itself may be practicable. This co-operation would have to be entirely in the field of planning and exchange of views since the actual supply of arms would still be expected to come from the United Kingdom, whose many other commitments would not allow of any great increase over the present flow.

Economic co-operation

The economic situation

56. The feature which all the countries of South-East Asia and the Far East have in common is the very low standard of living. Although the area is principally agricultural it can only feed itself on what from Western standards would be a semi-starvation level. Furthermore, India, a country with as many inhabitants as the rest of the countries of South-East Asia and the Far East combined (excluding China), is a net food importer. The general standard of nutrition of the area as a whole, low as it is, therefore depends largely on the ability of surplus food areas to provide for deficit areas. The troubles in Burma, Indo-China and Indonesia have seriously affected the surplus amounts of rice available for export and have aggravated the generally unhealthy economic situation of the area, resulting from the war.

57. In the field of economic development the Asian countries are without the resources or technical skill to embark on their own rehabilitation and improvement. They will therefore be forced to look elsewhere for help and their eyes are at present

turned towards the West.

58. For the West itself the area provides a field where capital investment may produce quick and profitable returns provided that the political stability of the non-Communist countries can be maintained. The need for technical assistance should provide openings for Western industry and commerce. A rising standard of living in Asia would provide large and steady markets for Western goods.

The economic possibilities

59. There are, therefore, three factors in our favour:—

(1) The East needs our assistance and may well acccept Western co-operation in the rehabilitation of the economic life of the area.
(2) Historic economic ties exist between East and West which render economic co-operation less suspect than attempts to promote greater political co-operation.
(3) The West is in a position to provide the technical help which the East requires in its reconstruction.

The interdependence of the area for food supplies is an incentive to greater regional co-operation. Pandit Nehru himself has now announced his conviction that India needs the help of European industry. If India, the key to South-East Asia, is prepared to examine the possibility of greater economic regional collaboration in which the West could also play its part, the other countries of the area would soon follow her lead.

60. The United Kingdom may be said to have been the pioneer of regional co-operation through the establishment in 1946 of the Special Commissioner's organisation in Singapore, subsequently absorbed by the Commissioner-General. Subsequently there was established the United Nations Economic Committee for Asia and the Far East (E.C.A.F.E.). Including as it does the Soviet Union in its membership, it is doubtful whether this organisation will really develop a healthy spirit of regional co-operation, though we are committed to its support.

The prospects for economic development

61. If the thesis is accepted that the most profitable line to pursue is the economic one, there still remains the problem of how to find from our slender resources sufficient for the development not only of India and Pakistan but of South-East Asia as a whole, especially at the present time when demands from the Colonial Empire are particularly heavy. The question is now being studied by the Far Eastern Official Committee and the results of this study cannot here be prejudged. This paper only attempts to set out the policy to be pursued. But it seems probable that although the demand by South-East Asia may well be enormous, it may be possible (especially if effective use is made of "Fourth Point assistance") to meet sufficient items for the whole venture to be considered a feasible proposition.

The prospects of the economic approach

62. Political differences between the countries of South-East Asia and the Far East and their unwillingness and inability to collaborate militarily, leave economic collaboration as the only form of greater unity which the countries of the area are likely to accept at present. But the habit of collaboration is a catching one and the settlement of economic difficulties, of common consultation and effort, may well

lead to greater political and military cohesion. In promoting greater economic collaboration, the West does not labour under the same handicap of suspicion of imperialism or selfish exploitation as it would were it to try to promote political or military unity. Regional collaboration in the economic field, if achieved, may well lead not only to a better understanding between the countries of Asia themselves, but also between East and West. It is therefore at present the only possible line to pursue in the direction of our long-term objective of political and military, as well as economic co-operation throughout the region in partnership with the West.

Conclusions

63. Assuming that the political and economic stability of South-East Asia and the Far East is of prime importance to the West, that this can best be brought about by greater regional collaboration and that it is for the United Kingdom to play the major rôle in bringing this regional collaboration into being, the following conclusions are reached on the course to pursue:—

(1) For the present our policy must confine itself to South-East Asia. Only if some stable system emerges there, will the countries of the Far East later attach themselves to it.

(2) In the Far East our main problem lies not with the inhabitants or Governments of the area, but with the United States whose policies we must endeavour to influence along lines acceptable to ourselves.

(3) In China we must try to keep a foot in the door in the hope that we shall be able to maintain China's contacts with the West and that we may be able to take advantage of any rift between Communist China and the Soviet Union.

(4) In South-East Asia, greater measure of regional co-operation is at present only practicable in the economic field. Though its own resources are insufficient to meet the large demands likely to be made, United Kingdom has the major rôle to play in promoting regional economic co-operation which, in turn may lead to regional collaboration in other fields. But she should play this rôle as unobtrusively as possible and encourage Asian countries to assume in initative where this can safely be done.

(5) In all fields—political, economic and military—the Commonwealth countries of Asia, with the United Kingdom and Australia and New Zealand, present a nucleus on which to build.

(6) South-East Asia is yet ripe for greater political collaboration either internally or with the West. Much can, however, be done along the lines suggested in paragraph 40.

(7) The security of the area is the most pressing problem, but for the time being we can only work within individual countries. Our general policy is laid down in paragraph 55.

(8) Only if we show our willingness and ability to bring about greater Asian solidarity, will the Americans be prepared to assist or to come into any regional arrangement. Convincing planning and some interim successes may, however, persuade the Americans to give practical interim aid which would further our ultimate aims.

(9) No plans will, however, be really successful without American participation and our main object must be to secure this.

197   CAB 128/16, CM 62(49)7   27 Oct 1949

'China: recognition of Chinese communist government': Cabinet
conclusions on the basis of UK policy in the region

[The People's Republic of China was officially proclaimed in Beijing on 1 Oct 1949. The
new regime was immediately recognised by the USSR and its satellites, and later by
Burma, India and, on 6 Jan 1950, by Britain despite US displeasure. Recognition posed
particular problems for Malaya: the colonial authorities feared that the reputation of the
MCP would be enhanced and that Chinese consuls posted to Malaya would act as a fifth
column for the PRC. For differing assessments by the FO and CO of the extent of the
PRC's threat to Malaya, see CAB 134/497 and FO 371/84478; for their *modus operandi* as
regards publicity towards communism in Malaya and China, see 202; on the problem of
Chinese consuls in Malaya, see 213.]

The Cabinet considered a memorandum by the Foreign Secretary (C.P. (49) 214) on
the question of the recognition of the Chinese Communist Government.

The Foreign Secretary said that the Communist Government of the People's
Republic of China had expressed a desire to enter into diplomatic relations with
foreign Powers; and the Soviet Union and their satellites had already accorded *de jure*
recognition to that Government. The case for recognising the new Government was
strong, but the first step must be to consult other Commonwealth Governments and
the Governments of the United States and other friendly Powers. Until these
consultations had taken place it would be premature to take any decision regarding
the date of recognition. Account must also be taken of the impact of recognition on
United Kingdom interests in the Far East, and this could be discussed at the
forthcoming Conference at Singapore of His Majesty's Representatives and Colonial
Governors in South-East Asia and the Far East.[1] He hoped it would be possible to
reach agreement on this matter with the United States Government; and, if it should
be decided to recognise the new Government, he thought it would be important to
ensure that the Indian Government took action at the same time. In the meantime,
he would feel bound to make it known that the recent statement on the subject made
by the Australian Deputy Prime Minister did not correctly represent the views of the
United Kingdom Government. It would be unwise to seek to make recognition
conditional upon the fulfilment of specific obligations.

In discussion, it was pointed out that *de jure* recognition of the Chinese
Communist Government would create a special problem in Malaya, since there
might be some disposition among the Chinese community to assume that this would
justify the cessation of punitive measures against the Communist bandits.

The Cabinet:—
Approved the recommendations made in C.P. (49) 214.

---

[1] The main conclusion of this conference, chaired by MacDonald from 2 to 4 Nov, was that HMG should
recognise communist China and at the same time intensify resistance to communism in SE Asia where the
immediate threat was very great (see CAB 129/37/3, CP(49)244, 26 Nov 1949).

198   CAB 128/16, CM62(49)8   27 Oct 1949
'South-East Asia and the Far East': Cabinet conclusions on general policy in the region

The Cabinet had before them a memorandum by the Foreign Secretary (C.P. (49) 207)[1] outlining the general policy which the United Kingdom Government should pursue in South-East Asia and the Far East. If the proposed lines of policy were approved, they would serve as a basis for the guidance of the forthcoming Conference at Singapore of His Majesty's Representatives and Colonial Governors in South-East Asia and the Far East.

The Chancellor of the Exchequer hoped that nothing would be said at this Conference to imply that this country would be able to continue to give financial or material aid to South-East Asia on the scale reached during the last few years. Commitments in respect of India, Pakistan, and to a lesser extent Burma and Ceylon, had been running at the rate of £200 million a year, and the present economic position of this country made it necessary to make substantial reductions in this expenditure in the future.[2] This was part of a general reduction of unrequited exports to various parts of the world; and it involved as a corollary the agreement of the United States Government to an integrated overseas investment policy. The extent to which the United States might be prepared to buttress the anti-Communist front in South-East Asia by undertaking capital investment had been discussed in a preliminary way during the recent Washington talks[3] and had been referred to a committee for detailed examination. It would shortly be necessary to have further discussions on this subject with the United States Government.

In discussion it was suggested that it should not be impracticable to maintain the political influence of the United Kingdom in South-East Asia while arranging for the United States to provide much of the capital investment that was required. Conditions in South-East Asia, and in certain parts of the world, were now so uncertain that loans could probably not be secured through the ordinary financial channels and large-scale capital investment by the United States Government might be required. The unfortunate experience which the United States Government had had in China had made them more receptive of suggestions for collaboration with this country in Asiatic affairs on the basis that the United Kingdom provided experience and the United States provided finance.

The Cabinet:—

(1) Approved the Foreign Secretary's proposals in C.P.(49)207 as a basis for the guidance of the Conference to be held at Singapore, subject to any necessary modifications to make clear the limited extent to which this country could undertake future financial commitments in South-East Asia.

(2) Took note that the Chancellor of the Exchequer was reviewing the whole field of overseas investment policy and would endeavour to secure early agreement on the subject with the United States Government.

---

[1] See 196, note.

[2] On 24 Oct Attlee had announced massive economies to control inflation.

[3] Cripps and Bevin had visited Washington in Sept; one result of their talks was an increase in US investment in Europe.

199   CO 537/4374, no 5   [Nov 1949]

'Note on tour of South-East Asia October 1949': report by Field
Marshal Sir W Slim[1] on the importance of civil action in counter-
insurgency   [Extract]

Minutes by O H Morris and W C Johnson[2]

. . .

Malaya

During my short visit to Malaya I had considerable opportunity for discussion with
Mr. Malcolm MacDonald, Sir Henry Gurney, Sir Franklin Gimson, Sir John
Harding,[3] Major-General Boucher,[4] and a number of civil and military officers. In
addition, I met a number of the leading Malay and Chinese politicians. I realise that
in so short a visit it is very hard to weigh all the factors and conditions affecting the
Malayan problem, but certain conclusions forced themselves upon me.

The first of these is that the supression [sic] of the Communist bandits is much
more a matter for civil than military action. The number of active bandits is not
large; I doubt if it is as large even as the accepted official intelligence estimates.
Military and Police action against the bandits has gradually pushed them out of the
more accessible districts and driven them to take refuge in the jungles on the edge of
the squatter areas. The Army has for a long period kept the Communist bandits on
the move and has inflicted minor losses on them. It is now extremely uncomfortable
to be a bandit in Malaya but the success of the Communists in China enables the
bandit leaders in Malaya to hold out the hope of the arrival of a Chinese Communist
Army in Malaya and thus keep their bands together and even recruit fresh members.
The sequence of action seems to be that a band having been located in an area, a
military force proceeds to beat through a wide expanse of jungle and locate the band.
Contact is usually made with one or two individual bandits acting as outposts but the
main body is able to evacuate its camp and disperse to rally again in some
pre-arranged area many miles away. The Army then laboriously repeats the process. I
had the trace of some of these operations plotted on the map and only too often the
result was a circle; the Army drove the bandits from one place to another until after a
few months the circle was complete and the bandits were back again more or less in
the area from which they had started. It seems to me that the Army can go on doing
this indefinitely, and so can the bandits. The only answer is that as the bandits are
driven by the Army from an area a real effective civil administration steps in and with
its Police and other forces takes complete administrative control of the area.

I did not realise before that very considerable portions of Malaya have not since the
war, and in some cases before it, been under effective administration. Before the war
this did not matter so much as these areas were very sparsely populated by the Sakai
Aborigines.[5] Now, however, very large Chinese populations are settled in these areas.

---

[1] Sir W Slim was CIGS, 1948–1952.

[2] W C Johnson was inspector-general of colonial police, 1948–1951.

[3] Sir J Harding was c-in-c, FARELF, 1949–1951.

[4] See 188, note 2.

[5] The term *sakai*, used by the security forces, implied the status of near slave and was resented by the
aborigines. It was later replaced by *asal* from the Malay word for origin.

These Chinese are referred to as squatters but for all practical purposes they are permanent inhabitants in Malaya, and they have not been under an effective civil administration. Roughly half the population of Malaya is Chinese and yet a civil official who can speak Chinese is extremely rare, and there are no uniformed Chinese constables. Before the war the Chinese population was supervised by a British official known as the Protector of the Chinese who had a small European staff. After the war it was decided that the Chinese population in Malaya would have to be recognised as citizens of Malaya. It was also decided that the post of Protector of the Chinese was inconsistent with the new idea; his organisation was therefore broken up and his officers drafted to other departments. As a result the civil administration has had no real touch with or control over a considerable portion of the vast Chinese population. Even now, when the necessity to build up an administration in the Chinese areas is recognised in the highest quarters, it is extremely difficult to produce anything effective because the senior British civil and Police officials have little knowledge of the Chinese, and most of the subordinate District Officers, who should be entrusted with the detailed local administration, are Malays who not only dislike the Chinese and are disliked by them, but are in some cases extremely nervous of entering squatter areas. An attempt is being made to gain administrative control by setting up Police stations in areas where they have never existed before, but as the whole of the Police are Malays this merely means that a small party of alien Police are dumped down in a population strange and often hostile to them.

All this is fully recognised by the High Commissioner and Chief Commissioner[6] but a number of the pre-war British Malayan civil and police officers are, I think, still obsessed with the idea that Malaya is a country for Malays only and that it is possible almost to ignore the Chinese. There is a also a tendency to regard the war against the Communist bandits as something that should be left to the Army. The Army is very willing to play its full share, but it is wasting its time unless urgent steps are being taken to bring the whole of Malaya under efficient civil administration. For a variety of reasons this does not seem to be making the progress that is needed, and it is essential, unless a serious situation is to arise within the next year or two, that a much more rapid progress should be made.

I would venture, with diffidence, to suggest that progress is needed very badly in two directions. Firstly, that the whole Malayan civil administration should be re-orientated so that it pays at least as much attention to the Chinese as to the Malays and has, for example, as many Chinese speaking officials as Malay speaking. The second line on which progress should be speeded up is in the Police. A great deal has been done in this respect already under the new Chief of Police, Mr. Gray, but he has an extremely difficult task not least because many of the pre-war senior British Police Officers have resented the introduction of new blood and have not given their full loyalty. What has to be done, in the Police force now, is to hold a balance between the need for local knowledge and the necessity to introduce modern police methods into what was a somewhat archaic Force. It seems to me that in the higher ranks preference should be given to the latter. It is more important that the general organisation should be on sound modern lines, e.g. there should be a proper central Headquarters for the Civil [? Criminal] Investigation Department,[7] than that the

---

[6] Slim is referring to the commissioner of police.

[7] Sir W Jenkin's reorganisation of the CID as the Intelligence Bureau in 1950 led to a clash with Gray and

most senior officers should have great local knowledge. Their task is to organise local knowledge as required on the second and lower levels. In fact, this local knowledge is only forthcoming from the old Malaya Police for one half of the population, and the new importation is not at as great a disadvantage as one would expect, when it comes to dealing with the Chinese half of the population, when both the new and the old start pretty well from scratch. It will, of course, be a matter of time, whatever energy is put into it, to build up a civil administration and a Police Force capable really of dealing with the Chinese, but there are some steps which could be taken to speed up progress. I would suggest consideration of the transfer, on suitable terms, of British and Chinese officers of the Hongkong Police. It seems also essential that a start should be made to recruit Chinese uniformed constables. The High Commissioner has made some headway in persuading Malayan politicians to accept the Chinese as citizens and to form parties containing both races. This is the only eventual hope for a united and peaceful Malaya, but I fear rather a long term policy.

A very important question in Malaya is whether the British recognise the Communist Government of China or not. From a purely local point of view it is probably advantageous not to recognise it. On the other hand I do not think recognition would have such disastrous effects as some people in Malaya would anticipate. Whether the Government is recognised or not, it is, and will be in fact, the Government of China and the Chinese population of Malaya will regard it as such. Recognition should enable us at any rate to have some diplomatic touch with the new Government and we might even in return for this recognition obtain for what it is worth some agreement on the [their] non-interference in Malaya. The only real danger in recognition that I can see is that it will lead to the establishment of Communist Chinese Consuls throughout Malaya. This could be a great danger in that they would be a means of supplying information, money, leaders and possibly arms to the bandits. I would suggest that, to lessen the possibilities of evil in this way, recognition of a Nationalist Government should be withdrawn some time before the Communist Government is recognised, if this is diplomatically feasible. It would thus be possible to close down the Nationalist Consuls and at any rate cause considerable considerable delay before they could be taken over by Communist Consuls. This delay should, if properly used, enable the Malayan authorities and Police to take such steps as are required to ham-string and possibly penetrate the new Communist Consuls.

In this note I have strayed considerably from the purely military aspect of the Malayan problem, but until it is recognised that the problem is by no means a military one, and that any military effort can only be subsidiary to and in support of a civil effort, we shall make no progress.

Minutes on 199

Mr. Paskin is away today and it is unlikely that he will be here tomorrow, but I should like him to see this Report, if at all possible, before the C.I.G.S. calls on the Secretary of State.

The paragraphs on Malaya put very clearly the salient features of the situation as

---

Jenkin's resignation in 1951, cf 249, note 6.

they have been known to us, and the Field Marshal says nothing surprising. It is good to see that he recognises that "the suppression of the Communist bandits is much more a matter for civil than military action". This is Sir Henry Gurney's view, and the Field Marshal recognises that the points he makes are familiar to the High Commissioner, who is taking action on them.

In particular, the High Commissioner is doing his utmost to bring administration to the squatter areas and to make Government more real to the mass of the Chinese people. The old Chinese Protectorate was a means whereby the Malayan Chinese were in touch with the administration, and this is now being achieved by the appointment of Assistant Secretaries for Chinese Affairs in the various States and by the establishment of Chinese Advisory Boards. Chinese-speaking officers are in charge of resettlement work which includes the establishment of an embryo form of local government, worked by the Chinese themselves. Some States are more forward in this work than others; Perak has taken the lead and is being followed by Selangor. The High Commissioner has also reported that a larger number of Administrative Officers are to learn Chinese. Recently it has been decided to recruit Chinese for the uniformed branch of the Police. 67 new Police Stations have been opened in squatter areas since the beginning of the year and more are planned.

I think that the progress that is being made both in administering the Chinese squatter areas and in re-orientating the administration so that it pays as much attention to the Chinese as to the Malays answers the first of the suggestions made by the C.I.G.S. As regards his recommendation that progress should be speeded up in the police, the forthcoming mission[8] should be valuable in advising on the structure and organisation of the force on a long term basis. It might be pointed out to the Field Marshal that the difficulty in Malaya has always been that the Chinese will not enlist in the uniformed branch and close contact with, and trust in the police is thus made impossible for half the population of Malaya. This situation may be remedied if in the future Chinese recruits *are* forthcoming for the uniformed branch.

Mr. Johnson should see.

O.H.M.
16.11.49

Seen. I raised the question of recruiting Chinese into the Police Force and was told very definitely that, other than for detective duties, they simply will not join—they can earn far more money outside for one thing. It is however a very important limitation at the present time.

I doubt whether Hong Kong could or should be asked to spare officers for Malaya.

W.C.J.
16.11.89

---

[8] Dissatisfaction with and within the Malayan police led to the appointment of the Police Mission to Malaya consisting of Sir Alexander Maxwell (chairman and until recently permanent under-secretary at the Home Office), J F Ferguson (chief constable of Kent, 1946–1958) and R L Jackson (secretary of the Metropolitan Police Office since 1946 and assistant commissioner CID at New Scotland Yard 1953–1963). The three men visited Malaya between 27 Nov 1949 and 12 Feb 1950. While broadly supportive of Gray's achievements, their *Report of the Police Mission to Malaya, March 1950* (Kuala Lumpur, 1950) drew attention to deficiencies in morale, in conditions of service, and in intelligence and the CID, to the lack of Chinese-speaking officers and the paucity of Chinese members in the uniformed branch, and to the priority given to paramilitary operations over 'normal policing' (see CO 537/5417).

200   T 220/233, ff 115   16 Nov 1949
'Financial assistance to Malaya for security measures': minute by J I C
Crombie

[Gurney's despatch no 10, 8 Sept 1949, requested a UK contribution of £5 million
towards internal security. The Treasury scrutinised the high commissioner's estimates in
close consultation with CO officials who, while accepting that Gurney's revenue estimates
were unduly pessimistic, nonetheless pressed very strongly for a UK grant of £3 million.]

It is quite clear that we must give Malaya financial help for 1950; we contemplated
last year that we should have to continue it beyond 1949–50.[1] The only question is
whether it should be £2 millions or £3 millions (plus the excess cost of British
troops).

On some fairly optimistic assumptions about Malaya's financial and economic
position, the figure might be kept at £2 millions, and the need for strict economy
would point in this direction, despite the risk of a subsequent Supplementary. On the
other side, there are strong political arguments (which themselves have economic
implications for us in view of Malaya's dollar earning capacity) in favour of acting
more generously and making the figure £3 millions (against Malaya's request for £5
millions).

I agree with Mr. Clough[2] that, on balance, the political arguments justify a
decision in favour of £3 millions. Two further points are relevant to this:—

(a) It is pretty clear that we shall have to continue to provide some help to Malaya
in 1951 also. If experience during 1950 shows that £3 millions has been on the
generous side, we shall have an opportunity of adjusting it in 1951.
(b) The 1950 forecast this Summer included provision for £5 millions; a decision
in favour of £3 millions will not add to our expected liabilities.[3]

---

[1] See 175, minute.   [2] A H Clough, Treasury since 1938.
[3] Sir B Gilbert, joint second secretary, Treasury, 1944–1956, noted (16 Nov): 'I think £3m. (against £5m.
in our forecasts and £5m. this year) is reasonable.' Sir S Cripps added (16 Nov): 'Let it be £3m.'

201   PREM 8/1407/1, EPC(49)152, annex   [Nov 1949]
'Economic and social development in South and South-East Asia and
the Far East': report by the Far East (Official) Committee. *Appendix* A
[Extract]

[This paper was the product of inter-departmental discussions, on which the CO was
represented throughout, and arose from CP(49)207 and the related Cabinet discussion
(see 196 and 198). Before being forwarded to ministers, the report was considered on 21
Nov by the Official Committee on Economic Development Overseas, chaired by Sir E N
Plowden, which recommended that it be used as a brief for UK representatives in
Washington talks about sterling balances and the encouragement of US overseas
investment. The CO brief advising Creech Jones's endorsement of the report drew his
attention particularly to paras 17 and 28(v) (see CO 537/4873, no 28, note for the
secretary of state, 5 Dec 1949). CP(49)207 and EP(49)152 formed the basis of the brief for
the UK delegation to the Colombo conference in Jan 1950.]

Introduction

In a paper submitted to Ministers by the Foreign Secretary on United Kingdom policy in South-East Asia and the Far East (C.P. (49) 207), which has been approved by the Cabinet, the general proposition is stated that "the United Kingdom has a particular position in Asia which is not enjoyed by other Western Powers, and that unless this position of advantage is used to bring about closer collaboration between East and West, there is a very real danger that the whole of Asia will become the servant of the Kremlin." The conclusion is reached that the aim of the United Kingdom should be to build up some sort of regional association in South-East Asia in partnership with like-minded Governments, including the United States of America. The immediate aim of a wider association of the West, including the Pacific members of the Commonwealth with the South-East Asia countries, would be to prevent the spread of Communism and to resist Russian expansion; its long-term object would be to create a system of friendly partnership between East and West and to improve economic and social conditions in South-East Asia and the Far East. The paper suggests that, since it is clear that the situation in South-East Asia will not allow of any attempt being made in the immediate future to bring about a greater degree of political co-operation on the lines that have been followed in Western Europe, the economic approach, rather than the political, offers a better chance of achieving our aim in the area. In the economic sphere there are three factors in our favour, namely, that the East need our assistance and may well accept Western co-operation in this sphere, that historic economic ties exist between East and West, and that the West is in a position to provide technical help. The paper states that the question of the economic approach is under study by the Far East (Official) Committee. In discussion the Cabinet issued a caveat to the effect that the United Kingdom contribution to the area in the economic sphere would from now on be strictly limited and that the aid we had already given to the area in the form of unrequited export could not be continued. The Cabinet also took note that the Chancellor of the Exchequer was reviewing the whole field of investment policy and would endeavour to secure early agreement on the subject with the United States Government.

2. The object of the present report,* which is the result of the economic study of the area foreshadowed in the Cabinet Paper (C.P. (49) 207), is to set out the case for helping development in South and South-East Asia. The report is intended to show that the case for limited help is sufficiently convincing on both political and economic grounds for Ministers to give it their support, and for us to have a reasonable hope of convincing the United States Government that our argument warrants their support also. We have in addition considered the means whereby development in this part of Asia might be financed.

3. We have had in mind the desirability of developing two parallel policies, which have the approval of both the United Kingdom and the United States Governments, namely, to maintain and, if possible, to improve the standard of living of economically backward peoples and to combat Communism. The Committee are very conscious that they have not been able to set out the case for action to help develop South and South-East Asia in a form which would make it possible to balance the cost against

---

* The countries concerned in this report are: Afghanistan, British North Borneo, Brunei, Burma, Ceylon, China, Hong Kong, India, Indo-China, Indonesia, Japan and South Korea, Malaya, Nepal, Pakistan, the Philippines, Sarawak, Thailand, and Tibet.

the results. The principal reason is that the necessary data are lacking: for some countries this could not be supplied even with the co-operation of the Governments concerned. Most of the Governments in this region have no comprehensive development plans for their countries; in any case, some could not be expected to work on such plans till order is restored. The result is that much of the argument which follows is *a priori*, while the projects specified in Appendix B[1] cannot be presented as being the result of close selection in relation to either needs or available resources.

4. The justification for presenting this report now is twofold: first, that within a reasonable period it would not be possible to undertake a substantially more critical examination; and secondly, that the United States State Department are pressing for United Kingdom views on development in this region since the United States Government may have funds available at an early date. We are anxious to steer American thinking on to lines which we regard as sound, bearing in mind that the question of development must be related to that of the sterling balances.

The political case for helping

5. Economic improvement will not in itself stop Communism. But failure by the West to encourage Governments in the area to embark on essential development will lead to a defeatist attitude in Asia from which Communism will be swift to profit. Communist Parties in the area have two weapons at their disposal, namely, the ideological appeal of Communism to the oppressed, and the material appeal of promises of assistance from the Union of Soviet Socialist Republics and her satellites which, even if ultimately unfulfilled, create a favourable impression when offered. This may be the last chance for the West to keep Asia out of the Communist camp since, despite the need for self-help and in some cases the readiness shown by countries to help themselves, it is clear that they cannot go far enough by themselves to forestall the danger. We must accordingly examine by what means and to what extent they can be helped. The political argument for helping them is strong. We must, however, see that the limited help which can be given is offered to those Governments who will thereby be most likely to be strengthened in their will and capacity to resist.

6. Various measures have been taken already by Governments in the area to initiate schemes of development. In this connection the United Nations Economic Commission for Asia and the Far East is helping to point the way to regional co-operation in development and to a greater realisation of the economic problems with which Governments of the area are faced. But if these Governments, assisted by the West do not continue and expand a programme designed to improve food supplies and basic services, there will be a progressive deterioration in the standard of living and an increase in human misery. There are conditions likely to accelerate the spread of Communist influence and to weaken the political position of the Governments at present in power. The increase in population alone will be sufficient to bring about this deterioration if further measures are not put in hand to raise productivity.

---

[1] Not printed.

The economic case for helping

7. The area is predominantly agricultural and is likely to remain so. Half the world's population lives in the area. Broad masses of the people are poverty stricken and their conditions of life are wretched, giving rise to considerable malnutrition and disease. Illiteracy is widespread. The most significant single economic factor is the pressure of population upon food supplies. The urgent problem is, therefore, to do everything possible to increase agricultural production, particularly rice production, for, apart from humanitarian reasons, we may in this way lessen the growing pressure of this area on the food production of the rest of the world.

8. Traditionally, this area in Asia has played a most important part in the pattern of world trade—thus Malaya and Indonesia were markets for European manufactures while their exports were not only of direct value to the European economy but were also part of the triangular trade structure which enabled Europe to obtain many of its requirements from the Western Hemisphere. This pattern has been distorted by the war which in general has led the area to rely on the Western Hemisphere for a disproportionately large share of its imports and at the same time to export as much as possible to the Western Hemisphere. The shape that future trade can take must depend in large part on the solution of the sterling-area dollar crisis. There is, however, no reason to doubt that as in the past there will be considerable scope for European, Commonwealth and American participation in trade with the area. Indeed, if development of basic services (particularly communications) is possible, it will have the effect of stimulating the trade of the area, which will in turn benefit the West.

The kind of development needed

9. The food problem, though serious, is not necessarily insoluble. Even without extending the area under cultivation in India and Pakistan, an improvement of $\frac{1}{2}$ cwt. per acre in the yield of food grains (which would bring the average up to the low figure of 6 cwt. per acre) would produce an extra 6 million tons of grain per year, of which 2 million tons would be rice. This is more than India is at present importing. Similar improvements are no doubt possible elsewhere in the area and to some extent might be achieved by modifying existing agricultural practices, though it would be over-optimistic to expect to solve the problem by this means alone.

10. In our surveys of South-East Asia countries we have paid particular attention to those aspects of each country's economy which are connected in the first instance with the food and population situation. Self-sufficiency in food production is not always a desirable or practical objective from an economic point of view, but it is a fact of political and strategic importance that the main food exporters in South-East Asia (*i.e.*, Burma, Thailand and French Indo-China) are vulnerable to Communist attack. If they came under Communist domination, food supplies for South-East Asia might be jeopardised. We have examined various development projects which would lead to increased production of basic food-stuffs for home consumption or export. There are in most countries in the area (particularly in India, Pakistan and Thailand) certain irrigation projects under consideration or in construction which are essential to this end. There are also transport (road, rail and seaport) projects which would accelerate the tempo of economic development and in particular increase food exports and facilitate internal distribution of food surpluses.

11. A brief survey of the countries in the area is attached at Appendix A. An

illustrative list of the type of project which it might be desirable to encourage in the area is attached at Appendix B. There are some countries in the area, notably Indo-China, Indonesia and Burma, where for the present little new development is possible owing to the unstable conditions existing there and where a large amount of rehabilitation will be required when conditions return to normal. Rehabilitation may yield a higher return than new development and may be as significant in building up political resistance to Communism. The salient fact which emerges from these country studies is that, in the long term, by reason of its size, population, low standards of living and strategic position, India presents the crucial problem in the area from the point of view of United States financial aid.

12. In the development of the area, technical assistance will play an important part particularly in such fields as the improvement of agricultural methods and crop yields. In this sphere we ourselves should have a substantial contribution to make, but we should also draw the attention of the United States to the needs of the area in connection with President Truman's Fourth Point programme of technical and [aid] to underdeveloped areas. (It is hoped that a United States Fourth Point appropriation will be made during the next Congressional session.) Technical assistance will, however, to a greater or less degree according to the type of activity involved, have to be accompanied by the necessary capital; on the other hand, such assistance, by improving technical standards, should make investment over the whole field increasingly attractive and correspondingly diminish the problem of raising finance.

13. The pressure of population in the area on available food supplies makes achievement of certain limited objectives all that can be expected in the short run. Anything more than this will be achieved only in the long term, and will depend mainly on the countries concerned helping themselves. Nevertheless, for reasons stated in paragraphs 18 and 19 below, the effort required to secure any substantial development would be beyond the resources likely to be available from the countries themselves without external assistance.

Criteria for granting financial assistance

14. In order to determine how external financial aid shall be used to the best advantage, it will be necessary to establish some general criteria for granting aid to any particular country for development. These criteria should be:—

(i)   Likely capacity to resist Communist penetration or attack.
(ii) Economic merit of the particular development schemes contemplated.
(iii) Ability to produce food or vital raw materials to the benefit of the region and of the world as a whole.
(iv) Extent to which a country is able to help itself as regards internal finance for development projects, *i.e.*, to raise taxes and to borrow locally (see paragraphs 15, 16 and 18 below).

15. Without any disposition on the part of the countries concerned to help themselves, any external assistance to them will be of little value and, indeed, would hardly be likely to be offered. Our aim should be to range on our side like-minded Governments in the area, who will take positive action to carry their people along with them. There is undoubtedly a considerable amount of potential investment resources in some of these countries which cannot be tapped until confidence has been established by the Governments concerned. External assistance should there-

fore be accompanied by appropriate measures by these Governments to raise money and resources internally for development. There is evidence that the need for such measures is realised in several of these countries. Efforts by the West to encourage the independent Governments to proceed still further must, however, take account of the fact that these countries prize their newly won independence and would resent any attempt by other Powers to dictate the course they should pursue. But they may be amenable to advice, especially if this is backed by the prospect of real assistance.

16. In many of the basic development schemes internal expenditure on wages will account for a very large proportion of the total cost, and in the initial stages it may well be that available local financial resources will not be adequate to meet the full internal cost of basic development necessary. In many oriental countries the private investor is not inclined to put his money in Government loans carrying low rates of interest. Moreover, in some countries the investors of former days are disappearing. This also applies to a greater or lesser degree to other countries in the area. While, therefore, it is most important that the Governments concerned should create conditions which will produce the maximum capital from local sources, and while there are indications that some Governments are aware of this need and are taking appropriate measures, some external finance will undoubtedly be required to meet a proportion of internal costs. Past experience has shown that in many cases as much as 80 per cent. or more of the cost of major public works may be incurred locally and that this burden is beyond what the Governments of Asia can shoulder. The use of external finance to meet internal costs would, of course, mean serious risks of inflation in the absence of sound financial policies by the Governments concerned; this method of financing local expenditure should be accepted only when it is impossible to finance it out of local taxation and borrowing.

Sources of external assistance

17. It is clear that the United Kingdom, with its existing heavy commitments, cannot assume the responsibility of doing more than it is already doing to contribute to the development of the area. Our own economic situation and indirectly our political influence in the whole area will be helped if we can continue our contribution, particularly in respect of dependent territories for which we have a special responsibility. But the total contribution in respect of dependent territories for which the United Kingdom is responsible and in respect of unrequited exports of capital goods to the area as a whole has been considerable and is, in fact, more than we can afford in the present circumstances. It follows that substantial aid to the area, if it is to be provided, must come from the United States, although any exceptional measures for United Kingdom dependent territories (whether or not undertaken in co-operation with the United States) would be primarily the responsibility of His Majesty's Government.

18. The case for a new approach to current investment in the Orient may be illustrated by the past history of investment in this area compared with the position existing to-day. During the 19th century and first half of the 20th century, for example, the United Kingdom was responsible for the Government of India. It was customary for that Government to raise rupee loans to finance the construction of railroads, irrigation barrages, canals and the like. The money thus obtained was expended on materials and labour in India, the Indian banks issuing rupees for this purpose. Similarly, arrangements were made for sterling Indian loans on the London

market to give, on the one hand, the necessary currency backing to the rupee and, on the other, to provide for goods on which the rupees paid out in India for labour, &c., could be spent. Generally, these rupee and sterling loans for public works carried a rate of interest of $2\frac{1}{2}$ per cent.—$3\frac{1}{2}$ per cent. and the projects were remunerative.

19.   To-day the United Kingdom is no longer in a position to invest in India or other countries on the 19th-century scale. This change has come at a time when power has been transferred in India and Ceylon; when people everywhere look for better, and not reduced, standards, and when the need for improved and extended public works, &c., is even more clamant that [?than] it was in the 19th century owing to the fact that population has risen sharply since then and is still rising. An alternative source of investment is, therefore, needed if development is to continue.

20.   There are four main possible sources of investment, *viz.*:—

(a) The International Bank and the Export-Import Bank.

(b) Public loans floated in the United Kingdom or the United States of America.

(c) Private investment.

(d) Use of the reserves and assets already held by the countries concerned (mostly in sterling). . . .[2]

Conclusions

28.   (i)   The Cabinet have endorsed a policy of promoting regional co-operation in South-East Asia and improving economic and social conditions in the area with the aim of checking Communism and Russian expansionism. They favour economic collaboration as a means to this end.

(ii)   The area under survey is under-developed and continues to need considerable assistance if it is to promote basic development schemes. These schemes should aim in particular at increasing the food supply in order to keep pace with increasing population.

(iii)   The area is under direct Communist attack and, unless some assistance from the West to like-minded Governments in the area towards initiating or expanding basic development schemes is forthcoming, there will be an increase in human misery and a progressive deterioration in the standard of living which will provide fertile soil for the spread of communism. A positive programme of development is likely to help strengthen Governments in the area against Communist propaganda.

(iv)   By reason of its size, population low standards of living and strategic position, India presents the crucial problem in the area of United States financial assistance.

(v)   The United Kingdom has done a great deal to assist the area. But there is at present no further possibility of any United Kingdom investment (except in the dependent territories) on any substantial scale and, indeed, the assistance which is now being given to these territories by release of sterling balances will have to be curtailed in the near future, although we shall try to get the United States to assume part of the burden which we must shed. Effective Western financial assistance could therefore only come from the United States or from international institutions largely financed by United States capital.

---

[2] Paras 21–27, which amplify points (a)–(d) in para 20, have not be printed here.

(vi)   Most of the countries in the area are independent. There is, therefore, no certain means of ensuring that United Kingdom and United States views of the form of desirable development will be in line with those of the Governments concerned, but, in so far as either the United Kingdom Government or the United States Government or both can hold out prospects of external assistance, their influence on the pattern of development in the countries concerned will be increased.

(vii)   Any external financial aid for basic development should, so far as possible, be balanced by appropriate measures by the Governments concerned to raise money for internal expenditure. Some countries may not, however, be able to raise all the finance required for internal expenditure in connection with any given scheme. In such cases, the possibility of external loans for this purpose should not be ruled out, due regard being had to any inflationary effects.

(viii) Possible sources of external assistance are the International Bank and the Export-Import Bank, public loans floated abroad, private investment and the use of assets already held. These should be used to the fullest practicable extent, but the aggregate to their contribution is unlikely to be sufficient to finance basic development on the necessary scale, and it will therefore be desirable to induce the United States to recognise the need for provision of additional finance.

(ix)   Technical assistance under President Truman's Fourth Point will be an important and essential element in assistance to this area, though in the field of development it will, of course, only be fully effective if it is accompanied by the necessary finance.

(x)   The criteria for determining whether a country should be granted external assistance should be based on an assessment of the extent to which it is vulnerable to communism, the general economic merit of the schemes proposed, whether it is able to produce food or vital raw materials to the benefit of the region and of the world as a whole and how far the country concerned can and will help itself.

(xi)   There are some countries, notably Indo-China, Indonesia, and Burma, where, when conditions return to normal, rehabilitation must precede new development. Rehabilitation may yield a higher return than new development and may be as significant in building up political resistance to communism.

Appendix A to 201: 'Country surveys: individual studies'[3]

The following paragraphs contain the salient points regarding those countries in the area which have been surveyed in detail (*e.g.*, Afghanistan, Burma, British Borneo, Ceylon, India, Indonesia, Malaya, Pakistan and Thailand, for which separate reports are available). Similarly Annex B is based on a selection of detailed development projects listed in the above reports (with the exception of Burma).

British Territories (Malaya, Hong Kong and British Borneo)
Among the countries studied by the Far East (Official) Committee in the present

---

[3] Only the section related to Malaya has been printed here.

survey, the British territories of Hong Kong and Malaya have forged ahead most in the field of economic and social development, and in these territories the standard of living is the highest in the area. In the Federation of Malaya and Singapore the social services are more advanced than in any other country in Asia. Hong Kong (whose economy has not formed the subject of a separate detailed study in this survey) also enjoys a high standard of living by comparison with neighbouring territories. The cost of maintaining the present services, however, has risen very sharply since the war and the territories are finding it difficult to find funds to meet the expansion which the people are now demanding. British Borneo, which has not advanced so far, is being developed politically and economically on lines fully in accordance with the needs of its population and with an eye to its possible future in the long term as a rice surplus area which can play its part in alleviating the food shortage in Asia. Brunei is producing about 2·7 million tons a year of mineral oil.

2. The economy of Malaya, including the entrepôt of Singapore, depends to such a large extent on exports of rubber and tin that it is extremely vulnerable to fluctuations in price and to American demand and purchasing policy. Recent declines in American purchases have emphasised this factor. The Malayan authorities are acutely aware of the problem which the dependence on two main commodities presents, but although the long-term aim is to create a more diversified economy to lessen this dependence, it is clear that these will continue to be the mainstay of the territories' economy. Every effort must, therefore, be made to increase the efficiency and lower the costs of production of the two major industries, and the replanting of rubber with high yielding clones is progressing as resources allow. Encouragement is being given to the expansion of secondary industries which aim at supplying consumer goods to the home market, as well as to other countries in the area. Rubber processing, oil and soap factories, a dry battery factory and a glass factory are already in operation and a cement factory is under consideration. This process of diversification of the economy is inevitably a long-term matter. Unless, therefore, earnings from rubber and tin can be maintained at a remunerative level the consequences for the Malayan economy, as a whole, will be most serious. Moreover, an economic crisis in Malaya would not only bring with it the severest internal political and economic strain, but by weakening one of the main areas of stability in the region would be bound to have far-reaching political and strategic consequences throughout the Far East. It is, therefore, essential that every effort should be made to avoid an economic crisis in Malaya. The Far East (Official) Committee fully endorsed from the general point of view of Far Eastern stability, the proposals which were accepted by Ministers and put forward in Washington in respect of rubber and tin at the time of the tripartite talks (W.D. (49) 28). It is worth noting that very considerable efforts have already been made to restore the Malayan economy since the war. Rehabilitation work in Malaya has already cost the United Kingdom and the local Governments very large sums of money and will continue to be a heavy financial burden. The measures necessary to defeat the present Communist campaign of violence are also a heavy drain on our resources. In addition development plans (opening up of new rice areas, drainage and irrigation schemes, hydro-electric power, &c.) are now in operation and under consideration and may cost in the neighbourhood of £50–£100 million over ten years, although it is unlikely that Malaya will ever be self-sufficient in food. . . .

202 CO 537/6089, no 17   Dec 1949

'Attitude to be adopted in publicity towards communism in Malaya and China': joint CO-FO note

1. Communist successes in China have in some measure instilled in the Chinese in Malaya a feeling of pride in the achievements of the Communist armies and of satisfaction that China will have a strong Government respected in the Counsels of the Nations. Recognition of a Communist Government in China will confirm this attitude of the Overseas Chinese and unless the publicity connected with it is handled carefully, the consequences may become serious by;

(a) confusing the mass of the Chinese population in Malaya by making them feel that recognition implies approval of Communism,

(b) boosting the morale and strengthening the resistance of the Communist bandits in Malaya,

(c) increasing the difficulties which the Malayan Administrations expect when Chinese Communist Consuls are appointed.

2. The problem has been carefully considered by the Commissioner General, the High Commissioner for the Federation of Malaya and the Governor of Singapore, in consultation with H.M. Ambassador to China, and the Officers Administering the Governments of North Borneo and Sarawak during the Conference of His Majesty's Representatives at Bukit Serene on the 2nd–4th November. Discussions have also taken place between the Foreign Office and Colonial Office, and Mr. Dening of the Foreign Office who took part in the Bukit Serene talks, has again been consulted. It has now been agreed in London that the following line should be taken.

3. The Chinese Communist Government must be distinguished from the Communist terrorist movement in Malaya, and it should not be suggested that the latter receives any aid from the Chinese Communist Government unless that Government engages in acts which prove the contrary.

4. It is desirable to keep separate the issues of Communist subversive activities in Malays and the relations of H.M.G. to the Communist Government of China. When Governments recognise each other it in no way means that they approve of each other's way of governing. What happens in China is the business of the inhabitants of China. If we recognise a Chinese Communist Government it is because it has become the effective Government of China.

5. This does not mean that we approve of Communism. For we consider Communism to be the means whereby the Russians seek to expand and to dominate all Asian territories. As such Communism is the enemy of all genuine nationalism, since it seeks the domination of nationalism by alien influence. This alien Russian influence has, through the agency of Communism, established itself in the countries of Eastern Europe, and it will seek to establish itself in China and elsewhere in Asia in the same way.

6. The danger to China is Russian penetration and domination. It is essential, until further notice to avoid any suggestion that any tendencies towards Titoism or independence of the Kremlin exist in the Chinese Government; such tendencies would be encouraged in practice rather by our stressing the Chinese Government's subservience to Russia, acquiescence in Russian exploitation of Manchuria, etc. At

present discreet references to conflicts of national interest between China and Russia should never suggest that the Chinese Communists are in any way standing up to the Kremlin. It is important to stress Russian attempts to dominate and exploit China; but for the present blame should be laid on the Kremlin.

7. For the sake of world opinion it is desirable to represent the struggle in Malaya as being directed against the Malayan Communist Party, and not as operations by Government against mere banditry. In Malaya, however, publicity should avoid writing-up international Communism, or emphasising the role which the Malayan Communist Party is playing in a world-wide Communist movement. The line should be that in Malaya Communism is not acceptable to the peoples of the country who are indeed overwhelmingly opposed to it. The Communists themselves have put themselves out of Court in Malaya on three grounds;

(i) They are a small and mostly alien minority seeking to impose their ideas against the wishes of the great majority in the country
(ii) they are attempting to do this by violent means, contrary to all democratic, constitutional and lawful practice
(iii) their violence is of a most morbid type consisting of intimidation, extortion and murder, and they have achieved nothing but death, destruction and distress.

8. The same line should apply, with due local modification, in North Borneo, Sarawak and Brunei as well as in the Federation of Malaya and Singapore.

9. This paper is being conveyed by the Foreign Office to its posts, as appropriate, and by the Colonial Office to the Governments of the South East Asia dependencies.

203 CO 537/4741, no 78   2 Dec 1949

[Malayan politics]: letter from Sir H Gurney to J J Paskin on a variety of recent developments

At the end of a week of meetings including Legislative Council and Rulers Conference, I thought I would let you have an omnibus letter on a variety of matters of interest.

Perhaps the most important development was the unanimous approval by Legislative Council on the 28th November of Zainal Abidin's[1] motion calling for compulsory teaching of Malay and English in Government and Government-aided primary schools. The Malays put up this motion as a test of Chinese sincerity without which it would be difficult to get Malay support for the opening of the citizenship door to be discussed by the Communities Liaison Committee at Penang on the 28th December. Two or three weeks ago the Chinese were accusing the Malays of trying to rush them and the Malays were accusing the Chinese of back-sliding, but after a good deal of talk we agreed that to take the motion on the 28th would give the Chinese reasonable time to get 100% Chinese support, which in fact they managed to do. There are of course many practical difficulties in carrying out this resolution but it

---

[1] Zainal Abidin bin Hj Abas, MCS, was at this time chief social welfare officer of the federation, unofficial member of the Legislative Council, secretary general of UMNO, 1947–1950, and a member of the Communities Liaison Committee.

would have seemed rather out of place to give much weight to these in the debate. As they have been such good boys the Chinese are now naturally expecting greater things in the citizenship line.

Dato Onn and Sainal [sic] Abidin are thinking on the lines of granting citizenship to every person born in the Federation. This is, of course, miles ahead of the rest of Malay opinion and I may add, of my opinion too. We are thinking on the lines of two generations of birth and of converting citizenship into whatever form of nationality it is open to us to create. On this complex question it will be useful to be able to pick the brains of Sir Alexander Maxwell[2] who is evidently an expert on it. Meanwhile, the Rulers yesterday agreed that we should amend the Federal Agreement so as to extend, for a further year, the two year period allowed for acquisition of citizenship without adequate knowledge of Malay, since for various reasons the full two years has not been available to applicants.

As to Dato Onn himself, the Mentris have for some time been wanting to have a meeting and a show-down with him in order to find where he was going in the matter of Malayan Nationality and to rebuke him for his Butterworth speech.[3] This meeting took place on the 29th when they made clear to him that he had no right to speak for the Malays on any subject unless he had first obtained the concurrence of the Rulers and the other Mentris. They pointed out to him that the Malays would be finished if he continued in the way he was going at the present. They told him that the question of Malayan Nationality must be put before the Rulers who should be persuaded that it was the correct course to follow and then, and only then, plans should be made to carry out the idea. They asked Onn to have his proposal produced in pamphlet form and distribute them to all U.M.N.O. branches and State Governments.

Onn appears to have capitulated and to have agreed to comply with these requests. The Mentris have on their side undertaken to do their best to persuade their Rulers on the Malayan Nationality question and to bring about a reconciliation between them and Onn. If the Rulers agree, a meeting will be called between the Rulers and Mentris and Onn. At present some of the Mentris are not sure how far they can rely on Onn to keep his word and I am not sure how far the Rulers will respond to the suggestion for a reconciliation. The interesting point is that the Mentris have taken absolutely the right line and that Onn has recognised this fact as well as the dangers of the course he has been adopting. I am told that in Johore itself opinion is swinging towards the Sultan's side and that the Sultan is not expected to have Onn back as Mentri even if the latter wants to come back.[4]

On the Chinese side Tan Cheng Lock has told me of his ideas on developing Trade Unions among the Chinese poorer classes as one way of combatting [sic] communism. At yesterday's Rulers Conference I put before them proposals for the administration of the rural Chinese which I did not think they would accept. But in fact they

---

[2] Sir Alexander Maxwell, permanent under-secretary at the Home Office, 1938–1948, was currently in Malaya as chairman of the Police Mission.

[3] At the UMNO general assembly in Butterworth (Province Wellesley) in Aug, Dato Onn had advocated a 'Malayan nationality' for all races to replace existing citizenship regulations. This proposal, representing a complete volte face since his opposition to the Malayan Union, further alienated Onn from the Malay rulers who resented his nationalist pretensions and challenges to their authority (see CO 537/4790).

[4] Onn's worsening relations with the Sultan of Johore had culminated with his resignation as *mentri besar* in Oct, see 182, note 2.

did, and this is very encouraging. The proposals are on the lines of those discussed at a meeting which Higham attended here and included the posting of a Chinese Affairs Officer as S.C.A. in each State containing a considerable number of Chinese, the posting of Chinese Officers to district offices to assist the District Officers in administering their Chinese population and the encouragement of Malay Officers to learn colloquial Chinese. They also agree that State Governments should insist on District Officers taking as much interest in their Chinese rural population as in anybody else. This is such a good step forward that when they jibbed at having the Colonial Prisoners Removal Act applied by Order by Council I agreed to give this matter some more thought. They also agreed that the Federal Unit of the Malayan Royal Naval Volunteer Reserve should retain the word 'Royal' in its title.

The surrendered bandits of various sorts who now number over one hundred and fifty, many of them very young, are, of course, creating a problem in that there is some evidence to justify a prosecution in some cases, but the danger of prosecution even in one case is that it might dry up the flow of surrenders. At the same time we can neither let these people off without punishment nor delay unduly taking them to court if they are to be taken to court at all. We therefore contemplate that before the end of the Emergency we shall set up special courts to deal with these people who may number many hundreds. I do not want to elaborate nor to make official proposals about it, but I thought that you would be interested to know the way our minds are working on the problem which will obviously be difficult.

I am sorry to say that on the question of the flag, the Rulers express preference for the third choice which is the one that looks like a red and yellow hammer and sickle on a pair of blue and white striped pyjamas, and would be suitable for a Turkish Colony in South America, so it may be some time before we shall reach finality on this controversial question. Meanwhile the three designs put up by the Committee have not been referred to any expert on flags, and I have been wondering whether the College of Arms or some other authority should be consulted at this stage.

You will be glad to know that so far as the public is concerned the Police Mission[5] has so far gone down very well. The Rulers have dropped their ideas about the inclusion of an old Malayan, and are putting up three Mentris to meet the Mission about the 23rd December. The Mission has had talks with myself, Newboult and Grey [sic] separately. The more I think of it the more I agree that it was right to keep the members of the mission entirely independent of any Malayan connection. I have been much impressed by Maxwell's grasp of the essentials of the problem.

---

[5] See 199, note 8.

204   CO 537/4741, no 76   5 Dec 1949
[Policy towards the Chinese community]: letter from Mr Creech Jones to Sir H Gurney

[This letter was drafted for Creech Jones's signature to follow up points raised in Slim's report (see 199).]

I was very impressed by the following passage in your speech to Legislative Council on the 29th September:

"A policy of purely defensive protection leaving the offensive and initative to the bandits would never succeed in these parts. Our main task is now to build up confidence and strength among the elements who have suffered under this Communist threat, to equip them with the protection, both moral and physical, which will fortify their power of resistance against any recurrence of this menace and to give full play to the natural forces of recovery to political health which are instinctive in all reasonable men. This task is an administrative one coupled with good sound police work on the ground and in touch with the people".

During the last few weeks I have also been reading with much interest a number of your despatches and letters in which you have reported measures which you have either introduced or which you have in mind in pursuance of your policy (which I am sure is right) of restoring a more direct administrative approach to the problems of the Chinese community in Malaya. The creation of Chinese Advisory Boards, the appointment of Assistant Secretaries for Chinese Affairs, and Assistant State Secretaries or Resettlement officers in the State Governments will I hope assist in restoring the confidence of the Chinese in the Government which was, in some measure, lost as a result of the dispersal amongst other Departments of the staff of the Chinese Protectorate. I have also followed with interest the development of the Malayan Chinese Association and the proceedings of the Communities Liaison Committee.

I have been very much encouraged by Malcolm MacDonald's reports of the progress, (hardly believable a year ago), which is now being made in that Committee in their search for ways and means of resolving communal differences and of creating a feeling of common interest and loyalty to Malaya. I am not under any illusion that this will be an easy or rapid process but I feel justified in hoping that the seeds of inter-community good-will which are now being sown will produce their fruit in the fullness of time.

In the meantime, you have your pressing administrative problems and, not least, your constant anxieties arising from the bandit situation, which not only involves such a heavy drain on the country's resources but is such an obstacle to the social progress of the people of all races. As to this, it is I think generally accepted that (apart, of course, from the constant pressure maintained by the police and security forces), the greatest single contribution which the Civil Government can make towards an early end of these troubled conditions, is by bringing the squatter areas under effective administrative control. I think that I am right in saying that this was perhaps the strongest single impression which was left in the mind of the Chief of the Imperial General Staff as a result of his recent visit to Malaya. I need hardly say how fully I recognise the difficulties with which you have to contend in achieving this—the shortage of Chinese speaking European officers, the fact that district administration (and particularly the administration of land) is in the hands of State Governments, the unsuitability of subordinate Malay district officers to administer Chinese areas (especially the remote squatter area, with bandit gangs in the offing), and the fact that practically the whole of the uniformed policy are Malays. In addition to these factors I am of course aware that a sympathetic approach to the administration of the Chinese does not come naturally to some of the senior officers of the M.C.S. who (as also some of the older members of the Police Force) find it difficult to adjust themselves to post war conditions and policies.[1]

It is against this background that I have noted with interest some of the steps which are being taken to tackle this problem such as the arrangements, which originated in Perak, for providing protection and for encouraging a rudimentary form of local Government,[2] in squatter areas, and the more recent decision to attempt to recruit Chinese into the uniformed branch of Police.

I am quite confident that it needs no words from me to impress upon you the anxiety of the Government here that nothing practicable should be left undone to restore peace in Malaya at the earliest possible date. Apart from our anxieties on Malaya's behalf, you should know that, in our present straitened circumstances—not only financially, but in the extended deployment of our armed forces—my colleagues are most anxious that our military commitments in Malaya should be reduced as soon as possible. It is against this background that I am writing to ask you, on the one hand, whether there is anything that the Colonial Office can do to assist you in the task of establishing effective administration in the squatter areas (e.g. by attempting to recruit Chinese speaking officers on a short term basis, or by arranging special courses in Chinese for selected officers to be sent home, or by finding instructors who could organise courses in Malaya itself). On the other hand, I should like to know whether you see any prospect of speeding up action in Malaya itself.

In this connection, since as you yourself have repeatedly stated, the establishment of effective administration in the scattered squatter areas is "an essential security measure" I was very much puzzled by paragraph 20 of your despatch (No.11) on Emergency Expenditure. If, as indicated in that paragraph, the building of access roads to these areas etc. is an essential element in the arrangements for bringing these areas under effective control, I found it difficult to understand why no financial provision was made for it. Am I right in assuming that, now that there has been a decision on the financial contribution to be made in 1950 by His Majesty's Government,[3] it will be possible to make the necessary provision for these vital services?

But perhaps the difficulty is that, in spite of all that you have done to imbue the State Governments with a proper sense of the importance and urgency of these measures, those Governments are failing to act with the speed and energy which the situation demands. If this is indeed the case, you can be assured of my support in any action which you would consider it proper for yourself or the Federal Government to take to ensure that State Governments face up to their responsibilities.

Again, reverting to your shortage of Chinese speaking administrators, I have been wondering whether the needs of the emergency could not be urged to persuade State Governments to recruit suitably qualified local Chinese into their administrations, even if the time is not yet ripe for their admission to the M.C.S. I am aware of the delicacy of this matter, and that—as a long term issue—you have been relying on the

---

[1] Rees-Williams wrote in his 'Report on short tour of Hong Kong, Singapore and the Federation of Malaya: October–November, 1949' that the European community 'still hark back to the "old days" seen through a rosy mist of nostalgia' (see CO 537/4870 no 1).

[2] This experiment in administration of squatter areas had been introduced by J L H Davis, formerly of Force 136 and currently assistant state secretary.

[3] See 200.

Communities Liaison Committee to produce an atmosphere favourable to this development. But, in the matter of establishing effective administration in the squatter areas, time presses.

205 CO 537/4741, no 83   31 Dec 1949
[Malay leadership and political responsibility]: letter from Sir H Gurney to J J Paskin suggesting moves towards a member system for the federal government

Many thanks for your letter of the 21st December (No. 51406/49) in which you ask for some indication of my views as to how far and by what means the various conflicting forces in Malay politics are susceptible to guidance or influence and to what ends our influence should be directed.

You will have seen in our November political report an account of the meeting on the 29th November between the Mentris and Dato Onn, when they had him on the mat for his attitude towards the Rulers, challenged him with endangering Malay unity and sought from him an assurance that he would formulate his ideas on Malayan "nationality" for submission to the Rulers with a view to obtaining both their approval and a reconciliation between the Rulers and Onn.[1] Onn agreed to do this and a meeting between himself and the Rulers will probably take place in February, when he will have had time to work on the result of the meeting of the Communities Liaison Committee held during the last few days of December in Penang. For this meeting I have given the Commissioner-General and Braddell, after discussion with them separately, my own ideas for the redrafting of the citizenship clauses of the Federation Agreement so as to the base citizenship by operation of law on two generations of birth and so admit at once some 250,000 non-Malays who do not qualify at present. Onn has been in favour of the out-and-out imaginative solution of the *jus soli*,[2] but this would at the moment frighten the vast majority of Malays into next week and even Tan Cheng Lock, in a recent talk with me, said that he thought it would be wiser to proceed by stages. The Malays have yet to concede the all-important point that Federal citizens must possess all the rights of citizenship, including entry for non-Malays into the Administration. Some of them still think that they might find it possible to open the citizenship door and so to wean the Chinese away from China and Chinese Consulates, while still confining certain privileges of citizenship to Malays only.

It thus looks as though the next few months will see a reconciliation between the Rulers and Onn on the basis of an opening of the citizenship door—how widely, I cannot at present say. The ideas we have put forward would, if adopted, go a long way towards removing the grievances of the British subjects of Penang on this score. If the Malays are not rushed over this issue, we are likely to get general acceptance. A recent attempt by a Malay named Hashim Ghani,[3] a Singapore lawyer's clerk, to

---

[1] See 203.
[2] *Jus soli* (literally law of the land) whereby citizenship would be automatically acquired by all persons born in Malaya.
[3] Hashim Ghani's Persatuan Melayu Semenanjong (Peninsular Malays Union, PMU) mounted a strong defence of Malay rights against 'surrenders' by Onn and later by Tunku Abdul Rahman.

launch a new political party at a public meeting in Kuala Lumpur, on a platform of Malaya for the Malays and in opposition to U.M.N.O., was a complete flop, partly on account of U.M.N.O. tactics in packing the meeting.

I feel that Onn has too much of the statesman in him not to appreciate that Malay political advance must be slow and steady. He is indeed always saying so to me. If he could be brought to saying it publicly, he would gain much support that he is in danger of losing. The "lousy" speech and his Butterworth capers of last July have not been forgotten. Now that he is no longer "senior" Mentri and yet has to carry them with him, he is for the moment more thoughtful.

When I invited him to represent the Federation at the Indonesian celebrations of independence at Batavia,[4] he said "thank you for giving me this grand opportunity. I feel really proud". He told me at the same time that he was thinking of going to Indonesia in January to see Hatta,[5] but vouchsafed no more.

We must remember that Onn's political experience in any position of responsibility is very short. He is learning and getting older, but I am very conscious of the importance of finding something for him to do.

In this connection, apart from municipal elections in Penang and Kuala Lumpur in 1950 or 1951, the conversion of antiquated things like Town Boards into municipal authorities, and preparations for elections to State Councils, it may be that the next step forward in the Federal field should be the appointment of Members (on the Kenya model). We have on Legislative Council ten official members who are European Government officers. There is much to be said for the appointment of local citizens of the calibre of Onn to 'portfolios' in displacement of some of these Departmental Heads, with a view at the same time to reorganising Executive Council on a basis that looks something like a cabinet of persons holding ministerial responsibility. I have as yet no firm proposals to put forward—and may have none for several months—and we should have to begin in a very limited way, but I propose to start some confidential discussions on this shortly. I am familiar with the Kenya and Tanganyika systems, which work, and with the new Gold Coast proposals,[6] which seem hardly likely to work, and I think I see most of the dangers. It is in the Federal 'Bureaucratic' machine that the Federal Government is most vulnerable to legitimate attack (e.g. Onn's idea of a Deputy High Commissioner) and it should be our aim to lead into the Federal Executive and Legislative Councils, *in positions of responsibility*,[7] the Malay and indeed non-Malay leaders who show themselves as competent and available. I see no reason why Onn should not carry out with success the duties of, say, Member for Health and Local Government, but I have a nasty feeling that he would ask for something like "Home Affairs", which would be impossible, and a less nasty feeling that the work involved in such a post would leave him little time for political leadership of the Malays in the face of the various

---

[4] On 27 Dec 1949 Queen Juliana signed the instruments of the transfer of sovereignty.

[5] Mohammed Hatta, vice-president, 1945–1956, and prime minister, 1949–1950, of Indonesia.

[6] Gurney had served in Kenya in 1921–1935 and on the East African Governors' Council in 1941–1944. As colonial secretary of the Gold Coast, 1944–1946, he had taken a particular interest in plans for a ministerial system. The 'new Gold Coast proposals' referred to here are those of the Coussey Committee which reported in Sept 1949; with respect to the executive it recommended that there should be seven Ministers drawn from the legislature and that the Executive Council should not be responsible to the governor but to the legislature (see BDEEP series B, vol I, R Rathbone, ed, *Ghana*, part I, 51–67).

[7] Emphasis in original.

disintegrating forces growing up in South East Asia. But this last must, I think, rest with the Mentris whose offices are after all political appointments.

This letter is largely thinking aloud, as an immediate reply to your enquiry, which I shall be better able to answer in a few weeks' time.

Meanwhile, there is no reason at all to think that the breach between the Sultans and Onn will widen in the near future. The indications are all in the direction of its being healed, if Onn is properly looked after both by ourselves and, as is now happening, by his brother Malay leaders.

206   PREM 8/1406/2   7 Mar 1950

[Director of operations]: minute by Mr Shinwell to Mr Attlee recommending the appointment of General Briggs   [Extract]

[After the general election in Feb, Attlee reconstructured his government, appointing Griffiths to the CO and Shinwell to the Ministry of Defence. Following this initiative by Shinwell, Briggs was appointed director of operations and arrived in Kuala Lumpur on 3 Apr 1950.]

Prime Minister

The present situation in Malaya has been giving the authorities on the spot considerable concern and an appreciation of the situation was recently called for. This was contained in the telegram SEACOS 24 dated 24th February.

2. The Chiefs of Staff have reviewed the whole position subsequent to the receipt of that telegram and have prepared a Report. They recommend the strengthening of our Forces in Malaya by moving the 26th Gurkha Infantry Brigade and one Spitfire Squadron from Hong Kong, the sending of the Squadron of Lincoln medium bombers, the transfer of a light bomber Squadron from Iraq and an increase in the strength of the Armoured Car Regiment and British Battalions already in Malaya.

3. In particular they recommend in addition to these purely military measures the appointment of an Army officer to the Civil post of Director of anti-Bandit Operations in Malaya as proposed by the High Commissioner and that urgent consideration be given to ways and means of resuming the repatriation of Chinese squatters from Malaya. Having doubts about the practicability and desirability of such an appointment I asked the Chiefs of Staff to come and discuss the matter with me this morning. I am satisfied as a result of this meeting with them that the proposed appointment is a step in the right direction and is one which will materially improve the combined operations of the Police and Military which under the existing arrangements have need for greater co-ordination. The individual whom the C.I.G.S. has approached for this appointment is Lieutenant General Sir Harold Briggs who commanded the Fifth Indian Division in the Western Desert and ended the war as G.O.C.-in-C. Burma. . . .

207 PREM 8/1406/2   8 Mar 1950
[Malayan operations and policies]: minute no PM(50)6 by Mr Griffiths to Mr Attlee

Prime Minister

I have seen the minute of the 7th March by the Minister of Defence[1] on the present situation in Malaya and I wish to say that I fully endorse the recommendations of the Chief of Staff in COS(50)84.

I note that the Minister of Defence had at first some doubts about the practicability and desirability of the appointment of an army officer in a civil capacity as Director of Anti-Bandit operations. I appreciate the difficulties of such an appointment and it is of course essential that no impression should be given that the normal administration of the police was being placed under military control or that the civil authorities are surrendering any of their responsibilities to the military. The High Commissioner himself attaches special importance to this. The crux of the matter is obviously going to be the personality of the officer selected and I am assured that the Chief of the Imperial General staff, in his approach to Sir Harold Briggs, had this point very much in mind.

From the point of view of Hong Kong, and in a lesser degree Malaya, the publicity line to be taken about troop and aircraft movements is of great importance. While nothing can stop the press learning about these moves it should as far as possible be represented that they are of a routine nature. Details of the publicity line must be agreed between the various authorities concerned in Hong Kong, Malaya and London.

The High Commissioner attaches the greatest importance to the resumption of repatriation of Chinese immigrants from Malaya back to their homes in South China. I well appreciate that the present moment is a difficult one in which to raise this with the Chinese Government but this question is already being thoroughly examined and I hope that the Foreign Office and the Colonial Office will shortly be able to report to Ministers on the position.

I support the recommendation that careful consideration should be given, in consultation with the Governor, to the timing of certain exchange control measures in Hong Kong that are likely to have political repercussions there in relation to the withdrawal of the Gurkha brigade. My Department are in communication with the Treasury on this and I am sending a copy of this minute to the Chancellor of the Exchequer as well as to the Foreign Secretary and Minister of Defence.

---

[1] See 206.

208 T 220/160   [Mar 1950]
'Economic and social policy in Malaya': CO note for the Treasury despatched on 18 Mar

1. Under British rule and largely as a result of British capital and enterprise, Malaya before the war was probably the most prosperous, relative to its population, of

all the countries in South East Asia and the educational and other social services provided had reached the highest level in the area.

2. The Japanese occupation left Malaya in a chaotic state. The people were close to starvation; trade and industry were at a standstill; the educational system had been completely destroyed; communications and basic services had been neglected, and crime and lawlessness flourished. At very great cost both to His Majesty's Government in the United Kingdom and to the Malayan Governments, the economic life of the country has been revived and basic services restored to pre-war level.

3. In accomplishing this measure of rehabilitation and as a policy for future progress, the aim of the Malayan Governments and of His Majesty's Government has been to proceed, as fast as limited financial and material resources and the high level of defence expenditure necessitated by communist banditry have allowed, with a positive policy of raising standards of living and of extending the social and basic services. Such progress is essential not only as a good thing in itself, but also as the only real long term way of creating conditions in which communism will not flourish.

4. In implementing this policy, the main efforts will be devoted to:—

(a) Economic measures to secure the long term prosperity of the country as a whole and of the individual inhabitants, and especially the production of more locally grown food.

(b) Education; to enable the inhabitants of all races to play their part in public administration and in the commercial, industrial and professional life of their country, and,

(c) Social Services.

The following paragraphs deal with these activities in more detail.

5. The economy of Malaya is almost entirely dependent on the production of tin and rubber and though one aim of policy is to lessen this dependence by the expansion and development of other products, it is clear that reliance on these two industries must continue for some years to come. Their continued prosperity is therefore vital for the interests of the country and of the people and is an important factor in countering communism in Malaya.

6. It may be remarked that, although much of the British capital invested in Malaya has been in tin and rubber, the local peoples also have an important stake in the two industries. The rubber industry employs about one million people on estates and small holdings. Many estates are owned by Chinese, while Malay small-holders in 1948 produced 43.7% of the total rubber production. In the tin industry only 50% of production comes from European owned mines. The remainder of the industry is largely under Chinese control. The tin and rubber industries are also important contributors to the revenues of Government by way of royalties, export and income taxes.

7. Positive measures by which the Malayan Governments and His Majesty's Government are assisting the rehabilitation of these industries are:—

(a) Loans to finance rehabilitation of estates and tin mines amounting to about £8.5 million, pending the payment of War Damage Compensation which will total nearly £20 millions for these industries alone.

(b) A grant of £121,786 from Colonial Development and Welfare Funds to provide replanting material of improved types for rubber small-holders.

(c) A grant of about £325,000 from Colonial Development and Welfare funds for the expansion of Geological Survey in the Federation (approved in principle).

8. The third product in importance in the Malayan economy is rice which is the staple diet of most of the inhabitants. Even before the war Malaya produced only about one-third of her requirements and though great efforts are being made to grow more rice locally, there is no prospect of Malaya achieving self-sufficiency. Over one-hundred-thousand acres of new rice lands have been brought into use since 1946, the cost of this expansion being met in part from a public loan floated in London. Further schemes now in train will provide for another eighty-five-thousand acres of new paddy land and improvements on two-hundred and eighty-three-thousand acres of existing land by 1953.

9. The production of palm oil and coconut oil is now back to pre-war level and future markets are assured under a long term contract with the Ministry of Food. Grants from Colonial Development and Welfare Funds have been made inter alia to finance research into the utilization of Malayan timbers; to establish a quarantine nursery for imported cocoa planting material, and to start a Fish Farming Research Institute at Penang. It is considered that the work of this Institute will lead to large scale expansion of marine and fresh water fish production which will contribute valuable additional proteins to the present diet of the people. A Colonial Development and Welfare Scheme for a Marine Fisheries Research Station at Singapore is under consideration. Schemes for large scale co-operatives to enable the Malay fishermen and peasant rice producers to enjoy more direct benefit from their labours are also under urgent consideration. A scheme is also in train for a rural economic survey of the Federation which will provide the necessary data on which plans for rural development may be based.

10. Improvements in basic services have been vigorously pushed ahead. Over $50 million have been spent on the rehabilitation of the Malayan railways and a further $50 million is to be spent for the same purpose from loan funds. Plans have been drawn up for the Government acquisition of all privately owned electricity undertakings, the development of hydro-electric power and the inter-connection of existing installations by grid transmission lines. The Colonial Development Corporation has invested £3,750,000 in these projects and it is estimated that a further £10 million will be required for their completion. One of the first tasks in Singapore was the rehabilitation of the docks. A great deal of this was done during the British Military Administration for which His Majesty's Government paid and restoration is now complete.

11. Malaya's resources cannot be developed to the full until more roads are provided in the backward areas, particularly those in the Eastern States. New roads are also needed to exploit the vast timber resources which are at present inaccessible, to bring outlying areas (which at present harbour and support large gangs of bandits) under effective administrative control; in connection with the colonization of new rice growing areas; and to meet strategic requirements. Plans have been drawn up for the improvement and extension of the present road system at a total cost of £10,500,000.

12. The aim of educational policy both in the Federation and in Singapore is to provide free primary education for children of all races. In June 1941, there were 263,000 pupils in schools. In January 1949, the number at schools in the Federation

stood at 566,000. Teachers under training in various colleges, schools and classes rose from 1,368 in 1947 to 2,748 in 1948 in the Federation alone. A six year development programme for the social services which has just been presented to the Federal Legislative Council includes among other items new colleges for men and women teachers, an extensive programme for the building of new English and vernacular schools and a new technical college, for which £565,000 has been provided from Colonial Development and Welfare Funds. In Singapore, a ten year educational programme has been recently supplemented by an "emergency school programme" which provides eighteen new temporary schools to be built in 1950.

13. In October, 1949, the University of Malaya, which will provide advanced education for 1,000 students, was formally constituted. A grant from Colonial Development and Welfare Funds of £1 million was made towards the cost of the University.

14. Medical and health services have been restored to pre-war level and plans for expansion have been drawn up in both Singapore and the Federation. Colonial Development and Welfare schemes have been made and are operating in connection with the investigation of the prevention of malaria. Colonial Development and Welfare funds are also being utilised to train social welfare workers. The six-year development plan provides for the construction of welfare centres, rural health centres, the extension of hospitals, the construction of clinics and the training of local health personnel. It is also planned to establish 50 community centres in rural areas.

15. There are two main factors restricting the pace of economic development and the expansion of social services. The first is the shortage of skilled manpower, the second is the limited financial resources available.

16. In present circumstances it is difficult to attract to Malaya the technicians and other skilled personnel which the country so sorely needs. The work of the Public Works Department and of the Drainage and Irrigation Department is particularly affected by the shortage of engineers. There is also a shortage of agriculture and veterinary specialists and of research workers needed for the surveys and pilot schemes which are necessary before the exact pattern of development in various spheres of activity can be foreseen. Many more teachers are necessary to implement the plans for the Education Services. To some extent these shortages of skilled personnel will be relieved by the increasing supply of locally trained men from the University of Malaya, the new Technical College, the new teacher training colleges, and the Malay Regiment, but only outside aid can ease the short term problem.

17. The financial position of the Federation is grave. A series of deficit budgets, necessitated by the large expenditure necessary on rehabilitation, on back pay which accrued to Government employees during the war, and on measures connected with the present emergency, has reduced the Federation's accumulated surplus balance from some £28 millions in April 1946 to about £6.5 million at the beginning of 1950. During this period expenditure of £15.5 millions has been financed by the issue of public loans and the Federation's public debt now stands at £35 million.

18. No diminuation [sic] in special internal security expenditure can be foreseen for some years ahead. In the two years 1949/50 this expenditure amounted to approximately £13 million, towards which His Majesty's Government made grants totalling £8 million. Any increases in taxation must be devoted to meeting this

expenditure in the future as a first charge on the Federation's resources. Revenue at present levels is scarcely sufficient to meet normal recurrent expenditure. The Social Services programme, modest though it is and drawn up with the financial situation in the Federation very much in mind will cost £6.4 million in capital expenditure over the next 6 years and will entail additional recurrent expenditure rising to £2 million a year. The programme of economic development, which is at present being prepared by the Federation Government, will be similarly limited by financial considerations. Public loans raised locally may be able to provide capital for some expansion of basic services of a revenue producing nature, but it is quite clear that only external assistance of a considerable order, whether by way of grants, loans or private investment, will be sufficient to overcome the financial limitations to progress.

19. An idea of the order of Government expenditure likely to be required for economic developments is given by the following figures:—

Colonization of new paddy areas 1951–1953	£4,500,000	
Development of Agriculture and Animal Husbandry	£3,500,000	(10 years)
Forestry Development	£1,500,000	(10 years)
Water Supply	£3,500,000	(10 years)
Road Developments	£10,500,000	(10 years)
Total	£23,500,000	

In addition large sums will be needed for bringing outlying areas under administrative control and for improvements of ports in the Federation, but no precise estimate of the amounts involved can yet be given. Private investment will be required in connection with the expansion and development of secondary industries.

20. The financial position of Singapore is sounder than that of the Federation and there has been a budget surplus each year since the resumption of Civil Government. A Government loan of $50 million was raised in Singapore in 1946 and has been expended on rehabilitation measures.

21. His Majesty's Government has given the Malayan Governments considerable financial assistance towards meeting their post-war difficulties. His Majesty's Government met the whole cost of the British Military Administration in Malaya up to April 1946, the net cost of which was estimated at £12 million. In addition the following financial help has been granted since April, 1946:—

(i) Contribution to Malayan War Damage Compensation	£20,000,000	
(ii) Direct contribution to internal security up to 1950	8,000,000	
(iii) Colonial Development and Welfare allocation	5,000,000	
(iv) Colonial Development and Welfare Central funds	1,300,000	
		(approx.)
(v) Additional cost of Imperial forces up to the end of 1949	4,000,000	
		(approx.)
Total	£38,300,000	

(vi) His Majesty's Government has also offered an interest free loan of up to £18½ million for the War Damage Compensation scheme and have allowed the Federation Government to raise a loan of £8 million on the London market.

209   CAB 21/2510, no 1A   27 Mar 1950
[Malayan operations]: minute from Mr Shinwell to Mr Attlee proposing a ministerial committee on Malaya

Prime Minister

As you are aware while I was at the War Office I was for a long time disquieted about the situation in Malaya. As a result of a talk I had with the Colonial Secretary at the time we obtained an assessment of the position from the Commissioner General. Since then it has been decided to send out General Briggs to co-ordinate the military and police campaign against the bandits.

2. The situation still remains so grave that in my view there is everything to be gained by setting up a Ministerial Committee of those primarily concerned, composed, say of the Colonial Secretary, the Secretary of State for War and possibly the Secretary of State for Air and myself. If you agree with the idea you may, of course, wish to add other Ministers.

3. The Committee should meet frequently to keep events in Malaya closely under review and to tender advice to you and the Defence Committee of any action considered necessary by the Committee in the light of the reports received from the scene of operations.

4. I have mentioned my suggestion to the Colonial Secretary—to whom I am sending a copy of this minute—who welcomes the proposal.

210   CAB 21/2510, no 5   1 Apr 1950
[Ministerial committee on Malaya]: personal minute (reply) no M.47/50 from Mr Attlee to Mr Shinwell

Minister of Defence

As I have already told you I agree in principle that a Ministerial Committee should be appointed to keep a watch on developments in Malaya on behalf of the Defence Committee, but I think that the composition which you propose in your minute of the 27th March[1] would overweight the military side. The balance could be redressed by omitting the Secretary of State for Air (he could be called in as required if important questions affecting the use of the Royal Air Force are to be discussed); and by adding the Secretary of State for Commonwealth Relations because Malaya is of special importance to the Australasian and Asiatic members of the Commonwealth, and the Minister of State (Mr. Younger)[2] because of the general Foreign Office interest in South East Asia. I shall be glad if you will preside over this Committee in your capacity as Deputy Chairman of the Defence Committee. The Cabinet Office and the Ministry of Defence will provide joint secretaries.

The terms of reference will be:—

"To keep the situation in Malaya under review and, reporting as required to

---

[1] See 209.
[2] Kenneth Younger, minister of state at the Foreign Office, 1950–1951.

the Defence Committee, to authorise such measures they may think necessary to preserve law and order in the Colony."[3]

---

[3] Chaired by Shinwell the Cabinet Malaya Committee met ten times between 19 Apr and 17 Oct 1950 and once in 1951 on 26 July (see also CAB 21/1681 and 1682, CAB 134/497, and PREM 8/1406/2).

211 CO 537/6092, nos 68–72   7 Apr 1950
[Colombo proposals for the economic development of SE Asia]: outward telegram no 151 from Mr Griffiths to Mr M J MacDonald on the line to be taken by the UK at the Commonwealth conference in May

[Led by Australia, Ceylon and India, the Commonwealth conference on foreign affairs at Colombo in Jan 1950 had agreed in principle to promote the economic development of S and SE Asia to guard against 'the menace of communism' (see CAB 129/38, CP(50)18, 22 Feb 1950). Since Bevin stressed Britain's financial constraints, attention swung to the central role which the USA might play, but, although many British dependencies required American investment, the CO accepted that it would be undesirable for them to fall within general schemes of US aid.]

H.M.G. have under urgent consideration the line to be taken by the United Kingdom delegation to the Commonwealth Conference, now to be held in Sydney in mid-May, to discuss the implementation of the Colombo resolutions for the development of South East Asia.

2. Line to be taken by U.K. delegation is that any significant development in non Colonial territories in South East Asia must depend, ultimately, on United States financial assistance. If there is Commonwealth agreement that possibilities of U.S. aid should be explored it is essential that countries concerned should be able to present a complete picture of their economic needs and prospects by August to enable a report on the needs of the area and the Commonwealth resources available to meet them to be drawn up, which might serve as a basis for the discussions with the U.S. These would take place after a further Conference in September, which it is envisaged will be attended not only by Commonwealth countries but also certain non Commonwealth countries in the area, who will be invited to prepare similar statements of their development needs, and to co-operate with Commonwealth in making a submission to the United States.

3. The position of the British non-selfgoverning territories in the region requires special consideration. No decision has yet been taken on the extent to which it will be desirable to seek U.S. assistance for these territories. It is impossible to say categorically that the scale of U.K. effort through C.D.W., C.D.C., and other means, will be entirely adequate to deal with the problem and that no external assistance from the United States is likely to be needed. Moreover, to take such a line would imply an exclusive attitude which would be politically undesirable. In all the circumstances I feel that it would be essential to agree that the British South East Asia territories should take a full part in the work of preparing a survey of developmental needs of the area for submission to the Americans, without prejudice to the question as to whether American assistance should subsequently be sought.

The decision on whether such assistance should be sought would of course have regard not only to the size and nature of the problem but also to the political factors involved in encouraging large scale American economic and political influence in these territories. In any case even if direct American financial assistance were not sought, we should always want to press for a co-operative attitude on the part of the United States in respect of rubber and tin purchases in view of the major contribution that these would make to South East Asia stability. Whatever the decision on the participation of the non self-governing territories in the general scheme of American assistance the territories will not of course be precluded from participating in existing U.S. schemes for assistance to undeveloped territories, offered through United Nations, or other Agencies, and would not therefore cut across particular projects mentioned in your telegram No. 67, to which I shall separately reply.

4. It is envisaged therefore, that if these ideas commend themselves to the Sydney Conference the British non self-governing territories in South East Asia will be asked to prepare development programmes on the same lines as other countries in the area. In these circumstances it will be of great assistance to have on the United Kingdom delegation a representative of these territories. I suggest that High Commissioners and Governors concerned should agree to elect one officer to represent all four territories on the U.K. Delegation. If acceptable to the Governors we consider that Benham[1] would be most suitable for this purpose, but in saying this we have no wish to restrict their choice. It is probable that the Colonial Office will also be represented on the delegation.

We should be grateful if you and the High Commissioner and the Governors concerned, to whom this telegram is being repeated, would telegraph any comments they have as soon as possible.

A separate telegram is being addressed to you regarding travelling arrangements of U.K. Delegation. I assume that you will make arrangements locally for booking air passages for yourself and Territories' representative.

---

[1] F C C Benham was economic adviser to the commissioner-general in SE Asia, 1947–1955; previously he had been economic adviser to the comptroller for development and welfare in the West Indies, 1942–1945, and professor of economics, University of London, 1945–1947; in 1955 he became professor of international economics, Royal Institute of International Affairs.

212   CO 537/6026, no 10   9 Apr 1950
[Constitutional development]: despatch no 6 from Sir H Gurney to Mr Griffiths proposing a member system

I have the honour to address you on the subject of constitutional development in the Federation of Malaya.

2. The new constitution provided in the Federation Agreement of 1948 has on the whole worked well. Any Federal constitution requires continual and sometimes laborious consultation between its various members, and it is always tempting in these circumstances for the Federal authority to assert itself by allowing the minimum exercise of power to the State components. My policy has been to build up the strength of the central Government by a maximum decentralisation to the units

through which the central Government must work, so that those units come to realise their own dependence upon the Federal authority and to look to it spontaneously for guidance and direction with confidence and goodwill. The desire for central control, so far as it may be necessary, then comes from the perimeter and not from the centre itself. This tendency is now at work and has of course been stimulated by the Emergency and by the binding force of resistance to Communist aggression. There is no evidence of any desire to amend the Agreement at the present time, except in regard to citizenship (as to which I shall be addressing you separately) and a few points of very minor importance.

3. It is, of course, still necessary to dispose of the Penang secessionists; and search is proceeding for a formula to govern the Federal Allocations to State and Settlement revenues, a problem which will assume increasing importance.

4. Within the constitution it now appears to me desirable to make as rapid progress as possible towards elections and to introduce a 'Member' system. I enclose for your information a copy of a memorandum[1] outlining my proposals, which was considered and agreed to by Executive Council last month. A similar memorandum was discussed with the Conference of Rulers in February, when Their Highnesses agreed to consult their Executive Councils on the issue of elections for State Councils and accepted the proposals for a member system on the understanding that any Asian Members to be appointed would be in the proportion of not less than three Malays to one Asian non-Malay.

5. In regard to elections, it is of course necessary to begin with municipal elections and a Committee appointed by the Legislative Council is now considering the draft of the necessary legislation. It is hoped to pass this by September and to hold the municipal elections in Penang, Kuala Lumpur and Malacca in 1951. At the same time steps are being taken towards the establishment of municipalities at Ipoh, Taiping, Seremban, Johore Bahru and Kota Bahru. Since the inhabitants of all these towns are mainly Chinese, municipal elections are the most practical method immediately available of giving the Chinese community an effective say in their own affairs without raising Malay-Chinese political issues.

6. Since it is proposed that only Federal citizens should be enfranchised (in the municipal as well as the Federal and State electoral systems), it is a necessary preliminary to extend citizenship to many who cannot possess it as the Agreement stands. Now that the Communities Liaison Committee has reached unanimous agreement that this should be done, it is hoped that it will be possible to pass the Bill making the desired amendments in the Agreement at about the same time as the Bill to provide for municipal elections.

7. In regard to the 'Member' system, I have little to add to the enclosed memorandum except that, after discussion with Dato Onn, I am considering the following alternative distribution, with which he agrees:—

Ex-Officio Members

Chief Secretary   Administration
                                             External Affairs
                                             Defence
                                             Civil Service

---

[1] Not printed.

| Attorney General | – |
| Financial Secretary | Finance, including Accountant General, Audit, Income Tax, War Damage, Estate Duty, Electricity. |

Official Members

Member for Home Affairs	Justice, Security, Immigration, Public Relations, Broadcasting.
Member for Economic Affairs	Trade and Industry, Imports & Exports, Customs, Statistics, Economic development.
Member for Education	Education, Museums.
Member for Health and Social Welfare	Medical and Health Services, Social Welfare.
Member for Agriculture & Forestry	Agriculture, Veterinary, Fisheries, Forestry, Drainage and Irrigation, Game.
Member for Communications	Posts, Telecommunications, Civil Aviation, Meteorological, Road Transport.
Member for Railways and Ports	Railways, Ports, Marine.
Member for Lands, Mines and Surveys.	Lands, Mines, Surveys, Geological Survey.
Member for Labour.	Labour, Trade Unions.
Member for Public Works	Public Works, Roads, Water and Water supplies.

8. In addition to the *ex-officio* members, the Member for Home Affairs and the Member for Economic Affairs would normally be appointed to Executive Council. It is generally desirable that all members of Executive Council should also be members of the Legislative Council, but as a temporary expedient I should propose to retain on Executive Council but not on the Legislative Council the Secretary for Chinese Affairs and also to appoint to Executive Council the Adviser on Malay States Affairs, who the Rulers have now agreed should be the keeper of the Rulers' Seal but has yet to be selected and appointed. To provide for European, Chinese and Indian unofficial representation Executive Council would also have to include unofficial members who are not 'Members'.

9. Dato Onn has informed me that he would not be prepared to accept an unofficial seat in the Legislative Council unless he were elected to it by the United Malay Nationalist Organization. He has recently propounded to me an idea for reconstituting the Legislative Council by allotting a number of unofficial seats to the United Malay Nationalist Organization, the Malayan Chinese Association and the Malayan Indian Association to be filled by election by each of these bodies respectively, leaving a proportion of seats to be filled by nomination.

10. At present the Malay unofficial seats are filled after consultation with the Malay Councillors' Association, a body comprising all the Malay members of the Council: and the Chinese and other unofficial members are appointed after consultation with and often virtual election by public bodies such as Chambers of Commerce and Mines.

11. Dato Onn's idea is for a Council of 84 members as follows:—

1	Speaker.
3	Ex-Officio members.
10	Official members.
11	State and Settlement members.
41	'Community' members.
1	Nominated Ceylonese.
1	" European.
1	" Eurasian.
4	Representatives of Commerce.
2	" " Mining.
3	" " Agriculture.
6	" " Labour.
84	

The 41 'Community' members would be:—

	Malays	Chinese	Indians
Penang	1	2	1
Malacca	1	1	
Perak	3	3	1
Selangor	2	2	1
Negri Sembilam	1	1	
Pahang	1	1	
Johore	3	2	1
Kedah	4	1	1
Kelantan	4		
Trengganu	2		
Perlis	1		
	23	13	5

12. The general effect of these proposals would be to increase the number of Malay unofficial members from 22 to 27; of Chinese from 16 to 18; of Indians from 5 to 8; and to reduce the number of European unofficial members from 8 to 4. Of the 23 Malay members 15 would be 'elected' by UMNO and 8 nominated, of the 13 Chinese 8 would be 'elected' by the Malayan Chinese Association and 5 nominated, and of the 5 Indians 3 would be 'Elected' by the Malayan Indian Association and 2 nominated. The allocation of the 41 seats is on a basis of one per 100,000 of the Commonwealth-born members of the respective Communities.

13. I set out these proposals to show the way in which Dato Onn's mind has been working, during some months in which he has had perhaps too little to do. They are so obviously objectionable, with their emphasis on communal politics, that I doubt whether he intends them as more than the product of an interesting study. They ignore the basis of Federal citizenship, to which in other connections he himself attaches such importance as a means of breaking down communal consciousness. I am not at present contemplating any change in the constitution of the Council, since the citizenship issue now under discussion must clearly be settled first.

14. In regard to the appointment of 'Members', I anticipate great difficulty in finding a suitable Chinese who would be willing to give up his professional or business interests for a much less remunerative political appointment carrying heavy responsibilities. I seriously doubt, indeed, whether the Chinese community themselves would wish to see a Chinese appointed to one of these posts in the near future. They would prefer that British officers should continue to occupy them.

15. I should therefore propose to introduce the system gradually, appointing in

the first instance two or three Malays to be Members—there are not more than that number of suitable Malays available, having regard to the necessity of filling State posts—and retaining the power of appointment in my own hands. The remaining Members would be for the time being the appropriate Heads of Departments, into whose hands the corresponding Secretariat machinery would gradually be decentralised, thus bringing into being the administrative pattern for a ministerial system.

16. I see nothing in these proposals involving any material change in the terms of service of expatriate Government officers.

17. I should be grateful if these proposals for the introduction of the 'Member' system could receive your early approval. I should propose to published them, when approved, in a paper laid before the Legislative Council, and the timing of this is important. On the 19th April the Council will approve the design for the Federation flag and will debate a paper on the Squatter problem. It is not yet clear when the Communities Liaison Committee's Agreed Views will be published, but I should hope shortly thereafter to put forward proposals for the setting up of a Rural Development Authority to assist in the economic development of the Malays, which is the obverse of the proposed citizenship concessions and a desirable accompaniment of the expenditure of public funds on Chinese squatters. Chapter II of the Draft Development Plan is now printed and will be issued before the end of this month. It would be helpful if I could be in a position to go ahead with the 'Member' system by the end of May.

18. Copies of this despatch are being sent to the Commissioner General and the Governor, Singapore, for their information.

213   CAB 129/39, CP(50)75   21 Apr 1950
'Chinese consuls in Malaya': joint Cabinet memorandum by Mr Griffiths and Mr Younger[1]

On 27th October the Cabinet approved the recommendation in C.P.(49) 214 that the impact of *de jure* recognition of the Chinese People's Government upon United Kingdom interests in the Far East should be considered at a conference of His Majesty's Representatives at Singapore under the chairmanship of the Commissioner-General for South East Asia (C.M.(49) 62nd Conclusions, Minute 7).[2] It was pointed out in the Cabinet's discussion that *de jure* recognition of the Central People's Government would create a special problem in Malaya, since there might be some disposition among the Chinese community to assume that this would justify the cessation of punitive measures against the Communist bandits.

2. At the Singapore Conference, which was held in November, 1949, it was appreciated that recognition meant that Chinese Communist Consuls would in due course have to be accepted in the Federation of Malaya and Singapore. It was realised that their appointment would create difficulties, but the view was taken that these difficulties should be dealt with *ad hoc* and not be held to justify delaying recognition. It was felt that though the appointment of Communist Consuls could not be long delayed, any possible delay should be contrived while the present

---

emergency existed. During the discussions which took place, His Majesty's Ambassador to China expressed the view that the appointment of Communist Consuls to Malaya would not involve any major accretion of strength to the Communist cause, since it was quite possible for China to send in agents through clandestine channels who, by operating underground, could be far more effective than Consuls, whose activities were bound to be restricted by their official position. He thought it possible that as a result of Communist successes in China attempts would in fact be made to step up the terrorist campaign in Malaya by subversive methods. Subsequent events seem to have borne out at any rate the second of these conclusions, for from our point of view there has been a marked deterioration in the situation during recent months.

3.   Though diplomatic relations between the United Kingdom and China have not yet been formally established, it had been the intention, once they were established, to ask the Central People's Government to accord formal recognition also to His Majesty's Consuls in China who, though still remaining at their posts, have not yet been accorded any official position by the new Government. His Majesty's Chargé d'Affaires was accordingly instructed to take up this matter on the conclusion of the preliminary and procedural talks, and, if the Central People's Government enquired whether reciprocal treatment would be accorded to Chinese Consuls, to inform them that the United Kingdom Government considered that the Central People's Government were entitled to take over all Chinese Consulates in British territories.

4.   Shortly after these instructions were issued the High Commissioner for the Federation of Malaya represented that, although he had reluctantly agreed to the recommendations of the Singapore Conference, the situation had now changed to such an extent that he could no longer find it possible to justify the acceptance of Chinese Consuls in the Federation until the emergency was over (there is no indication when this will be, but clearly it cannot be for many months). His view was based not so much on the difficulty of preventing direct contact between Chinese Consuls and the Malayan bandits—a risk which was foreseen and accepted at the Singapore Conference—but on the fact, which has only become apparent in recent months, that the mere prospect of the admission of Consuls has already had a most serious effect on the Chinese community in Malaya, and that their actual admission, after all the apprehensions which have been expressed by that community, might well have incalculable consequences on the course of the emergency. He pointed out that one of the main difficulties in coping with the bandit movement had been the hesitancy of the Chinese community, partly from fear of direct intimidation by the bandits, but equally from reluctance to commit themselves to the Government side until it was clear that the Government were going to win. This problem has been aggravated by Communist successes in China as well as by the continued and spirited resistance of the bandits. The High Commissioner reported that His Majesty's Government's recognition of the Central People's Government had also aroused considerable misgivings among the leaders of the Chinese community, but had in general been accepted as a fact of political realism. They had indeed come out more strongly than hitherto during the last few months against the bandits and had striven with some success to mobilise Chinese opinion more actively to the support of the Government. Several representative Chinese bodies had so far committed themselves to the support of the Government as to pass resolutions urging that Chinese Consults [sic] should not be appointed to Malaya.

5. The High Commissioner pointed out that it was absolutely essential, if the emergency was to be brought to a successful and reasonably rapid conclusion, to have not merely the passive acquiescence of the Chinese community, but their active support in denying supplies and shelter to the bandits and in giving information to the authorities about their movements. His conclusion was that the appointment of Chinese Communist Consuls would shake severely the confidence of the Chinese in the Government's determination to eliminate the bandits, that the Chinese might well decide that the time had come to make their peace with the other side and that they would consider that His Majesty's Government regarded the retention of British Consular posts in China as of greater importance than the security of the people of Malaya. The Commissioner-General, the Acting Governor of Singapore and the Commander-in-Chief, Far East Land Forces, support the High Commissioner's view of the dangers and consider his apprehension fully justified.

6. The crux of the situation in Malaya and Singapore appears to be the effect on the Chinese population of the appointment of Chinese Consuls of the People's Government. It has been reported to the Colonial Office that there are in fact three elements in the Chinese population. The merchant community and leading business men, many of whom are British subjects of long standing, are opposed to the People's Government. Left-wing sympathisers, fellow-travellers, principally school-masters, students and clerks, have been encouraged by recognition of the People's Government and are now trying to secure leadership of an [and] control over the overseas Chinese communities. The main body of overseas Chinese, however, are inclined to fear for the future and are more than ever anxious to sit on the fence.

7. In the policy which M. Stalin laid down as long ago as 1925 for the revolution in colonial territories, he stated that where there was a small proletariat and more or less developed industry the object must be to align the workers and the petty bourgeoisie against the imperialists *"and those elements of the bourgeoisie which work with it"*.[3] The destruction of the upper bourgeoisie is to develop from this process. The significance of this policy to the three elements of the overseas Chinese population needs to be considered. If action is to be taken to exclude Chinese Communist Consuls from Malaya which cannot fail to arouse the hostility of the Chinese People's Government, the latter may be expected to try to accentuate the cleavage between the various elements of the community. While it is encouraging to note that the section of the community which qualifies for the definition of upper bourgeoisie under the Stalin doctrine is coming out in more open support of the Government, it really has no other choice, since it will be the first to be eliminated if the Communists prevail. Unfortunately past experience with the Chinese has tended to show that the merchant and upper trading class is the least militant and usually non-resistant when it comes to open conflict with the Chinese national interest.

8. Again, experience of the Chinese people suggests that they will remain at least passively law-abiding citizens of a country which is to them foreign as long as they are not faced with the necessity of choosing to renounce their loyalty to the National Government of China (whether it be Communist or otherwise). A refusal to admit Chinese Consuls to Malaya is bound to cause a dispute betwen His Majesty's Government and the Chinese People's Government. This will have the effect of confronting the overseas Chinese in Malaya with the necessity of making a choice.

---

[3] Emphasis in original.

While those whose elimination would be the first object of any Communist regime may decide to burn their boats and declare their co-operation with British authority, it is possible that those who are sitting on the fence will be in even greater fear than before, while those who are in favour of the Chinese People's Government will become more active in their opposition to our authority. The consequences of such a development might therefore transcend the effect which may ensue from the acceptance of Chinese Communist Consuls in Malaya.

9. In view of the difficulties of this problem, examination has been given to suggestions that we should continue in some way to delay the appointment of Chinese Consuls indefinitely. These lack reality, because there is nothing that we can do, short of arbitrary discrimination, (which is bound to provoke retaliation) if, in the event, the Chinese People's Government should establish normal diplomatic relations and confirm the status of our Consuls in China. If they do not do so, the present position will, of course, be maintained, and no Chinese Consuls will go to Malaya. Equally, if they attempt to restrict the number of our Consulates in China or to restrict their functions, it should be possible to take action helpful to Malaya based on reciprocity. It is, however, necessary to consider what our position will be if and when normal diplomatic relations are established and the question of Consuls becomes a live issue. We are advised that, although there is an inherent right on the part of any Government to refuse to allow the appointment of Consuls to any given place, it is unusual to refuse to permit Consulates where they have existed before and where good reasons can be adduced for their continuance. It is the type of action which has hitherto only been taken by Governments such as the Soviet Government. It must be expected, therefore, that a refusal to permit the re-establishment of Chinese Consulates in Malaya and Singapore would lead to retaliation and the probable closing down of those Consulates to which we attach importance in China. It would also weaken our general case for objecting to similar action if taken against us in any other part of the world. It should here be noted that there are, in all, seventeen Chinese Consulates in the United Kingdom and dependent territories, as compared with thirteen British Consulates in China. Even if we should attempt to bargain on the basis of reciprocity, it is unlikely that the Chinese would be prepared to sacrifice their Consulates in Malaya and Singapore, where there are, in fact, large overseas Chinese communities. Thus, though it might be possible to contemplate a reduction in the number of our Consulates in China, it is unlikely that this would achieve any object.

10. The above considerations have been put to the authorities in Malaya and Hong Kong and H.M. Chargé d'Affaires in Peking.

11. H.M. Chargé d'Affaires holds the view that the normal and legitimate interest of the Chinese People's Government in Malaya are so great and so widespread that they would greatly resent a decision to exclude Consuls from that territory and that their resentment would be more bitter in view of the usual international practice outlined in paragraph 9 above. He considers that any public announcement of any decision to exclude Chinese Consuls from Malaya might well cause the Chinese People's Government to break off our negotiations for the establishment of diplomatic relations and to request the withdrawal from China of our diplomatic and Consular officers. He also feels that the question of Consular establishments could not be long postponed after the establishment of diplomatic relations (even if the Chinese do not raise this question in the preliminary negotiations) and that if they

were told (as opposed to any publicly announced decision) that their Consuls would be excluded from Malaya, they would ultimately demand the withdrawal of our Consuls from China, or even go so far as to discontinue diplomatic relations if these had by then been established. H.M. Chargé d'Affaires also points out that our policy has hitherto been to keep a foot in the still open Chinese door, in the hope of bringing influences to bear to prevent the formation of a solid Sino-Soviet bloc. This policy, he feels, would be nullified by the withdrawal of both Consular posts and diplomatic relations, and to a large extent delayed by the withdrawal of the former alone. Indeed, the consequences would be more far reaching, namely to increase Chinese dependence on the Soviet Union and the pace of Sino-Soviet co-operation. He goes on to express the view that it is possible that, if we fail to establish diplomatic relations, the Chinese People's Government might not wish to maintain diplomatic relations with the other Western and American countries. With these considerations in view, he concludes that we should try to maintain all our Consular posts in China, but that there seems no likelihood of doing that if we exclude Chinese Consuls from Malaya.

12. The general question of our relations with China is discussed in a separate paper (C.P.(50) 73), and the implications of any break in relations with the Chinese People's Government have been set forth in Part II thereof. It is also important to note that, if a decision to exclude Chinese Consuls from Malaya resulted in our own Consuls having to withdraw from China, it would be necessary to give prior intimation of this to our nationals in that country, to enable them to leave beforehand, should they wish to do so.

13. The Governor of Hong Kong regards anything that might jeopardise harmonious relations with whatever Chinese Government may be in power as contrary to Hong Kong's interests. But he doubts whether a decision by His Majesty's Government to refuse to accept Consuls in Malaya would, in fact, make either the Chinese People's Government or the local authorities in Kwangtung any less co-operative. On the long term view, he does not think it likely that the Chinese People's Government would be induced to make a major issue of the Hong Kong question because of any decision to exclude Chinese Consuls.

14. The High Commissioner for the Federation of Malaya does not consider that the exclusion of Chinese Consuls and the hostility of the Chinese People's Government, which would almost certainly follow, would have the adverse effects on the attitude of the Chinese community in Malaya suggested in paragraph 8 above. He considers that in any choice of loyalties the great majority of local Chinese would now choose loyalty to the Federation Government, because their feeling is directed against Communism both in Malaya and China, which has nothing to do with their loyalty to and affection for China itself. The Chinese would like to give positive backing to the Federation Government, but the High Commissioner agrees that they are restrained from so doing both by doubts as to the outcome of the emergency and fear of an ultimate British withdrawal. Readiness to admit Chinese Consuls would not only provide the Chinese with further grounds for such doubts and fears, but would also expose them to a powerful instrument for compelling their allegiance. They would, in fact, be left with no choice but to express their loyalty to the Chinese People's Government. Nor does the High Commissioner think that the Chinese fellow travellers in Malaya would be stimulated into more active opposition to the Government if relations between His Majesty's Government and the Chinese People's

Government were seriously to deteriorate as a result of the exclusion of Chinese Consuls, whereas the presence of Consuls would certainly encourage them to take a chance. The High Commissioner is confident that, if a decision were taken to exclude Consuls, the local Chinese would be able to increase and make effective their pro-Government hold over the majority of their community, who will see in this exclusion concrete evidence of British intentions, and who will, therefore, be more willing to give positive support to the Government against the Communist bandits.

15. The Commissioner-General and the Governor of Singapore strongly support these views of the High Commissioner.

Conclusion and recommendation

16. The considerations raised by this issue are strongly conflicting and most difficult to reconcile. Whatever decision is taken is bound to have important consequences on our policy in the Far East. In C.P.(50) 73 it is proposed that in the forthcoming discussions with the United States Secretary of State the whole field of our respective relations with China should be reviewed. We therefore recommend that a decision on this specific issue of Chinese Consuls in Malaya should be deferred until these discussions have taken place and their results have been reviewed in relation to this problem. A delay in reaching a decision will mean a prolongation of the present disquiet in the Chinese community in Malaya, but in view of the larger issues involved, this is unavoidable.

17. In the meantime, it should be possible to hold the position in Peking. The question of Consuls cannot be raised until both parties have agreed to exchange Ambassadors. The Central People's Government have as yet given no indication that they are ready to do so. Should they signify their readiness, H.M. Chargé d'Affaires has been instructed to take no action and to refer to London, and it should thus be possible to ensure that the question of Consuls is not raised until Ministers have had an opportunity to consider the matter after the talks with the United States Secretary of State.

214 CO 537/6089, no 5   26 Apr 1950

[Malaya and the sterling area]: minute by A Emanuel[1] to Sir H Poynton on the arguments in favour of Malaya's membership

With reference to your minute about briefing for your visit to the Far East,[2] I shall let you have my suggestions for points on which a brief might be useful as soon as possible.

Meanwhile, as you have specially mentioned the particular question of the arguments in favour of Malaya and Singapore being members of the sterling area, I think you may like to have a copy of a memorandum[3] which was prepared and circulated to the Supplies Conference, in which I have incorporated certain amendments suggested by the Treasury and the Board of Trade. The memorandum

---

[1] Assistant secretary, CO, 1948–1961.

[2] Sir H Poynton accompanied the secretary of state to the Far East in June, see 218.

[3] Not printed.

has also been revised so as to make it apply generally to the Colonies and not only to the West Indies. It was hoped that the Treasury and the Board of Trade would agree to this memorandum being sent to Colonial Governments for the guidance of their Public Relations Departments. The Treasury, however, though agreeing that, with the drafting amendments incorporated, it was a "reasonable exposition of doctrine" asked that we should ensure that no wide publicity was given to it as they thought that it would be especially harmful as some of the generalisations in the memorandum were broadcast out of their context. In the light of the Treasury's reaction and a similar reaction from the Board of Trade, it was decided not to send it out to the Colonies but to hold it in reserve as a statement which could be used on suitable occasions.

It seems to me that this is one suitable occasion, namely, to give you the full case for Colonial membership of the sterling area.

The specific case for Malaya has, however, been argued persuasively by Professor Benham[4] and I suggest you should see his broadcast which is at No. 6 on 96053/48–50, at present in action with Information Department. His memorandum, together with our general memorandum, seemed to me to give the whole story. I would sum it up as follows:—

(i) membership of the sterling area implies that a particular currency is convertible with all the currencies of the world with which sterling is convertible. As sterling is still the basis of half the world's trade this is itself very important. Before the war, of course, sterling was freely convertible and the aim is to make it freely convertible again.

(ii) small countries dependent on one or two crops or products are bound to have unstable currencies, with all the consequent disadvantages, unless they are automatically linked to stronger currency. Malaya is peculiarly liable to fluctuations caused through dependence on the American market for rubber and tin, and while in the long run a dollar reserve could no doubt be built up in good years so that convertibility with the dollar could be assured, this would only be at the expense of current imports.

(iii) so long as Malaya can obtain its requirements from the sterling area or soft currency sources, no hardship ensues by being a member of the sterling area. Before the war with no controls governing the use of sterling. Malaya naturally imported its requirements of consumer goods from the U.K., Europe and Japan, in return for exports to the dollar area. This is the natural pattern of trade. The inducement, however, to remain a member of the sterling area depends essentially on the U.K. in the long run being able to supply the goods that Malaya needs on a competitive basis with the U.S. Ultimately, therefore, the argument in favour of remaining a member of the sterling area must be the U.K.'s ability to provide the goods that Malaya wants in return for the dollars Malaya earns. People in Malaya will, therefore, only be convinced by the above if we are able to persuade them that they will, over the long period, get goods in return for their goods and that our efforts in the field of production and supply are adequate to maintain the value of sterling.

(iv) the general memorandum refers to the fact that Colonial Governments hold

---

[4] See 211, note 1.

their reserves in sterling and that H.M.G.'s assistance towards Colonial dependencies is only possible if the strength of sterling is maintained. As Malaya holds its currency reserves in the U.K., has had appreciable financial assistance from the U.K., and expects to get assistance in the future, these are also strong arguments in favour of Malaya remaining in the sterling area, though ultimately subordinate to the main question of ability to obtain imports in exchange for exports.

215 PREM 8/1406/2, MAL C(50)12   12 May 1950
'The present day situation and duties of the Malayan Communist Party': note by Mr Strachey for the Cabinet Malaya Committee commenting on a captured MCP document

[Produced in June 1949, captured some time later and transmitted to London in Nov, the MCP pamphlet *Present day situation and duties* reached the attention of ministers in May 1950.]

I circulate this note setting out my reactions to the captured document. "The Present Day Situation and Duties of the Malayan Communist Party"[1] in the hope that it will serve to stimulate discussion in the Malaya Committee. I do not suggest any specific action on our part until:—

(i)   We have had the opportunity to read further material and
(ii) the Secretary of State for the Colonies and myself have returned from Malaya.

I realise, of course, that the authorities in Malaya are fully aware that they are faced by the Communist insurrection and not a mere outbreak of banditry. But the captured document, by emphasising this fact, may help us to clear our minds on the combination of military and political methods necessary to break the insurrection.

1. *Communist motivation*
The document makes it clear that we are faced by a well organised and almost wholly political revolt in Malaya. Banditry and terrorist tactics are widely used, but merely as methods in an attempt to seize power by armed force on the part of the Malayan Communist Party. We should underrate the gravity of the situation if we supposed that the enemy's objective was anything less than the seizure of the full power of the State in Malaya.

2. *Military weakness*
The report gives an impression of considerable military weakness on the part of the communists, both relatively to the Government forces and absolutely.

3. *Political strength*
The document claims, with what degree of justification I am not in a position to judge, that the Malayan Communist Party has achieved a very appreciable degree of political strength, which we should not underrate.

---

[1] Not printed.

Evidence of military weakness

4.   (6E)* The Malayan Liberation Army, which is the military wing of the Malayan Communist Party, is stated to be dependent for supplies in general, and particularly for ammunition, on what it can capture from the Government forces. This admission in regard to ammunition is brought out much more strongly in the full document than in the summary. Considerable anxiety as to ammunition is expressed. I take it that our military authorities are fully alive to what would seem to be the paramount importance of denying ammunition to the enemy.

(7A) The Liberation Army is stated to depend for its ordinary supplies. i.e. food, on the support of the rural workers, evidently mainly the so-called Chinese squatters. It is evident from reports that if these squatters could be completely controlled or won over by our forces and freed from Communist terrorism, the Liberation Army could not exist.

The document contains throughout many admissions of the high degree of pressure exerted on the Liberation Army by our armed forces and indicates the difficulty of maintaining the Liberation Army's morale in these circumstances.

(6D) and other passages in the full document, make it clear that the main military objective of the Liberation Army is to secure a base, i.e. some area within Malaya into which our forces cannot penetrate and which can be administered by the Communists as the nucleus of a Communist State. This is standard Communist strategy in the initial stages of a Communist uprising; it was practised successfully in China and unsuccessfully in Greece. There is no claim that any real progress towards this first main objective of the Communists has been made in Malaya.

Evidence of political strength

5.   (8D) and other passages in the full document indicate that the Malayan Communist Party claims pretty general support from the Chinese rural population, i.e. the squatters: some, but much slighter, support from Chinese and Indian workers in the large scale plantations and mines, and growing support amongst the Malayan [Malay] populations. The claim to growing Malayan [Malay] support, unless it is quite unsubstantiated, is disturbing. On the other hand, the report admits that virtually no progress has been made with the city population, apparently either Malayan [Malay] or Chinese. The revolt, according to the document, is essentially a revolt of the unadministered rural areas.

(6C and 8B) An assertion is made that our efforts at suppression alienate "the rural masses", or as we call them the Chinese squatters, and drive them into the hands of the Communists. On the other hand, there is an admission, as in (8B), that the Communists' own operations may also alienate squatter populations and drive them into our hands. Thus we get the impression that the struggle is, in one important aspect, a struggle *for* the support of the Chinese rural squatters. This seems to suggest that we ought to be exceedingly careful to avoid punitive measures which hit the Chinese squatter population indiscriminately. It suggests that it is of importance for us always to appear in the role of protectors of the population against the Communists and their destructive and terrorist activities.

(7B) In this and many other passages the document emphasises the extreme importance for the Communists of denying us information as to the Liberation

*(References are throughout to the summary of the document prepared by the Foreign Office)

Army's movements. This again suggests that the struggle is in one essential aspect a struggle for the support of the Chinese squatters, and generally the rural population.

General purpose of the uprising

6. It is perfectly clear that the ultimate purpose of the uprising is to establish a Communist Government in Malaya. It is not suggested, however, that that purpose can be achieved by the efforts of the Malayan Communist Party alone. Reliance is placed on international success in the world wide Communist struggle for the capture of State power in Malaya. In the meanwhile, the present uprising is represented to some extent as a holding operation. The soldiers of the Liberation Army and the other active members of the Communist Party are exhorted to hold on, and fight on, in what would be a long and difficult holding operation. The purposes of this holding operation are:—

    (i)   To cripple Malaya as an economic asset for the West.

    (ii) To absorb the armed forces and other resources of the West.

Great reliance is placed on a new economic crisis in the capitalist world which will destroy the prosperity of Malaya and lower the standard of life of the population there. It is not too much to say that much of the argument of the pamphlet is based on the Marxist thesis of "increasing misery". It is assumed, that is to say, that the workings of Capitalism, in particular in an area such as Malaya, must steadily lower the standard of life of the population and increase its misery, thus driving the population into the hands of the Communists who alone will supply them with a leadership capable of improving their lot.

7. Conclusions

The main indications as to our best methods for breaking the revolt contained in the document appear to me to be as follows:—

We must seek to combine in the most skilful manner possible an intensification of our military pressure on the Liberation Army and on the Malayan Communist Party in general (it is quite clear that our military measures, though they may sometimes seem rather fruitless to us are exercising a heavy pressure on the enemy), with the most determined and sustained effort to falsify the Communist prediction of "increasing misery" for the people of Malaya. For in this way alone can we destroy the essential economic and political premise upon which the whole Malayan Communist Party's activities are evidently based.

It is evident that it may not always be easy to combine these two methods of breaking the revolt. Increasing military pressure may in the short run at any rate be difficult to combine with achieving a steady and satisfactory rate of social progress in the colony. Nevertheless, military or police measures for taking over the administration of the at present unadministered areas can be regarded as at any rate a pre-requisite of the orderly progress.

We emphasise, and rightly, the almost indispensable character of Malaya to us as a dollar earner. Should we not therefore be willing to expend considerable resources in sterling on Malaya, in order to develop her both economically and socially at the most rapid pace physically possible? Some of these resources will have to come from the United Kingdom, but some ought to come from Malaya itself by way of a better distribution of income. It is suggested that one of the most significant facts of which the Malaya Committee has been informed is that only about one quarter of the proper revenue is derived from the present rate of income tax in the colony. I take it that this means that it has hitherto been found impossible to collect anything like the taxes due from the rich Chinese and European merchants and employers of Malaya. This must mean that there are extreme inequalities in the distribution of income in Malaya. No doubt it would be highly unrealistic to think that anything approaching the same distribution of income as now exist [sic] in Great Britain could, or even should, be achieved in Malaya. Nevertheless, it is suggested that a steady removal of the extremes of riches and poverty there is one of the essential pre-requisites for a long term suppression of the revolt. And no better way, surely, of doing this than really collecting the income tax could be applied.

8. All this is really only to say that we all ought to recognise the fact that we are faced in Malaya with a determined and well organised Communist Party which rightly or wrongly considers itself strong enough to have passed to the decisive stage in its struggle for power, i.e. armed uprising. Subject to what the Secretary of State for the Colonies and myself may learn from our visit to Malaya, I cannot but feel we have more to gain than lose by publicly recognising this fact.

I do not think that we should suddenly come out with statements suggesting that we have just discovered from captured documents that we are faced in Malaya, not with sporadic bandit operations, but with a well organised Communist revolt. It is already pretty generally known or assumed that the Malayan situation is in fact a Communist uprising. We might lay ourselves open to sharp criticism if we suggested that we had only just discovered this fact. It seems probable that our proper course would be quietly to redirect our propaganda so that it is based on the true facts of the situation, namely that an armed Communist uprising exists in Malaya and that we are determined to break it. It does not seem to me that such a redirection of our propaganda would involve international complications or would drive the Malayan Chinese towards the Chinese peoples' Government. There seems to be little evidence that either Russia or China is giving much direct assistance to the Malayan uprising. If this is so, the Russians, and the Chinese Communist Government, would only be following precedent. Only a minumum amount of help, except in exceptional conditions, has been given to Communist Parties who have entered into armed struggle in various parts of the world. These parties are usually expected, on the whole, to fend for themselves. Russia has repeatedly shown herself, as in Spain before the war, and in Greece recently, ready to allow the uprising to be broken rather than to involve herself, when she does not feel in a position to do so safely.

216   CAB 21/1681, MAL C(50)23, Appendix   24 May 1950

'Federation plan for the elimination of the communist organisation and armed forces in Malaya' (the Briggs plan): report by COS for Cabinet Malaya Committee

[The Briggs plan, having been approved by the high commissioner, submitted to the BDCC(FE) on 24 May and noted by the COS, was considered by the Cabinet Malaya Committee on 17 July 1950 (see CAB 134/497, MAC C(50)8; also CO 537/5975 and PREM 8/1406/2).]

Outline of the problem

The Malayan Communist Party and the Communist armed forces in Malaya (the so-called "Malayan Races Liberation Army") rely very largely for food, money, information and propaganda on the Min Yuen (literally, "Peoples' Organisation") in the populated areas, particularly where Chinese predominate. These populated areas include towns and villages as well as uncontrolled squatter areas, unsupervised Chinese estates and small holdings, estate labour lines and timber kongsis. To end the Emergency it will therefore be necessary to eliminate both the Min Yuen and the M.R.L.A. The first task is primarily the responsibility of the Civil authorities, the second of the Services, mainly the Army.

2. The Min Yuen is able to exist and function in populated areas mainly because the population as a whole lacks confidence in the ability of the forces of law and order to protect them against gangster Communist extortion and terrorism. In consequence information, which is essential if the Min Yuen and the bandits are to be eliminated, is quite inadequate. This difficulty is enhanced by the use of the "cell" system in the Communist Party whereby members have little idea of the personalities or activities of corresponding cells.

3. In the long run security, and with it confidence and information, can only be restored and maintained:

(a) by demonstrating Britain's firm intention fulfil her obligations in defence of Malaya against both external attack and internal disorder;

(b) by extending effective administration and control of all populated areas which involves

(i) A large measure of squatter resettlement into compact groups,
(ii) A strengthening of the local administration,
(iii) Provision of road communication in isolated populated areas,
(iv) Setting up of Police Posts in these areas;

(c) by exploiting these measures with good propaganda, both constructive and destructive.

Outline plan

4. Broadly, the intention is to clear the country step by step, from South to North, by:—

(a) dominating the populated areas and building up a feeling of complete security in them, with the object of obtaining a steady and increasing flow of information from all sources;

(b) breaking up the Min Yuen within the populated areas;

(c) thereby isolating the bandits from their food and information supply organisation in the populated areas;

(d) and finally destroying the bandits by forcing them to attack us on our own ground.

Framework

5. To achieve these objects it is planned that in all States:—

(a) the Police Force will concentrate on fulfilling normal Police functions including the obtaining of intelligence through its Special Branch organisation in all populated areas;

(b) the Army will maintain in States in turn a framework of troops, deployed in close conjunction with the Police, to cover those populated areas which the Police cannot themselves adequately cover. This will entail the setting up of a series of strong points whereon patrols will be based;

(c) the administration will strengthen to the utmost extent possible their effective control of the populated areas by increasing, duplicating or trebling as necessary, the number of District Officers and other executive officers "in the field" to ensure that all populated areas are effectively administered; by making access roads to isolated populated areas where necessary; by establishing police posts in all populated areas brought under control; and by stepping up to the maximum extent possible within the limits of the manpower available in all areas where they are needed, the provision of the normal social services that go with effective administration, e.g. schools, medical and other services.

Striking forces

6. On this framework the Army will superimpose striking forces in each State in turn whose task will be to dominate the jungle up to about five hours journey from potential bandit supply areas. These forces will establish headquarters in populated areas, and will dominate the tracks on which the bandits rely to make contact with their information and supply organisation, thus forcing the bandits either to flight [?fight], disintegrate, or to leave the area. Increased offensive action by the R.A.F. against bandit targets will be taken as and when reasonably reliable information is received.

Maintenance of control

7. It is intended that the Administration and the Police network supported by a reduced number of troops will be strong enough to ensure that when the Army striking forces move on in due course to other States bandits will not be able to re-infiltrate successfully.

Action required by the civil authorities

8. A Federal War Council has been set up under the Chairmanship of the Director of Operations and includes the Chief Secretary, the G.O.C., Malaya, the A.O.C., Malaya, the Commissioner of Police and the Secretary for Defence. The Federal War Council is responsible, under the High Commissioner, for policy and the provision to State War Executive Committees of such resources as they need and are available.

9. In each State and Settlement a War Executive Committee has been set up, composed of the Mentri Besar and the British Adviser (or, in the Settlements, the Resident Commissioner), the Chief Police Officer, and Senior Army Commander. The War Executive Committee will be responsible for executive action in implementing the outline plan given above. Similar lower-level i.e. district committees are also being established.

Provision of additional district officers

10. The number of additional administrative officers required in districts is being

worked out at State level. As many as possible are being found by raiding the less immediately essential Government Services and transferring the officers thus made available. An enquiry as to the prospects of the early recruitment of a further thirty M.C.S. Officers has already been referred to the Colonial Office; and steps are being taken to bring forward next year's cadets to this.

Police

11.   Steps are also being taken by the Federal Government to recruit in the United Kingdom additional officers for Special Branch work from candidates who have had experience in the Indian Police, other Police Forces or in the Intelligence Branch of the Services. The total required is between 30 and 40. Police requirements for the expansion of the uniformed branch, including officers, are now being worked out. An Adviser on Special Branch work has been selected and will arrive in June.

Police wireless communications

12.   At present large numbers of Police Stations and Posts are dependent on telephone communication which can easily be cut; and many posts are without communications at all. It is intended to equip all Police posts with wireless transmitters and receivers as soon as possible. So far as equipment is concerned, an expert from the United Kingdom is now in the Federation going into the question and he is both improving the performance of the existing equipment and advising on the type of new equipment required. The manufacture of some of the necessary additional equipment has already begun in the United Kingdom and firm orders will be placed soon. An approach has also been made for assistance from the United States of America. Plans for the further enlargement of the organisation for training wireless operators and the practicability of providing instructors from local resources are under examination.

Road making

13.   The task of making access roads to isolated populated areas is a very big one and it will only be possible to carry it out if a large quantity of expensive mechanical road-making equipment, with its necessary maintenance backing, can be obtained. Details of the requirements have been furnished to London, the U.S. "Griffin" Mission[1] and the Sydney Conference.[2]

Squatter resettlement

14.   To bring all populated areas under effective administrative control will entail regrouping or resettling a large number of squatter communities, together with certain estate and mine labour lines. This is a major problem which will require considerable manpower and financial resources and the allocation of suitable land. It is hoped to find these resources from within the Federation and the land problem has already been resolved partly by the Legislative Council's approval of a White Paper on the squatter problem, and the provision by State and Settlement Governments of the necessary land. The provision of the necessary finance will necessitate the curtail-

---

[1] US aid survey mission to S E Asia appointed in Mar 1950 and led by R Allen Griffin.

[2] On economic development in S and S E Asia, May 1950, see 211 and 225, note 4.

ment of all normal Government expenditure and, in order to avoid the postponement of essential development schemes and social services, continued financial assistance will be required from the United Kingdom. If present plans are realised the essential resettlement programme necessary for security throughout the country will have been completed by the beginning of 1952.

Repatriation

15. There are at the present moment about 10,500 detainees and dependants awaiting repatriation. This number is increasing at the rate of about 350 a month. It may therefore be necessary to repatriate above 15,000 persons over the next two years and it is urgently necessary to start repatriation *now*. Not only will repatriation solve the present detention problem, but the raising of morale which will follow it cannot be overestimated. This is recognised locally as a problem of the very highest importance but its solution does not lie in the hands of the Federation Government.

Propaganda

16. A propaganda expert has been appointed to the Federal Government to co-ordinate the action of representatives in each State and Settlement in accordance with policy laid down by the Federal War Council under the general framework of Government policy. For day to day purposes these representatives will work under the guidance of State War Executive Committees.

Legal Action

17. Emergency Regulations are going to be passed by the Federal Government making the death penalty mandatory for convicted bandit food agents and money collectors with effect from 1st June. Existing Emergency Regulations can be revised and new regulations passed from time to time in the light of requirements. The great mass of people is prepared to accept almost anything directed to the early conclusion of the Emergency.

Finance

18. State Governments have now agreed to curtail normal expenditure and to make available the savings so obtained in State War Executive Committees for expenditure in connection with the Emergency. The Federal Finance Committee has also agreed to pass without delay requests for additional financial assistance for Emergency purposes put up in outline, but sufficient, form by the State War Executive Committees. Lump sums have already been voted to the State War Executive Committees of the more important States to enable them to proceed with certain types of Emergency work without prior approval.

Time table

19. The redeployment of troops is to be completed by 1st June, 1950, on which date operations of the Army striking forces will start in Johore. The redeployment of the administration and Police will be completed in Johore by this date and will follow in other States.

20. It is not expected that substantial results will accrue from these operations for the first two months. After that however, it is expected that the increased security

given to the population will result in an increasing flow of information which should lead to more effective action by the Security Forces.

21.   Intensive operations in Negri Sembilan will start on 1st August. Johore should be cleared by 1st November, after which the Army striking forces will move on to Pahang and Selangor simultaneously. It is hoped, though this may be optimistic, that South Pahang and Selangor will be cleared by 1st April, 1951.

22.   It is not practicable at this stage to forecast dates by which the remaining States and Settlements will be cleared. Much will depend on the progress that has been made in reinforcing the Police and administration, in repatriation or removal of detainees, in obtaining the assistance asked for to strengthen education services, in reaching political agreement on communal differences, and on the availability of mechanical equipment for road making.

Extent of the army commitment during the build-up of civil resources

23.   It will continue to be necessary to maintain a strong framework of troops in areas that have been successfully cleared by the striking forces to ensure that bandit activity does not recur before the civil administration and Police have completed their expansion and brought all populated areas under effective administrative control.

24.   It will be necessary to continue to maintain an Army striking force until the Malayan Communist Party organisation throughout the country has been completely broken. It is considered that this striking force, even in the later stages, can never be less than one brigade.

25.   Army forces available might be reduced as the programme for clearing Malaya State by State from South to North progresses. If all goes well it might be possible to consider some reduction of troops, without affecting the attainment of the aim, during 1951 and the possibility of a further reduction by 1952.

26.   The formation of a police para-military force is under immediate discussion with a view to assisting in the withdrawal of military forces as soon as possible after each State is cleared of bandits. This withdrawal must be gradual to conform with the provision of officers and N.C.Os and the training of the para-military units.

Other factors

27.   It will be appreciated that the elimination of the M.R.L.A. and the breaking up of the Malayan Communist Party are not solely dependent on the measures considered in this paper. External factors, including events in China and neighbouring States which may have political and economic repercussions in Malaya will have a considerable, even a determining, influence on the progress of the Emergency.

28.   Even if complete success is outwardly achieved, it must be recognised that for a very considerable time, particularly if any outside assistance even on a minor scale was forthcoming, there could be a rapid recrudescence of terrorist activity, (cf. the rapid build up of the resistance movement in 1942 at the height of Japanese occupational strength). For this reason the danger of relaxing security precautions and of prematurely withdrawing troops must be realised.

217 CO 537/6026, no 19   31 May 1950
[Member system]: outward telegram no 562 from Sir T Lloyd to Sir H Gurney commenting on the high commissioner's despatch

Following personal for Gurney from Lloyd. *Begins.*

I have just seen for the first time your secret despatch No. 6 of the 9th of April[1] about the introduction of a Membership system. As you may be discussing this with the Secretary of State, who was briefed on the subject before he left,[2] I am sending you at once my personal views. They are personal in that it has not (repeat not) been possible to consult any Minister as neither is available today.

2. I note from paragraph 4 of memorandum accompanying your despatch that your proposals do not (repeat not) involve any amendment of the Federal Constitution. Your intention therefore is to make headway, as has been done in Kenya and Northern Rhodesia, by developing a Membership system outside the Constitution in contrast to the arrangements made, or shortly to be made, in certain West Indian and West African territories where the Constitution already provides, or will soon be amended to provide, for a system of Ministers or Members. I see no objection to your proceeding outside the Federal Constitution, but since your intention is to progress as rapidly as may be possible to a system of elections to the Federal Legislative Council, it may be important to keep in mind even now the arrangements which will eventually have to be made in such matters as the method of appointment of unofficial Members and the arrangements for requiring them to resign in certain circumstances. Eventually the selection of unofficial Members ought to be made after consultation with (if not *in* consultation with) the Legislature or with leading political personages who are members of the Legislature, and although you wish at present to retain the power of appointment in your own hands you may think it well to start working towards the future by consulting whomsoever you think most suitable before you exercise that power. Similarly, although the time has not (repeat not) yet come to provide (as is done in some constitutions) that an unofficial Member must resign if a vote of no confidence in him is passed by say two-thirds of the total membership of the Legislature, you may wish to make it clear to all unofficials apptd [sic] as Members that you will expect them to resign if at any time you are satisfied that they no longer have the confidence of the Federal Legislative Council.

3. I think it is important that (as stated in paragraph 11 of memorandum enclosed in your despatch) all Executive Councillors should be members of Legislative Council and so be answerable there for the administration of Departments within their charge. That is the position even in Kenya and Northern Rhodesia. Would it not be possible (see paragraph 8 of your despatch) for Secretary for Chinese Affairs and Adviser on Malay States Affairs to be added to the Legislative Council so long as you require them temporarily on the Executive Council?

4. There is precedent in Kenya (as you will know) and in Northern Rhodesia for arrangement whereby Executive Council continues to include some persons who are not Members, and I see no objection to similar arrangement in the Federation though, as you implied in paragraph 10 of your memorandum, the desirable ultimate

---

[1] See 212.   [2] Griffiths visited Malaya with John Strachey in June, see 218 and 219.

aim is that the Executive Council should be composed entirely of persons with responsibility for Departments.

5. I have two comments on the distribution of responsibility among Members. Elsewhere (even in territories with the most advanced Constitutions) the charge of security is left to the Chief or Colonial Secretary. It might be awkward to have to take that responsibility away from the Member for Home Affairs if and when an unofficial was appointed to that Membership, and it might be better therefore to reallocate it now to the Chief Secretary or to some other Member (e.g. the one for Defence) who would almost certainly continue to be an official at a much later stage of constitutional development. My second comment is that for somewhat similar reasons responsibility for Justice might be left with the Member for Law and Order (i.e. the Attorney General), as is the case elsewhere.

6. I feel that (see paragraph 4 of your despatch) it is undesirable that the ratio of Malay to Asian non-Malay Members should come to be in any way regarded as sacrosanct. I realise the importance of starting on the understanding you mentioned, but would it not be possible to persuade the Malays to agree that this is temporary and subject to revision in the light of developments?

7. As stated in the brief given to the Secretary of State we feel it important that one of the unofficials appointed Members at the outset of the new arrangement should be a Chinese. If, as you fear, it proves impossible to find a suitable Chinese Member who is willing to take this on we hope that when announcing the introduction of the new system you would feel able to make a statement placing the onus for that situation upon the Chinese community themselves.

8. Your despatch is still being studied in the light of recent developments of Membership systems, or other similar arrangements, elsewhere and if we have any further comments I hope to be able to send these to you before the end of this week. *Ends.*

218 CO 537/5961, no 25   7 June 1950
[Constitutional development]: item 1 of minutes of fifteenth commissioner-general's conference at Bukit Serene attended by Mr Griffiths

(a) *Tempo of transition to self-government*
The Commissioner General reviewed the developments and stated that hitherto they had been working on the assumption that the strict merits of the case, and the best interests of the peoples of Malaya, required a transition period of a generation, say, 25 years, before the peoples of Malaya would be ready for complete self-government. This assumption, he said, was until recently generally accepted by all responsible Asian leaders. In London at the end of 1948, Dato Onn had said that he thought a period of about twenty-five years would be necessary. To Malayan Chinese and Indian leaders, and the more conservative Malays, this conception had been wholly acceptable. Dato Onn had, however, recently revised his views, and now spoke of a term of about fifteen years. The Dato thought that the process must be speeded up, and there is now a tendency among all responsible Asian leaders to accept the view that the transition to self-government will have to be accelerated.

2. *The Commissioner General* went on to say that in his opinion the process of development towards self-government will inevitably be accelerated by factors over which we shall have little or no control. These factors are:—

(i)   Within the next five or ten years a new generation of Malayan leaders will be coming to the fore, whose influence will be in favour of quickening the pace. He was thinking of students now in the United Kingdom, Australia and the University of Malaya. Many of them will come into politics and the administration and will want to move at a faster pace towards self-government than the present more conservative leaders have been contemplating. These new leaders will have the support of the politically conscious. Though large sections of the masses will not support them, as they are not interested in politics, they will not raise any opposition and the influence of the new generation of leaders in political circles five years hence is bound to be a factor favouring the acceleration of the pace towards self-government.

(ii)   The climate of opinion outside Malaya is likely to influence the pace of transition. Malaya, (with British Borneo) and Indo China are the only non-self-governing territories in South East Asia, and Indo China is likely to move towards complete self-government in the next two years. Malaya will then be left alone as a dependent territory, and the pressure of Asian opinion and also world opinion as expressed through U.N.O. will be irresistible upon Asian leaders in Malaya. If agitation in the direction of self-government is started, whatever the merits of the case may be, we shall have to agree, in conformity with local opinion, to a speeding up of the transition, extending the period as long as we wisely can to ensure the peoples are as fit as possible for the change. We must be mentally prepared, therefore, to accept a quickening of the pace, and if we were to resist the pace of change we should lose the present support of Asian leaders. It is vitally important that we should keep in step with them on this matter. We should not however, commit ourselves to a definite period of time.

(iii)   When the Emergency is ended it will be of vital importance to retain the support of the politically conscious people; if we lose that we should have them, and world opinion, against us. The secret of success is in pursuing a policy that always carries the agreement of the local Asian leaders, exercising our influence to slacken the pace, so that they may have time to fit themselves for their responsibilities, but accommodating ourselves to the requirements of the situa-tion. We must be in harmony with Asian leaders so that there is no discernable [sic] difference in views on which world opinion can take sides against us.

3. *The High Commissioner* thought the Commissioner General's analysis was correct, and emphasised the importance of keeping in step with Asian opinion in this matter. He thought it important that we should not set a time limit in which to satisfy the demands for self-government. It would be a great mistake to do so politically despite the apparent advantages. If Asian leaders spoke of a certain period, well and good, but it would be politically impossible for us to do so. He said he was not clear what self-government in Singapore meant. In the case of the Federation the State Governments rule themselves. The policy is to link up the Federation and Singapore, and if that is to be done what form will self-government take in Singapore? If we conceived of Singapore developing separately from the Federation as a strategic outpost of the Commonwealth like Malta there was a danger of handing

it over to the control of the Chinese. At what stage of development should we aim at the fusion of the two territories? His view was that it would have to come at a comparatively late stage, and they had still a long way to go in the Federation before public opinion would be ready to demand a constitutional link with Singapore. It was important to prevent the gap from widening between Singapore and the Federation.

4. *The Governor of Singapore* said that it was important to know whether we should encourage the transition towards self-government, or try to put a brake on the pace. It is much easier to retard development at an early stage. At a later stage when elected members have executive responsibilities it would be a much more difficult matter to do so. Should it be decided that the ultimate aim was the fusion of the two territories it would be possible to plan both administrative needs and political progress accordingly. The possibility of linking the two territories will be much easier if the Federation carries out a policy of decentralisation, Singapore could then fit into the structure as a City State, with complete control over its local affairs, its defence and external affairs being controlled by a central authority. It would be helpful if decentralisation on those lines could therefore proceed in the Federation.

5. *The Governor of Singapore* explained that political advance in Singapore was proceeding differently from that in the Federation. In Singapore they were concentrating on consolidating the electorate so that the elected leaders would have the full support of the people, and could later take up executive responsibility with the people's support. The governor understood that the Federation felt it necessary that executive responsibility should devolve on its leaders at an early stage rather than wait for members to become responsible to their electorate, because the advance to self-government through elections would come too slowly to satisfy the aspirations of their political leaders.

6. *The Commissioner General* thought it a great mistake to contemplate Singapore developing separately from the Federation. It is predominantly a Chinese city and might choose to dispose of itself in the international scene according to the wishes to [of] the Chinese majority, and might even become a satellite of China. To his mind this was unthinkable. Singapore was vital to the Federation both economically and strategically. Clearly the aim must be to bring Singapore into closer association with the Federation on a mutually satisfactory basis, so that Singapore could not be disposed of by its Chinese majority without the agreement of the Federation. A loose Federation of Malaya and Borneo would add a counter-poise to the Chinese element. He agreed with the views of the High Commissioner and Governor that Singapore must develop in union with the Federation.

7. *The Governor of Singapore* said that Singapore could not in fact exist independently. If it attempted so to exist it would fall under the influence of China, India or Indonesia and therefore the sooner they could move towards fusion with the Federation the better.

8. *The Secretary of State* said that this analysis had been very clear and helpful and corresponded with his own impressions during his tour. The old assumption that 25 years would be necessary before self-government could come was based on an estimate of the time needed to train the local peoples to the extent compatible with the responsibilities of self-government. This was a sound assumption if we were living in a normal peaceful world, but with conditions as they are today and especially in view of the control of China by the Communists, the tempo would have

to be increased. It would be unrealistic, unsafe and perhaps disastrous to work on the basis that 25 years was still available to us to accomplish the transition to self-government. He stated that two separate groups of people had asked that the terms of the Prime Minister's statement[1] about British intentions in Malaya should be made more specific. There were, firstly, Europeans and Chinese who thought we ought to say that we do not propose to leave Malaya under 25 years. He suspected that their reason was that they realised the demand for self-government was growing and that it would have to be satisfied before 25 years and they wished to prevent this by a declaration. The other group who pressed for a statement of this kind were students, although they wished for something more precise for very different reasons. They thought that a time limit of 10/15 years should be set to enable the steps towards self-government to be planned. The Secretary of State thought it likely that the young intelligentsia, many of them perhaps natural orators, might well play a bigger part than we anticipated in the political developments of the next ten years. He thought it dangerous to adhere to the old assumption and that we would be wise to accept the conclusion that the period for transition is likely to be a shorter, rather than a longer one.

9. *The Secretary of State* said that the crucial stage would come when the Emergency was ended. The Trades Unions in the Federation, especially, had made it clear that they were looking for advances when the Emergency was over and he thought we must be ready then to make very substantial advances in the political, economic and social standards of the people. The Trades Unions particularly look for advance in economic and social security, and he hoped that it would be possible for plans to be ready in the not too-distant future which would give a real indication of what is to come when the Emergency is over. He agreed that it was very important to keep in touch with Asian leadership, with students and Trades Union leaders. His impression was that the Trades Unions at present support the Government enthusiastically in the Emergency. The alternative to the present leadership is a more leftist one or worse. Self-government had a definite meaning for the Trade Unions in the way of better wages, and improved standard of living, increased opportunities and above all a promise of social security.

10. The second matter of importance to the Trades Unions was their request for an adviser from the U.K. Trade Unions to give them further guidance. They had asked for Mr. F. Dalley[2] whom they would like out here for several months. They also wanted facilities for adult education and he hoped it would be possible to help them by providing such facilities, and showing them that we were anxious to meet their needs. There had been a great advance in the lot of the masses at the end of the two world wars and he felt that the peoples of Malaya would look for a similar advance at the end of the Emergency. We must be ready with plans to meet their aspirations.

11. *The Secretary of State* said that he was more concerned about Singapore than the Federation. In the Federation, the people had roots; and although racial differences were more apparent on the surface in the Federation than Singapore, Singapore had a large and growing rootless proletariat. He wondered how great was the influence of the present political leaders with the masses in Singapore. If a crisis

---

[1] On 28 Mar reiterating his pledge of 13 Apr 1949, see 185, note 2 and 227, note 2.
[2] See 153, para 10 and note 2.

developed in our affairs with China, he thought it unlikely that the present leaders would have the support of the masses (as against the pull of Chinese nationalism.) The *Governor of Singapore* agreed with this view. The *Secretary of State* also thought Singapore Trade Unions needed more help than those in the Federation: they needed a central council, and if there was any dissension among them we should help to resolve it. There were also vital defence considerations in Singapore, and he agreed the Colony could not be left to independence on its own but he was doubtful when the fusion would become possible. Meantime, he wondered whether it would be possible to satisfy the political ambitions of Singapore through increasing the measure of self-government in the Municipality. Speaking with the Municipal Commissioners, who seemed to him to be a better cross-section of the peoples of Singapore than the Legislative Counsellors, the Commissioners had expressed their desire to achieve complete municipal self-government, and, the granting of city status to the municipality. He appreciated that it would be impossible to grant a charter until the City had a complete self-government with an elected Mayor, but he wondered if political aspirations in Singapore would be satisfied by the grant of self-government on the municipal level. The dominant thought in his mind was to be ready after the emergency so that we could give the people tangible evidence that we had a better alternative to offer.

12. The *Commissioner General* agreed as to the importance of maintaining the closest contact with students. The present University students were moderate and wise. With regard to the demand for adult education he stated that the Peoples Education Association was already doing excellent work in Singapore and would shortly be starting work in the Federation. Perhaps assistance might be forthcoming from the U.K. to help the P.E.A. to spread its influence. The *Commissioner General* said that he did not think that the grant of full self-government to the Municipality would satisfy the ambitions of the politically conscious people in Singapore. If they thought we were playing down the development of self-government in the Colony Councils by offering limited self-government to the Municipality it would certainly create an unfavourable reaction. A solution for political advance must be found in associating Singapore with the Federation in the advance towards self-government.

13. *The Governor of Singapore* stated that he was investigating the possibility of an Advisory Commission being sent out from the U.K. to advise on municipal development and the relationship between the Municipality and the Rural Board. It was likely that the Municipal Commissioners would pass a resolution asking for such a commission. Data, he said, was already being collected for a social security scheme in the Colony. The work of the P.E.A. was of the greatest value to the labouring classes as it provided an avenue of self-advancement which made a great appeal to them.

14. After further discussion on the need for a Trade Union Council in Singapore and the difficulties in the way, it was considered that if Mr. Dalley could be persuaded to come out he would be able to help in resolving the present difficulties and assist in the establishment of a Trades Union Council.

15. *The Commissioner General* said that political advance must be worked out between the Government and Asian leaders to enable them to agree on a common policy, and he suggested that he, the High Commissioner and the Governor might meet informally with four or five Asian leaders from the Federation and Singapore in an endeavour to reach agreement on the lines of political development which could

then be put before the Councils and public opinion. No one would be committed and an informal body such as proposed would stimulate thought and discussion, and lead to eventual action towards self-government. It would include a European and leaders of all communities, and would meet quite informally.

16. *The High Commissioner* said whatever solution was agreed upon for the fusion of the Federation and Singapore they had a very long way to go in the Federation before they would be ready for it. He was agreeable to and favoured the setting up of a very informal and flexible "study group". The *Commissioner General* said that it might be premature to try to bring the leaders of the Federation and Singapore together at once and suggested they might meet separately at first. He confirmed that the C.L.C. would continue, but he thought that it would not be an altogether appropriate body to handle political developments concerning the relations between the Federation and Singapore. The *Governor of Singapore* agreed that it was necessary to try and bring the leaders of the Federation and Singapore together. The discussion by Singapore leaders of the "member system" had made them realise the necessity for both territories keeping in step.

The *Commissioner General*, the *High Commissioner* and the *Governor* agreed to meet at an early date to have further talks on the possible functions of the C.L.C. in regard to the political issues reviewed today.

(b) *Communities Liaison Committee—proposals for citizenship*

17. The *Commissioner General* said he had been a little concerned at the way Malay opinion was moving in regard to acceptance of the C.L.C. proposals. However, he had recently seen Dato Onn, who said that he thought U.M.N.O. would accept the proposals in the modified form recommended by U.M.N.O.

18. The *High Commissioner* said that the Malays were showing displeasure at the treatment being given to squatters, and the Malay Press did not even publicise the Government's proposals to aid the Malays. He said it would do no good to bring pressure upon the Malays to accept the proposals; indeed this would have the opposite effect to that which we desired. He thought that U.M.N.O. would accept the modified proposals. He proposed as a next step that a Bill amending the Federation agreement and incorporating the modifications of the Malays should be introduced into the Legislative Council, and submitted to examination by a Select Committee with a strong Chinese representation. The *High Commissioner* said that he thought that the Chinese would accept the language test although, of course, they would protest. They were anxious, however, to secure Malay good-will, which was worth a lot to them. The M.C.A. suggestion for a Royal Commission was quite a recent one, to which he, the High Commissioner, was opposed. If they could not agree among themselves a Royal Commission would be unlikely to achieve success. Past experience had shown that one of the parties to a dispute of this nature always refused the recommendations of a Royal Commission. He thought that a middle way between the opposing viewpoints of the Malays and Chinese might develop in the Select Committee. The *Secretary of State* expressed the view that the appointment of the Royal Commission was not called for on this problem.

(c) *Introduction of the "Member" system;* (d) *Increase in number of elected members of Singapore Legislative Council*

19. *The High Commissioner* said that he was not anxious to rush the introduc-

tion of the "Member" system, but he had difficulty in understanding why Singapore should be embarrassed by its introduction in the Federation.

20. *The Governor of Singapore* said that European leaders in the Colony disliked the idea because it was an indication that we were accelerating the pace towards self-government. The Chinese members did not want the system. What they would like would be to see the unofficial element in the Executive Council enlarged by election from the Legislative Council of two of its members. He thought if this advance was introduced into Singapore at the same time as the "Member" System was introduced in the Federation, and the changes were carefully explained, then no demand would arise in Singapore for the "Member" System to be adopted there. It was important, however, that the two advances should take place simultaneously. If the changes in the Executive [and] Legislative Councils in Singapore were to take place before the introduction of the Member Systems in the Federation, then, when the latter system was introduced, the demand for a comparable constitutional advance in Singapore might arise. The Governor thought, however, that if the two were introduced simultaneously, Singapore would be satisfied for a period of four or five years to continue without the Member System. The *High Commissioner* agreed that the announcements of both advances should be simultaneous.

21. The Secretary of State agreed that there did not appear to be any demand in Singapore now for the introduction of the Member System, but he thought they might well ask for it later on when they saw it working in the Federation.

22. Sir Hilton Poynton stated that the Member System was most useful in developing responsibility among Legislative Council members. Under the Colonial system, when difficult local problems came up for decision, the Legislative Council members knew that finally the decision would have to be taken by the Governor and the Colonial Office, and they could sit back and avoid responsibility for taking a decision, and criticise the decisions of others. He thought it a great mistake for a territory to jump from Colonial system straight to self-government with no interim period for the development of responsibility among Legislative Council members. In his view a system which provided training in responsibility had an essential place. Ceylon had had a Member System for a long time before moving to self-government.

23. *The Governor of Singapore* said that he hoped that it would be possible to increase the elected members in the legislative Council to nine at the same time as the change was made in the composition of the Executive Council, and that both changes could be introduced before the elections next March. It was agreed that the announcement of the developments in each territory should be simultaneous, although the actual introduction of the "Member" System could come later in the Federation, if necessary.

24. *The High Commissioner* then mentioned his intention to allot six nominated seats for election by U.M.N.O. in order to give younger Malays an opportunity to be represented in the Legislative Council. He thought that the Rulers were likely to agree to this proposal which would be valuable in providing political education for younger Malays. The great objection was, of course, that it was communal politics, but it was purely a temporary expedient until elections could take place, and this aspect would be stressed in making the announcement. He said it was different to allot seats on a similar basis to the M.C.A., as agreement on the basis of the Federal Citizenship had not yet been reached, but if the M.C.A. wished it, he would see no objection to their being allowed to elect the two corresponding Chinese members.

25. *The Governor of Singapore* said it was very necessary to stress the temporary character of this proposal, as in Singapore the political leaders were strongly opposed to communal representation. He said that the announcement of the change in the Executive Council would be of very great value politically if it were made at the same time as the announcement of the increase in the number of elected members to the Legislative Council. There had been no public demand for a change in the Executive Council and the announcement would be received extremely well, and would be evidence of the sincerity of our desire to help in the advance towards self-government.

26. *The Secretary of State* said that on his return to London he would give a decision urgently on both the Singapore and the Federation proposals so that an announcement could be made simultaneously.

(e) *Closer association between the Federation and Singapore*

27. *The Commissioner General* was of the opinion that things seemed to be going more smoothly between the Federation and Singapore. It was essential to be clear in mind as to the form and nature of the eventual association, so that in the meantime political and other advances could be planned on suitable lines in the Federation and Singapore. Hitherto the problem of the Emergency and Federal Citizenship had taken precedence over that of bringing the two territories together. He considered that the time had now come for the first approaches in this direction to be made on a personal and informal basis with those whose opinions counted.

28. *The Governor of Singapore* said that at all costs we must not allow ourselves to be driven into the position where we have to say "we cannot grant you self-government because you are not yet united as one territory". He was in favour of talks between the Commissioner General and himself with unofficials to discuss what unofficials understood by self-government and how they would propose to bring Singapore and the Federation together in one constitution. The *Commissioner General* said that it should be made clear that nothing would be done without the agreement of the Federation. What was intended was not fusion of two separate entities, but rather a Federation for purposes of common defence, etc.

29. *The High Commissioner* said that in the Federation they were so preoccupied that they could not take the initiative in this matter for some time, but he could see every advantage if Singapore could say what form they think fusion with the Federation should take. The *Governor of Singapore* said that Singapore leaders were frightened of being rebuffed if they stated their views. He thought that discussions should start unofficially in Singapore and that those might eventually influence unofficial opinion in the Federation. He feared that there may be some divergence of opinion on financial matters between the Federation and Singapore. There had never been hitherto a vital difference between the Federation and Singapore that had not ultimately been settled by compromise, but if, now, a divergence arose it might serve more positively to emphasise the necessity for closer fusion. The *Commissioner General* considered that in any discussions in Singapore care must be taken to avoid the suggestion that after the Malays had made concessions to the Chinese in the Federation on Citizenship they were to be asked to make further concessions in favour of Chinese in Singapore.

219   CAB 129/40, CP(50)125   13 June 1950

'Preliminary report on a visit to Malaya and Singapore': Cabinet memorandum by Mr Griffiths

Introduction

1. I propose, with the Secretary of State for War, to circulate as soon as possible for the information of the Cabinet, a general report on our visit to Malaya. We shall also be bringing forward individual matters in detail to the Malaya Committee.

2. Meantime, I wish to let my colleagues have this summary of the matters arising out of my visit on which immediate action is required and is being taken.

The emergency

3. The Secretary of State for War and I are completely satisfied with General Brigg's [sic] operational plans.[1] They are based on full co-ordination of the military, police and civil forces. The military forces will clear the peninsula area by area, from south to north: the job of the police and civil administration will be to establish effective control in each area as it is cleared to enable the military forces to move on to the next. Operations under this plan began in Johore on 1st June.

4. No timed programme can be worked out for "operations" of this kind, and it will be a lengthy task. An indication is that General Briggs (i) does not expect to have cleared the two southernmost States of Johore and Negri Sembilan before November of this year, and (ii) he does not contemplate being able to release any troops from Malaya before April 1951 without seriously prejudicing his own campaign.

5. The speed of the plan depends entirely on the capacity of the civil administration to consolidate behind the military operations: and that in turn is mainly a question of personnel. It is vital to the success of the whole campaign that Malaya should receive, *within the next two to three months*, the civil reinforcements needed, particularly for the Police. The Police calculate, with their *present* strength, to be able to implement the Briggs Plan in the State of Johore and partly in Negri Sembilan: *they have no reserves to meet further phases of the Plan.*

Police reinforcements

6. The immediate Police requirements are:—

(i)   117 officers,
(ii) approximately 175 British n.c.os.

The officers needed are *trained* policemen (United Kingdom inspectors or sergeants), of 30–35 years, particularly those with C.I.D. experience. The Federation Government is prepared to offer permanent appointments or contracts. The Colonial Office will seek to recruit from every possible source, but the bulk of these men must come from the United Kingdom Police Forces. I am in touch with the Home Secretary and I hope that there will be no difficulty in meeting this need, which must be regarded as the first priority. The British n.c.os. required will be recruited through the Crown Agents in the ordinary way. The above requirements of officers and n.c.os. will enable the Police Force to meet their obligations under the first half of the Briggs Plan:

---

[1] For the Briggs plan, see 216.

there will be an additional demand for the second half but this will not be large.

7. In addition, General Briggs proposes to build up the Police "jungle squads" into 45 companies, which as a military branch of the Police will be able to relieve the military forces of internal security duties as the campaign progresses. He is not asking United Kingdom help on this, but has sought assistance from the Service Chiefs in the Far East in recruiting national servicemen (w.os. and n.c.os.), about to take their discharge, for service on contract with the Malayan Police as Police Lieutenants (platoon leaders) in the "jungle companies."

8. It is most desirable, particularly in view of the large reinforcements from outside, to increase the number of Asian officers in the Federal Police Force. For this purpose, a local police officer training college is needed. The Federation Government are preparing plans for this college as quickly as possible: the Commandant of the College and the Chief Instructor will have to be recruited from the United Kingdom and I shall seek the assistance of the Home Secretary as soon as firm proposals reach me from Malaya.

9. The Federation Government have agreed in principle that a regular police force of about 40,000 men must be maintained after the emergency.

Administrative reinforcements

10. The High Commissioner has asked that 25 administrative cadets allotted to Malaya this year should be sent out immediately without taking the usual year's training course. This is being arranged. About 15 of these officers were intended to be Chinese-speaking officers and they will be given a three months' intensive course in Cantonese before sailing. I am convinced of the need, both as part of the Briggs plan and for the future, for closer administrative coverage of the country at the "district officer" level, both in Chinese and Malayan areas. Future requirements are being reviewed on this basis; already, in addition to the 25 officers mentioned above, 30 others have been asked for by Malaya as immediate appointments.

Repatriation of Chinese detainees

11. I found all concerned in Malaya agreed, and I am convinced myself, that renewal of the repatriation of Chinese detainees to China is an *essential prerequisite* to the success of General Briggs's plan. The presence of detainees in ever increasing numbers:—

(i)   constitutes a most serious security risk,
(ii) wastes manpower on guard duties and, above all,
(iii) is a serious brake on information, through the Chinese population's fear of bandits still in the country in detention camps.

12. I discussed with the Commissioner-General, the High Commissioner and the Governor of Singapore, the prospects of resuming this traffic to China, through ordinary commercial channels. A first step might be made early in July, and I propose to take up this point immediately with the Foreign Secretary.

Information and propaganda

13. There is room for improvement in the Information Services in Malaya, although they are by no means ineffective at present. There is need however for better direction of effort against the Communists in both (a) general propaganda

work and (b) direct "psychological warfare" against the bandits. The latter is in its infancy, although a start has now been made by the appointment of a Public Relations Officer to General Briggs's staff and of a "propaganda section" of the C.I.D., which works in close co-operation with him.

14. I propose

(a) to investigate immediately the possibility of securing an anti-Communist propaganda expert for Malaya, whose appointment would be welcomed by the Federation Government;

(b) to see what additional financial assistance can be given to the Malayan Film Unit, since all concerned locally agree that films are the most effective medium;

(c) to pursue with the B.B.C. a suggestion that they post a permanent representative in Malaya, with a view to correcting the misleading impressions of the situation in Malaya sometimes given to the world by foreign correspondents who seldom move from Singapore.

15. There is little doubt that the most effective line of anti-Communist propaganda among the Chinese in Malaya is to play up the bad conditions of their relatives in China under the Communist régime. A certain amount of news of this kind is filtering through privately and is having a great effect: but it cannot be used in official propaganda in view of the present directive under which the local Information Officers work. I propose to re-examine this problem.

Financial and economic

16. I found among all concerned in Malaya, from the High Commissioner downwards, a keen appreciation of the need for developing the resources of the country and improving the standard of living, as a long-term counter to Communism. Despite the emergency, the Federation Government is being imaginative and farsighted. A draft development plan has been prepared for consideration by the Councils of the States and Settlements, and it is hoped will have reached the stage of approval by the central Legislative Council in July. A major feature of this plan is a scheme for the establishment of a Rural Development Authority which, though not exclusively for the Malay section of the community, is aimed at developing the economic potential of the rural areas which are predominantly Malay.

17. I am convinced that, if these plans are not to be jeopardised (and it is to my mind essential that we should be ready to put them into operation as soon as the emergency is ended, if not earlier), the Federation must have additional financial assistance from the United Kingdom. The £3 million contribution for 1950 from the Exchequer towards the cost of the emergency was based on an estimate made in August 1949 that the emergency might end during 1950, and is clearly inadequate. The Federation is in fact rapidly running into a serious financial crisis. I have discussed the whole question with the High Commissioner who will be putting the financial situation in detail before me by despatch very shortly; he thoroughly appreciates the need for counterbalancing any increased contribution from His Majesty's Government by the maximum possible increase in local taxation. It will be necessary to clear the Federation's request very quickly when the High Commissioner's despatch is received and, if the principle of further help is then accepted, I shall probably have to ask for a supplementary estimate during the present session of the House.

220 CAB 21/1681, MAL C(50)21   17 June 1950

'The military situation in Malaya': memorandum by Mr Strachey for Cabinet Malaya Committee

This paper is based upon an oral report on the military situation in Malaya which I gave to an informal meeting of the Army Council on 15th June. My colleagues will notice that the paper bears traces of this origin in its somewhat coloquial [sic] form. I hope that they will forgive this, but it was difficult to write an entirely fresh paper in the time available. So I thought they might prefer at this stage to have a paper which at least raised the main issues. They may wish me to prepare a more formal paper, with recommendations, in the light of discussions at this and future meetings of the Malayan Committee.

1. Military forces available

The responsible officers in Malaya, Generals Harding, Briggs and Urquhart,[1] take the view that the numbers of troops at their disposal, with the reinforcements now coming in, are adequate to deal with the situation as it is to-day. That situation might change but to carry on their present operations they have adequate numbers.

2. Weapons and equipment

The Command is a well found one, on the whole, in equipment and weapons. No doubt there are individual suggestions which can be made. One is the question of the American carbines. This we were able to clear up. The sanction of His Majesty's Government and of the American Government has now been obtained to the purchase of 1,000 M.2 carbines together with the appropriate scales of ammunition and spares. The provision of these carbines is, I think, in General Harding's opinion, on the whole a psychological point rather than one of prime military importance; but this weapon is superior to the Sten gun and there is a general feeling that it would give an immense psychological advantage if at any rate, a limited number of them were available enough to equip the leading man and perhaps one other in each patrolling section. What I should have thought was, on the whole, of greater real importance was the provision of Scout cars on a considerably greater scale, and that point is being examined.

3. Welfare

On the Welfare side, I have circulatated a sheaf of notes through my Department taking up a couple of dozen points, none of which are of tremendous individual importance, but which are, perhaps, of importance taken together. The outstanding welfare point is the married quarters. There is here a standard of comparison. We can judge how important it is by the different situations in the two theatres. In Malaya and Singapore it is going extremely well. Married officers and men see married quarters going up very rapidly and, although they are not living in them yet, they really think they will be living in them within twelve months. This is very satisfying

---

[1] General Sir John Harding was commander-in-chief, Far East Land Forces, 1949–1951; Lieutenant-General Sir Harold Briggs was director of operations, Malaya, 1950–1951; Major-General R W Urquhart was general officer commanding, Malaya, 1950–1952.

to officers, W.Os. and senior N.C.Os. in Malaya and Singapore. I should say that this is one of the main factors in their undoubtedly good morale. In Hong Kong, for quite understandable reasons, the picture is quite the reverse. Little or no material progress is being made and there is deep feeling about it and deep disappointment. If there is a way of breaking the log jam in Hong Kong and getting an appreciable start made with the married quarters programme it will make a very great difference to that part of the Command. I have circulated three specific suggestions from General Harding to the relevant sections of the War Office and I very much hope we can meet him on each of these points.

In the theatre as a whole there is a shortage of skilled engineer staff, particularly of civilian specialists such as architects, surveyors and draughtsmen. This shortage has been and continues to be a serious cause of delay in construction. I am examining what steps may be taken to recruit more of these civilians locally or from England.

All Commanders and medical authorities to whom I spoke agreed that the health of the Army in Malaya was extremely good, if anything better than that of the troops in the U.K. There is a shortage of general duty medical officers in the theatre which has not so far impaired the efficiency of medical attention but which I feel should be rectified to avoid any risks arising, e.g., from an epidemic. I am examining this point.

I inspected one of the three helicopters which have now arrived in the theatre to help in the evacuation of wounded. It will be some time before these have been fully tested and can be put into operation. They will certainly not enable a man wounded in the jungle to be lifted direct from the scene of action but they may, in many cases, shorten the period which he spends on a stretcher from days to hours.

One point which was brought to my attention everywhere concerned the provision of a suitable walking-out dress for the troops. I am putting before the Defence Committee a Paper asking for approval to go ahead with the issue of No. 1 and No. 3 dress—No. 3 dress being the new walking-out dress for tropical climates. In the meantime, I am examining a proposal to accelerate the provision of olive green suits of good material and workmanship.

4. *Military operations*

I should like under this heading to mention the matter of air strikes against the bandits. I think it is generally agreed that there is little prospect of killing bandits by air bombing on map squares of jungle. It is equally agreed, however, that bombing and, even more, rocket firing, has a profound moral effect on the bandits and can be used to move them from a particular area, in many cases, it is hoped, in a direction where our own patrols are waiting for them.

Under this heading also I should mention that a re-examination is taking place of the Command structure in Malaya to enable it to deal more effectively with the increased number of troops now available in the theatre and to have an adequate tie-up at all levels with the civil administration and police.

Coming to the question of the actual operations, what gives me great concern is a tendency to stalemate. The bandits, on the whole, can do us little *direct* harm—they are inflicting very few casualties. But they are involving us in this enormous commitment; and I do not believe that the Army alone, as such, can finish them off. In order to finish them off we have got to have a large military effort (which we have got), but we have also got to have an equally large police and administrative and political effort.

5. *The Briggs plan*[2]

That is what the Briggs Plan aims at—in that is its great element of hope. General Briggs is always emphasising that we cannot expect any sudden or overnight transformation in the situation. The only possible policy is a highly integrated combined operation. The obvious thing to do is to take one State at a time and get it and keep it permanently dominated. The lines of the Briggs Plan the Committee knows. The Secretary of State for the Colonies is pressing for the very considerably [sic] police and administrative reinforcements which, everyone agrees, are indispensable to the success of the Briggs Plan, and has put a Paper before the Cabinet. That does not concern me as a matter of direct departmental responsibility, but I should like to say a word about it from the point of view of the inter-action between the military and political sides of the emergency.

It seems to me that the (say) 4,000 bandits which the Army faces are, in a sense, not the main issue. I received the impression that at an earlier stage we had been to some extent misled by calling the enemy bandits. The armed forces opposed to us are simply the military arm of the Malayan Communist Party; it is the M.C.P. which is the real threat. There may even have been a certain tactical distortion of the situation because of the way we formulated our task as the clearing up of gangs of bandits. This may have led to a concentration on jungle patrols, etc., which inevitably pay comparatively small dividends for the effort involved, rather than to concentration on our real task. That task is to break the power of the M.C.P. Now the M.C.P. itself is not very vulnerable. It has gone underground; it has the experience behind it of two years of illegal work. I think that General Briggs would say that the vulnerable spot is the link between the M.C.P. and its forces in the jungle. That link is the Min Yuen, which is the commissariat, the logistic side of the Communist effort. It is the essence of the Briggs Plan that he attempts to break the back of the Min Yuen. Having saturated Johore State with military effort, not so much with emphasis on jungle patrolling, as by patrolling the edge of the jungle or squatter areas where bandits have to come out of the jungle in order either to munition and feed themselves or to attack us and do damage—they cannot damage us as long as they stay deep in the jungle—General Briggs proposes to set up a permanent net of police and administrative control. By this means the straggling squatter areas are to be either resettled or, at any rate, given an administration for the first time. The Secretary of State for the Colonies will I know be reporting to the Committee on the whole large and highly complex question of squatter resettlement.

6. *Politico-military aspects of the problem*

Perhaps the Committee will allow me to make a few remarks on the more political aspects of the problem, for these are, in fact, inextricably connected with the military aspects. In so doing, I shall inevitably express views on problems within the sphere of the Secretary of State for the Colonies. But I think I now know his views on most of these matters, and I do not think that the Committee will find that there are any wide differences in our conclusions.

The political essence of the problem is, in my view, the extent and the limits of popular support for the Communists. To take the extreme cases, if they had the full popular support of both the Malay and Chinese populations, our position would be

---

[2] See 216.

untenable. On the other hand, if there was no popular support for them there would be no problem for us. Therefore, what matters is the exact degree of support—and it is quite limited. There is virtually no popular support for the Communists among the Malay population,—we can arm the Malays pretty well indiscriminately. One of the most striking things we saw was the Kampong guards in the Malay areas armed with shot guns. In these areas the population was unquestionably on our side. In the Chinese areas, so I was told, though I did not see it myself, we are able to arm some Chinese in some places. So some of the Chinese population is quite keenly on the Government side. On the other hand, there are some areas, for example, some areas in Pahang, where, as all the soldiers and administrative people see it, the people are frankly on the side of the Communists. In these areas arms would go straight through to the bandits. It is a mixed situation politically and racially. The Malays (and to a large extent the Indians) are about 99% on our side, the Chinese are in some areas perhaps well over 50% on our side and in other areas well over 50% on the Communist side.

That leads us back again to General Briggs' concept of breaking the popular support for the rising; and you can only do that by police and administrative action rather than military action. However, the Army has got a great part to play in that especially, speaking quite frankly, as the police and the civil administration are not always strong. I think the Secretary of State for the Colonies will agree that at present the soldier often has to take the lead in the triumvirate, trying to do the job in each local area—these soldiers are usually brigadiers, sometimes lieut.-colonels. In each area there is the soldier, the local police officer and the District Officer of the Administration; sometimes one has the strong personality and sometimes another; but quite often it is the soldier who really has to push the job along, so that even on the police and administration side the Army is closely concerned.

7. Powers of detention

Here I come to a thing I stressed very strongly in Malaya. I was most reluctant to do it in view of the extremely loose talk which sections of the business community indulge in about "ruthlessness" and "total war" – phrases to which I cannot give any concrete meaning. Nevertheless, I was forced to the conclusion that there was one respect in which the Government was not being stringent enough with the rising. There is, I believe, one weapon partially lacking in the Government armoury: that is the power of preventative arrest, detention and internment. I should have said that power to put suspects into detention for the duration of the emergency was fully justified by the gravity of the situation—after the style of 18B in this country. Now they very nearly have that power. But they have not *effectively* got it, because they have committees of review, which have the power to release any suspect; and these committees do very frequently release suspects when they consider that the police have not got sufficient evidence against them. The knowledge of that possibility makes police action ineffective in some respects in Malaya. For the police, the District Officer and the military Commander in a district will not arrest suspects when they face the risk of these suspects being released in a few weeks by the Committees of review and so returning to the district and intimidating the authorities' informers who are the sole available sources of intelligence. After I left for Hong Kong some settlement was arranged—I don't know exactly its terms. There is quite a lot to be said on the other side. For example, the police are decidedly corrupt, and if you gave them sweeping powers of arrest on suspicion for the period of the emergency, many innocent people will be held. Nevertheless, many local administrators in Malaya consider that such a power would do more than anything else to break the emergency. I am inclined to think it would be worth it. Such police action is not the Army's business directly, but the Army is so concerned in putting an end to the emergency that I felt justified in pressing that view pretty strongly in Malaya.

8. *Character of the civil administration*

The civil administration struck me, and I think the Secretary of State for the Colonies would agree, as a curious one. For example, it was reluctant to use these "18B" powers: in this I thought it was being *too* liberal and weak. On the other hand, politically the Government and the administration seem to me not liberal enough in that they are not nearly active enough in forging ahead with the political development of the country. I formed the view that they were tending to wait until the end of the emergency. Democratic development has been complicated by the business of Chinese citizenship and I feel the Government should press on with that, even at some risk, pretty rapidly. And they should do so even more on the Trades Union side. It is not going badly. But I agree strongly with the view repeatedly expressed by the Secretary of State for the Colonies that the organization of a non-Communist Trades Union movement, which has taken in about 40 or 50,000 people, may in the end prove perhaps the most important single thing to be done. In this connection I arranged for the setting up of Joint Industrial Councils for the Asia civilian employees of the Army in both Malaya and Singapore. I saw their Trades Unions representatives and was well impressed by them.

7. [sic] *General conclusion*

Finally, if I had to sum up, I would feel no desperate concern about Malaya taken in isolation. In the long run we can suppress the rising and do the job, *if we are let alone to do it.* But we may only have a short time to settle the business in Malaya. If we look at the position in the rest of S.E. Asia, it is far from reassuring. Any further Communist successes there are almost certain to react in Malaya, and, therefore, I do not think, looking at the whole picture, that one can feel the same degree of confidence as by looking at Malaya itself.

We are bound to express in public perfect confidence in the outcome in Malaya—in part such confidence is justified looking at the Malayan situation in isolation. For the effect of any expression of a lack of confidence on the Chinese population would be appalling, especially as so much of it is on the fence. But, in fact, we must do every single thing in our power to influence the position in S.E. Asia as a whole in our favour if we are to be given the necessary conditions of success in Malaya. And in S.E. Asia as a whole the absolute condition of success appears to me to be that each Western nation concerned must come to terms with the genuine local, nationalist movement, even if this means the granting of full independence prematurely. The genuine nationalist movement in Malaya is only just starting: but it is starting, and we must come to terms with it.

221   CAB 128/17, CM 37(50)1   19 June 1950

'Malaya': Cabinet conclusions on reports by Mr Griffiths and Mr
Strachey following their visits to Malaya

1. The Cabinet had before them a memorandum by the Secretary of State for the
Colonies (C.P. (50) 125)[1] summarising the points on which immediate action was
required as a result of the visits which he and the Secretary of State for War had
recently made to Malaya. The Cabinet also had before them drafts of statements
which the two Secretaries of State proposed to make in the House of Commons on
the subject of their visit (C.P (50) 129 and 130).[2]

After opening statements by *the Secretary of State for the Colonies* and *the
Secretary of State for War*, the Cabinet had a general discussion under the following
heads:—

Reinforcement of police and administrative services
The essence of the new plan for dealing with the emergency was that the military
should clear areas successfully and that the civil administration should then move in
to hold the cleared areas and ensure that bandits did not return to them. For this
purpose it was essential that both the police and the administrative services should
be reinforced. The reinforcement of the administrative services was being handled by
the Colonial Office, by accelerating the posting of administrative cadets to Malaya.
For the police, the immediate requirements were: (i) 117 officers, preferably trained
policemen from the United Kingdom, and (ii) about 175 British non-commissioned
officers, who would be recruited through the Crown Agents in the ordinary way. In
addition, it was proposed to increase the police "jungle squads" by recruiting for
service under contract with the Malayan police national servicemen now serving in
Malaya who were about to take their discharge.

Ministers asked why the Malayan authorities expressed this preference for men
with police experience in the United Kingdom, when former members of the Indian
police were likely to be available, some of whom had long experience in dealing with
Asiatics. They were informed that this was due to the disturbance caused in the
Malayan police force some time ago by the introduction of men who had served in
the Palestine police. Existing members of the Malayan police had found that their
prospects of promotion had thereby been prejudiced; and it was thought that the
morale of the force would suffer from a second experiment of this kind. On the other
hand, the Cabinet were informed that it would be difficult to meet all the present
requirements from police forces in this country, especially as it would not be possible
for the Home Secretary to second a member of a provincial police force for a period
of service in Malaya. The urgent need of the Malayan police and the conditions of
service offered would, however, be brought to the attention of chief constables at a
conference over which the Home Secretary would preside. It was unlikely that
suitable recruits would be found from among those who were now being discharged
from police duties in Germany; for many of these men were already labouring under
a sense of grievance because their employment in Germany had been terminated
earlier than they had been led to expect.

---

[1] see 219.   [2] Not printed.

The Secretary of State for War strongly supported these proposals for the reinforcement of the police and the civil administration. The army in Malaya, though their morale was still good, had found it discouraging that areas which they had cleared of bandits had fallen back into disorder for lack of a strong civil administration; and, if the new plan for dealing with the emergency failed to prevent a repetition of this process, there was bound to be a serious deterioration in army morale.

It was the general view of the Cabinet that, while a determined effort should in the first instance be made to find the men required from the United Kingdom police, other sources should not be overlooked and former members of the Indian police service should, in particular, be considered. Too much attention should not be paid to the susceptibilities of the existing members of the Malayan police, since a recent investigation had shown that this force was in urgent need of reorganisation.

Repatriation of Chinese

There were now about 10,000 suspects detained in camps in Malaya and, because of the risk of mass escapes, it was important that large numbers of these detainees should be removed from Malaya as speedily as possible. Before September 1949 Chinese detainees were repatriated to China; but, now that China was under the control of a Communist Government, there were difficulties in continuing this policy and, if it proved impracticable, other alternatives would have to be considered. Deportation to Christmas Island had been suggested as one possibility, but this would have to be discussed with the Australian Government. The Secretary of State for the Colonies was proposing to discuss this problem with the Foreign Secretary.

The Secretary of State for War agreed that it was essential that some means should be found of removing from Malaya a substantial proportion of the suspects now under detention. Care should, however, be taken not to send to China any known members of the Malayan Communist Party, since they were likely to be picked out by the Communist authorities there and sent back after a time to Malaya. There seemed to be strong arguments in present circumstances for giving the authorities in Malaya even more drastic powers of detaining suspects and suspending for a time the operation of the appeal tribunal which had ordered the release of several suspects whom the police and civil authorities would have preferred to keep under continued detention.

Information and propaganda

There was room for improvement in the Information Services in Malaya; and *the Secretary of State for the Colonies* said that he was proposing to investigate immediately the possibility of securing the services of an anti-Communist expert for Malaya. Other detailed proposals for strengthening the Information Services would be discussed with the Malaya Committee.

The Secretary of State for War emphasised the importance of securing someone with a well-trained political mind to take charge of these Information Services. While there was need for the greatest severity in dealing with the current emergency, this should be coupled with an understanding of the nationalist movement in Malaya and a real desire to come to terms with it. It was also important that the person in charge of these Services should have a sympathetic understanding of the contribution which trade unionism could make towards future stability in Malaya.

Financial assistance

The Secretary of State for the Colonies said that the various measures proposed in his memorandum would involve a heavy financial burden, and it was important that Malaya should bear part of the cost. The Colonial Government recognised that they must raise further revenue, and were thinking of doing so by means of an increase in the export duty on rubber and tin. They did not favour an increase in income tax, for they lacked the necessary administrative machinery for collection.

The Chancellor of the Exchequer said that there were grave economic objections to an increase in these export duties, since this would have an adverse effect on the sale of rubber and tin in dollar markets. He would much prefer to see an increase in the rate of income tax, which would be fully justified on merits; and it should be possible to ease the administrative difficulties of collection by bringing Malayan officers over to this country for training in methods of tax-collection. Malayan producers of tin and rubber had been receiving high prices for their products; but they had been required to spend substantial sums in repairing war damage and in meeting the needs of the present emergency. He was therefore prepared to agree in principle that some further Exchequer assistance should be given to Malaya, so long as it was made a condition that the local Government developed effective machinery for direct taxation and undertook to finance, at the appropriate time, measures of economic and social improvement. With this in view he would wish to suggest some amendment of the reference to financial assistance which the Secretary of State for the Colonies was proposing to include in his forthcoming Parliamentary statement on Malaya.

Social reform

The Secretary of State for the Colonies said that a good deal was being done to reorganise the native trade unions on a non-Communist basis, and it was clear that the mass of the workers were opposed to the Communists. The trade unions were not, however, regarded with great favour by employers in Malaya, whether British or Chinese, and some further initiative on the part of the United Kingdom Government would be required if the development of the trade union movement in Malaya was to proceed with sufficient speed. He also believed that it would be necessary, as soon as the present emergency was over, to find means of accelerating the course of economic and social development in Malaya. Leading members of the European community there had pressed him to make a public statement that British rule in Malaya would be maintained for another twenty-five years. This he had declined to do. In the light of recent political developments in South-East Asia he agreed with the view now held by the Commissioner-General that Malaya's progress towards self-government would have to be accelerated and that the United Kingdom Government would be well-advised to put themselves in a position to announce considered plans for social and constitutional reform very soon after the end of the present emergency. The standard of living in Malaya was very low; and in the plans for its economic and social development first priority should be given to the improvement of agricultural methods, housing and education in rural areas. Too many of the European population were inclined to hope for a return to the conditions which existed in Malaya before the war. The Government would have to make it clear that they had different aims. They must, in particular, be able to demonstrate to the workers in Malaya that a non-Communist régime offered them greater opportunities for economic and social betterment than any Communist régime.

Amnesty
While they had been in Malaya the two Secretaries of State had discussed a suggestion made to them that many of the bandits might now be prepared to lay down their arms if an amnesty were granted. They were, however, satisfied that the offer of an amnesty at this stage would be regarded as a sign of weakness on the part of the Government. In view of the overrunning of Malaya by the Japanese during the war, it was essential to British prestige that the power of the British Forces to quell insurrection should be clearly demonstrated. The question of an amnesty could not usefully be considered until Johore, Negri Sembilan and Pahang had been effectively cleared of bandits.

Parliamentary statements
Following discussions between the Lord President and the Secretaries of State for the Colonies and War, it had already been announced that a statement would be made in the House of Commons by the Secretary of State for War as well as by the Colonial Secretary. Ministers agreed, however, that it would be preferable that the statement by the Secretary of State for War should be made by way of an addendum to the Colonial Secretary's statement. This would avoid having two separate statements on different days, and would make it possible for the Secretary of State for War to omit much of the material included in the draft circulated with C.P. (50) 130. Both statements should be made on Wednesday, 21st June.
    The Cabinet:—
    (1) Took note, with approval of C.P. (50) 125.
    (2) Invited the Secretary of State for the Colonies to make in the House of Commons on Wednesday, 21st June, a statement on the lines of the draft appended to C.P. (50) 129, to which the Secretary of State for War would add a shortened version of the statement appended to C.P. (50) 130.[3]
    (3) Invited the Malaya Committee to follow up in detail the proposals made in C.P. (50) 125 and in the Cabinet's discussion.[4]

---

[3] For the parliamentary statements of Griffiths and Strachey on their visits to Malaya and Hong Kong, see *H of C Debs*, vol 476, cols 1295–1308.   [4] See 222.

222   CAB 21/1681, MAL C 6(50)1   19 June 1950
'The civil situation in Malaya': Cabinet Malaya Committee minutes

The Minister of Defence[1] said that the preliminary Report by the Secretary of State for the Colonies on his visit to Malaya and Singapore had been discussed that morning at the Cabinet.[2] He thought therefore that it was not necessary to have any further general discussion of the problems, but that the Committee should rather consider in detail what immediate and practical action could be taken as a result of the visit. He could not help feeling that the Colonial Office had not been fully seized

---

[1] Mr Shinwell.   [2] See 219 and 221.

of the Malayan problem in its earlier stages; otherwise, he thought, much of the action which had been taken only recently would have been initiated a good deal earlier. He now wished to ask the Secretary of State for the Colonies to give the Committee his views on a number of specific questions:—

(i)   Was the Secretary of State for the Colonies satisfied that the civilian set-up and administration in Malaya were adequate for their task and had a proper appreciation of what needed doing? The task in Malaya was essentially one for the Colonial Office and the civil authorities; the army was only there to help the civil administration. But, in his capacity as Minister of Defence, he was very much concerned at the number of troops which were being tied up in Malaya, when they were badly needed to build up a strategic reserve in this country. This aspect of the question had become all the more important since the recent reinforcements had been sent to Malaya and since it had been made clear by General Briggs that no immediate and spectacular successes were to be hoped for there. This led him to his second question:—

(ii) Did the Secretary of State for the Colonies think that, as a result of the action which was now being put in hand, there was any hope of our being able to withdraw any substantial numbers of troops from Malaya by the beginning of 1951?

(iii) What were the facts about corruption in the Malayan Police, to which the Secretary of State for War had referred?

(iv) Were the Malayan authorities really making full use of their powers to deal with detainees etc? The Minister of Defence thought that we must be realistic and drastic in dealing with the question; it was no use detaining people and then letting them go back to their villages to spread terror among the inhabitants.

The background to the problem
The Secretary of State for the Colonies began by outlining the background to the present problems in Malaya. He reminded the Committee that Malaya had been occupied for four years and that occupation always left a number of grave problems in its wake. When the Japanese had surrendered there had been no British administration to take over, and the Communists had immediately stepped in and controlled the country for a number of weeks. As a result, we had had to make an entirely new start in Malaya, when we did get back there. The original plan for a Malayan Union had met with very strong political opposition and had had to be given up. The present constitution of the Malayan Federation was based on an agreement between the King and the Malayan rulers, signed in 1948. This being so, it was binding upon us, and the whole civilian administration of Malaya was conditioned by its terms. It would not be possible to make any change in the constitution of Malaya without the consent of the rulers, and we must not take any risk of alienating the Malays, who were at present very loyal.

The Secretary of State for the Colonies said that since General Briggs had taken up his appointment, the organisation of the campaign had been entirely overhauled. There was now a Federal War Council sitting in Kuala Lumpur, predided [sic] over by General Briggs, with the Chief Secretary, the General Officer Commanding, the Air Officer Commanding, the Commissioner of Police and the Secretary for Defence as members. This Council was responsible for directing the whole campaign throughout Malaya, and it had as its agents War Executive Committees in each State and Settlement. Before General Briggs had taken over, there had been no proper machinery for bringing together the heads of the different Services, but this organisation now existed and seemed to be meeting with no difficulties. The Secretary of State for the Colonies had formed the impression that personal relations at the top were very good and that General Briggs was fully accepted on all sides as being responsible for the conduct of the operations.

Police

The Secretary of State for the Colonies said that the Police organisation had also been non-existent when we returned to Malaya and had had to be built up from the start. The Commissioner of Police, Mr Gray, had been brought in from Palestine and had soon built up around him a body of key men in whom he had complete confidence. As was natural, a number of these officers also came from Palestine, and this had led to considerable discontent in the Police Force and eventually to the appointment of a Police Commission. Now, however, the worst of the difficulties at command level in the Police Force seemed to be over. The officers appointed by Mr. Gray had justified themselves and Mr. Gray himself was a vigorous and active officer who had made a very good impression on the Secretary of State for the Colonies. General Briggs also thought well of him and did not wish a change to be made in the post.

The Secretary of State for the Colonies said that the rank and file of the Police were at present mainly Malays. There was a great need for more Chinese in the Police Force, but the Chinese as a whole were reluctant to join. He himself had spoken to leading Chinese representatives and had asked them to do all they could to induce their compatriots to join the Police Force. The Malays in the Police Force were on the whole good at doing what they were told, but lacked initiative. It was therefore very important to have the right sort of officer in the middle ranks of the Police Force to direct them. For such officers the first qualification was incorruptibility, since there was no doubt that many rich Chinese were insuring against a possible Communist victory by secretly helping the bandits, and they would probably have no scruples in attempting to bribe the Police.

Treatment of detainees

The Secretary of State for the Colonies read out to the Committee a telegram from the High Commissioner for the Federation of Malaya (Number 573 of the 13th June) describing certain changes in the procedure to be followed by the Committees of Review. It was now proposed to refer to the Review Commission cases where the Committees of Review considered that release was justified either conditionally or on bond, but where the Police wished to press for continued detention. He thought that it was most important that the Malayan Government should not take into detention more suspects than it could be sure of holding. If any considerable number escaped from detention camps and returned to their villages, they would no doubt take their revenge of anybody who had informed against them and so dry up our sources of information. This was one reason why it was most important that as many detainees as possible should be repatriated to China.

In discussion of this question, the following points were made:—

(a) *The Secretary of State for War* said that he had inserted his reference to corruption of the Police because Sir Henry Gurney had given this as one reason why it was not advisable to take very wide powers to deal with detainees on the lines of Section 18(b) in this country during the war. About 90 per cent of the Police Force were Asian, and they were not above reporting people as suspects for personal reasons. Hence, any wide extension of the powers of detention would probably lead to considerable numbers of quite innocent people being detained. In any case, however, he thought, there could be no question of any particularly drastic treatment of detainees. The detainees were held as such because, by hypothesis, there was no actual evidence against them; they might well be innocent, and the most that we should do therefore was to keep them safely out of the way for the duration of the emergency.

(b) The Secretary of State for War said that he had been told by some administrative officers that at present they were unable to arrest numbers of people whom they had good reason to suspect, owing to the risk of these people being released by the Committees of Review and returning to their villages to make trouble. These officers had therefore suggested that the final decision whether a man should continue to be detained should rest not with the Committees of Review but with the Military and civilian authorities. *The Secretary of State for the Colonies* pointed out that the proportion of detainees released by the Committee of Review was not so large as had at one time been thought. These Committees had decided 1371 cases during April and May; in only ten of these cases was unconditional release ordered and in 197 cases there was release on bond.

(c) *General Brownjohn*[3] said that the Military and Police were often frustrated in their work by being unable to produce the evidence for arresting a suspect even if they had it. This effect was serious and cumulative. He thought that for this reason any tribunal which had the final decision whether a suspect should be detained or not must not be of a legalistic nature.

(d) The general feeling was that with a war actually in the country the conditions in Malaya were such that the final decision about the detention of any particular person should rest with the Executive, and that the Director of Operations should have a say in the matter. It was felt that the Committees of Review should be retained, but in an advisory capacity only. Where the Police agreed to the release of a detainee, no question would arise, and this would cover the majority of cases. In the small remainder (where the Committee of Review recommended the release of a man but the Police objected), the Federal Government must take the responsibility for the decision. *The Secretary of State for the Colonies* felt some doubts about the political implications of this, since the Chinese community would not, on this supposition, be represented on the tribunal which made the final decision. It was however, pointed out that the Chinese, together with the Malays, would continue to be represented on the Committees of Review, on which they would have the opportunity of making their opinions known.

The Committee:—

(1) Invited the Secretary of State for the Colonies, after consultation with the High Commissioner for the Federation of Malaya, to submit to them his views on the possibility of dealing with the detainees on the above lines.

---

[3] Vice chief of the imperial general staff, 1950–1955.

Place of detention for detainees
It was noted that the possible use of Christmas Island for detainees was being considered. The Australian Government would be interested in this, since an Australian company held a concession on the island; but the *Secretary of State for Commonwealth Relations*[4] said that he would wish to consider whether it would be necessary to seek the agreement of the Australian Government before sending detainees to the island or merely to inform them of our intention.

Future plan of campaign
The Secretary of State for the Colonies said that General Briggs' plan for regaining control State by State had now started in Johore. General Briggs had said that he had a sufficient organisation to clear and consolidate Johore and Negri Sembilan, and this operation should be completed by the beginning of November. The next two states to be tackled were Pahang and Selangor. These were believed to form the hard core of the bandit resistance, and by the time these states were tackled General Briggs would require further police reinforcements.

The Secretary of State for the Colonies said that everything possible was being done to ensure that these reinforcements became available in Malaya by the beginning of November. The Home Secretary was sending a circular to all Chief Constacles [sic] and speaking to them personally, urging them to do all they could to obtain suitable recruits, and an advertisement was also being issued.

Publicity
The Secretary of State for the Colonies said that he proposed to submit to the Committee at their next meeting a paper on publicity in Malaya. In the meanwhile, he had asked the Secretary of State for Commonwealth Relations, who had special experience in these matters, to suggest the name of a first-class expert to go to Malaya to take charge of our publicity there.

Summing up, *The Minister of Defence* assured the Secretary of State for Colonies and the Secretary of State for War that any criticisms and suggestions which the Committee had offered had been made solely with the object of helping them in their very difficult and important task. He was sure that much good would come out of their visit to Malaya and that the Committee fully appreciated what they had done already towards the solution of the Malayan problem.

The Committee:—
(2) Endorsed the appreciation expressed by the Minister of Defence.[5]

---

[4] Mr Gordon-Walker.
[5] The committee then turned to the military situation and considered Strachey's memo (see 220).

223   T 220/281, ff 69–79   18 Sept 1950
[UK financial assistance for the emergency]: letter from Mr Griffiths to Sir Stafford Cripps proposing a fixed percentage

I am writing to you about the question of His Majesty's Government's future financial contributions towards meeting the cost of the present Emergency in the Federation of Malaya.

2. You will remember that His Majesty's Government have already contributed to the Government of the Federation of Malaya the sums of £5 million in 1949 and of £3 million in this year towards Emergency expenditure.[1] These financial contributions of £5 million were made on a basis of need. That is to say after examination of financial estimates supplied by Malaya the amount of assistance required to enable the Federation Government to meet the cost of the Emergency and to fulfil its other essential commitments was calculated and a grant was agreed accordingly.

3. His Majesty's Government's contribution of £3 million for 1950 was originally calculated on the assumption that expenditure on the majority of Emergency items would be substantially less in the latter months of 1950, and that on average it would run during that year at half the rate of expenditure during the later part of 1949. This assumption was unfortunately falsified by events and the rate of Emergency expenditure necessary in 1950 has, in fact, considerably exceeded that of 1949. At the time of my visit to Malaya in June of this year it seemed clear therefore that[2] the Emergency situation would necessitate further substantial financial assistance from His Majesty's Government during 1950 and preliminary discussion between our two departments took place to determine the amount of such assistance.

4. As a result of these discussions it was agreed that a further contribution of £3 million for 1950 might be made on two understandings:—

(a) that it was the firm intention of the Government of the Federation to implement a programme of social and economic development, and
(b) that Malaya herself would take appropriate measures, largely to that end, to increase her revenues to the limit of her capacity.

The Federation Government's firm intention to fulfil the first of these conditions was demonstrated by the publication in Malaya of the Federation's Six Year Draft Social and Economic Development Plan which was approved in principle by Legislative Council in July. As regards the second condition, the further contribution of £3 million was made conditional on an assurance being given by the High Commissioner of the Federation that the rate of income tax on companies would be raised from 20 per cent to 40 per cent in 1951. The High Commissioner was quite prepared to give this assurance so far as the Federation alone was concerned but, because it is necessary for political[,] economic and administrative reasons that the rates of income tax in the Federation and in Singapore should be the same, the rate of tax could not be increased in the Federation without similar increases being effected in Singapore. The introduction of a rate of income tax on companies of 40 per cent in Singapore would almost certainly entail the use of the Governor's reserved powers to pass the necessary measures through Legislative Council and it therefore became necessary for me to discuss with the Governor the implications attaching to the use of his reserved powers in this context.

5. Meanwhile, however, as a result of the Korean situation, the prices of tin and rubber—on which the revenues of the Federation depend to a very great extent— have risen to a very high level which was unforeseen when the request for further financial assistance from His Majesty's Government for 1950 was made. As a result it

---

[1] See 175 and 200.
[2] Added in manuscript at this point in the letter is the sentence: 'It was represented that Malaya was running rapidly into a deficit.'

now seems reasonable to assume that the Government of the Federation of Malaya will be able to achieve a near balance in its 1950 Budget without further financial assistance. I do not therefore wish to pursue the question of a further financial contribution for 1950. It is the question of contributions towards the cost of the Emergency in 1951 and so long as the Emergency lasts that I now wish to raise.

6. As I mentioned above, His Majesty's Government's financial contributions to the cost of the Emergency have hitherto been made in the form of a deficiency grant. I now wish to suggest that future contributions should be in the form of a fixed percentage of certain Emergency expenditure.

7. I have given very careful consideration to the rival merits of these two forms of assistance. Frankly my first thoughts were that the practical difficulties to be overcome before a grant on a percentage basis would be acceptable to His Majesty's Government were insuperable. I have, however, since had an opportunity of reconsidering the whole matter in consultation with Sir H. Gurney, the High Commissioner of the Federation of Malaya, who is at present in England, and, in the light of further considerations raised by him, I have come to the conclusion that a form of computation on a percentage basis might be agreed which would not only be financially feasible but which would also be of very great political value to the Anti-Communist cause in Malaya today.

8. As you are aware it is accepted policy that the costs of internal security in Colonial territories must normally be regarded as a first charge on Colonial revenues. In the case of the Malayan Emergency, however, His Majesty's Government has always recognised the wider political implications involved and has agreed that the heavy financial burden of suppressing this outbreak of violence, which is part of a world-wide Communist movement directed at all freedom loving countries, should not be allowed to fall exclusively on Malaya merely because Malaya is in the unfortunate position of being in the front line against aggression. In recognition of Malaya's special position His Majesty's Government's financial contributions, though paid over as a deficiency grant, have been assessed on a liberal basis.

9. The method of contribution in the form of a deficiency grant has, however, been open to two serious objections which would not apply to contributions computed on the basis of a fixed percentage of Emergency expenditure. In the first place the deficiency grant method of contribution tends to frustrate attempts to secure the co-operation of public opinion and of unofficial members of Legislative Council in measures which must be taken to increase the local revenues. So long as His Majesty's Government contributes towards a deficit in the Federation Budget the Malayan people tend to think that the increased revenues which would result from their acceptance of a greater burden of taxation would not be turned to constructive account in a way which would allow them to reap some benefit from their sacrifices but would merely result in a reduction *pro tanto* in His Majesty's Government's Emergency assistance. This attitude is, I think, a product of the times when monies had to be used on necessary and urgent Emergency measures to the practical exclusion of any schemes for social development. I am, of course, aware that it is now His Majesty's Government's declared intention to make financial contributions dependent on the pushing ahead of plans for social and economic development in Malaya. I am assured, however, that the attitude will persist so long as deficiency grants continue; and to the extent that it cannot be removed, it must be taken into account in determining our policy. A contribution assessed on a percentage basis

would not be open to the objection discussed above. It would lend impetus to plans for long term social and economic schemes, for no longer would their financing be an uncertain and hand-to-mouth process for the Federation Government and it would give incentive to the Malayan taxpayer, who would be more assured that a reasonably high proportion of his taxes would be used to bring him tangible benefit.

10. The second and more important advantage of the percentage system is that the expression of His Majesty's Government's contribution as a percentage of emergency costs would be of the utmost value in impressing on Malayan opinion the co-operative nature of our task against Communist terrorism. It would emphasise that His Majesty's Government is solidly with the Malayan peoples in their struggle for peace and freedom and the rule of law in their land. One of my main aims in my recent visit to Malaya, was to drive this point home and I repeated it wherever I went. I think it was not without its effects on local confidence and morale. If I could be in a position soon to announce that His Majesty's Government had agreed to bear a fixed share of emergency costs, I am sure that the benefits of my own and of the War Minister's visits would not be lost and that my message would not be forgotten. We cannot afford to let political opportunity slip by in Malaya today. After talking to Sir Henry Gurney and in the light of my own experience, I am convinced that the psychological effect in Malaya of such an announcement, not only in the context of the emergency itself but in the wider context of the future relationship between Malaya and Britain, would be very great.

11. The proposal I wish to put forward is that His Majesty's Government should agree to bear fifty per cent of expenditure arising directly out of the emergency and incurred by the Federation Government so long as the emergency lasts, subject to a maximum contribution by His Majesty's Government of £5,000,000 in any one year.

12. Obviously it is of great importance to have an idea of the type of expenditure which constitutes "expenditure arising directly out of the emergency" for the purposes of the above formula, even though no precise definition can be given as circumstances are continually changing. For example when it becomes possible considerable expenditure will arise in connection with the repatriation of Chinese detainees. I attach however an extract from a secret despatch received from the High Commissioner which sets out the main items of emergency expenditure as it is at present running.[3] Subject to unforeseen additional items which would clearly fall within the definition of emergency expenditure, the expenditure of which we should have to take account would consist of the items listed in this extract. Thus it is not proposed that annually recurrent residual expenditure arising out of the emergency, e.g. pensions awarded in respect of death or disablement, should be classified as emergency expenditure for present purposes, nor would the phrase "emergency expenditure" include the cost of the expanding regular Police Force or the cost of normal military and defence expenditure. The High Commissioner also proposes that if my proposal were to come into effect the Federation Government would bear the full cost of the 5th and 6th Battalions of the Malay Regiment, the financing of which is still under discussion.

13. You will have gathered that for political reasons which I consider very important I am suggesting a basis whereby His Majesty's Government's contribution to the cost of the emergency would be computed without reference to the overall

---

[3] Not printed.

budgetary position of the Federation Government. I have given careful thought to the problems which are raised by this departure from the systems of deficiency grants. Clearly you will wish to know what agreement to a percentage basis is likely to mean both to the Federation and to His Majesty's Government in financial terms. Before I proceed to details, however, I must make it clear that I fully realize that my proposal should include some provisions to operate should unforeseen and substantial improvements in the Federation's financial position occur. If my proposal were agreed and it should happen in future years that, as a result of local measures to increase revenue, the budget workings of the Federation Government should in any year during which a contribution by His Majesty's Government was made, result in an excess of revenue over expenditure, I have agreed with the High Commissioner that the excess should be placed to the credit of a special reserve for development. This reserve would be used either in reduction of external financial assistance now being requested by the Federation under the Commonwealth proposals for economic aid to South East Asia, or, should the budgetary position of the Federation deteriorate, it would be used to finance that part of capital expenditure entailed by the Draft Development Plan for the years 1951–55 which it is proposed to meet from revenues.

14. The latest estimates of the 1951 budget workings of the Federation are already in the hands of your Officials. The Federation Government estimates that the outturn for 1951 will result in a deficit of Malayan \$67.9 million (£7.9 million). The estimate of budget outturn depends very largely on what assumptions are made regarding the average price of tin and rubber for 1951 and any such assumptions are, of course, highly tentative. The best advice available to me is that an assumption of Singapore prices of 85 cents (2/.08d) per lb for rubber and of £650 per ton for tin would not be unreasonable. On these assumptions and allowing for other adjustments which it is considered should be made, I am informed that the best estimate of the likely deficit on the 1951 budget is \$53.9 million (£6.3 million). This deficit is, however, estimated on the basis of Companies Tax being at 20 per cent. If the rate of Companies Tax were raised to 40 per cent, it is estimated that the deficit would be reduced by \$18 million to \$35.9 million.

15. Emergency expenditure as defined in paragraph 12 above, is estimated to amount to \$69.2 million (£8.07 million) for 1951. A grant of 50 per cent of this item—say \$35 million or about £4 million—would still leave a deficit of \$18.9 million to be found from increased taxation. I should of course ensure, in conjunction with the High Commissioner that steps to raise this extra revenue were actually taken. The deficit of \$18.9 million could in fact be eliminated by raising the Companies rate of Tax from 20 per cent to 40 per cent (the local Income Tax Department's estimate of additional receipts likely to result from such an increase is \$18 million) and such an increase to 40 per cent would fulfil the condition on which His Majesty's Government agreed to make a further financial contribution of £3 million to the Federation this year. (See paragraph 4 above).

16. However, as I have said, a rate of Companies Tax of 40 per cent could only be achieved in the Federation of Malaya if I instructed the Governor of Singapore to use his reserved powers to secure a similar increase in that Colony. Such instructions could only be issued at the present time at the risk of seriously prejudicing the smooth working of Singapore's Constitution and of raising bitter feeling between Singapore and the Federation, on the grounds that Singapore was being forced to

adopt a measure which was not in itself necessary so far as the interest[s] of the Colony alone are concerned. The use of reserved powers in this context is not, therefore, a step which I should wish to take if it can be reasonably avoided. On the other hand a rise in Companies rate of Tax to 30 per cent could probably be passed through Legislative Council in Singapore without the use of reserved powers and, even if reserved powers had to be used to secure this increase, the political implications would not be so serious as those attending the use of reserved powers to enforce an increase to 40 per cent. I should therefore prefer that immediate steps to increase revenue in the Federation of Malaya should take the form of an increase in Companies rate of Tax to 30 per cent and of the imposition of increased export duties on rubber and tin. The High Commissioner is in full agreement with these proposals. Together they would certainly yield not less than a straight increase in Companies Tax to 40 per cent.

17. I do not wish to under-estimate the importance of pushing on with increases in income tax. Income Tax must form the mainstay of revenue structure because obviously revenue derived from widely fluctuating prices of primary commodities can never be secure. I therefore regard the level of Companies rate of Tax of 30 per cent as only a step towards the short term aim of raising Companies Tax to 40 per cent in both Malayan territories. I consider, however, that it would be tactical, while present prices for rubber and tin are so abnormally high, to take this interim step to 30 per cent and to increase export duties rather than to go straight away to 40 per cent and to risk the political trouble which a sudden doubling of the rate of Companies Tax in Singapore would entail. I hope therefore that you will be able to agree that for 1951 an increase in Companies rate of Tax to 30 per cent and increases in export duties of tin and rubber together could be regarded as fulfilling the revenue raising condition attached to further emergency contributions by His Majesty's Government.

18. As regards increased taxation in future years, it is quite clear that still further efforts will be required in Malaya. The Federation's Development Plan will call for additional revenue over present levels of $33 million a year even if all emergency expenditure were to stop tomorrow, and this figure of $33 million will be increased by about another $8 million a year if the 5th and 6th Battalions of the Malay Regiment are to be a commitment of the Federation Government as a result of the acceptance of my present proposals. The Legislative Council in conferring their unanimous approval on this plan have accepted the principle that additional financial burdens must be shouldered if it is ever to be translated into reality and as soon as additional income tax staff can be found to overcome present administrative difficulties, the Federation Government will therefore be able to set about finding the additional revenue necessary by increasing personal rates of income tax as well as by increasing Companies rate.

19. I know that in present times when the resources of the United Kingdom are stretched to the utmost, every further financial commitment considered by His Majesty's Government must be justified to the hilt. However, I do not have to remind you of the paramount importance of Malaya as the chief dollar earner of the sterling area today. On ground of hard economic reality even if on no other, we cannot risk any avoidable prolongation of the Malayan emergency with its ever present threat of disruption of production. The proposals I have made will, I am certain, constitute a realistic and constructive method of handling the situation, both from Malaya's and His Majesty's Government's point of view.

20. I should be very grateful if a decision could be reached on this matter in time for an announcement to be made on the subject of His Majesty's Government's contribution for 1951 by the 30th September, not only because an early announcement would be of greatest psychological effect but also because an announcement by this date would enable the Federation Government to incorporate an estimate of His Majesty's Government's assistance in their 1951 Budget, which is already before the Finance Committee of Legislative Council. I am sorry to have to press you like this but Sir Henry Gurney only arrived in this country on the 5th and I felt it necessary for the matter to be fully discussed with him before putting forward my proposals.

224 T 220/281, ff 101–103   29 Sept 1950
[UK financial contributions for the emergency]: letter (reply) from Mr Gaitskell to Mr Griffiths

[By this time Cripps was very ill and Gaitskell, minister of state for economic affairs at the Treasury, deputised for him. On 20 Oct 1950 Cripps resigned as chancellor of the Exchequer and was succeeded by Gaitskell.]

I have given very careful consideration to the proposal in your letter of the 18th September[1] that in 1951 and thereafter H.M.G. should agree to make grants to the Federal Government of Malaya in the form of a fixed percentage of certain emergency expenditure. Although I can see the argument in favour of the proposal I am afraid I do not feel able to accept it. Our own resources are already severely strained, particularly by the requirements of the new defence programme, and in these circumstances it would to my mind be quite impossible to justify a grant from the U.K. Exchequer which did not have regard to Malaya's financial position. You yourself have accepted the validity of this principle in that you agree that there is no case for a further grant to Malaya for the year 1950. I appreciate that according to present estimates the Federal Government will be faced with a deficit of £6.3 millions in 1951 if Company Profits tax remains at 20 per cent. You have proposed, however, to press the Federal Government to increase Company Income Tax to 30 per cent and to make certain increases in the export duties on tin and rubber. You do not give any details of the increased export taxes you have in mind, but I should hope they would be of a significant amount. If allowance is made for the yield from such increased taxes and also for certain other practicable adjustments the deficit should be reduced to a negligible amount. In that event the greater part if not all of the grant of £4 millions which would become payable under the scheme you have suggested would be in excess of requirements. I appreciate that it is part of your proposals that any surplus of revenue over expenditure would be carried to a special reserve to be used to finance the development plan put forward by the Federation as Malaya's part in the scheme for economic aid to South-East Asia. It has already been agreed, however, that the external financing of the development plan for Malaya, other than what is provided by way of market and International Bank loans, should be found by grants from the Colonial Development and Welfare Fund. The provision of additional finance by the transfer of sums voted from the U.K. Exchequer for

---

[1] See 223.

emergency assistance would entail overlapping and would to my mind be quite undesirable. Moreover, as I myself pointed out at the Conference, we really ought not to provide external finance except in so far as it is needed to deal with any worsening of the balance of payments. Any other course is inflationary in character.

I appreciate your view that a system of grants from H.M.G. on a sharing basis would offer certain political advantages and in particular that it would impress on Malayan opinion the co-operative nature of our fight against the terrorists. The large number of British troops, including many National Servicemen, who are now taking part in the campaign in Malaya should, however, surely be sufficient evidence in itself of our co-operation. Incidentally, you will not have overlooked that H.M.G. are bearing the full cost (£36 millions up to date) of the British Forces employed in Malaya. Even excluding "normal" expenditure, H.M.G. has incurred up-to-date direct extra expenditure amounting to over £12 millions in connection with the emergency in Malaya. This compares favourably with the figure of $24 millions (under £3 millions) which, according to the High Commissioner's dispatch of the 9th June, is the estimated annual amount of additional taxation raised by the Federal Government. There should, therefore, be no room for doubt that the people of this country are playing a full part in co-operating with Malaya in her fight against terrorism.

On the evidence at present available, therefore, I am afraid that I cannot see my way to promise any specific grant from H.M.G. for 1951. I appreciate, however, that at this date any estimates of probable revenue and expenditure during the coming year are necessarily speculative. I suggest, therefore, that the whole question be re-examined at some later date, say in June next year, when we shall have a clearer picture of Malaya's financial position over the year 1951.

225   T 220/282, ff 1–7   24 Oct 1950
[UK financial assistance for the emergency]: letter (reply) from Mr Griffiths to Mr Gaitskell

1. I have been studying your letter of the 29th September[1] in reply to mine of 18th September,[2] about H.M.G.'s financial assistance towards the cost of the emergency in the Federation of Malaya.

2. I know that you will wish me to be quite frank and I must say at once that I find your letter very disappointing, particularly since it cannot be reconciled with the attitude which was so firmly adopted by your predecessor and which has hitherto formed the whole basis of our approach to this subject.

3. When I came back from Malaya in the early part of this year one of my first tasks was to submit to your predecessor the question of further financial assistance from His Majesty's Government towards the cost of the emergency during the current year. At that time it appeared that a substantial measure of assistance, in addition to that already given, would be required during 1950. The Chancellor's attitude, while being sympathetic, was quite firm on two prerequisites. The first was that the Government of the Federation should take steps to impose taxation to a reasonable limit of its capacity: the second was that the Federation should press on with development.

---

[1] See 224.   [2] See 223.

4. I accepted these conditions the more readily since they were entirely in accordance with the conclusions I had myself already reached as a result of my visit to Malaya. I want to emphasise, however, that the whole approach along these lines was based on the very definite personal attitude of the Chancellor himself. The impetus, in other words, came from your side at least as much as from mine.

5. It was recognised from the outset that the two conditions were inseparable. That is to say, it was realised that the primary aim of increased taxation in the Federation at the present time must be to finance the heavy programme of development, rather than to provide funds for other purposes. This approach was accepted here as being both right in itself and psychologically necessary, if a taxation drive in the Federation was to have any hope of enthusiastic local support. This did not mean, of course, the abandonment of all hope that increased taxation would help in greater measure to meet the cost of the emergency, but it did mean that His Majesty's Government were willing to continue to give generous help in lightening the financial burden of the emergency, in order that the Federation's own financial resources could be increasingly devoted to its own development. I cannot too strongly emphasise this point which I regard as absolutely fundamental. On the 22nd June, in full agreement with your predecessor, I made a statement in the House,[3] and I should like to quote the following passage:—

> "The Federation of Malaya put to me a request for further financial assistance towards the emergency, in order that those plans should not be hampered. On the understanding that it is the firm intention of the Government of the Federation to implement such a programme of social and economic development, and provided that Malaya herself will take appropriate measures, largely to that end, to increase her revenues to the limit of her capacity—as I am sure she will—His Majesty's Government will certainly be prepared to give further assistance in this effort by the people of Malaya to destroy Communist banditry in their country. The amount and form of that help are now under consideration."

6. This statement was, of course, made in the context of proposed further assistance during the current year, for which it has now been agreed not to press; but that does not in any way alter the fact that His Majesty's Government are publicly pledged by my statement to the general attitude I have described. This view can be further strengthened, if necessary, by quoting the following passage from my telegram No. 824 sent on the 24th of June to the Government of the Federation with the approval of your Department:—

> "This condition that essential development work should proceed as rapidly as is feasible during the current year is made possible by the further grant now approved and I am prepared to give you an assurance that Emergency assistance in subsequent years will be designed to give sufficient help to enable you to take all exceptional emergency measures without delay and to make appropriate provision from Malayan revenues for necessary social and economic developments."

7. It was against this background that the proposals made in my letter of the 18th

---

[3] See 221, note 3; the statement was made on 21 June not 22 June.

September were put forward. I am afraid that in your reply this background has been ignored, with the result that my proposals seem to have been misunderstood. Thus, the main proposal that future financial aid from His Majesty's Government should be on a percentage basis was made with the intention of realising the objectives which I had thought had been accepted between us. This proposal would not have relieved the Federation from bearing a heavy share of the cost of the emergency, more particularly as it left the Federation the whole burden of carrying the greatly expanded regular Police Force. Nor, of course, would it have saved the Federation from increased expenditure if the cost of the emergency as a whole had risen. It would, however, have given the Federation a firm basis on which to tackle the inseparable questions of taxation and development and would have demonstrated unmistakably His Majesty's Government's determination to fulfil the pledges they had already given. Similarly, my proposal that any increased surpluses should be devoted specifically to development was [put] forward against the background I have described. From what I have said I hope I have made it clear that I was not attempting to introduce a device for securing disguised development grants from His Majesty's Government, but was seeking to ensure, in accordance with your predecessor's conditions, that any increased local financial resources, insofar as they would not be spent on the emergency in accordance with the percentage basis, would be specifically reserved for development and not diverted to other purposes. I quite realise, of course, that any development grants to territories in this area for the implementation of the "Sydney" Plan[4] will be by means of the Colonial Development and Welfare vote. It seems probable, however, that such development grants as we may be able to extend to the South-East Asia territories under the proposed new Colonial Development and Welfare Act will go largely to the Borneo territories and not to the Federation of Malaya or Singapore. When I spoke in this connection of a diminution of external assistance, I had in mind the very substantial programme for external loans which the Federation have included in their "Sydney" Plan.

8. Since receiving your letter I have been pursuing with the Federation Government the question of an increase in the rate of export duty on rubber. But for this reason I should have replied to your letter earlier. Incidentally, I should make it clear in this connection that the sum of $24,000,000 referred to in the second paragraph of your letter was the estimated annual yield from new taxation measures already in force when the High Commissioner's despatch of 9th June was written, and took no account of proposed further increases. The Federation Government have responded most satisfactorily and the latest information I have indicates that substantial additional revenue is expected to accrue as a result of the revised rates which it is intended to introduce as from 1st January, 1951. No more than approximate estimates of such additional revenue are yet possible, but these seem to indicate that the new rates would produce increases of the order of £5 million per annum at a price of 1/10d. per lb. for rubber, rising steeply to £35 million per annum at a price of 3/3d. per lb. It must of course be regarded as very unlikely that a price as high as the latter figure will be maintained throughout the whole of 1951; and I should mention that the Federation's proposals will provide that where forward

---

[4] The 'Sydney' plan was produced by the Commonwealth Consultative Committee on Economic Development in South and South-East Asia which, following up the Colombo Conference of Jan 1950, met in Sydney in May 1950 (see CAB 129/40, CP(50)123, 16 June 1950).

contracts have been made and formally registered with the Government the price taken for the purpose of export duty will be that fixed by the contract. And since it is known that forward contracts covering a large proportion of the 1951 crop have been concluded at prices between 90 cents and 1 dollar a lb. the full effect of the new scale cannot be reflected in 1951.

9. I am satisfied that there is no cause for an increased export duty on tin, the present duty being roughly comparable to that about to be imposed on rubber, but it does remain the intention to make every endeavour to raise the rate of company tax, both in the Federation and Singapore, from 20% to 30%.

10. These expected increases in revenue do not, in my view, undermine the case for emergency assistance on a percentage basis on the lines, and for the purpose, which I have described. Indeed, I still think that this represents the only clear and safe way of securing that local support which is so vitally necessary, both for increased taxation and for a whole-hearted development policy. So long as His Majesty's Government's emergency assistance continues to be calculated purely on a basis of need, I fear it will be hard to persuade public opinion in the Federation that increases in taxation will not be used merely to reduce His Majesty's Government's emergency assistance in future. That would not only frustrate local initiative, but would undoubtedly be regarded as a breach of faith. It would be held—and I do not know how we could answer the charge—that the Federation having fulfilled their side of the bargain, His Majesty's Government were using this very fact as a means of not fulfilling theirs.

11. If however, in spite of these considerations you are still unable to accept the principle of grants on the percentage basis proposed in my letter of the 18th of September it is imperative that I should be authorised to make an early statement in the House to the effect that, while the amount of His Majesty's Government's future contribution cannot at present be assessed, the question of a grant in respect of 1951 will be sympathetically considered by His Majesty's Government, when the financial position is a little clearer, in the light of pledges already given, and against the background of His Majesty's Government's desire to make it possible for the Federation during that and subsequent years to proceed as rapidly as possible with measures for social and economic development.

12. It will also be necessary for the Government of the Federation to make a similar statement not later than the 1st November, on which day it is proposed to announce the intention to increase export duty on rubber as from the 1st January, 1951. My latest advice from the Federation is quite emphatic that, if the impression is created that increased taxation will not in the main be used for development, the increased export duty on rubber will give rise to opposition and resentment which may well make it very difficult to put through the proposed increase in the rate of company tax.

13. The time will come, of course, when these statements will have to be put into practice. In other words, His Majesty's Government will have to consider the question of emergency assistance in 1951, whether the question is to be decided on a percentage basis or on any other basis, in accordance with their declared intention that the major part of the proceeds of increased taxation shall be devoted to development. I realise that this may mean that the Federation may be able, in addition to financing current development, to build up their surplus balances, perhaps to an appreciable extent. Provided, however, that the balances thus achieved

are earmarked specifically for future development, I believe this would be an excellent thing from the point of His Majesty's Government as well as Malaya. The proceeds of the rubber export tax, during this period of very high prices, must be regarded as something of a windfall, and it seems to me to be excellent if some of this can be kept back to form a capital fund for financing development in the future. This will both have an anti-inflationary effect when that is most needed, and will reduce Malaya's subsequent need for external assistance for development.

14. This brings me to the argument in your letter about the balance of payments. I should be the last to deny that the question of the balance of payments is relevant to the question of external assistance, but I do deny that at any given moment the balance of payments position can be taken as a reliable index of the amount of external assistance required. As I think I have shown, it is not the case that the Federation will be failing to take all necessary and possible steps to utilise local financial resources. In such circumstances as these, I contend that it is quite admissible for the Federation to build up a reserve for later expenditure on development (and thus to show some net increase in sterling balances for the time being) and at the same time to seek external assistance in connection with the emergency. The point is that the creation of the development reserve, besides helping to defeat inflation, will reduce the need for external assistance to finance development in the future. It might equally be admissible that there should be certain accumulations of reserves in private hands. Thus, the rubber and tin industries might well take the opportunity afforded by high prices to build up reserves which will enable them to undertake future development in their own sphere and thus to strengthen their position against the more doubtful days to come. In the case of the tin industry it is indeed necessary that this building up of reserves should be undertaken now, since the prospecting which is required to assure the future of the industry cannot at present be undertaken owing to the disturbed state of the country. Provided the industries in question are making their full contribution towards public revenues, I could by no means agree that the existence of these reserves should debar the Federation from seeking external assistance in other fields. There is also the very important fact that, owing to the high prices now ruling, the industries have to carry much higher working capital than ever before. I know for a fact that the rubber dealers in Malaya are seriously embarrassed by this development.

15. Finally, I should point out that under the proposals advocated in my letter of the 18th September the Federation Government would be willing to accept the whole cost of the establishment of the 5th and 6th Battalions of the Malay Regiment. It is not clear from your letter that you realise that this would constitute an additional burden on Malayan finances, for which no allowance was made in the various calculations in my letter of 18th September. If my proposals are not to be accepted, and if the whole question of His Majesty's Government's future emergency assistance is therefore to remain unsettled, this question will be thrown back into the melting pot.

16. I greatly hope you will be able to let me have a reply to this letter in time to enable me to authorise the Government of the Federation of Malaya to make a statement, as mentioned above, not later than 1st November.

226 CAB 21/1682, DO(50)92   24 Oct 1950

'Present situation in Malaya': joint memorandum by Mr Shinwell and Mr Strachey for Cabinet Defence Committee

The Committee will recall that in accordance with the Briggs' Plan[1] operations in Johore began on the 1st June this year. Although it was not expected that substantial benefits would result from these operations for the first two months, it was expected that after that period the increased sense of security which, it was hoped, would be given to the civil population would result in an ever-increasing flow of information to the authorities and that this would in turn lead to more effective action by the Security Forces. The plan was that Johore should be cleared by the 1st November, 1950, after which the Army striking forces would move on to Pahang and Negri Sembilan simultaneously. The present position is that Johore has not been cleared and the latest Colonial Office reports indicate that the total number of incidents reported for the month of September exceed those of previous months—particularly in Johore.

2. We view the present situation in Malaya with grave anxiety for two reasons:—

(1) There are at the moment 21 infantry battalions, the 3rd Royal Marine Commando Brigade and 2 Armoured Car Regiments, making a total of approximately 40,000 troops stationed in Malaya. Commitments elsewhere make it extremely difficult, if not impossible, to retain such a large force in Malaya until the end of 1951.

(2) We have always maintained that the successful conclusion of operations again[st] the guerrillas in Malaya is a vital step in the "cold war" against communism in the Far East. The Malayan campaign is not isolated, and must be considered in relation to the Far East theatre as a whole. The successes of the United Nations force in Korea will lose a great deal of their value in the Far East if the position in Malaya does not show a sensible improvement. Meanwhile, the French campaign in Indo-China is going far from well.

3. Broadly speaking all that the Army can do is to hold the position. It is unlikely that any change of military methods can radically alter the situation. There seems to be no possibility of seeing an end to the emergency unless the Civil Administration in Malaya can in particular succeed in preventing the return of bandits to areas which have already been cleared, and unless it can in general and in the long run produce a political and economic situation in Malaya in which a Communist guerrilla rising cannot win enough popular support to maintain itself. Until this has been achieved troops cannot be withdrawn without detriment to the situation. We appreciate that the Civilian Administration are having great difficulties in carrying out the functions assigned to them under the Briggs' Plan. There is a great shortage of staff and there is also still in Malaya, both among the Civil and Administrative population a considerable resistance to progress and a nostalgia for pre-war conditions. Nevertheless, in our view the above situation calls for an appreciation by the authorities on the spot of the present military and political situation in Malaya. We understand that the Secretary of State for the Colonies is preparing a memorandum, consulting as

---

[1] see 216.

necessary with the Foreign Office, giving the political background and
of the Civil Administration. We suggest that this memorandum shoun
together with our memorandum.

Recommendation
4. We recommend that the Committee should invite the Chiefs of Staff to request
the British Defence Co-ordination Committee, Far East, to submit an immediate
appreciation of the present political and military situation in Malaya.

227 PREM 8/1406/2, DO(50)94   15 Nov 1950
'Political and economic background to the situation in Malaya': memorandum by Mr Griffiths for Cabinet Defence Committee

I was invited by the Malaya Committee to submit to the Defence Committee a paper
giving the political and economic background to the present situation, for consideration in conjunction with the memorandum by the Minister of Defence and the
Secretary of State for War (D.O. (50) 92)[1] and the appreciation of the current
situation by the Acting High Commissioner and the British Defence Co-ordination
Committee (Far East) which is to be circulated.

2. There has always been general acceptance of the thesis in paragraph 3 of D.O.
(50) 92 that the emergency can only be brought effectively to an end when the
Federation Government can bring about conditions in which the bandits can be
prevented from returning to areas which have been cleared by the military and can
produce a political and economic situation in the country in which the bandits find it
impossible to maintain an armed rising on any appreciable scale.

3. The central problem facing the civil authorities is one of restoring full
confidence among the general population. The confidence both of the Malay and
Chinese communities was to some extent lost as a result of our military defeat in
1942. Post-war developments, notably the establishment of the Malayan Union and
the subsequent abandonment of that policy, had a serious effect on the attitude of the
two major communities to the British connection.

The Malays and the relationship of the federal and state governments
4. Malay political pressure forced us to abandon the plans for a strong central
Government with wide executive powers which were embodied in the Malayan Union
and a measure of legislative and an even greater measure of executive authority were
restored to the Malay States by the 1948 Federation Agreement. The Malay States, in
combination, are a powerful force, and the Federal machine can only work with their
confidence and goodwill. There is no doubt that, although the Malays themselves are
strongly anti-Communist, the suspicion and distrust of the Malays regarding British
intentions was at one time such that the State Governments were most resentful of
any attempt by the Federal Government to intervene in State matters, particularly
where this intervention took the form of pressure to devote resources to the
resettlement of the Chinese rural population, resources that in the Malay view

---

[1] See 226.

should more properly have been devoted to the betterment of Malay conditions. The High Commissioner's policy has been, in my view quite rightly, to ensure that the desire for central control should come from the perimeter and not from the centre itself and results have justified his decision not to force the pace unduly in the early stages. It has now been possible, largely as a result of the High Commissioner's tact and patience in dealing with the State Governments, to set up State and District War Executive Councils and Committees with wide powers of executive decision and I am confident that the machinery of government has during recent months become much better adapted to "war" purposes and that much, though not all, of the former Malay suspicion has been overcome. There still remains, to a great extent, the difficulty of securing effective action by a State and District Administration which is in many respects inexperienced and is largely staffed by Malays; the administrative machine has been strengthened already by the addition of more British administrative and police officers, and will improve still further as reinforcements arrive; but, as I explain in paragraph 18, political considerations make it essential that the influx of British officers should at least be matched by increased opportunities for the training and advancement of Asians.

Government must secure the confidence of the Chinese

5. The question of securing the confidence of the Chinese population has been and continues to be an intractable one. I deal in more detail with the Chinese problem in paragraphs 16–17, and I need only say here that until Government can demonstrate not only its willingness but its ability to protect those Chinese who are ready to take a stand against the Communists and to give information to the security forces, we shall be unable to obtain in sufficient volume the intelligence which is vital to the success of military and police operations.

Nationalism and the communal problem

6. A further aspect of the problem of confidence, with which I deal below, is that we must, while taking strong measures against the Communist bandits, at the same time do nothing to frustrate the healthy desire of all communities to take a greater part in the Government of their country. We must show that our intention is not only to restore law and order but also to ensure for the peoples of Malaya higher standards of living and the satisfaction of their legitimate nationalist aspirations.

7. In a country where, of a total population of just over 5 million, $2\frac{1}{2}$ million are Malays, just under 2 million Chinese and the balance mainly Indians, the communal problem is of peculiar difficulty. Taking Singapore and the Federation together the Chinese population slightly predominates. During the last 18 months the Malay rate of natural increase has become slightly greater than that of the Chinese and this trend has had a fortunate effect on the communal situation.

8. The Chinese population of Malaya has assumed significant proportions only during the present century; immigrants were attracted from Southern China by the prospects of work and prosperity in the tin mines and in commerce and the Chinese claim, not without reason, that the economic development of the country would never have been brought to its present pitch but for their industry. The Malays, on the other hand, are in general easy-going and until before the last war were content to share in the prosperity which the Chinese and Europeans had brought to their country. Both Malay and Chinese nationalism were aroused during the Japanese

occupation and the Malay is no longer content to see the economic life of his country in the virtual control of what he regards as an alien community; he is afraid of the country coming increasingly under the domination of the dynamic Chinese and is not unnaturally reluctant to accord the Chinese full political rights or to surrender the "special position" of the Malays which is guaranteed by the 1948 Federation Agreement. The Chinese, on the other hand, regard the present arrangements, under which no more than about one-third of their number qualify for Federation citizenship and they are not admitted to the higher ranks of the administration, as inequitable, particularly as the majority have beeen born in the Federation and have no intention of returning to China.

9. The major political problem confronting the administration is the fusion of these two nationalisms, which if they develop separately will almost certainly lead to a conflict[,] into a Malayan nationalism which will have as its object the building of a Malayan nation of different races, to be ultimately a self-governing member of the British Commonwealth. It is noteworthy that the present emergency, which is almost exclusively directed by Chinese Communist bandits of alien origin, has so far not brought about any serious communal trouble. It is, indeed, most encouraging that the community leaders—Malay, Chinese, Indian, Ceylonese and European— have spontaneously created an unofficial body, known as the communities' liaison committee with Mr. Malcolm MacDonald as "liaison officer." The Committee have seized the vital fact that before real unity can be achieved the Malays must agree to give increased political and civil rights to the Chinese and Indians while the Chinese must be brought to renounce their political ties with their Chinese homeland and accept an undivided loyalty to Malaya. During the summer the Committee published agreed proposals for the admission of larger numbers of non-Malays to Federal Citizenship, at the same time making suggestions for assisting the Malays to greater participation in the economic life of the country.

Communism in the Federation

10. The situation is further complicated by the attitude of the Malayan Communist Party. Captured documents prove that the M.C.P. is an orthodox Stalinist party. Overwhelmingly Chinese in composition, it is far from being, despite its pretensions, the expression of a genuine Malayan Nationalist movement. The permanent armed force of Communists consists only of 3–5,000 men, and relies very largely for food, money, information and propaganda on the Min Yuen ("People's Organisation") in the populated areas. It is the breaking up of the Min Yuen, which is Communist controlled, if not Communist, and which certainly musters many thousands of supporters, which is one of the primary responsibilities of the civil authorities. The size of the active bandit force is limited by supply considerations rather than by lack of recruits, and the indications are that casualties are quickly replaced, either by volunteers or pressed men from the Min Yuen. Not unnaturally the M.C.P. manifestos carefully mask the Chinese nature of the movement and its appeal is deliberately directed towards all the communites, the "British imperialists" being made the chief object of propaganda attack. Links with the Chinese Communist Party have been up to the present very tenuous and there is virtually no evidence of direct assistance from outside to the M.C.P. Indeed the indications were at one time of a certain tension between the two Communist Parties, the C.C.P. expecting loyal Chinese to return and prosecute the revolution in China, while the M.C.P. regarded

as traitors any who have attempted so to return. However, these divergencies will no doubt be resolved. There has been a very limited response from the Malays and Indians to the M.C.P. appeal but there are no signs of any danger of a widespread extension of doctrinaire communism outside the Chinese community or that the M.C.P. will succeed in uniting Malayans of all communities against us. To the vast majority of the Malays, indeed, Mohammedan in faith, communism is distasteful; while, to all but a small proportion of the Chinese, the M.C.P. stands only for brutality, banditry and ruthless suppression and intimidation of all those who refuse to support the terrorist movement. Of the 1,180 civilian victims of the disorders, 800 have been Chinese. This does not mean that some of the Utopian promises put forward by the M.C.P. do not have a general appeal, particularly to the under privileged. I think, however, that there is no danger that our present policy of declared determination to stamp out the Communist bandits will be interpreted in Malaya as opposition to true nationalism, provided we continue to pursue with energy the political, economic and social policies described later in this paper. I am confident that the vast majority of the population of all communities, even though many of the Chinese are still unwilling to come out into the open against the M.C.P., are opposed to a way of life so closely associated in their minds with indiscriminate violence.

Indonesia and Malay nationalism

11. I should mention here a development that may become significant in future. Many of the Malays in the Federation are descendants of comparatively recent immigrants from Indonesia. They have not unnaturally been stimulated by recent events in that country and there is a section of Malay extremists in the Federation that regards Malaya's destiny as that of an independent component of a Greater Indonesia. This section is as yet comparatively small and uninfluential, and the more responsible Malay leaders are strongly opposed to it, though they are a little disturbed at the appeal that such a doctrine might have should the Malays fail to build up their economic position in the Federation. There is as yet no official Indonesian Government support for these Malay extremists, but I feel it right that my colleagues should know of this matter, and that there have also been indications recently of Indonesian interest (which have, of course, been officially disclaimed) in Sarawak and North Borneo. We may thus, in future, be faced with Malay nationalism fed from Indonesia, just as we may be faced with more active support from China for the Chinese Nationalist movement.

Political and constitutional measures designed to satisfy nationalist aspirations

12. As I indicated in paragraph 9 the responsible leaders of the communities have seen the imperative need for a closer integration of the communities and the Federation Government have been quick to guide this movement and to ensure that the initiative gained is not dissipated. Legislation will shortly be introduced to extend Federal citizenship to an increased number of non-Malays. It should not be thought that these proposals have been accepted by the Malays without some heartburning; at one stage Dato Onn, the President of the United Malays National Organisation, had to resign in order to secure the agreement of the Organisation to this relaxation of the present citizenship laws. But it now seems certain that Malay opinion will accept the proposed changes which, although they will not have any considerable immediate

effect, will mean that in the course of time anyone born in the Federation and owing loyalty to the country will become a Federal Citizen.

13. Steps are now being taken towards greater Asian participation in the government of their own country. It is intended to introduce elections, first to Municipal Councils, then to State and Settlement Councils, and ultimately to the Federal Legislative Council itself. The whole process will occupy two or three years, but legislation for municipal elections has already been passed and the committee on State elections in Johore has reported. More rapid progress towards Federal elections is unlikely, partly because it is considered that a normal democratic structure should be built up by stages, partly because the Emergency makes the compilation of an electoral register a matter of some difficulty and partly because it is hoped that the franchise for Federal elections will be on the basis of the wider citizenship proposals mentioned in paragraph 12 above.

14. Without waiting for the introduction of the electoral principle the High Commissioner, with my full agreement, has announced his intention of inviting a number of "unofficials" to accept office as "Members." Each Member will be responsible to the High Commissioner for the department or group of departments placed in his charge, and will answer for them in the Legislative Council and will in effect assume Ministerial responsibility. It is significant that the Malays, who are not yet prepared to admit members of the other communities as members of the Malayan Civil Service, have nevertheless agreed to the appointment of Chinese and Indian members. I attach importance also to the readiness of the Asian leaders to suggest that a European "unofficial" should be appointed a Member: the part that can be played in the Malaya of the future by a public-spirited European community should not be underrated, and the High Commissioner, with my encouragement, is devoting much of his influence in this country to impressing on the London commercial interests the importance of sending out to Malaya public-spirited men prepared to take a real interest in the country and its peoples and to welcome the new spirit abroad in Asia.

15. A further important development is that the High Commissioner is to cease to be the President of the Legislative Council and his place will be taken by an unofficial member appointed as Speaker.

The Chinese problem

16. I must here elaborate a little on the problem of the Chinese. The Chinese in Malaya have not in the past played an active part in local politics, but as I have said above, their sense of Chinese nationalism was developed during the Japanese occupation. Many of them, particularly the comparatively recent immigrants, still retain strong family links with their homes in South China. They are not unnaturally deeply influenced by events in China and in the rest of the Far East and one of the greatest dangers to Malaya lies in the fact that their political sensitivity is effected by external as much as by internal events. There is, particularly among the young people, a feeling that the new Chinese Government has restored to China a prestige and power that had been squandered by the corruption and inefficiency of the K.M.T. In this sense therefore the Communist success in China has undoubtedly been a stimulus to Chinese national pride. The only effective counter to this sentiment is to give the young people of Malaya a constructive and Malayan nationalism to inspire them and this is one of the declared objects of the Federation Government's

educational, social and economic policy. But I must emphasise that there is no popular support for the M.C.P. There is intimidation, and this is deeply ingrained in the Chinese character. The Federation Government's policy is to be both imaginative and strong. It must demonstrate its strength not only by vigorous action at home, but by showing that it can make its will effective in external matters, it is in this context that it is so important that the Government must show that it can repatriate to China the thousands of detainees now held in camps in Malaya, a subject with which I deal in D.O. (50) 93.

17. Events in Korea have had little repercussion in the Federation, though there undoubtedly has been some improvement in the morale of the anti-Communists as a result of the United Nations victory there. A United Nations defeat in Korea would have had the most serious results and the consequences of the involvement of China in the Korean war would of course be grave. At the moment the Chinese interest is concentrated more closely on Formosa and Indo-China. The Chinese know well that if there is a French collapse in Indo-China then Siam is unlikely to avoid going into the Communist camp and the enemy would be at the gates. It is not easy for any Chinese to come out openly against the Communists while the external situation is so uncertain and I cannot too strongly emphasise the importance to Malaya of the position in Indo-China being held. As regards Formosa, the improvement in the situation there and a failure of the Chinese Government to launch an attack, have undoubtedly encouraged the strong anti-Communist elements in Malaya and have in that sense been of direct benefit to us.

The future and self-government

18. The fear of Communist China is not only short-term but long-term. It is known to be our policy that Malaya should, by gradual steps, progress towards self-government within the Commonwealth. The whole outlook of the Malayan Chinese is to some extent conditioned by the fear that self-government may involve the withdrawal of protection against Communist China. In order to allay these fears, statements were made by the Prime Minister on 13th April, 1949, and again on 28th March, 1950,[2] making it clear that it was our firm intention to implement the policy of steady democratic progress towards self-government within the Commonwealth and that we shall not be deflected from that policy and have no intention of relinquishing our responsibility for the defence of Malaya and the protection of its law-abiding people by all means at our disposal. I cannot with any confidence hazard a guess at how long this progress of development towards self-government will take. At one stage the view was generally held that twenty-five years would not be too high an estimate and the Malay Sultans have made it quite clear that in their view (which is obviously not entirely disinterested) Britain cannot withdraw from Malaya within the foreseeable future. Post-war events have shown, however, that the danger lies in

---

[2] For Attlee's parliamentary statement of 13 Apr 1949, see 185, note 2. The prime minister made a further statement on 28 Mar 1950: 'I gave a clear statement of His Majesty's Government's policy to the House on the 13th April last, and it is our firm intention to implement the policy which I then affirmed of steady democratic progress towards self-government within the Commonwealth. We shall not be diverted from that policy and have no intention of relinquishing our responsibility for the defence of Malaya and the protection of its law-abiding people by all means at our disposal.' When Gammans pressed the prime minister for 'something a bit more red-blooded than that', Attlee repeated his statement of 13 Apr 1949 (see *H of C Debs*, vol, 473, cols 180–181).

too slow rather than in too rapid progress, and I returned from my visit to Malaya convinced that it would be unrealistic to think in terms of such a long period. At the same time the political leaders of Malaya have been and are well placed to observe the experiences of other Asian countries. The tendency has undoubtedly been to create a sense of realism and to temper nationalist thought with a distrust of those who clamour for early independence at all costs. The High Commissioner considers that this will continue to be the trend so long as Government avoids coming into conflict with the nationalist or other progressive forces and shows itself ready to continue with a steady advance in this direction. It is true that even those leaders who are most seized of the necessity of progress by degrees are often unreasonably critical of certain aspects of British policy. For example Dato Onn has recently made one or two statements criticising the reinforcement of the administrative and police services by large numbers of European officers; and these criticisms are voiced more irresponsibly by the student body in this country. I am satisfied that these criticisms are not widespread and that it is essential to send European officers to deal with the emergency. But they give added urgency to the measures that are being taken to ensure that Asians, and in particular the Malays, are given training to fit them to hold a greater proportion of the senior posts in the Administration.

19. The political progress that is being made and is planned shows that the Federation Government are fully seized of the importance of meeting nationalist aspirations. We shall have to go further in the next few years in staffing the administrative and technical services with Asians, but here we are at the moment checked by the communal difficulty. The Malays alone have at present the right to enter the higher branches of the administration and there are insufficient trained Malays for this work. One of the most difficult tasks facing the High Commissioner is to persuade the Malays that they must accept the other communities into the senior branches of the Government service, and this will be difficult until arrangements are made for the Malays to receive the education and training which will enable them to compete on equal terms with the Chinese and Indians.

Economic and social problems

20. The Federation Government submitted to the recent meeting of the Commonwealth Consultative Committee their Development Plan for the next six years, a plan largely based on a programme which has already been published in Malaya and received the warm approval of the Legislative Council. The total plan envisages Government expenditure of some £45 million over the period 1951–57, of which 29 per cent. is to be devoted to the development of the social services, 24 per cent. to agriculture, 24 per cent. to transport, 22 per cent. to fuel and power, and 1 per cent. to industry and mining. The financial resources of the Federation Government have, of course, been strained to breaking point by the exigencies of the emergency, and until recently, despite direct grants totalling £8 million from His Majesty's Government towards the cost of the emergency, it proved impossible to undertake any substantial expansion of social services. In the summer the Federation Government put to me a further request for financial assistance and, after discussion with the Chancellor of the Exchequer, I informed Parliament on 21st June that, "on the understanding that it is the firm intention of the Government of the Federation to implement a programme of social and economic development, and provided that Malaya herself would take appropriate measures, largely to that end, to increase her

revenues to the limit of her own capacity, His Majesty's Government will certainly be prepared to give further assistance in this effort by the people of Malaya to destroy Communist banditry in their own country. The amount and form of that help are now under consideration." Since then the almost unprecedented boom in tin and rubber has put a different complexion on the financial situation, though it is still the view of the Federation Government that further assistance will be required during 1951. I am at present engaged in discussions with the Chancellor of the Exchequer on this question.[3] Already the Federation Government have shown their willingness to increase their revenues by announcing a substantial increase of the export duty on rubber. It is impossible to predict how much additional revenue will actually accrue during the next financial year, but, assuming an average price of $1 (Malayan) a lb. during the period, the increase might be as much as £12 million. It is further the intention of the Federation Government to increase the company rate of income tax from 20 per cent. to 30 per cent.

21. Before the war Malaya was a prosperous country, indeed, by general oriental standards it was an extremely prosperous one and the national income per head is still greater than that of any other country in the region. During the war it suffered much physical destruction, the repair of which swallowed up the greater part of its accumulated savings. An even more serious loss was that of the lives of some of its best citizens and with this may be coupled the loss by many thousands of children of their educational opportunities. The cost of rehabilitation and of the emergency, even allowing for the grants and other assistance which have been given by His Majesty's Government, have been a grievous burden on the country's resources, to the temporary exclusion of almost all expenditure on development. The country is still precariously dependent on its two primary products, rubber and tin, and although there is at the moment an almost unexampled boom in these commodities, past experience has shown that this exceptional prosperity may not endure.

22. The emphasis of the Development Plan is on a diversification of the economy to minimise to some extent the country's dependence on tin and rubber; on increased food production; on the improvement of educational and social services so that the people may be fitted to take a fuller share in the development and prosperity of their land; and on the improvement of the economic status of the smallholders, who form the backbone of the rural population. This latter is of particular importance in present circumstances. There are in the Federation, for example, some 350,000 rubber small-holdings, averaging 3 acres each, on which the trees are old and yields are falling. Although it would result in a three-fold increase of yield in rubber per acre, the smallholders cannot replace the old trees with high-yielding types. Quite apart from the technical difficulties of replanting part of a small-holding, they cannot afford to lose half of their present income by destroying some of their existing trees, as the new ones would take seven years before beginning to yield. The Government proposes to assist the small-holders by clearing new land, planting it with high-yielding rubber and possibly other crops. In other cases, small-holdings can be grouped together and part of the area replanted. A Rural and Industrial Development Authority has already been set up, under the Chairmanship of Dato Onn, which will initiate schemes for helping small-holders and fishermen to market and process their products by co-operative methods without recourse to the

---

[3] See 223, 224, 225, 228 and 229.

middlemen, who, at the moment, take off an undue proportion of the profits. The Colonial Development Corporation are interested in schemes for assisting small-holders and there is a possibility that E.C.A. may also be induced to assist. These schemes are all of vital importance since it is only through them that the backward Malay peasantry can be placed on a really sound economic footing and the present Chinese, Indian and European domination of the economic field can be relaxed. At the same time both the Federal and State Governments are incurring heavy expenditure on the regrouping and resettlement of the Chinese rural population ("squatters"), who must be given an effective stake in the country if they are to be shown that we have a better alternative to offer than communism. As I indicated in paragraph 10 above, there are certain points in the Communist programme, such as the division of the large estates, social insurance, &c., which make a natural appeal to the under-privileged. I am convinced that if the Development programme goes ahead we have an effective answer to this appeal. There is, in fact, land for all in Malaya, since all land belongs to the State; but we must ensure that people are in a position to make use of the land and this the programme put forward by the Federation Government will do. Any failure to meet the time-table would be disastrous, particularly in view of the unavoidable delays which have already occurred due to the emergency. It is absolutely necessary that the finance necessary for meeting these plans should be readily available.

23. A further burning issue is that of debt among both town and country dwellers. Some 80 per cent. of the Malay small-holders and fishermen are in the hands of Chinese and Indian money lenders, and the town-dwellers are often in an even worse plight. Until this vicious circle can be broken there will be no firm basis for prosperity and contentment. The solution lies in progress in co-operative development and in more stringent legislation for the control of money-lending, and the High Commissioner assures me that this question is to be tackled energetically.

24. I circulated to the Malaya Committee on 14th July an account of the measures that had been taken and were contemplated for raising the social standards in Malaya (MAL (C) (50) 26), and I need only, in this memorandum, give a very broad indication of the policy of the Federation Government.

25. In the communal circumstances I have already described the supreme importance of educating the Chinese community to acquire a Malayan outlook and of giving the relatively backward Malays the knowledge and training necessary to bring them to terms of equality with the other communities needs no emphasis. The Chinese have already, with commendable statesmanship, agreed that State education should be in English and Malay, with Chinese as only an optional subject. The next step forward, which is being recommended by a Committee of Malays and European officials under the Chairmanship of Mr. Leonard Barnes,[4] will, it is hoped, be the

---

[4] Leonard Barnes, author of *Empire or democracy: a study of the colonial question* (London, 1939), had been closely involved in the shaping of Labour's colonial policy since his return from farming and journalism in South Africa in 1933. His report on Malay education recommended the creation of an integrated system of national schools where the medium of instruction would be either Malay or English. Meanwhile, however, the Fenn-Wu report on Chinese education proposed improvements in the Chinese school system. The two reports fanned communal controversy which did not abate when the government largely ignored Fenn-Wu and based its Education Ordinance of 1952 on the Barnes report. See Federation of Malaya, *Report of the Committee on Malay Education*, Kuala Lumpur, 1951 (the Barnes Report) and *Chinese Schools and the Education of Chinese Malayans: The Report of a Mission Invited by the*

establishment of non-communal primary schools in which the media of instruction will be English and Malay. Eventually these primary schools will cover the whole school population. But the process is bound to be slow, and the High Commissioner considers that the emphasis must be on quality rather than on quantity, since it is only by insisting on high standards that we shall offer the Chinese a reasonable alternative to the present undesirable vernacular private schools. At present less than a half of the children of school age receive any education whatsoever, and progress over the next few years will do little more than maintain the present position as regards numbers owing to the growth of the population.

26. The basis of the Federation's labour policy is to stimulate the formation of strong trade unions, and in the meantime, while trade unionism is in its infancy, to provide effective alternatives for collective bargaining. The number of trade unions in existence at the beginning of 1948 was 289, with a total membership of 200,000. Nearly half of these unions were under the direct control of the Communist Pan-Malayan Federation of Trade Unions. With the onset of the emergency the Federation of Trade Unions disintegrated, and by the beginning of 1949 the number of registered trade unions had fallen to 161 with a total membership of 70,000. The rank and file of the workers were disillusioned and their condition still persists. By the end of 1949 the number of trade unions had risen to 169, but the total membership had fallen as low as 42,000. The situation is improving slowly but steadily and the Department of the Trade Union Adviser is available to give guidance and has achieved a great deal of useful work. A Malayan Trade Union Council has been established this year; it has applied for membership of the I.C.T.F.U. (which has now established a regional Office in Singapore) and maintains close links with the T.U.C. I hope that Mr. F.W. Dalley[6] will be able to visit the Federation early next year to advise on the most effective methods of developing the council's activities and arrange for the local training of trade union leaders and officers. Some employers have up to the present shown a reluctance to conduct negotiations with representatives of the trade unions, preferring to deal direct with their employees; but the Government, through its Labout [sic] Department, is making steady progress in the "education" of employers in the advantages of trade union methods.

27. Among many items in the Government's labour policy I should like to draw special attention to the intention to establish an employment exchange system and to the decision taken recently to establish a provident fund for the lower paid employees to which compulsory contributions are made by both parties.

Summary

28. I have not attempted in this paper to do more than indicate the major problems facing the Federation Government, problems which, for the main part, would exist, though not in such an acute form, quite apart from the emergency. The emergency itself has, of course, meant that to the constitutional, political, economic and social problems has been added a tremendous burden of administrative work. One of the major emergency tasks of the civil authorities is that of resettling or

---

Federation Government to Study the Problem of the Education of Chinese in Malaya, Kuala Lumpur, 1951 (the Fenn-Wu Report).

[5] F W Dalley, a member of the CO Labour Advisory Committee, had reported two years earlier on Malayan trade unions, see 153, para 10 and note 2.

regrouping some 300,000 Chinese rural dwellers who previously have been under no proper administrative or police control and who have been, during the emergency, entirely at the mercy of intimidation and exploitation by the Communists. A full report on the progress made in this operation will shortly be available and will be circulated to the Malaya Committee.

29. The main conclusion that emerges from my paper is that the task of the civil authorities is complicated not only by international political and constitutional stresses, but by external factors outside the control of the Federation Government. Internal constructive policies designed to give the Chinese a greater share in the political and administrative life of the country and to extend Government services to the rural Chinese population must be expedited, but we cannot do this in a manner that shows any disregard for the legitimate aspirations of the relatively backward Malays. Indeed, without the good-will of the Malays we cannot hope to make progress or to achieve a wholesome settlement in Malaya. The administration has to overcome apprehensions and mistrust engendered as a result of the events of 1942 and developments since the reoccupation, and in particular this sentiment is at the base of the present constitutional arrangements, which, giving as they do so much authority and power to the individual State Governments, make the task of administration, even in favourable circumstances, a difficult one. A further factor is that our policy towards the Chinese Communist bandits and their voluntary and involuntary supporters must have regard to the general feelings of the Chinese community; a policy of greater ruthlessness would alienate the sympathies of the vast majority of those Chinese who are inherently friendly to our cause and this would outweigh any immediate practical gain.

30. Externally, the Federation Government has to contend not only with the reactions of the population, and in particular the Chinese, to events in China, Korea and Indo China, but their actions are to a large extent negatived by their present inability to repatriate the 10,000 detainees, with perhaps twice as many dependants, to China. A solution of this particular problem is vital to any rapid and substantial progress in Malaya.

31. Finally, I have given an account of the various nationalist trends in the Federation and of the steps that the Federation Government is taking to bring these trends together and fuse them into a common Malayan nationalism. As I have tried to show, political action alone is not enough to achieve this and it is essential that by a progressive economic and social policy we should show the peoples of Malaya that we do not intend to keep them longer than absolutely necessary in a dependent status, but that our firm intention is to lead them towards self-government within the Commonwealth and to bring them higher standards of living, as rapidly as practicable. I am convinced that our policies in Malaya in all these fields are essentially sound and that the Federation Government have the will and the ability to carry them into effect. Although emergency measures must take first priority at the present they cannot be allowed to impede progress in these other fields, since it is only by such firmness that we shall offer a real alternative to communism.

228   T 220/282, ff 150–154   15 Nov 1950
[UK financial assistance for the emergency]: letter (reply) from Mr
Gaitskell to Mr Griffiths

I am sorry that my letter of the 29th September, about financial assistance to Malaya,
should have caused you so much disappointment.[1] I have gone into the points raised
in your reply with some care.

My first concern, naturally, was with your suggestion that I was reversing a policy
initiated by my predecessor. It is certainly the case that he took a special interest in
this matter; but a second reading of the several directions which he gave to officials
here has convinced me that had he been able to answer your letter of 29th [18th]
September[2] he would have done so in terms little, if any, different from mine. You
will also agree, I hope, that the financial position of the Federation has shown itself
liable to such rapid changes that it would be unreasonable to maintain that any
policy once enunciated should never be modified. When my predecessor was
considering with you the terms of the statement to be made in the House on the
22nd June[3] he was under the impression that the Federation was about to run into
severe and continuing financial difficulties. He had before him at the time your
report to the Cabinet of 13th June[4] in which you said "The Federation is in fact
rapidly running into a financial crisis". I think, therefore, that Stafford's initiative, in
offering assistance on conditions, can only be taken against that background; his
minutes at the time do not envisage a contrary basis and therefore do not indicate
what his attitude would have been had he known that the financial crisis would fail to
materialise—as eventually occurred from causes which nobody could have predicted.
However, he clarified his views on this point at a later date when he instructed his
officials on the line to be taken over the abortive proposal to grant £3 m. in 1950. On
the 23rd July, he minuted that he was prepared to assist Malaya with her exceptional
anti-bandit costs, but only on certain conditions, one of which was that any excess
over $60 m. in the Federation Government's reserve balance at the end of the year
(and in future years) should be carried over and count against the amount of any
grant from H.M.G. in the following year. This condition was, in fact, communicated
to the High Commissioner in Emergency Telegram No. 834 sent next day, to which
you refer in your letter. Thus I feel pretty sure that Stafford's offer, which related
only to the year 1950, had regard to Malaya's financial position as we then
understood it, and that there was never any intention to give assistance in any
circumstances provided only that the conditions about taxation and development
were fulfilled. For similar reasons I cannot regard the statement made in the House
on the 22nd June, to which you refer, as committing H.M.G. to any further grant to
Malaya either for 1950 or subsequently unless a specific need could be shown. That
this was understood by the Malayan Government themselves is demonstrated by
their own decision later in the year, in the light of their more buoyant revenue
position, not to ask for any further grant for 1950.

The question is therefore whether we should depart from the "deficit" basis of
grants hitherto followed, in favour of a system under which H.M.G. would pay part of
the cost of the anti-bandit campaign irrespective of Malaya's own financial position. I

---

[1] See 224 & 225.   [2] See 223.   [3] See 225, note 3.   [4] See 219.

recognise that, as you say, an arrangement on these lines might provide an additional inducement to the people of Malaya to accept increases in taxation. But against the background of our own strained economic position, and with the additional burden of rearmament now upon us, such an approach seems to me to be altogether unrealistic. I feel strongly that any further grants to Malaya must, as hitherto, be related to need, and that any other arrangements would be quite unjustified. This in no way reflects any retraction from our willingness as ever to give Malaya all the assistance that may be shown to be necessary, both for the effective operation of the anti-bandit campaign and to enable her to go ahead with her plan of economic and social development. In this connection it would be wrong to ignore the very considerable contribution His Majesty's Government have already made in recognition of the mutual nature of our struggle against terrorism. So far as military aid is concerned, we shall continue to provide whatever troops are required to the extent to which our resources will allow. At this stage, however, it is by no means clear that Malaya will need any further financial grant from H.M.G. for 1951; in fact, with the yield that may be expected from the recently increased rubber duties, it would be reasonable to believe that so far from being in deficit in 1951 Malayan revenues will show an overall surplus. I appreciate, however, that any estimate of Malaya's financial position in 1951 must at this stage be largely conjectural and, as I have already promised, I shall be very ready to give further consideration to the whole question in the light of the position obtaining say in June next year.

I hope, in view of what I have said above, that you will be able to agree that we should not go further than this at present. I should naturally be very willing to discuss the whole matter with you if you desired.

229   T 220/282, ff 211–212   28 Nov 1950
'Aid to Malaya': minute by A H Clough[1] of a meeting between Mr Gaitskell and Mr Griffiths about UK financial assistance

At this morning's discussion between the Chancellor and the Colonial Secretary, the Chancellor said that while he could not agree to the proposal that H.M.G. should pay a fixed proportion of the cost of Malaya's emergency measures, he would be willing to consider a contribution towards the cost of some specific item of expenditure in furtherance of the campaign, e.g. the cost of raising the 5th and 6th Battalions Malay Regiment.

We have discussed this question further with Sir H. Gurney, the High Commissioner, and with representatives of the Colonial Office. The Federal Government have already raised at their expense 4 Battalions of the Malay Regiment, and the Chiefs of Staff have recommended the raising of two more Battalions—i.e. the 5th and 6th Battalions. The High Commissioner is strongly in favour of this proposal as going part of the way to enable Malaya to defend herself against outside attack in the event of the British troops having to be withdrawn. The raising of these Units would, too, be a very popular move in Malaya. The War Office have indicated, however, that they would be unwilling to accept the cost of these Units as a charge against Army Votes,

---

[1] A H Clough, Treasury from 1938 (from War Office); under-secretary from 1951.

and the Federal Government have hitherto felt that they could not provide the finance necessary to equip them.

We accordingly suggested that H.M.G. might meet the cost of raising these two Battalions (i.e. the cost of clothing, arms, vehicles and other equipment, but not of their accommodation) on the understanding that the Federal Government would meet the cost of their maintenance. The High Commissioner and the Colonial Office would be fully content with a settlement on this basis and, in the view of the High Commissioner, it would give great satisfaction in Malaya. He asked, however, that we should also give an assurance that H.M.G. would still be willing to come to Malaya's assistance if need be—e.g. if Malaya's revenues were badly hit owing to a major fall in commodity prices. We see no objection to such a promise. Indeed we should feel bound to give such help if the need arose even without such a promise.

The High Commissioner has asked, too, that in the event of it being necessary to seek further aid from H.M.G., we should not close the door to the possibility of such aid taking the form of our sharing the cost of some part of the emergency campaign.

The arrangement now proposed is much more advantageous to H.M.G. than the sharing the cost proposal originally put forward, especially as our contribution will be in the form of a final capital payment and will not carry a continuing liability. We understand that if approval is given for the raising of these two additional Battalions, the first (i.e the 5th Battalion) would be completed by about the end of 1951, and the other (the 6th Battalion) in 1952. On present prices the amount of H.M.G.'s contribution on the basis proposed would be of the order of £1¼ million.

Recommended:—

That the Chancellor should approve an arrangement on the lines suggested above. If this is approved we will agree with the Colonial Office the terms of a statement announcing the decision.

230   PREM 8/1406/2   11 Dec 1950

'The Malayan situation and the Far East': minute by Mr Strachey to Mr Attlee urging the appointment of a regional supremo

[The prime minister and other ministers discussed Malayan operations with General Briggs on 25 Nov and 1 Dec 1950, and regretted the slow progress in implementing his plan. At the same time the military position in Korea was deteriorating rapidly; China had entered the war and, fearful that President Truman was contemplating the resort to nuclear weapons, Attlee flew to Washington on the night of 3 Dec. He returned to London on 11 Dec, the day Strachey sent him this top secret and personal memorandum, and the next day reported to Cabinet before making a short statement in parliament (see CAB 128/18, CM 85(50)3, 12 Dec 1950). Though reassured by Attlee's account of his talks with Truman, ministers would continue to express anxiety that American retaliation against the Chinese might provoke an attack on Hong Kong and a southerly drive through Indo-China to Malaya. Meanwhile, as contingency plans were prepared lest Thailand succumbed to communists (see 231), Strachey's worries about leadership and regional organization gained currency (see FO 371/93009 and 93010).]

Prime Minister

As a result of our two meetings with General Briggs I have made a suggestion in regard to the higher direction of our affairs in Malaya in particular, and in the Far East generally, to the Minister of Defence, the Secretary of State for the Colonies and the Chief of the Imperial General Staff.

Each of them desired to think the matter over. Since then I have again spoken to
the Minister of Defence in the light of the repercussions on the whole of the Far East,
including Malaya, which the grave turn of events in Korea must be expected to have.
The Minister of Defence agreed that, in view of the new urgency of the situation, it
would be best if I put the suggestion, which I have already made to him, to you in
writing, which I am accordingly doing in this minute. I apologise for its length, but I
feel that I must set out the conclusions which I have reached on the Malayan
emergency.

Consideration of my suggestion inevitably involves matters outside the military
side of affairs in Malaya. But that is because the military and civil aspects of the
struggle are inextricably intertwined. I have put my view of the characteristics of our
regime in Malaya to the Secretary of State for the Colonies. I do not think that he will
think it wrong of me to put my view to you for what it is worth: for after all vital
considerations for the Army are involved.

What disturbed me about our two recent meetings on Malaya was that the only
concrete suggestion of importance which emerged was that of the mass deportation
of detainees to China. I am all in favour of this move if the Foreign Office will agree
to it and if, in general, it is found to be practicable. But I find it very difficult to share
the optimism which some of our officials in Malaya feel as to its effect. I very much
doubt whether this move, useful as it no doubt will be, provides anything like a
solution to our growing difficulties in Malaya.

Our objectives in Malaya
Nevertheless, I am in full agreement with the general objectives as set out, for
example, in the Colonial Secretary's admirable paper (DO. (50)94,[1] which we are
pursuing in Malaya. I have no particular comments or criticisms in this respect and I
feel that if only we can reach our declared objectives in time all will yet be well.

I do, however, feel acute concern lest we fail because of a certain lack of vigour
with which our representatives in Malaya are attempting to move towards these
declared objectives. As I see it, what is indispensable for our regime in Malaya is a
combination of:—

(a) great firmness and vigour on the part of the governing authorities on the military and police side; in fact, ruthlessness where ruthlessness in [is] necessary; but
(b) equal firmness and vigour in pressing on with the economic and political
development of the country.

The Colonial Secretary, in his paper, has set out the successive steps by which we
seek to promote such economic and political developments, i.e. the introduction of a
measure of democracy by way of local, then State, and finally Federal elections: the
fostering of a healthy non-Communist trades unionism which can raise the standard
of life of the now large wage-earning population: rural development, including, as an
emergency measure, the resettlement of the Chinese squatters, while laying equal
emphasis on assisting the Malayan peasant, etc., etc. This programme would amount
in the end to the development of a Malaya, not only prosperous (indeed rich) as it is
today, but one in which that prosperity was shared by the mass of the population, and
which was steadily developing, through the co-operation of the Malays and the

---

[1] See 227.

Chinese, into a self-governing community, we trust and believe within the Commonwealth.

Character of the British regime in Malaya

Our governing authorities in the Malayan Peninsula (including Singapore) seem to
me to fall short of what is indispensable in both the above respects. On the one hand,
our authorities (I am speaking here of the Civil power—the Army can fundamentally
do no more than act in its support) are not firm, vigorous, or even ruthless enough
in their prosecution of the measures necessary to break the armed Communist
rising. For example, I formed the view while in Malaya that they have been too
squeamish in the use of their powers to detain suspects for the period of the
emergency. I raised the matter repeatedly, but I do not know to what extent it has
been remedied. In this respect our authorities are, in my view, almost too "liberal", if
one understands the word "liberal" in a very old-fashioned 'laissez faire' sort of way.

No doubt this tenderness for civil rights does our authorities credit, but I am
reluctantly forced to the view that it is inappropriate in present circumstances.
Moreover, it is, in my view, motivated not only by an honourable desire to preserve
civil liberties, but also by a certain langour and inability to believe that the easy going
Malayan world of 15 or 20 years ago has irrevocably disappeared.

Moreover, and this is my major criticism, this out of place, and out of date, form of
liberalism is joined, in our Malayan regime, by a disastrously conservative bias in
regard to the political, democratic and economic development of the country.

Lip service is, of course, paid to our declared objectives in Malaya, but there is
intense reluctance on the part of, especially, the middle rank of officials and
administrators to carry out the actual steps which it is necessary to take in order to
begin the implementation of our plans.

For example, there is strong opposition, which I came across when I was in
Malaya, to the growth of trades unionism. Mr. Brasier [sic], the Government's
Labour Adviser, is illuminating on this subject. Many officials, naturally perhaps,
cannot help believing that their real function is to assist in the production of the
maximum possible amount of tin and rubber at the lowest possible price. They find it
impossible to feel that they ought to be supporting something, such as an increase in
the rubber workers wages, which must increase costs of production. In general, I
found a deep belief that the Government ought to do nothing contrary to the
interests of the rubber growers and tin producers. In the same way the administrators are, at heart, very reluctant to see democratic development or, in the case of
some of them, a growing collaboration between the Malays and the Chinese. They
cannot conceive that it can really be right for us to foster a Malayan Nationalist
movement which, while anti-Communist, will undoubtedly wish, in the course of
time, to take over effective power in Malaya (while, we hope and believe, remaining
within the Commonwealth). I cannot really doubt that the proposal to defer all major
political changes till the end of the emergency which was made in General Briggs'
recent appreciation (COS(50)468) was a reflection of this view, however cogent may
have been the reasons, such as deflection of administrative effort, given for it. In a
word, our authorities in Malaya still hanker for the old colonialism and do not really
believe in anything else.

Thus we have a combination of relative inertia on the part of the Civil power in its
effort to break the Communist rebellion, with a bias against those political,

economic and democratic developments which can alone produce a Malayan community capability of itself resisting Communism. This most unfortunate combination of characteristics on the part of our regime is tending to make us lose the struggle in Malaya. I do not think I am going too far in saying that.

Proposed appointment of a British high commissioner for the Far East
I make the following suggestion to meet this situation. Clearly we cannot change the nature of the Malayan regime from London. The key seems to me to lie in the appointment of some man of the right type with supreme powers in Malaya in particular, and over our Far Eastern interests in general. By a man of the right type I mean a man who, on the one hand, is prepared and is capable of carrying on a most rigorous and even ruthless police and military action and yet, at the same time, is genuinely determined to press on with the political, economic and democratic development of Malaya. A man who is, at one and the same time, strong and yet is genuinely and at heart in sympathy with the new Nationalism of Asia. It is very hard to find a man who combines these two qualities. The only man I can think of who has this combination of qualities is Mountbatten. There are, no doubt, all sorts of objections and difficulties about putting Mountbatten in charge, but for my part, I see little to hope for unless we can appoint a man of his stature and background.

The alternative is to let matters go on as they are going, and at present they are going towards our defeat rather than our victory.

The question arises, of course, of the actual post and powers Mountbatten should be given if he were sent out. I suggest that he should be made British High Commissioner for the Far East taking over the present post of our High Commissioner for South East Asia. Further, the powers of this post, the title of which might be changed as above, would be enlarged both geographically and in regard to Malaya. In regard to Malaya the new High Commissioner should be given specific powers over the Governor of Singapore and the High Commissioner in Malaya, and at the same time, should be given the supreme operational command in the military sphere.

I suggest that there would be advantage in giving a man like Mountbatten the same type of commission throughout the Far East that the present High Commissioner enjoys in South East Asia. The Korean setback is only too likely to produce a prolonged crisis in the Far East during which the advice of a British representative of Mountbatten's standing, a man fully able to hold his own with General MacArthur for example, would surely be of use.

In making this suggestion I realise the danger of seeming to criticise Malcolm MacDonald. He is one of my friends since Oxford days and I should hate to do this. I formed the opinion while in Malaya that he had done an admirable job but he specifically told me that he did not wish for enlarged powers and he certainly (and rightly over the past few years) has not conceived of his job as that of a Supreme Commander. Indeed I do not think he would be wiling to undertake such a task. In any case I understand that he is to be transferred to another post in a little over a year's time. Would it not be possible to give him a year's leave between the two jobs without any slur whatever on his capacities? I know how much he has felt the strain of Malaya.

The Minister of Defence has suggested that if you think there is anything in this proposal, you might wish to call a meeting of himself, the Secretary of State for the Colonies, the Chief of the Imperial General Staff and myself to discuss it.

231   PREM 8/1406/2, DO(51)16   23 Feb 1951

'Preparations for the defence of Malaya': COS note for Cabinet Defence Committee on the plan to occupy Songkhla in the event of Thailand falling to communists[1]

Attached at Annex I is a Report[2] examining and making certain recommendations on a number of propsals which have been made by the British Defence Co-ordination Committee, Far East, for the occupation by British Forces of a defensive position (the Songkhla position) on Siamese soil in the Kra Isthmus in the event of Siam coming under Communist domination.

2. We have already informed the British Defence Co-ordination Committee, Far East, that, pending Ministerial approval, they should begin to prepare detailed plans for the occupation of the Songkhla position in various possible circumstances. The occupation of the Songkhla position in sufficient time to allow of its development is of vital importance to the defence of Malaya. It is admitted that if the internal security situation is not under control, the Allied Forces on the Kra position might be in a difficult situation. The advantages gained by the move forward are, however, such that this is a risk worth taking. Although we accept the fact that four months would be required to prepare the Songkhla position itself before it was directly threatened, nevertheless, it is important that plans should also be made to seize and hold the position under adverse conditions in which there might be little or no time for preparation. In these latter circumstances, a decision would have to be taken at the time as to whether this was or was not a justifiable operation of war. The Foreign Office cannot agree to any delegation of responsibility to the British Defence Co-ordination Committee, Far East, which might involve initiating action against Siam. While it is agreed that military plans should be prepared to cover all contingencies, responsibility should devolve solely upon His Majesty's Government. The Foreign Office view is that United Kingdom forces could enter Siam only on the invitation of the Siamese Government or else to meet a clear and imminent threat to the security of Malaya. There is the possibility that in certain circumstances the Siamese Government might ask His Majesty's Government for military assistance. It might not be possible to provide more than sea cover although it might be to our advantage to send a token force to Bangkok. The great advantage of a request by the Siamese for assistance would be that it would enable us to take the opportunity of manning the Songkhla position. It might even be a practicable military proposition to send our ground forces farther north than the Songkhla position, which could then become the limit of our withdrawal. We agree with the British Defence Co-ordination Committee, Far East, that the greatest importance attaches to the Kra Isthmus and consider that it must be the aim of United Kingdom policy in this area to forestall any possible Communist move to seize the position.

Recommendation
3. We recommend that the Defence Committee should approve the report at Annex and agree:—

---

[1] This paper by the COS was considered by the Cabinet Defence Committee on 28 Feb 1951 (DO 4(51)1).
[2] Not printed.

(a) That the occupation of the Songkhla position, in sufficient time to allow of its development, is of vital importance in the defence of Malaya:

(b) that the Commanders-in-Chief, Far East, should be instructed to prepare detailed plans for the occupation of the Songkhla position, bearing in mind the various circumstances in which occupation might take place;

(c) that the Foreign Office and His Majesty's Embassy, Bangkok, should keep in close touch with a view to ensuring—

(i) that everything possible is done, in collaboration with the United States Government, to ensure that an anti-Communist Government remains in power in Siam,

(ii) that in any event, whatever the course of internal developments in Siam, circumstances which would constitute a clear and imminent threat to the security of Malaya are promptly recognised, so that the timely occupation of the Songkhla position may, in such circumstances, be authorised.

232　PREM 8/1406/2, GEN 345/5,　　　　　　　27 Feb 1951
[Briggs plan]: Cabinet Office summary of a meeting at 10 Downing Street on 26 Feb called by Mr Attlee to consider the plan's slow progress

[Amongst those present were: Attlee, Shinwell (Defence), Griffiths (CO), Younger (minister of state, FO), Sir W Slim (chief of imperial general staff), Sir J Slessor (chief of air staff), Sir W Elliot (deputy secretary, military, to Cabinet), R H Scott (FO) and J D Higham (CO).]

The Prime Minister said that he had called the meeting because the Briggs Plan seemed to be progressing only very slowly. No State in Malaya had yet been fully cleared, and large numbers of troops seemed to be tied up there for an indefinite period.

The Chief of the Imperial General Staff said that the situation had undoubtedly improved in some ways; for instance, a record number of bandits had been killed since the beginning of the year. But he agreed that the Briggs Plan was progressing very slowly, and that at the present rate of progress no end could be foreseen to our military commitments in Malaya. The main task, however, was not the purely military problem of killing bandits in the jungle; it was rather to re-establish law and order in the squatter districts and the settled areas and to break up the organisation which was sustaining the bandits, and this was a matter for the civilian authorities and the police. The Chiefs of Staff felt that perhaps there was not enough vigour or sense of urgency being applied to this problem; and they recalled that practically all the efforts to impart more drive into the operations had been initiated from the United Kingdom end rather than from Malaya.

The Secretary of State for the Colonies referred to the Appreciation of the present situation contained in a note which had been circulated to his colleagues. This Appreciation listed some of the steps which had been taken in recent months under the direction of the Federal War Council. This Council now included a planter in its membership of four. It had the fullest possible authority and powers, and could make available any necessary funds without reference to the Legislative Council. Among its recent measures were the issue of regulations for directing man-power and for the collective punishment of villages which failed to supply information to the security forces. Under these regulations a whole village had recently been removed in its entirety, because it was known to be a centre of activity for helping the bandits. But it remained extremely difficult to uproot the cleverly-hidden underground organisation of the bandits, largely through lack of adequate intelligence.

As regards recruitment, the needs of Malaya had very largely been met, but fresh demands were still coming in. The greatest difficulty was over the supply of "Police Lieutenants", partly because the conditions of service in Malaya were not really attractive. There were also considerable technical difficulties about the secondment of such officers from home police forces, but it was hoped that these had now been surmounted.

The Colonial Secretary shared the disappointment which had been expressed at the progress of the Briggs Plan. Even Johore had not yet been completely cleared, and on the whole he thought that the situation was neither better nor worse than it was a year ago.

The Minister of Defence said that no substantial progress had been made in Malaya. The number of incidents fluctuated from month to month, but there was no sustained downward tendency. The powers of the Malayan Government were now admittedly adequate; but were they being fully used and was there any real leadership? He had no complaints to make about General Briggs, but he thought that more drive was needed at the top. He felt also that the military and civil authorities might be letting themselves to some extent be deterred from sufficiently drastic action by too great a regard for the susceptibilities of the planters and by a desire not to interfere with the amenities of normal life.

The Minister of Defence suggested that a new psychological approach to the problem and a wider and more vigorous outlook were needed. The Malayan troubles were only [one] aspect of the whole Far Eastern question; if, for instance, the Government of Siam proved unable to control the Communists in that country, the northern frontier of Malaya would be seriously threatened.

Mr. R.H. Scott said that, if unlimited time and man-power were available, our present policy would be adequate; but the time factor was vital and more ruthless action was needed. The prime need was the restoration of law and order, and to this, such other advantages as constitutional progress and dollar earnings must, if necessary, be sacrificed for the time being. He thought that constitutional progress must be suspended for the present (exept in the purely municipal sphere). More encouragement should be given to those Chinese who were willing to co-operate in the running of the country, and we should be more drastic in dealing with those who refused to co-operate. The present constitution was too heavily weighted in favour of the Malays. The British territories in South-East Asia should be treated more as a unit, and the present very complex chain of command should be simplified. Help should be sought from the Governments of Australia and India, both of whom were vitally interested in restoring the peace in Malaya, even though this might mean giving them some voice in our policy there. Perhaps the most important thing of all was to set aside immediately large areas in North Borneo for the reception of Chinese deportees and to give this operation the highest possible priority. The proposed dumping of Chinese detainees *en masse* on the coasts of China should be held in reserve; this would amount practically to an act of war and in any case could only be carried out once.

In further discussion, the following points were made:—

(a) The changes of fortune in Korea would probably have less effect on the Chinese in Malaya than events in Indo-China, which was much nearer at hand.

(b) If constitutional progress was suspended, this fact would certainly be exploited by the Communists, who would renew the cry of Colonialism.

(c) We had been compelled to enter into an Agreement with the Sultans in 1948, but this Agreement was in some ways not at all satisfactory. It admittedly favoured the Malays, and the Chinese, for instance, were debarred by it from entry into the higher Civil Service. It would be desirable to bring more Chinese into the administration, so far as this could be done without offending the Malays. The Chinese were unfortunately very reluctant to join the police in Malaya except in the C.I.D. Branch.

(d) The Malay Sultans were as a whole ineffective and largely a burden on the country. They still, however, exercised a strong religious influence over the Malays; and the recent riots in Singapore showed how inflammable Moslem feeling was.[1]

(e) The need for more drive and vigour in the conduct of Malayan affairs was generally agreed, but it was not yet clear how this could be best achieved. It was felt to be desirable that as a next step the Commissioner-General for South-East Asia should be called home for consultation as soon as possible. The High Commissioner for the Federation of Malaya should not at this stage be brought into these discussions.

(f) *The Secretary of State for the Colonies* stated that General Briggs' present appointment in Malaya terminated early in April. It was understood that he would be willing to remain for a further six months or so, and there was general agreement that he should be invited to do so.

The Meeting:—

(1) Invited the Minister of State to arrange for the Commissioner-General for South-East Asia to fly to England for consultation as soon as possible.

(2) Invited the Secretary of State for the Colonies to extend General Briggs' appointment for six months.

---

[1] On 11–13 Dec 1950 Moslem riots (known as the Maria Hertogh or Nadra riots) resulted in 18 deaths and 173 other casualties (see *Report of the Singapore Riots Inquiry Commission*, Singapore, 1951).

233 PREM 8/1406/2, GEN 345/7   9 Mar 1951

[Briggs plan]: Cabinet Office summary of a further meeting at 10 Downing Street on 8 Mar called by Mr Attlee to consider the plan's slow progress

[The meeting was attended by Attlee, Morrison (FO), Shinwell (Defence), Griffiths (CO), MacDonald, Sir A Sanders (deputy chief of air staff), Sir G Creasy (vice-chief of naval staff), Sir K McLean (military secretary to secretary of state for war, 1949–1951; chief secretary, Ministry of Defence, 1951–1952), Sir J Harding (c-in-c, Far East Land Forces), R H Scott (FO), J J Paskin and J D Higham (CO).]

The Meeting had before them a note by the Joint Secretaries (GEN. 345/6) covering a Progress Report by the Director of Operations, Malaya, dated 15th February, 1951, together with a note by the Colonial Office on certain points in it.

The Commissioner-General for South-East Asia said that there had been some limited improvement in the situation during the last few months. More information was now being received about bandit activities, the troops were making more contacts with them, and the morale of the people was improving. This improvement was due partly to military action and to the new and better disposition of the troops in the priority areas since last November, and partly to greater drive in the civil administration and the successful progress of resettlement. Nevertheless, it was generally agreed that the process of clearing the country would inevitably be slow. Malaya was a guerrilla's paradise, with three-quarters of the country covered by thick jungle, and the Communist victories elsewhere in Asia had made the Chinese less ready to co-operate.

The Commissioner-General said that, shortly before his departure for London, Sir Henry Gurney and Sir Harold Briggs had expressed to him their view that the situation was not likely to improve sufficiently during the present year to permit the release of any British troops unless these could be replaced from elsewhere. General Harding and he himself, however, thought that if the situation elsewhere in South-East Asia could be held (and this was a big 'if') and if present progress was maintained in Malaya, it should be possible to start to release some British troops in the autumn of 1951 and perhaps more early in 1952. The possibility was being considered of obtaining troops for Malaya from both Fiji and East Africa; the former political objections to the use of these troops had now disappeared and they would be very welcome.

Resettlement was now going well. Much had already been done, and it was hoped that resettlement in the priority areas would be completed by 1st May. But there was still a shortage of administrative and resettlement officers. If these could be obtained, either from the African Colonies or by other means, the completion of resettlement in the non-priority areas would be brought much nearer. Owing to our success in resettling the squatters, the bandits were now turning their attention more to estates and mines. The Government were therefore concentrating the workers on the mines and estates in order to protect them from the bandits. It was hoped that such concentration might be complete by 1st May, though it could never be entirely effective, since the workers were bound to scatter during the day time and so to become vulnerable to bandit activities.

The greatest difficulty at the moment was recruitment for the Police. The vacancies for police officers had now been reduced to 18, of which 11 were under offer, but there still remained a shortage of over 200 Police Lieutenants, and this was really the crux of the situation. Without these non-commissioned officers, it was impossible to train or make full use of the special constables or to form jungle squads and so to release British Troops from jungle operations. The Secretary of State for the Colonies had recently come to an arrangement with the Home Secretary by which it would be possible to second members of home police services to Malaya for a period of three years on attractive terms. Such secondment should supply the right type of non-commissioned officer, since men with authority and the power to control others were needed, and it was hoped that about 100 Police Lieutenants might be obtained from this source. Of the remaining 100, some 20 or 30 might possibly be obtained from Gurkha ex-officers in Nepal. There had also been a suggestion that young men doing their National Service in the Army might be asked to volunteer for this work, but some doubt had been expressed whether young men of this type would carry the necessary weight and authority. There was also great difficulty in recruiting for the rank and file of the police, since the boom in rubber had made wages in the rubber industry much more attractive. The Malayan Government were doing their best to meet this situation by raising the pay of the police and by using their powers of direction to bring men into the force. There was also the possibility of recruiting some 2,500 Gurkhas from Burma for the Malayan police, and His Majesty's Ambassador in Rangoon had been asked to pursue this with vigour.

The Commissioner-General said that the problem of Chinese detainees still remained very serious, since the Peking Government had now stopped their return to Southern China. As a result, the removal of the detainees to British North Borneo was now the only solution of the problem. Two islands in this area were being surveyed at the moment. There was strong opposition in North Borneo, both in official and unofficial circles, to the removal there of the detainees. But this was a necessary move; and, as soon as the survey of the islands was completed, he proposed to issue a direction to the Governor of North Borneo to accept the detainees and make the necessary arrangements for them. He himself would then visit North Borneo and explain the need for this action.

As regards the higher direction of the emergency, the Commissioner-General said that the Federal War Council was now functioning satisfactorily, and that Sir Henry Gurney and General Briggs were working well together on it as Chairman and Vice-Chairman. He agreed, however, that the position had not always been so satisfactory. It was not until after his last visit to London that Sir Henry Gurney had sat on the War Council. Until that time he had tended to be somewhat divorced from the operational side of the emergency, which he had left to General Briggs, and to concentrate rather on economic and social questions and on political reform. It was, he thought, partly dissatisfaction at the results of this situation and at a certain lack of drive in the civil administration that had led General Briggs to suggest resigning, a suggestion which he had later withdrawn. The Commissioner-General was convinced, however, that the situation had now definitely improved in this respect; the Federal War Council, with Sir Henry Gurney in the Chair, was now a streamlined and efficient body for the conduct of the emergency and he did not think that General Briggs would now have any complaint on the score of a lack of drive. In addition to the Federal War Council, there was also a Malaya and Borneo Defence Council, with the Commissioner-General in the Chair. General Briggs attended its meetings regularly. Atlhough this Council was largely concerned with preparations against a possible general war, it also interested itself very directly in the emergency in Malaya, since it fully appreciated the vital need for clearing up the emergency and releasing the British troops there before any general war broke out. The Defence Council had wide powers and could take suitable action if at any time General Briggs felt that there was undue slowness on the part of the civil administration in Malaya.

General Harding confirmed the view that, if progress in Malaya continued and the position outside Malaya could be held, it should be possible to start a programme of phased withdrawal of British troops from Malaya in the autumn of 1951. No definite decision on this point could be given at the moment, but the possibility should be kept constantly under review. He thought it important to obtain troops from Fiji and

East Africa. The troops now in Malaya were only sufficient for its defence in case of war. They could not be withdrawn in a hurry without greatly damaging public morale, and therefore the replacement of any British troops which might be withdrawn must in any event be continued. He thought that volunteers from National Service recruits would not be suitable as Police Lieutenants, but that they might be very useful in the rank of corporal for training and supervising special constables. As regards the higher direction of the emergency, he thought that the Malaya and Borneo Council had not yet had a chance of proving its value, but that if it was sufficiently active and had enough executive powers it should be very useful both as regards the Malayan emergency and in preparation for a possible war. From the general defence point of view, it would be very valuable if the Federation of Malaya could be more closely integrated with Singapore, thus avoiding duplication of channels.

In discussion, the following points were made:—

(a) There was general concern about the slowness of our progress in Malaya and of the operation of the Briggs Plan. It was recalled that, in the middle of 1949, the authorities in Malaya had expressed the hope that the emergency should be cleared up by the end of that year. Since that time, however, the sweeping victories of the Communists in China had greatly raised the morale of the bandits and had driven large numbers of Chinese in Malaya to "reinsure" with them. The recognition of the Communist Government of China by His Majesty's Government (though clearly necessary in the light of the general world situation) had also had unfortunate repercussions in Malaya.

(b) It was also now clear that the time-table originally put forward by General Briggs for the operation of his Plan could not be maintained. But General Briggs had now been in Malaya for about a year, and had put forward a new tentative time-table in the light of his experience there. Under this, it was hoped that Malaya would be cleared up to the middle of the peninsula by the end of 1951 after which the northern half could be tackled. But all progress in Malaya must still be largely conditioned by events outside.

(c) It was noted that in spite of the considerable number of bandits that had been killed by the troops their total numbers remained more or less stationary. This was explained by the fact that the bandits could always obtain as many new recruits as they needed to fill up their numbers, by press-gang or other methods. Their supply of arms and ammunition came from the large caches which they had maintained since the end of the Japanese war; there was no evidence that they were receiving arms or ammunition from outside sources.

(d) *The Commissioner-General for South-East Asia* emphatically repudiated any suggestion that the planters were lacking in co-operation or that military operations were in any way impeded by a desire to avoid interfering with production of rubber etc. He thought, on the contrary that the planters were in all cases most eager to have their neighbourhood cleared of bandits and welcomed military action there.

(e) It had not yet proved possible to clear Johore entirely of bandits, as envisaged in the original Briggs Plan, as it was impossible to draw a cordon round the State or to isolate it completely. In spite of progress with resettlement, there were also still over 500,000 squatters remaining in the priority areas.

(f) One favourable feature of the situation in Malaya was that the Nationalist Movement had been kept solidly on the British side. This had been a great help in

Malaya itself and also very valuable for its effect on Indian opinion.
lay with Sir Henry Gurney.

(g) *General Harding* said that he was fully satisfied with the
serving under him in Malaya. There was now good co-operatio.
military, the civil administration and the police, who had joint Ope.   ...s
down to district level. He thought that any lack of drive in the civil administration
might be due to the fact that so many administrative officers, both British and Malay,
had been prisoners of war for nearly four years, which had naturally impaired their
health and vigour. *The Foreign Secretary* suggested that it might be possible to
secure for service in Malaya some of the British administrative officers who were now
becoming redundant in Libya and Eritrea. He thought that everything possible
should be done to stimulate the vigour, and if necessary ruthlessness, or [of] all our
actions in Malaya.

The Meeting:—

(1) Invited the Foreign Secretary and the Secretary of State for the Colonies to
consider further the possibility of obtaining British administrative officers for
Malaya from the former Italian Colonies.

(2) Agreed to meet again on Monday, 12th March at 3.45 p.m.

234 PREM 8/1406/2, GEN 345/8   13 Mar 1951
[Briggs plan]: Cabinet Office summary of a meeting resumed on 12
Mar to consider the progress of the plan

The Meeting resumed discussion of the situation in Malaya,[1] with special reference to
the Progress Report by the Director of Operations (GEN. 345/6).

Progress of the Briggs plan
General Harding said that he appreciated the disappointment which had been
expressed over the slow progress of the Briggs Plan, and particularly over the fact
that Johore had not yet been completely cleared of bandits. He thought, however,
that there was perhaps some misconception about the original intention of the Plan
There existed all over Malaya a network of organised Communist cells, in towns,
villages and estates, which supplied and supported the bandits. The bandit companies
themselves were very active and mobile, and count [could] not be confined to one
State. General Briggs had therefore planned to spread a framework of security forces
all over Malaya, which would contain the bandits and their supporters and prevent
them from becoming even more troublesome. The remainder of the troops, once this
framework had been provided, were concentrated in the South of the peninsula. The
progress of the military operations was closely tied up with that of the resettlement
programme, the establishment of police posts and the improvement of communications. As this programme was achieved in each State, it was hoped that it would
become possible to hold down bandit activities there with the framework troops only,
leaving the mobile units to proceed to another State. But General Harding
emphasised that it had never been hoped that any one State could be completely
cleared of bandit activity; and the Briggs Plan could not be said to have failed merely

---

[1] See 233.

ɔecause incidents were still occurring in Johore. Johore was a particularly difficult State to control; it contained a very large proportion of the squatters in the whole of Malaya, who had to be resettled; and it was the nearest State to Singapore, which the bandits used as an exchange centre for their communications. It was now hoped that Johore would be "cleared" by the beginning of May, i.e. that it would then be possible to hold down bandit activity there with only the framework troops, leaving the reserve to move on northwards. This date was six months later than had been hoped; but military success depended on the progress of resettlement of squatters, and this work had been considerably held up by lack of man-power. The situation was now improving as regards the supply of resettlement officers, who had been concentrated in the priority areas. Besides the resettlement of squatters, there was also the question of regrouping the estate and mine workers, which was proceeding in parallel. It was hoped that this work also would be completed in the priority areas by 1st May, 1951. But there would always remain the difficulty that there would still be some sympathisers with the bandits both among resettled squatter communities and estate labour, who would provide the bandits with small quantities of food and money. To prevent this called for vigilance and efficiency on the part of the police, and this again depended on adequate supervision.

Recruitment of administrative officers

The Secretary of State for the Colonies said that he had discussed with the Minister of State the possibility of obtaining British administrative officers for Malaya from the former Italian Colonies. It appeared that there were a few members of the Colonial Service, who had been seconded to Cyrenaica and Tripolitania, and their release was being discussed. A few more administrative officers might become available from the former Italian Colonies, but there were not likely to be many. A more promising source was the British Zone of Germany, where about 1,000 officers were expected shortly to become redundant. A representative of the Colonial Office and an officer from Malaya were shortly going to Germany to examine this possibility further.

The Secretary of State for the Colonies said that one difficulty was that nobody could be forced to go from the United Kingdom to serve in Malaya; but he thought that in Malaya itself the Government might make more use of its powers of direction in order to draft members of the planting and mining communities into Government Service, even if this meant a check to production.

The Commissioner-General for South-East Asia doubted whether much would be gained by this; most of the able-bodied Europeans on the estates and the mines were already doing very good work in charge of Special Constables etc. in addition to their normal jobs. He said that as regards the vital problem of resettlement, one of the main difficulties was to keep in proper contact with the Chinese population. They had already recruited some 200 Chinese Assistant Resettlement Officers, and European officers were doing special short courses in Chinese. Some Chinese officers had been obtained by conscription. It was difficult to obtain the right type of Chinese by voluntary methods, since they could do better for themselves outside the Government Services. Other sources outside Malaya were also being tapped, including consulates and trading-posts which were closing down in China. Missionaries from China would be useful for social work, but they were unfortunately rather chary of undertaking Government work, even in the welfare fields.

Replacement of British troops in Malaya
The Chief of the Imperial General Staff said that the British troops in Malaya were badly needed elsewhere, and he thought that they might well be replaced by native troops from the African Colonies, who would be very suitable for the Malayan type of jungle warfare. There was also the possibility of a battalion from Fiji. There had previously been political objections to the use of such troops in Malaya, but he understood that these had now disappeared, since the Malays were now being fully used in the new battalions of the Malay Regiment. He appreciated that in some of the African Colonies there were no more troops than were required for internal security; but if some of these troops were taken from these Colonies for Malaya, it should not be difficult to raise new battalions locally. The recruitment of volunteers from India and Pakistan, which had been suggested, would not be likely to commend itself to the Governments of those countries.

The Secretary of State for the Colonies agreed in principle with the use of African and Fijian troops in Malaya; but it would be necessary to examine the local political implications, and suitable financial arrangements would have to be made.

Other points
(a) It was noted that in a recent ambush in Johore a party of 100 bandits was reported to have been engaged; and it was suggested that the security forces should have been aware of so large a concentration of bandits, which was a good deal bigger than their usual practice. It was however explained that, though the local commander would no doubt know that such a force of bandits existed within a certain area, there were many hundreds of square miles of jungle into which they could easily disappear. It was also very easy to make a mistake about the numbers of a bandit body, since it was almost impossible to count the numbers of attackers accurately in a jungle ambush.

(b) It was clear that the bandits were deliberately using minor incidents, e.g. the burning of a lorry, as a decoy to lure the security troops into an ambush. The success of these ambushes suggested some lack of vigilance on the part of the troops, but such incidents were almost bound to arise when the troops were tired out after long and arduous jungle patrols

(c) Of the captured bandits, those who had committed murder had been hanged, and full publicity had been given to this. Others were being used as sources of information about the bandits and for propaganda purposes.

The Meeting:—
Agreed in principle that African and Fijian troops should be used to replace British troops in Malaya; and invited the Secretary of State for the Colonies, in concert with the War Office, to examine the practical problems involved.[2]

---

[2] By the end of Mar the proposal to use East African troops had been agreed with all the governors concerned. See also 238, para 3.

235 CO 967/145 19 Mar 1951
[Gurney offers to resign]: letter from Sir H Gurney to Sir T Lloyd

[Gurney had been on the verge of relinquishing office on at least one previous occasion. In May 1949, believing that he was constitutionally unable to carry out the prime minister's instructions in the matter of advising the Sultan of Selangor to reprieve an Indian sentenced to the death penalty, Gurney had offered his resignation which Attlee had immediately declined, informing the high commissioner, through Lord Listowel, that he retained full confidence in his judgment (see CO 537/4770, nos 8 and 10). The following year, when the CO suspected that Gurney may have acted unprofessionally in taking the deputy leader of the opposition into his confidence, Lloyd had advised against administering any rebuke because the high commissioner was 'particularly sensitive, almost touchy' (see 183–184 and minute from Lloyd to Rees-Williams, 1 Apr 1949, CO 537/4741). The private and personal letter (the original was sent in manuscript) reproduced here, which was written to Lloyd after the Downing Street talks, is in a different class and reveals the real strain the high commissioner was under by this time.]

Malcolm MacDonald looked in here yesterday and told me of the impatience and dissatisfaction felt and expressed to him by certain Ministers at the slow rate of progress of the Malayan campaign.[1]

I agree that if there is not a marked improvement in the operational field in say, six months' time, it will be very desirable to have a change of High Commissioner.

When officers are invited by Ministers to criticise my conduct of affairs, for which I am responsible, it seems right that I should be informed as to what takes place. From the fact of such consultations and from the absence of any information from London about them, I must be forgiven if I feel that there is in certain quarters a lack of confidence in myself.

The situation here is a delicate one politically. To keep all the various elements including the Services moving forward smoothly and to maintain progress in the political, economic and social fields are a fairly difficult operation, which leaves me little time to keep others informed of what is happening. Perhaps I am at fault in this respect and it is as much my fault as anyone else's that when an appreciation of the 'situation in Malaya' is required, the request for it is sent to the B.D.C.C. or anybody but myself. Such appreciations are written by people sitting in offices in Singapore or perhaps written by General Briggs and transmitted through Service channels to London, and they have seldom appeared to me to be either complete or accurate.

It is also a little discouraging to have such complete silence from the C.O. on certain matters which are important here. I sent a despatch on the Member system six weeks ago and have had no reply to it nor any sign of interest. I have recently asked twice for a reply to the Penang Secession Petition,[2] now over a year old, but have heard nothing. The same applies to Foster-Sutton's date of appointment.[3]

As you know, I was reluctant to take this on and only did so when pressed on grounds of public duty (as in Palestine). These grounds clearly no longer apply, and

---

[1] See 233 and 234.

[2] Since 1946, when the Straits Settlements of Singapore, Penang and Malacca had been dismantled and Penang had lost its free-port status, secession from the rest of Malaya had been advocated by those Chinese and Indians of Penang, who feared for their rights as British subjects and their future within a Malay-dominated Federation.

[3] S W Foster-Sutton served in Malaya as attorney-general, 1948–1950, officer administering government, Sept–Dec 1950, and chief justice, 1950–1951.

my reluctance to continue under present conditions is strengthened by the inability of my wife to join me here for reasons of health. If I felt able to continue at full stretch for some years—and the situation here requires and will require 100% output of energy—and if I were less conscious of lack of confidence in certain quarters in London, I should think it a mistake to change. But under present strains three years is probably long enough for anybody and Jews do not forget.[4] Fantastic though that may sound, I have good reason for thinking so.

Thus it may be advisable that I should be permitted to relinquish office towards the end of the year when Briggs leaves, which would provide the opportunity for the appointment as High Commissioner of a suitable Services candidate. I think he will need to possess some unusual qualities if he is going to hold together the Malay and Chinese & Indian politicians, the Rulers, planters & Services as well as defeat the Communists, without repatriation to China.

In case you should misunderstand what I have written, let me say that I fully acknowledge and appreciate the support given me by the Secretary of State and yourself. That support should not be strained too far. The short fact is that when a man is entrusted with the job of finishing off Communist banditry in Malaya and appears unable to do it, there are bound to be demands that somebody else should be brought in. Cf. de Lattre.[5] I hope therefore that the advocates of that course may be told that I shall be glad to facilitate their wishes and shall remain silent. I desire no further appointment.

You may like to show this to the Secretary of State, but otherwise perhaps it would be best to keep its contents to yourself. It requires no reply.

---

[4] This reference, presumably to Gurney's time in Palestine, is inexplicable.

[5] General de Lattre de Tassigny had arrived in Vietnam in Dec 1950 to assume the dual function of high commissioner and commander-in-chief; his prime task was to save Hanoi and by June 1951 he had halted the Vietminh offensive in Tonkin. Illness, however, forced him to return to Paris where he died on 11 Jan 1952.

236 CO 967/145   5 Apr 1951
[Gurney's offer of resignation]: letter (reply) from Sir T Lloyd to Sir H Gurney

[Considering Gurney's letter 'disturbing' and regretful that the high commissioner had not been included in the party which had travelled from SE Asia for the Downing Street talks (but see 232, para(e)), Lloyd consulted Griffiths before despatching a 'sympathetic and reassuring reply'.]

Thank you for your manuscript letter of the 19th of March.[1] It took some time on the way as I did not receive it until Friday last, the 30th of March. You said that it needed no reply but I should not be content to leave such a letter answered. I have shown it, as you said I might, to the Secretary of State (but to no one else outside my Private Office) and this reply is sent with his approval and authority.

Let me start with an apology (for the fault would be mine) if you have got the impression that these last Ministerial talks were intended from the beginning to be

---

[1] See 235.

an inquisition into *your* conduct of affairs. If they had been so intended I should have advised, and the Secretary of State would I feel sure have agreed, that you ought to be invited here to take part in them. The intention of the talks was the much wider one not merely of discussing the Malayan campaign but of examining the whole situation in that part of the world in the broader context of its relation to, and effect upon, defence requirements elsewhere. In the course of that examination there was inevitably—you saw for yourself from the talks last autumn how these things happen—criticism by other Ministers of the conduct of civil administration not only in the Federation but in other parts of South East Asia. I do not worry unduly about that so long as the Secretary of State of the day retains complete confidence, and expresses it, in the particular person responsible to him. Both Mr. Griffiths and Malcolm MacDonald (as I hope he told you) did in quite unqualified terms make plain to other Ministers the confidence they have in you personally, in your handling of the political problems of the Federation, and in your determination to ensure that economic and social progress without which the direct campaign against banditry could not fully succeed.

I have said that I hope that Malcolm MacDonald made all this plain to you. He was asked to do so but if in fact he failed to convince you of the Secretary of State's continuing confidence in your administration the reason must, I am sure, be that we failed to impress the point sufficiently upon him and that is our fault.

The Secretary of State has asked me to give you this personal message. He greatly appreciates the terms in which you wrote to me and in particular your offer to tender your resignation (for that is what I take you to mean) and to "remain silent" if in say six months there has not been a marked improvement in the operational field. Mr. Griffiths recognises the high principles and unselfish motives which prompted that offer which would of course make it that much the easier for him should he at any time come to the conclusion that there ought to be a change of High Commissioner. But that, as I have tried to make plain, is not his view now. On the contrary, he feels that only someone with the confidence, which you have, of the leaders of all races in Malaya could hope at the same time both to achieve success on the civil side of the campaign and to lead the Federation in the way it must go politically and in the social and economic fields. Should Mr. Griffiths at any time feel that there ought to be a change of High Commissioner he would not hesitate at once to tell you, particularly now that you have made your position so plain. He asks you to believe that nothing of the sort is now in his mind. So long as there is no lack of confidence between the two of you it would, as you said in your letter, be a mistake to change and you still have the Secretary of State's full confidence. He looks forward to your continuing for so far ahead as can now be foreseen the admirable work which you are doing in and for Malaya and he hopes that during the next few months that work will receive its due reward in an ever increasing measure of success in the anti-banditry campaign and in a realisation of the Briggs plan.

237 CO 537/7262, no 51   28 Apr 1951

[Executive and Legislative Councils]: letter from Sir H Gurney to J D
Higham on recent constitutional innovations   [Extract]

[The member system, which had been proposed in Apr 1950 (see 212), was approved by
the Legislative Council in Jan 1951.]

Since our monthly Political Reports are of rather limited scope, you may like to have
some further information about the introduction of the Member system on the 9th
April and the first meeting of the new Legislative Council this week.

The six new Members have settled in very well and are already working as
members of the team. Dato Onn has expressed to me his great satisfaction with the
way in which this development has taken place, and other official members have
commented on the remarkable difference in atmosphere in Executive Council now
that almost all its members are responsible for duties of their own. This is indeed
very noticeable to me and what was often an apathetic, if not critical, attitude on the
part of some has been transformed into one of very live keenness both to do their
own job well and to understand their colleagues' difficulties. It is too much to expect
that this spirit should continue for long without serious difficulties arising, but it is
of course natural and proper that this should be so.

The new Members' appearance in Legislative Council was welcomed in speeches
from all sides of the Council, which, apart from being out of order, must have been
an encouragement to the Members themselves. Mr. Ponnodurai, who is the rather
questionable Secretary of the Penang Secession Committee and now represents the
Settlement Council in place of Lee Tiang Keng, took the opportunity of announcing
that he was considering seceding from the Committee. In this connection, it is really
time that a reply was sent to the Penang Secession petition.[1]

The member elected by the Malacca Settlement Council is the Resident Commissioner himself, and it was interesting to see him putting questions to Mead as
Member for Works and Housing. This is all rather up-side-down, but I thought it
might show the Malay members that if Malay Government officers can sit as
unofficial members others can do so as well.

I have not sent you any report about the composition of the new Legislative
Council and I appreciate your not having asked for one. We have got rid of about a
dozen passengers from the old Council and replaced them with stronger members,
most of whom were nominated by U.M.N.O. It was on Dato Onn's suggestion that we
have put Aziz of the Utusan Melayu on the Council since he is one of our most
ill-informed critics.[2] I had hoped to send him to England as one of the two
journalists shortly to go there, but Singapore has selected his brother, also of the
Utusan, so that we must continue to put up with Aziz at this end. He moved a motion

---

[1] See 235, note 2.

[2] In 1953 Abdul Aziz bin Ishak was invited to the coronation in London as representative of the Malayan
press, but, after he published pejorative comments about members of the British establishment, Templer
reputedly called him 'a rat and a rotten journalist whose name stinks in South East Asia'. As minister of
agriculture and co-operatives, 1955–1962, Abdul Aziz opposed the location of British military bases in
Malaya after independence. His brother, Yusoff bin Ishak, was the founder-editor of *Utusan Melayu* in
1939.

about the dispossession of Malays from the land required for the Fisheries Research Station at Penang and was, I think, surprised to find that after debate there was no single supporter for him in the House.

The fact that the 61 unofficial members are a stronger body of individuals than previously is an additional reason why I am glad that we did not delay in strengthening the official side as we have done. Another satisfactory feature is the spontaneous and loyal support being given by senior Government officers to the new set-up, including the ex-officio members and particularly del Tufo, who has been shorn of a good deal of his responsibilities but yet has worked very hard and tactfully to plan and start up the new machine on the administrative levels.

Spencer has also made his mark both in Legislative Council and outside and I am greatly impressed by his ability as a speaker and as a practical economist. This is another example to Malaya of the value of importation. . . .

238   CO 537/7263, no 31   22 May 1951
'Malaya': minute by Mr Shinwell to Mr Attlee on the emergency situation

Prime Minister

Since I spoke to you on 2nd May on the present situation in Malaya,[1] I have had further consultations on this subject with the Secretary of State for the Colonies, the Secretary of State for War, and with the C.I.G.S. The following is a summary of the main points which have been brought out in these consultations:—

1. The position in Malaya cannot be judged solely on the statistics of incidence and casualties shown in the weekly returns. A better test of the position is the frequency with which information comes in from local inhabitants. Judging from this criterion we are making real but slow progress. There is general agreement that in the past month there has been a slight improvement in the overall situation.

2. Resettlement is complete in the main priority area and nearing completion in the remaining priority areas and there is evidence that the operation is seriously hampering the Communists, particularly the Min Yuen.

3. On the military side, slow progress is evident and the Commander-in-Chief, Far East, has recently stated that if progress in the programme for raising the 5th Battalion Malaya [Malay] Regiment and the Police Jungle companies is maintained, reductions in the garrison might start this autumn. (In this connection you will recall that at your meeting with the High Commissioner for the Federation of Malaya on 13th March[2] this year it was agreed in principle that African and Fijian troops should be used to replace British troops in Malaya subject to an examination of the local political implications and the making of suitable financial arrangements). A paper is being prepared for the Defence Committee on this subject asking for approval in principle to the despatch of two Battalions of King's African Rifles for active service in Malaya.

---

[1] At that time Shinwell called the situation 'still very disturbing'.
[2] Shinwell is actually referring to the meeting with the commissioner-general on 12 Mar, see 234.

4. The real enemy is not the jungle bandit but the Min Yuen in the towns who finance supplies and direct the bandits. Against this our main weapons are Intelligence, the C.I.D. and Police. The recruiting of Police Officers and the reorganization of the Police Force has made great progress but is hampered by a lack of suitable personnel.

5. The reorganization of the C.I.D. and Special Branch of the Police has been in progress for some months and the latest information indicates that the Police Intelligence Organization is better geared to cope with the increasing supply of information.[3] A large proportion of contacts between the security forces and the bandits is now directly due to information supplied by the civil population.

The Secretary of State for the Colonies has suggested that it would be useful for the authorities in Malaya to be asked to prepare a form of appreciation of the situation at the end of May, which would enable us to review progress during the three months since our discussions at the beginning of March with the Commissioner General and General Harding.

I agree with this suggestion and, subject to your comments, I propose to discuss with the Secretary of State for the Colonies how this can best be done.[4]

I am sending copies of this minute to the Secretary of State for the Colonies and the Secretary of State for War.

---

[3] See 199, note 7.　　　　[4] On 22 May Attlee agreed that such an appreciation be prepared, see 239.

239　CO 537/7263, no 38A　　　　4 June 1951
'Federation of Malaya—combined appreciation of the emergency situation': joint memorandum by Sir H Gurney and Lieutenant-General Sir H Briggs

In a campaign such as this, where pitched battles between organised armies do not occur and where success depends on the morale of and the help given by the population and the breaking of Communist morale and organisation, one is left to judge the situation by a combination of varying factors.

Perhaps the greatest weight can be given to the factors of Communist surrenders and of the information and assistance forthcoming from the Chinese population as a result of their coming "off the fence". Other factors include the number of Communist casualties and arrests, battle contacts by our troops and the successful prevention of supplies, arms and ammunition reaching the enemy.

2. There is a definite feeling among local Army, Police and Administrative officers, to which we subscribe, that the cumulative effects of our measures are bringing us, or have brought us, to the turning point of the campaign. We believe this improvement will continue, especially if the development of events in the Far East, particularly in Korea and Indo-China, continues to be favourable.

3. Owing to resettlement, in which approximately 240,000 people have now been resettled, and to our increased successes, public opinion generally is feeling more confident and secure and the flow of information is increasing daily, leading to further successes. While it cannot yet be said that the Chinese are no longer "sitting on the fence", our policy of committing them to our side by getting them to join our

Home Guard organisation, which they are doing in very great numbers, is bearing good fruit.

4. The figure of bandit surrenders, given in the Appendix[1] (for the period of 3 months March–May compared with the preceding 3 months) is encouraging as it shows an increase of approximately 180% whilst the total bandit casualties show an increase of 42%, 683 bandits having been definitely accounted for during the whole six months. There has been a similar increase in arrests of bandit supporters, which two factors must be affecting bandit morale.

5. Resettlement of squatters in SOUTH MALAYA, and, to a lesser extent, the regrouping of labour, is sufficiently advanced to permit a strict measure of food control which is now to be applied. Together with this measure an intensified offensive is now to be undertaken by the Army, Police, Intelligence and Propaganda Services, aimed at both the bandits and their MIN YUEN[2] cells in these areas. (NOT TO BE DISCLOSED). Full results may not be forthcoming for three months.

6. Information is to hand to show that the Communists in SOUTH MALAYA have been making an all-out offensive since January, allowing no rest periods to their platoons as before, in order to dislocate our general plan which is well known to them. To counteract the shortage of food resulting from resettlement they have established many food dumps, and this accounts for the large increase in such dumps being discovered by Security Forces as shown in the Appendix. Food shortage also accounts for the increase of incidents which are vital to them if their morale is to remain high.

7. In the Southern areas especially bandit incidents are of a more serious nature in the form of disrupting our economy, ambushing Security Force patrols and attacking Special Constable posts. The latter leads frequently to the loss of arms, which is serious. Unfortunately the training and discipline of these Special Constables, who are essential for the security of planters, is weak and has suffered from lack of officers to supervise them. Every step possible is being taken to improve this but Police Lieutenants are still deplorably short—about 180.

8. Improvement in Police Intelligence is now very noticeable but there is still much to be done to make this our first line of attack as it must be. Propaganda is paying good dividends and is doing much to strengthen morale and lower that of the enemy.

Police Jungle Companies are now beginning to become operative but need more experience and training before becoming fully effective. By the end of the year 20 out of the 45 should be operative. Gurkhas to augment these are beginning to arrive from Burma.

Much concern is caused by the need for training and supervision of the Police and, in particular, the Special Constables. Operational demands and lack of the full quota of trained officers, Police Lieutenants and Inspectors make this a slow and difficult matter.

Slowly a Chinese element, essential for dealing with a Chinese population, is being brought into the Force.

The arms situation is satisfactory but the shortage of clothing for so large a force

---

[1] Not printed.
[2] The *Min Yuen*, or 'Masses Organization', provided the MRLA with food, funds, recruits and information and were vital to the communists' campaign.

still exists and tends to lower morale. The efficiency of Police Jungle Companies will be impaired until the prototype wireless set, now being tested, can be manufactured and sent out.

This unavoidable slowness in promoting Police efficiency is our most serious obstacle to the quick success of operations.

9. Repatriation of detainees to China has, on the whole, gone well in spite of many difficulties. During April and May approximately 2,000, including families, have left for China. A further 850 are expected to leave on June 20th.

10. Our main deficiency in supplies is again barbed wire, owing to the inability of the Crown Agents to produce even our original requirements. The demand grows daily and is most pressing. So far we have only been able to get a promise of 500 tons from Japan as against our existing requirement of 2,900 tons.

Building materials have greatly increased in price under pressure of demand and a scheme for controlling them is under consideration with the Government of Singapore. Building is already controlled. The supply of timber is to some extent affected by bandit activity.

11. The Malay Regiment is 40 officers short. This is serious because there is no purpose in proceeding to recruit for the 6th Battalion until this shortage is made good. Approval of our proposals for better terms of service and permanence with the Regiment would be helpful.

12. Medical services, particularly in the Chinese settlements, are required, but we are 40 doctors short. This has recently been discussed here with the Chief Medical Officer of the Colonial Office, who appreciates that in this campaign a syringe may be as important as a gun. The British Red Cross Society is beginning to give valuable assistance, and it is gratifying that the Church Missionary Society has now decided to bring in missionary workers from China.

13. The Appendix sets out statistics for the three months March–May.

240 CO 537/7303, no 10 13 June 1951
[Dato Onn and the Independence of Malaya Party]: letter from Sir H Gurney to J D Higham discussing Onn's intentions

In connection with Dato Onn's recent announcement of his intention to form an Independent Malaya Party [sic] embracing all communities, I thought you might like to know what is in his mind. I had a long and frank talk with him today in which he explained that his first object is to free himself from the inactive and purely conservative elements in UMNO who have been obstructing his efforts to admit non-Malays into UMNO and who are in his view merely a dead weight in any political party.

As the leader of a new non-communal party he felt sure of taking with him the live and active elements of UMNO and also the kampong Malays. This would be a shock to UMNO from which it would be unlikely to recover but he had no intention of yielding to probable pressure to continue as President, and his son Hussein would probably resign as Secretary General. He thought that UMNO would then break down into purely state organisations and indeed that was largely the condition of affairs now. It had been impossible to effect any real central control. None of the non-Malay leaders would be prepared to take on the Presidency and the party would therefore probably disintegrate.

I asked him whether he did not think it possible for him to continue to lead UMNO as well as the I.M.P. but he said that he was utterly tired of the sabotaging of his efforts by diehards in UMNO. On the other hand, he had offered leadership of the I.M.P. to Tan Cheng Lock but the latter was becoming more and more nervous and would not take it on. He added that he thought the present M.C.A. leaders were losing their influence among the Chinese and he agreed with my view that this was largely because of the amounts of money that many had accumulated during the past two years. He said that the press reports of his first statement referring to independence in seven years were incorrect, but he had not contradicted them because that might have made confusion worse. In any case, independence was not the object. The object was the good of the people to which independence was only a means. The main question was what should be done with self-government when you got it. He thought that this was far more widely realised among the Malays, particularly the kampong Malays, than was generally supposed and he would have great faith in the horse sense of the ordinary kampong Malay. Nor had he said anything to the press about Singapore being merged in the Federation. Union with Singapore could not come about for many years but in the meantime everything possible must be done to prevent the two territories drifting apart, and the I.M.P. would cover Singapore as well as the Federation. The I.M.P. would probably absorb the Labour Party and C.C. Tan with his Progressive Party would probably not like this at all as the Progressives would be swamped.

We then went on to discuss how the I.M.P. might secure seats in the Legislative Council, a point which I raised myself because the UMNO nominees have recently been put in for three years. I said that I hoped that we could come to some understanding within the constitution whereby the majority of the unofficial seats could be in effect held by parties, rather than adhering to the rather vague understandings which we are at present. He took this point and said that he had been thinking of it himself but had not yet formed any definite ideas except that a better geographical representation was needed than the present one which brought in, for example, no Chinese from Johore.

I then spoke to him about the vital part played by the Malays in the defence of Malaya against communism; but for them the country would today have been communist, and we had therefore to consider carefully any proposition which might so deeply split the Malays as to weaken their strength in the present struggle. He said that he had no fear of that and added in passing that he wished that sometimes some Chairmen of rubber and tin companies could pay some tribute to the Malays who were guarding their properties as well as the tributes so commonly paid to their managers and staffs, tributes with which incidentally he himself entirely agreed. This is a point worth mentioning in London at any suitable opportunity.

We then got on to discussing R.I.D.A. development plans and some of his work as Member for Home Affairs. It is I think a measure of his stature that he is quite happy to see himself performing all these various tricks at the same time. There are of course official limits to the versatility of a member of the government and in this connection the European members of the Legislative Council are sending a deputation to see me tomorrow, no doubt to ask whether Dato Onn's pronouncements represent Government policy. The answer to this is quite easy and so long as

Dato Onn keeps me frankly in the picture as to what he is doing, his presence in the Government will remain a source of strength rather than otherwise. But his decision to break with UMNO is a major one which may have far-reaching consequences, such as a building up of a strong rulers' party from the middle elements of UMNO who are largely government officers and may thus come into conflict with the I.M.P.

Meanwhile Dato Onn will have to move the second reading of the Citizenship Bill in Legislative Council next month and his speech on that occasion may well be an interesting one.

241 CO 537/7303, no 12   22 June 1951
[Dato Onn and the IMP]: inward telegram no 537 from Sir H Gurney to Mr Griffiths

Following for Higham.

My letter 13th June[1] despatched by Colonial Office mail No. 97 on 15th June gives you the background and should have reached you by now.

2. Onn has told me that Press reports of his first statement referring to independence in 7 years were incorrect, but he had not contradicted them because that might have made the confusion worse. This needs careful handling in conversation with the Press, since any suggestion, particularly from official sources, that he did not mean what he is reported to have said would be an invitation to him to confirm it. Best line is to advise waiting until new party itself is in a position to announce its programme. I do not think this will state any time limit.

3. Onn did not consult anybody before making this statement and has put himself in the wrong with U.M.N.O. through this omission. Our line is to persuade him of the advantage of continuing to lead U.M.N.O. as well as forming new party, which is, of course, in no way an unhealthy development, but not to be godfathered on to me (see 'Observer') except in so far as I have never made any secret of the view that a united party would be a move in the right direction, getting away from communal politics.

4. Onn's immediate purpose is to stimulate into activity the ultra conservative Malays who, in his own words, are always moaning about the backward state of the Malays, but never do anything but obstruct.

5. I have given paragraph 3 and paragraph 4 off [sic] to local correspondent of the 'Manchester Guardian'.

6. You should know that on 15th June, all European members came to me to protest against Onn's reported statement, seeing that he is a member of the Government. I explained the situation to them and they agreed to wait and see whether he would himself amplify or modify it. Desirable that the general line is therefore that too much importance should not be attached to a Press report of a conversation at the present time.[2]

---

[1] See 240.

[2] Replying to this telegram on 6 July, Higham informed Gurney: 'The Secretary of State read it with much interest. His own feeling is that Dato Onn represents the only real hope of the Malayan peoples breaking away from Race and turning to Party. Clearly, however, not all the Malays are happy about this development and although you quoted Onn as saying that he had no fear of a deep split I am rather anxious about the outcome of U.M.N.O.'s General assembly' (CO 537/7303, no 13). See 244.

242   CO 537/7263, no 42   6 July 1951
[Review of progress in the emergency]: memorandum by Mr Griffiths commenting on the appreciation by Gurney and Briggs[1]

While the Appreciation by the High Commissioner and the Director of Operations discloses several factors from which we may draw a measure of encouragement, we should not be justified in reaching any general conclusion other than that the situation is still most serious. Nor do I consider that the Appreciation attempts to conceal this fact, although we can detect a note of hopefulness in it, particularly as regards the increasing support which is being given by the Chinese population and increased confidence of public opinion. I am well aware that the feeling of confidence is by no means shared by sections of the planting and mining communities, who continue to bear a very heavy burden and, seeing the situation from a particular rather than a comprehensive viewpoint, can observe little signs [sic] of improvement. The most recent weekly reports show that the statistics of incidents, casualties, etc., do not materially differ from those reported in the Appendix to the Appreciation, and that Johore, which, with a few other States, has so far received priority treatment, still remains one of the worst affected areas in the whole Federation. In these circumstances I think that we must reconcile ourselves to the fact that we cannot contemplate reducing the number of troops deployed against the terrorists for some time ahead. Nevertheless the increasing flow of information and the greater, though still small number of surrenders, are important indications that the intensive military and civil effort has begun to make an impression on the enemy.

2.   Of the positive measures which can be taken to speed up the process of getting the situation under control there can be no doubt that the principal need is still to increase the efficiency of the police. The main difficulty here is the recruitment of Police Lieutenants. The Appreciation speaks of a shortage of 180 but since this was written further men have been flown out and these, together with others ready to leave, will reduce the deficit to about 100. A total of 450 Police Lieutenants have now been recruited by the Crown Agents for the Colonies. The recent appeal to the Home Police Forces has been disappointing and the present indication is that it will yield only some 40 recruits in all. The position may be improved a little by an appeal to members of the British South African Police in Southern Rhodesia, which it is hoped that the Secretary of State for Commonwealth Relations will support; but the numbers obtainable from that source must be small.

3.   I have considered whether an improvement in the terms offered would be likely to produce any great improvement. The pay drawn by a married Police Lieutenant amounts, after deduction of Malayan Income Tax, and including separation allowance, to just over £1,000 à year, and at the end of three years' service he draws a gratuity of £240. The chief bar to recruiting is the fact that, owing to the scarcity of accommodation, it is not possible for Police Lieutenants to take their wives and families with them. I believe that members of the Home Police might volunteer in greater numbers if the tour of secondment, now three years, were halved and I have asked the High Commissioner to consider this suggestion urgently and also to review once more the possibility of building accommodation for families

---

[1] See 239. Griffiths sent Shinwell his memo and appreciation in response to 238.

of these men. In the light of his reply I will again consider the question of improved financial inducements, but I think it unlikely that anything that can be done in this direction will bring in sufficient recruits to meet our total need.

4. I recently approached the Secretary of State for War and the First Lord of the Admiralty, informing them that there seemed little prospect of meeting Malaya's full requirement of Police Lieutenants by recruiting from the general public and the Home Police Forces and asking whether they would agree to the secondment of Regular Troops, particularly Commando N.C.Os, to fill vacancies. I am aware that this is a request which it may be difficult to meet but in view of the gravity of the situation I trust that it may be given sympathetic consideration.

5. The shortage of doctors is also serious and is, of course, not confined to Malaya; it is general throughout the Colonial territories. I propose to discuss this with my Chief Medical Officer, who is expected back shortly from a visit to Malaya and other territories.

6. The High Commissioner and Director of Operations mention certain shortages of supplies, in particular clothing, barbed wire and wireless sets for the police jungle companies. There has been a great improvement recently in the clothing situation, owing mainly to the provision of jungle green uniforms from War Office stocks and the prospect of early supplies of khaki drill and shirting from India. Stocks of clothing in Malaya are now at a reasonable level and once supplies start to come from India and other sources stocks will be sufficient to prevent any hold-up in new recruiting, and to meet normal replacement needs.

7. It has recently been possible to place considerable orders for barbed wire with promises of delivery in from one to four months and the position no longer gives cause for concern.

8. Malaya are being urged to complete local tests of wireless sets for police jungle companies. Present indications are that the firm responsible will not be able to start supply until four to five months from the date of approval of the prototype and that it may be 12 months before the complete order can be delivered. This situation is clearly most unsatisfactory and I am having urgent enquiries made to see if a considerable improvement can be effected.

243   FO 371/93010, no 75   Aug 1951

'Commissioner-General, S E Asia': CO note of an inter-departmental meeting with the FO on 14 Aug to discuss the current workings and future of the office

[Unease about British leadership in the region and knowledge that MacDonald's term would expire in May 1952 provoked discussion within and between departments as to the future of the office. On the FO side, whereas R H Scott suggested radical reorganisation, both M E Dening and M J Creswell (FO counsellor, Singapore, 1949–1951) preferred to maintain the essence of the existing system, and it was their views that shaped the FO memorandum which formed the basis of inter-departmental talks on 14 Aug 1951. After this meeting a number of alternatives to MacDonald were considered, although it was felt that 'we could do a good deal worse than keep Mr MacDonald on, if he really wanted to stay.' When parliament was dissolved in Sept it was agreed to postpone decision until after the general election.]

Mr. Ashley Clarke, Mr. R.H. Scott and Mr. Dalton Murray of the Foreign Office came to discuss this subject with Mr. Paskin at 4.15 p.m. on the 14th August. Mr. R.H. Scott produced a copy of a Memorandum[1] which had been prepared in the Foreign Office in which the conclusion is reached that no radical change in the functions or organisation of the Commissioner-General's office is desirable at present. Mr. Paskin confirmed that this was also the Colonial Office view and suggested that the two departments might now prepare a joint paper for Ministers, covering both the future of the Commissioner-General and the appointment of a successor to Mr. MacDonald. He explained that although Mr. MacDonald was not due to leave Malaya until May 1952, the decision on his successor might affect the choice of a new Governor of Singapore, and from the Colonial Office point of view it would therefore be desirable to reach a decision about Mr. MacDonald's successor as early as possible. He suggested that the aim should be to agree a joint paper at the official level for discussion between Sir T. Lloyd and Sir W. Strang[2] before the latter goes on leave about the middle of September so that the matter would be ripe for submission to Ministers by the time the Secretary of State for the Colonies is available at the beginning of October.

After discussion it was agreed that the choice of a Commissioner-General need not be deferred pending a decision on the proposal that in the event of a major war or an immediate threat to Malaya the Commissioner-General's powers of direction in matters of defence should be transferred to the Military Commander. At the same time it was desirable to hasten settlement of that issue and we should press Mr. MacDonald for a reply about the end of August.

The meeting went on to consider the type of person who would be suitable to take Mr. MacDonald's place. It was agreed that he must be a man of high rank whose status was widely known; that he must be politically-minded and appreciative of developing political tendencies in South East Asia; he must be capable of dealing effectively and tactfully with such a variety of persons as local unofficial leaders, the Governors and High Commissioner, the local Heads of the Services and Ministers of foreign and Commonwealth Governments, particularly those of Burma, Siam, India and Australia. He must be publicity conscious and informally accessible to members of all communities; but this accessibility must not be allowed in any way to constitute an embarrassment to the High Commissioner and the Governors. The Commissioner-General should therefore be a person of considerable tact. If possible he should have previous experience of foreign affairs and this was more important than first hand knowledge of the Far East and of South East Asia. As the job is a strenuous one in a difficult climate Mr. Scott suggested that the man appointed should, if possible, be under 55. The appointment could be for a three year tour, with a possibility of extension.

It was agreed that the type of person required was one generally similar to Mr. MacDonald, but it was desirable to have a man who would be prepared to give a strong lead in an emergency. It was suggested that a man of the type of but younger than Lord Tedder[3] or Sir Archibald Nye[4] would be suitable.

---

[1] 'Memorandum. Commission-General, Singapore', 9 Aug 1951, FO 371/93010, no 74.

[2] Permanent under-secretary of state, FO, 1949–1953.

[3] Lord Tedder (1890–1967) marshal of the Royal Air Force, had been deputy supreme allied commander (under Eisenhower), 1943–1945, and chief of the air staff, 1946–1950. He was currently serving as chairman of the British Joint Services Mission, Washington, and UK representative on the standing group of the Military Committee of NATO, 1950–1951.   [4] See 151, note 2.

On a subsidiary point, it was agreed that it would be desirable to arrange for the next Commissioner-General to work in Singapore, although it might still be undesirable for him to reside there.

244 CO 537/7297, no 18   29 Aug 1951
[Tunku Abdul Rahman and the leadership of UMNO]: letter from Sir H Gurney to J D Higham

[At the 6th annual general assembly of UMNO, held in Kuala Lumpur on 25–26 Aug, Dato Onn resigned as president and Tunku Abdul Rahman was elected in his place. The in-coming president pledged to do his utmost for the welfare of the Malays and promised that, in spite of his royal blood, he would struggle with commoners for the independence of a Malaya governed by the Malays themselves. In his farewell speech Onn warned Malays that the era of privileges had ended and they should not delude themselves into believing that independence could be achieved by any one racial group or section of the people. On 16 Sept 1951 and with the support of some prominent non-Malays, Onn formally launched the Independence of Malaya Party in a blaze of publicity. It was later decided that membership of UMNO and IMP were incompatible, see 271.]

Further to my letter of the 14th August, in which I said that I proposed to recommend Tunku Abdul Rahman for transfer to the Colonial Legal Service, I do not think that this will now arise.

He was elected President of U.M.N.O. on the 25th August, the other runners having scratched, and I had a long talk with him yesterday. He hopes to retire from the Kedah service with his pension and practise in chambers (with a Chinese lawyer) in Penang, but his retirement depends at the moment on some rather complicated legal questions as to whether our new Pensions Ordinance takes away any right he may have had in Kedah to calculate his age and service on the Muslim calendar.

He told me that since he did not know for certain that he was going to be elected, he had not prepared his Presidential speech in any written form, with the result that he was badly misreported in the Press. I said I was glad to hear this (as it had appeared under headlines 'Kill the Federation'). He explained that while he naturally had to talk about independence to satisfy some of his followers, he had no intention of making this a main feature of the new U.M.N.O. programme, which would aim rather at getting practical advantages for the Malays, such as land in the towns on favourable terms.

We discussed this for some time and I pointed out the obvious weaknesses of these ideas of how to make things still easier for the Malays at other people's expense.

I am afraid that he will not be the sort of leader who will be capable of holding U.M.N.O. together in any important controversy. He will not of course be persona grata to the Rulers, and sooner or later these differences will have to be faced.

Dato Onn made two courageous and fairly moderate speeches at the U.M.N.O. meeting and has I think retained the hopes, if not the trust of most of the U.M.N.O. leaders. He answered his critics effectively and I do not at the moment see signs of any major split among the Malays. Abdul Rahman and Onn do not, I think, like each other, but many Malays will be in both I.M.P. and U.M.N.O., with a foot in each.

Hussein bin Onn[1] is carryng on for the time being as Secretary General, and I took the opportunity of telling Abdul Rahman that I thought it time U.M.N.O. published some accounts. He agreed.

---

[1] Son of Onn bin Jaafar, leader of UMNO Youth, 1946–1950; secretary general, UMNO, 1950–1951; prime minister of Malaysia, 1976–1981.

245   CO 1022/148, no 10   [Oct 1951]
[Gurney's 'political will']: a note by Sir H Gurney expressing his frustration with the Chinese community

[The manuscript original of what M V del Tufo (chief secretary, Federation of Malaya) called Gurney's 'political will' was found amongst the high commissioner's private papers and known to have been written two days before his death. Del Tufo handed it to Lyttelton during the secretary of state's visit to Malaya in Dec 1951 together with the following comments of his own: 'This is an extraordinary document because Gurney had no anti-Chinese bias whatever. Indeed he had a very considerable sympathy for their point of view. The note of exasperation which runs through this document was most untypical of Gurney and shows how far he was moving towards an attitude of firmness—if not actual toughness—towards the Chinese.']

The attack of the M.C.P. was always directed at the Chinese, to obtain their support through racial sympathy and intimidation. Three years ago it was made clear to the M.C.A. leaders that unless they provided an alternative standard to which loyal Chinese could rally, the Communists would win. The answer was that the rural Chinese, the peasants, who are the real target, must first be protected. With the help of the M.C.A. the whole vast scheme of resettlement has now been almost finished and labour forces regrouped. Into these settlements and into trade unions and into schools the M.C.P. are trying hard to penetrate and are succeeding. If they are allowed to continue this unopposed by any Chinese effort whatever, the whole of the Chinese rural population will soon come under Communist domination. These people are looking for leaders to help them to resist. But what has happened?

(a) the Government wished to recruit up to 10,000 Chinese for service in the Police. There was full prior consultation with leading Chinese, but as soon as the men were called up, the cry was all for exemptions, 6000 decamped to Singapore and several other thousands to China.
(b) Everyone knows that the M.R.L.A. and Min Yuen are today being financed and supplied by Chinese. Everyone knows that with a few notable exceptions the Chinese themselves have done absolutely nothing to help their own people resist Communism, which is today rampant in schools and among the young uneducated generation. How many Chinese schools fly the Federation flag?
(c) The wealth amassed by the Chinese in Malaya is enormous, and all of it will be lost unless something is done by the Chinese themselves and quickly. The British Government will not be prepared to go on protecting people who are completely unwilling to do anything to help themselves.
(d) A feeling of resentment is growing up among all other communities at the apparent reluctance of the Chinese to help. These people live comfortably and devote themselves wholly to making money. They can spend $4 million on

celebrations in Singapore but can spare nothing for the M.C.A. anti-Communist efforts.

(e) Chinese labour forces lie wide open to Communism. There is no encouragement to them to join Trade Unions, which are mainly Indian-led.

2. A year ago there were [. . .] armed Communists in Johore. Now there are [. . .].[1] There are nearly 400,000 Chinese in Johore.

3. Leading Chinese have contented themselves with living in luxury in Singapore etc. and criticising the Police and security forces for causing injustices. These injustices are deplorable but are the fault not of the Police but of those Chinese who know the truth and will not tell it. The longer this goes on, the more injustices there will be and the greater the opening to Communist propaganda.

4. Positive measures:—

(a) full time central organisation;
(b) raise $2 million.
(c) men in every settlement.
(d) men in every school.
(e) A.P. squads paid by results.
(f) work with S.C.A.'s.

---

[1] Numbers of armed communists left blank in original with a footnote reading: 'Figures withheld on security grounds.'

246 FO 371/93118, no 2　　　　　　　　　　　　　　6 Oct 1951
[Assassination of Sir Henry Gurney on 6 Oct]: inward telegram no 951 from M V del Tufo to Mr Griffiths

My immediately preceding telegram.

The High Commissioner's car with Sir Henry and Lady Gurney in the back of the car and the Private Secretary[1] in front with a Malay driver was proceeding to Frasers Hill[2] escorted by one Land Rover and one armoured scout car. Police wireless van, which was also part of the convoy, unfortunately had broken down about eight miles short of ambush position. Party was ambushed at 1.15 p.m. about two miles short of the Gap. Driver of the car was hit in the head on the first outburst of fire. Private Secretary managed to stop the car from falling over the edge of a precipitous slope on the left of the road and brought it to a standstill. Heavy automatic fire was directed from front right and rear both against the High Commissioner's car and the Land Rover after first burst of fire. Gurney opened the door of the car and stepped out and was immediately shot down by heavy automatic fire. Scout car drove up behind and with difficulty pushed past the High Commissioner's car to fetch help from the Gap police station. Intermittent fire continued at any sight of movement for about ten minutes, at the end of which a bugle was blown and the bandits withdrew. Lady Gurney and the Private Secretary remained in the car until the firing ceased when they crawled out and found Gurney's body in the ditch on the right side of the road.

---

[1] D J Staples was Gurney's private secretary.
[2] Fraser's Hill, a hill resort 65 miles to the north of Kuala Lumpur.

Officer in charge of the scout car returned about 20 minutes later on foot with reinforcements from the Gap Police Station, bandits having felled a tree across the road above the site of the ambush. Armoured vehicles from Kuala Kubu arrived on the scene about 2.15 p.m. and engaged in follow-up operations.

2. Hogan[3] and wife were following the High Commissioner's party in their own car and were about half a mile behind at the time of the ambush. They stopped when they heard firing in front. After a few minutes telecommunication van (which had been passed by the High Commissioner's party) appeared from the opposite direction and it was possible to tap the overhead telephone wires and communicate with Kuala Kubu. Ambush position was some half a mile long and clearly carefully prepared. Estimated size of bandit party was 20. Full investigation into the circumstances is being made.

---

[3] M J P Hogan, attorney-general, Malaya, 1950–1955.

247   CO 1022/148, no 2   30 Oct 1951
[Stalemate in Malaya]: savingram no 83 from M V del Tufo[1] to Mr Lyttelton on meetings with the rulers, *mentris besar* and Chinese leaders, 25–28 Oct 1951   [Extract]

On the 25th October, I met Their Highnesses the Rulers at a routine meeting of the Conference of Rulers and the opportunity was taken by each of Their Highnesses in turn to speak on various matters connected with the emergency. There was no room for doubt as to Their Highnesses anxiety about the slowness of the progress which is being made and their desire to see more severe action, including deportation on a large scale, taken against the Chinese. The suggestions which were put forward are being examined but they contained little if anything which has not been considered before. Some of them incidentally indicated a deplorable lack of appreciation of the realities of the situation.

On the following day a meeting of Mentri Mentri Besar, Resident Commissioners and British Advisers was held under my chairmanship. The Commissioner-General, who was in Kuala Lumpur on other business, was able to attend for an hour and a half in the morning. The Director of Operations, the Acting Chief Secretary, the Attorney General and the Secretary for Defence were also present. At this meeting, at which, of course no Chinese were present, there was clear evidence of the intensity of the Malay feeling against the Chinese and a number of proposals were put forward for pursuing a "tougher" policy towards them, including operations under Emergency Regulation 17D[2] against "black" areas, large-scale deportation, and the sequestration of property of persons who can be shown in some definitive way, to have failed to co-operate with the Government, for instance, by failing to supply information which must have been in their possession. The latter proposal, which presents some novel difficulties, is being examined by the Attorney-General. It was agreed that the most urgent need was for more Chinese in the Police Force. All were agreed that until this

---

[1] Now officer administering the government.
[2] See 188, note 6.

was achieved relations between the Force and the Chinese public could never be satisfactory nor could Government expect to secure the information and co-operation which are essential if the emergency is to be brought to an early end. . . .

It will be apparent from the preceding paragraphs that it has become of the greatest urgency that it should be brought home to the Chinese leaders that they must exert their influence with the Chinese community so that there may be a radical change in their attitude towards Government and towards the efforts being made to eliminate Communist banditry. This is, as you will realise, a most formidable task and I will not attempt in this report to go into the reasons for the present non-cooperative attitude of the great bulk of the Chinese beyond saying that they include the following:—

(a) The fact that banditry is endemic in China where also there is no tradition of an uncorrupt Police Force to whom it is the practice to take information or from whom protection can be expected.

(b) The fact that the rank and file of the Police Force is almost entirely composed of Malays who do not speak Chinese and who, generally speaking, are unsympathetic to Chinese.

(c) The fact that the contacts both in quantity and in quality between the purely Chinese speaking population and the Administration still leave much to be desired. (Proposals for strengthening the Chinese Affairs Department are now under active consideration.)

(d) The uncertainty which is felt about the future in South East Asia and the ability of the United Kingdom to defend Malaya in the event of war. Recollections of 1941/42 and of the years of Japanese occupation which followed are still a vivid memory.

(e) The close ties linking the Chinese in Malaya with those in South China and the knowledge that open co-operation with the federation Government is likely to bring serious trouble—loss of property and possibly loss of life—to relations in China.

(f) The failure to understand the reasons for His Majesty's Government's recognition of Communist China and the fear that, sooner, or later, Communist Consuls will be appointed to Malaya who will report back to Peking the activities of Chinese in Malaya.

A meeting was accordingly arranged on Sunday, 28th October and copies of a note of the more important matters discussed will be sent by the next bag. The Chinese who attended came from all parts of the Federation and from Singapore but, with the possible exception of Dato Tan Cheng Lock, there are no Chinese whose names are both known and respected throughout the country. Their influence is purely local and is often restricted to a single town. A national appeal is therefore likely to achieve little or no result and efforts will have to be made at State and Settlement and at District levels. The various proposals mentioned at the meeting are now being considered by Government and by the Chinese and it is proposed to hold a further meeting with them in two or three weeks' time. . . .

248 PREM 11/122 30 Oct 1951
[Secretary of state's visit to Malaya]: minute PM(51)1 from Mr Lyttelton to Mr Churchill

[At the general election on 25 Oct the Conservative party won an overall majority of 17. Churchill formed his government on 27 Oct and appointed Lyttelton to the Colonial Office. Lyttelton informed Cabinet of his intention to visit Malaya on the day he wrote this minute (see CAB 128/23, CC 1(51)8, 30 Oct 1951).]

Prime Minister

The Malayan problem appears to me to be the first priority here. A new High Commissioner for the Federation has to be appointed and partly for reasons of health a suitable man will be difficult to find from the Colonial Service. Sir Rob Lockhart,[1] the newly appointment Director of Operations, is leaving to succeed Harold Briggs on the 6th November. The Governor of Singapore retires in April, and MacDonald's term of office is due to end in May, 1952.

It therefore seems to me important that I should visit Malaya as soon as possible and I would propose to leave for Singapore about the 25th November for a short visit in order to see and judge for myself. I should thus be present at a time when new arrangements, both civil and tactical, are first under discussion by the men newly appointed and should be able to make recommendations more surely to you and my colleagues. It so happens that there is to be about that time a meeting of all the Governors of the area and the British representatives in other South East Asian and Far Eastern territories, including India. It would clearly be most valuable for me to meet them and I have hopes that this could be arranged.

I would also hope to take this opportunity to go to Hong Kong for a few days, which is particularly desirable because my predecessor was unable to visit Hong Kong when he went to Malaya in May, 1950, and this caused a good deal of feeling in Hong Kong.[2]

---

[1] General Sir Robert Lockhart had retired in 1948, having been army commander, India, 1945–1947, and commander-in-chief, Indian Army, for four months after partition. He was made director of operations, Malaya, in Dec 1951, and, on the appointment of Templer, became deputy director, Feb 1952 – Mar 1953.
[2] Churchill minuted in reply (5 Nov): 'I highly approve of your wish to see the Singapore situation on the spot. We do not think the [parliamentary] Session will end before December 4 or 5. We cannot afford to reduce our majority. Unless a special pair can be obtained for you the various functionaries you have to meet should rearrange their dates to suit you' (PREM 11/122).

249 FO 371/93011, no 87 31 Oct 1951
[Foreign Office interests in and views on Malaya]: minute by R H Scott to Mr Eden briefing him for a meeting with Sir R Lockhart on 1 Nov

General Sir Rob Lockhart's[1] call on the Secretary of State to-morrow afternoon, Thursday, November 1st, at 4.30, will give the Secretary of State an opportunity to emphasise to him the great importance attached by the Foreign Office to his task in Malaya.

---

[1] See 248, note 1.

2. The Secretary of State may care to say that the pinning down of British forces in Malaya weakens our position throughout the world; the disturbed condition of Malaya makes it difficult to move foward with any assurance in planning with other interested powers for the defence of South East Asia in war; and the threat to Malaya's export trade is a factor of great importance to the sterling bloc.

Foreign Office interest

3. There are five ways in which the Foreign Office has been and is able to help the authorities in Malaya:

(a) By obtaining Siamese co-operation on the Northern border;
(b) In connection with the deportation of undesirable Chinese from Malaya to China (this is effected on a small but useful scale through shipping companies and not through any formal arrangements with the Chinese Government);
(c) By providing anti-Communist propaganda material for use in Malaya, particularly with the Chinese;
(d) By ensuring that United States opinion is properly informed about events in Malaya and by trying to secure United States material assistance when necessary;
(e) By ensuring that events in Malaya are properly understood in other Asian countries.[2]

4. The Foreign Secretary of course shares the general responsibility of H.M. Government for the conduct of affairs in Malaya. In addition the Foreign Office has had a direct interest in Malayan policy since April 1950 when the Malaya Committee of the Cabinet was set up consisting of the Minister of Defence (in the Chair), the Colonial Secretary, the Secretary of State for Commonwealth Relations, the Secretary of State for War and the Minister of State.[3] This Committee has however met irregularly and only once this year though there have been meetings of Ministers under the Prime Minister, at which the Foreign Secretary was represented, when Mr. Malcolm MacDonald visited London in the spring.[4]

5. A number of members of the Foreign Service serve in the Commission-General in Singapore under Mr. Malcolm MacDonald, the Commissioner-General, though they have to be a little careful in expressing views on internal Malayan policy which is not strictly within their province.

Situation in Malaya

6. The war in Malaya has sharpened in recent months though those who are responsible for the conduct of the campaign continue to hope for early improvement. These hopes have been disappointed in the past and they may be disappointed again.

7. Though very large numbers of troops and police are now employed in Malaya, it is basically a political and administrative rather than a purely military problem. Political, in the sense that (a) it is necessary to enlist the support of the Chinese community (the present constitution which is weighted in favour of the Malays and the Sultans has made many Chinese rather apathetic), and (b) it is affected by developments outside the country and by the policies of foreign countries such as

---

[2] These five points were considered by the commissioner-general's conference at Bukit Serene in late Nov 1951, immediately prior to Lyttelton's visit to Malaya.
[3] See 209–210.   [4] See 232–234.

China, India, Indonesia and Siam (the success or failure of the new Chinese Government has direct repercussions in Malaya). Administrative, in the sense that army sweeps to clear any given area can have only temporary effect unless their gains are consolidated by an effective administrative and police organisation afterwards. It has proved very difficult to recruit the necessary staff and in particular junior police officers of the right types.

8. The problem is complicated also by friction between the Malays and the Chinese who are about equal in number (about $2\frac{1}{2}$ million each)[5].

9. Finally it is complicated by a lack of clarity in the chain of command and a multiplicity of authorities with somewhat ill-defined and overlapping responsibilities.

General Lockhart

10. He is going to Malaya to take up the appointment of Director of Operations in succession to General Sir Harold Briggs. The Director of Operations is a civilian official responsible to the High Commissioner for Malaya and his task is to see that the efforts of the Army, Police and Civilian Departments are brought together in a centrally directed campaign against the Malayan Communist Party.

11. General Lockhart is being brought from retirement, having ended his career as the first Commander-in-Chief of the Indian Army after partitition. He had previously been an Army Commander in India from 1945.

12. He takes over in Malaya at a difficult time. General Briggs is the third leading figure to leave the Malayan scene within recent weeks. Sir Harold [sic] Gurney, the High Commissioner, was murdered last month shortly after the resignation of Sir William Jenkin, the Director of Intelligence of the Federation Police Force,[6] who resigned, I understand, as the result of failure to secure approval for recommendations which he had made in the field of intelligence.

13. Malaya is a country of somewhat lax standards in which personalities play a most important part and in which personal jealousies are not absent. General Lockhart's task is of the first importance and he will need the fullest support of H.M. Government to give him a fair chance of success.

---

[5] The approximate figures usually cited at this time were: $2\frac{1}{2}$ million Malays, 2 million Chinese and $\frac{1}{2}$ million Indians.

[6] Sir William Jenkin (formerly superintendent, Indian Police Service, and deputy director, Intelligence Bureau, Home Department, Government of India) was brought out of retirement in May 1950 to advise on the reorganization of the Malayan CID. Towards the end of 1950 he became director of intelligence but submitted his resignation on 1 Sept 1951.

250 FO 371/116969, no 14   5 Nov 1951
[Proposal to appoint a soldier as high commissioner]: inward telegram from Mr M J MacDonald to Sir T Lloyd   **[Extract]**

[In 1955, when Sir H Caccia of the FO put foward the name of Field Marshal Sir J Harding as successor to MacDonald, Lloyd sent him a copy of this extract to indicate MacDonald's views when Lloyd himself had previously 'suggested Harding as a possible High Commissioner for the Federation of Malaya after the death of Henry Gurney' (FO 371/116969, no 14, Lloyd to Caccia, 18 Apr 1955).]

. . . I am averse to the appointment of any of the soldiers you mention. None of them would be likely to understand adequately the need to continue Gurney's political and social policy. If they failed to do so important sections of Asian opinion, who at present support us, would be at least partially alienated. Of the soldiers who you mention, Harding[1] would be best, but there are the two following objections to him:—

(a) When here, he always tended to underestimate the importance of the political and social, as distinct from the military and police aspects of our anti-terrorist campaign, and I do not (repeat not) think that he would manage this side of things with wisdom or success.

(b) His appointment would probably be awkward for General Keightley,[2] not on personal but on professional grounds. My hunch is that a principal defect in our campaign against the terrorists at present is on the military and police operational side. In strict confidence I believe that Keightley wishes for some changes in this respect and I personally hope that he will succeed in getting Lockhart to take a somewhat different view in certain respects from that of Briggs. He might be handicapped in doing this if Harding were the High Commissioner for he would presumably have less opportunity to influence high military policy in the Federation. . . .

---

[1] See 220, note 1.
[2] General Sir Charles Keightley, commander in chief, British Army of the Rhine, 1948–1951, Far East Land forces, 1951–1953, and Middle East Land Forces, 1953–1956.

251   CO 1022/39, no 3   15 Nov 1951
'Emergency in Malaya': CO record of a meeting between Mr Lyttelton and a delegation representing British business interests in Malaya

[This record was drafted by the delegation and later amended by the CO. Present at the meeting were: Mr Lyttelton, Mr Lennox-Boyd, Sir H Poynton, Sir G Clauson, J J Paskin, T C Jerrom, A S Gann (CO); Mr Hamilton, Sir Sydney Palmer, Mr Ascoli, Mr Anderson, Mr Egmont Hake, Mr Eyles (Rubber Growers' Association); Mr Glenister, Mr Ivan Spens, Mr Rich, Mr Kiddle (Malayan Chamber of Mines); Mr Potts, Mr Shearn (Association of British Malaya); Mr Karsten, Mr Wilson (Rubber Trade Association of London); Mr Cockburn (Eastern Exchange Banks Association); Mr Holyoak, Mr Crosley (British Association of Straits Merchants); Lieutenant-Commander C C Powell (Incorporated Society of Planters). On the same day the representatives had a separate meeting with Lyttelton.]

The leader of the Delegation (Mr A.P. Hamilton) in his opening remarks thanked the Secretary of State for receiving the members of the Delegation, and after stressing the ever increasing gravity of the emergency which had deteriorated still further in the past few days, he said that he hoped that H.M. Government fully appreciated the seriousness of the position and would from now on tackle the problem with a firmer and more realistic attitude.

He said the Delegation had come in the hope that they might be of some assistance to the Secretary of State preparatory to his coming visit to Malaya.

The Secretary of State informed the Delegation that it was the Government's intention to give the emergency the very first priority, indeed he felt "a state of emergency" (which implied something of a short duration) was now the wrong term to apply to the position in Malaya. He felt that the "near war" nature of events in Malaya had in the past been insufficiently emphasised. He fully realised that the position recently had been deteriorating, and he thought it would be unwise to suggest that whatever efforts they made they could hope to bring about any rapid or early improvement.

While the suppression of terrorism was obviously the task of first priority due attention must be devoted to Asian claims for political and social advancement: we must give the Asian population in Malaya some incentive to fight for as well as trying to convince them that the defeat of the terrorists was number one priority.

He was inclined to the view that a further declaration of H.M. Government's policy towards Malaya might perhaps be useful, but in view of all that had been said in the past, very careful consideration would have to be given to the form it should take.

There was full realisation at the Colonial Office that more vigorous measures were needed to deal with the present position and he was looking forward to hearing from the Delegation what suggestions they had to offer.

Asked whether the Delegation felt that the "Briggs Plan" was the correct line of approach, to adopt in dealing with the situation, the general view was that it was the correct approach, but some criticism was expressed of its administration, especially of the shortage of manpower required to carry it out. It was felt by others that the "Briggs Plan" by itself was insufficient, and sterner measures were now required.

The feeling was also expressed that the civil administration had not been in the past whole-heartedly behind the "Briggs Plan". Administrators had been all too occupied with the development of social welfare schemes and this had caused a drain on available man-power when all energy should have been devoted entirely to the fight against banditry.

The Delegation was in favour of much stronger action against those of whatever race or nationality, who were known to be supporting the bandits with funds. They felt that the present system of long drawn out trials and appeals was thoroughly bad and was not understood by the Asian population. They pressed for some quicker form of justice, the results of which should be widely advertised.

The Minister of State asked whether business interests would welcome the introduction of Martial Law, and he was told that they had been given to understand in the past that this action would be undesirable; some members of the Delegation had however an open mind on this matter and felt that they were not really in a position to judge.

On the other hand they did press most strongly for the appointment of someone of the very highest prestige, possessing very much greater powers than had been given to the late High Commissioner or to General Briggs, they felt also that it was essential that these powers should extend not only over Federal matter but should also cover the States and Settlements. As was mentioned by the leader of the Delegation in his opening remarks, they had in mind "someone like Alexander".[1]

On the question of armoured vehicles, the *Secretary of State* confirmed that the vehicles referred to in the House of Lords on the previous day (numbering 341) would be despatched without delay and that a substantial proportion would be ready

---

[1] Field Marshal Lord Alexander of Tunis (1891–1969); commander in chief, Middle East, 1942–1943, North Africa, 1943, Allied Armies in Italy, 1943–1944; supreme allied commander, Mediterranean theatre, 1944–1945; governor-general, Canada, 1946–1952; minister of defence, 1952–1954.

by the end of the year.[2] He said he was in favour of more protection of this nature for members of the Armed Forces and Police. The Secretary of State was questioned regarding the adequacy of the supply of armoured vehicles. The Delegation thought that if the seriousness of the situation had been appreciated sooner very much larger quantities of such equipment would have been made available when it was first requested.

The Secretary of State stated that he understood that General Briggs had said that all his demands for equipment had been met to the full. The Delegation said this might have been the case a year ago, but was it in fact true to-day?

It was suggested by one member of the Delegation that an approach through diplomatic channels, should be made to the United States of America to provide a token of assistance; for example, it had been suggested that one or two of their ships might patrol off the coast, and a few of their "G" men might co-operate with the local C.I.D. The effect of this would be to show the Chinese in particular that America was determined to ensure that Malaya was not going to fall into the hands of the Communists.

Mr. Paskin said that the suggestion in question was already under consideration by the Federation Government.

On the question of reinforcements for the bandits, it was generally agreed that they were obtaining their new recruits from inside the country rather than from outside sources.

The complaint was voiced that the direction of man-power had been half-hearted. Apart from that, although about 150,000 Malays had taken service mainly without direction in the Police and Military Forces, the number of Chinese was negligible. The Secretary of State was urged to bring this aspect home, as forcibly as possible to any leading Chinese he might meet during his coming visit. The Delegation laid stress on the dangers which would inevitably ensue from a policy whereby in a attempt to relieve the man-power shortage, Europeans were taken away from Estates and Mines. A policy such as this would only result in a further deterioration in supervision and eventual chaos.

The present position regarding European Staffs was that many of the older and more experienced men had left Malaya, and it was extremely difficult to persuade young men to go out, as they were doubtful whether there was any future for them in Malaya.

Amongst other matters mentioned were the inability to proceed with Rubber replanting programmes, and the almost total lack of any prospecting for tin ore during the last 20 years.

Mention was also made of the extreme difficulty the Tin Industry was experiencing in obtaining supplies of steel.

In conclusion the *Secretary of State* said that many of the particular difficulties to which attention had been drawn would diminish once it was clear that the Government campaign against terrorism was succeeding; if we could get over the hump of the struggle the individual problems would gradually fall into place. He thanked the Delegation for their attendance and said that he had found the views expressed by the respresentatives interesting and useful; he looked forward to meeting the Delegation again on his return.

---

[2] Colonel Gray, commissioner of Malayan Police, had opposed the armouring of police vehicles largely on the grounds that it would reduce police mobility and morale.

252   CAB 129/48, C(51)26   20 Nov 1951
'The situation in Malaya': Cabinet memorandum by Mr Lyttelton.
Annexes I–III

I was invited (C.C.(51) 5th Conclusions, Minute 3)[1] to submit a memorandum on the situation in Malaya. I have recently received an appreciation by the retiring Director of Operations, Lieutenant-General Sir Harold Briggs. This was considered by the British Defence Co-ordination Committee (Far East) and I attach in Annex I a summary of their conclusions.

A note on the present situation prepared in the Colonial Office is in Annex II; and a statement of the forces engaged in Malaya and the cost of their maintenance in Annex III.

While in Malaya I propose to pay particular attention to the following aspects of the situation:—

(a) How to reassure the planters and miners of our determination and ability to support them by all means in our power, and to bring the anti-Communist campaign to a successful conclusion.

(b) How to secure the active co-operation of the Chinese, if necessary by a more forceful policy towards those who fail to "come off the fence".

(c) How to settle disagreements between the military and police authorities. This may involve the replacement of the Commissioner of Police.

(d) How to improve the organisation and training of the police force.

(e) Who should succeed Sir Henry Gurney as High Commissioner for the Federation of Malaya and Mr. Malcolm MacDonald as Commissioner-General, South East Asia.

(f) How the division of responsibilities between the various authorities could be improved.

I will, of course, report fully to my colleagues on my return from Malaya.

Annex I to 252: Conclusions of the British Defence Co-ordination Committee (Far East) (telegram dated 15th November 1951)

1. Our main conclusions are:—

(a) Although the Briggs Plan is fundamentally sound and has achieved a certain measure of success, the Communist hold on Malaya is as strong, if not stronger, today than it ever has been. This fact must be faced.

(b) The crux of the problem is the winning of the confidence and loyalty of the bulk of the Chinese population to an extent that they are willing to join with us actively in the fight against Communist terrorism.

(c) Confidence of the Chinese generally will not be gained until they feel safe from internal Communist pressure and external Chinese attack.

---

[1] Churchill, 'disturbed at the high cost of our military commitments in Malaya', had asked Lyttelton to submit to Cabinet before his departure 'an appreciation of the present position and his proposals for remedying it' (CAB 128/23, CC 5(51)3, 8 Nov 1951; see also WO 216/446 and CO 1022/34, nos 2 and 3).

(d) Confidence of the Chinese in their safety from internal Communist pressure will only be engendered if police efficiency is improved.

(e)We must take every necessary step to organise and train sufficient Chinese as settlement guards, police, members of jungle squads, etc.

2.　The first priority is the reorganization and build up of the police force. During this time, the ring must be held by the army, for which purpose it is assumed that no reduction in present strength will be made.

3.　The action required to be pressed forward in Malaya includes:—

(a) The reorganisation of the police.

(b) Expansion of the Chinese resettlement guards and the formation of the Chinese element of the police force.

(c) Completion of the revision of the citizenship constitution.

(d) Action to associate the Chinese with local government.

(e) Improvement of conditions in the settlements.

(f) Expansion of Chinese Affairs Department at the centre and in the field.

4.　Action in which we press for the assistance of the United Kingdom:—

(a) Selection and provision of the best available technical advice and professional leadership to achieve reorganisation and build up of the police force and its specialist agencies.

(b) The provision of outstanding police lieutenants.

(c) No reduction in the military forces at present in Malaya.

(d) Support for the build up of the Malaya [sic] Regiment, in particular, British officers.

Annex II to 252: 'The situation in Malaya': CO memorandum

The enemy is the Malayan Communist Party, which is almost exclusively Chinese. The "whole-time" enemy force, operating in the jungle and highly elusive, is only a few thousand strong; but there is an insidious and numerous underground operating wherever there is a Chinese element in the general population. This underground powerfully assists the main force and by the intimidation and murder of peaceable labourers and squatters is able to secure the supplies, shelter and information which that force requires. The 500,000 Chinese squatters until recently living in isolated areas, and without any form of police protection or any form of settled Government, have been the main source from which the communists have been able to derive supplies. Almost equally vulnerable to Communist attacks has been the considerable number of estate labourers living outside any defended perimeter.

2.　The intention of the Briggs Plan has been by isolating the regular bandit forces from the Chinese civilian population, to cut the enemy lines of communication to break up the underground cells, and to force the enemy to fight harder for his very existence on ground of our own choosing. These tasks are primarily the affair of the Government and its police forces rather than of the military, and the military cannot be used in any decisive way until the enemy has been forced from his jungle fastness by lack of supplies and the police are able to provide the fullest information of enemy movements. Some 350,000 squatters have now been resettled—in itself a considerable administrative achievement—and progress in regrouping estate labour has also been made. The first stage of the Briggs Plan is thus nearing completion. The immediate problem now is to ensure that the new settlements, which had to be put up in the greatest haste are provided as a matter of urgency not only with adequate protection against direct attack and subversive infiltration but with fullest opportunities to become reasonably prosperous and contented communities, convinced of being much better off as the result of resettlement and willing, therefore, to give increasing and positive help to Government. Unless this is done we may have done little more than present to the enemy an easy target for attack, infiltration and propaganda. This is not an enemy to be despised, and he has so far shown himself capable of matching every move of ours by a counter-move which, if unchecked, can vitiate the whole of our operations.

3. Simultaneously with this consolidation of the resettlement operation, must come a new drive to bring more of the Chinese population actively on to our side. After nearly $3\frac{1}{2}$ years of warfare, we are still not within prospect of a definite break in the Communist ranks. Without active co-operation from the Chinese—not only from the leaders but from people of all classes—we shall not be able to secure any rapid conclusion of the conflict. While the Malays, to whom a Communist victory would mean Chinese hegemony in Malaya, have come forward in their tens of thousands to fight the enemy, the Chinese—although they have been the main sufferers at the terrorists' hands, having lost 1,200 civilians out of a total of 1,700 killed—have made no comparable response. The Malayan-Chinese Association has done excellent work, but its leaders are unlikely on present showing to rally the people openly behind them. The reasons for Chinese reluctance to show by deeds their abhorrence of the terrorists are not far to seek; they arise not only from Chinese tradition and character, but from events outside as well as inside Malaya. Previous attempts to compel Chinese co-operation have been largely abortive, and it was felt that a policy of sanctions against non-co-operators could not be adopted until we could offer these people a greater protection in their towns and villages. This we should now be able to do in greater measure, and though one may have considerable sympathy with the ordinary Chinese living in daily fear of Communist racketeers and assassins, there well may be scope for a more active policy. Some Chinese leaders do, in fact, now feel that the Government should increasingly issue instructions and enforce compliance instead of relying on voluntary co-operation. Certain Chinese leaders have also set on foot an organisation working within the Chinese community itself, whose object would be to stimulate a more positive reaction against Communism, and which will work in ways best suited to the Chinese mentality. The existence of this organisation is, at least for the present, of the highest secrecy. The Malayan Authorities have already outlined certain methods by which the desired objective may be furthered. It will, however, be necessary that any measures adopted should not be such as to give the appearance of a bias against the Chinese; that the sympathy of the Chinese community should not be alienated by unnecessary harshness; and that the Chinese should be convinced of our intention, and that of the other communities in Malaya, of admitting more freely to the rights of Malayan citizenship those who show their loyalty. The main advantages of increased Chinese co-operation would be an increased supply of information and more recruits to the uniformed policy forces. It is difficult to police a country which is nearly half Chinese with a force which is 95% Malay, and which cannot speak the language of the peoples it purports to control.

4. Annex III shows the cost in man-power and money of the Malayan Campaign.

Malaya's United States dollar earnings in 1950 were $350,000,000 out of total sterling area earnings of $1,285,000,000, but rubber production has fallen substantially in the past year and some estates are now unworked because of terrorist activity. The vital replanting and maintenance is virtually at a standstill, and prospecting for tin was barely resumed after the re-occupation of the country when it had to be suspended because of the lack of law and order. The present output of tin cannot be maintained, let alone increased unless prospecting is resumed and fresh reserves of ore discovered in the next year or two. There has recently been an intensification of Communist attempts to break the economy of the country by large scale and brutal intimidation of labour.

5.   No one can foresee when the world situation may demand a reduction of the garrison, although in present circumstances such a move would be bound to have a most serious effect. The police force, which has undergone tremendous numerical expansion, is still far from adequate in organisation and training to meet its full responsibilities, and until a great improvement has been effected the maintenance of military forces at their present strength will be necessary. The British Defence Co-ordination Committee consider that no further reduction in the total number of army units can be made before Spring, 1953, at the earliest. Recently there have been acute differences of opinion in Malaya regarding police policy, and the Director of Operations has now been given direct authority over police administration and training. The Acting High Commissioner, with the agreement of the Commissioner-General, the Director of Operations and the Army Commander-in-Chief has also recommended that the Commissioner of Police should be asked to resign. The Inspector General of Colonial Police will visit Malaya with the Secretary of State and remain for some time to advise the local authorities on what measure of police reorganisation may be necessary.

6.   Malay exasperation at the apparent inability of the Chinese to help positively in countering the continuing high level of terrorist activity is liable to produce a dangerous state of communal tension. This is another reason why we must strive to make the Chinese take an increasingly active part in fighting Communist terrorism. Their help is essential not only to bring the campaign to a more rapid conclusion but also to avoid serious communal disorders which would place a further and grievous strain on the British forces. Moreover if the emergency were to end without the active co-operation of the Chinese, the hope of building a single Malayan people might never be realised.

Annex III to 252: Forces engaged in Malaya

The fighting forces currently engaged in Malaya (and foreseen reinforcements) are:—

(1) 7 British infantry battalions
     8 Gurkha battalions
     3 Colonial battalions
(2) 2 Royal Armoured Corps Regiments
(3) 4 battalions Malay Regiment
     (5th battalion being raised)
     Malayan Police Forces

(4) Malayan Scouts (4 Squadrons)
(5) 10 R.A.F. Squadrons (114 aircraft)
(6) 2 Royal Australian Air Force Squadrons
    (14 aircraft)
(7) 1 Frigate, 6 Minesweepers and 2 Motor Launches.

Further details are included in the Appendix. Additional forces are being raised by the Malayan Government.

2. The cost of the forces has been calculated on alternative bases:—

(i)   The cost of maintaining and operating the forces including base forces and of recurring charges but excluding capital costs.
(ii) The extra cost involved in having these forces engaged in operations.

3. The estimated expenditure in a full year is:—

	Cost of Maintenance		*Extra cost*
	£m.		£m.
Royal Navy	1.7		0.4
Army—United Kingdom forces	21.0		2.5
Other forces	10.0		1.0
R.A.F. And R.A.A.F.	15.8	(£.09m. of which is borne by Australia)	4.5
	48.5		8.4

APPENDIX

The forces expected to be engaged in the Malaya emergency operations in 1952/53 are:—

Royal Navy
    Third R.M. Commando Brigade   120 officers
                                                          2,000 other ranks

    1 Frigate
    6 "Algerine" Minesweepers
    2 Seaward Defence Motor Launches

Army
    12 Lancers
    13/18th Hussars
    7 British Infantry battalions
    8 Gurkha Infantry battalions
      Malaya Scouts
    2 K.A.R. battalions   }   In relief of Third Commando Brigade which is due
    1 Fiji battalion   }   to be withdrawn next Spring

R.A.F.
    2 Day Fighter/Ground attack squadrons   32 aircraft

2 Light Bomber squadrons	20	aircraft
3 Transport squadrons	24	"
1 Flying Boat squadron	5	"
1 Photographic Reconnaissance squadron	8	"
1 Air Observation Post squadron	20	"
R.A.F. and W.R.A.F. strength	6,300	
Malayan airmen	1,100	

Australian Air Force

1 Medium Bomber squadron	8	aircraft
1 Transport squadron	6	"

Malayan forces (forces raised as at 30th September, 1951)

    4 battalions Malay Regiment.
23,000 Regular Police
38,000 Special Constables
175,000 part-time Auxiliary Police and Home Guard

4. It is difficult to estimate next year's expenditure by the Federation of Malaya. In 1951 the extra cost to the Federation Government arising from the emergency and excluding the cost of services of a normal and permanent nature is about £13.8 m. The major part of this is in respect of police forces (£5.6 m.) and resettlement of Chinese squatters (£4.8 m.). The full cost to the Federation of all police, defence and Emergency measures is about £29 m. (out of total Government expenditure of £66 m.).

253 CAB 128/23, CC 10(51)2   22 Nov 1951

'Malaya': Cabinet conclusions on the current situation and Mr Lyttelton's forthcoming visit

The Cabinet had before them a memorandum (C.(51)26) by the Secretary of State for the Colonies on the situation in Malaya.[1]

The Colonial Secretary drew particular attention to the existing division of responsibility between the various British authorities in Malaya. One of the primary purposes of his forthcoming visit was to find means of securing stronger direction and more unified control of the campaign for restoring law and order. His present bias was in favour of concentrating in the hands of a single individual the powers of Governor-General and Commander-in-Chief. He would not, however, ask the Cabinet to take a final decision on this point until he had been able to see the conditions on the spot.

The Chief of the Imperial General Staff[2] said that, while the police and military were already under unified command for operational purposes, he would favour more radical measures for unified control on the lines suggested by the Colonial Secretary. The situation in Malaya would not, in his view, be remedied until the civil administration was strong enough to ensure stable government.

---

[1] See 252   [2] Field Marshal Sir W Slim.

The Parliamentary Under-Secretary of State for Foreign Affairs[3] said that, in adopting a more forceful policy towards the Chinese as recommended in paragraph (b) of C.(51)26, care should be taken to avoid alienating the sympathies of Chinese communities elsewhere in South-East Asia. *The Colonial Secretary* said that this was largely a matter of timing: it would clearly be inexpedient to take a stronger line with the Chinese in Malaya until we could show that we were in a position to protect them from the bandits.

The Cabinet:—

Took note of C.(51)26; and invited the Colonial Secretary to submit his further recommendations immediately after his return from his forthcoming visit to Malaya.

---

[3] Lord Reading, parliamentary under-secretary of state for foreign affairs, 1951–1953.

254   CO 1022/81, no 7   3 Dec 1951
[Lyttelton's statement to the Malayan press]: outward telegram no 83 from J D Higham to A M MacKintosh requesting clarification of Mr Lyttelton's statement   [Extract]

[Lyttelton left London on 26 Nov accompanied by Hugh Fraser (his parliamentary private secretary), J J Paskin and A MacKintosh. The party landed at Singapore on 29 Nov where, as he recalled, his initial statement—'to restore law and order is the first thing'—was interpreted by local journalists as 'Secretary of State denies constitutional change'. See *The memoirs of Lord Chandos* (London, 1962) p 364.]

1. The Prime Minister is being asked on Wednesday whether Secretary of State's statement on November 29th that political progress was not an integral part of the struggle against militant Communism in Malaya represents H.M.G.'s policy.[1]

2. We have seen Reuter and Times report of statement referred to and Times report of December 2nd from Kuala Lumpur in which the Secretary of State corrected his earlier announcement and said that political and social advancement were essential parts of the war against militant Communism but the military effort had been lagging; it was a matter of emphasis.

3. We are proposing reply to the effect that the Hon. Member will by now have seen press reports correcting the statement to which he refers. . . .

---

[1] The parliamentary question was put down by Woodrow Wyatt, Labour MP for Aston division of Birmingham 1945–1955, who had been personal assistant to Sir Stafford Cripps during the Cabinet Mission to India in 1946.

255   CO 1022/81, no 8   4 Dec 1951
[Lyttelton's statement to the Malayan press]: inward telegram (reply) no 1189 from A M MacKintosh to J D Higham

Your personal telegram no. 83.[1]

---

[1] See 254.

Following for Higham from MacKintosh.

Begins. S. of S. has never made any statement or implication to the effect of your first paragraph. He has stressed that political and social progress are essentially part of the struggle against militant communism in Malaya, but that emphasis changes from time to time, and at present it is on the operational side, that the main effort is required. Without success there, progress in other ways is bound to be slower and more difficult. S. of S. has not corrected his original statement, but has expanded it.

2. A reply should be on these lines, but should begin with categorical denial of statement attributed to him in your first paragraph. [*Ends*]

256 PREM 11/639, f 51   8 Dec 1951

[Reorganisation of Malayan government]: inward telegram no 1214 from Mr Lyttelton to Mr Churchill

Following personal for the Prime Minister from the Secretary of State for the Colonies No. 4. *Begins.*

I have subjected the subject of the chain of command and responsibility to intense and careful study and I have definitely reached the conclusion that the place where a personage of the calibre we discussed is required must be Kuala Lumpur as (Headquarters of the) High Commission of the Federation. My advisers agree.

(If, for example, Singapore was included at this stage in his orbit, the effect would be disastrous on Malayan opinion. Malays would regard it as a step towards a fusion with Singapore, for which time is not ripe. They fear Chinese domination since half the population of the Federation is already Chinese and 90% of the population of Singapore is Chinese. In addition, Singapore is far too far from the centre of operations to serve as a headquarters).

2. This High Commissioner would assume entire responsibility for both military operations and civil administration. He would be called the High Commissioner and Director of Operations.

3. Under him would be

(a) a Deputy Director of Operations (Lockhart)[1] and
(b) a Civil Authority to be designated Deputy High Commissioner.

I would recommend for this post the ablest of the younger Colonial Governors and I have a man in mind. The post is essential to the successful direction of the whole since, without a Civil Deputy of this standing, the new High Commissioner would become hopelessly overloaded with civil affairs which are bedevilled by the existence of eleven Governments within the Federation.

4. These conclusions would have been part of my report on my return but I am advised that to create post of Deputy High Commissioner with seat on the Executive and Legislative Councils involves amendments to the Federal Agreement to which Rulers must be assenting parties. I am further advised that unless I put this proposal to the Rulers myself it may easily not receive their assent.[2]

---

[1] See 248, note 1.
[2] Churchill agreed to this, subject to Cabinet confirmation.

5. I am, therefore, arranging to fly here from Hong Kong to see them again. I will try to keep the position fluid until I see you. But local politics are very complicated and political actions of some pieces of the jigsaw unpredictable. I would therefore like to have your authority to clinch the matter if, when I see the Rulers, there seems a serious danger in delay. I reiterate my confidence that this is the right set up.

6. The position of Malcolm MacDonald can await discussion until I get home. He will have no executive powers in this new set up and his activities would be mainly diplomatic. Obviously a discussion with Anthony[3] is necessary on his future role if any.

7. Was neither hurt nor shaken by our mishap but it was a close call.[4] Expect to reach England 20th

Oliver

Ends.
This telegram should be seen by Minister of State and Lloyd.

---

[3] Anthony Eden, foreign secretary.
[4] The RAF Valetta transporting Lyttelton's party to Penang crash-landed on touching down.

257   CAB 129/48, C(51)59   21 Dec 1951
'Malaya': Cabinet memorandum by Mr Lyttelton. *Appendices I–XV*

[Lyttelton drafted his report in Kuala Lumpur. He later commented that the number and size of its appendices 'demonstrated how inadequate were the instruments of our policy at that time' (*The memoirs of Lord Chandos*, London, 1962, p 379). He arrived back in London on 21 Dec and discussed Malayan problems with Churchill and Montgomery over lunch at Chequers on 23 Dec (see 258). Cabinet considered Lyttelton's report on 28 Dec and gave 'general support for the Colonial Secretary's approach to the problems of restoring order in Malaya'. It also appointed a committee to examine the report in detail and make recommendations for Cabinet approval in the second half of Jan 1952. The committee consisted of: Lord Salisbury (chairman, lord privy seal), Sir David Maxwell Fyfe (home secretary), Lyttelton, Macmillan (minister of housing and local government) and Lord Swinton (chancellor of the Duchy of Lancaster) (CAB 128/23, CC 20(51)1, 28 Dec 1951, see also 266).]

I append my report on the Federation of Malaya and its "Emergency." My recommendations are to be found as follows:—

		Paragraphs
1.	The Chain of Command and Responsibility	34–47
2.	Federal War Council and Cabinet	48–50
3.	Police	51–62
4.	Home Guard	63–69
5.	Protection of Resettlement Areas	70
6.	Education	71–75
7.	Malayan Civil Service	76–83
8.	General Conclusions	84–94
9.	Malay Regiment	Appx. X

The report has a number of rather long appendices. They are:—

I.—Itinerary and Sources of Information.

II.—Text of Broadcast in Singapore on 11th December, 1951.

III.—Federal and State Councils, &c.

IV.—Armoured Vehicles for the Police.

V.—Arms, Clothing and Equipment Urgently required by the Police.

VI.—Earth-Shifting Equipment.

VII.—Chemical Defoliation of Roadside Jungle.

VIII.—Language Teaching.

IX.—Intelligence Services and Related Counter-Measures.

X.—Terms of Employment of British Officers and Other Ranks posted or seconded for service with the Malay Regiment.

XI.—Detention and Repatriation

XII.—Man-power and National Service.

XIII.—Tax Evasion.

XIV.—Financial Devolution.

XV.—Extension of Service Beyond Retiring Age.

These are added mainly for the benefit of the new High Commissioner, when he is appointed, in the hope that they will save him work and enable him to dispense with many of the investigations in which I have necessarily been involved. I have no wish to burden my colleagues with studying these appendices: they will, however, perhaps agree that their range and detail demonstrate how inadequate are the instruments of our policy.

Malaya: general description

The country

1. The territory of the Federation of Malaya is not large, about the size of England without Wales: the population is about that of Wales without England.

2. The country is divided from north to south by a dorsal range rising in places to 7,000 feet. Three-quarters of the whole area of the country is covered with dense jungle. Little light penetrates to the jungle where it is thickest. Because of this the aboriginal who lives in the jungle is stunted; and, to give another example, the Malayan elephant is a much smaller animal than the Indian. A man would have to be fit and tough to cut his way through the jungle at a greater rate than five miles between dawn and dusk.

3. No-one can fail to notice the splendid roads which interlace the country, particularly in the west. They are testimonals to British rule. Often the jungle comes down to the verge of the roads. Roads crossing the spinal barrier from west to east are few.

4. The last geographical feature worthy of mention is the numerous rivers: their waters are discoloured by the erosion of the rich soil and alluvial.

5. Broadly speaking, there are no seasons; the temperature does not rise much above 90 degrees; it rains a little almost every day, a lot once a week and still more during the monsoons; the humidity is high. Europeans easily stand the climate for about two years at a time without losing energy or health, but it is a mistake to prolong any tour of duty beyond two years without leave.

6. Rubber (the most important industry) is grown all over the Federation, but the rich tin alluvials in the plains, caused by the erosion of the central range, are almost all found on the western side of the main watershed.

The people

7. The population is mainly Malay, Chinese and Indian (chiefly Tamils), though there are smaller communities of Cingalese and Eurasians. The numbers are approximately as follows:—

Malays	2,500,000
Chinese	2,000,000
Indians	500,000
Others	70,000
	5,070,000

The European population to-day is about 10,000. It is very rarely that a European remains in the country when he retires. Before the war the Malays, who at one time or another have all come from the territories now constituting Indonesia, were regarded as indigenous; while the Chinese and Indian communities were regarded as immigrants, most of whom would at some time in their lives return to their native lands. There are, however, considerable Chinese communities in Penang and Malacca (and in Singapore) who are proud to call themselves "King's Chinese." They have been in Malaya for many generations, are British subjects (fervently loyal and devoted to the Crown) and can speak only English. They are deeply anxious not to have their British citizenship diluted, so to speak, by inclusion in any United Malaya. They would not tolerate separation from the British Commonwealth.

8. The Malays are for the most part farmers, growing rice and vegetables and producing rubber, copra, palm-oil and oil-seed and small quantities of pineapple. They are rarely found in commerce and industry.

9. The Indians, mostly Tamils, provide a good deal of the unskilled labour of the country, many tapping rubber and a few working in the dredging or hydraulicing of tin.

10. The Chinese, on the other hand, are found in all the activities of the country—in rubber and tin, as common labourers, as agriculturalists, as proprietors of rubber estates (20 per cent. of the rubber on smallholdings and 17 per cent. of that on estates is Chinese owned) and of the mines (40 per cent. of the production of tin is Chinese owned), as merchants, as contractors, as shopkeepers (of whom they constitute much the greater part), as bankers and as traders. Every year they gain greater economic strength and increase their hold over the wealth of the country.

There are many rich Chinese in the Federation, highly sophisticated, urbane, shrewd, politically aloof and inscrutable. They are mostly absentee landlords with no following in the villages or among the mass of their fellow-countrymen. Many live in Singapore, where their touch with the Chinese in the plantations or mines of the Federation is still more distant. It is amusing and stimulating to argue or negotiate with them but they are generally politicians without constituencies, leaders without followers, remote from the problem, trimming adroitly, ready sometimes with advice and almost always with criticism, but not prepared to lead or even to exhort.

The constitutional pattern

11. Even before the war the constitutional and administrative position in Malaya was complex: immediately after the war an attempt was made to simplify it by the creation of the Malayan Union. This, however, met with such opposition from the Malays that it was rescinded (perhaps too readily) and replaced by the present

Federation Agreement, under which the Malays have greater executive authority than before the war, at any rate in the former Federated States.

12. In many important matters, such as defence, internal security, economic and financial policy, labour policy and immigration, both legislative and executive authority rests with the Federal Government. In other matters, including health, education, agriculture and land, all executive authority and a measure of legislative authority rests with the nine State and two Settlement Governments,* although the Federal Government retains legislative authority over all questions of common concern.

13. Both the Federal and the State Governments have Legislative and Executive Councils. The Federal Legislative Council (with a large unofficial majority) consists entirely of nominated members, as do all the other Legislative and Executive Councils.

14. In April this year a Member system[†] of Government was introduced, under which the responsibility for the different Departments of Government was divided between nine Members (excluding the High Commissioner, the Chief Secretary and the Financial Secretary), of whom six are unofficials. In each State the chief executive (Mentri Besar) is a Malay nominated by the Ruler.

15. In the Federal sphere no expenditure outside the provision of the annual budget may be incurred without the authority of the Finance Committee which, under the Financial Secretary, consists entirely of unofficials.

16. The position of the British in Malaya is based upon treaties with the Malay Rulers. The influence of the British has now in fact to be exercised by persuasion rather than direction. Their power is nevertheless very great and in the last resort their influence prevails. Apart from this, and the limited representation of the other races on the various Councils, political power is in the hands of the Malays. It is exercised through the Rulers and Mentri Besars in the States and through the Malay preponderence [sic] on all Councils. The High Commissioner has the usual reserved power to override his Legislative and Executive Councils in the interests of public order and good government.

17. Thus, partly, from the heterogeneous nature of the population, and partly because of the existence of the Malay Rules, a political pattern has been formed ill-adapted to the needs of a small country at any time, least of all at a time of political convulsion and emergency. The most striking way in which the complexity of this pattern can be expressed is to say that the Federal Government has very often to work through eleven other Governments.

18. We cannot now re-shuffle all the cards. Some, but not all, of the administrative tangle to which I shall refer in the course of this paper is due to these causes, but the administration, like the country, is covered with jungle.

Political organisations

19. The most important Malay political body is the United Malay National Organisation (U.M.N.O.), whose President was until recently Dato Onn,[º] then the most influential figure in Malayan politics. In September this year, however, after

---

* The States are Johore, Kedah, Kelantan, Negri Sembilan, Pahang, Perak, Perlis, Selangor and Trengganu. The Settlements are Malacca and Penang and Province Wellesley.
[†] This curious nomenclature describes the half-way stage to a Cabinet or Ministerial system.
[º] "Dato" is an honorific title.

breaking with U.M.N.O., he formed the Independence of Malaya Party (I.M.P.) and thereby lost nearly all of his Malay support. U.M.N.O. aims at "Malaya for the Malays" and has consistently stood for preservation of the "special position" of the Malays under the Federation Agreement. This position is reflected, for example, in the admission of all Malays to Federal Citizenship, whereas not more than one-third of the Chinese qualify for it.

20.   I.M.P. marks a clean break with the tradition of racial separation in Malayan politics and has as its slogan "Unity, Freedom, Independence and Equality for All." Dato Onn has said that it aims at independence within ten years and he refuses to commit himself on the question whether an independent Malaya would remain within the Commonwealth. I.M.P. has been strongly supported by the Chinese and Indians but has found little favour among the Malays. Dato Onn is a volatile but clever politician. By European standards he is at worst unreliable and at best fitful. Despite his loss of Malay support he is still a force in the land. I have had two long talks with him and I am fairly sure that he favours the inclusion of a united Malaya in the British Commonwealth. He is certainly ready to say so in private.

21.   The main Chinese political party, the Malayan Chinese Association, aims at acquiring for the Chinese equal rights in the Federation. It represents in the main only the middle classes and has little influence on the great body of the Chinese peasant population. Its President, Dato Tan Cheng Lock, is a garrulous old man whose philosophy is woolly, though his intentions are good.

22.   The rôle of the Indian parties, the Malayan Indian Congress and the Federation of Indian Organisations, has never been clearly defined, and internal dissensions have so far prevented the development of any effective Indian political policy.

23.   The only European organisations which need to be mentioned are those representing the planters and miners. Their aims are industrial rather than political and they are chiefly preoccupied with restoring conditions in which their members can once more carry on their businesses undeterred by the threat of violence.

The Emergency

The enemy

24.   The history of the Emergency is too recent to make it worth while to retrace it: we are concerned with the problem as it is posed to-day. It cannot be too strongly emphasised that the Emergency is almost entirely concentrated in the Federation and is outside the Colony of Singapore. The Singapore police have the usual task of watching and suppressing subversion and Communist cells. There is no military and hardly any para-military problem in Singapore.

25.   If the present situation had to be summed up in a sentence it would run: "You cannot win the war without the help of the population, and the Chinese population in particular, and you cannot get the support of the population without at least beginning to win the war." It is therefore clear that we must organise a much heavier and more concentrated impact upon the enemy and key up the machine at once.

26.   It is, however, necessary that the word "enemy" should be defined. The Communist organisation is headed by a Secretary-General, with two or three staff officers. It is not known, but it is believed, that this central body is located somewhere in Pahang. The war is waged with two instruments, propaganda and

armed forces. The Min Yuen, or People's Movement (probably numbering about 10,000) is used for both: the armed bandits are recruited from them in the villages and it is the Min Yuen who penetrate the Resettlement Areas, the schools, the villages and the Trade Unions with Communist doctrine. They also find supplies for the armed forces and undertake small ambushes.

27. The Communist organisation is widely decentralised. It works through State units and is again devolved down to Districts and even to villages. The armed forces themselves are divided into twelve or thirteen regiments. Regimental Headquarters usually operate at the State level. The operational unit is seldom much larger than 10 or 12 men up to a platoon. They used to undertake larger operations but these have apparently been abandoned because of the heavy losses which they entailed. The total estimated strength of the armed bandits is between 3,000 and 5,000 but, owing to the paucity of information, it is not clear how much of this force is committed to active fighting and how much is held in reserve.

28. It is the general opinion that Communist efficiency has greatly improved and that a formidable instrument, both for propaganda and for war, has been forged. Propaganda again is an "overcoat" term: some of it is driven home by harrying the population at the point of a gun, the rest of it by peaceful and insidious means. One of the most serious features of the whole problem is the amount of protection money and payment in kind which are being made daily to the bandits. On the one hand, the rich Chinese are known to be paying large sums of money to prevent their estates and mines from being attacked; on the other, the Chinese labourer is passing food and clothing or stolen rubber and tin to the bandits through the wire of the Resettlement Areas or directly in the fields of jungle generally from fear but sometimes from sympathy. The European companies and single Europeans are not paying directly, but I fear that many know that indirectly they are receiving protection in this way. For example, the Shell Company has a large fleet fleet [sic] of oil tanker lorries: they are seldom, if ever, attacked. The reason appears to be that the retailer who depends for his livelihood on selling the oil is paying the protection money.

29. Such is the present picture of the enemy tactics but, if we are successful in increasing our victories over the bandits, the Communists may well elect to go underground. Thus, in parallel with the "military" impact mentioned at the beginning of this section, we must quickly forge much more effective weapons for the warfare of ideas.

The rôle of the army.

30. I have everywhere been impressed by the efficiency and bearing of the British troops and their commanders. Throughout the Federation they are engaged in joint operations with the police and civil authorities and are fighting a trying campaign with great courage and efficiency. The National Service men are proving themselves first class, both in combat with the enemy and in their resilience to the climate. Morale is uniformly high. The armed forces are contributing to the campaign against the bandits almost all that can be expected of them.

31. Except in certain small and remote districts along the Siamese frontier, they have prevented the enemy from gaining military control of areas outside the jungle. They have broken his larger offensive in Johore and elsewhere and have forced him to operate in platoons or smaller units. If the present pressure of the British forces is

not relaxed, Communist military action can at least be contained within this reduced compass.

32. This is vital, but it must be recognised that the war has now nearly reached a deadlock. In spite of the considerable casualties inflicted upon the bandits their operational strength remains virtually constant.

33. This deadlock must be broken. Part of my main proposals concerns the creation of trained Police Forces and Home Guards. For this training, Police and Special Constables will have to be withdrawn; and during their absence the Army will have to bear a serious additional burden of static defence. I have discussed this matter with the Commander-in-Chief Land Forces, Far East, who combines outstanding military ability with a firm grasp of the political situation, both in Singapore and Malaya as a whole. I have obtained from him an assurance of his fullest co-operation during this difficult transitional period. I believe that, once the training and re-training of the Police and para-military forces have been completed, police action, including the better provision of information, will render military action gradually more effective and, I hope, ultimately unnecessary.

Measure proposed and reasons

The chain of command and responsibility

34. This in my view has been unsound: the idea of having, in effect, two heads at the summit, one for military operations and the other for civil administration, in a condition of affairs that differs from both war and peace, must inevitably lead either to conflict between the authorities or to long drawn-out discussions to reach an accommodation and compromise between two points of view. In my opinion the most effective single measure to be taken is the unification and concentration of command and responsibility in one man.

35. A note on the civil administration is necessary here. Partly from the highly complicated jigsaw puzzle through or around which it must work, partly from its pre-war traditions of conscientious but unhurried administration, partly from over-centralisation in the Poona-like society of Kuala Lumpur, partly from the host of new problems which almost daily crowd in upon an overstrained service, a Government machine has grown up of which I am critical.

36. Owing to this strain inexperienced Government officers are sent straight out on to the ground—and a good District Officer is worth more than a battalion. The central authority thus finds it necessary to issue more and more directions. In this way the central authority becomes itself desk-bound, clogged with paper and remote. I was told by one man in a district which I reached from Kuala Lumpur in forty-five by Auster, that I was almost the only man from Kuala Lumpur (apart from the High Commissioner and the Director of Operations) whom he had seen since the Emergency began.

37. A cold wind must blow some of the paper out of these Government offices. Only an experienced, forceful and ruthless administrator will succeed in creating a system equal to its task. That system must be closely knit, muscular, quick and instant; delay must be abhorrent; action not distasteful.

38. I must add that the Malayan Civil Service includes many men of great ability, knowledge and energy, devoted to their work. It is not in the main the material but the system which is at fault.

39. It early became quite clear to me that, if one man was to be entrusted with both civil and military responsibilities, it would be necessary to appoint a Deputy High Commissioner to handle the great bulk of the civil administration. Otherwise, the head man would quickly be immersed in the paper jungle and never be able to turn his attention to the real jungle and its menace.

40. Unfortunately, an amendment of the Federation Agreement is involved, but I have succeeded in obtaining the agreement of the Rulers to this. Their Highnesses are suspicious of any alteration and, for reasons into which I need not enter, negotiations with them were extremely delicate.

Deputy director of operations

41. If any alterations are required in the directive appointing the Deputy Director of Operations (the present document appointing the Director of Operations would appear adequate), they should be made only after discussions between the new High Commissioner and General Lockhart.

42. The "G" Branch of the Deputy Director of Operations can and should be small, but a Director of Intelligence and an intelligence staff (as far as possible drawn from military and police headquarters) should be added. Through them the Deputy Director of Operations would be able to direct, co-ordinate and distribute intelligence derived from the two main sources—the police and military intelligence branches. The present structure is noticeably faulty at this point.

43. I recommend, therefore, the appointment of one man, to be styled High Commissioner and Director of Operations, with a Deputy Director of Operations on one side and a Deputy High Commissioner on the other.

44. I have carefully studied whether there should be an extension of the area of the High Commissioner's responsibility so as to include other territories, and where his headquarters should be. I must strongly advise that his responsibility should be confined to the Federation and that his headquarters should be in Kuala Lumpur.

45. The Malays are fearful that the increasing Chinese population, and their growing hold on the wealth and economy of the country, will soon destroy the present political strength of their race. All the Rulers, who are by no means a negligible force and are entrenched behind the Federation Agreement, would be bitterly opposed to such a step.

45. On the other hand, the Chinese in Singapore are to-day apprehensive of being drawn into a bigger unit in which their future might be determined by Malays. Furthermore, they are hardly involved in the Emergency. If this spirit of isolation is smug, it is at least deeply ingrained.

47. Finally, not only is Kuala Lumpur the seat of civil government: it is also nearest to the centre of the fighting. The Deputy Director of Operations must have his headquarters there. If the necessary cohesion is to be gained there can, in my opinion, be no doubt that the High Commissioner must also have his headquarters at Kuala Lumpur.

Federal War Council and Cabinet

48. The proposed appointment of a High Commissioner, charged with both civil and "military" responsibilities, and the other measures which I have described, should ensure quick and ultimately decisive action in the Emergency. We must avoid the risk of this "cutting edge" being blunted by the complex of Councils and

Committees which exists in the Federation to-day. The Federal and State Legislative and Executive Councils are normal and necessary parts of the constitutional machinary [sic] prescribed in the Federation Agreement, and there can be no question of making any radical changes in their functions or composition.

49. The Federal War Council, on the other hand, is an "Emergency" growth and I have devoted some thought to its place in the general pattern—in particular to the possibility of reducing the number of these bodies by combining the War Council with the Executive Council. This Council has grown to its present size as a result of a demand from the various principal communities to be associated with the higher direction of the war. Even though, as at present constituted, it is an impossibly cumbrous body for practical purposes, it serves two very useful ends. On the one hand it satisfies, at any rate partially, the aspirations of the leaders of the various communites; and on the other hand it associates them with what must frequently be distasteful measures. I am satisfied that at present there are insuperable political difficulties in the way of increasing the membership of the Executive Council to embrace that of the War Council, or of reducing the membership of that Council to the number prescribed for the Executive Council. I have agreed that this Council should remain as a separate body. I have, however, arranged that an inner "War Cabinet" should be set up, consisting of the High Commissioner, his Civil and Operational Deputies, the Chief Secretary and four prominent Asiatics. The remaining members of the Council can usefully be employed on other Committees to deal with such matters as man-power, education, resettlement, &c.

50. I am also satisfied that the devolution to State War Executive Committees has proved itself. I have met the members of three of these Committees and have been impressed by their keenness and capacity for gearing the military and civilian efforts in their respective States.

Police

51. Urgent and drastic action is called for. The Emergency is in essence a Police rather than a military task. More troops would add little to the impact. While some of the Police are being drawn back from the ground for training more troops would doubtless be useful, but I am satisfied that this difficulty can be surmounted by temporary measures and by stepping up the present operations for a short time in the areas principally affected.

52. The figures for Johore are typical. At the beginning of 1951 it was estimated that there were 780 armed bandits in the State; during the year altogether 309 armed bandits and Min Yuen have been killed or captured or have surrendered; to-day there are estimated to be still 750 armed bandits in the field.

53. In short, I do not recommend any increase in tropps [sic] but concur in the British Defence Coordination Committee (Far East) Summary S.E.A.C.O.S. 242 of 15th November, paragraph 16:—

> "There must therefore be no further reduction in the total number of army units in Malaya before the Spring of 1953 at the earliest. After that any reduction must depend on the success or otherwise of the campaign over the next twelve months. The Spring of 1953 is selected as a date as it is necessary to plan far ahead and an unexpected reduction in troops at short notice has repercussions throughout the country as plans are readjusted. We are

especially concerned with the recent change of tactics of the bandits in attacking convoys which must make additional demands on armoured car units and a requirement for a considerable increase in armoured personnel carrying vehicles."

54. The organisation of the Police is in utter disorder and even the Regular Force is inefficient. For example, soon after my arrival I tried to obtain both the "state" (or numerical composition) of the Force on the one hand and its deployment on the other. After cross-examination I could obtain no satisfactory answer under either heading. No detailed allocation of establishment has been laid down below State level; the Chief Police Officer in each State has a free hand to make what use he wishes of the officers and men posted to him. It is difficult to believe that in the absence of authorised establishments there can be rational planning of expansion or that the needs in man-power can be gauged, requests for additional officers and technicians justified and priority for building programmes (particularly permanent buildings) decided.

55. I have now been supplied with the following figures. They give an accurate general picture, but in detail they must be accepted with reserve:—

Officers				1948	December 1951
Gazetted Officers	...	...	...	150	561
Inspectors (Asian)		...	...	188	614
Police Lieutenants (Europeans)			...	...	743
Other Ranks					
Regulars	...	...	...	...	9,888	19,704
Special Constables		...	...	...	38,466

56. Of the Special Constables approximately 24,000 are employed on estates and mines and on guards. The remainder are used to augment the normal Police formations of all kinds and the Jungle Companies (3,500 strong). Some 2,300 Auxiliary Police are organised to perform voluntary part-time duty. The Regular Police are also concerned with the arming and training of part of another large force of part-time Police (amounting now to about 100,000) and Home Guards. Officering, training, housing and supplying have fallen behind—indeed, they are now out of all relation to this expansion.

57. Owing to the Emergency this huge Force has been totally committed—and in a haphazard manner. For example, the total density of officers over the whole Force, including the large staff employed at headquarters, the Asian Inspectors and the newly-engaged European Police Lieutenants, is roughly 1 in 30 of the full-time force. On the other hand, the density of officers in the 24,000 Special Constables performing duties on estates and mines is apparently only 1 in 480. Again, of the 561 Gazetted Officers only 170 can be regarded as fully trained and the Police Lieutenants are not trained Police Officers in any sense: few of them know the language. In the Army it is considered desirable to have a larger density of officers in untrained than in trained forces. This does not mean that the Special Constabulary should, even when untrained, have more officers than the Regular Police Force; but they should certainly have many more than at present or than will be required when they have been trained.

58. As well as being unled, the Special Constabulary are almost entirely untrained: they are mere levies.

59. Unfortunately, there is another very serious aspect of the disorganisation of the Police. The Government has wide emergency powers of mass arrest and detention without trial. No doubt these powers must sometimes be used, but a properly organised and trained Police Force should be able to focus arrest on the guilty and reduce the numbers detained on suspicion without trial.

60. The figures are at present profoundly disquieting. A guess is that perhaps 200,000 persons have been so detained for less than 28 days. It is known that 25,000 persons have been detained for 28 days or more. Of these less than 800 have been prosecuted. After deportation and release there are still 6,000 detained without trial. A trained Police Force should be able to make great, even startling, reductions in these numbers.

61. I propose, therefore, to relieve the Commissioner of Police, who is a gallant officer but without the necessary grasp of organisation in these exceptional circumstances, and to replace him with the best that can be found. I have already arranged for a thorough examination of all possible sources from which a replacement can be drawn. The Home Office are being most helpful in this search.

62. When the new Commissioner has been appointed I shall arrange for the Regular Police Force and the C.I.D. to be treated as one distinct Force, and for the Special Constabulary to be separately organised. Both Forces will be commanded by the Commissioner of Police.

63. My proposals for the Home Guard follow.

Home Guard

6. It is axiomatic that we must gain the support and help of the Chinese population and involve them much more deeply in the struggle.

65. One of the great weaknesses to-day, which is unfortunately bound to persist for a long time, is that the Police—both the Regular Force and the Special Constabulary—are overwhelmingly Malay, while the bandits and those whom they are terrorising are overwhelmingly Chinese.* In the face of this handicap it is hard to gain the confidence of the population, to increase the flow of intelligence and to concert the proper counter-measures.

66. The Chinese will not volunteer since they at present enjoy high wages and good opportunities for trade and are not attracted, as are the Malays, by the rates of pay in the Regular Police Force. They are not satisfied that the British will stay in Malaya; they harbour some patriotism towards the Chinese People's Government even if they are not themselves Communists; and they feel marked men if they voluntarily join any section of the Police. When conscription was first introduced many young Chinese liable for service took to the jungle or left the country.

67. I am, however, satisfied from the success which has attended direction into the Regular Police this year that the Chinese can with equal success be directed into a Home Guard if the rôle of that Force is the protection of Chinese lives and property in the towns and of the Resettlement Areas into which their countrymen have been concentrated outside the towns. I would hazard the guess that they will serve loyally.

---

* Out of a total of 38,466 Special Constables only 1,860 are Chinese. Since the Emergency began, 2,578 bandits have been killed: of these 2,409 were Chinese.

Some risks will attend arming these guards but I am sure that they must be accepted.

68. The formation of a Chinese Home Guard should, however, be looked upon only as a first step to trying to gain much more Chinese support and to enlisting much larger numbers of them in the Police.

69. Although a beginning has been made there is at present no discernible framework or organisation of the Home Guard. I have discussed the matter with the Deputy Director of Operations and have suggested the name of an officer already in the country for the post of Inspector-General. The Deputy Director of Operations is busy examining the measures necessary to expand the Home Guard and make it into a coherent force under his hand. Only those serving full time will be paid.

Protection of resettlement areas

70. This subject has already largely been covered under the headings "Police" and "Home Guard," but I am arranging that better wire fences and better lighting of the perimeter of these areas should be regarded as urgent. I saw a well wired and lighted fence at Pertang in Negri Sembilan: it is ironical that this village, which is notorious for a sullen population in sympathy with the bandits, should be better protected than many of the areas which are far more favourable to our cause.

Education

71. There is no compulsory primary education in Malaya although the Government is already committed to the principle. The cost would be about $20 million per annum, say, £2,140,000.

72. More serious than the money required is the strain on man-power and materials involved in this programme. Nevertheless, there is scope for ingenuity and I am satisfied that the Government of the Federation should act rapidly. I shall try to animate it and produce action.

73. It would, in my opinion, be wrong to regard the effect of primary education only as a long-term weapon in the war of ideas. Children coming back from school convert their parents to our way of thinking—instances could be cited—and provide some answer to the propaganda being whispered to them from the jungle.

74. Again, a most important feature of primary education is to bring the races together while they are children and to teach them a common language.

75. In the long-term war of ideas, which we must win if we are to see a peaceful country and one which can some day be entrusted with self-government within the British Commonwealth, it is obvious that education and the impartial administration of the law must take first place.

Malayan Civil Service

76. The high standard of local administration set by District Officers and the members of the professional departments, such as the Medical, Education and Engineering Departments, is in danger.

77. The housing shortage is disastrous. I found an officer with his wife and two children, recently returned from leave, who had been posted to a new district and would have had to live over a Chinese shop (where trade was thought to extend beyond inanimate commodities) if the British Adviser had not crowded them into his own house. These conditions are widespread and when better known in England will make recruitment almost impossible.

78. Again, armed with a pay code unsuited to to-day's conditions, the Establishment Officers have fought a successful rearguard action. Exasperation over the rigid attitude adopted by the central authority is spreading. Recruitment is sluggish and there are now some 500 unfilled vacancies in the Service.

79. The high cost of living and of sending children home for education makes it imperative to revise the system of expatriate allowances.

80. Finally, there are doubts whether the British will remain long enough in the country to provide a career for young men. I tried in the broadcast which I made in Singapore to reassure opinion upon this.

81. Further measures covering the whole Colonial Service, such as interchange of officers and guaranteed employment and pensions, are in hand but must take some time to complete since they will involve all Colonial Governments.

82. Reverting to the local problems, I insisted that a Board should be set up to study the necessary changes. It is directed to report to me by 31st January and is now at work.

83. I need hardly add how vital is this problem. If the Service disintegrates under our hands—and it is no exaggeration to say that that might happen—then the changes of achieving any of our long-term aims would indeed be finally destroyed.

General conclusions

84. It appears to me that the objective of one day building a united Malayan nation within the British Commonwealth and Empire should not be abandoned. I believe that the ever-improving communications of our century—Singapore will soon be less than 24 hours by Comet from London—the rapidity with which news and propaganda can now be spread, and above all the increasing education and literacy of all people make it impossible to hold any other policy than the creation of new Dominions, self-Governing but part of the Commonwealth owing allegiance to the Crown.

85. Fifty million islanders shorn of so much of their economic power can no longer by themselves expect to hold dominion over palm and pine on the nineteenth century model of power and paternalism which made us the greatest nation in the world. We may regain our pinnacle of fame and power by the pursuit of this new policy.

86. Nevertheless, in Malaya to-day there is only one reason to expect that we can achieve a united nation. All the others are at present against us. The factors against the idea in this plural and heterogeneous society are formidable. The Malays are a simple, agricultural people, the Chinese a sophisticated one with centuries of experience upon which to draw. They are at once agricultural, commercial and industrial and will continue to gain a bigger hold on the wealth of the country. Of all the religions likely to appeal to a Chinaman the Muslim faith is, perhaps, the last. Under its code he could not open his shop or work his mine on Fridays but must needs pray. The consequent loss of profit and increase in overheads is unacceptable to his realistic temperament. His staple and favourite diet, pork, would be taboo. Again, of the Chinese who are not Communists many have a patriotic sentiment for China, some for the Chinese People's Republic and others for the Kuo Min Tang.

87. These are the fundamental difficulties: the immediate obstacles are hardly less. Today 95 per cent. of the bandits are Chinese, while more than 90 per cent. of

the police are Malays. Apart from the British influence, political power is in the hands of the Malays and economic power is increasingly passing to the Chinese. Nor is the broad pattern—two million Chinese, two and a half million Malays and half a million Indians—so simple as it sounds. The States of Kelantan and Kedah, for example, contain one-third of the whole Malay population. These States look to the British to keep Malaya for the Malays. In Johore, half the population is Chinese, half Malay and other races. Their voice is less clear.

88. On the other hand, the one favourable factor is the absence of any obdurate hostility between the two races like that between Jew and Arab. In small bodies, on the Executive and Legislative Councils, in the Universities, the races mix easily and without constraint. Both set high store on good manners and have a predilection to smile rather than to frown.

89. These are indeed slender foundations upon which to build and it is easy to feel that we might not be vouchsafed the time. Genuine partnership between the races will, in my opinion, take more than a generation and can come about then only if inter-racial schools are quickly established.

90. In these plural societies the policy of our predecessors—of using self-government as an instrument for creating unity—is an example of political immaturity amounting to folly.

91. In plural societies self-government must be the expression, not the instrument of unity. If a young man and a young woman of different races were highly suspicious of one another, we should hardly oblige them to marry by ordinance and expect harmony. Even when they love one another, marriage is not invariably a guarantee of harmony, or even of continuity. In seeking to create a Dominion like Canada, in which the British Protestant and the French Catholic are ruled by a single government, there is the ever-present danger of creating a Palestine in which unitary government tends only to increase the fissiparous forces at work.

92. These fears haunt the various races; none of them in their heart of hearts wish to see us go. They still believe in British justice. We must not break down their belief. The King's Chinese and the Malay States openly express these sentiments in fervent phrases. Other Chinese imply it. All know that we are their hope and stand-by.

93. I say, therefore, that we must persist. I believe that with patience and wisdom there is a reasonable chance—if we are given the time—of reaching our goal, a united Malayan nation within the British Commonwealth and Empire.

94. To go too quickly now to impose self-government, would be to condemn the whole country to confusion, and almost certainly to civil war, and to throw the Malays into the arms of the Indonesians. We must adapt the old saw of one of the wisest political peoples of their day: *"Festina lente."*

Appendix I to 257: Itinerary and sources of information

1. *29th November to 1st December—Bukit Serene Johore*
By air from London to Singapore and thence by road to Bukit Serene.

   (a) Consultations with Commissioner-General, South East Asia; Governors of Singapore, North Borneo and Sarawak; Officer Administering the Government of the Federation of Malaya; Commanders-in-Chief, Far East; retiring and incoming Directors of Operations; and other senior Service Commanders and Government officials.

(b) Meeting with unofficial members of the Executive Councils of the Federation and Singapore.

(c) Meetings with Johore State War Executive Committee; principal officials and Police Officers; military commanders; and unofficials (planters and business men of all races) in the State.

(d) Visits by road to Resettlement Areas and Police Stations and meetings there with Police Officers and other ranks; Resettlement Officers; and local military commanders.

2. *2nd to 8th December—Kuala Lumpur*

By road from Bukit Serene to Singapore and thence by air to Kuala Lumpur.

(a) Consultations with Officer Administering the Government of the Federation and his senior officials; Director of Operations; G.O.C., Malaya, and other senior Service Commanders; Commissioner of Police and other senior Police and C.I.D. Officers; Mentri Mentri Besar of the Malay States; British Advisers of most of the States; and District Officers and Police Officers on the ground in a number of States.

(b) Meetings with the Malay Rulers; Executive Council of the Federation; and Federal War Council.

(c) Meetings with representatives of United Malay National Organisation; Malayan Chinese Association; Malayan Indian Congress and Federation of Indian Organisation; Malayan Trades Union Council; Federated Malay States Chamber of Mines; All-Malayan Chinese Mining Association; Rubber Producers' Council; Incorporated Society of Planters; Malayan Estate Owners' Association; and United Planting Association of Malaya.

(d) Private talks with Officer Administering the Government of the Federation; Director of Operations; Commissioner of Police; retiring Director of Intelligence; G.O.C., Malaya; Commandant, the Malay Regiment; President of the Independence of Malaya Party; President of the Malayan Chinese Association; Trades Union Adviser to the Federal Government; representatives of the Malayan Civil Servants' Association; and leaders of the European planting and mining communities.

(e) Visits to:—

(i) Combined Operations Room for the State of Selangor for a meeting with the Selangor State War Executive Committee.

(ii) By Austor [sic] over typically dense, mountainous Malayan jungle to Bentong in Pahang, one of the areas most seriously affected by bandit operations, where there were meetings with Mentri Besar; British Adviser; local District Officer; local military commander; Chief Police Officer for the State; representatives of the Malay, Chinese and Indian communities; Malayan kampong guards and Chinese Home Guards; Resettlement Officers; planters; and other officials and unofficials.

(iii) Combined Operations Room at Federal Police Headquarters, where there were discussions with Commissioner of Police and other senior Police and C.I.D. Officers.

(iv)   Malayan Military Headquarters for talks with G.O.C., Malaya, and other senior Service Commanders.

(v)   Police Depot to see something of Police training.

(vi)   By air to Ipoh in Perak, the State in which the bandit menace is at present at its worst, for meetings with State War Executive Committee; Mentri Besar; British Adviser; local military commanders and Police Officers; local officials of the civil administration; and representatives of the various racial, planting, mining and business communities.

(vii)   By air to Penang to meet Resident Commissioner and his staff; senior local Police Officers and military commanders; and members of all local racial and business communities.

(viii)   By Auster to Negri Sembilan, to meet Mentri Besar; British Adviser; Chief Police Officer and other local Police Officers; local military commander; local planters and miners; (including visit to a tin mine), and heads of the nine small States constituting the Federation of Negri Sembilan; to see Resettlement Areas and Police Stations; and to visit a Battalion of the Suffolk Regiment at Kajang.

3. *15th December—Bukit Serene, Johore*

By air from Hong Kong to Singapore and thence by road to Bukit Serene. Final consultations with the Commissioner-General, South East Asia.

4. *16th to 19th December–Kuala Lumpur*

By road from Bukit Serene to Singapore and thence by air to Kuala Lumpur.

(a)   Final consultations with Officer Administering the Government of the Federation and his senior officials and Director of Operations.

(b)   Visit by air to Kota Bahru in Kelantan to see a typical predominantly Malay State.

Appendix II to 257: Text of broadcast in Singapore on 11th December 1951

1.   I have tried to see as much as I could during the short time that I have been in the country. It has to be a short time because action is required at once. I have been in the States of Johore, Pahang, Selangor, Negri Sembilan and Perak and in the Settlement of Penang and now I am back in Singapore. I have given the problem of the Emergency intense study.

2.   First of all, let me express my admiration for the courage of the many ordinary people, Malay, Chinese and Indian, growing rice, tapping rubber or mining tin, who go about their daily life not knowing what may befall them. Amid them all the Europeans have set their own splendid example of continuing courage. Nor can anyone who has recently been in touch with what I may call "the front line" help saying a word of gratitude to the women, who are steadfastly suffering all these anxieties and dangers.

3.   I have tried, as far as possible, to see everybody that I could. I have seen representatives of all the communities. I have talked to District Officers, planters and miners, policemen, soldiers, Resettlement Officers and Home Guards. I have listened to many voices. But the problems are many and there is no one answer.

4.   I have seen something of the British, Gurkha and Malay troops and their

commanders, the Royal Navy and the Royal Air Force with its Australian contingent.

5.　This is warfare which makes heavy demands upon troops, especially those used to northern climes. Yet day by day they are showing to the inhabitants of this country and to the world an example of discipline, courage and humour. The National Service man has proved himself beyond all expectation.

6.　In short, I have been engaged, so to speak, upon reconnaissance. This must be followed by plans and plans must be followed by immediate action. When I get home I shall address a State document to the Prime Minister and the Cabinet to obtain their agreement and their help. I must therefore excuse myself from going into detail now but there is much that I can say. I shall report that the main headings under which the immediate problem should be attacked are these.

7.　First, the over-all direction of our forces, military and civil, against the enemy. It is not an easy problem. Let me put it this way. War is a matter of violence; the art of administration is a matter of reflection and of check and counter-check. These two widely different activities have to be geared so that they move in concert and express themselves in immediate impact upon the enemy. I cannot go into the measures which I shall propose to secure this end. They will not be long delayed.

8.　Second, the re-organisation and training of the Police is urgent. They are doing a stout-hearted job in face of trial and difficulties but we must now achieve a much higher state of training in the Special Constabulary and create a Reserve of trained police.

9.　Third, Education. Too many do not have a clear enough idea of what they are fighting for. They must be taught, and one of the ways in which it can be done is by pressing foward with the project for compulsory primary education. It is not only the war of arms that must be won: education must help us to win the war of ideas. Of course, the effects of education are most striking in the long term but even at the beginning the children who go back to their parents from school are living evidence of another way of life to set against that which is being whispered to them from the jungle.

10.　Fourth, a much higher measure of protection of the resettlement areas must be achieved, and achieved quickly.

11.　Fifth, the organisation of a Home Guard. We must move now to enlist in the Home Guard a large number of Chinese in the towns and in the Resettlement Areas to defend their homes and their fellow countrymen. I have seen such a Home Guard working in Pahang and I am encouraged to think, from this small instance, that the object can be achieved.

12.　Sixth, we must tackle the problem of the great strain under which the Civil Service is at present suffering. We must review their terms of service and strive to maintain the high standards which have always been set. We must recruit the best here and at home.

13.　These are the main subjects upon which we must concentrate our attention and our energies. There is a host of smaller but highly important details which we must tackle at the same time. My report to the Cabinet will contain a massive appendix. I cannot go through all the subjects but can mention only a few upon which action must be taken at once. For example, armoured vehicles. There must be sufficient armoured vehicles to enable the civil authorities, the Police, the planters and miners to move about upon their duties in vehicles which enable them to hit back if they are attacked. I cannot subscribe to the theory that protecting a man from rifle-fire reduces his fighting spirit. Another subject is the officering of the Malay Regiment. This will require consultation with my colleagues. There is also the important matter of increasing—and rapidly increasing—the number of Government officers who can speak Malay and Chinese. There is the question of the appropriate weapons for issue to planters and miners. The propaganda system appears to require careful scrutiny. These are a few instances among many.

14.   On my return to England I shall wish to be kept in close touch with all these important matters, and shall closely watch their development.

15.   In solving these problems we must look for help to the great Colony of Singapore. We must look to all races here, and particularly to the enlightened and educated Chinese. We must look to those who are proud to call themselves the "King's Chinese", who have been here for many generations and whose descendants will be living here long after the present problems are forgotten.

16.   I have already said that this is a war of ideas as well as of arms. We have to see that our philosophy opens up to the peoples of Malaya the prospect of a finer and freer life than that which our enemies are now trying to instil.

17.   The ideal for which all communities in the Federation of Malaya must strive is a united Malayan nation. When this has been achieved that nation will carry the responsibilities and enjoy the advantages of self-government. Then, we confidently hope, Malaya will add strength to the British Commonwealth, the greatest association of free peoples of which history tells.

18.   Political advancement, economic development, social services and amenities are rungs in the ladder. Today, however, we have to place emphasis on the immediate menace. We must ask who are the enemies of those ideals? Who are the enemies of political advancement? What is delaying progress towards it? The answer is Communism. The answer is the terrorists. The answer is the Min Yuen and those who, partly from fear and partly from sympathy, create a passive but no less serious obstacle to victory. All these in greater or lesser degree betray our ideal and upon them we must unite in visiting, under the law, the full severity which their betrayal merits. Only so will victory be gained.

19.   Without victory and a state of law and order, which it alone can bring, political advancement becomes a hollow mockery to everyone and not least to the worker in field, in mine and in factory. The first duty of every government in every country is to ensure and protect liberty. Freedom from fear is the first human liberty.

20.   The pursuit of the ideal of a united Malaya will demand great political wisdom and the exercise of those rarest of human virtues, patience and forbearance.

21.   The British believe that they have a mission in Malaya and they will not lay it aside until they are convinced that terrorism has been killed and buried and that a true partnership of all communities can lead to true and stable self-government. The road to this partnership will certainly be long—it may well be very long—and it runs through jungle and ravine. But we will protect it, we will stay, we will never quit until our aims—and they are common to all races—have been achieved.

22.   I believe, too, that when self-government has been attained the British have a place and a part to play in Malaya together with their fellow-citizens of the other races. Let all Britons know, therefore, that there is a future open to them in Malaya—first, in bringing about the partnership of all the communities, and thereafter in the united and self-governing Malaya which will emerge.

23.   In conclusion, I want to turn back to the subject of the Emergency. I cannot

promise you speedy success. I can—and do—promise you speedy action. Only with your help can the war be won but I end by saying that if we act together my confidence and my faith is that law and order and freedom from fear can be regained and restored.

Appendix III to 257: Federal and state councils, etc

1. *Federal Legislative Council*

The Federal Legislative Council has 75 members, of whom 14 are officials, 9 are the Presidents of the Councils of State of each of the nine Malay States, 2 are representatives of the Settlement Councils of Penang and Malacca and 50 are unofficials. The unofficial members are all nominated. They are selected to represent different interests—employers, labour, industry, commerce, etc. The racial composition of the Council is at present:—

34 Malays	(3 officials, 9 Presidents of State Councils, 22 unofficials)
17 British	(10 officials, 7 unofficials)
16 Chinese	(1 official, 15 unofficials)
5 Indians	
2 Ceylonese	
1 Eurasian	

(*Note*: When a Deputy High Commissioner is appointed it is the intention that he will normally preside over the Legislative Council, thus relieving the High Commissioner of this duty).

2. *The Federal Executive Council*

This Council consists of the High Commissioner, three ex officio members (the Chief Secretary, the Attorney-General and the Financial Secretary), four other official members (one of whom, the Member for Home Affairs, is a Malay) and seven unofficial members (at present two Malaya [sic], two Chinese, one European, one Indian and one Ceylonese). It has recently been decided to increase the membership of the Council from 14 to not more than 19.

3. *A Federal War Council* was set up in April, 1950, under the Chairmanship of the Director of Operations, the other members being the Chief Secretary, the G.O.C., the A.O.C., the Commissioner of Police, the Secretary for Defence and the R.N. Liaison Officer (when required).

Its functions were to be to decide on operational policy and to put it into effect.

In October, 1950, the Council was expanded by the addition of two Malay unofficials (Keeper of the Rulers' Seal and Dato Onn), a Chinese unofficial (Dato Tan Cheng Lock) and a European unofficial (Mr. G.D. Treble, a Pahang planter). At the same time the High Commissioner assumed the Chairmanship.

After the death of Sir Henry Gurney in October, 1951, there was an insistent demand for the expansion of the Council to include much wider representation of the various communities and interests. It now consists of all the members of Executive Council (except one who lives in Penang), together with a few extra unofficial members—representatives of all communities particularly affected by the Emergency—making a total of 20. Its functions have necessarily changed with its change of character and it is now purely advisory on important matters of war policy. For this reason the Service Chiefs (including the Commissioner of Police) are no longer members, their executive responsibility being represented by the Director of Operations. Its composition, by races, is at present as follows:—

	Officials (including "Members")	Unofficials
Europeans	8	3
Malays	1	3
Chinese		3
Indian		1
Ceylonese		1

4. *State and Settlement Legislative and Executive Councils*
In each State and Settlement there are Legislative and Executive Councils (the former with unofficial majorities) roughly reflecting the composition, but on a smaller scale and with necessary local variations, of the corresponding Federal bodies.

5. *State War Executive Committees*
These bodies were set up in 1950 at the instance of the Director of Operations to facilitate the carrying out of his instructions and to avoid the unacceptable delays which were inevitable when action was taken through the normal civil authorities. They consist of the Mentri Besar, British Adviser, Chief Police Officer and senior military officer in the area, each of whom is responsible for executive action in his own sphere.

6. *District War Executive Committees*
Similar bodies have been set up in Districts or Police circles (which cover several Districts). Their composition varies but the basic membership includes the District Officer, the Officer Commanding the Police and the local Military Commander.

7. The War Executive Committees thus provide a direct chain of command from the Director of Operations down to District level.

Appendix IV to 257: Armoured vehicles for the police

The "procurement" of armoured vehicles has not been properly organised and requests had been made for vehicles which, I fear, will prove unsuitable. The orders were also too small. Accordingly I gave instructions that a Committee should be set up to go into this question. The Committee contained representatives of the civil administration, Police and Army. Its report is attached.

REPORT

1. *Types*
Armoured vehicles are needed solely for protection against roadside ambushes. For this three types are required:—

(i) for carrying numbers of men travelling on dangerous roads or when called out on operations;
(ii) for escorting soft vehicles; and
(iii) for carrying individual officers travelling on duty in dangerous areas.

2. *Specifications*
Ideal specifications of these three types of vehicles would be:—

(i) *Troop-Carrying Vehicles.* Fully armoured to carry driver and 10 men. Quick
and easy means of exit. Ports from which small arms can be fired. Weight not to
exceed 5½ tons in order that vehicles may negotiate bad roads and weak bridges.
(ii) *Escort Vehicles.* Fully armoured. Accommodation for driver and two men.
Revolving turret and L.M.G. mounting.
(iii) *Vehicles for carrying individual officers.* Fully armoured. Accommodation for
driver and two men. Required for all purpose travel and should therefore provide a
modicum of comfort.

All the above should be fitted with run-flat tyres and be provided with a full scaling
of spare parts.

3. *Numbers required*
The following numbers are based on optimum requirements and take no account of
limiting factors of finance or availability of vehicles:—

(i) *Troops Carrying Vehicles*   902
    Scale of issue: 1 to each Police Station
                  with 20 men and over.
                  2 to each District H.Q.
                  3 to each Contingent H.Q.
                  4 to each Jungle Company.
                  10% reserve.
(ii) *Escort Vehicles*   206
    Scale of issue: 2 to each District H.Q.
                  2 to each Contingent H.Q.
                  10% reserve.

Note: This number is not required for present purposes but envisages the need for
escorting civil food convoys if food control measures prove successful.

(iii) *Individual Transport Vehicles*   502
    Scale of issue: 1 to each O.C. Division
                  1 to each O.C.P.D.
                  1 to each O.S.P.C.
                  1 to each P/Lt stationed on estates or mines.
                  3 to each Contingent H.Q.
                  8 to each Police H.Q.
                  1 to each Jungle Company
                  10% reserve.

                                                  Total   1610

4. *Availability*
It is realised that it may not be possible to obtain vehicles answering all the
specifications given in paragraph 2. For instance it would not be possible to obtain a
fully armoured vehicle capable of carrying 11 men and weighing only 5½ tons. The
aim must therefore to be procure the most suitable vehicles available which offer the
best delivery dates.
    5. The ideal vehicle would be one which is capable of performing all 3 duties
efficiently. In this respect consideration has been given to modifying a G.M.C. A.P.C.
by armouring the top and back of the driver's cab and installing an armoured casing

in the rear of the vehicle sufficient to give protection to one man and from which he can fire an L.M.G.

6. This type of vehicle would not, however, offer as high a standard of efficiency as having one type of vehicle to be used as a troop-carrier and another type capable of being used in the dual role of an escort vehicle and for the transportation of individuals, as the specifications of these last two types of vehicles are very similar.

7. The most suitable type of vehicle available for use as a troop-carrying vehicle is the G.M.C. A.P.C. suitably modified. Modifications required are armouring of the roof and rear of the driver's cab and raising the sides and rear of the back of the vehicle 12″ with armour plate.

150 of these vehicles are now in the country and will be modified as required. 341 are on order and should be modified before being shipped.

A further 411 will be needed to meet the full requirements stated above. If they are not available in the United Kingdom enquiries will be necessary in Canada, where they are or have been manufactured.

8. The most suitable type of vehicle known at present that could be used in the dual role of an escort vehicle and for the transportation of individuals is probably the G.M.C. Scout Car. It is not known whether they are in fact available or still in production but enquiries should also be made in Canada about this type of vehicle.

The Police have at present only 26 (Ford Lynx) of this type of vehicle. On the above figures 682 are therefore required but if a dual purpose vehicle could be obtained, the total requirements could probably be reduced.

9. Other vehicles which have been considered are:—

(a) *Humber Scout Cars.* These are unsuitable as no spares are available.

(b) *Daimler Scout Cars/Ford Lynx.* These vehicles carry only a driver and 1 other and need to be modified to provide top protection and a turret. Spares position of Ford Lynx is unknown.

(c) *Morris Armoured Scout Cars.* These are mechanically unsound and the spares position is unsatisfactory.

(d) *"OXLEY" type on a Ford V8 Chassis.* It is considered that in order to armour this vehicle effectively, the weight of armour would be too much for the chassis and suspension. However, if tests on the prototype prove to be satisfactory this vehicle could be considered to provide transportation for individuals but would not be satisfactory as an escort vehicle.

(e) *Armoured Land Rovers.* The weight of armour is too much for the carrying and tractive capacity of the vehicle.

(f) *Saloons converted by partial armouring as used by Estate and Mines managers.* The intensive use to which Police vehicles are put would entail constant mechanical breakdowns, since these vehicles are not built to carry armour and the weight imposes too great a strain.

10. *Maintenance*

As armoured vehicles require more maintenance than soft vehicles, an increase of armoured vehicles for the Police Force on the scale suggested will impose a very heavy strain indeed on Police maintenance facilities. A variety of makes of vehicles should therefore be avoided, if possible. The provision of GMC APCs and GMC Scout Cars would be the ideal solution from this point of view since they are the same vehicle mechanically and both maintenance and supply of spare parts would be greatly simplified.

11. *Summary*

(a) 341 GMC APCs now on order require modification before being shipped. A further 411 GMC APCs suitably modified are required. These vehicles are considered the most suitable as troop carriers.

(b) 180 further vehicles are required for escort duties.

(c) 502 vehicles are required for transportation of individuals.

(d) GMC Scout Cars will satisfy (b) and (c) above if available.

(e) If GMC APCs and GMC Scout Cars are not available either in the United Kingdom or in Canada in sufficient numbers, vehicles should be provided which would meet required specifications as nearly as possible such as the Ford Lynx (if spares are available) for escort duties and the "OXLEY" (if proved satisfactory in tests) or any similar vehicle for transporting individuals.

(f) All vehicles should be fitted with run flat tyres and have a full scaling of spares.

(g) Results of enquiries into costs and availability may entail modification of programme.

Appendix V to 257: Arms, clothing and equipment urgently required by the police and obtainable only from the United States of America

Requirements	*Reasons why unobtainable from sterling sources.*
1. 1,000,000 yards Kahki cellular shirting or twill *or* Khaki drill.	Estimated consumption of Khaki clothing in 1952 is:— 787,000 yds. cellular shirting 846,000 yds. Khaki Drill. Indian mills are the normal suppliers but delivery prospects from India are bad because of internal difficulties. Alternative sources of supply have been found which should largely satisfy Khaki drill requirements during 1952, and enquiries are now being made in the United Kingdom about the supply of cellular shirting, or of twill or Khaki drill in lieu. If Khaki cellular shirting cannot be obtained in the United Kingdom it may be necessary to order up to a million yards of it in the United States.
2. 12,000 carbines M.I. and 4,000,000 rounds .300 ammunition.	These weapons have proved to be ideal for jungle warfare, being easily handled and giving a high rate of accurate fire. Supplies can be obtained only from the United States of America. The numbers asked for will be sufficient to enable demands of estates and mines for this type of weapon to be met.

3. 500 Pump Guns and   These guns are considered an essential part of Police
   125,000 rounds of   Jungle Company equipment. They would greatly
   steel plated   increase fire power of Coys. They can be obtained only
   ammunition.   from the U.S.A.

Appendix VI to 257: Earth-shifting equipment

1. 20 caterpillar tractors (10 Type D.7 and 10 Type D.B.) have been ordered from the Caterpillar Tractor Company Ltd. of the United States. These orders received the support of two American Missions (the Griffin and Melby Missions) which visited Malaya in 1950. The tractors were originally needed because the building of new roads and improvement of existing ones was a very urgent economic necessity in Malaya; and the Economic Cooperation Administration have endorsed the supply of the tractors on economic grounds. Owing, however, to the needs of the United States re-armament programme, supply cannot be met unless these tractors are given operational priority by the Defence Department (a "D.O. rating".)

2. The urgency of the construction of new roads in Malaya is now military, and economic considerations are secondary. Unless the road-building programme can be pushed ahead (for which the tractors are essential) the campaign against the Communists will be seriously impeded. Among vital projects which are an *immediate* military need are:—

(a) Mountain roads to set up V.H.F. wireless stations for the Police network. This network, comprising 18 stations in all, will link the huge number of Police Stations built and under construction as part of the plan for defeating the Communists. They are situated on mountains and over 50 miles of new mountain roads are required. Because of lack of plant only one or two of these roads have so far been completed.

(b) Approach roads to Resettlement Areas. Several hundred miles of road are required for squatter resettlement schemes. Many miles are already being built but, because of lack of plant, the bulk remain to be started. The resettlement schemes are the vital core of the "Briggs Plan", and unless these areas are linked with the main communication arteries it will remain very difficult indeed to supervise and protect them.

(c) Operational Trunk Roads. Over 100 milkes of operational roads suitable for military vehicles in all weathers are required. For lack of plant most of these roads have not yet been started. The Temerloh-Maran Road, for example, reduces the distance from east to west coast by 72 miles. This road is necessary not only for long-term strategic purposes but also for the present Emergency. Another road, 65 miles long, will open up the Malay [sic]-Siam border to military and police traffic and greatly facilitate the control of this vital frontier, across which terrorists can at present pass into the relative sanctuary of Siam.

3. The War Office and Foreign Office are taking this matter up vigorously but if they are unsuccessful it is hoped that the Prime Minister will agree to press the matter at the highest level. An assurance could be given to the Americans that this equipment, if supplied, would be used in the first place only for work of immediate importance to the anti-communist campaign.

4. Other road-making equipment now in Malaya or due to arrive there shortly will be quite useless unless these tractors can be supplied.

5. It is also urgent for the prosecution of the anti-communist campaign that more tracks should be driven through the jungle. For this additional equipment will be necessary. I am arranging to have these means examined and will as soon as possible submit proposals for obtaining the required equipment.

Appendix VII to 257: Chemical defoliation of roadside jungle

1. It is agreed on all hands that the risks of ambush by bandits can be greatly reduced by defoliation of roadside jungle. A certain amount of this is already being done by hand but the process is slow and costly and the vegetation quickly grows again. Chemical defoliation would, it is believed, be much more effective.

2. Experiments on a small scale have been carried out using two recently discovered hormone weed killers (2, 4-D and 2, 4, 5-T) with Sodium tri-chloracetate in various combinations.

3. Tests began on the 17th September, 1951, by means of hand sprays, and within ten days the foliage was dead. Three months later no significant regeneration had taken place and the original growths are generally dead. Current observations strongly support the view that there will not be regeneration of any plant growth sufficient to provide cover for the enemy for six months, and probably for one year, after treatment.

4. For the most effective treatment the current costs of the chemicals involved is equivalent to $190.00 (£22) per acre. On the assumption that it will be desirable to clear roadsides to a depth of 100 yards on either side (=72.7 acres per mile) the cost of the chemicals per mile of road will be $13,780 (£1607). With further experimental work it is believed that the dose can probably be reduced to give a cost of chemicals of $55.00 (£6) per acre, or $4,000 (£133) per mile of road. The cost of cutting by hand varies between $300–$450 per acre for three slashings a year depending on the denseness of the growth. A shorter distance than 100 yards may have to be accepted. The savings are therefore massive.

5. On the 14th December attempts were made to use a "TIFA" fogging machine for practical roadside tests. This is the only spraying equipment available in the country but it proved unsuitable because the solution emulsified. Other possible measures are being explored.

6. Messrs. Imperial Chemical Industries, Malaya, Ltd, have conducted the foregoing experiments and they report that a combination of chemicals has now been found which will meet the purpose. While these chemicals have been successfully applied by hand the advantages to be derived by this method of control by chemicals can be fully realized only by means of large-scale mechanical methods of application. It is now therefore an engineering problem. I.C.I. Ltd. and Plant Protection Ltd. in England have been kept fully informed by I.C.I. (Malaya) and they have been asked to carry out trials of all types of spraying equipment.

7. There are three main uses for this chemical method of control:—

(a) rail and roadside clearance in dangerous areas (likely ambush positions);
(b) clearance of perimeters of resettlement areas, etc.; and
(c) destruction of crops grown by, or for, the bandits in remote jungle areas.

(a) and (b) require mechanical means of application though (b) can possibly be done by hand spraying. For (c) the Federation Government has ordered through I.C.I. (Malaya) Ltd. two sets of Spray rigs for use in Auster aircraft. This is the only purpose yet in mind for application by aircraft. Earliest date of delivery is February/March, 1952, and despatch by air has been requested.

8. *Summary*

(a) A suitable combination of chemicals has been found and supplies are available from sterling sources.

(b) The cost of chemicals (taking no account of the cost of application) compares favourably with the cost of slashing by hand.

(c) Mechanical methods for large-scale application have not yet been determined. This is now the main problem.

(d) I.C.I. Ltd. and Plant Protection Ltd. have details of experiments carried out and have been requested (through I.C.I., Malaya) to carry out research for suitable mechanical equipment.

Appendix VIII to 257: Language teaching

1. As part of their training in order to qualify for confirmation, officers of the Malayan Civil Service and gazetted officers of the Malayan Police Service are normally required to pass examinations in Malay, Chinese or Tamil within $2\frac{1}{2}$ to 3 years of appointment.

2. During the past three years officers of the Malayan Police Service have been confirmed in their appointments on the recommendation of the Commissioner of Police, Federation of Malaya, or the Commissioner of Police, Singapore, whether they have passed the prescribed examinations in language or not, since it has been held that in Emergency conditions they do not have opportunities for study.

3. Of the 194 Malayan Civil Service officers recruited from 1946 to 1951 inclusive, 114 have passed the test in one or other of the prescribed languages. Of the 519 Police Officers recruited during the same period, 163 have passed lower standard Malay.

4. The figures in the preceding paragraph include all officers serving in both the Federation of Malaya and Singapore, since the Malayan Establishment provides expatriate officers for both territories, and officers on the common establishment are liable for service in either administration.

5. Officers selected to learn a Chinese dialect are normally sent to China for 18 months to 2 years. Since 1946 28 Malayan Civil Service cadets and one Assistant Superintendent of Police (on probation) have been sent to China. Of these, 9 Malayan Civil Service cadets and the Police Officer are still there.

6. Two intensive courses in colloquial Cantonese and Hokkien were organised at Cameron Highlands in July/August, 1951. Each course takes 12 officers and lasts 6 months. 20 Police and 4 Malayan Civil Service officers attended the first two courses, and the same numbers are to attend the second two courses, which are due to begin in January/February, 1952.

7. Evening classes in Malay were started in Kuala Lumpur in June, 1951, to teach Police Officers stationed in the neighbourhood. These classes will be continued in 1952.

8. Cadets appointed since January, 1950, have in most cases been required to undertake full-time duties in the field and have not had normal opportunities for study. The majority of those appointed in 1950 have, however, now been released from special Emergency duties, and steps must be taken to ensure that the remainder, after serving 9 to 12 months in Emergency posts, have suitable opportunities for taking up the study of both language and law.

9. Police Lieutenants, being temporary officers, are not required by their terms of service to pass any examinations. Of the 837 recruited up to date, 112 have passed some examination in Malay. This is not enough, however, and I have therefore arranged for examination of the possibility of awarding bonuses to them as an inducement to learn Malay.

Appendix IX to 257: Intelligence services and related counter-measures

I *Intelligence services*

A. *Intelligence against the enemy*

The importance of intelligence in the Malayan campaign cannot be exaggerated. Every police operation is in large measure an intelligence task and the Malayan campaign is in essence a police operation. In a country covered with dense jungle, where evasion is easy and contact with the enemy cannot be made without secret information, it is essential that intelligence should be gained from the Communist forces without their knowing. Intelligence, therefore, to use semi-technical language, must be "live" as well as "blown" or "dead". It must come from sources whose "pumping" is unknown to the Communists.

At present, the opposite occurs. The bulk of our reliable information is obtained not from agents or police friends or contacts but instead from corpses, prisoners of war and captured documents. This process builds up an interesting academic or even strategic picture. It would be most useful in fighting regular troops in formal battle, but it is of much less value against a mobile, intelligent and localised guerilla force.

The provision of more "live" as opposed to "blown" or "dead" information must be the task of the Police Force. In this, until recent months, they have failed. They have been handicapped by post-war reorganisation, shortage of Asiatic officers, expansion of the Uniformed Force and the striking fact that more than 90 per cent of the enemy are Chinese while 95 per cent of the Police are Malay. In addition, the C.I.D. Special Branch formerly operating from Singapore and serving both Singapore and the Federation has on two different occasions been separated from the main Police Forces, with unfortunate results. The reorganisation of the Federation Police C.I.D. by Sir William Jenkin, although starting with the handicap of having few if any agents and contacts, and its re-integration with the main Federation Police Force, seem to have established a firmer framework and already military commanders report an increased flow of information.

Nevertheless, it would be foolish to expect any profound improvement even with an increased and more efficient C.I.D. until the basic police training of all ranks of the regular, uniformed police is improved. It is mainly on the uniformed police that C.I.D. counter-measures must be based. Without the firm base of a Police Force in close touch with the people, penetration of enemy organisations becomes most difficult. In Malaya, little or no deep penetration of the enemy has been achieved.

To-day, many of the regular Police Force, far from being policemen capable of carrying out their share of investigations and of acquiring intimate local knowledge, are little more than static, para-military guards—which throws an extra burden on the C.I.D. In addition, weaknesses exist in the intelligence filing system at lower levels. Thus little is done at police stations to identify and arrest thousands of wanted persons classified by the C.I.D. as active Communists.

Improvements are likely to take some little time to achieve. Meanwhile, as the efficiency of police intelligence improves, intelligence can and is being collected in the following ways.

(a) aggressive patrolling by police and military;
(b) Police round-ups and security checks;
(c) aggressive patrolling by jungle squads and companies;
(d) deep patrolling by Malay Scouts;
(e) reconnaissance by air; and
(f) interrogation of suspects and captured bandits.

It should also be possible for the C.I.D. to concentrate on specific targets in certain areas. At the moment a special C.I.D. investigation is being launched against the Min Yuen. This investigation, however, is still in the course of being planned. It should also be possible to appoint special investigation teams aimed at certain individuals—that is, to hunt down individual men from Communist higher formations through their families, properties, sweethearts, etc. This will be undertaken shortly.

Recommendations:—

(1) more Chinese must be recruited or directed for all Regular branches of the Police and given chances of promotion;
(2) more training in basic police and intelligence methods must be given to all police branches irrespective of race;
(3) the question of new techniques for penetrating the jungle by aerial photography should be examined;
(4) the gaining of intelligence from the aboriginal tribes should be investigated; and
(5) the training of agents should be accelerated where this is possible and they should be used against specific targets under C.I.D. arrangements.

B. *Security of our own forces*

Because over 150,000 persons have been absorbed into the Security Forces, some risks in recruitment have been taken without proper screening. Efforts must therefore be made to tighten up our own security arrangements. If the Malayan Communist Party at any time succeeded in bringing about a civil war in certain regions, many unforeseen misfortunes would befall us. The growing efficiency of the enemy must be combated more vigorously on our home ground. Recent disquieting incidents have been the suspected purloining of ammunition from lighters in Singapore; the sale of arms by Special Constables and Home Guards; the penetration of Home Guards by the Min Yuen; the treachery of a Sakai chief tracker; the disclosure of a Communist cell in King's House, Kuala Lumpur; and the infiltration into the Chinese schools of Communist teachers and literature. At every level and in every Service Department normal security precautions must be tightened up.

Recommendation:—
A conference should be held of the chiefs of the Services and Police and the heads of
the Government Departments concerned to consider the problem and set up suitable
machinery in Kuala Lumpur and in Singapore to deal with internal security of our
own forces. Trade Union organisations should be consulted at a later stage.

C. *Use and control of intelligence by field forces*
At lower levels this is largely a matter of harmonious relations between soldiers and
policemen. These in general seem to exist. C.I.D. personnel and intelligence files are
usually available to the military down to battalion level. At the centre, however, a
more purposeful use might be made of intelligence. The Deputy Director of
Operations should establish an Intelligence staff to deal with the various aspects of
intelligence and guide the intelligence campaign in the direction which his plan
demands. This is, perhaps, all the more necessary owing to the slender resources
available. He should be able to issue general directives to the C.I.D., Internal
Security Forces, "black" propaganda and subversive organisations as they grow up
under his command. For this purpose he should be given a Directory of Military
Intelligence or Director of the Intelligence Bureau. Whether this man should be a
soldier or a policeman is immaterial, though the balance might be in favour of a
policeman.

Recommendations:—

(a) that a Director of the Intelligence Bureau be appointed to the Deputy Director
of Operations; and
(b) that the main Operations and Information Room be located at the headquarters of the Deputy Director of Operations.

D. *Auxiliary intelligence instruments*

1. *Propaganda and Information Department*
(Information Department, Film Unit, Public and Press Relations, Radio, etc.). This
Department is in a confusion of divided loyalties and responsibilities and must be
entirely reorganised under one head. At present it is inefficient. The vernacular press
is ill served by it. The Film Unit, whilst possessing 63 mobile vans and a film studio,
has so far failed to produce any propaganda films of importance. Because Dato Onn is
the Member in Charge of these services, reorganisation may prove difficult, but such
is the importance of this weapon that means must be found for undertaking
complete reorganisation under one chief who is a trained propagandist.

2. *Special Emergency Information Department.*
This deals with psychological
warfare and is under the control of the Deputy Director of Operations. It does good
work in straight propaganda. It is short of staff, makes use of Chinese Affairs
Department staff half-time at lower levels or borrows staff from the Information
Department proper.

3. *"Black" or Counterfeit Propaganda Department.*
This Department hardly exists,
but could do useful work. Its chief concern is the sporadic production at long
intervals of a bogus Communist newspaper. The Department is very much under-

staffed. Occasional hours are devoted to it by the head of the Special Emergency Information Department. It employs one Chinese cyclostyler full-time and enjoys the part time co-operation of one Chinese literary expert.

4. *Subversive Activities (Military).* This Department existed for a short time but was abandoned. It could do useful work with suitable staff.

Recommendations—

(a) the whole information and propaganda machine must be drastically reorganised and put under one head, who is a propagandist;
(b) the film studio must be reorganised for the production of local propaganda films;
(c) the present Special Information section should perhaps be removed from the Deputy Director of Operations to the general Propaganda and Information Department while the new chief of the whole Propaganda Department creates an efficient liaison between himself and the Deputy Director of Operations; and
(d) the Black Propaganda Department and the Subversive Activities Section should be increased, given expert chiefs and placed under the control of the Director of the Intelligence Bureau to the Deputy Director of Operations.

Conclusion
Until the Regular Police are re-trained as policemen and until all Police Branches have a complement of Chinese personnel, progress in intelligence work will remain patchy and haphazard. At present it is only the information got from the bodies of dead bandits or from prisoners which saves the face of our Intelligence Services. If the Malayan Communist Party decided to become clandestine and concentrate on political action, the intelligence canvas would be blank indeed.

The existing instrument of police intelligence is inadequate. It must be developed.

II *Subversive activities*

It is suggested that a special subversive section should be set up under the Deputy Director of Operations, with one or two units in the field. For political as well as security reasons it is important that such a section should be secret and under his personal control.

Recommendations:—

(a) a subversive section to be placed under the direct command of the Deputy Director of Operations;
(b) the Deputy Director of Operations to submit an establishment for such a section; and
(c) suitable persons to be recruited for it in Malaya and the United Kingdom.

III *Deception tactics*

One of the major assets of the Communists is undoubtedly their local intelligence services. This strength might be turned against them, and their own intelligence network used to feed them with false information. This can be done only in the

Districts as the enemy have now streamlined their command down to companies and platoons. This disadvantage is, however, almost outweighed by the fact that in the nature of things bandit maquis or guerilla forces are vulnerable to rumour and liable to exhaust themselves in the panic to which that leads.

Deception should be organised with the chief objects of:—

(1) discrediting the bandits' sources of intelligence in the Min Yuen by the infusion of information soon proved to be false or valueless; and

(2) harrying the bandits by spreading signs and rumours which will force them to keep on the move.

These steps may not result in killing bandits but by intensive deception the morale of individual units in desperately tough country can be profoundly shaken if they are constantly kept on the move.

Recommendations:—

(a) that this matter be considered by the Deputy Director of Operations;

(b) that, if he is agreeable, a small expert cadre from the United Kingdom be put under his command; and

(c) that a school for local army and police officers be opened at his Headquarters.

Appendix X to 257: Terms of employment of British officers and other ranks posted or seconded for service with the Malay Regiment

1. The type of British officer so far being obtained for the Malay Regiment is not up to the standard required to maintain British prestige. It has been represented to me that this situation has arisen as a result of difficulties in the conditions on which British officers are assigned for duty with the Regiment.

2. At my request I was given the annexed memorandum on the question at issue between the Federation Government and the War Office.

3. This discloses a system which should not be accepted. It is therefore necessary that the whole matter should be urgently re-examined and I propose to discuss it with the Secretary of State for War early in the New Year.

MEMORANDUM

1. It is accepted by the War Office that the system of posting British personnel to the Malay Regiment is not sound. As long ago as November, 1949, the Colonial Office said "Though the War Office have power to post officers and men compulsorily for service under Colonial Governments they are not prepared to make a regular practice of this, but only to do it temporarily to prevent the breakdown of a Force through lack of volunteers. The present rates of additional pay have not been in operation very long. If they do not produce sufficient volunteers it will be necessary to review them irrespective of whether officers and men are provided by formal secondment or on loan as at present."

2. The Regiment is at present about 40 officers below strength and no officers are yet available for the 6th Battalion or for any further expansion beyond that Battalion. Special additional pay has recently been authorised to encourage officers to

volunteer. This additional pay, which will presumably be subject to United Kingdom tax, was authorised without reference to the Federation Government and there are a number of points which are not clear. G.H.Q. FARELF have been asked to state how they propose to interpret the War Office instructions.

3.   Other points which affect the position are:—

(a) *Secondment or posting.* The War Office seem to have abandoned the idea of secondment, presumably because there are few if any officers prepared to be seconded on present terms of service. The Federation has always pressed for definite secondment terms which would assure the Federation of the services of officers for definite periods and also incidentally permit the introduction of certain obligations on the part of the officer. For example, before the war officers were required to qualify in Malay within a given period. There appears to be no reason why a clause should not be included in terms of secondment to the effect that normal British service conditions would apply should circumstances at any future time necessitate the assumption of responsibility for the Malay Regiment by the Army Council.

(b) *Income Tax.* If secondment terms were re-introduced officers would be paid directly by the Federation Government and liable to pay the local and not United Kingdom income tax. In May, 1949, the Federation reluctantly agreed to accept the proposal that British personnel serving with the Regiment should draw their emoluments from British Army funds and should be liable to pay United Kingdom income tax.

(c) *Housing.* Apart from the severe shortage of accommodation (Government or Army) which in any case deters officers from volunteering, there is a fundamental divergence of opinion between the War Office and the Federation Government as regards the housing arrangements. The Federation view is that officers should pay the Federation Government rate for the class of quarters occupied. The War Office fear (quite unnecessarily in present circumstances) that this will mean the granting of preferential treatment to officers and other ranks serving with the Malay Regiment over those serving with British Regiments. The War Office therefore consider that "to avoid complications likely to arise" entitlement to quarters should be based so far as is possible on British Army scales and rent charged at current British Army rates for unfurnished quarters. In practice the Federation view has been adopted.

(d) *Passages.* Although the original conditions of service put forward by the Federation Government in August, 1948, it was proposed that British personnel should be granted free passages for themselves and their families in accordance with regulations in force for other British Army personnel serving in Malaya, the Commandant has recently recommended that British personnel posted or seconded for service with the Regiment should be permitted to travel to and from Malaya by civilian passenger steamers. It is understood that the War Office rarely grant this privilege to officers and other ranks who would normally travel by troop-ship because a passage by troop-ship is cheaper than one by passenger liner.

(e) *Leave.* The Federation has proposed that the Government leave regulations applicable to expatriate officers should be applied to British Army personnel serving with the Regiment. The War Office is not prepared to accept this, stating that "it would be detrimental to the individual's health if he were permitted to accumulate terminal leave at the expense of his annual leave".

(f) *Inter-tour leave pay.* Early this year the War Office informed G.H.Q. FARELF that officers who wished to return for a second tour must revert to the home stablishment [sic] with effect from the date of embarkation from Malaya. Prior to this ruling officers who proceeded on leave between tours were retained on the pool establishment of the Regiment. This permitted them to continued to draw language pay, additional pay, pay of temporary rank if held and, for a period of 61 days, local overseas allowance. Under the War Office ruling, such officers lose language pay, additional pay and local overseas allowance with effect from the date of embarkation and may only, as a concession, receive pay of temporary rank for 61 days from the same date. It is believed that instructions have been issued permitting officers serving with the RWAFF to draw additional allowances during periods of inter-tour leave.

Appendix XI to 257: Detention and repatriation

1. The Federation Emergency Regulations provide for detention under two separate sections. Under Section 17(1) individuals may be detained for a period not exceeding two years. Anyone detained under this Section has the right to object to the detention order. If he does so his case is considered by a Committee of Review. People detained under this Section may also ask for their cases to be reviewed by the Chief Secretary after they have been in detention for 18 months.

2. Under Section 17D detention orders can be made covering all the inhabitants of a stated area, or one or more of those inhabitants as may be named, if the High Commissioner believes them to be guilty of having helped the terrorists, or of having failed to disclose information to the police. There is no right of appeal against detention orders made under this Section.

3. Persons detained under either Section may be deported from the Federation, provided that they are not Federal citizens or British subjects born in Malaya.

4. The numbers of persons detained under these Sections are:—

	Reg. 17(1)	*Reg. 17D*	*Total*
(a) Total number of persons detained for more than 28 days at any time since the start of the Emergency	25,641	10,118	35,759
(b) Total number repatriated to China	11,261	879	12,140
(c) Total number still detained (December 1951)	6,341	2,263	8,604

Of the 25,641 persons detained under Regulation 17(1), 22,667 were Chinese, 1,753 Malays and 1,099 Indians.

5. At my second meeting with the Conference of Rulers on the 16th December it was agreed that up to 5,000 detained persons might be sent to an island off the coast of North Borneo. It is accepted that they cannot stay in North Borneo permanently and must ultimately be re-absorbed in Malaya or repatriated to China. Their final disposal may cause difficulty and the establishment of camps in North Borneo will be expensive, but it is considered necessary to accept these disadvantages to give some

satisfaction to the Malays, who have pressed strongly for the removal from Malaya of as many Chinese as can be expelled. A survey team will be sent to make the necessary arrangements in North Borneo.

6. I have repeatedly impressed upon the authorities in Malaya the need for using either Section 17(1) or Section 17D only with the greatest circumspection. I am addressing a memorandum on this subject to the Officer Administering the Government of the Federation and shall impress upon him the great need for releasing with the utmost speed those who, after examination, are found to be guiltless. Section 17D may no doubt have to be used occasionally but it is a measure of Draconian severity and the authorities must be very sure of their ground before applying it.

Appendix XII to 257: Manpower and national service

I append a memorandum which I have had from the Government of the Federation of Malaya.

I am not satisfied that the present system works satisfactorily. I am told that, under the first National Service Bill, the Police were swamped with directed men and that the call-up was therefore stopped. This has of course led to inexplicable anomalies and injustices.

I am addressing a note to the Federation Government to ascertain whether my information on this is correct and whether, if more men are likely to be called up than are required, the Government will consider introducing some kind of ballot.

MEMORANDUM

1. Under the Emergency Regulations men aged 18 to 23 inclusive are at present directed into the Federation Police Force.

2. Monthly requirements, based on police training facilities, have been met throughout 1951. There has been a concurrent increase in the voluntary recruitment of Malays. Prevention of widespread invasion, chiefly by Chinese, has proved impossible because registration was not introduced simultaneously in all parts of the Federation, let alone Singapore, and because certificates of registration were not issued.

3. The scheme will run down early in 1952, when, it is estimated, 5,000 men will have been directed, including 2,500 Chinese, against the initial request for 6,000 (i.e. to give one Chinese in ten in the Police.)

4. In concert with the Singapore Government, which has agreed that the Federation's Comptroller of Manpower should in war be Comptroller for Singapore, too, twin National Service Bills are now being drafted, which will provide for registration of all men aged 18 to 54, and for direction for (a) Local Forces, (b) Police Force, (c) civil defence forces, (d) labour.

5. There will be no mention in the Bills of exemption of aliens. This is essential since a high proportion of the Chinese population are neither British subjects nor Federal citizens. Exemption of aliens from particular types of service flows from the legislation governing the Forces; and similar procedures concerning, for example, U.S. citizens and Dominion subjects, will be ironed out administratively, as has been done successfully over direction into the Federation Police Force.

6. Industry of all races has been consulted and Advisory Manpower Committees set up. They will report to the Malayan Manpower Sub-Committee, which is also responsible for examining bids for manpower. Present information suggests that Malaya may be unable to meet Service requirements for European officers, skilled men and technicians.

7. The new legislation will be introduced into the Legislatures early in 1952 and the machine tested over two age groups, to meet requirements in the Federation for further police and in Singapore for the Local Forces.

8. Major legislative difficulties which may be possible of solution only by Defence Regulations are (a) direction in one territory for service in the other and (b) direction into His Majesty's Forces otherwise than by the expedient of initial direction into the Local Forces.

9. The major practical difficulty is prevention of evasion. It would become minor with Chinese co-operation, which the Chinese allege would be forthcoming if (a) police pay was increased and (b) after completion of service a directed man automatically became a Federal citizen.

Appendix XIII to 257: Tax evasion

1. There is widespread evasion of income tax in Malaya, mainly because of the peculiarities of Chinese accounting and book-keeping and of the shortage of expert income tax staff. The main burden of taxation therefore falls upon the European commercial and official community and the Chinese pay far less than their due share. The result is that the whole system of taxation is in danger of being brought into comptempt [sic]. The political dangers of this are obvious.

2. It is estimated that at least 20% of trading profits escape tax by reasons of deliberate evasion, and the figure may well be much higher.

3. Evasion by the Chinese is roughly of two types:—

(1) The simple type, which probably includes 90% of Chinese traders. Here the trader, who probably does not know his actual profit, under-states his income without any deliberate intention to defraud. His conception of income is what is left after he has lived out of his business.

(2) The second type of evader is the wealthier Chinese trader. This type, with an income of anything over £6,000 a year, practises deliberate evasion of a kind most difficult to detect.

4. The only way of dealing with the latter type is to have a staff of qualified experts engaged full-time on the investigation of these complex cases. Successful prosecutions would no doubt have a salutary effect on other persons engaged in similar malpractices, but thorough investigation of the affairs of such a taxpayer may extend over many months. At present there seems very little prospect of engaging permanent officers for this work but a start could be made by sending a small team of experts to Malaya for long enough to give such advice as would make it possible to bring two or three exemplary prosecutions. The formation of such a team is now being taken up urgently with the Treasury and the Board of Inland Revenue.

Appendix XIV to 257: Financial devolution

1. Under the Federation of Malaya Agreement of 1948 there is already consider-able financial devolution by the Federal Government to State Governments. This is accompanied by annual block grants from Federal revenue.

2. Further devolution of financial responsibility to local authorities would, however, help in the prosecution of the campaign against the bandits, and at my request arrangements for it are now being examined by the Federation Government.

Appendix XV to 257: Extension of service beyond retiring age

1. The age at which an officer in Government Service is required to retire is 55 years. There are probably a number of competent officers who would be willing to continue to serve beyond that age and who would still be sufficiently fit and active to do good work.

2. The Federation Government has been asked to examine the possibility of encouraging selected officers to continue to serve after they have reached the age of compulsory retirement.

3. I have also asked the Federation Government to comb out of office jobs as many trained and experienced officers as possible for work "on the ground".

258   PREM 11/121   27 Dec 1951
[Lyttelton's plan for Malaya]: letter from Field Marshal Lord Montgomery to Mr Lyttelton following discussions at Chequers on 23 Dec

[Field-Marshal Lord Montgomery of Alamein (formerly CIGS, 1946–1948 and chairman of the Western European Commanders in Chief Committee, 1948–1951) was deputy-supreme allied commander, Europe, 1951–1958. He had already written to Field-Marshal Slim stressing the need for 'the men' to 'electrify Malaya' (PREM 11/121, 3 Dec 1951). In his *Memoirs* (p 379) Lyttelton recalled receiving on the day after the Chequers meeting a letter from Montgomery which, he claimed, was 'the only one from him which I have ever received' but which was a good deal shorter than document 258: 'Dear Lyttelton, *Malaya*: We must have a plan. Secondly, we must have a man. When we have a plan and a man, we shall succeed: not otherwise. Yours sincerely, (signed) Montgomery (F.M.)'.]

I was delighted to meet you at Chequers on 23rd December and to hear some more of your views about the situation in Malaya. Since then I have pondered long over that problem.

2. In general, I am disturbed about the whole situation in our Colonial Empire. It has drifted down hill since the war, chiefly because of two useless Secretaries of State for the Colonies: Creech-Jones and Griffiths.

Your advent seems to me to be exactly what is needed. You clearly are the man to put things right and you have the necessary courage to do so: which your two predecessors did not.

3. Your plan to put in a good man to succeed Gurney as High Commissioner or Governor of the Malayan Federation is good. And so is the man you have selected. I have no doubt whatever that he will carry out the necessary organisational reforms

in the Federation and will put things on a good footing in that territory. It is long overdue. And that will be *one* step towards what is necessary.

4. But the measures you propose to take in Malaya are, so it seems to me, only the first and very essential step in the Master Plan for South-East Asia *as a whole*.

The contrast between the East and West, between Communism and Democracy, between evil and Christianity, is approaching its climax; the next two years, 1952 and 1953, will be critical for the West.

The main objectives of Stalin today are in Asia; it is *there* that he can do us the greatest harm at the present time; it is *there* that we are not organised to handle the threat that is maturing against us.

China is already gone.

Indo-China is holding out stoutly, but the issue there is by no means certain; and General de Lattre is a very sick man in Paris and is unlikely to return to Indo-China.

Burma is in grave danger; only a very small effort would gather that country into the Communist fold.

There remains the rest of South-East Asia, South of the line Tonkin-Burma.

If that area goes, the West will be in grave danger.

5. I hold the view that British affairs and interests in the Far East, in Honkong [sic] and in the whole of South-East Asia, should be placed in the charge of one man: a sort of over-all Governor General or High Commissioner. He should be skilled in organisation and in political matters.

Working with him would be an over-all Commander-in-Chief of all the fighting Services in the Far East.

6. The over-all Governor General would hold the post now held by Malcolm Macdonald, but he would need greatly increased powers; if his mandate was only to coordinate, he would never achieve the results needed.

I say "Now held by Malcolm Macdonald" because in my view a new man is needed in that post.

I do not see how a man can live for 5 years on the Equator and still retain his energy, drive and power of decision. Macdonald commands no confidence among the Commanders-in-Chief in the Far East; they all say he has doubtless done much good work in the past, but that he has now "had it" and should go. Their main complaint against him is that he never makes a decision and seems unable to do so.

Macdonald must have known the appalling state of affairs in the Malayan Federation, and the complete lack of sound organisation in the Governmental Machine at Kuala Lumper [sic].

He must have know that the Police Force under Gray in the Federation was in a hopeless state.

He must have known, after the Hertogh riots,[1] that the Colony Police Force in Singapore was in a poor state.

He should have known that Del Tufo and Gray in Kuala Lumper [sic] and Blythe, the Colonial Secretary in Singapore, were not fit for their jobs. I have already given you my opinion of Del Tufo and Gray.

Blythe, as Colonial Secretary in Singapore is responsible for the administration of the Colony; it was he who should have made certain that the Colony Police had taken

---

[1] See 232, note 1.

all steps to ensure no trouble when the Hertogh case was before the Courts. In fact, very serious riots resulted.

I doubt if the Governor of Singapore is any good.

7. Why has Macdonald taken no action to put things right?

Why has he allowed such a state of affairs to continue for so long?

Why were these things not found out by the Government until a Minister goes out there and finds out for himself: as you did?

Many other people, including myself, have known all about these things for a long time.

Why, indeed!

In my view, it is because Macdonald has lived for five years on the Equator; he has lost his ability to grasp rapidly the essentials of a problem and to do something about it quickly.

In these very critical days we surely cannot have such men holding high positions of immense importance.

8. One further point.

I do not myself see how Singapore Colony can be seperated [sic] from the Malayan Federation in the fight against Communism and banditry in that part of South-East Asia.

It may be necessary to have two Governors, one for each territory; on that point I am possibly not qualified to express an opinion.

But the two Governors should surely be under the over-all direction of the over-all Governor General I refer to in paragraph 5 above.

It is that over-all Governor General (at present the Commissioner General) who has, or should have, the call on the fighting Services.

9. Finally, what I have endeavoured to outline in this letter is that we should treat South-East Asia as one entity and have *one* Master Plan for British interests and affairs in the whole area.

We should give *one* Governor General the task of carrying out the political, administrative and strategical policy of H.M.G. in that area.

All individual Governors should be under the guidance and control of that *one* Governor General.

Only in this way will we succeed in hanging-on to South-East Asia against the gigantic threat that is slowly but surely being developed against it.

10. I must admit that I have not yet read your Report; all the matters I mention may become clear to me when I have done so.

At the moment, and without having read the Report, my concern is that we may take only the first step in South-East Asia and may neglect to ensure that that first step is part of a Master Plan or Grand Design for the whole area.

11. As we all three discussed the problem at Chequers on Sunday last I am sending a copy of this letter to the Prime Minister. I thought you would agree to my doing so.

259 PREM 11/639   4 Jan 1952

[Appointment of Templer]: telegram no T6/52 from Mr Lyttelton to
Mr Churchill

[In addition to the names Lyttelton mentions here, the following had been suggested as
possible candidates for the Malayan job: General Sir J Harding, Marshal of the RAF, Sir A
Harris (c-in-c Bomber Command, 1942–1945, who had retired to South Africa), General
Sir B Robertson (c-in-c Middle East Land Forces, 1950–1953), and Field-Marshal W
Slim.]

Following personal for Prime Minister from Secretary of State for the Colonies.

I have now seen and spent more than an hour each with Portal, who refused,
Bourne and Scobie,[1] and three hours with Templer. There is no doubt in my mind
that we should appoint Templer who would accept if offered as a two year
assignment. He asks also that Slim should be told before decision is taken.

2. My opinion of Templer is strongly reinforced by Montgomery whom I have also
seen again. Templer would have been his own selection.

3. Templer is 53 and at present General Officer Commanding Eastern Command.
Previously he was Vice Chief of the Imperial General Staff and before that Director of
Military Intelligence. He is regarded in the Army as outstanding man of his age and is
likely to be C.I.G.S. in three or four years time. He has very good brains, is quick and
decisive and is interested in all political aspects of problems. His imagination is
obviously fired by prospect of possibly being entrusted with the job.

4. It would be very helpful to have your authority to appoint him forthwith
especially as I am getting cables saying that delay is adversely commented on in
Malaya and contrasted with my promises of immediate action. I do not take this too
seriously but after long search and interviews with all likely candidates Templer is in
my opinion the only one in the field.

A very happy New Year.[2]

---

[1] Marshal of the RAF Lord Portal, chief of air staff, 1940–1945; Lieutenant-General G C Bourne later
became GOC Malaya, 1954–1956; Lieutenant-General Sir R Scobie, GOC Greece, 1944–1946, retired 1947.
[2] Churchill received Lyttelton's telegram on board the *Queen Mary* which docked at New York on 4 Jan.
Accompanied by Slim, amongst others, he was on his way to talks with President Truman and would later
go to Ottawa, returning to Washington to Address Congress on 17 Jan. Churchill replied to Lyttelton on 4
Jan: 'C.I.G.S [Slim] is telling Templer to fly to Ottawa by 12th where Alex [Lord Alexander,
governor-general of Canada, see 251, note 1] and I can have some talks with him. I have every wish to
endorse your choice, which Slim strongly recommends, but I must see him first. Orders are being given
accordingly.'

260 PREM 11/169   4 Jan 1952

[Appointment of Templer]: letter from Field Marshal Lord Montgomery
to Mr Churchill. *Enclosure*: 'Success in Malaya', note by Montgomery
(M/222, 2 Jan 1952)

I saw Oliver Lyttelton at the Colonial Office at 1600 hrs yesterday, 3 January.

I gave him the attached paper M/222 entitled 'Success in Malaya'.

I thought you might like to have a copy.

2. He agrees with this paper and said that the clean-up has started.

3. He agrees that the long-term aim must be to unite all British interests out there into a Dominion of S.E. Asia, under one Governor General. This cannot be done quickly; it will take time; but it is the long-term aim towards which we must move. It may be possible to unite the Malayan Federation and Singapore Colony quicker than the rest.

4. He considers that Macdonald must stay on for a few months, with less powers than at present.

I gave it as my opinion he should go when his present tenure ends in May.

5. I gave it as my opinion that Robertson,[1] having said he didn't want to face the task in Malaya, the most vital task today in the Empire, should receive no further employment under the Crown.

When his tenure in the Middle East ends, he should be retired. A soldier must do his duty.

6. I think the selection of Templer to go to Malaya as High Commissioner is excellent. I have the very highest opinion of his qualities. He was in charge of my Military Government in Germany during the last stages of the war and after it ended; he was my V.C.I.G.S. at the War Office. He will do the job well in Malaya.

Enclosure to 260

1. No one doubts the urgency of restoring law and order, and good Government, in Malaya. It is vital from every point of view: economic, military, political, and from the viewpoint of the contest between East and West.

If the present conditions are allowed to continue much longer the situation may well get beyond a solution; futhermore the younger type of planter, if he stays at all, will probably take to drink and will cease to be of value to us in the struggle.

2. The problem has been studied by the Secretary of State for the Colonies; the measures necessary to begin to put things right are clearly set out in his Report.[2]

But to determine what must be done is only half the answer, and the easiest half; that of itself will not achieve success.

In all this welter of trouble "the man" is what counts.

The second half of the answer is to produce good men, really good men, who have the courage to issue the necessary orders, the drive to insist that those orders are carried out, and the determination and will-power to see the thing through to the end.

3. Such men do not exist today in the Malayan Federation or in Singapore Colony.

The seven key appointments are the following:—

The Commissioner General in S.E. Asia
The High Commissioner in Malaya
The Chief Secretary in Malaya
The Commissioner of Police in Malaya
The Governor of Singapore

---

[1] See, 259, note.   [2] See 257.

The Colonial Secretary, Singapore
The Chief of Police, Singapore

Let us look at the present holders of these appointments.

4. *Commissioner general*
I have given my views on Malcolm Macdonald in my letter to the Secretary of State for the Colonies dated 27 December, 1951.[3] He is a "waffler"; he appears still to have great vitality but what actually happens is that he talks for a long time and gives out no clear doctrine at the end. He has the emotional approach to every problem and is unduly influenced by his emotion. He is afraid to take action which he thinks may be unpopular.

5. *High commissioner in Malaya*
It was commonly supposed that GURNEY was good. It is natural that after his murder he should have had a build-up; but this was really not justified. He was certainly a very good Chief Secretary in Palestine in 1946/47. But in Malaya he concentrated on the political problem; he never was able to handle the bandit problem; he did not understand how to keep law and order in the Federation, and he was unable to give clear guidance and direction. The state of affairs under his regime has been exposed by the Secretary of State.

6. *The chief secretary in Malaya*
The Malayan Civil Service (European) is divided into Malay, Chinese and Labour Officers, speaking Malay, Chinese and Tamil. DEL TUFO is a Labour Officer, with no administrative experience in the districts. His parentage is I believe Maltese-Ceylon-burgher. He has no power of command and gives out no inspiration. He is, of course, quite useless as Chief Secretary. He is now acting as High Commissioner.

7. *Commissioner of police in Malaya*
GRAY was a Commando officer under me during the 1939/45 war; he has great energy but does not know how to use it.
 No one in his senses could imagine him as a good Commissioner of Police.
 When he was appointed I was C.I.G.S. and I protested to Creech Jones.

8. *Governor of Singapore*
GIMSON is a worthy soul.
 But he was a prisoner in Japanese hands in the war.
 He has now "had it", and he admits it.

9. *Colonial secretary, Singapore*
BLYTHE[4] is the type of Colonial Civil Servant who will never take any action which he thinks is likely to be unpopular.
 His unfitness for his job was proved at the time of HERTOGH riots in Singapore.[5] He is a Chinese Protectorate officer and as such has had little or no real

---

[3] See 258.   [4] See 140, note 1.   [5] See 232, note 1.

administrative experience: though as adviser on Chinese matters he may be quite competent.

He is not fit to be Colonial Secretary in Singapore.

10. *Chief of police, Singapore*[6]
I do not know him. But from what happened during the HERTOGH riots it is clear he cannot be much good.

11. The above personalities present a sorry picture. Can anyone wonder that the situation in Malaya got out of hand as soon as the clouds appeared on the horizon? Can anyone in his senses think it will ever be put right with such an outfit in control in the Malayan Federation and Singapore Colony?

A complete clean-out is wanted.

And unless we have the courage to make the clean-out, there will be no success. We will then be able to blame no one but ourselves.

12. The first and really urgent need is to put a really high class man into the Malayan Federation as High Commissioner, and give him a first class Chief Secretary and a first class Commissioner of Police.

The best selection for High Commissioner would be a man with administrative experience and one who understands the Governmental and military machine. It is doubtful if a first class civilian can be found with these qualities and one who could handle the present emergency. It therefore seems that a first class soldier is necessary. In selecting this soldier, availability must not be considered; once the man is agreed he must be made available. Any soldier who pleads he is tired and exhausted and therefore cannot face it, should be considered as unfit to hold his present job, and be relegated to retired pay. We are faced with a crisis and all must do their duty: or be discarded.

13. A really high class man cannot be asked to serve under Macdonald.

It is fundamental that Macdonald must go, and with him must also go all those mentioned in para 3 above: gradually of course.

14. There is no alternative to success in Malaya.

We know what is required to be done.

We must now collect the men to do it.

If we are not prepared to do this, we had better get ready to lose that part of the Colonial Empire and suffer all the repercussions that would follow: and we will most certainly do so.

---

[6] A E Wiltshire had been acting commissioner of police at the time of the Hertogh riots; he became commissioner of police, Aden, in 1962.

261   CO 1022/304, no 2   9 Jan 1952
[Reorganisation of government]: inward telegram no 7 from Mr Fraser to Mr Lyttelton

[Hugh Fraser, parliamentary private secretary to Lyttelton 1951–1954, accompanied the secretary of state to Malaya and stayed on until mid-Jan to examine local problems.]

Following personal for S. of S. from Sakai.

Congratulations on your choice of Templer.

2. Final conclusions, after as mature thought as I am able, are that the acutest problem here is neither in the spheres of politics, military or even police but in that of general administration.

3. Neither the civil nor emergency administration is working effectively.

4. Whatever improvements can be made at the centre, and at the moment the Central Secretariat is indeed overworked in some branches, understaffed and not sufficiently geared to the emergency, fact will remain that present constitution makes Kuala Lumpur a mill grinding too much air (repeat air). Balloonism in Kuala Lumpur must be tethered to the ground and, simultaneously, States streamlined into action. Neither does Kuala Lumpur's writ nor even that of the D. of O.[1] run smoothly or swiftly in the States. On one hand central machine takes too long to answer queries from regions or to permit initiative; or on the other, local State Governments have natural but obstructive antipathy to the centre.

5. I would, therefore, suggest *firstly* that War Council and Executive Council be merged, not in the next six months as is proposed, but as soon as possible. *Secondly*, that British Advisers be ordered to insist that the central decisions are more swiftly executed and that they be called in for monthly meetings with the High Commissioner: it is notable that fourth of these in three (repeat three) years is to be called this month. *Thirdly*, that more use be made of Mentri Besar at the centre and, if possible, on the Executive Sub-Committees of proposed Inner Cabinet. *Fourthly*, that either the new G.O.C. Malaya be chosen for appointment as Deputy Director of Operations (with H.C. as Director, I do not believe that this is politically impossible) or that the present D.D.O. be given liaison Officers to pursue decisions in the States. *Fifthly*, to avoid overloading and friction at the centre, in view of the arrival of a Deputy High Commissioner, that the post of Chief Secretary be abolished and replaced by a person to be called Secretary for Defence and Assistant (repeat Assistant) Chief Secretary, or some such title. *Sixthly*, that this post be filled by one of the British Advisers to effect a psychological link with the territories.

6. Understand that some of this may necessitate constitutional changes but, as you know, atmosphere has changed greatly in favour of action in the last months, opposition of Rulers should not be extreme and, in the first glory of Templer's arrival, this and more could be accomplished.

7. Would suggest, with complete confidence, Corry[2] for suggested post, Watherstone's promotion to Singapore and David[3] as a B.A.

8. Arriving 19.00 hours on Thursday, 10th January. Please inform Laura.

9. Malcolm [MacDonald] has seen this telegram and agrees with most of it. He will telegraph comments in the next two or three days.[4] Regards.

---

[1] Director of operations.
[2] W C S Corry entered the MCS in 1923, became British adviser, Pahang, in 1948 and retired in 1953.
[3] E David entered the MCS in 1931 and became officiating secretary for defence and internal security in 1951; he was seconded to the CO in 1953.
[4] See 264.

262 PREM 11/639   12 Jan 1952
[The task in Malaya]: minute by Sir G Templer to Mr Churchill

[Flying to Ottawa at Churchill's request, Templer had two hours with the prime minister on 11 Jan. He gave this account of their conversation to Lord Moran, Churchill's physician: 'Winston began: "I am an old man. I shall probably not see you again. I may be sending you to your death." When he said this he almost broke down. And then he said to me: "Ask for power, go on asking for it, and then—then never use it." ' (Moran's diary, 11 Jan 1952, cited in Lord Moran, *Winston Churchill: the struggle for survival 1940–1965* (London, 1968 ed) p 387).]

Prime Minister

You asked me to let you have a short note on the job for which you intend to recommend me.

The problem is a fresh one to me, and I have had little time to study it. I am however firm in my mind on the following five points:—

1. *Directive by H.M.G.* The general object is obvious—*viz* to restore law and order, and to bring back peace to the Federation. In order that this object may be achieved, I am clear as to what must happen from the purely military point of view. I am not at all clear as to what H.M.G. is aiming at from the political point of view. Is it a "united Malayan nation"? And if so, what exactly does this mean? Does it mean a merging of Malays and Chinese in one community—as a long term project?

I must have a clear policy to work on. I want to be given a directive from H.M.G.—not so that I should shelter behind that directive—but rather that I can use it publicly to impress H.M.G.'s purpose.

It should also state plainly that the British are not going to be kicked out of Malaya; and that there is still a great future for the British in that country.

2. *The men to do the job.* This is of primary importance. You have given me your assurance that I shall have your support in getting good men—civilians and soldiers—for certain key appointments.

3. *The higher set-up in Malaya.* I am to be responsible both for Civil Government and for the direction of military operations. I will not abrogate this latter responsibility to anyone else, and I must therefore handle that aspect as a soldier, and with the operational set up which I consider necessary for the purpose. When I have got out there, it may well be found by me that the present "Lockhart set-up" in [sic] not the best.

4. *Relationships with Singapore.* My appointment covers the Malayan Federation alone. The Colony of Singapore will be entirely outside my jurisdiction: I feel this is right.

At the same time I believe that some much closer integration (or whatever it may be) of the Malayan police with the Singapore police is necessary. This will be difficult and unpopular.

5. *Higher Defence Organisation in the Far East.* This concerns my position *vis à vis* that organisation. It is unsatisfactory. The matter is already under examination in the Colonial Office and in the Chiefs of Staff Committee in London.

263   PREM 11/639   14 Jan 1952

[The task in Malaya]: minute by Sir G Templer to Mr Churchill on the first meeting of the Cabinet Malaya Committee

Prime Minister

You asked for my comments on the First Meeting of the Malayan Committee[1] held on the 10th January. They are these:—

(1) *C.I.D.* I cannot believe that it is efficient to have two Bureaux—one in the Federation and one in Singapore. When the new Head of the Police is appointed, I expect he will have strong views.

(2) *Officering of the Malay Regiment.* I want to increase the Malay Regiment very considerably, for two main reasons:—

     (a) It is a necessary step on the way to Dominion status.[2]

     (b) I hope it will enable British troops to be released for Europe in due course.

It cannot be done without sufficient good British officers, in spite of the additional flow of young Malay officers which I hope to produce.

Very few officers—good or indifferent—will volunteer today for Colonial Forces anywhere, because of the bad financial terms. Gone are the days when the young officer could recoup his financial position by a couple of years "bush whacking".

There are two alternatives:—

     (a) To improve the terms for all Colonial Forces.

     (b) To treat the Malay Regiment in isolation because of the overriding importance of the problem.

If we are to get the officers on a voluntary basis, one of the two must be adopted. Even so, in my opinion, we shall not see results quickly enough, and for some time therefore officers must be ordered to go. Can they be spared? War Office must say, but in my opinion they must be. And I know Field Marshal Montgomery considers they can be.

This question is most urgent.

(3) *Tax evasion.* This is just another example of the lack of proper law and order. We must bring these people up with a jerk. I press strongly for even one expert team at once to enable me to nail a few outstanding cases, and prove to the remainder that the game is not worth the candle.

(4) *Commissioner general, South East Asia.* I do not myself see the virtue of extending Mr. Malcolm Macdonald's appointment by three or four months.

(5) *My relationship with commanders in chief, Far East.* Before giving any opinion, I would prefer to see the report which is being produced. I do not think there would be any real problem if I were made an additional member of the British Defence Coordination Committee, Far East. This meets in Singapore from time to time. Mr. Macdonald is the Chairman, and the Chiefs of Staff, Far East, are members.

---

[1] see 257, note; for the committee's report, see 266.

[2] Churchill wrote in the margin at this point in the minute: 'There is no hurry about this surely!' He later forwarded Templer's minute to Lyttelton.

264   CO 1022/60, no 2   14 Jan 1952
[Reorganisation of government]: inward telegram no 12 from Mr M J
MacDonald to Mr Lyttelton

Following secret and personal for Secretary of State, from MacDonald.

Telegram No. 7[1] containing personal message to you from Sakai.

This telegram is one of many indications of how useful and helpful was Fraser's stay in Malaya. We are all very grateful to you and him for making it possible.

2.   I agree with Fraser that acute problems do not, at present, lie in either political or military spheres. I suggest, however, that police problem is just as acute and urgent as that of general administration and that this should be given equal priority. We can make no headway against terrorists until the Police Force and Police Intelligence are much more efficient than they are now. It is of prime importance to get the right man to head the police as early as possible.

3.   On the question of administration, I agree generally with paragraphs 3, 4, 5 and 7 of telegram under reference except

(a) on one or two details with which I need not bother you but which I will discuss with new High Commissioner on his arrival and
(b) suggestion that Chief Secretaryship should be abolished.

4.   Regarding this latter suggestion, it would seem difficult to have a post called Assistant Chief Secretary when there is no Chief Secretary. I think that we should either stick to your plan and have a Deputy High Commissioner, a Chief Secretary and a Secretary for Defence, or (if that seems to be "overloading" the hierarchy) abandon the idea of having a Deputy High Commissioner and have a Chief Secretary with an Assistant Chief Secretary who is also Secretary for Defence.

5.   On balance I am in favour of having a Deputy High Commissioner assisted by a Chief Secretary and a separate Secretary for Defence. Arguments for this are that

(a) On merits, new top man will need assistance on the civil side by someone with status of a deputy;
(b) plan has been accepted by the Cabinet in London and is now expected by the Rulers and public here.

6.   On reflection, I feel, however, that there would be difficulty and perhaps considerable criticism of a plan which resulted more or less all at once in:

(a) arrival of a new High Commissioner and Director of Operations from [?outside] Malaya;
(b) arrival of a Deputy High Commissioner from outside Malaya;
(c) resignation and departure of del Tufo, and his replacement in the Secretariat by a man like Corry without recent experience of central administration;
(d) a new Commissioner of Police from outside Malaya.

(Corrupt groups)[2] these changes, public might feel apprehensive at such a complete change of team at the top, especially as Lockhart is still regarded as also a new man who has yet to learn his job and who has so far not (repeat not) made any distinct

---

[1] See 261.   [2] ie phrase garbled in transmission.

impression. On merits of the case there is also, of course, a lot to be said for keeping in the high up hierarchy at least one man who provides experience of and continuity with previous administration. This leads me to the view that we should, perhaps, reconsider del Tufo's position and contemplate making him, at least for a short time, Deputy High Commissioner. I realise his defects and am frequently worried at their impact on the situation. But he has many good qualities, and if new High Commissioner keeps him under control bringing out his good points and helping to suppress his bad ones, this is worth serious consideration. I do not think he should remain Deputy High Commissioner for long. Perhaps he could be temporarily appointed for say six months or a year until new High Commissioner has thoroughly learnt his job. del Tufo could then resign and be replaced.

7. If you think there is merit in this suggestion but that del Tufo really is not adequate for Deputy's post, a possible alternative is that question of appointing a Deputy should be postponed. The new High Commissioner might be asked to consider the matter and advise you on it after he has arrived, in the meantime del Tufo continuing as Chief Secretary, taking on rather more duties than that officer would so as to relieve the High Commissioner. I doubt whether this plan could work for long because the new High Commissioner will really need, on political side, much more relief than a man with the status of a mere Chief Secretary can properly give him.

265   CO 1022/22, no 1   16 Jan 1952
[Reorganisation of government]: memorandum by Mr Fraser for Mr
Lyttelton   [Extract]

[Hugh Fraser's report followed up points mentioned in Lyttelton's Cabinet paper (see 257). It is divided into three sections covering: instruments of government, aspects of emergency policy, and general external considerations affecting the emergency.]

Instruments of government

(i) *The federal structure*
In principle the administration of the Federation could be comparatively simple. In practice the Federation is cursed with a written Federal Constitution, primarily devised not as an instrument of administration but as a political compromise, with the Central Government safeguarding non-Malay and the States Malay interests.

As a result, far from simplicity there emerges a caricature of government not dissimilar to a cartoon of a constitutional monarch and of an unelected House of Commons attempting to administer through eleven suspicious Houses of Lords, led by eleven more or less recalcitrant Lord Chancellors. Frustration results locally and at the centre. On the one hand Kuala Lumpur, lacking the constant advice or experience of people in the field, tends to become academic, perfectionist and unpractical, overworked and so bogged down in its paper constructions as to make it chronically short of staff, while State Governments, by complaint, obstruction and jealousy of local privilege, distort and delay the execution of Federal policy. These processes apply more especially to the civil administration but reflect also in the conduct of the emergency machine. Whatever the future may hold, the immediate necessity is to gear more closely the central and provincial administrations. Real and psychological rifts are unfortunately widened by the inability of a chair-bound and overworked central hierarchy to leave K.L.

By leadership, visitations and, if needs be, cajolery or direction, the new High Commissioner will undoubtedly remedy most of these defects. But certain improvements should, perhaps, be made of a more statutory order:—

1. By means of more frequent conferences between the eleven British Advisers and Residents, the High Commissioner and the Director of Operations and their staffs, a two-way traffic of ideas could be established, and clearer and firmer directions could be issued, with all the benefits of permitting more local initiative within a strategic framework. It is notable that during the last three years only four such conferences have been held.

2. Similarly, more use might be made of the alternate monthly conferences of the State Prime Ministers whereby, by a mixture of high flattery and cajolery, they could be urged into swifter action and into participation in some of the proposed Executive Committees of the Central Government.

3. The ablest of the British Advisers, Mr. W.C.S. Corry,[1] might be given the post either of Chief Secretary or of Defence Secretary in the Federal Government. He could assist in bringing both the central administration down to earth and the more recalcitrant British Advisers or State Prime Ministers to heel. Some such appointment has been requested by the Sultans. His local experience would be of much value at the centre.

4. Finally, should the State Governments prove unco-operative, it is well to recall that the reserve powers of the British Advisers in tendering official advice, tantamount to instructions, have not been used except on two minor occasions and that the very threat of their use might concentrate the minds of Sultans who daily become more fearful of their futures.

(ii) *The central machine*

The reorganisation of central government and the institution of an inner "Cabinet" with executive Committees proceeds. Of the two processes, that concerning executive Committees seems to be the more satisfactory, as the so-called grouping of the inner "Cabinet" is already sprawling into a Committee not of seven but of eleven or twelve persons. This, however, is not perhaps of supreme importance as real and final power can never rest with any nominated cabinet, but only with the High Commissioner or his deputy.

What seems to be of more vital importance is that WAR COUNCIL should be absorbed by EXCO as quickly as possible. Until this is done, and the talk is now of doing it in six months or so, the split personality of the Government regarding the emergency will continue. Simultaneously, I believe it is important that whilst the members for Government departments of government [sic] should be regrouped into ad hoc executive committees responsible to His Excellency or his deputy in "Cabinet", the departments themselves should be regrouped, on the one hand under a Secretary of Defence responsible to the Director of Operations or his deputy, and on the other under a Secretary Assistant to the Civilian Deputy High Commissioner.

---

[1] see 261, note 2.

At the moment, and this is confirmed by General Lockhart, within groups of departments 'the right hand knows not what the left is doing'. This policy might or might not make the post of Chief Secretary redundant. If it is kept, it is perhaps worth noting that there will be no official Residence for its holder.

Until the whole Federal system is working more expeditiously I see little chance of reducing essential administration staff in K.L. At the moment both the Defence Secretariat and the Establishments staff are short of officers. . . .

266 CAB 129/49, C(52)16, Annex   26 Jan 1952
'Report by the Committee on Malaya': Cabinet note by Lord Salisbury

We were invited by the Cabinet on 28th December, 1951 (C.C. (51) 20th Conclusions, Minute 1), to consider in detail the report on Malaya (C. (51) 59)[1] by the Secretary of State for the Colonies. We endorse the recommendations in this report and draw the attention of the Cabinet to the particular points set out below. Action on many matters of detail within the competence of the Secretary of State for the Colonies is, we understand, already proceeding.

Responsibilities of the high commissioner
2. The Chiefs of Staff and the Commanders-in-Chief, Far East, have agreed that the High Commissioner must have complete operational control of all the forces in the Federation, and be empowered to issue operational orders to the G.O.C., Malaya, without reference to the Commanders-in-Chief. These must, however, continue to be responsible for the morale, discipline, training and administration of their respective forces. In order to ensure the closest consultation between the High Commissioner and the Commanders-in-Chief (who are, of course, responsible for the whole Far Eastern theatre) it has been agreed that Sir G. Templer should be invited to attend all meetings of the British Defence Co-ordination Comittee (Far East) at which the internal or external defence of Malaya are to be discussed or when he himself expresses a wish to attend.

3. We agree with the strong recommendations of the Secretary of State for the Colonies (paragraphs 44 to 47 of C. (51) 59) that the High Commissioner's responsibility should be confined to the Federation. Although our policy must be to bring Singapore and the Federation into closer union as rapidly as circumstances permit, there would be the most severe reactions—both from the Malays in the Federation and the Chinese in Singapore—to any attempt to force the pace. If there were weighty practical advantages in putting these two territories under one head, then the risk of upsetting local opinion might have had to be accepted. Our view is, on the contrary, that the practical advantages are in favour of a High Commissioner for the Federation alone. This limitation of the High Commissioner's responsibilities has, on the whole, been received with understanding by the Press.

Federal War Council and Cabinet
4. Although it would be desirable to simplify the complicated pattern of Government in the Federation by amalgamating the Federal War Council with the

---

[1] See 257.

Executive Council, it is not possible to press this measure without some regard to local political factors. The new High Commissioner is seized of the importance attached by Ministers to this simplification of the administrative machine. The acting High Commissioner has been informed that General Templer will wish to consider the possibility of an early merger very soon after his arrival. The establishment of an inner "War Cabinet" (paragraph 49 of C. (51) 59) will ensure that the urgent tasks of the campaign are pressed ahead with resolution and the minimum of delay.

Commissioner-general South-East Asia

5. The Commissioner-General has a dual responsibility. He answers to the Secretary of State for Foreign Affairs for the "better co-ordination of measures for the maintenance and protection of His Majesty's interest" in the foreign countries in South-East Asia, and is responsible for advising His Majesty's Government on general problems of foreign affairs within his area. He is specifically charged with constant watch over the food situation in the area and regional intelligence and information.

6. The Commissioner-General is also His Majesty's principal representative in the Colonial and Protected Territories of South-East Asia (Federation of Malaya, Singapore, Sarawak, North Borneo and Brunei). His published instructions direct him to promote the co-ordination of policy and administration between the Governments in his area of authority. He has no administrative functions in any territory however, though he can issue directions on "defence matters" to the High Commissioners and Governors. His defence advisers are the Commanders-in-Chief, Far East, and he forms with them the British Defence Co-ordination Committee, Far East, of which he is Chairman. His present instructions tell him that "Defence" includes all measures necessary for dealing with the Emergency in Malaya; but the Colonial Secretary is arranging for this arrangement to be ended, since the High Commissioner alone must have full responsibility within the Federation. It is, however, desirable that the power of direction should be retained for general defence purposes to ensure that all the Colonial Governments in the area march in step in their preparations against aggression.

7. We have considered whether there is any real justification for retaining the appointment of Commissioner-General. The Foreign Office would wish to retain a "listening post" in Singapore, but do not regard the retention of a high-powered Commissioner-General as essential, and they are concerned at the high cost of the present organisation. It would, however, create an unfortunate impression both in the Far East and elsewhere if at this time we were to take a step which might be held to indicate a lessening of our determination to maintain our position in the area. We have also taken into account the very great personal prestige and popularity which Mr. Malcolm MacDonald enjoys in South-East Asia, and the considerable local feeling against his giving up the appointment, together with the great assistance that he would be able to give the new High Commissioner and the new Governor of Singapore. Our conclusion is that there would be advantage in his remaining as Commissioner-General, South-East Asia, for three or four months after the normal expiry of his appointment in May, and that the continuation of the post of Commissioner-General, South-East Asia, when Mr. Malcolm MacDonald finally leaves it, should be decided in the light of events nearer that time. The Secretary of State for the Colonies has undertaken to look into the present cost of the Commissioner-General's organisation, which appears unduly high.

Police and C.I.D.

8.   While we do not advocate the immediate amalgamation of the police forces of the Federation of Malaya and Singapore, since the separate administrations must have a large measure of control over their own forces, we consider that there might be an advantage—since there are many intelligence problems in common—in establishing a unified C.I.D. under the Commissioner of Police in the Federation. This is essentially a problem to be studied by the authorities in the Federation and Singapore in the first place, but we would urge that, if the practical advantages of amalgamation are seen to be considerable, political considerations should not be allowed to weigh too heavily against the implementation of such a scheme. It is in any case desirable that the closest liaison should be maintained between the separate C.I.D.s.

British officers for the Malay Regiment (Appendix X of C. (51) 59)

9.   The present standard of British officers in the Malay Regiment is not satisfactory. Although they receive additional pay the number of volunteers has not been sufficient and it has been necessary to post on a compulsory basis. A short while ago special much higher rates of additional pay were approved for volunteers and it is not yet possible to say whether these new rates will prove sufficient inducement. We have, however, asked the Secretary of State for the Colonies and the Secretary of State for War to re-examine the question as a matter of urgency.

10.   Whether, however, the majority of officers are found on a voluntary or compulsory basis, there must remain the difficulty of providing the number of officers needed of the quality which has been asked for. British Regiments and Battalions are already considerably below the strength in regular officers needed for efficiency and can stand no further depletion. A scheme is being examined for attracting ex-Indian Army officers to accept Short Service engagements for the Malay Regiment.

Tax evasion

11.   We have noted the danger that the whole system of taxation for Malaya may be brought into contempt by the widespread evasion of income tax, and we reinforce the request (Appendix XIII of C. (51) 59) that a staff of qualified experts should be sent for a period to Malaya to carry out an investigation of some of the more complex cases, and collect material for exemplary prosecutions.

Recommendations

12.   We recommend that the Cabinet should give general approval to proposals contained in the report on Malaya by the Secretary of State for the Colonies, and in particular should:—

(a) endorse the decision to appoint a High Commissioner with full responsibility for both the civil administration and military operations within the Federation;
(b) agree that the term of office of the present Commissioner-General, South-East Asia, should be extended for three or four months after he is due to be relieved in May, but that consideration as to whether he is eventually to be relieved or the post abolished should be deferred for the time being;
(c) agree that the High Commissioner and the Governor of Singapore should

consider the most efficient way of integrating the two police forces and in particular the C.I.D.s;

(d) take note that the Secretary of State for the Colonies and the Secretary of State for War are considering the proposals for improving the number and standard of British officers in the Malay Regiment, and invite them to submit the result of their consultation to the Minister of Defence;

(e) take note that the Secretary of State for the Colonies will be asking the Chancellor of the Exchequer to assist the Malayan Governments in combating income tax evasion by the temporary loan of an expert investigation staff.[2]

---

[2] Cabinet approved these recommendations on 5 Feb (CAB 128/26, CC 10(52)6).

---

267 CO 1022/61, no 7   29 Jan 1952
[Closer association of British territories]: savingram no 9 from Mr M J MacDonald to CO reporting recent discussions. *Minutes* by J D Higham and J J Paskin

My previous Savingrams on the subject of closer political association between the Federation of Malaya and the Colony of Singapore.

2. I am now able to report further steps which have been taken in this matter. On December 18th, 1951, Gimson and I had another confidential talk with the group of unofficial Singapore Legislative Councillors at Government House. I reported on

(a) my talks with Dato Onn as reported to you in Savingrams nos. 171 and 181 of 1951. I pointed out, however, that Dato Onn's influence had recently (but perhaps temporarily) declined somewhat amongst the Malays though it had increased amongst non-Malays; and said that this made it important that in further discussions with Federation representatives on the subject we should be sure to include representatives of important shades of Malay opinion which Dato Onn and his I.M.P. colleagues no longer fully represent.

(b) my discussions with Hone and Abell[1] in which they said that opinion in Sarawak and North Borneo would probably be more favourable to close association between these two territories if at the same time it involved closer association with at least Singapore and probably the Federation also. I expressed the view that people in Singapore might also feel that association with the Borneo territories would in some ways be an easier move than association with the Federation, and said that, if those present agreed, it might therefore be wise to establish early informal contacts between not only legislators of Singapore and the Federation but also legislators of the three Borneo territories.

3. C.C. Tan[2] then reported on a development which had taken place during the visit to the Festival of Britain of Singapore, Malayan and Bornean representatives. He

---

[1] Sir Ralph Hone, governor of North Borneo, 1949–1954; Sir Anthony Abell, governor of Sarawak, 1950–1959.

[2] C C Tan, lawyer; founder-member of the Progressive Party, 1947; member of the Singapore Legislative Council, 1948–1955, and Singapore Executive Council, 1951–1955; leader of the Liberal Socialist Party, 1956–1959; returned to legal practice in 1959.

said that this group quickly found themselves working as close friends and associates together in the discussions which took place with other colonial representatives on general colonial questions. In fact very cordial relations had been established, particularly between the representatives of Singapore, Sarawak and North Borneo. Before they left London they all expressed a strong desire to renew their meetings from time to time in South East Asia. Mr. Tan said that he thought this a helpful and important development. He agreed that closer association between Singapore and the Federation could be helped if it also envisaged closer association with the Borneo territories. Mr. Tan Chin Tuan,[3] who had been in London as well, supported this view.

4. The whole discussion then widened into consideration of the possibility of taking gradual steps towards a closer association between all the British territories in South East Asia. Those present were unanimous that we should advance judiciously and gradually but definitely in this direction. After an interesting talk it was agreed that:

(a) the first step should be an informal meeting in Borneo of representatives of the various Legislatures in British South East Asia. I expressed the view that the Governors of North Borneo and Sarawak would welcome and facilitate this, and undertook to approach them with a view to an invitation being issued from Borneo.

(b) after that the informal week-end gathering at Port Dickson which we had contemplated, and which I mentioned in my Savingrams Nos. 171 and 181, should be held. Representatives of the Borneo territories also should be invited to this.

5. I have since mentioned these proposals to Mr. del Tufo, who agrees that they are a wise method of procedure.

6. Two weeks ago I put the proposals to Mr. Calder, the Chief Secretary in North Borneo, when he stayed with me at Bukit Serene. He welcomed them and said that he felt sure that the Governor and Legislative Councillors in North Borneo would play their part. He will discuss the matter with the Governor on his return. He pointed out to me that a branch of the Commonwealth Parliamentary Association has recently been formed in Jesselton, and that it would therefore be appropriate for this organisation to act as the host in North Borneo.

7. I discussed the matter this week with the Governor of Sarawak in Kuching, and he enthusiastically supports the plan. I have now addressed communications to the two Borneo Governors in order that action may be taken with a view to the first meeting in Borneo being organised in the near future.

Minutes on 267

Mr. Paskin
. . . Mr. MacDonald has reported during recent months that his intention was, as the next step in accustoming unofficials of both the Federation and Singapore to think along lines of closer association, that informal discussions should be held, and that later a weekend conference of members of the two Legislatures should be organised. Later, an informal working party would be set up.

Mr. MacDonald's present savingram shows that the intention now is to bring in

---

[3] Member of Progressive Party and deputy president of Singapore Legislative Council.

the Borneo territories and to hold the first informal meeting of Legislative Councillors in Borneo.

While we have always hoped that the South East Asia territories would eventually come together in some form of federation, and perhaps become a dominion of South East Asia, we have hitherto felt that it would be difficult to associate the more backward Borneo territories (particularly Sarawak where the tradition of Malay domination lingered in Dyak and Chinese minds) with more sophisticated Singapore and Federation. No-one is better aware of these dangers than Mr. MacDonald and I don't think we need say anything to him at this stage beyond a brief acknowledgement to (7). Draft herewith.

J.D.H.
6.2.52

While we were in Malaya, the Commissioner General indicated that unofficial opinion in Singapore and the Federation was veering towards this new approach to the problem of bringing the various governments of the area into some form of closer association.

Since the new initiative seems to have been taken by the Unofficial Members of Council in Singapore with whom Mr. M. MacDonald's discussions have been conducted, it is quite clear that the line of approach will have to be explored. But I must confess that I am not very optimistic of its producing any useful results without a longer delay than we had been hoping would be the case.

Hitherto the approach has been to attempt to bring into some form of closer association:—

(a) the Governments of Singapore and the Federation; and
(b) the Governments of the 3 territories in Borneo.

There have been times within the last 3 years when we have permitted ourselves to hope that each of these 2 separate groupings might be achieved before the expiration of the term of office of the present Commissioner General. But in the course of the last year or so we have really given up any such expectations. The possibility of a further closer association—i.e., between the territories in group (a) and the territories in group (b)—has hitherto been regarded as a matter for the more distant future.

About a year ago there seemed almost a possibility that Singapore and the Federation might perhaps be brought together at the time when Sir F. Gimson's term of office was due to expire; but there was then a recession in the feelings of the Unofficial Members and the project seemed to fade into the more distant future.

As regards the Borneo territories, steps had been taken to pave the way for a closer political association by closer departmental association in matters of common concern, such as meteorology, the Judiciary, etc., but at the Commissioner General's Governors' Conference in January, 1949 there was something approaching a revolt on the part of Sir E. Twining and Sir C. Arden-Clarke[4] against what they regarded as a dangerous "forcing of the pace" on the part of the Commissioner General's organisation. This resulted in a recommendation ((c) on page 7 of no. (1) on

---

[4] Sir Edward Twining, governor of North Borneo, 1946–1949; Sir Charles Arden-Clarke, governor of Sarawak, 1946–1949.

58922/49) that "implementation of such plans should not be unduly hurried", and this recommendation was endorsed in the Secretary of State's despatch at no. (2) on that file. It is true that that conclusion was reached two years ago and that there are now new Governors in North Borneo and Sarawak. Even so, having regard to the very backward conditions in North Borneo and Sarawak, by comparison with conditions in Singapore and the Federation, and the repeated protests against unduly hurrying the process of administrative and political development in North Borneo and Sarawak, it is surprising to learn that it is now felt that more rapid progress in bringing about a closer association between Singapore and the Federation can be achieved by attempting at the same time to bring in these relatively backward territories.

Nevertheless, as I have said above, since the approach to this problem throughout has been on the basis of attempting to stimulate some initiative on the part of Unofficial Members of Council, and since it is they who have suggested this new approach, it is clear that it has to be tried.

J.J.P.
7.2.52

268   PREM 11/639, ff 20–22   1 Feb 1952

[Templer's instructions]: directive issued by Mr Lyttelton on behalf of HMG

> [The draft directive was amended several times in the light of discussions with Templer, the chiefs of staff and the Malayan authorities (cf CO 1022/102). The final version was approved by Lyttelton on 31 Jan and by Churchill on 1 Feb. On 4 Feb it was sent to Templer who took it with him when he departed for Malaya the next day. The text was released at his swearing-in ceremony in Kuala Lumpur on 7 Feb. The document printed here is the version approved by Churchill on 1 Feb. Like Attlee's statement on 13 Apr 1949 (see 185, no 1), it strikes a balance between long-term constitutional aims and immediate military needs. In response to those who accused the government of precipitate action or unrealistic idealism, Lyttelton pointed out that 'if we are to maintain our present position in Asia we must make no bones about the ultimate aim of our policy' (CO 1022/82, no 13, Lyttelton to Amery, 14 Mar 1952, commenting on a letter from Lady Clementi).]

The policy of His Majesty's Government in the United Kingdom is that Malaya should in due course[1] become a fully self-governing nation. His Majesty's Government confidently hope that nation will be within the British Commonwealth.

2.   In assisting the peoples of Malaya to achieve this object, you will at all times be guided by the declaration of policy expressed in the preamble of the Federation of Malaya Agreement and by the statement of the special responsibilities of the High Commissioner contained in Section 19 of that Agreement.

3.   To achieve a united Malayan nation there must be a common form of citizenship for all who regard the Federation or any part of it as their real home and the object of their loyalty.[2]

---

[1] The phrase 'in due course' was inserted at the request of Templer but to the regret of Lloyd who felt that 'the addition is meaningless in practice but the words would have a dampening effect on Malaya' (CO 1022/102, minute by Lloyd to Lyttelton, 31 Jan 1952).

[2] The CO had originally included in this paragraph the words: 'All Federal citizens must enjoy the same

4.   It will be your duty to guide the peoples of Malaya towards the attainment of these objectives and to promote such political progress of the country as will, without prejudicing the campaign against the terrorists, further our democratic aims in Malaya.[3]

5.   The ideal of a united Malayan nation does not involve the sacrifice by any community of its traditional culture and customs, but before it can be fully realised the Malays must be encouraged and assisted to play a full part in the economic life of the country, so that the present uneven economic balance may be redressed. It will be your duty to foster this process to the best of your ability.

6.   His Majesty's Government believe that the British have a mission to fulfil in the achievement of these objects, and that, even after self-government has been attained, the British in Malaya will have a worthy and continuing part to play in the life of the country.

7.   Communist terrorism is retarding the political advancement and economic development of the country and the welfare of its peoples. Your primary task in Malaya must, therefore, be the restoration of law and order, so that this barrier to progress may be removed. Without victory and the state of law and order which it alone can bring, there can be no freedom from fear, which is the first human liberty.

8.   In furtherance of your task, not only will you fulfil the normal functions of High Commissioner, but you will assume complete operational command over all armed forces assigned to operations in the Federation and will be empowered to issue operational orders to their Commanders without reference to the Commanders-in-Chief, Far East. You should establish the closest consultation between yourself and the Commanders-in-Chief, Far East, in matters of common concern.

9.   You may assure the Malayan peoples of all communities that they can count on the powerful and continuing assistance of His Majesty's Government not only in the immediate task of defeating the terrorists but in the longer term objective of forging a united Malayan nation. His Majesty's Government will not lay aside their responsibilities in Malaya until they are satisfied that Communist terrorism has been defeated and that the partnership of all communities, which alone can lead to true and stable self-government, has been firmly established.

---

civic rights and have the same responsibilities.' This phrase was later deleted on the advice of the Malayan government though to the regret of the CO.

[3] The passage 'and to promote . . . aims in Malaya' was included at the request of the Malayan government.

269   CO 1022/60, no 3   28 Feb 1952

[Reorganisation of government]: inward telegram no 286 from Sir G Templer to Mr Lyttelton on new measures

I have now made up my mind as to the present reorganisation of the Government Administrative H.Q. machine, and I propose to give effect to this re-organisation from 1st March.

2.   The principal change will be the merging of the functions of the Federal War Council with those of the Federal Executive Council, which will then become the sole instrument of the Federal Government's policy. I propose, at the same time, to expand membership of the Executive Council to the full number of 20 permitted by

the recent amendment to the Federation Agreement. I have considered the advisability of keeping one or two vacancies on the Executive Council up my sleeve, but have decided against this on the grounds that existing vacancies would be found to invite agitation for representation (or increased representation) of one or other community or sectional interest. I propose, therefore, to fill all the vacancies, there are five, at once. It is necessary, however, that at least two of these vacancies should be filled by Malays, since an undertaking was given at the time when agreement was sought to the amendment of the Federation Agreement that proportional management of the Executive Council would be maintained. I propose to appoint General Lockhart, Deputy Director of Operations, and Mr. J.D. Hodgkinson, Member for Industrial and Social Relations, to two of the five vacancies.[1] The reason for Lockhart's appointment is obvious, and I need make no comment here. Hodgkinson's appointment arises from the increasing importance of his portfolio, which now includes direction of manpower. The remaining three vacancies I propose to fill as follows:—

Raja Uda, Mentri Besar Salangor, [sic][2] on whom the Rulers place considerable reliance, but who is a man of virtue, breadth of vision and liberal views.

Tengku Abdul Rahman. Although his appointment will be a personal one and not as President U.M.N.O., it will, in reality, recognise the desirability of representation on the Council of the views of U.M.N.O. Onn, with whom I have discussed these appointments, accepts the necessity for this. If U.M.N.O. were to be left out at this stage, there is little doubt that the party would go into strong opposition to the Government, and this would be dangerous development at a time when unity of purpose on the part of all communities is a first essential. The inclusion of U.M.N.O. is all the more important now that there are signs of cementing and [sic] extension beyond Kuala Lumpur of the alliance which was formed between the M.C.A. and U.M.N.O. for the purpose of the recent municipal elections.[3]

Mr. Leona Yew Koh, [sic][4] a Chinese leader of much strength of character and with a large following, whose advice on the Federal War Council has been valuable. He lives in Perak.

All these five new appointments will be for a period of one year in the first instance. All, except Lockhart, are already Members of the Federal Legislative Councils.

3. There are only four members of the Federal War Council who will not find a place on the new Federal Executive Council. These are:—

The Keeper of the Rulers' Seal.
Dato Sir Cheng Lock Tan.
Mr. Treble.[5]
Mr. Facer.[6]

---

[1] J D Hodgkinson entered the MCS in 1930 and had been acting British adviser of Johore.

[2] Raja Uda was Mentri Besar, Selangor, 1949–1953.

[3] The Selangor branches of UMNO and the MCA formed an electoral alliance for the purpose of defeating the IMP in the Kuala Lumpur municipal elections, Feb 1952. In combination UMNO and MCA won nine of the twelve seats contested, while the IMP captured only two; the remaining seat was won by an independent candidate.

[4] Leong Yew Koh, a leader of the Perak Chinese Chamber of Commerce and of the MCA, had escaped an assassination attempt.

[5] G D Treble, a Pahang planter, had been brought onto the war council by Gurney in 1950.

[6] H H Facer was a leading member of the Rubber Growers' Association, see 149.

I have explained the reason for the discontinuance of the War Council to the first three, and they appreciate that it is not possible to find room for them on the new Federal Executive Council. I propose to see Facer shortly. The last two were representatives of planters' opinion on the Federal War Council, and it may be that there will be some public criticism of the re-organisation on the grounds that this opinion will no longer be sufficiently represented. However, Mead,[7] the Member for Works, has definitely decided that he cannot continue in office after the 1st April, and I propose to replace him by the appointment of R.B. Carey.[8] The latter is a member of the Rubber Producers' Council, and his appointment should go a long way to allay such criticism. Although his appointment will not be effective until the 1st April, it is very necessary, in order to forestall planters' criticism, that it should be announced along with other appointments effective on 1st March, and this will be done.

4. I propose to keep in being the existing Director of Operations Committee with extended membership and scope; I shall myself preside over this committee whenever possible. Its new composition will be as follows:—

Director of Operations (myself).
Deputy Director of Operations.
Chief Secretary.
Secretary for Defence.
Director of Intelligence (when I get him).
G.O.C.
A.O.C.
Commissioner of Police.

The Committee will sit at least three times a week, but the three members last mentioned above will attend only about once a week, when matters of a strictly "operational" nature are under examination. Apart from "operations" in the strict sense, the Committee will undertake direction of all those controls and activities which are necessitated solely on account of the emergency, and which would not form part of the functions of the government in normal times. It will operate within the policy determined in the Executive Council, and will refer to the Executive Council for policy decisions when these are required.

5. My immediately following telegram contains text of a press release which I propose to issue on Saturday. I should be glad to have by Friday any comments you may have on it.

6. You will note that this draft release omits any reference to the Operations Committee. This is deliberate. This Committee, operating through S.W.E.C.S. and D.W.E.C.S., should be able to ensure speedy consideration and implementation of controls and activities directly connected with the emergency and will, so to speak, by-pass the cumbersome Government machine which is imposed by the present Constitutional system. The Director of Operations' Committee, and S.W.E.C.S. and D.W.E.C.S., already exist, and are tacitly accepted by the Rulers and politicians as a temporary necessity of the emergency; but I believe it would be politically unwise to draw attention in a public statement to any extension of the use of this system.

---

[7] J D Mead, a leading mining engineer in Malaya since 1930, was a member of the federal executive and legislative councils, 1948–1951, and member for works and housing in 1951–1952.

[8] R B Carey was member for works from 1952 to 1955 when Sardon bin Jubir became minister for works, posts and telecommunications.

7. An Executive Council of 20 is obviously an unwieldy body, and I have considered the suggestion that there should be established some form of inner Cabinet; this would have to contain, apart from myself, the Deputy High Commissioner and Deputy Director of Operations, the three Ex-Officio Members, and at least four Asiatics; and the advice of Secretary for Chinese Affairs and Member for Economic Affairs would often be required. Such a body would not have any constitutional standing, and I believe that its existence might well be resented by those members of the Executive Council who were not included. Moreover, need for a small working body will not be so great if extended use can quietly be made of the Director of Operations' Committee. I have, for these reasons, discarded the idea of an inner-Cabinet. It may well be, however, that it will prove necessary to establish one or more committees of Members of the Executive Council in order to relieve the Council of routine work and to ensure that, in respect of some other matters, closer consideration than is possible in a large assembly. These committees would be composed of those Members of the Executive Council particularly concerned with groups of subjects with which each would deal; their decisions would be subject to confirmation by the full Council. I propose, however, to postpone further examination of this proposal until after experience has been gained of the working of the enlarged Executive Council.

Particular stress is laid in the last paragraph of the draft press release on the continuing functions of Chief Secretary, since it is necessary to counter the impression gained in some quarters that the status of the post and the importance of duties attached to it have suffered on account of the creation of temporary post of Deputy High Commissioner. It is very necessary that the post of Chief Secretary should be built up. Not only will he remain responsible for all Civil Service matters, but he will have a specially important task of co-ordinating the work of the Director of Operations' Committee with that of various members of the Government.

9. I apologise for the length of this telegram, but issues contained in it are important.

270 CO 1022/298, no 6   12 Mar 1952

[Political progress]: inward telegram no 348 from Sir G Templer to Mr Lyttelton indicating the line on elections which he proposed to take in his forthcoming speech to the Legislative Council. *Minutes* by A S Gann, T C Jerrom[1] and J D Higham

It is, I understand, customary for the President of the Federal Legislative Council to make an address at the opening meeting of the new session, and for this address to include statements indicating the Government's intentions for the forthcoming year. I propose, therefore, to give such an address in general terms when the new session opens on 19th March. This address, which will be fairly lengthy, will indicate the manner in which it is proposed that my directive should be implemented. The draft which I have prepared, is, I believe, entirely in accord with Her Majesty's

---

[1] Gann and Jerrom were CO principals; Jerrom was seconded to British Guiana as deputy chief secretary in 1954 and returned to the CO as an assistant secretary in 1957.

Government's policy, and it was gone through yesterday by the Executive Council, and approved, subject to certain minor modifications. I am sending you a copy of the draft by air mail, but there are three passages which I think I must clear with you by telegram. I am telegraphing separately about two of them, one relating to income tax evasion, and the other about a Federation Army.

2. The third passage is on the subject of political progress. During the last few weeks I have had a number of discussions with Onn, Thuraisingham and others about responsible local government, during which I have urged the desirability of establishing such Government at the earliest possible moment, at what I described in these private conversations as "the parish pump level". They did not dissent to the need for this and, indeed, have given the proposal their support. On the 7th March the Singapore Standard came out with a critical editorial based on an article in the Eton [? London] Observer, stating it was my intention that progress in responsible Government should be limited to the parish pump level. This attracted a good deal of attention, and in order to check further press comments at that time I issued a statement that, although I did not propose to comment then, I would include the subject in my address at the opening of the new Session.

3. The relevant passage of what I propose to say on the subject reads as follows in the draft which was put before the Executive Council yesterday:—*Begins.*

> "I now turn to the question of political progress. Ten days or so ago I was criticised in a newspaper for saying that I would confine political progress to the Parish pump level. Who gave that information to the newspaper in question I have no idea, since I had been careful not to make any statement whatsoever on this subject until I could make a considered one at the opening of this new session of the Federal Legislative Council. I am, of course, aware of the responsibilities placed on all of us in regard to the election of members to the several legislatures, by the penultimate sentence in the preamble to the Federation Agreement.[2] But, I am a firm believer in first things first. Or, to put it another way, that it is politically unsound and structurally impossible to put the roof on the building until the foundations of it are well and truly laid, and until the uprights or, anyway, the corner posts, are in position and firmly fixed. I believe it right to ensure that truly responsible local government at Rural community and Municipal Council levels is firmly established, and as quickly as possible. Not for one moment would I suggest that this should be postponed in any way at all because the so called 'emergency' is upon us. On the contrary, it is all the more necessary—because of the emergency—to press on with this measure. I firmly believe, from the bottom of my heart, in the principle of responsible local government by local people. I will do all in my power to foster this and the quicker we can start on it the better. That is the firm foundation on which political progress must be based.

---

[2] *Viz*: 'And whereas it is the desire of His Majesty and Their Highnesses that progress should be made towards eventual self-government and, as a first step to that end, His Majesty and Their Highnesses have agreed that, as soon as circumstances and local conditions will permit, legislation should be introduced for the election of members to the several legislatures to be established pursuant to this Agreement'. The Federation of Malaya Agreement, 21 Jan 1948, in J de V Allen, A J Stockwell and L R Wright, eds, *A Collection of treaties and other documents affecting the states of Malaysia 1761–1963*, II, p 101. See 293, para (a) 2(a).

If it is not based on this principle, what is the future?

You remember the wise man who built his house upon a rock "and the rains descended, and the floods came, and the winds blew and beat upon that house and it fell not, for it was founded upon a rock"; and you remember the foolish man built his house upon sand "and the rains descended, and the floods came, and the winds blew and beat upon that house; and it fell and great was the fall of it". *Ends.*

This passage attracted more comments from the members of the Executive Council than any other in the draft address and there was criticism, principally from H.S. Lee, and Onn, that the second sentence[3] left as it stood, disposed too abruptly of the question of elections to the State and Federal Legislatures, and gave the impression that the matter would be shelved indefinitely. One quarter was anxious that there should also be included a sentence indicating my intention to bring about "a more territorially representative distribution of membership of the State and Settlement Councils and the Federal Legislative Council until such time as the franchise can be extended throughout the Federation for the election of Members of these several Legislatures."

4. To meet these points I am contemplating the inclusion subject to agreement, of the following at the end of the second [fourth] sentence of the original draft; "and we should not put out of mind the arrangements it will be necessary to make to give effect to this purpose as soon as circumstances and local conditions will permit; there may also be a case meantime for a more territorially representative distribution of membership of these Legislatures".

Minutes on 270

. . . It seems to me that the statement at (6) might have a discouraging effect, although the principle of building a firm foundation of local government is clearly sound. If a reference to definite proposals for holding State elections in Johore next year could be included, the sincerity of HMG's directive would be better demonstrated. I suppose the High Commissioner must, however, finally decide this point.

A.S.G.
14.3.52

Mr. Higham
Personally I am inclined to agree with Mr. Gann that our policy in Malaya should be to press on with State elections regardless of the difficulties involved and I do not myself entirely accept the theory that one must work upwards gradually from the "parish level". But I think that Gen. Templer's line of policy on this has been discussed here and generally agreed.

T.C.J.
15.3.52

---

[3] For 'second' read 'fourth'; see first sentence of para 4 of telegram.

Sir T Lloyd
I think that no positive undertakings have been given by previous Governments or High Commissioners in this matter of elections, but you should see Mr Griffiths' reply to a P.Q. on the 16th Nov 1950[4] (tab X on 52243/29/PQ1).

This question was raised in the House of Lords Debate recently. Lord Munster's statement (col. 361) was supported by Lord Ogmore (col. 364).[5]

While I agree that it is better to start from the parish level, I am sure that, at the present stage of development it is not possible to insist on a completely orderly development from the rudiments to the ultimate perfection of Leg. Co. elections, and I agree with the draft prepared by Mr. Jerrom and Mr. Gann.[6]

As the statement is to be made on Wednesday, a telegram should issue as soon as possible on Monday.

J.D.H.
15.3.52

---

[4] On 16 Nov 1950 James Griffiths issued a written parliamentary statement about elections: 'Great importance is attached to the introduction of elections to the Federal Legislative Council of Malaya as soon as practicable, but it is intended that the electoral system should first be introduced for certain local authorities. This has already been provided for in legislation recently passed by the Federal Legislative Council. It is proposed that the next step should be elections for the State and Settlement Councils, and finally for the Federal Legislature. I understand this is the desire of the leaders of the local communities who have carefully considered this matter' (*H of C Debs*, vol 480, col 205).
[5] See *H of L Debs*, vol 175, cols 299–365, 27 Feb 1952.
[6] For the final version of this passage in Templer's statement, see 280.

---

271 CO 1022/183, no 10   Apr 1952
[UMNO affairs]: report by the Pan Malayan Review of Intelligence no 4/52 of UMNO's general assembly, 29–30 Mar   [Extract]

. . . A. *Malay and Indonesian affairs*

U.M.N.O.

24. The half-yearly general assembly of U.M.N.O. was held in Kuala Lumpur on 29th–30th March, 1952. In his presidential address, Tengku ABDUL RAHMAN referred to the position of the organisation at the time he took over the presidentship, and the great responsibility which he had to shoulder in attaining independence for Malaya. He recalled the meeting he had had with Mr. Lyttelton,[1] who had assured him that Malaya would be granted independence as soon as the present Emergency had ended, and the people were united. He then mentioned the remarkable success of the Kuala Lumpur U.M.N.O./M.C.A. merger in the recent Municipal Elections and exhorted members to extend the alliance and promote friendly relationship with non-Malays in the other States.[2] He referred to the informal discussions which he had had with Chinese leaders and the assurance given him that there would be no interference with the privileges of the Malays either in respect of Malay reservations or appointments to the Medical Auxiliary Service. With regard to the Federation Army proposal, he said that, provided the Malay Regiment

---

[1] ie during Lyttelton's visit to Malaya, Dec 1951.   [2] See 269, note 3.

was expanded, it should not be opposed. He did not, however, agree that members of the Police and Military Forces, who were not qualified to become Federal Citizens, should be entitied to do so after three years' service as recommended by the Select Committee. He thought that such persons should not be permitted to join any of the armed forces. He appealed for all possible assistance to Malay members of the Security Forces and their families who were in distress and urged that every effort should be made to secure the release of Malays under detention.

25. During the meeting a resolution was passed requesting H.M. the Queen and the Malay Rulers to reserve the post of Deputy High Commissioner for the Malays. Other resolutions were adopted urging Government to proclaim the formation of an interim Government to make arrangements for the independence of Malaya within three years from the date of proclamation, to ensure that Malay members of the Police Force serve only in Malaya, to appoint suitable Malays to protect the interests of the Sakai[3] and to form a committee to investigate the cases of persons detained under the Emergency Regulations. It was also agreed that U.M.N.O. divisions should urge their State and Settlement Governments to hold public elections and that U.M.N.O. members who joined political organisations—such as I.M.P.—whose policies were in conflict with those of U.M.N.O., should automatically be expelled. . . .[4]

---

[3] A term for non-Muslim aborigines or forest dwellers, see 199, note 5.
[4] This marked the end of Dato Onn's links with UMNO.

272   CO 1022/85, no 13   10 Apr 1952
[Visit of Dr Purcell and Mr Carnell[1] to Malaya]: letter from J D Higham to D C MacGillivray. *Enclosure*: note of discussion with Purcell and Carnell on 6 Mar 1952

I think you should see the enclosed note of a discussion which took place recently between Victor Purcell, F.G. Carnell, Paskin and myself. Purcell, I am sure, needs no introduction to you, but you may not know that he acts as honorary adviser to M.C.A. Carnell lectures in Colonial Administration at Oxford and was in Malaya earlier this year by invitation from Penang M.C.A. to discuss constitutional reform. The meeting here was quite informal and at the suggestion of Purcell and Carnell; but I think it is important that you should be aware, unofficially, of ideas about constitutional reform which are being canvassed in M.C.A. circles. The only thing I have to add to the information contained in the note is that both Purcell and Carnell were warned here that in order not to offend Malay opinion they would have to impress on any Chinese with whom they discussed their suggestions the need for very careful timing. We made it quite clear that our feeling in London was that the present time would be inauspicious for the M.C.A. to put forward any "official programme" based on these ideas.

---

[1] Victor Purcell, MCS 1921–1946, was appointed lecturer in far eastern history, Cambridge, in 1949; Francis Carnell, lecturer in colonial administration at Oxford, was the author of, *inter alia*, 'Malayan citizenship legislation', *International and Comparative Law Quarterly* (Oct 1952).

We shall, of course, welcome any comments which you may care to make for our guidance should there be any further discussions with Purcell.[2]

Enclosure to 272

Dr. Purcell and *Mr. Carnell* called on the 6th March to discuss this subject with *Mr. Paskin* and *Mr. Higham.*

In reply to an enquiry by *Mr. Paskin, Mr. Carnell* confirmed that he had been in touch with *Mrs. Oon*[3] and M.C.A., and they had a general idea of the suggestions he would put forward; he was not, however, in any official relationship with M.C.A. *Dr. Purcell* said that he acted as adviser to M.C.A. It was confirmed that neither *Mr. Carnell* not *Dr. Purcell* were authorised, or did act as representatives of M.C.A. in this country.

Mr. Carnell went on to say that the basis of his idea was to devise some scheme for such a measure of Parliamentary government in Malaya as would act as an adequate dynamic against the Communist ideology. His own view was that Parliamentary Government was the only dynamic of this type in view, and that under the present policy the prospects for development of Parliamentary Government in Malaya were obviously bleak. He went on to touch on the basic factors of the communal problem, and said that his attention has been concentrated on the question how the Chinese could be given greater political power without swamping the Malays. Progress in this direction has been very small to date, and in his view the nature of the Federation is frustrating such progress. It was clear that in the West Coast States (e.g. Selangor where—according to *Mr. Carnell*—only about 24% of the inhabitants are Malays) the Malays would maintain their resistance to the admission of Chinese to citizenship in substantial numbers. He felt that this sort of thing inhibited what would otherwise be a natural development towards unitary Governments in Malaya as a whole; the Malays would be bound to defend their political powers State by State.

In an effort to overcome this difficulty *Mr. Carnell* proposes that the States should be formed into two groups, Northern and Southern. The Northern Group would include Perlis, Kedah, Kelantan, Senangor [sic], Perak, and Trongganu, but Penang would be detached from this group and joined with Singapore. The Southern Group would contain the remaining States together with Malacca. There would be two Regional Governments which would have powers rather similar to those of the present State Governments. According to the best estimate he could make the Northern Group of States would contain a Malaysian [sic] majority of about 490,000 people and the Southern Group about 350,000. He advocated that the boundaries of constituencies for election to the Regional Governments should be drawn (as had proved satisfactory in Ceylon) with due regard to the racial basis. He thought that it would be possible for boundaries to be so drawn that the Malays would not be swamped in the elections. It was also in his view by far the best means of getting the communal factor out of politics at the lower level. The Regions would have

---

[2] Purcell and Carnell left for Malaya in Aug 1952. Perhaps because he had received an incorrect signal from MI5 that Purcell was coming out as 'a paid troublemaker', Templer took an instant dislike to Purcell and the feeling was reciprocated, each man pursuing a personal vendetta against the other.

[3] Mrs B H Oon, a lawyer in Penang, was an unofficial member of the Federal Legislative Council.

Legislative and Executive Councils etcetera and the present States would become something like local authorities. The first stage in the scheme would be to establish Regional Governments, and the second to use the elected bodies of the Regional Governments as Electoral Colleges for Federal Legislative Council. The franchise would be open to anybody born in Malaya.

Mr. Higham enquired whether the natural increase of the Chinese population would not throw the calculation about majorities out in a comparatively short time. Mr. Carnell admitted that there was some doubt in this connection, but Dr. Purcell thought that on a basis of Smith's[4] calculations of populations growth [sic] in Malaya the Malaysian [sic] majority in the two Regions might be safe for ten years or so which was as far as one could look ahead in a matter of this sort. Mr. Carnell made it clear that it would be essential to detach Penang from the Northern Region so as to exclude its large Chinese population.

Dr. Purcell went on to explain his personal position as honorary adviser to M.C.A. He said that at present the leaders of the Party were in a state of some confusion about their political programme, and they very much wanted to reach agreement on this. They were, of course, very short of good leadership and were therefore open to suggestions put forward by anybody in whom they trusted. In his view the Chinese as a whole were strongly opposed to the present political developments at State level. If the M.C.A. could find what they regarded as a just interim solution they would be prepared to fight for it; they realised that such a solution must include safeguards for the Malays, but it must also provide for a very substantial increase in Chinese political power in the country.

In discussion between Mr. Paskin, Dr. Purcell and Mr. Carnell, it was agreed that whatever resulted from further discussions between Mr. Carnell, Dr. Purcell, Mrs. Oon and M.C.A. there should be no reference to the fact that the matter had been discussed in the Colonial Office. Any scheme put forward must be advanced by unofficial leaders, preferably as a result of consultation between Chinese and Malay leaders, but quite independently of any Government agency.

Mr. Higham asked how far the mass of the Chinese were really interested in political development and how far a scheme of this sort would satisfy them. Mr. Purcell claimed that such a scheme might satisfy a substantial body of Chinese opinion, and even if it was only partially successful it would be an advance on the present position. Mr. Carnell agreed and said that Government should do anything possible to get away from the present fragmentary growth of elections with mushroom political parties.

Mr. Higham enquired Mr. Carnell's opinion on the Kuala Lumpur elections; Mr. Carnell thought that they proved once again that communal feeling is the real driving force in Malaya.

Mr. Carnell said that he thought his scheme might ultimately help in the future association between Malaya and Singapore.

Mr. Paskin said that even if a scheme of this sort were thought to be sound, as to which he had doubts, it would obviously take a very long time to work out and get acceptance. It would, in effect, be going back once more for something like a fresh start. Dr. Purcell said that he assumed that the only alternative to such a scheme was

---

[4] T E Smith had entered the MCS in 1940; his *Population growth in Malaya* (Institute of International Affairs) was published in 1952.

to pursue the present policy. In his opinion the Malays regard this as a progressive invasion of their rights, and the Chinese as giving them nothing at all. There was, therefore, no real chance of getting Chinese support in the Emergency. The Government was undoubtedly unpopular with the Chinese community as a whole; this could be judged by many instances, even the Government lottery was heavily undersubscribed while the M.C.A. lottery was over-subscribed. *Dr. Purcell* went on to point out that the Federation Agreement has not even united the Malays behind the Government, and really seems to have gained us very little. Mr. Higham thought that it might be a mistake to initiate a scheme of the sort put forward by *Mr. Carnell* before the Malays could see more prospect of entry on a large scale to the economic life of the country through R.I.D.A. and similar openings. *Dr. Purcell* agreed that anything that could be done to redress the economic balance would have important political consequences, but he pointed out that the scheme could not come forward for a long time in any case and that by then R.I.D.A and similar projects might have made substantial progress.

Mr. Paskin reverted to the question how many of the Chinese in Malaya really care at all about these political developments and whether the so-called "leaders" really carry much weight with the mass of their compatriots. *Dr. Purcell* said that in his view they all cared, in an instinctive sort of way, and once they saw that the way towards real political progress for Chinese community was open they would take a much greater share in the practical work. *Dr. Purcell* said that in his view the Chinese leaders had very considerable influence, admittedly largely as advisers and intermediaries between their people and Government, but he thought they could influence large numbers of their fellow countrymen.

Mr. Carnell returned to his contention that the present State structure inhibits further political progress and *Dr. Purcell* agreed that it was not realistic to expect the Malays to go much further in granting citizenship to the Chinese under the present conditions. *Mr. Higham* made the point that this was not the best moment to run a major risk of antagonizing the Sultans, but *Dr. Purcell* thought that the Sultans were not much use anyhow. In any case the scheme would be Chinese sponsored, and if it evoked an adequate response from both Chinese and Malays the Sultans could hardly blame us. The present structure of the Federation was very open to attack both from above and below, and in his view there was a very substantial body of opinion in Malaya, among all the communities, which would be ready to listen to and probably to support radical proposals for political reorganisation.

Mr. Paskin pointed out that it had taken over two and a half years to work out the present pattern of citizenship; it was admittedly a compromise and the Chinese naturally objected to the provisions under which they had become subjects of rulers before they could become Federal citizens. But progress was being made and the general aim of our policy must be to let all the favourable tendencies to greater co-operation between the comunities work themselves out gradually. The Colonial Office had not accepted the abolition of the Malayan Union and creation of a Federation without misgivings, but we had little alternative in view of the extremely strong advice which came from all those on the spot. It might well be politically impossible at this stage to support another radical change of the structure of the country. But *Dr. Purcell* and *Mr. Carnell* were acting quite independently, constructive ideas were needed in Malaya, and there was nothing to stop their ideas being discussed locally and put forward if they receive adequate support.

Dr. Purcell and *Mr. Carnell* said that they quite understood the position of the Colonial Office and promised to keep us informed from time to time of further developments in their discussions.

273   CO 1022/355, no 1   6 May 1952
[Rural development]: letter from O A Spencer[1] to H T Bourdillon[2] on proposals for a land bank and a development bank

RIDA, for some months past, has been considering the question of providing long-term loans to smallholders for the purchase, development and improvement of their holdings and has come to the conclusion that the only practicable method of doing this on any considerable scale is through a Land Bank. The Authority, however, is of the opinion that neither its resources nor staff are adequate or suitable for this purpose and it will be unsatisfactory to saddle it with the responsibility for making long-term loans of a commercial character in addition to its other functions.

RIDA has therefore recommended to Government that a Land Bank should be established which should work in association with the Authority but would not be part of it. A figure of $25 million has been mentioned as a first estimate of the capital likely to be required to start the Land Bank. It is intended of course to earn revenue from interest on loans and that this should be sufficient to pay interest on the capital advanced to the Bank by Government or borrowed from other sources.

I may mention that the problem of providing credit facilities for smallholders has been under review for some years past. In 1947, the Secretary of State forwarded to Governments a report of the Colonial Economic Advisory Committee, on the subject of the facilities available for the supply of short and long term credit to agriculturists in the Colonies, with the request that Governments should consider existing arrangements in the light of the report. A Committee was set up to consider whether the machinery for agricultural credit in Malaya was adequate and to consider generally the problem of rural indebtedness. The Report of the Committee, the Boyd Report[3], was published in 1948 and although it was pretty widely distributed and commented upon, no tangible results appear to have been produced from the Committee's recommendations.

The 1947 Committee was sceptical concerning the need for or the advisability of lending money to smallholders in the form of long term loans and stressed the necessity for thrift, rather than credit, to be encouraged by the formation of rural co-operative societies. If any assistance was to be given at all, the Committee thought that it should be through the medium of co-operative societies. An exception, however, was made in the case of the replanting of rubber smallholdings, an urgent problem to which the Committee drew attention. This problem, as you know, has now been provided for after much controversy by separate and special legislation and

---

[1] O A Spencer, economic adviser and development commissioner, British Guiana, 1945; served in Malaya as economic secretary, 1950, member for economic affairs, 1951, and minister for economic affairs, 1955–1956; economic adviser and head of the CO's economic section, 1956–1960.
[2] Bourdillon was now head of the CO's Finance Department.
[3] Robert Boyd, MCS 1913–1948, was reconstruction adviser in the Department of Co-operation, Malayan Union and Singapore 1946–1948.

the replanting cess. The Committee also referred to the possibility of the present Planters' Loans Board being replaced by a Land Bank or an Agricultural Co-operative Bank and recommended that Government should assist in the formation of such a Bank with capital subscribed by the public, to provide long term finance for agriculture at low rates of interest. The Planters' Loans Board, incorporated in 1915, with a revolving capital of $4 million provided by Government, was primarily intended to serve large estates, no loans of less than $5,000 being considered. Due apparently to the difficulty of raising local loans, this idea was dropped.

Since then two other ideas have arisen. The first is the question of setting up a *Development Bank* in the Federation. It seems clear to me that for political and other reasons we in this country must increasingly look "inwards" for supply of venture capital both for new enterprises and for the extension of existing ones. The suspicion with which the London capital market regards Malayan securities can be read by a glance at the interest rates which most of them are currently yielding. Even when full allowance is made for the ups and downs to which the rubber and tin industries have historically been subject, it is clear that these market valuations are heavily weighted against Malaya as a field for the investment of private funds. Investors obviously consider us a "bad risk". In the meantime the habit of forming private companies to take over businesses which before the war would have been run as a "kongsi"[4] is growing apace here and I think it likely that in the next ten years or so there will be many opportunities for the employment of capital for new industrial or agricultural undertakings which in easier times might have raised funds in one of the recognised money markets.

All this marries up with the second of the two ideas to which I have referred, which is that this country should not go on spending the entire proceeds of its export duty from tin (which is really in the nature of a royalty) as though it were recurrent revenue of a permanent character. In fact (as we all know) it is really part of the proceeds of an exhausting asset and therefore should strictly be treated—at least to some extent—as a capital fund. This matter was brought up in the Budget debate last year and on behalf of the Treasury I said that we accepted in principle the idea of setting aside part of the proceeds from Tin Export Duty for capital measures. The persons who were fostering this notion did envisage that any money which was so set aside would be invested in gilt-edged securities and that the *interest* therefrom (as opposed to the principal) treated as true Government revenue. This is not my idea at all. I think that the liquid capital obtained by the exploitation of our tin reserves should itself be turned, through some investment medium, into another productive asset of a different kind, e.g. in the form of new agricultural development, plants, factories, etc. Accordingly, it seems to me that this would be a good time and opportunity to set up a Development Bank which would be owned by the Government and financed by part of the proceeds of our tin revenue. Obviously as an initial measure we should have to draw a substantial sum outright from our accumulated surplus balances carried forward from last year.

Although I have said in the previous paragraph that this Development Bank would be a State owned corporation I would add that I would not personally be averse to other commercial banks participating in it. In this way indeed we might obtain two advantages, the first being that of additional capital over and above the moiety

---

[4] *Kongsi* was a Chinese business cooperative.

originally contributed by the Government, and the second that of more skilled management, since if any of the major banks participated in the Development Bank they would surely be willing and anxious to second to it experienced managerial staff solely to get the new organisation off to a sound start. They would also presumably be prepared to use their own branches as agencies for the new bank and this too would be very advantageous.

However the purpose of this letter is to solicit the favour of your views on this subject in general and in particular whether you think the Development Bank and the Land Bank could be inaugurated together as twin enterprises under a common management or perhaps as two departments of one undertaking, or whether you feel they must be absolutely separated ab initio.

The second purpose is to enquire whether you could get anyone for us on secondment from a Bank or similar institution who would come out, study the situation and draw up specific detailed proposals for us. If suitable such a person might well be invited to stay on in a managerial capacity. This is not a firm indent as I have as yet no financial authority to cover such an engagement but I hope the Standing Committee on Finance would vote the necessary funds if a man were available. I should however be grateful for any advice you can offer on this score.[5]

---

[5] See 278.

274   CO 1022/485, no 2   9 May 1952
[Economic development plan]: letter from O A Spencer to J D Higham suggesting a World Bank mission to Malaya. *Enclosure*: memorandum by Spencer, 'Revision of the development plan of the Federation of Malaya' (23 Apr)

I recently brought up the question of the revision of the Development Plan of the Federation of Malaya in Executive Council. I enclose a copy of the Executive Council paper in question. I am anxious to revise the whole plan but there are obvious difficulties to say nothing of the need to concentrate on the emergency and Council advised that the work of revision should be undertaken at a later date when a clearer picture of the needs and prospects of the Federation can be developed. His Excellency concurred on this view. This matter therefore is to be brought up again to Council in six months' time.

I also asked in Council whether Members felt we might explore the possibility of getting the services of a team of experts to undertake a general survey of the Federation's economic potential and in fact revise the Development Plan for us—in close consultation of course with the Members concerned. The Deputy High Commissioner is in favour of this as it might be of political as well as of practical value. He tells me also that Jamaica has been negotiating with the Colonial Office over the past eighteen months for a mission of the International Bank to visit Jamaica. The mission consisting of seven experts in economics, agriculture, engineering and social services was reported to be arriving on 2nd March and will be making "an independent and objective study of the development requirements of Jamaica, particularly in consideration of its growing population." The Deputy High

Commissioner has written to Newton[1] in Jamaica to ask for preliminary impressions on the calibre of the experts and the probable value of their report.

The purpose of this letter is to seek your own views on this tentative proposal for a mission to come to Malaya to do a survey on our economic potential with the object of putting up a revised Plan of Development. You have most probably studied our Draft Development Plan and I imagine you will agree with me that a drastic revision of this "Plan" is needed. But it would help immensely if we could get some detailed expert assistance in reassessing our needs and resources more accurately and in drawing up a proper and comprehensive Plan within the limits of those resources. From the Administrative angle our ordinary staff are too completely absorbed to spare the time to make really detailed plans; while they are often too close to the ground to take a detached view of the problem anyway—which is essential. Politically also such a revision is, I think, most desirable. Even without outside help, we shall have to attempt it somehow although it will put our Departmental staffs to some strain. Whether we need an International Bank team similar to that now in Jamaica or something else I can hardly say and must await your advice, but I am sure we need some outside help. (You will already have seen our Savingram No. 855/52 asking for an F.A.O. Rice Mission to study the rice situation here and to recommend a comprehensive national policy for rice.)

Perhaps you would discuss this in the Office and let us know your views on the practicabilities of this idea.[2]

Enclosure to 274

Council at its meeting on 11th March, 1952, advised that a report should be tabled in the Legislative Council on the progress made in the Development Plan of the Federation of Malaya showing in particular how far it had been slowed down by the Emergency and other factors. Members have already received a memorandum on this subject, requesting that the Heads of Departments in their portfolios should complete by 1st June next certain printed forms giving a detailed account of the financial and physical progress of each scheme or project administered by them

2.   There have been two essays in planning: the *Draft Development Plan* produced between the end of 1949 and mid 1950, and the Federation of Malaya section of the *Columbo Plan* for Co-operative Economic Development in South and South East Asia, produced in September, 1950. The Colombo Plan thus includes not merely the Draft Development Plan but also certain additional items so that it represents the latest attempt by this Government to set down a master plan of development for the six-year period 1950–55. A meeting of the Colombo Plan Consultative Committee was held last month in Karachi to prepare the Annual Report on the Colombo Plan, and the Hon'ble Dato' Onn bin Ja'afar represented the Federation at the Ministers' meeting. The Report of the Consultative Committee will be published on 1st May and will be circulated to Council. It contains a brief section on the progress made in the development plan of the Federation of Malaya.

3.   While a Progress Report, such as that which is now in preparation is necessary to show up the extent to which the original plan has been affected by the Emergency

---

[1] Robert Newton was financial secretary in Jamaica, 1949–1953.   [2] See 275.

etc., it is also important *to revise the Plan as a whole*. The Development Plan of the Federation as contained in the Draft Development Plan (the "Yellow Book") and modified by the Federation section of the Colombo Plan, has not really been satisfactorily recorded in these two documents. The Yellow Book sets out the long term objective of the Federation's development planning in too broad a form on the one hand, while it gives whole lists of detailed projects which are supposed to be undertaken by each Department of Government on the other. An attempt must be made to weave some composed and balanced pattern into this coat of many colours. Moreover, certain of the assumptions on which the Draft Development Plan were based have now been proved wrong. It was assumed, for example, that there would be a gradual and progressive lightening of the Emergency, that the country's financial resources would continue to be about the same and that the prices of its raw materials would tend to fall. With the knowledge and experience available when the Draft Development Plan was prepared, and the limited time available for its preparation, the line taken was undoubtedly the only one possible.

4. The present plan is also too rigid. Planning is a continuous process and what matters most under present uncertain conditions at any given time, whether it be this year or ten years from now, is not to have a huge list of estimated expenditure year by year for ten years ahead on all sorts of schemes, (which figures humanly speaking cannot possibly come true), but to know what the *objectives and priorities* of Government are; what it is already doing to attain them and what it intends to do next.

5. Specifically therefore, what is required is, firstly, *a general statement of the Policy and Objectives of each Department of Government* with particular emphasis on what is aimed at by the end of a specific period which, in the case of the Colombo Plan, is 1957. The *"Policy"* statement should set out clearly the guiding principles and fundamental long term aims of each Department's policy. The statement of *"Objectives"* should next indicate wherever possible in concrete terms, what specific short term practical targets it is proposed to set, say, for the period 1952–57. Thus, for example, Departments associated with social services should endeavour to state their short term objectives as so many school-places, hospital beds or other units of service amenities, per State, or per thousand of population and so forth. Departments concerned with production should consider what national output in terms of tons of rubber, tin, rice, copra etc. should be aimed at in the same period. It will undoubtedly be difficult, and in some cases impossible, for Departments to record what their objectives are in such a precise manner, but if a Development Plan is not to be a mere bag of bones in the form of a collection of disconnected schemes (however worthy these are individually) some flesh must be put on it by making clear to everyone—and not least to the peoples of this country—just what sort of Malaya (expressed in some understandable economic and social terms) it is proposed to develop. In this connection members concerned should endeavour to be sure that the plans and policies of their various Departments fit in with each other where appropriate and that as far as possible the whole "front" is advancing in step so to speak.

6. Next, a specific statement is then required of the schemes, policies and devices by which the "objectives" previously stated are to be attained. For the most part this will consist of a reference to existing schemes, but in some cases it will necessarily involve, on the one hand, proposing entirely new schemes which are not already in

the existing Development Plan, and possibly, on the other, in discarding some old schemes which no longer conform with Government policy.

7. The basic material required for the revision of the Development Plan, to conform to the criteria suggested above, will of course consist of the Progress Report on the various schemes already undertaken or contemplated, which the Heads of Departments are now preparing.

8. If the above suggestions, in connection with the necessity for and the manner by which the Development Plan of the Federation of Malaya should be revised, are accepted, the question arises as to *when* this revision should be undertaken. A picture of what this Government wants to do in the various fields of social and economic development of the country, and of the resources available with which to do it, is undoubtedly much clearer today than it was in the middle of 1950 when the Draft Development Plan was prepared. It is, however, probable that a yet clearer picture will have developed in six months' time. By then, for example, the future of rubber may be assessed more accurately; it may by then be possible to know whether the acute building problems with which the Government is faced are likely to be solved within a reasonable period of time; there may be a better indication of this country's prospects of importing and producing more rice; there should also by then be a better idea of what the implementation of the resettlement policy will cost; it may be possible to gauge more accurately the price at which R.I.D.A and the Housing Trust will operate; and by then it may be possible to determine a new pattern for the educational and medical and health services of this country. Further, at the present time, it is not considered desirable to involve the administration in any work that can be avoided. The P.W.D. and many other Departments are fully occupied on Emergency work and it is certainly undesirable to distract their effort from this vital work. Moreover, and perhaps the most crucial point of all, the course of the Emergency is at present by no means clear and few Departments are in a position to know as yet what their capacity for developmental work will be in the next few years. The P.W.D. for example, is unable to forecast with any degree of accuracy what Emergency and defence demands would be made on them, and similarly the Forest and Geological Survey Departments are unable to determine when their officers will be able to venture into the jungle for the performance of their normal duties.

9. For these reasons there is the danger that a revision of the Development Plan of the Federation of Malaya undertaken too soon, might produce another plan which would exist on paper only. On the other hand, it is important to have a balanced and revised plan "on the ice" at an early date so that full advantage may be taken of any lightening of the Emergency which enables more normal Development work to be tackled.

10. To summarise: since the middle of 1950, when the Draft Development Plan was prepared, improved knowledge and experience has been available on the policies and objectives of Government in regard to development planning. It has become necessary therefore to revise the Development Plan of the Federation of Malaya. It is proposed that this revision be undertaken to conform with certain accepted criteria. It is suggested also that six months hence would be the most appropriate time for this work to be started.

11. The attention of Council is drawn to these proposals which are submitted for information and advice.

275 CO 1022/485, no 3 26 May 1952
[Economic development plan]: letter (reply) from J D Higham to O A Spencer

We are not much attracted by the idea in your letter of the 9th May[1] that an International Bank (or other) Mission might be induced to visit Malaya to advise you about the revision of your Development Plan. It is, of course, our policy to encourage interest by the Bank in Colonial development and to induce them to send teams to any part of the Commonwealth in which the possibility of Bank investment may arise. But we do not regard such visits as being a substitute for local planning by Colonial Governments, nor indeed as a suitable method of providing basic data for such planning. It is rather the other way round; the Bank is normally invited to come in when local plans are complete and the investment "gap" is more or less clearly established.

There is unanimous agreement here that, although outside advice may help, the job of drawing up a comprehensive development plan is one which can only satisfactorily be done by people actually engaged in development work on the spot with an intimate knowledge of local conditions; and of course development must depend on the basic economic policies of Government. The case of Jamaica, mentioned by you, affords no real parallel with what you have apparently in mind. There the Development Plan had already been carefully revised—this, indeed, was an essential preliminary to the visit of the Mission—and a big factor in deciding the Governor and the Colonial Office to ask for a visit was that unofficial opinion might more readily be brought to face certain unpalatable facts of economic life if these facts were stated by an independent authority.

We fully appreciate that your staff may already be stretched to the limit, but, as I have said, we really do feel convinced that if a revision of the Development Plan is to be made, it must be done locally. What we would suggest is that you should try to get the services of Freddy Benham[2] for a month or two. While he might not be able to help much with detailed planning, he would in our opinion be well qualified to have a look at the present validity of the basic principles upon which your present planning is founded. If his recommendations were adopted by Government we feel that the filling in of the outlines must be left to the Government Departments which would have to execute the plans.

We do not, however, rule out the desirability of getting an International Bank team to go out to Malaya to look at your Development Plan when it has been revised (and, of course, to look round for specific projects in which they might be willing to assist). If you think that this would help at any stage, we should be only too ready to pursue the idea.

---

[1] See 274.   [2] Economic adviser to the commissioner-general, 1947–1955.

276 CO 1022/61, no 15   10 June 1952

[Closer association of British territories]: inward savingram no 73 from Mr M J MacDonald to the CO. *Minutes* by J D Higham and Sir T Lloyd

My Savingram no. 49 and its predecessors about closer association between the Federation and Singapore.

2. I refrained from sending this further Savingram until the Minutes of the Meeting between the Members of the various local Commonwealth Parliamentary Association branches and potential branches held on April 23rd were circulated. They have recently appeared and I attach a copy in case you have not seen them.[1]

3. It was encouraging that the two Borneo territories as well as the Federation accepted Singapore's invitation to send eight members to Mr. Nicoll's[2] Installation and to the meeting. As the Minutes report, there was wide agreement that (a) Members of the Malayan and Bornean branches of the Commonwealth Parliamentary Association should meet from time to time; (b) a central organisation with a central office could with advantage be established in Singapore; and (c) an approach should be made to the headquarters of the Commonwealth Parliamentary Association in London to see whether the branches here could form a Regional Organisation.

4. In addition to the business meeting in the afternoon, a formal dinner party was held in the evening and was attended by Mr. Nicoll and myself as well as by the Members of the Singapore Legislative Council and the visiting Legislative Councillors from the Federation and Borneo. There was much favourable discussion at it of the project for periodic meetings. We shall now therefore consider plans for the next meeting.

5. A short while ago the local newspapers reported a statement by Sir Franklin Gimson in Yorkshire to the effect that Singapore and the Federation should be merged. Since then a number of prominent personalities in Singapore and the Federation have publicly expressed their agreement with this. Amongst others C.C. Tan[3] has done so and has suggested that there should ultimately be one self-governing unit in the Commonwealth consisting of Singapore, the Federation and the Territories of British Borneo, though he stated that closer association between Singapore and the Federation should wait until various rather formidable difficulties have been overcome. It is noticeable that the favourable commentators in Singapore and the Federation are all Chinese, Indians and other non-Malays. The crux of the decision will probably lie finally with the Malays of the Federation, most of whom will undoubtedly be extremely cautious in their approach to the question of closer association. Nevertheless, opinion amongst them is moving. It is generally known that Dato Onn favours ultimate closer association not only between the Federation and Singapore but also with the Borneo territories, and he hinted at this in a speech which he made at an I.M.P. gathering in Penang two or three weeks ago. More presently representative Malay opinion will not easily be so forthcoming. It has been persuaded to make some valuable concessions to the non-Malays recently on such

---

[1] Not printed but see 267.
[2] John F Nicoll, colonial secretary of Hong Kong, 1949–1952, and governor of Singapore, 1952–1955.
[3] See 267, note 2.

questions as citizenship, land holding for squatters, admission of Chinese to Government Service, etc.; and we must be careful not to test it too hardly all at once.

6. The recent expressions of opinion by C.C. Tan and others on closer association are the result of our private and informal talks with them during recent months. I do not propose to make any public statement on the matter in spite of urgings by the Press, because it is best at this stage that the public initiative should be left with the Asian leaders. In a recent off-the-record discussion with about twenty leading British, Asian and American journalists I said frankly that our long-term aim in British South-East Asia is the creation of a self-governing dominion of all these territories within the Commonwealth. The journalists and I discussed this at length and they all seemed to be in agreement with the proposal. I shall keep judicious contact with them on this subject, and hope that the newspapers will give helpful support to the project when that becomes timely.

7. As I say, the main difficulty will almost certainly come from the Malays in the Federation, although the Chinese in Singapore may also prove difficult when the time comes to consider the conditions of association between these two territories. I do not, repeat not, think that we can rush the matter. We shall make surer progress if we employ the tactics of gradualism, and the Commonwealth Parliamentary Association will be an extremely useful instrument for aiding our purpose.

Minutes on 276

1. One of the main "Colonial" reasons for keeping the office of Commissioner-General in being, and in particular for asking the present holder to stay, has been Mr. MacDonald's peculiar qualifications for promoting closer association of all the territories in South-East Asia. The interests of the territories are in many cases so difficult to reconcile that great qualities of diplomacy will be required if progress is to be made, and Mr. MacDonald's influence with the Unofficial Leaders and his charm and address at the conference table will be difficult to replace. At least one of the Governors (Sir R. Hone) has said recently that if Mr. MacDonald goes progress towards a Dominion of South-East Asia will be retarded.

2. On the other hand it is encouraging to see that the Commonwealth Parliamentary Associations of the four territories have now decided to hold periodic meetings in the four capitals with Singapore as a centre, and it may be that now that "the ice has been broken" the presence of a cementing personality will not be so badly needed. Indeed, there may be some advantage in the Chair at these discussions being taken by different persons (i.e. the Governor or High Commissioner of the host territory). I do not think it could now be said that the retention of a Commissioner-General is *vital* to the future of "closer association".

3. The attitude of the Unofficials, both in the Federation and, more particularly, in Singapore, shown in (15), is a distinct advance on earlier form.

J.D.H.
23.6.52

Secretary of state
You should, I think, see Mr. MacDonald's saving telegram at No. 15, paragraph 5 of which gives broadly the same picture as General Templer gave us, so far as the

Federation is concerned, of local feeling on the question of closer political association between Singapore and the Federation. The one substantial difference between the two is that whereas Mr. MacDonald feels that opinion among Malays is moving in favour of closer association, General Templer doubted whether there had been any such progress during his time in the peninsula.

No exception could I think be taken, even by the Commonwealth Relations Office, to Mr. MacDonald's off the record remark reported . . . in paragraph 6 of No. 15.

Submitted for information.

T.I.K.L.
25.6.52

277 CO 1022/81, no 24   27 July 1952

[Pace of constitutional advance and talks with Onn]: inward telegram 909 from Sir G Templer to Mr Lyttelton. Minutes by T C Jerrom,[1] J D Higham and Sir T Lloyd

The comments which you made about self-government in the course of the debate in the House on 17th July[2] have, naturally, been the subject of considerable public and press comment here. Generally, this has been in support of what you said, although Tunku Abdul Rahman has been severely critical and Malay press has pooh-poohed the suggestion that racial strife would at once ensue if self-government was granted immediately. Dato Onn gave support in public to your views, but made suggestion that pace of preparations for self-government should be accelerated. Thuraisingham, in public comment on your speech, suggested setting up of a Consultative Committee in Malaya of representatives of all interests "to consider various problems which arise out of Her Majesty's Government's declared policy to progress towards independence in Malaya". Subsequently, he sent a letter to Onn suggesting that the latter should put this suggestion to you during the course of his present stay in London. It is, therefore, possible that Onn will seek an interview with you for discussion of this proposal.

2. In his letter to Onn, Thuraisingham suggested that proposed Committee should be under an Asian chairman and might consider *inter alia* the following points:—

(1) Whether a definite date should now be set for independence.
(2) The position of Malays *vis à vis* the other races in an independent Malaya.
(3) Whether the aim should be independence within the Commonwealth or outside it.
(4) The form of Government to be aimed at.
(5) The position of Rulers when independence is achieved.

He stated that the object of his suggestion is to focus attention on the reality of the

---

[1] See 270, note 1.
[2] *H of C Debs*, vol 503, cols 2378–2396, 17 July 1952. Lyttelton stressed that self-government would depend on the achievement of stability in Malaya.

goal, to stop speculation, and to prepare a plan of progress towards independence which could form the object of public study both here and in the United Kingdom.

3.   I need hardly say that I give no support to this proposal, and consider that Onn and Thuraisingham should be ridden off it, if they attempt to pursue it. The divergence of energy and thought at this time to what could only be largely theoretical discussions about future constitutional changes would inevitably detract from the emergency effort, and this detraction would not be counterbalanced by any resulting expansion of anti Communist feeling. On the contrary, such discussion is more likely to arouse ill feeling between the Rulers, the Malays, the Chinese and others, and would open gaps in our ranks which the Communists would not be slow to exploit. Moreover, my advisers and I are of the opinion that there is little real demand for discussions on independence from the people of Malaya as a whole. This opinion would seem to be supported by recent public reaction to your recent comment in the House. I do not think, therefore, that in putting forward his suggestion, Thuraisingham can claim to speak for any strong body of opinion, and I doubt whether, in the absence of any public backing, either he or Onn will wish to press it. Indeed, it may well be that Onn will not put it forward in discussions with you.

4.   Should he do so, however, I suggest that the following points might be made:—

(i)   Our first task is to end the emergency as soon as possible, and any steps which would militate against the measures which we are taking to achieve this purpose obviously cannot be countenanced. One of the most important of these measures is the uniting of all races and classes in a common effort by the creation of a greater sence [sic] of Malayan loyalty and unity. The proposed Committee would obviously have to be representative of all communities and, until there is that greater sense of loyalty and unity, discussion in such a Committee would be more likely to accentuate the conflict of the present viewpoints than reconcile them. The present public controversy over the Immigration Bill is evidence of this. The result, therefore, of setting up a Committee, might well be

(a) seriously to aggravate racial feelings, particularly between Malays and Chinese;

(b) to weaken support which is now being given whole-heartedly by the Rulers to the Government of the Federation in fighting the emergency; the Rulers might well feel that the Committee was a threat to their constitutional position, and their instinctive dislike of Chinese and distrust of Chinese ambitions may harden into a greater reluctance to admit Chinese to full citizenship; their attitude would evitably affect the loyalty of Malays as a whole, and you well know to what extent we are dependent on Malays for both Army and Police;

(c) to have an unsettling effect on Europeans of all classes; all, including Government Servants, would be concerned about their future prospects and their work would be adversely affected accordingly; and

(d) to divert the attention of all communities from emergency effort towards jockeying for position in future set up.

(ii)   the country lacks political leader with real political experience and, with the possible exception of M.C.A., there is no properly organised responsible political party with a coherent political programme. The first step necessary to political advancement, and so to independence, is political education; this I believe can best be begun by experience in local politics. That is to say at village, town, and State level. It is true that, so far, little has been achieved in this direction, but I propose to bring presure on the States and Settlements to take early action in this direction. Local Government is within Dato Onn's portfolio and he himself can therefore do much by pressing on with the implementation of recently enacted Local Councils Law and by securing an early overhaul of Town Board Legislation and organisation. The political parties which will emerge from this more active political life, will themselves largely determine to [sic] time of independence, and they would hardly feel bound by proposals put forward at this stage by any committee.

5. I propose to have a talk wth Thuraisingham on these matters and try to find out what is really at the back of his mind. I suspect it is his political ego. I shall wait before seeing him until I learn result of your interview, if any, with Dato Onn.

Minutes on 277

Mr. Higham
I have spoken to Mr. MacKintosh[3] who will show the Secretary of State a copy of the telegram at 24 this evening.

It is I suppose unnecessary to comment on the details of Thuraisingham's proposals. The important point is that they show an utter lack of understanding of the realities of political evolution in Malaya. From this and other recent indications it does appear that there is some danger that Thuraisingham may adopt an irresponsible attitude.

As you know my own feeling is that crux lies in the last sub-paragraph of paragraph 4 of the telegram, and particularly in the planning of State or Settlement elections. It is not clear exactly what X of the telegram implies,[4] but you will remember that when he was in this country last month General Templer took the view that nothing should be done to expedite State elections until considerable progress had been made at municipal and village level. He was apparently doing all that he could to persuade the local political leaders to take an active part in these elections, and felt that by this means responsible political parties might be developed.

But it is arguable that it is useless to expect political leaders in a country like Malaya to devote their efforts to elections at these lower levels, if only because they could not rally permanent support among the people for clearly defined and separate policies in local government. Can reasonably coherent and solid political parties develop of themselves without being directly harnessed to representative institutions at least at the State or Settlement level?

T.C.J.
28.7.52

---

[3] Angus MacKintosh was at this time principal private secretary to the secretary of state.
[4] This refers to 'early action in this direction' in para 4 (ii) of Templer's telegram.

Mr. Paskin

No meeting between the Secretary of State and Dato Onn has yet been arranged, though I hope that it may be possible to fix something. I have put Dato Onn in direct touch with Mr. MacKintosh.

I agree with Mr. Jerrom throughout, particularly at X.[5] While, from a purely practical point of view, I am sure that Malayan politicians would do well to keep their noses to the grindstone of local administration, I very much doubt whether they will be content with this for long and I think it would be wise to allow them somewhat wider scope by encouraging elections to State Councils. The State Councils themselves are such unsatisfactory organs of Government that I should have thought there would be some practical advantage in introducing elections to them, since this might mean a salutary change of personnel and might stimulate more local interest in the proceedings of these Councils. I feel, too, that elections to State Councils might absorb the energies and blunt the wider aspirations of some politicians who may, if they're not given an outlet in this way, become more clamorous about wider issues of national independence etc.

Dato Thuraisingham may feel that the proposals in 24 can be regarded as an extension of the work of the Communities Liaison Committee of which of course he was chairman.[6] No doubt he envisages himself as chairman of the Committee he now proposes, to study the problems of independence. The Communities Liaison Committee however, although an appropriate body to discuss community relationships would be quite the wrong forum for the discussion of high political matters such as the date for independence. In any case the C.L.C. was an unofficial body and I take it that what is now proposed is a Government sponsored committee of Asian unofficials.

If the matter is raised by Dato Onn the Secretary of State might take the general line (in order not to be so completely negative as is suggested in paragraph 4 of 24) that most of these topics are in the first place matters for discussion between political leaders, that in particular he welcomes any discussions between the communities on the future relationships of those communities and their place in the future Malayan State, but that he thinks the time has not come when it would be appropriate for a Government sponsored committee with such specific terms of reference to be set up.[7]

                                                                                 J.D.H.
                                                                                 30.7.52

Secretary of State

I do not regard the High Commissioner's telegram as being too negative. General Templer's first point, i.e. the one made in paragraph 4 (i) of No. 24, seems to me to be an extremely good one and the most should, I suggest, be made of it in any talk with Dato Onn.

I am not so happy about paragraph 4(ii) of the High Commissioner's telegram. That line of argument seems to me unlikely to impress Dato Onn.

If Dato Onn does have a talk with you, you may wish the Department or Mr.

---

[5] This refers to the last paragraph of Jerrom's minute
[6] See 171, note 1, and 195, sections 4 & 5.
[7] Paskin noted (30 July): 'I agree'.

MacKintosh to be present, and to make some sort of note, as the High Commissioner proposes (see paragraph 5 of No. 24) to await the result of your talk, if any, with Dato Onn before himself taking up these matters on Dato's return to Malaya.[8]

T.I.K.L.

30.7.52

---

[8] Following a half-hour talk with Onn on 7 Aug, Lyttelton recorded that Onn 'suggested a Consultative Committee to determine what he was pleased to call a flexible blue print for future self-government or independence. He mentioned that there should be no definite date and ten or fifteen years was one of his phrases. I was non-committal and chilly upon this and said we must concentrate on State Elections as next step. I should judge that this could satisfy him since he did not press Committee again'. On 14 Aug Lyttelton had a further three quarters of an hour with Onn who this time did not raise the question of a consultative committee but urged the appointment of more Malays to the civil service. He struck Lyttelton as 'a motherless politician who is in search of a grievance and finds a suitable one elusive' (CO 1022/81, nos 28 and 29).

278   CO 1022/355, no 3   14 Aug 1952
[Rural development]: letter (reply) from R J Vile[1] to O A Spencer

We are very conscious of a sad delay in replying to your letter to Bourdillon of 6th May about the proposals for a Land Bank and a Development Bank in the Federation of Malaya.[2] We were hoping for an opportunity of discussing it with you during your present visit, but I gather that your time in [sic] likely to be fully taken up by the rubber talks; and in any case Bourdillon and Higham have now gone away on leave. In the circumstances it might be best if I put down on paper our first reactions.

Perhaps the first thing I ought to say is that we entirely agree with your idea that such revenues as the proceeds of export duty on tin should not be entirely regarded as recurrent revenue of a permanent character. We further agree with your view that the right way of using these revenues for capital purposes is not to invest them in gilt-edged securities but to employ them in new development in the Federation. We had very much the same idea when we suggested to Godsall,[3] in our discussions with him at the beginning of the year, the creation of a Development Fund into which surplus revenues from "impermanent sources" could in future be paid. I think Godsall liked the idea at the time, and it was subsequently incorporated in an official despatch; but of course the subsequent fall in rubber prices may have made the rapid accumulation of such a fund a much more remote possibility than we then hoped.

This conclusion does not seem, however, to lead inevitably to the further conclusion that the right thing to do is to set up a Development Bank on the lines you have in mind. I may have misunderstood your fifth paragraph, but it rather appears that there is quite a lot of money in the Federation seeking local investment. If this is so, then at first sight that would appear rather to weaken in your case one of the main arguments in favour of government participation in industrial development—namely, the lack of private capital which is ready to come forward for

---

[1] Principal in the CO.   [2] See 273.

[3] W D Godsall was financial secretary of the Malayan Union, 1946–1948, and of the Federation of Malaya, 1948–1953.

that purpose. Be that as it may, we do feel that it ought to be pretty clearly established, before a Colonial Government goes in for a development of this kind, that the possibilities of industrial development are there, that private capital on a sufficient scale is not available, and that if capital were to be found industrial development would not still be frustrated for other reasons. If, on the other hand, it is reasonably established that these conditions are present, then it is our view that government participation in industrial development may have a lot to be said for it—provided, of course, that it is undertaken in such a way that it is free from political influence and really does help the industries which need help. Perhaps you will let us hear again when you have thought further about the Development Bank idea. We may then be able to give you some helpful guidance from our knowledge and experience of other territories (I expect, incidentally, that MacGillivray will have told you all about the proposals for an Industrial Development Corporation in Jamaica), but until your ideas have moved rather further forward we hesitate to give you a lot of material which may be irrelevant.

Now for the Land Bank. Here again, I expect MacGillivray will have told you about the Jamaican proposals for an Agricultural Development Corporation. We are definitely inclined to think that the Land Bank, if established, should be separate from the Development Bank. It is clear from the first paragraph of your letter that you are thinking of long term loans for agricultural purposes and not of short-term credit for small holders (a need which, in our view, can best be met through properly organised credit societies, as is being done successfully in Perlis). On the subject of the Land Bank, perhaps the most helpful suggestion which I can pass on to you at this stage, from Surridge,[4] is that you should get from the Agricultural Credit Department of the Reserve Bank of India (in Bombay) its recent bulletin on Land Mortgage Banks. We would have sent you a copy ourselves, but I am afraid we only have one in the whole office. If you feel inclined to follow the Indian pattern, a party from Malaya might perhaps be sent later on to Madras to study the Indian system on the spot. It is very possible that Madras would be willing to train people from Malaya so that they could go back and run a Land Mortgage Bank in the Federation, but I am afraid it is very unlikely that anybody suitable could be found in the U.K. for this purpose.

I am sorry that we cannot be more constructive. It may be easier for us to be helpful when your ideas are a little more advanced. That is not to say, of course, that we did not welcome your letter. We were very glad indeed that you consulted us, and we shall be equally glad to be kept in touch with developments. Meanwhile, I hope I have given you something to go on, however slight.

---

[4] B J Surridge was adviser on co-operatives to the secretary of state for the colonies, 1947–1964.

279 CO 1022/183, no 16   Oct 1952

[UMNO affairs]: report by the Pan Malayan Review of Intelligence 10/52 on UMNO's general assembly, 12–15 Sept, and central executive committee, 9 Oct   [Extract]

[UMNO appeared to be adopting an increasingly militant stand but intelligence reports suggested that Tunku Abdul Rahman's leadership was not secure. While UMNO's youth wing urged him to espouse a more radical course, moderates were threatening to withdraw from the party and join up with Dato Onn. On the first day of UMNO's general assembly, Templer confided in Lyttelton that he and MacGillivray had had secret talks with Nik Kamil, Raja Uda and Dato Mahmud about the possibility of launching a new political party open to all federal citizens of all communities, and that 'Tengku Abdul Rahman would be jockeyed out of it' (CO 1022/298, no 280.]

. . . A. *Malay and Indonesian affairs*

U.M.N.O. general assembly

14. The United Malay National Organisation held its seventh assembly at Butterworth, Province Wellesley, from 12th to 15th September, 1952.

15. The first day was given up to the 4th annual general meeting of the U.M.N.O. Youth League, which was presided over by Dato ABDUL RAZAK, the U.M.N.O. [Deputy] President.

16. In declaring the meeting open, Tengku ABDUL RAHMAN said that there was a time when Government had contemplated proscribing the League, and that had this come to pass they would all have shared the same fate. He reminded members that it was the Youth League which had changed the U.M.N.O. slogan from "Hidop Malaya" [sic] to "Merdeka",[1] and it was also this League which had suggested that an interim Government for Malaya be proclaimed. He commented however that, on the whole, the Organisation was not strong enough to realise their aspirations at the present time, and in conclusion exhorted members of the Youth League to work wholeheartedly within the U.M.N.O. Constitution so that the independence of Malaya, which they cherished, could be achieved within the shortest possible time. Che' SARDON ZUBIR, the leader of the League, then delivered a short and inspiring speech.

17. In course of discussion the following motions were adopted:—

(a) U.M.N.O. should ask the Federation Government to decrease the number of British Officers in the Police Force, and fill their places with Malays.
(b) U.M.N.O. should ask the Federation Government to build hostels at suitable places for children of members of the Federation Police and the Malay Regiment serving in the Jungle.
(c) Members of the Special Constabulary and the Home Guard should be equipped with up-to-date weapons.
(d) U.M.N.O. should hold a lottery on a large scale as soon as possible.
(e) U.M.N.O. should prepare a "blue print" for the interim Government of Malaya.
(f) U.M.N.O. should enforce "Party Discipline" amongst its members.

18. In the election of office-bearers for 1952/53, Che' SARDON ZUBIR, Haji

---

[1] *Hidup Melayu* means 'long live the Malays'. *Merdeka* means 'independence'.

AHMAD bin Haji ABDULLAH[2] and Dato ABDUL RAZAK became President, Vice-President and Chairman respectively.

19. The second day was taken up by the Women's section of U.M.N.O. This meeting was declared open by the wife of the RAJA of Perlis. Hajah ZAIN binti SULEIMAN, the President, then spoke. In her address, she emphasised the need for the U.M.N.O. Women's League to stand on its own legs instead of being dependent on the parent body. It was time, she thought, that the League worked independently. She exhorted the members to work more vigorously for the attainment of the independence of Malaya. A resolution that U.M.N.O. should be asked to establish the U.M.N.O. Young Women's League, Malaya (Perikatan Wanita U.M.N.O., Malaya) was then adopted. Hajan ZAIN was re-elected President.

20. The third and fourth days saw the U.M.N.O. general assembly proper. It was declared open by His Highness the Sultan of Perak who, in a brief speech, stated that they should all co-operate with the U.M.N.O. and make it a more progressive national organisation. He hoped that they would be benefitted [sic] by their deliberations and prayed that their toil and labour would pay them handsome dividends. A message from the Sultan of Pahang was then read.

21. When U.M.N.O. commenced deliberations later in the day, Tengku ABDUL RAHMAN gave a lengthy presidential speech. He said he was glad that there was an increase in membership and that additional branches of the organisation had been formed in various parts of the country. He mentioned that certain quarters did not like U.M.N.O. and cited the rumour of the intended banning of the Youth League. The United Malay National Organisation was made up of the youths', women's and men's sections and if they were to be separated the parent body would die. He did not subscribe to the belief that Government would ban the Youth League but feared that some members were disloyal to U.M.N.O. He was convinced that the Malays were keen to be members but held back because they did not understand the objects of U.M.N.O. He urged the Committee members to keep in constant touch with the people in their respective States and Settlements. He touched on his apprehensions over finance and appealed for contributions. He then spoke about the Malay detainees,[3] their pitiable condition and the establishment of the Detainees and Families Welfare Committee which he hoped would be able to do a great deal for them. When he spoke about the creation of an independent and free Malaya, he said that this was indeed a difficult problem. Independence could not be achieved with ease; the Malays must work hard, energetically and wholeheartedly for it. He had frequently been asked why he had not announced a "blue print" for the interim Government of Malaya, and to this question he was proud to reply that the programme was complete, but that there were several conditions which must first be fulfilled before he would publicly announce it. He was happy at the U.M.N.O./M.C.A. friendship and was looking forward to more substantial help from the association. He mentioned his surprise at Mr. Lyttelton's statement in Parliament last July that if Malaya were given independence now there would be chaos within a few months[4] and referred to his comment on it at the time. He had been greatly shocked by the visit of

---

[2] Hj Ahmad bin Hj Abdullah was vice-president of UMNO Youth, 1952–1953.

[3] Malay detainees included radicals such as Ishak bin Hj Mohamed who had been arrested at the start of the emergency. In Dec 1951 1,753 Malays had been held in detention, see 257, appendix XI.

[4] See 277, note 2.

Dr. Purcell to this country[5] because he felt that if the Chinese thought that they had been wronged they were at liberty to discuss the matter with the Malays; there was no reason to ventilate their grievances through a third party. Referring to important and high appointments in this country, including the M.C.S., he urged that the matter should be considered by the Rulers.

22.   The business of the meeting then commenced with Haji MOHAMED NOH bin OMAR[6] in the chair. It was resolved that U.M.N.O.:—

(a) should draft as soon as possible a "blueprint" for the interim Government of Malaya;

(b) viewed with regret the Press reports that Dr. Purcell had been asked to investigate the position of the Chinese in this country without investigating that of the other communities. It considered that any report on one community could only place the other communities in an unfavourable light in the eyes of the world and might be the cause of conflict between the communities;

(c) at this meeting protested against the proposal of the Federation Government to open the Malayan Civil Service as widely as possible to non-Malays;

(d) should establish a young women's league to be known as the Perikatan Wanita U.M.N.O.—Malaya;

(e) should hold a welfare lottery on a large scale early;

(f) should urge the Federation and Singapore Governments to bring the Malay detainees to trial as soon as possible.

(g) should instruct State branches to hold fun-fairs, etc., for the purpose of collecting money for the erection of the U.M.N.O. Headquarters;

(h) agreed that the Rulers, through the Keeper of the Rulers' Seal, should consult U.M.N.O. in matters pertaining to the Federal Agreement before any decision was taken with the Federation Government;

(i) should urge the authorities to establish an Islamic College;

(j) should send U.M.N.O. youth delegations, from time to time, to various countries to observe the activities of the youth movements in those countries.

23.   In the election of office bearers for 1952/53, Tengku ABDUL RAHMAN, Dato ABDUL RAZAK and C.M. YUSUF[7] became President, Deputy President and Vice President respectively.

24.   In an adjournment speech Che' RAMLI bin Haji TAHIR[8] of Kuala Lumpur drew attention to the fact that the Federal Councillors nominated by U.M.N.O., had failed to bring up for discussion any decisions made at their deliberations in the Federal Council. He felt that they were making use of U.M.N.O. as a stepping stone and suggested that they should be ousted from office and replaced by those who had the interests of U.M.N.O. at heart. At the close of the meeting it was resolved that U.M.N.O. should enforce "Party Discipline" amongst its members.

---

[5] See 272.

[6] Hj Mohamed Noh bin Omar, member of Johore state council and executive council since 1948; nominated member of the federal legislative council, 1952–1957; permanent chairman of UMNO's general assembly, 1952–1957.

[7] C M Yusuf, member of Perak's state council and executive council since 1948; member of the federal legislative council; founder-member of UMNO.

[8] Mohd. Ramli bin Hj Tahir had been a journalist on *Majlis* and the first secretary of the Selangor Malay Association, founded in 1938.

U.M.N.O. central executive committee

25. The Central Executive Committee held a meeting in Kuala Lumpur on 9th October 1952. In the course of discussions it was agreed:—

(a) To form an U.M.N.O. Political Committee one of whose functions would be to promote closer liaison between U.M.N.O. and the M.C.A. and subsequently with other political organisations in the Federation. Also agreed upon was the proposed round-table conference with the M.C.A.[9]

(b) To take steps in implementing the resolutions passed at the Seventh U.M.N.O. General Assembly held recently at Butterworth.

(c) To appoint a 7-man Finance Committee one of whose duties would be to go into the question of running an U.M.N.O. Welfare lottery. Included in the Committee was MOHAMED SOPIEE bin Sheikh IBRAHIM,[10] an U.M.N.O. non-member.

(d) That the Central Executive Committee should meet before, instead of after, a meeting of the Federal Legislative Council as was done in the past.

(e) To enforce Party Discipline on all officials and members.

(f) To approach the Malay Rulers to allocate a certain quota of M.C.S. appointments to the Malays and to accept other Asians outside this quota.

26. In conclusion the meeting welcomed the proposal of Tengku ABDUL RAHMAN to attend the Asian Conference for World Federation in Hiroshima on 3rd November 1952.

---

[9] It was eventually agreed that the Tunku should invite *all* political parties to a round-table conference to consider the question of independence.

[10] Mohamed Sopiee bin Sheikh Ibrahim was chairman of the Pan-Malayan Labour Party.

280 CO 1022/298, no 30   18 Oct 1952

[Elections]: letter from D C MacGillivray to J D Higham on current plans. *Minutes* by A S Gann, T C Jerrom and J D Higham

I did see the article in the "New Statesman and Nation" of the 13th September headed "The Brakes are on in Malaya" to which you have referred in your leter SEA.213/290/01 of the 23rd September. I agree with you that it is an unbalanced article; it gives an entirely wrong impression of present policy. It is sheer nonsense to suggest that "The current political drift—with the Emergency as a convenient pretext—is back towards the paternalistic forms of indirect rule used during the 19th Century." The writer has deliberately ignored the passage in the High Commissioner's very first address to the Legislative Council on 19th March this year[1] which I quote below for ease of reference:—

> "I am, of course, aware of the responsibility placed on all of us in regard to the election of members to the several legislatures by the penultimate sentence in the Preamble to the Federation Agreement, and we should not put out of mind the arrangements which it will be necessary to make to give effect to

---

[1] See 270.

this purpose as soon as circumstances and local conditions will permit; there may also be a case meantime for securing a more territorially representative distribution of the membership of these legislatures. But I am a firm believer in first things first. Or, to put it another way, that it is politically unsound and structurally impossible to put the roof on a building until the foundations of the house are well and truly laid and until the uprights, or anyway the corner posts are in position and firmly fixed. I believe it right to ensure that truly responsible local government at the rural community and Municipal Council levels is firmly established and as quickly as possible. Not for one moment would I suggest that this should be postponed in any way at all because the so-called Emergency is upon us. On the contrary, it is all the more necessary—because of the Emergency—to press on with this measure. I firmly believe, from the bottom of my heart, in the principle of responsible local government by local people. I will do all in my power to foster this and the quicker we can start on it the better. That is the firm foundation on which political progress must be based. If it is not based on this principle what is the future?

It was once related of a wise man who built his house upon a rock that the rain descended, and the floods came, and the winds blew and beat upon that house; and it fell not; for it was founded upon a rock. It was also related of the foolish man who built his house upon the sand, that the rain descended; and the floods came; and the winds blew and beat upon that house; and it fell and great was the fall of it."

The Secretary of State has recently written to the High Commissioner to say that if he should come under fire in this matter of elections he would propose to say that the High Commissioner hopes to have Municipal Councils elected in the twenty-three major towns by 1st July, 1953, and that the State and Settlement elected Councils will follow as quickly as arrangements can be made. To this the High Commissioner has replied suggesting a rather less definite line. The wording he has proposed is as follows:—

"We hope to have Municipal Councils elected in some twenty of the major towns by the middle of next year. We also hope that at least some of the States/Settlements will follow soon afterwards with their own elections."

In any statement which the Secretary of State makes I suggest it would be well worth while stressing the passage in July last of the Local Councils Ordinance, an entirely new piece of legislation which did not form part of the previous "phased programme" to which Derrick Sington refers in the "New Statesman" article and which he declares has now been abandoned. This is legislation which can be claimed to be a distinct and definite advance on the previous programme in that it introduces the principle of responsible local government at the small community level and establishes widespread training grounds, in rural areas as well as urban, for the practice of the basic principles of democratic government, in the use of electoral machinery, etc. Decisions have now been taken as to the manner and extent of financial assistance to these Local Councils, (see Appendix A to this letter)[2] and the

---

[2] Appendices not printed.

State Governments have been urged to establish a number in each State. Present indications are that a total of about sixty areas will have been gazetted as Local Council areas within the next six weeks and the Councils elected in time for them to prepare their little budgets for a first financial year beginning 1st January, 1953. This is the date by which it is anticipated the majority of these first Councils will have been effectively established under the July legislation and will begin to administer their own affairs. A good deal of supervision and guidance by the District Officers will, of course, be necessary at the outset, and it would therefore be unwise to attempt to start with a much greater number.

I suggest also that it would be worth mentioning the appointment of Bedale[3] with the following terms of reference:—

(a) To confer with and advise the existing Municipalities of Georgetown (Penang), Malacca and Kuala Lumpur.
(b) To examine the position in regard to the 19 larger Town Boards throughout the Federation with a view to their conversion into Town Councils.
(c) To advise on the establishment of Local Councils under the Local Councils Ordinance.
(d) To make recommendations concerning the local government of areas not included in categories (a), (b), and (c) above.
(e) To report generally on the future structure and functions of local government throughout the Federation and to make recommendations as to the necessary permanent machinery for control and guidance at Federal and State level.

Bedale is being very active and is doing much to stimulate interest in his subject. He has already visited both Settlements and most of the States, and he expects to put in his report by the end of December.

We are also doing all we can to obtain early implementation of the recommendation in paragraph 49 of the Report of the Select Committee appointed in 1950 "to advise the Government on the policy to be incorporated in legislation to provide for elections to Local Government authorities". This recommendation was that there should be a Town Council with a majority of elected members in respect of every town having a population of approximately 10,000 or over. Nineteen towns were mentioned in that Report. One of these was Batu Arang in Selangor; the population of Batu Arang has greatly declined during the last two years; it has been a hot-bed of communism and is regarded as not suited at present for elected Town Council status. Another, Ayer Itam, is really a suburb of Penang and Bedale is of opinion, and I think the Settlement Government agrees, that it is better included in the Municipal area of Penang. Four of the remaining seventeen are in Johore: three of these—Johore Bahru, Bandar Penggaram and Bandar Maharani, are to have elections early in December and arrangements are being made by the State Government to hold elections early in 1953 in the fourth—Kluang—and also in Segamat. The Selangor Government is pushing ahead with elections for Klang and Port Swettenham, and it is likely that these two areas will be combined in a single local government unit and given municipal status at the outset. It is probable that Selangor will also establish

---

[3] Harold T Bedale, town clerk of Hornsey, started examining local government on 20 Aug and submitted his report on 29 Dec 1952 (see Harold Bedale, *Establishment Organisation and Supervision of Local Authorities in the Federation of Malaya*, Kuala Lumpur, 1953, and CO 1022/299).

an elected Town Council for Kajang. Trengganu proposes to hold elections in January for a Town Council in Kuala Trengganu. Action is not so advanced elsewhere but it is likely that elected Town Councils will be established in at least six other towns—Seremban, Kuala Pilah, Butterworth, Bukit Mertajam, Kota Bahru, and Kuantan—by the middle of next year. Perak, where there are four towns with a population in excess of 10,000—Ipoh, Taiping, Telak Anson and Kampar—and Kedah, where there are two—Alor Star and Sungei Patani—are showing some reluctance and it may be that elections in respect of these six towns will not be held until the latter part of 1953. In short, in addition to the elected Municipal Councils of Penang, Malacca and Kuala Lumpur, there should by the second half of 1953 be a majority of elected members sitting on the local government bodies administering the affairs of twenty large urban areas.

One difficulty arises in the case of some of these Town Councils. At present two of them, Bukit Mertajam and Butterworth, are part of the Rural Board area of Province Wellesley and will have first to be excised therefrom, leaving the remaining parts of Province Wellesley to be administered by the existing Rural Board. Most of the other proposed Town Councils form part, the central part, of existing Town Boards administering a number of geographically separate locations of an urban or semi-urban nature each with a population ranging from five hundred to ten thousand. With the excision of the largest and central unit from these Town Boards and the establishment of that unit as an independent Town Council, there will be left the problem of administration of the remaining smaller outlying areas. Some of these will be suitable for Local Council status at once. Others will probably have to continue to be administered under a truncated Town Board with the District Officer in the chair and a nominated membership, until such time as they have sufficiently developed to justify Local Council status; while so administered, some arrangements will have to be made for them to obtain from the Town Council, against payment, the services which are at present shared among all the areas constituting the present Town Board area and which cannot be economically split up. This is a matter to which Bedale is giving particular attention and which he will treat in his report.

As regards elections to State Councils there is little progress to report, and, in my view, if we achieve elections in one or two of the States/Settlements by the end of 1954 we shall have done well. The State Governments themselves show no desire to push ahead with these and there is little public demand for them. Even in the Settlements there is a real reluctance to take any action. In Malacca there has been recently a public debate on the matter and you will be interested to see from the enclosed press cutting (Appendix B) that the proposal that elections should be held in the near future was rejected by a large majority. Both in the States and in the Settlements, the attitude is taken that it is first best to obtain experience in the Town Councils, and that only when elected Town Councils have been well established should attention be given to State elections. This feeling was very well expressed by H.E. Mackenzie[4] in the State Council of Johore in December, 1950, and I enclose (Appendix C) a copy of the record of what he said.

It has always been expected that Johore would be the first State to hold elections to the Council of State, and, as you probably know, a Select Committee was appointed

---

[4] Harold E MacKenzie was a rubber planter in Malaya, 1926–1955; member of Johore State and Executive Councils, 1948–1955; and chairman, Federation of Malaya Welfare Council, 1954–1955.

by the Council of State in June 1950 to make recommendations upon the policy to be incorporated in legislation to provide for the election of such members. The Committee, under the chairmanship of Hodgkinson[5] who was then acting British Adviser, prepared an excellent Report in September 1950 and this was adopted in the Council of State in March of the following year. Resolutions were then passed adopting the recommendations contained in the Report (subject to possible amendment at the later date of paragraph 32 of the Report which related to qualifications of members of the Council) and that the first election should be held in the year 1952. An amendment substituting 1953 for 1952 was defeated.

I have recently asked Hodgkinson to report what the present position is and he now writes to tell me that since the debate in March, 1952, no further action has been taken and that the matter would appear to have been sidetracked by the proposals for Town Council elections, and more recently, for implementing the Local Councils Ordinance. He says that he understands it to be the Mentri Besar's hope, once the Town Councils have held their elections and got going in 1953, to bring forward again the question of elections to the Council of State, and that he is anxious not to make a start with the latter until there is background experience from the elected Town Councils. He is thinking in terms of elections to the Council of State in 1954. Hodgkinson adds that, with the very considerable difficulties likely to arise in practice over the sloughing off by newly elected Town Councils of their Town Board areas, he doubts whether it will be possible to advance this programme. I intend, however, to discuss this with the Mentri Besar and the British Adviser shortly and to press for elections to the Council of State before the end of 1953, or at least early in 1954.

Mention might also be made by the Secretary of State, at any date after the publication of the Federation of Malaya Agreement (Amendment) Bill, of the intention of the High Commissioner to appoint a Speaker of the Federal Legislative Council in place of himself as President. The Bill will probably be published during the second week in November, but it will not be possible to secure its passage until the January meeting. As you will see from another letter which I am writing to you about this, the proposal is to appoint Dato Mahmud[6] as Speaker about July of next year, after he has had a period of training in the House of Commons.

The "brake on the creation of representative institutions" is not being put on from the top. It is, however, undoubtedly being applied at State level with the support of a considerable body of public opinion, and it will need constant pressure from the top to get these brakes released.

Minutes on 280

Mr. Jerrom
Mr. Higham
. . . 2. I think we can be well satisfied with the progress that is being made in the field of local government; but Mr. MacGillivray's remarks about State/Settlement

---

[5] See 269, note 1.

[6] Dato Mahmud bin Mat, educated at Malay College, Kuala Kangsar; entered government service, 1912; promoted to MCS, 1927; *mentri besar* of Pahang, 1948; member for lands, mines and communications, 1951–1953; first Speaker, Federal Legislative Council, 1953–1955.

elections . . . are to my mind far less encouraging. Johore is not expected to hold elections before 1954, and the most we are promised, by the High Commissioner, . . . are elections in one State and one Settlement during that year. This strikes me as slow progress for Johore, where the report of the Select Committee laying down election policy and constituency divisions was adopted early last year; while there is no mention at all of definite planning having even been started in any of the other eight States, or in either of the Settlements. As Mr. MacGillivray admits, the brakes *are* on: at State and not at Federal level, but it is understandable that a not very well informed outsider should fail to appreciate the distinction. One such outsider contributed to "New Statesman"; many others may be getting the same false impression.

3. At this stage, I think it would be timely to look broadly at our policy in Malaya and to attempt to clear our ideas on the subject of elections with their attendant problems. Our long term policy for Malaya, as laid down in the Directive given to Sir G. Templer, is that she should become a self-governing member of the Commonwealth; presumably because, setting aside all motives of altruism, we realise that in the long run only an independent State which has chosen voluntarily to associate itself with the free way of life can form an effective bastion against the spread of Communism in South East Asia. Hence that democratic institutions must be built up, and elections must take place at both State and Federal level in Malaya, is not in question. We merely have to consider the timing of these developments and the forms they should take. The present view of both the High Commissioner and Mr. MacGillivray appears to be that elections for the State/Settlement Councils are of course essential and must come soon; but if the State and Settlement Governments are not enthusiastic, nothing very much can be done to hurry them; and anyway, to make a start in Johore and one Settlement the year after next will be satisfactory. At this pace it may take years to introduce elections at State level throughout the Federation; and the development of Federal elections would follow after that.

4. There are several good reasons for not attempting to go any faster than this. The Emergency is not yet over and its end is not in sight. The majority of the population are not yet ready for elections by any ideal standards. Such parties as exist are confused, and the only real public support they have is dictated by communal loyalties. There is no real demand from the people for elections and political advance. Even amongst political leaders, there is little enthusiasm for swift advance; the Chinese would first prefer to see a further extension of citizenship rights in the direction of Jus Soli;[7] and although the U.M.N.O. Malays may call for quick progress, it is with the motive of preserving Malay political supremecy [sic]. As our policy is to build a "united Malayan nation", we cannot endorse the communal motives of either group. Yet the Independence of Malaya Party, standing in the middle and professing to be non-communal, shows every sign of being on its last legs, its leadership divided and its following non-existent. Mr. MacGillivray, in Appendices 'B' and 'C' to his letter, offers some evidence of the lack of public demand for elections. There is a report of a public debate in Malacca at which the time was held not to be ripe for Settlement Council elections; the Chinese speaker who carried the meeting quoted similar arguments to those I have mentioned above (except that his fifth one need hardly be taken seriously); an Indian and a Malay spoke in favour of elections, and I

---

[7] According to *jus soli* citizenship would be automatically acquired by all persons born in Malaya.

think there is little doubt that the vote went on purely communal grounds. There is also a report of part of a speech by Mr. H.E. Mackenzie in Johore which stresses the wisdom of going slow and educating the people through local elections.

5. I think that there are, however, some reasons which ought to be stated for going, if not fast, then at least faster than is at present intended. There are three main arguments:—

(a) During recent months there has been a decline in the volume of terrorism and we know that the Communists are now planning to concentrate on gaining public support, which they hope to do by directing their attacks solely against their known enemies, and by propaganda and penetration building up a "united front". Communist policy in creating a "united front" is traditionally to bring together all the more progressive political elements in the country on a platform which is deceivingly non-Communist; in Western countries the rallying point may be a fairly mild liberal-socialist programme; in Malaya it would almost certainly be self-government. The Communist attack is two-pronged, military and political, and the Communists hope that their opponents will strive so hard to defend themselves against the one that they will increase their vulnerability to the other. Just at the moment we can say that there is no strong public demand for early elections in Malaya; but such a demand could easily be created. I think there is a real danger of that demand growing suddenly and soon. This may sound fanciful, but it should be remembered, first, that the outbreak of the Emergency itself was hardly foreseen by government; and secondly, that it is already about a year since the M.C.P's new policy was formulated. The dangers of a popular demand for elections being created by the Communists rather than by us do not need stressing. Government would be placed in the embarrassing position of fearing that to go ahead with what it had planned would give the appearance of weakly making concessions to a Communist-inspired movement. It has always been a trump card in our hand that the most elastic imagination was needed to see Communist terrorism in Malaya as a national uprising. But on a demand for self-government the Communists, who because of the position of China already have a hold on the Chinese, might also gain Malay support and thus achieve what has never been achieved before: a united front of Malays and Chinese against the Government. This, I think, is the nature of the threat which is contained in the M.C.P's new policy; and to delay the grant of elections, or to proceed at a leisurely pace (and it must be admitted that to think in terms of elections in two-elevenths of the country the year after next is rather leisurely) may lead to the "public demand" for elections which is at present so weak becoming rather stronger and of such a character that Government must resist it.

(b) Just as the people really do not know what they want, nor can political parties develop any strength, clarity of purpose, or above all leadership until elections at least on State level are established, so that they are given scope to develop policies and attract men of good calibre. Local Council elections do not give the requisite opportunities; the issues are too small, and the offices too minor. I need not elaborate this point as it has already been made in Mr. Higham's minute of 30th July on SEA 31/1/01.[8]

---

[8] See 277, minute by J D Higham.

(c) We do not know how long it will be before Malaya becomes independent, but in the present political atmosphere of the world it may be sooner than we would wish. Clearly our whole policy will have failed unless, when this does happen, she stays in the Commonwealth or at least remains, to put it very simply, on our side. Becoming independent contains many dangers for a country particularly if it involves at the same time the too sudden introduction of the forms of parliamentary democracy. If Malaya is to be saved from the weaknesses of Burma and Indonesia we must see that she is given as much experience of self-government as possible before she achieves her independent status.[9] As the time at our disposal may turn out to be limited, I think this means that we should advance as quickly as possible to the stage of State, Settlement and Federal Council elections while conditions are still comparatively favourable. The experience that a country really needs is of national self-government rather than of local self-government, and it seems to me more important to give Malaya as long a period as possible as a self-governing "Colony" than to go too slowly and carefully in the initial stages.

6. The conclusion I draw from the arguments given above is that the sooner all the States and Settlements start to work on their plans for elections, and as soon as Johore, which so far as I know is the only State to have plans already made, puts them into effect, the better it will be. There are practical difficulties to this policy, to which the two most important are that the Emergency still continues and is at its worst in Johore, and simply that the State and Settlement Governments don't want to hurry. Neither of these should be insuperable, however; the Johore Council of State was willing to accept, a year ago, that elections need not await the ending of the Emergency. The report of its Select Committee says:

> "The mechanical arrangements for an election will require considerable manpower, though much of it may be occupied only for the actual voting day. We are not unaware of the present Emergency calls on manpower but we do nevertheless trust that this will not be allowed to delay the implementation of our recommendation".

Elections might have to be postponed in particularly troubled constituencies, but I do not think that the M.C.P. would attempt to interfere by terrorism with the conduct of an election, as to do so would be quite out of accord with its present policy. As for the other big obstacle—the reluctance to advance of the Malay State oligarchies—I cannot help feeling that their opposition would not last long in the face of a really vigorous and determined approach by the High Commissioner. In the last resort the Rulers and their supporters cannot stand without British help. Such popular backing as they have comes from the Malays, who are the people who would most favour early elections. On this issue I do not think the State Governments can really offer much resistence.

7. What seems to me a much more important subject for consideration is that, before a start is made in holding any elections anywhere above municipal level, at least two important policy decisions will have to be made, both of which are directly connected with the delicate question of communal relationships. They are, firstly, what is to be the franchise? And secondly, is there to be any attempt to secure

---

[9] Higham added in the margin at this point: 'I would not regard this as a reason for greater speed'.

representation on a communal basis? These are not questions which can be decided here and now on a minute sheet, but I think it is worth while trying to clear our minds on the issues involved.

8.   Theoretically, there are three possible bases on which the franchises might be awarded: to citizens of the Federation; to citizens of the Federation and citizens of U.K. and Colonies; or to all adult residents. In practice, the third alternative would have to be ruled out straight away, as it would be quite unacceptable to the Malays; although it is worth noting that it is the franchise which has been adopted in the Local Councils Ordinance. The choice will therefore lie between restricting the electorate to citizens of the Federation, or admitting also those citizens of U.K. and Colonies who are not eligible for citizenship of the Federation. There might also be a move in some States to give the vote only to subjects of the Ruler, but it is interesting that the Johore Select Committee recommended including "other Federal citizens" who had been resident in the State for at least 1 of the 2 years preceding registration as an elector. It seems logical that, if citizenship of the Federation is to mean anything at all, it should be the one and only qualification of the franchise in Federal elections, and although the States could make an equally logical case for restricting the vote in State elections to State nationals, it would be simpler if they were all prepared to make the small concession that Johore has agreed to. There seems to be no particular reason why citizens of U.K. and Colonies who are not citizens of the Federation should be entitled to vote in either State or Federal elections, yet they are at present given the franchise in municipal elections. The experience of Singapore suggests that such a provision may open the door to "birds of passage", particularly Indians, who become entitled to vote and to stand for election on account of a qualification which they can have obtained without previously setting foot in Malaya. On the other hand, some form of concession might be thought desirable to citizens of the U.K. and Colonies who move into the Federation from Singapore—mostly Chinese. Clearly there are several points of detail which would have to be settled in agreement with all communities; but as the citizenship legislation represents the best possible compromise which could be reached on who amongst the non-Malays might be regarded as sufficiently assimilated to the life of the Federation to be regarded as Malayans I think, despite the confusion of franchises at present existing for local elections, that citizenship must be the principal and probably the only, qualification for the vote in State/Settlement and Federal elections.

9.   Probably the most difficult question of all which will have to be settled after the franchise has been decided, is whether constituencies are to be drawn on a purely territorial basis, or whether any attempt is to be made to create constituencies in each of which the voters of one community are in a large majority. It could be argued that the latter course would eliminate the communal issue from electoral contests and hence foster the growth of non-communal parties offering alternative programmes in Malay, Chinese and Indian constituencies alike. On the other hand, an artificial rigidity would be imparted into the system by virtually fixing in advance the representation which each race would have. Further, by introducing a mild form of segregation into politics, communal representation would in fact reduce the chances of developing by assimilation a "united Malayan nation", and would hence be contrary to our policy. The Johore Select Committee favours territorial constituencies which would result in some having a fairly equally divided communal

composition, but in which most States, and in the Federation as a whole, the Malays would have a majority of voters, particularly as only about 60% of the Chinese are citizens. Both communities might be prepared to accept such an arrangement, the Malays being satisfied by this assured majority, and the Chinese hoping to expand their population, increase their number of citizens and secure an extension of citizenship rights later on. They would no doubt renew their plea for immediate Jus Soli, but this could no more be accepted in connection with elections than it could be in connection with immigration. A form of proportional representation to protect minorities, a communal second chamber, or a provision giving the Ruler or High Commissioner power to nominate additional councillors to restore a balance of representation where necessary, might be considered as possible concessions. We cannot of course decide here or now what course should be adopted, but personally I think we should be against communal representation if possible, provided that there appears to be a reasonable chance of non-communal parties developing on issues cutting across racial questions.

10. In this minute, prompted by Mr. MacGillivray's observations at (30), I have tried to suggest that there is a case for making a vigorous attempt to override local reluctance in Malaya to plan and hold elections in all States and Settlements as soon as possible, and to start thinking about Federal elections. I have also attempted to summarise some of the problems which will have to be faced before elections are held, and to offer some first thoughts about them. Even if you agree with the above, I don't think it should form the basis of a reply to (30); but I think we should consider discussing the whole question with Sir G. Templer during his forthcoming visit to this country. We might inform Mr. MacGillivray so, and I attach a brief draft reply for conson [consideration].

A.S.G.
4.11.52.

Mr. Higham
I have not had time to study this in the detail which it demands and will therefore confine myself to a few general remarks, which would no doubt need some qualification on further discussion.

It seems to me that here we are dealing with a crucial political issue which is certain to have a profound effect on communal relations in Malaya and may well set the pattern (or lack of pattern) in development of those relations for years to come. It is therefore of the utmost importance that we should discuss it fully with the High Commissioner or Deputy High Commissioner before any action is taken which is likely to remove or greatly to reduce our power to influence developments.

Very briefly my own views are:—

(a) that our general policy should be to hasten State/Settlement elections rather than to let the pace be dictated by those at present in power or to wait until there is a widespread public demand—which may well be exploited by the Communists;
(b) that State/Settlement elections will raise extremely difficult communal problems and that these must ultimately be settled on a Federal basis. I cannot see how the idea of "experimenting" in one or two States/Settlements can work satisfactorily because the basic decisions (e.g. franchise; the drawing up of constituencies; the balance between official, unofficial nominated, and unofficial elected membership)

must surely be common to all States, and probably to both States and Settlements. To take an example, political decisions on these points which would be acceptable in Johore might be anything but acceptable in Selangor with its large Chinese majority;

(c) that these two approaches, (1) Federal and (2) by experiment in one or two States/Settlements, should now be considered and a decision reached in favour of one or the other—or in favour of any other practicable or alternative course;

(d) if the Federal approach is decided on it will presumably entail long and arduous negotiations, as in the case of the new code of citizenship, and in my view the sooner a start is made the better. It will take a good deal of time and can run on parallel to the "practical training in democracy" which we hope for through the Municipal and Local Council elections.

(e) To sum up: my feeling is that we have been thinking too much about the holding of elections and too little of the political struggle which must accompany or precede them: that the best course may be to face up to this political struggle and have it out on a Federal basis before the elections: that this will take a long time and produce some fireworks, but that subject to the High Commissioner's views the present time may be as favourable as any to make a start.

I agree with Mr. Gann that the question should appear on the agenda for General Templer's visit, though it may well fall to Mr. MacGillivray rather than to General Templer to handle these problems in future. If you agree, I will discuss it in an exploratory way and without stating any definite views during my visit to Kuala Lumpur.

T.C.J.

7.11.52

Mr. Paskin

1. You should see Mr. MacGillivray's letter at (30), and subsequent minutes before we meet General Templer. Mr. Gann's minute of the 4th November is in my view a very penetrating analysis of the possible dangers of not pressing ahead more rapidly with State Elections. I do not think his arguments are of necessity conclusively in favour of more rapid progress; but they are, at the very least, good theoretical points. I am not myself convinced that the right answer to Communist "United Front" tactics is to press ahead with State Elections, since premature elections might only mean that the Communists would be able to make mischief with greater effect. I suggest, however, that the following points (some of which, of course, have a significance outside the field of Elections) might be put to General Templer:

(a) We know that there is no pressure from "respectable" leaders of any community for earlier State Elections. But what weight is to be attached to U.M.N.O. calls for more rapid political progress; in particular what is the danger of the Communists achieving some political success and popular support (particularly among the Malays) by building up a "United Front" which might strongly press for early State and Federal Elections?

(b) If the above is a danger, is the best way of meeting it by hastening Elections, or are there other ways of meeting these political aspirations?

(c) The State Councils themselves are apparently not entirely satisfactory organs of Government; is it not possible that Elections might mean a salutary change of personnel and might stimulate more local interest in the proceedings of these Councils?

(d) While, from a purely practical point of view, Malayan politicians would do well to "keep their noses to the grindstone" on local administration, is it not possible that Elections to State Councils might absorb the energies and blunt the wider aspirations of some politicians who may, if they are not given an outlet in this way, become more clamorous about wider issues of national independence?

(e) Might it not be advisable to press ahead more rapidly in the relatively quiet States than in Johore?

(f) What is the basis for the franchise and for the delineation of constituencies? If we go ahead with elections in one State only, can it be assumed that other States will adopt a broadly similar basis of franchise? Will it not be essential to have this basis agreed by all the States before Elections are held in any one? Similarly as regards constituencies, must it not be settled throughout the Fedeeration whether constituencies are to be drawn on a communal or a territorial basis?

In many ways I hope that progress can go ahead at the speed indicated in Mr. MacGillivray's letter, but I think that we should have General Templer's reactions to the above points before the present time-table is finally endorsed.[10]

J.D.H.
29.11.52

---

[10] Not all the points listed in Higham's minute (notably [f]) were put to Templer during his visit to London. Rather than offer positive opinions themselves, CO officials decided to ask MacGillivray for his views on the more important questions raised in these minutes, see 290.

281   T 220/493, IF 242/23/01B   17 Nov 1952

[Expansion of Malaya's land forces]: despatch no 2311/52 from Sir G Templer to Mr Lyttelton on the need for an adequate Malayan army as an essential pre-requisite for independence

I have the honour to address you on the expansion of the Federation Land Forces and to set out my proposals for the next few years together with some of the considerations involved.

2. It is the policy of Her Majesty's Government to lead the Federation of Malaya towards self-government within the Commonwealth. While it is not possible in present conditions to estimate the rate of progress towards this goal and to aim at any specific date on which this status will be achieved, preparatory measures must be initiated in all necessary fields. One of these is defence—from the point of view of both external agression [sic] and internal security. There is a lesson to be learnt here from India on the one hand and from Burma on the other. The problems which attended the grant of independence to the Indian continent were vast and complex; partition with all the political, religious and communal sources of strife which it presented might have reduced India to a state of chaos in a very brief time. That this danger was averted, that it was possible to carry out mass movements of population with such comparatively small bloodshed as to confound the prophets, that the new

Governments were able to establish and sustain their authority was in my view due to one thing and one thing only—the existence of a large, well-trained and disciplined Indian army with the best traditions behind it. By contrast the grant of independence to Burma, whose problems should have been susceptible to more straight-forward solution, plunged the country into chaos from which it is only now beginning to emerge for lack of a proper instrument to maintain law and order. I am convinced that an essential pre-requisite to the grant of independence to Malaya is the formation of an adequate Malayan army to support the civil authority and the foundations of that Army cannot be laid too soon. Although the Malay Regiment was formed as long ago as 1934, it only consisted in 1948 of two battalions while the Malayan army of the future must not only be very much larger in size but also different in composition. It must be a balanced force and it must be composed of men of all races who have made Malaya their home.

3. The outbreak of the Emergency in 1948 and the demand which ensued upon Imperial Army units naturally led to proposals to expand the Local Forces in order to reduce as far as possible the commitment upon Imperial troops. In the circumstances and the need to produce quick results it was inevitable that the programme was based on the expansion of the existing regular force—the Malay Regiment. The programme provided for an expansion to six battalions of which five are now in existence and the sixth will form at the end of this year.

4. Such was the position when I assumed office and I gave early consideration to the steps which should be taken for the further development of a Malayan Army concurrently with the discussions which were already in train between your predecessor and the Commissioner-General (in which connection I invite reference to Mr. Griffiths' Top Secret despatch No. 9 of the 5th October, 1951). There were certain political factors to be taken into account. On the one hand the sincere and progressive endeavours being made by all community leaders to promote and inculcate a Malayan consciousness among all races together with the considerations mentioned in para. 2 above pointed to an early need to open the ranks of the Army to all races. The responsibility for all to share in the defence of their country is clearly an important ingredient of a truly Malayan outlook. On the other hand Their Highnesses the Rulers with all their liberal appreciation of the need for assimilating the other races on equal terms with Malays into a Malayan nation could not but have certain misgivings regarding the pace to be set in planning this assimilation—more particularly in view of the predominantly Chinese character of the militant Communist movement and the apparent lack of response from the Chinese population generally to rally actively to the side of the Government. In these circumstances, proposals for multi-racial units in the Federation Army would only be acceptable to them if the Malay preponderance in the Armed Forces was maintained by a further expansion of the Malay Regiment.

5. There is a limit to the size of the regular Armed Forces which the Federation with its small population can afford to maintain. Moreover if the most effective results are to be produced with the maximum of economy, the defence of the Federation and Singapore must be regarded as one, and even if co-ordination cannot at present extend to the maintenance of joint regular forces, the plans for developing separate forces should be closely integrated. The point is not of immediate importance since Singapore has not up to now planned the raising of any regular land forces, but it will require to be borne in mind when the time comes.

6. In the light of the above considerations my proposals envisage the raising of new units of the Federation Army to provide for the following regular forces to be in existence by the end of 1955:—

9 battalions of The Malay Regiment.
3 battalions of The Federation Regiment.
1 Armoured Car Regiment (H.Q. and three squadrons).
1 Signal squadron.
1 Squadron Field Engineers.

With the exception of the Malay Regiment, all these units will be open to British Subjects and Federal citizens. Further subsidiary units will be required in due course, but in the long term, the nucleus of what is required will be found in the British Army units which employ locally enlisted personnel. The statement attached at Annexure A[1] sets out the phased programme for raising these local regular forces.

7. The required legislation has been enacted in the shape of the Federation Regiment Ordinance, 1952, and the Military Forces Ordinance, 1952. The latter Ordinance confers authority on the High Commissioner-in-Council to raise whatever forces are required for the defence of the Federation. Sooner or later it will be desirable to enact a proper Army Act with all the necessary provisions to cover the Regular and Volunteer Forces.

8. Apart from the ability of the Federation Government to finance this programme which is discussed in para. 11 below, the major difficulty in expanding the Forces at the rate proposed lies in the shortage of officers and non-commissioned officers. The 300% expansion of the Malay Regiment which has taken place during the last four years has severely strained their resources in this respect already while the additional 12 companies to be raised between February, 1953, and February, 1954, and which will ultimately form the 7th, 8th and 9th bns. will leave no margin at all for assistance to the other units proposed to be found from this source. My long term plan for meeting this deficiency is twofold; firstly a potential officers training wing, which has already been opened, to give pre-OCTU training to which potential officers have been recruited direct. From there they will proceed to the National Service school at Eaton Hall (the Federation has been given 54 places for the course beginning next May). The best of the output will go on to Sandhurst with a view to being given regular commissions, the rest will be granted short service commissions after successfully completing the course at Eaton Hall. In time I hope to see established in Malaya a military college at which the necessary training can be given in this country. Secondly, I have started a Boys Company to which boys of 14 will be admitted for a good 4 years English education under military discipline. These will provide the potential officers and warrant officers required by the Federation Army in the future. These plans however will take some years to produce substantial results and in the interim period we shall require increased assistance from the British Army. I have already received a promise from the War Office of the additional officers required to cover the further 12 companies of the Malay Regiment to be raised during the next 18 months. I shall require additional assistance to cover the commitments of the other units included in the programme. A detailed statement will be prepared shortly but a preliminary examination indicates that if the proposed

---

[1] Annexures not printed.

timetable is followed officer requirements can be met from existing and promised resources with a 10% deficiency until July, 1953, rising to 23% in November, 1953, and 36% in August, 1954. The deficiency will decline until September, 1955, when it will be 22% and December, 1955, when it will be 13%. For British Other Ranks the corresponding deficiencies by percentages will be even greater. I draw your attention to this factor because it will be one of the major difficulties to be overcome and at a later stage I may require to invite your assistance in negotiations with the War Office.

9.   The maintenance and administrative backing for the Federation Army also present a problem. By arrangements recently concluded with the War Office the maintenance of the Malay Regiment (including the additional 12 companies in the expansion programme) has now been accepted as a British Army commitment on a per capita charge to the Federation Government. I have yet to obtain the consent of the War Office to providing the initial equipment required for the Federation Regiment and the Federation Armoured Corps and to the subsequent maintenance of these units on the same basis as the Malay Regiment. The resources of the British Army in Malaya are considerably strained in this respect already and in general it appears that the maintenance of additional units of the Federation Army could only be undertaken if accompanied by a withdrawal of a corresponding strength of British Army units. Provided that there is no radical change for the worse in the present "cold war" in South East Asia during the next couple of years I see no reason why this reservation should not be accepted and it will afford a relief to the War Office which may incline them to regard more favourably the additional demands for British personnel which our expansion entails.

10.   The picture would not be complete without some reference to the proposed Volunteer Land Forces. The present plans embrace a Light Anti-aircraft Battery, Engineers Regiment, Field Survey Squadrons, Signal Squadrons, Reconnaissance Corps, Transport Companies, Recovery unit and Provost Company with a total strength of 155 officers and 3659 other ranks. To this will probably be added in due course Port Companies and a Pioneer Group. These units, which would be mobilised on the outbreak of war, are designed to supply the additional backing required for the Imperial Army in Malaya in war time. Firm endorsement of these plans awaits the reply to my Savingram No. 34 of the 5th January, 1952 in which certain assurances were sought from the War Office in regard to provision of equipment and maintenance.

11.   I now turn to the question of financing this expansion. At Annexure B to this despatch is a statement of the approximate expenditure which will be required during the next three years. This shows a capital expenditure of some $70 millions and a recurrent expenditure rising to about $44 million in 1955. In the present financial position of the Federation and in view of the heavy expenditure to which it is committed in combatting [sic] the Emergency it is clearly going to be extremely difficult to find the funds required. Moreover the increasing demands for expansion of the social services (which are in themselves our most potent weapon against Communism) and the delay in this expansion which has been forced on the country by the division of resources to prosecute the Emergency campaign present a conflicting claim against future available funds which it will be most unwise to resist. Although I am satisfied that the present modest plans for the Federation Army command universal public support, they are unlikely to be so acceptable if they have to be implemented at the expense of education, health and other social services.

There is moreover a growing feeling in unofficial quarters that the price which the Federation is being called upon to pay through being in the front line of the battle against World Communism is larger than this country should reasonably be expected to meet. This feeling is not necessarily focussed on further financial assistance from Her Majesty's Government; it looks to the wider front of the democratic countries lined up against Communism and in particular to the United States. I have already referred to this in the telegraphic correspondence resting with your secret and personal telegram 163 and in the event the Finance Committee made no mention in their Report of the possibility of obtaining financial assistance from America. But the question may still well be raised in the Legislative Council since it is felt that there is no reason why Malaya should be excluded from the very substantial help which America is giving to the anti-Communist front all over the world and not least in Asia. A very small share of that assistance would go a long way to meet Malaya's difficulties and to ease the burden on this country which is increasing with the recession in rubber prices. There are those too who will point to the terms of the Federation Agreement whereunder Her Majesty's Government has accepted the responsibility of defending the Federation and who will ask why the burden of this responsibility should be shifted.

12. In regard to recurrent expenditure, all these arguments must fall to the ground. An independent Federation of Malaya will have to maintain and finance its own armed services and there must be a gradual acceptance of the increasing annual commitment on that account during the years leading up to the attainment of self-government. It is one of the responsibilities of an independent country to allocate a certain proportion of its annual revenue to defence and this responsibility will have to be recognised and accepted. The position respecting the initial capital expenditure required to raise these forces is however different and here I think there are good grounds for a grant in aid. You will recollect that on my visit to London in June this year I put forward certain proposals for assistance from Her Majesty's Government towards the cost of the Armed Forces in the Federation and although the question was left in abeyance pending a review of the general budgetary position of the Federation, I should like to renew this request now that a decision has been taken not to approach the Chancellor for financial assistance towards the general budget deficit of the Federation in 1953. A grant of £8 millions spread over the next two years would approximately meet the foreseen capital expenditure on the expansion of the Local Forces and would not only be welcomed as a very timely gesture but would also be a very real and substantial indication of the genuine intention of Her Majesty's Government to assist the Federation in taking the preparatory steps towards self-government in the foreseeable future. Much of its value would be lost if it were associated with any general assistance made necessary by the Federation's inability to pay its way but if granted for this specific purpose the return in political goodwill would, I am sure, be very considerable.

13. To sum up, I am certain that the programme I have outlined for the expansion of the local Forces is an essential preliminary to the attainment of self-government and that if it is to keep pace with political development no time can be lost in giving effect to it. Assistance will be required from Her Majesty's Government in finance on the lines I have indicated and in the loan of additional officers and Other Ranks seconded from the British Army, and I shall be glad to receive assurance that this assistance will be forthcoming. Without it I see little

possibility of achieving my object. If financial assistance could take the form I have indicated in the above paragraph and I could make an early announcement of it, the political benefit would be very great.

14. I am sending copies of this despatch to the Commissioner-General and the Governor of Singapore.

282   CO 1022/485, no 8   26 Nov 1952
[Economic development plan]: letter (reply) from O A Spencer to J D Higham

May I refer to your letter of 26th May (SEA. 261/1/01)[1] on the subject of the possibility of inviting an International Bank (or other) Mission to Malaya to do a survey of our economic potential with the object of preparing a revised Development Plan for the Federation of Malaya. We deferred further consideration of this at the time as Executive Council decided that the question of any revision of the Plan should be put "on the ice" for several months; recently however we have brought the matter up once more and have considered it afresh.

I must say at once, however, that I find myself unable to agree with the view that, although outside advice may help, the job of drawing up a comprehensive development plan is one which can only satisfactorily be done by those actually engaged on the spot with an intimate knowledge of local conditions, after which consideration may be given to the question of an outside mission. Obviously the development plan must incorporate the experience, advice and reflections of those who really know the problem on the spot. No one questions that. But it is no less important that it should be detached in its appreciation of fundamentals and it is useful if it can introduce a breath of fresh air as well. This argument alone suggests that planning should not be entirely a local matter.

But the compelling consideration which leads me to dissent from your proposed procedure is that we think it amounts to putting the cart before the horse. In our view the first requirement is a basic survey of the country's economy and a reappraisal in general but comprehensive terms of the country's economic needs viewed in the light of the resources likely to be available to meet them. From this the survey should proceed to a studied appreciation of existing special, economic and fiscal policies, appraising them in relation to the objectives generally agreed upon, and of the resources in men, money and materials likely to be available now and in the future. In the course of this study we should like particular attention to be given to the attainment of a correct balance between economic and social development and also the more specialised question of the diversification of the local economy—a study which would comprehend the twin questions of industrialisation and the role to be played by external capital.

Once this basic structure has been completed and [sic] detailed task of filling in the thousand and one particular schemes and projects which constitute the practical manifestation of the development plan can proceed on a sound and intelligent basis. The trouble is that our existing Draft Development Plan is not based on any such

---

[1] See 275.

thought-out basis or set of principles: it is simply a huge schedule of projects which each department wants to undertake. Assuming that these all conform to the approved policy of the departments, they may well be quite sound seen in the narrow context of a purely departmental view. But they may well be thoroughly unsound, unbalanced, ill-timed, or even impractical in a host of different ways when considered not from the individual departmental angle, but as part of a comprehensive plan for the country as a whole. It is this welding of departmental plans into one national plan and pattern with which we are most concerned, and to do this we must start off with a basic examination of the economic and social needs of the situation and compare them with resources likely to be available. Such a basic study cannot be satisfactorily undertaken within the Government, partly because all the senior and responsible Members of the Government are too heavily loaded with day to day executive duties, and partly because each of them is of necessity committed in some degree to the existing policies which must come up for review. With all the confidence in the world in the strength and ability of this administration, we think it asking too much to expect Members and Heads of Departments to embrace with alacrity the undertaking of a detached re-examination and critical analysis of the various public policies to which their departments are already committed, particularly when in some cases they themselves individually may have actively sponsored them. The basic survey must therefore be of an entirely independent character although it will of course have to draw extensively on local advice and evidence, which will be easy to ensure. In the United Kingdom a corresponding situation could be met by an independent Commission; but in this country there is simply not available, outside the ranks of Government, sufficient experience and talent to enable us to get up such a body. Benham, as you say, would be thoroughly suitable and would be entirely acceptable to us; he is, however, only one man and we are quite clear in our minds what we require is a team and not one individual, however distinguished; in any case I understand that he intends to retire from the public service in February and to spend the next six months or so revising his well known text book on Economics. He will therefore not be available for work of this sort until October, 1953.

In your letter you mentioned the case of Jamaica. On this I naturally rely on the Deputy High Commissioner and he points out that, while it is true that a big factor in deciding the Governor and the Colonial Office to ask for an International Bank Mission was that unofficial opinion might more readily be brought to face certain unpalatable facts of economic life if these facts were presented by an independent authority, it was largely fortuitous that the Development Plan was revised *before* the Mission arrived in Jamaica. In fact it had been revised on a purely official level and by the Treasury alone; and this revision had not been debated in the Legislature, nor had it even been presented to the Executive Council before the arrival of the Bank Mission. Furthermore, what the Jamaican Government had in mind when the proposal to invite the Bank Mission was made, was that an enquiry carried out by an authoritative international body would not only help further planning, but that the International Bank's report might further encourage investment of private capital in Jamaica. The Deputy High Commissioner agrees that, if there is to be a background economic survey, it should be made before any attempt is made to revise our Development Plan.

Our views in this matter have been strongly confirmed as a result of consultation with Sir Sydney Caine. As you know, Sir Sydney was head of the International Bank Mission which visited Ceylon in September last year, at the request of the Ceylon Government, to survey the development potentialities of Ceylon with special consideration to certain fields of economic activity specified by the Ceylon Government. We have just seen the Bank Mission's Report, published last September simultaneously in Colombo and Washington. It is a most comprehensive document and is just the sort of thing which we have in mind in Malaya. Sir Sydney admits that he himself had some doubts in the past about some of the Bank Missions to other countries, but now considers that one has to judge them ad hoc in relation to particular circumstances. In the case of Ceylon, he thought that it was a job worth attempting for two main reasons: firstly, there had been no general assessment of Ceylon's economic position by any Commission or other enquiry for a very long time; secondly, he suspected that in the political circumstances of Ceylon, there was a tendency for a great many different development projects to be put up by different political factions or energetic ministers, and that it would help the Government to get some kind of comprehensive and objective survey free from political pressures and prejudices. Very much the same reasoning would apply to Malaya and Sir Sydney believes, as we do, that the kind of team that he had in Ceylon, could analyse the basic factors and relate the different projects to one another in a consistent and integrated programme of development in a way better than any group drawn from the local administration, or any one man however able.

Coming to the question whether such a mission is best organised by the International Bank or some other institution, Sir Sydney Caine suggests three reasons in favour of a Mission from the International Bank which commend themselves to us: first, the Bank will pay most of the cost; second, the Bank is probably in a better position than any other organisation today to command experts of every nationality; third, there has been, in a number of countries to which the Bank has hitherto sent Missions, a very considerable political advantage in organising such a Mission through the International Bank. The International Bank still has a reputation for impartiality which is natural enough as the undeveloped countries are directly represented on it. To these arguments, we would add a fourth: that the International Bank is regarded as having no axe to grind. A report by the Bank which indicated opportunities for investors in Malaya is much more likely to create confidence on the part of potential investors than is a report by a mission appointed by H.M.G. or this Government, which might well be suspected of prejudice by observers and investors in the United States and elsewhere. As is pointed out so clearly in the talk which Poynton gave at the Ministry of Defence "Defence Day" on 22nd October we can no longer look to the United Kingdom for substantial new investments.

I have gone into this at some length because I would not like you to think that we come to a conclusion which is at variance with yours without careful consideration and considerable discussion amongst ourselves. Having thought over the matter, however, we have come to the view that some form of independent study, preferably sponsored by an undertaking such as the International Bank which might be able to influence the attitude of independent observers and capital interests, is a necessary prerequisite to the revision of our development plan. We do not wish to rule out the possibility of a mission locally appointed and selected with your assistance, provided the members were of the right standing and calibre. But we think a mission with an international flavour and some Asian expert participation would be favoured locally—although we would certainly always stipulate a British Chairman. The survey should, we think, be modelled on the one undertaken for Ceylon by the Caine Mission and its emphasis should be on the diversification of the economy, industrialisation, and the attainment of a correct balance between social and economic development.

We have not raised this matter again in Executive Council since the previous discussion earlier in the year which I have referred to above, but we should like to bring it up again, at the latest, early in the new year, when we must take a decision as to the future policy and procedure.

This letter has been drafted as a result of close consultation with the Chief Secretary and the Deputy High Commissioner; it has also been considered by the High Commissioner personally and he has authorised me to say that the views contained therein have his approval. We should therefore be glad if you would reconsider your attitude in this matter in the light of the above arguments and hope you will feel able to assist us in carrying out these proposals.[2]

---

[2] Persuaded by Spencer, the CO approached the Treasury which then took up the matter with Sir Edmund Hall-Patch, British representative at the IBRD, Washington. After a small exploratory mission to Malaya, Hall-Patch transmitted to Eugene R Black (president, IBRD) a formal request from the British and Malayan governments for a World Bank survey. Black accepted this on 3 Sept 1953.

283 CO 1022/86, no 3   3 Dec 1952
'Political talk with General Templer': CO minute of discussion with Templer on political advance

An informal meeting was held at 10.30 a.m. on 3rd December, 1952 in Mr. Paskin's room. The following were present: General Sir Gerald Templer, Mr J.J. Paskin, Mr. J.D. Higham, Mr. A.S. Gann.

General discussion took place about the political future of Malaya. General Templer said that he had called for proposals for the reconstitution of the Federal Legislative Council (still on a nominated basis, but with more attention paid to the distribution of seats geographically) by 1st July, 1953. He then outlined a tentative time-table for the development of self-government as he thought it might come about. Elections to town and local councils would get well under way during 1953. Elections for one State Council (presumably Johore) and one Settlement Council would take place in 1954, and the remaining States and Settlement might follow in 1955. A period of about two years consolidation would probably then be necessary before there could be Federal Legislative Council elections; these might come during the period 1956 to 1958. He imagined at least a further two years would elapse after this before there could be any form of national self-government with a proper cabinet. This would place the earliest possible date for self-government at 1960.

General Templer emphasised that there was no popular demand for the type of progress outlined above and no real desire for independence amongst any community in Malaya. The country lacked political leaders and there were no political parties of the type required to operate successfully a parliamentary system. He mentioned particularly the political ineptitude of the Malays and said he was worried about the extremist pro-Indonesian trends in U.M.N.O. Communist penetration of the Malays was, he thought, one of the greatest of current dangers. He felt that the present need was for a strong Malayan centre party with a non-communal platform. The only hope for leadership was from a handful of Malays now in senior Government positions.

It was generally agreed that there were many fundamental points requiring early consideration, such as the future position of the States and the Malay Rulers, the franchise for State and Federal elections, the policy to be adopted in delineating constituency boundaries, having regard to the communal issue; and the position of Singapore. General Templer felt that there would be advantage in having some definite constitutional goal at which to aim, and it was agreed that some form of "blue-print" for a self-governing Malaya should be drawn up by the end of 1953. This could at least be used as a cock-shy. As the visit of a constitutional expert to Malaya would undoubtedly lead to disharmony, it might be best if Mr. Hogan,[1] the Federation Attorney-General were given two or three months extension of his next home leave during which time he would be able to formulate his ideas in consultation with a constitutional expert. Mr. Higham was consulting Sir K. Roberts-Wray about a suitable team-mate for Mr. Hogan.

---

[1] It was agreed that Michael Hogan (attorney-general of the Federation) should extend his home leave and, in conjunction with the CO and professor K C Wheare (Gladstone professor of government and public administration at Oxford), should draw up a number of alternative plans for the future constitution of Malaya.

284   CO 1022/245, no 16   8 Dec 1952
'Communist tactics in South East Asia and measures to meet them': inward saving telegram no 98 from Mr M J MacDonald to FO reporting discussions at the commissioner-general's conference, 4–9 Dec

[The annual conference of the UK diplomatic representatives, colonial governors and service chiefs in South-East Asia was held at Bukit Serene (Johore Bahru), chaired by MacDonald and attended by Lord Reading, parliamentary under-secretary for foreign affairs.]

The Conference noted that in the four years since the Communists in 1948 intensified or went over to methods of violence in Indo-China, Malaya, the Philippines, Burma and at one time Indonesia, they have nowhere scored any decisive success. Behind the defensive barrier created by United Nations troops in Korea and by the French Union forces in Indo-China, the Communist elements have in fact been contained so far in South East Asia. Moreover some encouragement may be derived from a growing but still insufficient realisation among the South East Asian leaders of the danger which Communism represents and from the greater international interest in South East Asia which has been built up in various spheres in the past three years.

2.   The Conference was informed that in Malaya, the Philippines and Burma, this year has shown improvement in the sense of the diminution and decreased effectiveness of Communist violence. There is no reason yet to suppose that in these three countries violence will be abandoned but there are signs of increasing

emphasis on "constitutional" methods. This may be a reflection of a general policy in which the Moscow Economic Conference and Peking Peace Conference were stages. Such a change of emphasis would call for even greater vigilance and fresh or more intensive counter-measures in the economic, political, social and psychological fields.

3. The minor regional improvements recorded by no means counter balance the growing strength of Communist China; and that country's solidarity with the Soviet Union and its satellites contrasts sharply with the complete lack of mutual cooperation between the individually weak countries of South East Asia and the as yet ineffective coordination of planning and effort between the Western Powers in this area.

4. Apart from the military aspects of the present situation dealt with in my telegrams Nos. 97 Saving, 680 and 681, the Conference considered in particular measures:—

(a) to mitigate the possible dangers and repercussions of the Ceylon rubber-rice deal with China (see my telegram No. 105 Saving),

(b) to counter a possible Communist trade campaign (see my telegram No. 95 Saving),

(c) to win over labour and youth and preserve them from Communist penetration,

(d) to keep track of Communist activities.

5. As regards paragraph 4(c) above, much is being done to counter Communist penetration into Trade Unions in the British Dependent Territories by the Police, Trades Union Advisers and Labour Officers. As regards Burma, Siam and Indonesia, the Conference recognised the importance of the work in this sphere of the Labour Adviser to this Commission General. It was felt that every encouragement should be given to visits of Asian Trade Union leaders to the United Kingdom and that Burma in particular was a promising field for return visits. A recommendation regarding a possible T.U.C. adviser in Indonesia will follow in a separate telegram.

6. In the view of the Conference the Communist penetration of schools, colleges and universities is perhaps the greatest long-term danger and the schools controlled by the Chinese communities are a particularly serious problem. The Governments of the British Dependent Territories are pushing ahead with programmes for setting up more State schools, establishing control over Chinese schools and revising school textbooks etc.

7. In this and other connexions the Conference was impressed by the tributes paid to the work of the British Council, particularly in the foreign countries, and considers that in South East Asia (as well as in India and Japan) this organisation is likely to be our strongest weapon in the educational and cultural sphere if its activities can be increased under the right type of personnel. Although well aware of the difficulty of providing further funds for this purpose, the Conference strongly recommends that every effort be made to expand the work of the Council in these countries. Activities of particular value are for example those in the fields of teacher training, university teaching, the provision of scholarships for Asian students in Britain and the provision of appropriately equipped centres of interest in British institutions and culture.

8. As regards paragraph 4(d) above, the Conference noted with approval the work

already in progress in the exchange of security intelligence with the appropriate governmental institutions in the foreign territories of South East Asia and hoped that every opportunity would be taken of expanding this form of liaison. The technical question of travel control with the object of hampering the holding of Communist conferences was discussed and will be dealt with by despatch.

Foreign Office please pass to Colonial Office and Commonwealth Relations Office.

285   CO 1022/56, no 35   10 Dec 1952
[Collective punishment]: letter from Mr Lyttelton to Mr Grimond in support of Templer's methods

[Templer's imposition of collective punishment upon villages which refused to co-operate with the authorities provoked both protest and applause in Britain. A notable case was the curfew placed on Tanjong Malim, which was some 55 miles north of Kuala Lumpur. Towards the end of Nov, Jo Grimond, chief whip of the Liberal Party, wrote to Lyttelton for further information and was reassured by this reply, which, he said, 'was most useful and made quite an impression on a good many people who obviously know nothing about conditions in Malaya' (CO 1022/56, no 42).]

Thank you for your letter of the 25th November about collective punishment in Malaya. This is a subject about which a great deal has been said and written during the past few months and I welcome your asking for the facts.

Collective measures were first used by General Templer at Tanjong Malim in March of this year. There had been a long series of terrorist outrages in this area, culminating in the murder of an Assistant District Officer[1] and eleven others when they were on their way to repair the village water supply. On only three occasions during the previous six months had any information been given to the Police by local people. It was clear that the terrorists had a hold on this community and that the people of Tanjong Malim were not prepared to accept the common responsibility for the preservation of law and order on which all decent government rests. The High Commissioner consequently visited the village and imposed a twenty-two hour house curfew, at the same time ordering the collection of all surplus rice and the introduction of a strict rationing scheme. These restrictions remained in force for thirteen days.

These measures had a punitive element but this was by no means their sole purpose. By curtailing the movement of villagers to a minimum the Security Forces were helped in their operations, and by cutting down the amount of rice in circulation supplies were denied to the terrorists. The restrictions were accompanied by certain positive measures, such as the re-organisation of the district administration, the reinforcement of the Security Forces and the founding of a Home Guard unit. In addition, "Operation Question" made its first appearance—the distribution to each household of questionnaires by means of which information about the terrorists in the locality could be given to the authorities in conditions of complete confidence (thus eliminating any fear of reprisal).[2] There was therefore a great deal more to the action taken at Tanjong Malim than mere punishment.

---

[1] Michael Codner, one of the heroes from the 'Wooden Horse' escape from a German prison camp.
[2] But, commenting on Templer's letter to Lyttelton of 13 May, a CO official minuted that the questionnaire exercise had been 'a flop' (CO 1022/54, Jerrom to Higham, 21 May 1952).

Similar measures were applied at Pekan Jabi in Johore at the end of October after a number of incidents. Villagers were known to be supplying food to the terrorists and they gave no information to the Police. A 22-hour curfew for an "Operation Question" was followed by a modified curfew and a reduction in the rice ration lasting one month. Here again the reason for the action was largely operational.

A recent case which can perhaps be more appropriately described as "collective punishment" than those mentioned above was the action taken by General Templer at Permatang Tinggi in August. In this small village of only nineteen families a Chinese Assistant Resettlement Officer was murdered in a coffee shop in front of several witnesses; but no one was willing to volunteer any information to the Police. This was in line with the village's record of non-cooperation. The High Commissioner personally warned the villagers that unless information was given by a specified time they would all be detained and the village (but not their belongings) would be destroyed. No information was forthcoming and the threatened action was therefore taken. There was no disturbance and personal property was disposed of according to the instructions of its owners. This is a bare summary of what took place: you may be interested to read a more detailed account of the operation showing the care and scrupulousness with which it was carried out. I therefore enclose a copy of part of a report[3] prepared for the High Commissioner and quoted by him at his recent press conference here.

General Templer made it quite clear at the press conference that he strongly dislikes imposing collective punishments. "But", he said "what evidence we can get on this very difficult question shows that on the rare occasions on which they have been used they have been justified by their results."

I need hardly add that on all these occasions he has acted with my full support.

---

[3] Not printed.

286 CO 1022/86   10 Dec 1952

[Closer association of British territories]: minute by J J Paskin to Sir T Lloyd on discussions with Sir G Templer and COS   [Extract]

. . . Sir G. Templer . . . wishes to raise with the Secretary of State the question of closer Constitutional association between the Federation and Singapore. There was a good deal of discussion on this matter at a meeting of the Chiefs of Staff yesterday afternoon. The Chiefs of Staff were most concerned at Sir G. Templer's statement that the prospects of closer association between these two territories has greatly receded during the 12 months since he has been in Malaya. The Chiefs of Staff thereupon decided that they themselves would embark upon a study as to the scope of unification which *they* would like to see in South East Asia, from the strategic point of view. (By this I understood them to mean a study on whether the aim should be a "South East Asia dominion" including the Malayan *and* Borneo territories).

To my astonishment Sir G. Templer asked me, at the meeting of the C.O.S., whether there was any Colonial Office policy on the matter. I was quite taken aback by this question but I had to explain that from 1945 onwards it *has* been Colonial Office policy that there should be closer association between (a) the Federation and

Singapore, and (b) the three Borneo territories; and that there was also a "hope" that there would ultimately be a union of the Malayan *and* the Borneo territories.

I then had to explain that it had always been the view of those on the spot that, as regards the Federation and Singapore, it would be necessary for the impetus to come from Malaya itself and that it would be for the authorities there to stimulate local unofficial opinion in the respective territories (by whatever means were thought best) to get closer together and if possible for themselves to formulate proposals.

I explained that the first attempt at getting local opinion moving in the right direction was the Commissioner-General's "Communities Liaison Committee", but that this Committee had now ceased to function. The most recent line had been the establishment of local branches of the Commonwealth Parliamentary Association, with a regional Association in Singapore, which would provide a meeting house for unofficial members of the Legislative Councils (including those from the Borneo territories).[1]

Sir G. Templer said that this was all very well but, the way things were going, we might find that the Federation might be ready for full self-government, *before* Singapore and the Federation were ready to get together. Had not therefore the time now come for some forthright declaration of policy from London which would jolt the local political leaders into taking this matter seriously? I replied that the advice from Malaya in the past had been on the lines that this would hamper rather than help; but if he now felt such a declaration *would* help, the proper course would be for him to get together with the Governor of Singapore and make a joint recommendation to the Secretary of State. Sir G. Templer's retort to this was a "surprised" question whether policy on this matter lay with the Secretary of State or with him and the Governor of Singapore?

Almost immediately afterwards Sir G. Templer made the comment that closer union between Singapore and the Federation would mean tearing up the present Federation Agreement (which he himself has repeatedly told us could not be contemplated at present— or indeed that nothing should be done to make the Malays fear that any such move was in the wind).

The discussion was all very confused and in parts inconsistent, but it served to show how disturbed Sir G. Templer's mind is about the lack of progress in getting the two territories together.[2]

---

[1] See 267 and 276.

[2] Paskin spoke on the lines of this minute when the future relationship between the Federation and Singapore—and ultimately between the Malayan and Borneo territories as a whole—was considered at a meeting between Lyttelton, Templer and CO officials in the evening of 10 Dec. During this discussion Templer outlined his programme for local and state elections 'which he thought would lead up to the first Legislative Council Election by about 1958' and 'asked for guidance on what would happen after that'. The agenda also included: 'Action necessary if Indo-China falls'; 'The use of tear gas to "flush" blocks of jungle'; 'Expansion of the Federation army and a grant from HMG'; 'Recruitment'; and 'Code of discipline for the police' (see CO 1022/493, no 31).

287 CO 1022/107, no 12 3 Jan 1953

[Reform of the MCS]: despatch no 5/53 from Sir D MacGillivray

[With the improvement in internal security attention shifted to constitutional and political issues in 1953. The principal matters were: elections to state and settlement councils, reform of the Federal Legislative Council, extension of the member system, and closer association with Singapore. In addition, the 'Malayanisation' of the federal armed forces and civil administration were under active consideration.]

I have the honour to inform you that at a special meeting of the Conference of Rulers held on 6th November, 1952, Their Highnesses accepted the recommendations of a Committee of Mentri Mentri Besar appointed at an earlier meeting of the Conference and agreed to the admission of Asians of other than the Malay race to the Malayan Civil Service.

2. Hitherto, as you aware, the Rulers have jealously preserved the Administrative Services from the intrusion of officers of any race other than Malay or British. Their Highnesses have now accepted the argument that Federal Citizenship must carry with it the privilege of eligibility to take part in all branches of the public service but on the condition that, for the present, the position of the Malays should be safeguarded by means of a quota. The proposals agreed were as follows:—

(i) That non-Malay Federal Citizens should be admitted to the Malayan Civil Service on a quota basis.
(ii) That the quota should be four Malays to one non-Malay Asian Federal Citizen.
(iii) That all Asian candidates, Malay or non-Malay, recommended for appointment to the Malayan Civil Service should be selected by a Selection Board, consisting of:—

The Chief Secretary as Chairman
One representative from the former Unfederated Malay States
One representative from the former Federated Malay States, and the
Malayan Establishment Officer.

(iv) That any Federal Citizen who was a member of the Malayan Civil Service should, subject to the approval of the Secretary of State, automatically cease to be a member of that Service if, for any cause, he ceased to be a Federal Citizen.

3. It was agreed also that in the event of Asians being appointed to the Malayan Civil Service in the Colony of Singapore they should not thereby become eligible for service in any part of the Federation. The High Commissioner felt that he could not oppose Their Highnesses' view on this point in view of the fact that the Federation Government has no control over the numbers who might be so appointed in Singapore and that the proportion of Malays among such appointments would almost certainly be negligible. In any case even if Asian officers are appointed to the Malayan Civil Service in the Colony of Singapore it is unlikely that they will be Federal Citizens.

4. As a condition of this relaxation of the former rule, Their Highnesses requested that a special Committee should be set up to examine and make recommendations regarding the economic position of the Malays and also that certain steps should be taken to encourage the higher education of Malays with the object of bringing their

economic and educational status to a level more closely approximating to that of the other races in Malaya. The conclusions reached at the Conference of Rulers were communicated to the Federal Executive Council on the 14th November, 1952, and were endorsed. Some of the Asian members of the Executive Council expressed the view, however, that the quota should be more favourable to the non-Malay Asians. The special Committee has now started work under the Chairmanship of the Mentri Besar, Perak, Dato Panglima Bukit Gantang.

5. Applications for appointment to the Malayan Civil Service under the new scheme are now being invited and the recommendations of the Selection Board will be forwarded to you in due course.

6. I am sending a copy of this despatch to the Governor of Singapore.

288 CO 1022/61, no 19   20 Jan 1953
[Closer association of British territories]: minute by J D Higham to J J Paskin   [Extract]

[On 17 Dec 1952 the secretary of the Joint Planning Staff, Ministry of Defence, asked the CO for a paper on political objectives in British territories in SE Asia, paying particular attention to the questions of: (a) policy as regards granting self-government to the territories concerned, (b) expected dates at which they would be ready for this step, and (c) plans for combining some or all of them, especially the possible union of Malaya and Singapore. J D Higham, who was about to be seconded to the Singapore government, addressed the third of these issues in this minute. For further developments, see 292 and 293.]

. . . 4. In replying to (c) I would begin by referring to the Secretary of State's Despatch of the 12th November, 1949, transmitting the Royal Instructions to the Commissioner-General, and particularly to the following passage:

> "In the course of time some closer political co-operation may be desirable, and you will advise the Secretary of State for the Colonies on this question from time to time . . . You are directed . . . to promote the co-ordination of policy and administration between the Governments in your area of authority . . .".

The draft could go on to quote the 1946 White Paper (Cmd. 6724), which stated that it was not part of H.M.G.'s policy to "preclude or prejudice in any way the fusion of Singapore and the Malayan Union in a wider union at a later date should it be considered that such a course were desirable". In the 1947 White Paper (Cmd. 7171) it was stated that H.M.G. still held this view and believed "that the question of Singapore joining in a Federation should be considered on its merits and in the light of local opinion at an appropriate time."

5. The following remarks may be of assistance when the redraft is prepared. They relate both to Questions (b) and (c). The hope when the Malayan Union and the Colony of Singapore were established was that fusion would be possible within a few years; similarly it had been hoped in respect of the Borneo territories that fusion of Sarawak and North Borneo under one Governor would be possible when the first Governors relinquished their appointments. It has been accepted policy, reaffirmed by the successive Secretaries of State, that the initiative for a closer association of

Malaya and Singapore must come from the two territories and there should be no question of imposing unification from Whitehall. Although it is generally accepted by responsible Asians that some form of closer association must come, and e.g. the Pan-Malayan Labour Party and, I think, the Independence of Malaya Party have included closer association as one of the planks in their programme, the trouble is, as the draft points out, that despite this lip service to the ideal, there is at present no *desire* for closer association and the short term interest of the two territories often differ. The danger of letting matters drift is that Singapore in particular may advance so rapidly along the paths of parliamentary democracy, with all the outward trappings of "self-government", that, with the passage of time, it may become increasingly difficult for the two territories to come together. At the same time I am certain that to attempt to force the pace before the Malays have come to feel that they have some chance of making good in the economic and professional fields, would only cause a revulsion of Malay feelings with all the security consequences that that would entail, and possibly throw the Malays into the arms of Indonesia. This is a point that should be brought home forcibly to the Joint Planners.

6. As far as Borneo is concerned, the original difficulty of making much progress towards greater administative and political integration was the extremely sharp reaction that might have been expected in Sarawak to any break with old traditions. The anti-cession element was then a force to be reckoned with, and it was agreed at several Governors' Conferences that the political pace had to be set by Sarawak; North Borneo, under Sir Ralph Hone, was much more ready to consider schemes for increased co-operation. In fact, until communications are vastly improved, there would probably be no administrative gain in bringing the two territories under one Governor since it would be still necessary to maintain substantial Secretariats, etc. in each territory. The problem of bringing Brunei into the scheme of things is also intractable, though, of course, the Governor of Sarawak is also High Commissioner for Brunei. It has not even been possible, despite the administrative advantages, to amalgamate the Brunei and Sarawak constabulary in order to ensure uniformity of police control in the oil fields.

7. Our original conception was, of course, that on the one hand Malaya and Singapore would come together and on the other the three Borneo territories, and that the two blocks might then merge into some sort of confederation. This idea of a South-East Asia Dominion has never been, as far as I can trace, publicly stated as authoritative British policy, but, as the draft points out, Mr. Malcolm MacDonald "let the cat out of the bag" as recently as the summer of 1952 in an off-the-record talk to journalists.

8. There have, in fact, been indications that a closer union may be more acceptable if it is approached on the basis of the territories all coming together at the same time rather than forming into Malayan and Borneo blocs. It would be easier for the Malays perhaps to swallow the idea of a Federation including not only the almost undiluted Chinese Colony of Singapore, but also the less Chinese dominated Borneo Territories. Singapore might find it easier to bargain for suitable terms of entry into a Greater Federation if other territories, which had also been Colonies in their own right, were to come in at the same time. On the other hand the Dyaks in Sarawak have no love for the Malays and might well resent any attempt to force them into a confederation in which the Malay element would be relatively so much more important than it is in Sarawak.

9. The new approach to the question of closer association, i.e. the approach involving all the territories together rather than the two separate blocks, seems to be going well enough. (See 15 and 17 on SEA.19/4/01); but progress is desperately slow and without some clearer agenda there may be no progress at all, and although it was agreed, when Sir G. Templer discussed the question with the Secretary of State recently (see Mr. Gann's Minute of the 11th December on SEA.31/1/07) that the present time would be inappropriate for any positive action, I am not happy to leave the matter entirely in abeyance. In the first place, as I indicated above, there is the danger that Singapore will become so set in her present ways that she will only consent to enter a Greater Malaya on terms unacceptable to the Federation; and secondly—and even more urgently—there is danger in leaving the thinly populated, under-developed Borneo Territories out on a limb, adjacent to a potentially acquisitive Indonesia. I can see little future for a self-governing Sarawak or North Borneo, or even for a self-governing Colony of British Borneo plus Brunei. The Federation and Singapore themselves are, in all conscience, small enough in size and population when compared with their neighbours. (Indonesia, population some 70 million; Siam 18 million; Burma 17 million; Indo-China 27 million; Philippines 20 million). I think that all possible means should be used to forward the idea of a British South-East Asia Dominion, and I think that the next step should be to ask the Commissioner-General's views on whether he and the Governors concerned would now recommend a more positive statement about the aim of our policy than has hitherto been vouchsafed. What I have in mind is an arranged question and answer in Parliament. The reply need not be too specific; it could talk about our ultimate hopes rather than about our definite intentions; and it could refer to the over-riding importance of ensuring that in any such Greater Federation the interests of all sections of the community should be adequately safeguarded. I think too that the Commissioner-General should be asked to try and find out what the present views of Asian leaders are, and the terms on which each territory would be prepared to come into some form of closer association. I know that e.g. C.C. Tan has been giving very careful study to various forms of federal constitution, and I think, if we could get some idea of what people on the spot feel to be real difficulties and minimum desiderata, we might then have a basis to do some preliminary thought in this office. At the moment I do not feel that we have enough information on which to base a further study of the problem. It might also be timely to enquire what plans are being devised for increased central control of the Governments in wartime. At one stage it was contemplated that a considerable degree of administrative and even legislative integration might be achieved by means of a central "War Cabinet" with the Commissioner-General in the Chair.

289   CO 1022/463, ff 7–9   22 Jan 1953

[Economic position of Malays]: minute by T C Jerrom on his recent visit to Malaya

I discussed this subject with a number of officials and others during my visit to the Federation in November and December, and it may be of use to record on this file my random impressions.

2. I think it is fair to say that there is now a widespread realisation in Malaya of the tremendous importance of improving the economic position of the Malays. But amongst the more educated members of the community there is also a growing realisation of the difficulty of the problems involved. My own feeling is that it is unlikely that the Malays can ever be successfully "encouraged and assisted" (to quote General Templer's Directive)[1] to play a much fuller part in the economic life of the country than they do at present. This is, of course, no argument for letting things drift. On the contrary it is to my mind all the more important that the whole subject should be fully ventilated without further delay, and that any constructive measures which can be introduced should be introduced at once. The other side of the picture, i.e. the possible political repercusions of a failure to achieve any great success in improving the economic position of the Malays must be considered separately as one of the basic political problems of Malaya.

3. Among suggestions made to me by District Officers, Malays and senior officers in Kuala Lumpur were those referred to briefly below:—

(a) *Education.* It seems to be generally agreed that from the long term point of view the greatest possible assistance which Government could give the Malays would be the provision (either free or at low cost) of English education and technical education for the greatest possible number of young Malays. Most of those with whom I discussed this had boys in mind, and the idea of widespread higher education for Malay girls would probably get a patchy acceptance at present; my own view is that while it must be carefully handled the education of girls has a special importance from the long term point of view as one of the best antidotes to the old family customs which have a bad effect on young Malays.

(b) *Rural development teams.* I came across one or two little R.I.D.A. and other schemes in the kampongs; as is, I suppose, to be expected, they had been started in rather a haphazard way and are now in considerable difficulties. Several of the people I talked to in Perak thought that before devoting a lot of time and money to individual schemes of this sort, it would be far better to set up development teams to gather basic information about kampong economy and the rural life of the Malays. This information would serve as a basis for properly thought out plans of economic development which would take account of all local conditions. One District Officer thought that all the Government Departments directly concerned with rural life should send representatives to make up a development team; I pointed out that a detailed investigation of this sort over a wide area would involve a tremendous expenditure of time and effort, but he still thought that it was the only sensible way of attacking the problems of the rural areas.

(c) *New Malay enterprises.* I found a fairly general feeling of disillusionment among Europeans about the chances of Malays by themselves developing new enterprises on a profitable basis, even if they were dealing with new products which had not yet attracted the Chinese. I did not discuss this subject very fully, but I think that many Europeans have a feeling at the back of their minds that if the Malays did succeed in getting into any enterprise from which substantial profits could be derived they would be unable to keep out the Chinese; whatever the position might be on the surface, in a short time the Malays concerned would

---

[1] See 268, para 5.

be in the hands of Chinese financiers. Someone suggested that in the early stages joint Malaya-Government enterprises would be the only way of ensuring that the Chinese did not get in under the surface, and another idea was that joint Malay-European commercial enterprises might be possible.

(d) *Entry of Malays into existing trades, etc.* Here again the picture left in my mind was a pretty sombre one. Dato Onn, who was admittedly in a depressed mood when I saw him, said plainly that the Malays could never compete effectively with the Chinese because they did not understand bribery. This is no doubt a gross over-simplification of the problem, but my own feeling is that there is none the less some measure of truth in it. The fact seems to be that as a people the Malays are simply lacking in the nous, or whatever one likes to call it, which is necessary to trade successfully in competition with the Chinese; and if one assumes that the Chinese will continue to improve their technique there is little hope that the Malays will ever be able to catch up.

(e) *Fragmentation of land.* To the outsider it looks as if fragmentation of land holding under the Moslem law of inheritance has a bad effect on the rural economy. I was considerably surprised when a Malay A.D.O. in Perak suggested that it might be possible within a few years to secure an amendment of the Moslem law, which would avoid the automatic division of small plots of land in this way. I know nothing about this subject but my own first reaction would be that any attempt, even by the Moslem religious authorities themselves, to amend the inheritance laws would run into pretty heavy opposition.

(f) *Parental influences.* Several people pointed out the contrast between the Malay and Chinese attitude towards parenthood. It is a subject on which generalizations must always be extremely suspect, but it is perhaps fair to say that amongst a reasonable proportion of the Chinese community parents take a keen interest in the ambitions and material progress of their children, and are prepared to go to considerable trouble and expense to help their children obtain a good education, or a reasonable opening in trade. Among the Malays on the other hand I was told that there is far more tendency to make economic use of their children at an early age and to disregared the future interests of the children in favour of the immediate interests of the family.

(g) *Health.* Several people suggested to me that indifferent health was a most important factor which retarded the economic advancement of the Malays. This is clearly a matter of great importance, but it is not one on which I am competent to comment. Using the word health in its widest sense I suppose it might even be held to cover traits in the Malay personality e.g. those which give rise to something like a national inferiority complex among them. My own feeling is that this inferiority complex (if that is what it is) is perhaps the most important factor affecting the wellbeing of the Malays as a people. But many other aspects of the health position among the Malays might justify detailed investigation.

In conclusion I should note my own impression that the Federation Government may have exposed themselves to rather an awkward situation in appointing a Committee under the Chairmanship of Bukit Gantang and with Dato Onn as a Member to consider the economic position of the Malays. I think it is quite likely that the Committee will recommend legislative action which would in effect involve discrimination against the Chinese and other communities, and if this demand comes forward at a time when Malay opinion generally in the country is restive, the Federation Government may be in an awkward position.

I suggest that the papers in Sir G. Maxwell's P.F.[2] attached should be copied to this file, which should then be noted to be brought up for discussion with Mr. Hogan as part of his general consideration of the political future of Malaya.[3]

---

[2] ie Sir George Maxwell's personal file. Former Malayan civil servant and tireless lobbyist in retirement, Maxwell was in correspondence with the CO about the position of Malays in commerce. For Maxwell, see part I of this volume, 73, note 1.

[3] See 283, note 1.

290   CO 1022/298, no 34   23 Jan 1953

[Elections]: letter (reply) from J J Paskin to Sir D MacGillivray.
Minutes by A S Gann, T C Jerrom and A M Mackintosh

Higham, unfortunately, was unable before leaving us last Tuesday, to reply to your letter of 18th October.[1] It therefore falls to me to thank you for the comprehensive and useful survey of the Elections position contained in that letter. We are encouraged by all we have heard about the progress of local elections, and look forward to seeing the Bedale Report.[2]

2. We had a word with the High Commissioner while he was here and I understood from him that your hope was that other States and Settlements would follow pretty fast on the heels of Johore and Penang, and that the objective was to have all these elections completed or at least in an advanced state of preparation, by the end of 1955.[3] We quite realise that constant pressure from the top will be needed to keep to such a timetable and we are glad to notice that you intended to press for elections to the Johore Council of State before the end of 1953 or at least early in 1954. We had mentioned to the High Commissioner our feeling that such pressure might well be necessary as a counter to Communist tactics of building up a "United Front" which might press for early Federal elections. I see from paragraph 3 of the December Political Intelligence Report that there is a danger of this, but I do not know to what extent the tactics are regarded as a real threat to which it will be necessary to pay attention in deciding on your election timetable.

3. The question is sometimes asked here why Johore should be selected as the pace-maker and it is suggested that it might be simpler to start in one of the less complicated and quieter States. This is a possibility you have no doubt considered and there are obvious advantages in going ahead in a State where the public is conditioned to the idea of elections and a lot of spade work has been done as in Johore. This is the line we take in answering such questions, hinting that in practice there will be little, if any, advantage in point of time in disturbing your present plans to start with Johore and Penang. But if you have anything to add on this point, we should like to know your views.

4. This brings me to a question that arises out of your intention to start with one State and one Settlement, and then to spread the net wider until it covers the whole Federation. Put briefly, the question is: Are you going to attempt to get a

---

[1] See 280   [2] See *ibid*, note 3   [3] see 283.

Federation-wide agreement on general principles, such as the basis for the franchise, the delineation of constituencies and the composition of councils before the starting pistol is fired in Johore and/or Penang? Decisions were reached in the Report of the Select Committee set up by the Johore Council [of] State in 1950 on these questions; but I do not know how far this report would still be acceptable, or whether it would be regarded as [an] acceptable basis by all the States and Settlements. Would you contemplate agreeing to any substantial divergencies of policy between the States, or would you feel it necessary to insist on at least a considerable degree of uniformity? I imagine that in Selangor, for example, there might well be difficulties in accepting the Johore basis, since the Malays are probably already outnumbered by other Federal citizens and the drawing of constituencies might involve a good deal of controversy.

We will, of course, have a word with Hogan about this when we see him, and I do not want to trouble you to reply at any great length; but if you can at your leisure let us know how your ideas are forming on this particular aspect of the election problem, it would be most helpful to us.

Minutes on the reply to 290

Mr. Jerrom
In reply to (34) Sir D. MacGillivray has sent, with (35), a copy of a paper which was to be considered by the Conference of Federation Executives on 17th March.[4] This paper, which forms the second enclosure, sets out the general principles on which it is hoped all States and Settlements will agree to conduct their Council elections when the time comes. This clears up one important point about which we were doubtful by indicating that the Government hopes to obtain Federation-wide agreement on questions of franchise, composition of Councils and delineation of constituencies before the first State/Settlement Council elections take place next year.

2. The proposals are based on the report of the Johore Select Committee, which is behind (19) on 52243/29/50. Briefly the main points are as follows:—

(a) "The basis of elected representation should be territorial and not communal."
(b) The franchise should be given to all Federal citizens. (This includes Federal citizens who are not nationals of the State in which they are living, or who, in a settlement, are not British subjects; although in these cases a residence qualification will be required.)
(c) There should be a majority of official plus nominated members over elected members so long as the Executive Council remains a nominated body. But wherever a State/Settlement constitution is amended to allow an elected element in the Executive Council, it will be sufficient if officials plus those unofficials (nominated or elected) who are also members of Executive Council form the majority.

3. I think we can regard (a) and (b) above as eminently satisfactory, and (c) is a

---

[4] Neither item 35 nor its enclosure is printed here but their contentes are summarised in Gann's minute.

common sense arrangement designed to ensure that the Councils cannot stalemate the Governments, while at the same time providing for a half-way house towards responsible government in the fullest sense. But these are of course simply the proposals put forward by the Federation Government. We do not yet know what was the outcome of the discussion by the Conference of Federation Executives (which consists of the Mentri[s] Besar and the Resident Commissioners), but even if they approved the memorandum, the real test will come when it is considered by the various Governments and debated in the existing Councils.

4. I think the Federation Government is wise in putting forward its proposals in this way and basing them on a report which has already been approved by one State Council. We have already considered in the Department the various objections which might arise, and we can now only wait to see how far they are seized upon by the States. It will be interesting to learn, for example, the reactions of the Government of Selangor. I feel it is important that we should be kept informed of developments, particularly in view of the forthcoming talks with Mr. Hogan, and it would perhaps do no harm to reply to (35) as in the short draft opposite, which might be for Mr. MacKintosh's signature.

A.S.G.
20.3.53

Mr. MacKintosh

You may wish to glance at the minutes from 4 November onwards,[5] (34) and (35). The enclosure to (35) is a very sketchy piece of work and it is clear that the Federation Govt. have plunged into this without the prolonged cerebration we rather expected. In fact they seem to be relying almost entirely on the out of date Johore Report.

A minor point is that in Singapore candidates seeking election have to have lived in the Colony for 3 years and there has been a recent attempt to raise this to 7 years.

T.C.J.
23.3.53

Mr. Puskin

I think that in replying to (35) we ought to make some reference to two points upon which Mr. Jerrom has rightly seized on page 2 of the enclosure and in the list attached to it respectively. I have therefore re-drafted the reply for your signature. You may well think that my additions are jeujune and unnecessary but I thought that it might do no harm if I let you know in particular the sort of consideration which seems to me to be involved in the question of the numbers of constituencies in the various States and Settlements.

As I had already told you, I have been led by reading (30),[6] (34) and (35) and the minutes from that of the 4th November, 1952, onwards, to wonder whether we have ever explicitly put to ourselves the choice between treating the Federation now and in the future as if it were always going to be a true federal state or taking every opportunity to guide developments in the direction of unitary government. The first would mean leaving substantial powers in the hands of the State authorities and would make it comparatively unimportant to secure uniformity amongst them in

---

[5] See 280, minutes.   [6] See 280.

legislation, executive action, etc. The States and Settlements would retain a degree of sovereignty and their Legislatures would have to be regarded as coordinate with the Federal Legislature and not subordinate to it. If, however, our aim is to integrate the States and Settlements, reducing the status of their Legislatures to that of County Councils and subordinating them to a unitary central government, then we should presumably never lose an opportunity to stamp upon the whole Federation a common pattern of law and procedure. I am diffident about expressing an opinion from so little knowledge but I should have thought that it would be better for Malaya in the long run if we could guide the country away from federal towards unitary government. In that case it seems to me that it would be worth while doing all we can to build up the same structure of local government (including the State Councils) throughout the Federation.

A.M.M.
30.5.53

291 CO 1022/450, no 16 Feb 1953

'General priorities of a district officer (in order of priority)': monthly administrative report (Appendix 'A') by Sir G Templer. *Minute* by T C Jerrom

1. The District Officer is the natural and single leader in his district. He must make sure not only that he acts as a leader, but that everyone in his district realises that that is his job.

2. The District Officer must be the central and binding force in relation to all administrative, police and military effort in his district. It is his responsibility to co-ordinate and encourage all measures taken by the police and the military, to sort out any differences which occur between these two and to provide the direction and advice which both need in their relation to the general aim of Government. He must, therefore, continue to act as the Chairman of DWEC.

3. Operation "Service" in the broadest sense of the word.

4. The inauguration and guidance of elected Local Councils, and, where practicable, elected Town or Municipal Councils.

5. Full assistance to the District Information Officer (when appointed) in the education of the people in the broadest sense of the word. This includes the fostering of Civics Courses, Youth Service Teams, Meetings of Penghulus and Officers in charge of Police Stations, etc. It must also include the promotion in all ways of our new Education Policy.

6. Improvements to Malay kampong life, e.g. in water supplies, bridle paths, the provision of electric light (in those cases where the electric mains are handy) and in the establishment of Community Centres.

7. Land administration generally.

8. Continuing to raise the standard in the New Villages until they reach the general position outlined in Appendix 'B'.

Minute on 291

... Gen. Templer is very anxious to strengthen the District Administration and stimulate leadership in the Districts. Since Malaya now needs a modern system of local government with elected councils the position is somewhat confused, also some of the District Officers. But my own feeling is that the High Commissioner's personal interest and support has already done a lot to raise their standing. The best of them are successfully combining autocratic rule with the new democratic processes in a typically Malayan way.

T.C.J.
27.3.53

292   CO 1022/91, no 23   5 Mar 1953
[Closer association of British territories]: minute by J J Paskin to Sir T Lloyd

Arising out of some remarks made by Sir G. Templer, at a meeting of the C.O.S. which he attended in November, the C.O.S. have directed the J.P.S. to prepare a paper on long term defence policy in South East Asia, taking into account the policy as regards constitutional development in the territories in that area. To assist them in preparing their paper the J.P.S. have put to us the questions in No. 3 on this file,[1] which we have attempted to answer in the draft opposite. As will be seen, we have altered the order of questions (b) and (c) for obvious reasons.[2]

2. The proposed answer to question (c) is, I am afraid, rather long. But it has deliberately been cast in the form of an historical review of the development of policy for the reason that, on several occasions in the past few years, not only the C.O.S. here, but also the Commanders-in-Chief Committee in Singapore, have shown themselves impatient of the doctrine that a policy of closer association between Singapore and the Federation can only be achieved by a judicious process of stimulating the development of a climate of public opinion which would be favourable to this development. They have in fact from time to time been inclined to the view that what was required was a robust and forceful directive from H.M.G. It will be recalled that Sir G. Templer also spoke on these lines at his last talk with the Secretary of State at the end of his visit here in November. For this reason, it seems to me that a useful purpose would be served by placing on record, with the Chiefs of Staff, a review on the lines suggested as a reply to their question (c).

3. From what was said by Sir G. Templer himself while he was here, which has been confirmed by what we have heard from many other sources, the attainment of a policy of closer association between Singapore and the Federation seems farther away now than at any time during the past six years. Indeed the antipathy between Singapore and the Federation is perhaps now even stronger in official than in unofficial circles. Indeed it has reached the point at which Sir J. Nicoll and Sir D. MacGillivray are reported to have expressed the view that it would be better to leave the two territories to drift further apart instead of constantly attempting to keep

---

[1] See 288, note.   [2] For the final version of this paper, see 293.

them in step in such matters as local taxation, conditions of service, etc. The kind of exasperation which is caused by these constant sources of friction between Singapore and the Federation is illustrated by an extract from a letter written by Sir G. Templer to the Secretary of State on the 7th February.[3]

4. This picture of a constantly widening breach between Singapore and the Federation is so different from the optimistic account given in the Commissioner General's latest report on this subject (as recently as the 10th June, 1952)[4] that it seems to me that, on this ground alone, the Secretary of State would be justified in asking the Commissioner General, the Governor of Singapore and the High Commissioner for the Federation to put their heads together and attempt to assess the situation and the question whether it is possible to do anything to rectify it.

5. But quite apart from this, there have been other recent developments which, to my mind, make it almost imperative that these three authorities should be asked to get together to consider the situation.

6. In paragraph 9 of his minute of the 20th January,[5] Mr. Higham has expressed the apprehension that "Singapore will become so set in her present ways that she will only consent to enter a greater Malaya on terms unacceptable to the Federation". I also, for some time, have been concerned that Singapore seemed to be developing along lines which appeared to be so exclusively aimed at "self-government for Singapore" that it would become increasingly difficult to find a basis acceptable to both territories, for a wider federation. This concern of mine has been considerably increased by the receipt, since the date of Mr. Higham's minute, of Sir J. Nicoll's letters of the 19th January and 23rd February at Nos. 20 and 21 on SEA 31/249/01.[6] I had previously written to Sir J. Nicoll (my letter of the 9th December at No. 19 on that file) in which I had expressed the view that what was really wanted, from the point of view of facilitating some form of political association with the present Federation, was the transfer to the City Council of as many as possible of the purely *local* functions of the Singapore Government. I have always felt that a process of this kind would make the solid Chinese Singapore pill much easier for the Malays of the Federation to swallow. Sir J. Nicoll, in his letter of the 3rd February, rejects this thesis in favour of a proposal, which he has already been pursuing with unofficials in Singapore, that the present Legislative and City Councils should be merged into one. (I am commenting further on that letter in a minute on SEA 31/249/01 in order to confine the discussion on this file to matters strictly relevant to the theme of an ultimate political association between Singapore and the Federation).

7. In the last paragraph of that letter Sir J. Nicoll says that it would be unwise at this stage to raise the issue of constitutional association with the Federation; and that "we must get agreement first on the proper set up in Singapore".

8. I must say that I find it difficult to accept this thesis for two reasons. The first is that it seems to me that, in considering the line of constitutional development in Singapore, it would be unwise to get committed to a line which would make the problem of political association with the Federation even more intractable than it is at present. Secondly, this process might well involve more painful adjustments in Singapore itself when the time comes for working out concrete proposals for a union with the Federation.

---

[3] See CO 1022/61, no 22.   [4] See 276.
[5] See 288.
                                                               [6] Also at CO 1022/91.

9. I have referred to this as an "intractable problem" and it is so for two separate kinds of reasons. In the first place we have a very long way to go yet before the relationship between the Malays and the Chinese in the Federation itself can develop into anything more than a very uneasy association, so that the Malays would certainly still be extremely uneasy at the prospect of a closer political association with the solid Chinese mass of Singapore. On the other side of the picture, in present circumstances in the Federation, political association would be very unattractive to the prosperous Chinese business community in Singapore.

10. The other reason why this is an intractable problem is that, in so far as local politicians in the Federation have thought about it at all, I feel sure (and Mr. David[7] agrees) that they will have abeen thinking of it in terms of Singapore becoming another unit in the greater Federation, in rather the kind of position which is at present occupied by Penang and Malacca. I am sure that this would be completely unacceptable to Singapore where the local politicians, I should expect, will be thinking in terms of some "fifty-fifty" arrangement as between themselves as one unit and the existing Federation as a whole as another unit. Even, therefore, when the politicians in the two territories can be brought to the point of facing up to the practical issues of some form of political association, it will be a very difficult problem indeed to evolve a form of association which will be satisfactory to both parties.

11. These considerations seem to me another reason for asking the Commissioner General, the Governor and the High Commissioner to take stock of the ultimate objective.

12. But it is not only in Singapore that ideas of constitutional changes are simmering. When he was here in November, Sir G. Templer several times said that he felt that it was high time to look ahead to constitutional changes which he felt would be necessary in the Federation when the time comes for the *election* of members of the Federal Legislative Council. He felt that any ventilation of this question in Malaya itself, or even a visit to Malaya by some constitutional expert, the object of whose visit would be difficult to camouflage, would create such alarm in the minds of the Malays that it would be out of the question. The conclusion which we ultimately reached was that advantage should be taken of Mr. Hogan's impending arrival on leave to get his mind working on this problem so that (possibly with an extension of leave) while he was here, and with the assistance of some constitutional expert, he should work out proposals for the amendment of the Federal constitution. Here again it seems to me that, in working out these proposals, Mr. Hogan should have in mind the objective of a political union between Singapore and the Federation.

13. I must say that it seems to me that unless more positive guidance can be given, the present process of "philosophical" stimulation of unofficial opinion in favour of political association between Singapore and the Federation might go on for ever without producing any very practical results. Since the demise of the Communities Liaison Committee, this process, judging from Mr. MacDonald's savingram at No. 15 on SEA 19/4/01,[8] seems to have been confined to Singapore (and a smaller extent to the Borneo territories) and to have been completely neglected in

---

[7] E David, MCS since 1931, officiated as secretary for defence and internal security 1951–1953 when he was seconded to the CO; appointed chief secretary, Hong Kong, 1955.   [8] See 276.

the Federation. It has also always seemed to me that the idea that something useful in this direction would emerge, in the measurable future, from meetings of the various local branches of the Commonwealth Parliamentary Association (leading towards a possible union of all the Malayan and Borneo territories) is something of a pipe dream.

14. (In this connection it is interesting to see from the Commissioner General's savingram at No. 4 on SEA 19/5/01[9] that Mr. MacDonald and Sir A. Abell have now come to the conclusion that the "atmosphere" is becoming favourable to pursue the idea of some form of union between the Borneo territories *alone*. See also now Sir R. Hone's savingram at No. 5 on same file).

15. It will be recalled that when, in Sir H. Gurney's days, the best way of creating the desired favourable climate of opinion was canvassed, Sir H. Gurney consistently took the line that neither he nor any officials of the Federation Government should appear to be involved in any such discussions. From what I have said in paragraph 12 above, Sir G. Templer may well take the same view. But what I am proposing is not at present any overt involvement of the High Commissioner, but rather that he and Mr. MacDonald and Sir J. Nicoll should get together behind closed doors to take stock of the whole position. Apart from other considerations, this would I think be salutary for Sir G. Templer who, from the remarks which he made when he was here in November, seems to have very little, if any, notion of what has been going on for the last four or five years on this theme. Moreover we know that Sir G. Templer is himself very much wedded to the idea of an *early* association of Singapore with the Federation, and the injection of his forceful and practical personality into such discussions might well have a stimulating effect also on Mr. MacDonald and Sir J. Nicoll. Indeed, from this point of view, there is much to be said for the view that, instead of allowing the colonial functions of the Commissioner General to lapse when Mr. MacDonald's term of office expires, he should be replaced by someone with the kind of forceful and direct approach which has been displayed by Sir G. Templer.

16. But it also seems to me that if any such discussions are to get anywhere, they should be directed to providing answers to as specific a set of questions as can be devised, and I have tried my hand at producing a questionnaire at No. 27 on SEA 19/4/01 which is the appropriate file for pursuing these matters.

17. As I mentioned to you, my original idea was to send out that questionnaire to the Commissioner General, the High Commissioner and the Governor in time for them to have a preliminary meeting before Sir J. Nicoll comes on leave at the end of March—really so that he could see for himself the red light in the course on which he is embarking. In my discussion with you, however, it was agreed that a preferable course would be for you to send a letter to Sir J. Nicoll sounding a word of warning against getting too positively committed on the theme of his letters of the 19th January and 3rd February, and telling him that we should like to discuss these matters with him during the course of his leave. For this purpose I submit a draft for your signature on SEA 31/249/01. The questionnaire at No. 21 on SEA 19/4/01 could then be kept back to be brought into these discussions, and not sent out to Mr. MacDonald and Sir G. Templer until after we had run over the ground with Sir J. Nicoll.

18. But, in connection with the enquiries which Mr. Hogan is being asked to

---

[9] At CO 1022/63, no 4.

undertake (paragraph 12 above) we should I think discuss with him the general question of our ultimate objective in Malaya and Singapore, not only in order that he may have these matters in mind but also because his intimate knowledge of the political scene in the Federation will help us in deciding how to present this matter when putting it to the Commissioner General and the others.

19. If these general ideas are accepted then the immediate action is:—

(a) to send the memorandum at No. 7 on this file to the C.O.S. Secretariat; and
(b) to write to Sir J. Nicoll as in draft on SEA 31/249/01.

P.S. I find that I have omitted to mention one further aspect of this matter. We have been talking about the difficulties of creating a favourable climate of opinion amongst the prominent unofficials of the two territories. But it is not only the unofficials who are parochially-minded; we have it not only from Sir G. Templer, but from many others, that the virus of separatism is rampant amongst officials also. Indeed, when he was here, Sir G. Templer said (no doubt hyperbolically) that he and MacGillivray on the one hand, and Sir J. Nicoll on the other, were about the only people in official circles in the Federation and Singapore who could ever agree: all their respective officials were constantly at loggerheads. An example of this has recently come to my notice in a batch of minutes of the M.B.D.C. and its sub-committees which have recently arrived. A committee had been considering for a very long time the issue whether, in the event of war, the various Pan-Malayan "controllers" who would (theoretically) get their "directions" from the Commission-er General, should have executive authority in each of the territories, or whether the executive authority should rest with their "deputies" in the two territories, who would have a separate allegiance to their respective Governments. The representa-tives of the Federation and Singapore having registered complete disagreement on this issue in the committee, the matter was referred to the M.B.D.C. itself for a decision. But the difference of view persisted in the M.B.D.C. so that, instead of coming to a decision, that body has referred the matter to another (newly constituted) committee which has recently been set up. And so the talk goes on. It is for this reason that I have inserted point 6 in my draft questionnaire on SEA 19/4/01. (I have not modified that point to take account of Sir D. MacGillivray's letter at No. 26 on that file).

293   CO 1022/91, no 25   10 Mar 1953
'Political objectives in British territories of South East Asia': CO memorandum for the Joint Planning Staff, Ministry of Defence

(a) *"The policy as regards granting self-government to the territories concerned."*
1. The British Colonial and Protected Territories in South East Asia are covered by the following general statement of policy made by the Secretary of State for the Colonies in the House of Commons on 14th November, 1951:—

> "Certain broad lines of policy are accepted by all sections of the House as being above party politics. These have been clearly stated by my predecessors from both the main parties. Two of them are fundamental. First, we all aim at

helping the colonial territories to attain self-government within the British Commonwealth. To that end we are seeking as rapidly as possible to build up in each territory the institutions which its circumstances require."

2. As regards particular territories, the following quotations are relevant:—

Federation of Malaya
(a) Preamble to the Federation Agreement, 1948 (which was subsequently incorporated into the Federal Constitution):—

> "And whereas it is the desire of His Majesty and Their Highnesses that progress should be made towards eventual self-government and, as a first step to that end, His Majesty and Their Highnesses have agreed that, as soon as circumstances and local conditions will permit, legislation should be introduced for the election of members to the several legislatures to be established pursuant to this Agreement:".

(b) Directive issued to Sir General Templer (February 1952):—

> "The policy of His Majesty's Government in the United Kingdom is that Malaya should in due course become a fully self-governing nation. His Majesty's Government confidently hope that that nation will be within the British Commonwealth".

Sarawak
Preamble to the Sarawak Constitution Ordinance, 1941 reaffirmed, after the cession of the territory, by the Sarawak Letters Patent, 1946:—

> "8. That the goal of self-government shall always be kept in mind, that the people of Sarawak shall be entrusted in due course with the governance of themselves and that continuous efforts shall be made to hasten the reaching of this goal by educating them, in the obligations, the responsibilities and privileges of citizenship".

3. Although there has not been any authoritative statement to this effect, it has not hitherto been contemplated that any one of these territories should obtain complete self-government by itself. The conception has always been that, as minimum prior requirements, (a) the Federation of Malaya and Singapore, and (b) the three territories in Borneo, should be brought into some form of constitutional association. Further information about the difficulty of achieving these requirements, and also of achieving some form of Constitutional relationship between groups (a) and (b), is given in the next section of this paper.

(c) *"Any plans which may exist for combining some or all of them, and in particular the difficulties involved in welding Singapore and Malaya first into a single dependent and subsequently a self-governing territory."*[1]
There are no "plans".

There are however general policies which we have hitherto not been able to achieve. These policies, and the difficulties in the way of their achievement can perhaps best be indicated by a brief review of events since 1946.

---

[1] See 292, para 1 for an explanation of why question (c) is positioned here before question (b).

2. The Malayan Union, as created in 1946, combined the nine Malay States, and the British Settlements of Penang and Malacca, under a single administration. Singapore was excluded because its addition, with such a large Chinese population, would have made the Union unacceptable to the Malay population of the mainland. It was hoped that, within a few years, the Union could be extended to include Singapore but in order to avoid an adverse reaction from the Malays, no explicit statement was made to this effect. Instead the following passage was included in Cmd. 6724:—

> "It is recognised, however, that there were and will be close ties between Singapore and the mainland, and it is no part of the policy of His Majesty's Government to preclude or prejudice in any way the fusion of Singapore and the Malayan Union [in] a wider union at a later date should it be considered that such a course were desirable".

3. In the event, the Malayan Union proved to be so unacceptable to the Malays that they embarked upon a policy of non-cooperation and, in due course, after prolonged negotiations, the Union was replaced by the present Federation in February, 1948.

4. This experience confirmed the Colonial Office in its view that it would be useless to attempt to *impose* a fusion of Singapore with the Mainland. The policy was not abandoned, but the Commissioner General, and the other authorities concerned, were charged with the task of attempting to create a climate of public opinion which would be favourable to its adoption. If possible the initiative was to appear to come from local leaders of public opinion. This is reflected in the following passages in Instructions issued to the Commissioner General in November, 1949:—

> "2. You are directed by the Royal Instructions to promote the co-ordination of policy and administration between the Governments in your area of authority."

> * * *

> "3. In the course of time some closer political co-operation may also be desirable, and you will advise the Secretary of State for the Colonies in this question from time to time."

5. The first organised attempt to create a favourable climate of opinion was the setting up of the Communities Liaison Committee in which, although not a member, the Commissioner General was able to exercise influence. The purpose of this committee was to bring the leaders of the various racial communities together in an endeavour to break down their mutual distrust. Considerable progress was in fact achieved in reaching agreement upon (e.g.) the qualifications for Federal Citizenship.

6. At one time the progress made seemed sufficient to warrant a hope that, even if the time were not yet ripe for a fusion of the constitutions of Singapore and the Federation, it might be possible for the posts of Governor of Singapore, and High Commissioner for the Federation to be merged, with deputies in each territory. But when Sir H. Gurney was last on leave (September, 1950) he was emphatically of the opinion that the burden of responsibility resting on the High Commissioner, as a result of the emergency situation, made this impracticable.

7. In due course, owing to the continuance of the "Emergency" in the Federation, and to the progressive absorption of many of the members of the Communities

Liaison Committee in the responsibilities of office in the Federation, the Committee ceased to meet, and the prospect of closer association between Singapore and the Federation definitely receded. The current view (March, 1953) is that conditions are less favourable for the early realisation of this policy than they have been for some years and that, in spite of an acceptance, by some prominent Singapore politicians, of the idea of fusion with the Federation, the formulation of any practical basis for a fusion, which would be acceptable to them, would be a matter of extreme difficulty. One of the reasons for this is the extent to which the wealth of the Federation has been dissipiated in combatting [sic] communist terrorism.

8. *The territories in Borneo.* In 1946 it was the definite (though not overtly declared) hope that the two newly created Colonies of North Borneo and Sarawak and the State of Brunei would in due course be brought under some form of unified administration. A public declaration to that effect at that time would have had a bad effect on public opinion in Sarawak, and would have played into the hands of the "anti-cessionists" whose campaign was in full swing. Moreover, both North Borneo and Sarawak (and especially North Borneo) had been badly devastated, and several years of physical reconstruction and administrative consolidation lay ahead. Nevertheless, in order to pave the way for political union, a policy of close association (and where suitable combination) between the various Departments of Governments was embarked upon. But in January, 1949 the two Governments complained that the pace was being forced beyond the capacity of the two administrations, and a modified policy of slower progress was agreed upon. (In this connection however see now paragraph 12 below.)

9. As indicated above, we had been looking towards:—

(a) the closer association of Singapore and the Federation of Malaya, which it was hoped would be realised in a relatively short time;
(b) the closer association of North Borneo, Sarawak and Brunei, which however was not considered to be attainable—as a matter of administration apart from political considerations—for a considerable number of years; and
(c) ultimately, some form of political association between the Malayan and Borneo groups of territories.

10. When however it became apparent that no progress was being made towards the closer political association of Singapore and the Federation of Malaya, and that the Communities Liaison Committee had ceased to perform a useful purpose, a new approach was sought. It was suggested, on the one hand, that the Malays of the Federation would find it easier to join in a wider Association which would include the non-Chinese dominated territories in Borneo, than to combine with the solid Chinese mass of Singapore. On the other hand, it might be easier to devise terms on which Singapore could join if other territories, also of Colonial status, were to be included.

11. It was accordingly decided in December, 1951 that advantage should be taken of the formation in South East Asia of branches of the Commonwealth Parliamentary Association, to attempt to bring together, in periodical meetings, the leading politicians of all these territories, and thus to foster the idea of a political Association of *all* the South East Asian territories in a single group. So far, however, very little progress has been made on these lines apart from the ventilation of the idea of such an association.

12. On the other hand the Commissioner General has recently reported that, following a successful meeting of the branch of the Commonwealth Parliamentary Association at Jesselton in January, it has been agreed between him and the Governors of North Borneo and Sarawak that there now seems some prospect of progress being made towards closer co-operation between the three territories in Borneo. A Council of representatives of these three territories, with the Commissioner General in the chair, is accordingly being set up to further this object. If and when the "atmosphere" of the discussions on the Council make it possible, the question of federation between the three territories will be considered.

13. It has sometimes been suggested that the requirements of the situation might be met by giving the Commissioner General authority over the Governments of all the territories in his area. Except, however, in matters of defence, this is not at present practicable, for the following reason. By Article 17 of the Federation Agreement it is provided that "The executive authority of the Federation shall be exercised by the High Commissioner either directly or through officers subordinate to him". There is no reference to the Commissioner General either in the Federation Agreement or in the Agreements with the individual States. Even therefore if it were desired to confer authority on the Commissioner General, in the Government of the Federation, there would be no constitutional means of achieving this without a substantial amendment of the Federation Agreement for which the political climate is not favourable.

14. For this, if for no other, reason the simplest means of achieving a measure of unification of the Governments of the Federation and Singapore—short of some form of constitutional fusion—would be by the appointment of one person as Governor of Singapore and High Commissioner for the Federation. Even this step would be a matter of some political delicacy and, as a matter of practical politics, it could only be done with the concurrence of the Malay Rulers and of the leading politicians in the two territories. Apart from this consideration, the political and administrative problems of each of the two territories are at present sufficient to engage the full time attention of a separate Governor and High Commissioner. (In this connection see paragraph 6 above).

15. As regards matters of defence, Article 4 of the Federation Agreement provides as follows:—

"His Majesty shall have complete control of the defence and of all the external affairs of the Federation and undertakes to protect the Malay States from external hostile attacks and, for this and other similar purposes, His Majesty's Forces and persons authorised by or on behalf of His Majesty's Government shall at all times be allowed free access to the Malay States and to employ all necessary means of opposing such attacks."

By virtue of this provision, it has been possible to confer on the Commissioner General, powers of direction, in matters of defence, over the High Commissioner in the Federation, as well as over the Governors of the Colonies in the area. The view has hitherto been held that, even in time of war, the High Commissioner and the Governors would remain the executive authorities in their respective territories, which would have to be governed in accordance with the provisions of their respective constitutions. In the ultimate resort the capacity of the High Commissioner and the Governors to give effect to directions issued by the Commissioner General derives from their "reserved powers". In this connection however it has been noted that, at a meeting of the M.B.D.C. in January last, the Commissioner General stated that he would re-open the question whether, in time of war, the High Commissioner and the Governor should continue to operate under existing constitutional machinery or that "their powers should be transferred to a Civil Head to be appointed at the time". It is not known in the Colonial Office what arrangements the Commissioner General may have in mind.

16. The Governor of Singapore is expected here on leave at the end of March. These matters are then to be discussed with him and it may be that, possibly in the light of the report of the committee of representatives of the two Governments, under the chairmanship of the Commissioner General, the latter and the High Commissioner and the Governor will be asked by the Secretary of State to review the question whether some form of political union between Singapore and the Federation is likely to be attainable within a measurable period, and whether a new approach to this problem might produce more positive results than the tactics which have been followed hitherto. It has recently been reported from Malaya that in consequence of frequent and acute differences of opinion, on various matters of policy affecting both territories, the Governments of Singapore and the Federation are considering a proposal that a committee of representatives of the two Governments, under the Chairmanship of the Commissioner General, should be set up, to define the subjects on which co-ordinated action is (a) imperative, and (b) desirable; and to consider what machinery should be established for consultation on such subjects and to ensure unison in action.

(b) *"Expected date at which they will be ready for this step"*
It is not possible to give any reliable estimate.

It is possible that in (say) eight to ten years' time the development of political institutions may have reached a stage at which it may be possible to contemplate, without undue despondency, the assumption by a Malayan Government, or even by a combined Government of the Malayan and Borneo territories, of a substantial measure of local autonomy. It is to be hoped that the pressure of external events, or the exigencies of internal politics, will not lead to an irresistible demand for this step in a shorter period, and that, indeed, we shall have a substantially longer period within which to create the conditions necessary for a reasonably stable administration. It is however clear that the pace of constitutional development in Malaya will depend on many factors, some of which are outside the control of H.M.G.

(d) *"The probable attitude of individual or combined territories to the stationing of United Kingdom forces within their borders and the maintenance there of United Kingdom bases, after they have achieved self-government"*
There is no present reason to doubt that the local politicians, both in Singapore and the Federation, are fully conscious of the strategic importance of Malaya and of the impossibility of a successful defence of the area without outside assistance. In particular they are assumed to be conscious of the importance of the Singapore naval base and of the impossibility of defending that base without adequate depth on the mainland. Neither the Malays nor the Malayan Chinese would relish the domination of Malaya either by China or by Indonesia. Provided therefore that the attainment of self-government is not attended by any local feeling hostile to this county, it is

considered to be a reasonable assumption that, even after Malaya had achieved self-government, they would still look to us (rather than to India or elsewhere) for the outside assistance necessary; they would count on our retention of the naval base; and would agree to the stationing in Malaya of such U.K. forces as would serve to reassure them of a successful defence against external aggression.

294   CO 1022/86, no 5   14 Mar 1953
[Training Malayan politicians]: letter from Sir D MacGillivray to Sir T Lloyd suggesting the extension of the member system and the appointment of a working committee to examine the question of federal elections

[With improvements in internal security, Templer and MacGillivray were anxious to retain the political initiative by adjusting the membership of the Federal Executive and Legislative Councils so as to incorporate a range of political interests and provide what they saw as a training ground for national leaders.]

The periods of appointment of the members of the Legislative Council expire at the end of January next year and there is a general expectation that there will then take place some reconstitution of membership, both because the present membership is regarded by some as ill-balanced in the aspect of territorial representation, and because it is thought that the time would be appropriate for some further advance along the road to self-government. With the improvement in the conditions of the Emergency political matters are receiving greater attention and, should this improvement suffer no setback, there can be little doubt that the pressure for swifter progress towards self-government will increase greatly during the next twelve months. Strangely enough the pressure emanates mainly from outside Malaya, but outside pressure makes its impression within. The High Commissioner now feels strongly that we must keep the initiative in this matter, and that if we should wait until next year the feeling in favour of some early action may have gathered such strength that, by that time, we would be constrained by public opinion to concede a greater measure of advance than in our own judgment would be wise. He has, therefore, asked me to examine the possibility of the introduction of a limited step forward on the 1st October this year, a step forward to a point which could be held until elections to the Legislative Council are introduced following upon the completion of State and Settlement elections in 1955.[1] I have, accordingly, been giving some thought to this matter and have had some preliminary informal discussions with Dato Onn and two or three others among the unofficials.

It is fairly evident that the greatest immediate need is for a wider training ground for the Asian politicians who will, within the next decade, be required to play an increasingly prominent part in the government of Malaya. The Membership system, now nearly two years old,[2] has been a considerable success, but it provides for the training of only a very limited number of Asians in the art of government, and these few for whom it has provided this opportunity are none of them young and cannot

---

[1] See 283.   [2] See 237.

look forward to very many more years in positions of authority. Like beech trees, they are stately, but nothing is growing under them. The primary present need is, therefore, for a testing ground for the younger men who must take their place. The High Commissioner has, therefore, tentatively mooted the idea of the creation of a number of deputy Members whose position would correspond roughly to that of Parliamentary Under-Secretaries of State in the United Kingdom. They would not be members of the Executive Council, but they would sit in the Legislative Council and would support the Members in their work therein and in their offices. If this measure should be accompanied by an increase in the number of unofficials holding portfolios, it should be possible to get a total of nearly twenty unofficials holding office, some as Members and others as Deputy Members, and thereby provide the training ground which is an urgent necessity if, within a few years, Malaya is to go forward to an elected Legislative Council and a Party system.

It would be possible, without any further amendment to the Federation Agreement, and merely by obtaining the approval of the Legislative Council to the payment of salaries, to increase the number of Members of the Executive Council by one (which might be a new portfolio for Local Government, Town Planning and Housing) and to place unofficials in charge of two of the portfolios now held by officials (Industrial and Social Relations and Railways and Ports), thus bringing the number of Memberships held by unofficials up to nine, of whom probably eight would be held by Asians. It would also be possible, without amendment to the Federation Agreement, to appoint deputies to these nine Members and also to the Member for Economic Affairs, making a total of ten deputies. It would not, however, be possible to obtain from the existing members of the Legislative Council ten men who would be suitable for appointment as deputies, and to whom the appointment would be likely to be acceptable. The salary attached to the position of deputy would not be as high as that of a Member, and there would be few of the present Legislative Councillors suitable for appointment who would be prepared, in exchange for this salary, to lay down their present business interests. There is, however, likely to be a number of younger men, not now in the Legislative Council, who would like an opportunity for political experience. If, therefore, this proposal to appoint deputies should be proceeded with, it would be necessary to consider an enlargement in the membership of the present nominated Legislative Council and, in order to effect this, an amendment to Article 36 (2) of the Federation Agreement would have to be made. If, therefore, the High Commissioner's target date—1st October, 1953—is to be attained, it will be necessary to introduce amending legislation at the July meeting of the Legislative Council and to lose no time now in prior examination of the proposal with the various authorities who will have to be consulted. I have, therefore, sent a secret and personal letter to the Mentri Mentri Besar and have asked them to discuss this tentative suggestion when they meet together here next week. I enclose a copy of this letter.[3] If the idea should not meet with strong opposition from them, the High Commissioner would wish to put it before the Rulers at their next Conference at the end of April. To do this, it would be necessary to circulate a paper in advance of the Conference. I shall therefore be very grateful if you will let me have your reactions to this proposal as early as possible.

I mentioned in the first sentence of this letter that some people regard the present

---

[3] Not printed.

representation in the Legislative Council as being ill-balanced in its territorial aspect. Moreover, it is also ill-balanced in its racial aspect since the proportion of Chinese Federal Citizens in Malaya is now, on account of the citizenship laws of last year, far higher than formerly and is no longer reflected in the present small number of Chinese in the Legislative Council. Dato Onn, for one, is very keen to bring about an early adjustment and to put representation in the present nominated Legislative Council on a new basis. Indeed, he thinks that this also might be done by the 1st October, I have, however, pointed out to him that the period of appointment of the present members of the Legislative Council does not expire until next year and that it would not be possible to ask these members to agree to an earlier termination especially since they are in receipt of the monthly allowance of $500. Onn has accepted this, but he is likely to press for an adjustment of the basis of representation when the Council is reappointed early next year. There would certainly be some advantage in such an adjustment; first so as to meet the Chinese claim for more seats; and, secondly, to bring about a more equitable territorial distribution. At present Trengganu has no seat, Kelantan, Kedah, Pahang and Malacca each have one, Johore only three, whereas Penang has ten, and Selangor twenty-one from out of a total number of 50 Unofficial seats. Presumably when the time comes for elections to these Unofficial seats it will be necessary to allot a number to each State and Settlement on the basis of population figures. Trengganu, Kelantan, Kedah, Pahang and Malacca can then expect to obtain their fair share and it would be desirable, therefore, that, meantime, some representatives of these States should be given opportunity to gain experience in the nominated Council.

I do, however, see real difficulty in bringing about a complete revision of the present basis of representation in time to give effect to it by the end of January next year. The present formula for representation was arrived at only after much argument in the Constitution Working Committee and proved to be the most contentious and difficult of the problems which that Committee had to contend with. Many authorities would have to be consulted, including the Rulers' Conference, representative organs of the tin and rubber industries, various political parties, Chambers of Commerce and others. Moreover, I believe that it would be unwise to embark upon such consultations with a view to obtaining a measure of agreement on a new formula for distribution of seats in a new nominated Legislative Council which, it would be assumed, would have the full life of three years envisaged by Article 42 (1) of the Federation Agreement. The knowledge of such consultation would almost certainly lead to a campaign by UMNO and certain sections of the English and Malay Press for the very early introduction of elections. The High Commissioner's view, with which I agree, is that it will be necessary to await the completion of elections to State and Settlement Councils before there can be an elected element in the Legislative Council, and that then this elected element will be the product of some Electoral College system. Many, however, will not take this view and will press for elections to the Federal Legislature even before those to State and Settlement Councils have been completed. In any case I am sure that it will be necessary to proceed to a Federal Legislature with an elected element as soon as State and Settlement elections are over, and it may not be possible or desirable to wait until the new Legislative Council nominated in February, 1954, had run its full course of three years.

What I suggest, therefore, is that, at the time of the announcement of the intention to create posts of Deputy Members and to increase the number of Memberships held by unofficials, an announcement, which would perhaps best be made at the time of the publication—probably early in July—of a Bill amending the Federation Agreement in order to give effect to this, there would also be announced an intention to appoint a Working Committee to examine the question of elections to the Federal Legislature and to make recommendations which would include one as to the date when these elections should be introduced. Such a Committee would have to consult with many representative bodies, including State and Settlement Governments, and it would, I am sure, be many months before it could complete its work. Should the Committee be appointed this autumn it is not likely, therefore, that it would be in a position to report before the spring of next year. It would, therefore, be stated, when making the announcement of the intention to appoint this Committee, that the life of the present nominated Legislative Council would be extended for one year from the end of January, 1954, without change in the present formula for the distribution of seats, in order to allow time for the Working Committee to report and for its recommendations to be considered and decisions taken thereon. This arrangement would, I think, be readily accepted, and I doubt if even Dato Onn would then press for a change in the present formula in order to appoint a new nominated Legislative Council for so short a period. I think it highly probable that the Working Committee would recommend that elections to the Federal Legislature must be delayed until those to the State and Settlement Councils had been completed, and that, therefore, the life of the nominated Council should be extended for a further limited period beyond January, 1955.

As to composition of this Working Committee, I think it would be desirable that it should not contain any outside element. A committee of eight or ten selected from among the members of the present Legislative Council, other than officials, presided over by Hogan, might be the best.

If an announcement is to be made in July, as proposed above, to the effect that it is intended to appoint such a Committee, the High Commissioner would wish to discuss this proposal with the Rulers at the Rulers' Conference at the end of April when putting to them the other proposal in regard to the appointment of deputies, etc. The next Rulers' Conference after that will not take place until mid-August. We would be glad, therefore, to have your reactions also to this proposal as early as possible.

If you consider that these proposals raise issues of such consequence that they should be discussed in detail before they are taken to the Rulers' Conference, the High Commissioner would be willing that I should pay a brief visit to London for this purpose and also so that the proposals might be worked out there in somewhat greater detail in consultation with Hogan. I might also take the opportunity to discuss the problem of relations with Singapore which has recently been giving us cause for some concern—my letter of 26th February to Paskin refers. There would also be other matters which I could usefully take up. If, therefore, you are of the opinion that a brief visit (say ten days) during the middle of April would be useful, you will no doubt tell me by telegram.[4]

---

[4] Lyttelton approved the proposals contained in this letter and MacGillivray was informed that there was no need to come to London for further discussions. MacGillivray meanwhile consulted the Rulers and *mentris besar* (see CO 1022/86, nos 11 and 20).

295   CO 1022/86, no 20, enclosure C   6 Apr 1953
[National conference]: note by Sir D MacGillivray for the CO on the political developments leading to this initiative

['The political tempo is increasing rapidly', MacGillivray informed Lloyd in the letter accompanying this note. Local demands at this stage focused upon reform of the Federal Legislative Council rather than the Executive Council. The 'National Conference' was an attempt by officials and Malayan moderates to slow down what they regarded as the precipitate pace being forced by the Alliance, and particularly UMNO, and to provide a multi-racial alternative to the ill-fated IMP. But this initiative provoked the Alliance to issue a 'blue print' and prepare a 'National Congress' (see 297, enclosure). In order to head off confrontation, the government announced its intention to appoint a working committee to examine the possibility of holding federal elections earlier than the timetable suggested by MacGillivray on 14 Mar (see 294 and 298).]

For some months there has been a growing uneasiness among those whom I might call "moderates" among the Malays, mainly those of the official class, on account of the Malay political disunity which has become increasingly pronounced since Dato Onn broke with U.M.N.O. and formed the I.M.P. and also on account of the irresponsible and extreme nationalist leadership of U.M.N.O.[1] At the same time there has been a realisation that I.M.P. was premature and that its leaders are losing support. There has also been distrust of the M.C.A.-U.M.N.O. Alliance, a distrust which, with the success of this Alliance at the Kuala Lumpur Municipal and the Johore Town Council elections last December, has developed into fear of its influence, partly on the part of those Malays who are outside U.M.N.O. (notably Onn and some of the Mentri Mentri Besar), partly by the Indians, Ceylonese and Eurasians, and partly by those Chinese (mainly in Penang and Ipoh) who have no use for the M.C.A. In October, Malcolm MacDonald had a talk on the subject of Malay disunity with Onn, Thuraisingham and Nik Kamil at Bukit Serene and this led to a subsequent reconciliation between Onn and Bukit Gantang on the latter's return from London later that month. A little while after that the High Commissioner himself had a talk with Raja Uda, Bukit Gantang and Nik Kamil and expressed to them his own concern at the lack of political leadership among the Malays.

2. From all this there emerged a series of meetings of a group of community leaders under the chairmanship of Bukit Gantang. The first of these meetings was held at Ipoh at the end of January and was attended by Onn, Nik Kamil, Thuraisingham, Yong Shook Lin,[2] Heah Joo Seang,[3] Y.C. Kang,[4] Chin Swee Onn[5] and Shelley.[6] The early part of the meeting was also attended by Malcolm MacDonald, and, according to a note of record which he then made, it seems that everyone present was more or less agreed that:—

---

[1] See 279, note.
[2] Yong Shook Lin, a founder-member of the MCA and a member of the federal legislative council, was a friend of Dato Onn and an early supporter of the IMP.
[3] Heah Joo Seang, a Penang millionaire rubber dealer, would become vice-president of Onn's Party Negara in 1955 before eventually throwing in his lot with the MCA and Alliance.
[4] Y C Kang, a Perak businessman who was appointed by the MCA in 1952 as its 'agent-general' to examine the living conditions in New Villages and resettlement projects.
[5] Chin Swee Onn was a Perak businessman and MCA member.
[6] Gilbert Shelley was elected president of the Eurasian Union of Malaya in 1950.

(i)   The present diversity of political parties in the Federation was extremely unfortunate and had a bad effect on inter-communal co-operation and unity; and there was an urgent need for a reduction in the number of parties engaging in politics, and for the maximum possible co-operation between the principal communal leaders.

(ii)   Communal organisations like U.M.N.O. and the M.C.A. should be concerned primarily with social welfare, cultural and similar activities, and should be as far as possible non-political. (Two or three members pointed out that this is probably an ideal which cannot be fully realised in practice, and that to some extent at least communal organisations cannot avoid political activity.)

(iii)   The U.M.N.O.-M.C.A. Alliance is not a helpful movement because:—

(a)   in it the U.M.N.O. is in fact subordinate to the M.C.A.;
(b)   the M.C.A. leaders are concerned almost exclusively with promoting Chinese interests;
(c)   many of them are primarily interested in forwarding the cause of the K.M.T.

(iv)   The I.M.P. has the right spirit and aims, but owing to certain circumstances does not command the support of a number of important Malay and other community leaders who share its spirit and aims.

3.   There was, however, some divergence of opinion as to what action should be taken to bring about a change in the political party set-up. The original idea had been that a number of the "moderates" among the Malays should endeavour to capture the leadership of U.M.N.O. and it had been suggested that Nik Kamil should secure the leadership of the Kelantan Branch and Bukit Gantang that of the Perak Branch, and that one or the other of them should then endeavour to oust Tunku Abdul Rahman from the Presidency of the party at the annual elections in September. Indeed, apparently in pursuit of this aim, Bukit Gantang successfully stood for the Presidency of the Perak Branch in February. Onn was, however, in favour of the early formation of a new political party, while Thuraisingham was in favour of the calling of a conference by the Government of the Federation to consider the steps which should now be taken towards self-government.

4.   No conclusion was reached at this first meeting of the Group and at a subsequent meeting held in Kuala Lumpur on the 12th–13th February, attended by the same people but with the addition of Narayanan,[7] the Trade Union leader, it was agreed to form a new central inter-communal political organisation in which all the responsible community leaders and as many community organisations as possible would unite and co-operate for the achievement of national purposes. If all went well this Organisation was to be formed some time in the latter half of 1953, i.e. after the annual elections for the Presidency of U.M.N.O. The following points were brought out during this meeting:—

(a)   The I.M.P. would probably dissolve itself and urge all its members to join the new Organisation. The I.M.P. leaders would join it en masse.
(b)   It was hoped that the Pan-Malayan Labour Party[8] would adopt a friendly and co-operative attitude towards a new Organisation, whose aims would be purely

---

[7] P P Narayanan, president, MTUC, 1950–1952.　　　　　[8] This was led by Mohd Sopiee, see 279, note 10.

political; though it may wish to retain its separate identity for the purpose of advocating socialism in economic affairs.

(c) The Ceylonese and Eurasian Associations would probably support the new Organisation, and it was hoped that the Malayan Indian Congress would do likewise.

(d) Bukit Gantang and Nik Kamil hoped, by the latter part of the year, to influence the U.M.N.O. so that it too would support the new Organisation. Whether they would succeed would depend on whether their policy could replace that of Tunku Abdul Rahman in the U.M.N.O. If they were not able to do that, they and the Malays who followed their lead would nevertheless join and support the new Organisation.

(e) It was recognised that it would be more difficult to secure co-operation from the M.C.A., since some of the present M.C.A. leaders are likely to guard jealously (a) the independence of the M.C.A. and (b) its right to participate in a big way in politics. It was hoped, however, to detach at least some of the most important M.C.A. leaders and to gain their adherence to the new Organisation.

5. A discussion then took place as to the means of achieving this new Organisation and a sub-Committee was appointed to prepare a draft constitution for submission at the next meeting. It was, however, agreed at the second meeting of the Group that there should be held an early conference of various existing political bodies and communal associations to consider the problem of co-operation between these various bodies for the achievement of their common declared purpose, i.e. the creation of a united and free Malayan nation. The calling of this Conference by the Group would, they thought, ensure that (a) the members of the Group gained the initiative in its organisation and (b) that they and their friends would predominate in the conference. The proclaimed purpose of the conference would be as stated above, but it was hoped that in the course of its discussions it would be possible to launch the idea of forming a new political Organisation and to secure support for this.

6. The Group met again in Kuala Lumpur on the 16th March and considered the reports of its two committees. Meantime, the M.C.A. and U.M.N.O. had made a statement that they proposed to convene a National Congress of all political parties to discuss the steps to be taken towards independence. It was, therefore, necessary for the Group to act quickly, and they decided at the meeting on the 16th March not to wait until the autumn but to take immediate steps to form a new political Organisation. They considered that the meeting of the Legislative Council that week offered a suitable moment for them to act, and that the occasion of the debate on the High Commissioner's speech would provide an opportunity to launch their proposal to hold the Conference. They therefore approached the remaining Mentri Mentri Besar who were then in Kuala Lumpur attending the meeting of the Legislative Council and secured the agreement of all but Perlis and Pahang to join them in their enterprise. They also thought it prudent to get a European to join their Group, and having first approach Carey, without success, they then secured the allegiance of W.N. MacLeod (of Neill and Bell the Chartered Accountants).[9] The statement which they then issued to the Press on the evening of the 19th March appeared in the

---

[9] William MacLeod, practising accountant in Malaya since 1946; member of the Federal Legislative Council, 1953–1955; would later join Party Negara.

newspapers on the morning of the debate on the High Commissioner's speech. A copy of this statement is enclosed, along with the Hansard records of the speeches made that day during the debate by Thuraisingham, Onn, and Tunku Abdul Rahman.[10] The statement was not signed by Onn because the Group had decided that since U.M.N.O.-M.C.A. had not be consulted and were not being invited to sign the statement, no leader of any political party should be directly associated with it. Onn was to keep in the background, but at the appropriate moment was to drop I.M.P. and come forward as the leader of the new political Organisation.

7. The decision to hold a Conference considerably annoyed U.M.N.O. and, to a less extent, the M.C.A., since thereby the initiative had been taken out of the hands of the Alliance. At first there were indications that they might both decline an invitation to attend; but it was reported in the newspapers on Easter Sunday that they had decided to accept an invitation on one condition, and that is that the Conference Committee will allow only political organisations to vote at the meeting. It is reported further that this had been stated in a joint declaration signed by Tunku Abdul Rahman and Sir Chen Lock Tan, the respective Presidents of the two organisations. The statement went on that the Alliance shared wholeheartedly the fundamental aims of the Conference, but maintained that it would be controlled by the high Government officials and individuals not representing any sections of the people. "The M.C.A.-U.M.N.O. consider that the desire for a united Malayan nation and self-government must spring from the people themselves" and that "any Conference to be convened with that object must be representative of the people". On the following day, the Pan-Malayan Labour Party decided to take the same line and announced that they would only attend the Conference if it consisted of "accredited representatives of democratic political organisations whose voting power alone shall prevail at the Conference". They criticised the Conference because "it appears to have been inspired by Colonial and Imperial interests". Dato Onn, who has publicly given support to the proposal to hold the Conference, and who is known to be behind the whole proposal, has been under pretty heavy criticism and has even been described in a letter to the Press as a "British stooge".

8. We thus have the line-up of those who were represented in the Group discussions, and, on the other side, the three political parties who were not consulted in regard to the convening of the Conference i.e. the M.C.A., the U.M.N.O. and the Pan-Malayan Labour Party.

9. Within a week of the issue of the statement calling the Conference, Onn made a provocative and unwise speech in which he foretold a conflict of racial interests and attempted to link the M.C.A. with the Chinese Chambers of Commerce and the Kuo Min Tang. He is reported to have stated that the Malayan Chinese were endeavouring to turn Malaya into the "20th Province of China"; the prepared record of his speech contained no such statement but he admits to having made it in answer to a question. It was, however, a speech which aroused much criticism from many quarters in that, although its whole sense has been grossly distorted by the Press, it was one which could not possibly be regarded, even without this distortion, as conducive to racial harmony. Following this, there came a report prominently featured in "The Straits Times" that Bukit Gantang had strongly criticised the M.C.A.-U.M.N.O. Alliance in a public speech.

---

[10] Not printed.

10. The U.M.N.O. held a Party meeting at Malacca over the Easter weekend. There they decided to expel Bukit Gantang from the Party and to call upon the Federation Government to introduce Federal elections by 1954. They produced what they alleged to be the agreed M.C.A.-U.M.N.O. blue print for these elections. Enclosed is a copy of this as reported in the Press.[11] It is also reported that it was decided that should the Federation Government reject the proposal for elections by 1954, the representatives of U.M.N.O. and the M.C.A. should resign from the Federal Legislative Council.

---

[11] Not printed but see 297, enclosure.

---

296   CO 1022/86, no 25   14 Apr 1953
[Political leadership]: letter from J D Higham to J J Paskin giving his impressions of the Alliance leaders   [Extract]

. . . The atmosphere in the Federation is completely different, stimulating and constructive.[1] And yet the officers there are no better material—but they are keen and enthusiastic, while our people look forward only to leave, transfer or retirement. We went up to Malacca for Easter and stayed part of the time with Wisdom,[2] part with Cheng Lock. It was very delightful there, but "Sleepy Hollow" was quite lively with the U.M.N.O. General Meeting.[3] We were invited to a dinner given to Abdul Rahman by the M.C.A., and I found myself in somewhat unwanted eminence between the two "allies". Poor Cheng Lock, who is by no means the dodderer Templer thinks, is now, as you know, in uneasy and unwilling wedlock with the Tungku, and is quite well aware that he is in the unenviable position of the young lady of Riga. I think there is little doubt that U.M.N.O., despite their fine liberal professions, will turn on their allies once they have used them to force the pace for federal elections. What weight should be attached to U.N.M.O. fulminations I don't really know. You will remember that Templer discounted them as a political force when we saw him in December,[4] but it is my impression that U.M.N.O. has gained in prestige and power and that, ragtag and bobtail as they are, they enjoy considerable actual and potential support that could only too easily be whipped up by a little agitation to a "crusade" of considerable nuisance value. The Indonesian elements in particular, are dangerous. Mind you, I think, U.M.N.O. are right to ask for Federal elections before State elections—you will never get real leaders taking an interest in State elections: and while it would be ideal if we could build up from the bottom methodically I don't think things work out that way and it would be as well to set a target for Federal elections in, say 1955. . . .

---

[1] Higham, now posted to Singapore, is comparing the Federation with Singapore.
[2] G E C Wisdom, after twenty years in the service of the Gold Coast government, was transferred to Malaya in 1946 and appointed resident commissioner of Malacca in 1949.
[3] See 295, para 10.   [4] See 283.

297   CO 1022/86, no 23   17 Apr 1953

[Alliance constitutional plans]: letter from Sir D MacGillivray to Mr
M J MacDonald. *Enclosure* "A": 'MCA-UMNO blue print'

Many thanks for your letter of the 9th April commenting on the documents I sent
you regarding elections to State and Settlement Councils. I agree fully with all you
have written there.

Things are moving fast and it is certainly going to be a problem to keep the
initiative. Tan Siew Sin has two particularly nasty motions down for debate on the
6th May, one seeking a resolution of the Council deploring Onn's recent speech as
one calculated to exacerbate racial feeling,[1] and the other seeking endorsement of
the view that Government servants and Government executives should be prohibited
from participating in politics. The latter is, of course, directed against Bukit
Gantang. We are now considering how to deal with these.

H.S. Lee came to see me early this week before leaving for Tokyo. He was very
incensed at Onn's public attack on him and thought it was particularly bad form on
the part of Onn to do this while Lee himself was absent in London. He said that this
was the second occasion on which Onn had attacked him while he was away from the
country. It is perhaps as well that he will still be away when Tan Siew Sin's motions
are debated. Lee then told me that the M.C.A. and U.M.N.O. had had four meetings
before reaching agreement on their blue-print for a new Federal Constitution. I had
only seen a Press report of this blue-print, so Lee let me have a copy of it in the form
finally agreed to between the M.C.A and U.M.N.O. Lee said that he himself was the
architect of this blue-print and that he had followed closely the Gold Coast
Constitution. He also said that U.M.N.O. had wanted something far more advanced
immediately, and that it was only after much argument that U.M.N.O. had agreed to
accept the M.C.A. proposals. He added that the procedure which had been agreed to
by the Alliance was first to get this blue-print accepted at the half-yearly general
meeting of U.M.N.O. (and you will see from the Press that this first step had been
achieved), then to get it accepted at a general meeting of the M.C.A. (this has not yet
been convened), and, after that, to convene a "National Congress" to which all
political organisations in the Federation would be invited, and before which this
blue-print would be laid for acceptance. Should this National Congress accept the
blue-print, then it would be presented to the Rulers and to the High Commissioner.
He said that the M.C.A. would undoubtedly accept this blue-print at the general
meeting which it would hold shortly, but that their plan for the calling of a National
Congress had now been somewhat upset by the manoeuvre of Bukit Gantang, Onn
and company in calling a Conference on the 27th April. He went on to say that the
Alliance realised that it would not be possible to get their blue-print endorsed by the
Rulers and the High Commissioner and accepted by H.M. Government, and then to
pass the necessary legislation and take the essential administrative measures in time
for elections to be held early next year, and that, therefore, it would be necessary to
extend the life of the present nominated Council on its expiry at the end of January,
1954. What they propose is that elections should be held in December, 1954, to a new
Federal Council which would be summoned to meet for the first time in February,

---

[1] See 295, para 9.

1955. Lee added that he thought that, if this blue-print, having now been adopted by U.M.N.O., should be accepted by the Rulers and H.M. Government, it would be possible to hold the situation for a period of four years from February, 1955 without making any further advance. If the blue-print were not accepted, however, he felt certain that U.M.N.O. would press strongly for a greater measures of self-government at a far earlier date.

In commenting on a point of detail in this blue-print I said that I thought there would have to be four *ex-officio* members, the fourth being the Secretary for Defence, having regard to the High Commissioner's special responsibility for defence. Lee accepted this.

You will note that it is proposed that the franchise should not be limited to subjects or [? of] the Rulers and federal citizens, but should be extended to any person born in the Federation and ordinarily resident therein for the last five years. In accepting this, U.M.N.O. have, of course, gone much further than the Malays were prepared to go when amendments were made last year to the citizenship clauses of the Federation Agreement.[2]

The intention is, apparently, though it is not clear from the documents, that after the election of the 44 members, the High Commissioner should have consultation with the leaders of the successful party or parties and then select the names of 12 from out of the elected members for appointment to the Executive Council. These appointments by the High Commissioner would then require ratification by the Legislative Council on a resolution on which only the elected members would be entitled to vote. Of these twelve, nine would hold portfolios and three would be without portfolios. In addition to these twelve elected members there would be three "special Members" to be appointed by the High Commissioner to the Executive Council from among the nominated members of the Legislative Council.

Lee explained that he contemplated the appointment of Under-Secretaries to the elected members of Executive Council holding portfolios, since this was also provided in the Gold Coast Constitution.

What we are at present endeavouring to ensure is that no "National Congress" is convened by any political organisation or group of organisations with a view to reaching agreement upon a blue print for presentation to the High Commissioner and the Rulers. I feel that, unless such a Congress had guidance, it is unlikely that it would be able to present anything which would be acceptable to the Rulers and to H.M. Government, and that the effect of rejection of its proposals might be very bad. As you say, we must retain the initiative in this matter and ourselves convene a Conference for study of the problem, and we must see that that Conference is presided over by the Chief Secretary or the Attorney-General, or at least that it includes one or both of these officials in its membership. Apart from these officials, however, the Conference should, I think, consist of representatives of the various political organisations plus a number of representatives of State and Settlement Governments. We are therefore putting to the Rulers' Conference on the 30th April a paper of which I enclose a copy[3] and, so as to forestall any calling of a "National

---

[2] The Federation of Malaya Agreement (Amendment) Ordinance, Aug 1952, relaxed the citizenship provisions and allowed the acquisition of federal citizenship through either citizenship of the UK and colonies or state (ie Malay state) nationality. Eligibility for the latter was laid down in the state nationality enactments.   [3] Not printed.

Congress" by any political organisation for the purpose of drawing up a new Constitution, it will probably be necessary to make an announcement shortly after the Rulers' Conference of our intention to convene a Constitution Working Party. The Mentri Mentri Besar will have seen this paper before attending the Conference on the 27th April[4] which has been called by Bukit Gantang, and it is not likely, therefore, that, prior to discussion with the Rulers on the 30th, they will support any suggestion for the convening of a National Congress if this suggestion should be made on the 27th.

P.S. Thuraisingham has just told me that on the 26th April there is to be a meeting of the Perak U.M.N.O. to pass a vote of confidence in Bukit Gantang; that a fortnight later there is to be a further meeting of the Perak U.M.N.O. to pass a vote of no confidence in Abdul Rahman; and that on the 15th May there is to be a meeting of the M.C.A. for the expulsion from the M.C.A. of Shook Lin, Y.C. Kang and Chee Swee Onn.[5] They all seem to have forgotten that the motto of the Federation is "Unity in Strength".

Enclosure "A" to 297

Legislative Assembly

I.   There shall be a Legislative Assembly in and for the Federation of Malaya consisting of the following members:—

(a) Three *Ex-Officio* Members namely the Chief Secretary, the Attorney-General and the Financial Secretary;
(b) The nine Official Members namely the nine Presidents of the Councils of State;
(c) One representative from each of the Settlement Councils of Penang and Malacca;
(d) Two Members to be nominated by the European Chamber of Commerce;
Two Members to be nominated by the Associated Chinese Chamber of Commerce;
One Member to be nominated by the Indian Chamber of Commerce; and
One Member to be nominated by the Malay Chamber of Commerce;
(e) Two Members to be nominated by the F.M.S. Chamber of Mines; and
Two Members to be nominated by the All Malayan Chinese Chamber Association;
(f) Five Members to be nominated by the Rubber Producers' Council;
(g) Two Members to represent Husbandry and Agriculture other than rubber;
(h) 44 Elected Members.

II. There shall be a Speaker and a Deputy Speaker to be elected by the Legislative Assembly from the Elected Members.

Constituency

III. Each State or Settlement is a Constituency and the number of Elected Members for each Constituency is determined by the population of that Constituency.

---

[4] For an account of the conference, see 298.   [5] See 295, notes 2, 4 & 5.

Qualifications for electors
IV. (a) Subjects of the Rulers of the Malay States;
    (b) Federal Citizens;
    (c) Any person born in any part of the territories now comprising the Federation of Malaya and ordinarily resident in the Federation of Malaya for the last five years;
    (d) British subjects born in Singapore and ordinarily resident in the Federation of Malaya for the last five years.

Tenure of office
V. The tenure of office of members shall be 4 years, but the High Commissioner may at any time, by Proclamation published in the Gazette, prologue [? prorogue] or dissolve the Assembly.

Voting
VI. When the High Commissioner submits the name or names of the representative members of the Executive Council for approval by the Assembly, only the Elected Members have the right to vote.

Qualifications for candidates
VII. The candidate must be:—

(a) a registered elector, and
(b) a subject of any of the Rulers of the Malay States or a Federal Citizen.

Executive Council
I. There shall be an Executive Council in and for the Federation of Malaya consisting of the following Members:—

(a) The High Commissioner as President;
(b) 3 *Ex-Officio* Members namely the Chief Secretary, the Attorney-General and the Financial Secretary;
(c) Not less than 12 Representative Members;
(d) 1 Representative from the Mentri Mentri Besar;
(e) 3 Special Members to be appointed by name by the High Commissioner.

All the names of the Members of the Executive Council except the High Commissioner, the 3 *Ex-Officio* Members, the Representative from the Mentri Mentri Besar and the 3 Special Members, shall be submitted to the Legislative Assembly for approval and no Member whose name has not been so approved shall sit in the Executive Council.

Leader of the government business
II. (a) There shall be a Leader of Government Business in the Legislative Assembly (hereinafter called "the Leader of Government Business"), who shall be elected by a majority of the Members of the Executive Council from among their own number.
    (b) The Leader of Government Business shall have such powers and duties, as the High Commissioner acting in his discretion, may determine.

Tenure of office

III. (a) The tenure of office of the Members of the Executive Council shall be 4 years.

(b) The Legislative Assembly may, by resolution in favour of which there are cast the votes of not less than two thirds of all the Members of the Legislative Assembly, request the High Commissioner to revoke the appointment of any Special or Representative Member of the Executive Council.

(c) Upon receipt from the Speaker or other Member presiding [over] the Legislative Assembly, of a copy of any such resolution, the High Commissioner shall, revoke any such appointment; and thereupon the seat of any such member shall become vacant.

(d) If the High Commissioner, acting in his discretion, shall consider that any Representative or Special Member has failed to carry out any policy or decision of the Executive Council, the appointment of such member may be revoked; and if the Executive Council shall so resolve, the High Commissioner shall revoke such appointment, and thereupon the seat of any such member shall become vacant.

Qualifications

IV. (a) No person shall be a Member of the Executive Council, other than the High Commissioner, unless he is a Member of the Legislative Assembly.

(b) (For other details and procedure in connection with the above, follow the Gold Coast Constitution as closely as possible.)

298 CO 1022/86, no 27 1 May 1953

[Federal elections]: inward telegram no 456 from Sir G Templer to Mr Lyttelton proposing an early announcement of the intention to appoint a working party to examine the question

In his secret and personal telegram No. 41 Lloyd informed MacGillivray that you had approved the arrangements in the latter's letter of 14th March[1] which included the proposal that an announcement should be made of my intention to appoint a working party to examine the question of elections to the Federal Legislature. Subsequent developments have been reported in MacGillivray's letters of 7th April to Lloyd[2] and 17th April to Paskin,[3] and you will see from these that there has been considerable political activity. The present position is that both U.M.N.O. and M.C.A. have formally adopted their blueprint for elections to the Federal Legislature, and despite the outcome of the conference of 27th April to which I refer below have declared that they still intend to convene a national congress to examine this blueprint with a view to its presentation to Her Majesty's Government and Rulers for (corrupt group ?acceptance). The conference called by Bukit Gantang group for 27th April was boycotted by the U.M.N.O.-M.C.A. Alliance and by Pan Malayan Labour

---

[1] See 294. [2] This letter accompanied document 295.
[3] This letter accompanied document 297.

Party. It was attended by all other political organisations[4] and in accordance with previously announced intention, a resolution was passed appointing a committee to examine steps which should be taken to build a united self-governing nation and to report back to a further conference to be convened in three months time.[5] This committee is to be composed of one representative of each political organisation attending, the seven Mentri Besar attending and three others to be coopted. It was agreed that should the U.M.N.O.-M.C.A. wish to send representatives to join this Committee they would be allowed to do so despite their boycott of the conference. The Alliance has, however, indicated in public that they do not intend to take advantage of this offer. Feeling between these two groups is running pretty high and may become much higher next week when the motion deploring Dato Onn's speech of (corrupt group ?25th March) is debated.

2. All this rather bitter rivalry and jockeying for leadership in the present demand for constitutional advancement is likely to go on in the absence of any declaration of intention on the part of Her Majesty's Government and the Rulers seriously to examine the question of elections to the Legislative Council. Moreover, unless an early announcement of such intention is made, there is the danger that Her Majesty's Government would at least appear to have lost the initiative in the matter and it might later be represented that action had eventually been taken only under "Nationalist" pressure. I have come to the conclusion, therefore, that the sooner an announcement is made the better, and in this view I was supported by the Rulers in conference today. My immediately following telegram gives the text of announcement as agreed in that conference. I should like to put this text before the Executive Council on Tuesday and, subject to their advice, to get the Deputy High Commissioner to make an announcement in the Legislative Council on 6th or 7th May. I shall be grateful to learn whether you agree with this timing and with the text.[6]

3. I note, relevant to Paskin's personal telegram No. 51 that Nicoll is of the opinion that if such an announcement comes before the announcement of appointment of the commission to consider constitutional development in Singapore, it would be embarrassing to him.[7] I shall be grateful if you will explain to him the situation which has developed here and the virtual necessity for a very early announcement. When he understands that this announcement is only of the

---

[4] It was attended by the IMP, MIC, Malayan Indian Association, Selangor Pakistan Association, and Straits Chinese British Association.

[5] The working committee submitted its report to the National Conference in Sept 1953. The MIC withdrew at this point and, failing to create a broad-based front matching the Alliance, the National Conference gave way to the Party Negara which was launched by Dato Onn in Feb 1954.

[6] The CO approved and on 6 May MacGillivray announced British intentions in the Federal Legislative Council. The committee's composition (46 members with Hogan as chairman) was made public on 15 July, as were its terms of reference: 'to examine the question of elections to the Federal Legislative Council and constitutional changes in the Federal Government arising therefrom; and to make recommendations'. Opposition was not pre-empted, however, since the Alliance sponsored the 'National Convention' which, meeting in Oct, adopted, a 'blue print' based upon the document drafted earlier in the year by UMNO and MCA, see 297, enclosure.

[7] Having retired from a career in the diplomatic sevice in 1950, Sir George Rendel was re-employed on a number of commissions. He was chairman of the commission on constitutional development in Singapore, 1953–1954, which recommended the creation of a legislative assembly with a majority of elected members and a council of ministers in place of the executive council. Elections to implement the new constitution were held in 1955.

intention to appoint a working party, and that it will inevitably be some months before composition of this working party and its plans can be announced, I hope he will feel that it will not be a great embarrassment. I will certainly consult with him later in regard to the timing of the subsequent announcement.

4. The Rulers also approved today the proposals in regard to the expansion of the system with the modification that ten out of nineteen posts proposed should be held by Malays, a modification which I accepted. I shall now consult the Executive Council in regard to this proposal but since there is not the same urgency for an announcement in regard to this, I propose to delay it until after my visit to London.

299 CO 1022/86, no 35   18 May 1953
'Constitutional development in the Federation of Malaya': CO note of a meeting with Sir G Templer

[This meeting (attended by Lloyd, Templer, Hogan, Paskin and MacKintosh) indicates the extent to which the political tempo had quickened since Templer's talks at the CO in Nov–Dec 1952, see 283.]

Sir G. Templer said that his original hope was that it would be possible to have elections in all States/Settlements by the end of 1955 and then allow two years (or at the least one year) to elapse before elections to the Federal Legislative Council were introduced. He had thought that an electoral college system, using the State Councils as electoral colleges, would be most suitable, but had since been advised that this might unduly strengthen the position of the States. He now doubted whether it would be possible to delay Federal elections for so long, and was concerned about the likelihood that we should be forced to hold them earlier and that the first elected Council would include many undesirable or completely inexperienced members. He said that there were at present no signs of the emergence of new political leaders, and that the older leaders such as Dato Onn were so unpopular that they might well fail to secure seats in an election.

Sir T. Lloyd said that if experience in other territories was a guide a number of middle-class professional people would come forward when elections were intro-duced. *Mr. Hogan* felt that it might be best from the point of view of building up a strong Central Government to have Federal elections before State elections. *Sir T. Lloyd* said that experience indicated that better results would have been obtained in other territories if elections had been introduced more slowly, and without suggesting any rigid attitude to the problem in Malaya he thought that the best course would be to work as gradually as possible towards an elected Federal Legislative Council.

The meeting then discussed the position of Deputy Members appointed under the new scheme.[1] *Mr. Hogan* said that these Deputy Members would probably wish to take part in State elections, and he did not see how they could fairly be prevented from doing so. Without them it might be impossible to get political activity going on sound lines in the States. Even established political leaders such as Dato Onn might

---

[1] See 294, paragraph 2.

wish to seek election in their States. It was agreed that there was bound to be a certain amount of confusion and that it might prove necessary to have Federal elections at about the same time as State elections, but on the whole it would be better to try to carry through State elections first.

Sir T. Lloyd mentioned that a circular had been sent to Colonial territories giving guidance on the conditions under which U.K. civil servants were released to take part in politics and enquired about the position in Malaya. Sir G. Templer pointed out that it was essential to allow such releases in Malaya since the only potential Malay political leaders were officials, and unless special arrangements were made to release them the Malays would complain of political discrimination. Sir T. Lloyd agreed that in the early stages it might be necessary to treat this matter specially, but he thought that the position of middle and senior grade civil servants who entered politics would become impossible once a party political system was in operation. Perhaps the best course would be to allow all but the most senior civil servants to enter politics for the present, but to keep in mind the desirability of drawing the line rather lower down as soon as possible.

300   CO 1022/61, no 40   18 May 1953
'Closer association between the Federation of Malaya and Singapore': CO note of a meeting with Sir G Templer and Sir J Nicoll[1]

Sir G. Templer said that a year ago he thought it might be possible to make some early movement towards closer association, but he felt that during the last year feeling in both territories had become more opposed to the idea. He thought that the aim of our policy must be some sort of Federation, but that Singapore would have to have a special position, not only for political reasons but in view of its special strategic[2] and commercial importance. The Malays were afraid of the power which the Singapore Chinese would exercise in any Federation and the Singapore Chinese were afraid of getting involved in the troubles of the Federation; these fears could not be overcome by a straightforward union. He felt that a definite lead from London was necessary.

Sir J. Nicoll agreed with Sir. Gerald Templer that local feeling had become more opposed to closer association, and constitutional advance would make it even more difficult. He hoped that the Joint Federation-Singapore Co-ordination Committee[3] would accept the need for political power to pass to some inter-territorial body, perhaps on the lines of the East African High Commission. Sir Thomas Lloyd and Mr. Paskin expressed doubts about the suitability of the East African High Commission as a mode, both because conditions in East Africa were quite different from those in Malaya and also because the East African High Commission was not in

---

[1] Only the list of those who attended (ie Lloyd, Templer, Nicoll, Hogan, Paskin. MacKintosh and Jerrom) and the six conclusions were included in the final version of this minute.

[2] See 293. On 15 Jan, reinforcing the conclusions of the CO meeting, Lyttelton referred MacDonald to the recent conclusions of the chiefs of staff that 'it is of the utmost importance that the two territories should not be under separate governments' (CO 1022/61, no 46).

[3] It was set up under MacDonald to improve links between the two territories and especially to examine ways of bringing about their closer political association. See part III of this volume, 324.

itself wholly satisfactory. *Sir T. Lloyd* mentioned that a useful account of the working of the East African High Commission had recently been prepared and would be of interest to Malaya. There was the fundamental difficulty that no inter-territorial authority could exercise much real authority without financial power.[4]

Sir J. Nicoll doubted whether it would be possible to make much progress with political union at present. He thought that it would be more fruitful to try to get working agreement on common economic interests such as transport. *Sir G. Templer* thought even this would present difficulties and mentioned the present inclination in the Federation to build up Port Swettenham as a possible competitor with Singapore. *Sir J. Nicoll* thought it was possible that industries would develop in Southern Johore in close contact with Singapore and felt that if the right approach was made industrial development, communications, trade departments, customs, etc. should present valuable opportunities for collaboration. There was of course already need for defence co-ordination. He referred to item (iii) in the Joint Co-ordination Committee's terms of reference which authorised it to consider means by which co-ordination could be more effectively achieved by modifications of the existing constitutions of the two territories, and said that from the political point of view this was the crucial issue.

The meeting considered the questions prepared by the Colonial Office (copy enclosed at (38))[5] and *Mr. Hogan* asked what action should be taken about question 4 from the point of view of linking the two territorial committees with the Joint Co-ordination Committee.[6] He felt that this might be the moment for more decisive action, and was rather doubtful whether the three committees would be linked together closely enough to deal adequately with the whole problem.

After further discussion it was agreed that it seemed that the most we could hope for at present was a very loose type of Federation but we must aim at the closest form of association between the Federation and Singapore which we could get local opinion to accept. Paragraph (iii) of terms of reference of the Joint Co-ordination Committee should provide the Commissioner General with an opportunity to guide that Committee towards consideration of the basic problems involved. This should lead to the Constitution Committee in Federation and Commission in Singapore being associated with this study in due course.

Sir Thomas Lloyd felt that this was not the moment for a plain statement of policy by H.M.G., but that such a statement might be prepared and used at a suitable opportunity. The statement might take the form of noting the operations of the local committees, expressing the hope that attention would be given to closer association of the territories in the future interests of all their people, and saying that H.M.G. would welcome any action of this sort. Mr. Malcolm MacDonald should be given a copy of the draft statement of policy but no decision as to its issue would be made until we saw how things developed locally as a result of Mr. MacDonald's action.

Sir J. Nicoll hoped that the Joint Co-ordination Committee would consider the constitutional question fairly soon, but Sir G. Templer was not sure that this would be possible.

---

[4] Writing to MacDonald on 16 June, Paskin elaborated the point about the discouraging experiences of the East African High Commission and the Central African Council (CO 1022/61, no 47).

[5] Not printed. This questionnaire of twelve items was prepared by the CO in Mar and used as a basis for the discussions on 18 May.

[6] ie Hogan's committee on federal elections and the Rendel Commission, see 298, notes 6 and 7.

It was agreed that it was important that the terms of reference of both the territorial committees should be sufficiently wide to enable them to participate in the study of closer association, although this might involve difficulty *via-à-vis* the Rulers in the Federation.

With reference to item 5 of the questionnaire, it was agreed that there was little that could be done at present to stimulate public opinion in the territories. It was also decided that items 7 to 12 of the questionnaire[7] could be left for the present, and that it would be best to deal only with the Federation and Singapore at this juncture and make no reference to the Borneo territories.

Conclusions

1. Our objective should still be the closest political association between Singapore and the Federation that we can get local opinion to accept.

2. The setting up of the joint Federation/Singapore Co-ordination Committee under the Chairmanship of the Commissioner-General, and of a Constitutional Committee in the Federation and a Commission in Singapore, provides us with an opportunity which has not existed before, and which it would be folly not to seize, to attempt to achieve this objective.

3. The Commissioner-General should be requested to steer the Joint Co-ordination Committee towards expressing the view that some form of political association between Singapore and the Federation is necessary; and means should then be found of associating the Constitution Committee in the Federation, and the Commission in Singapore in a further study of the best means of achieving this objective, and of the form that the association should take.

4. The terms of reference of the two territorial commissions should be so drawn as to permit them to undertake such a joint study.

5. The time is not yet ripe for a statement of policy by H.M.G., but one should be drafted ready for issue when the right psychological moment is reached in the deliberation of the Joint Co-ordination Committee.

6. In case an intermediate solution on the lines of the East African High Commission should be proposed, the Commissioner-General and the two Governments should be furnished with a memorandum indicating the disadvantages which experience has shown to exist in that form of inter-territorial association.

---

[7] ie aspects of constitutional and political association.

---

301   CAB 134/898, FE (0)(53)6   13 June 1953

'Political effects that a deterioration of the situation in Indo-China might have in British colonial and protected territories': CO memorandum for the Far East (Official) Committee   [Extract]

[On 19 Feb 1953 the Cabinet appointed a committee under Eden to consider the defence of Malaya in the event of a French collapse in Indo-China leading to a communist victory in Thailand. Its recommendations were approved by Cabinet on 31 Mar 1954 (see CAB 128/26/1, CC 13(53)2, and CAB 128/27, CC 23(54)5; CAB 129/67, C(54)117 is also relevant but has been retained). Meanwhile, on 13 May, the Far East (Official) Committee, chaired by R H Scott, commissioned a series of investigations by the CO, CRO, Treasury and

Board of Trade into the economic and political implications of communist successes in mainland South-East Asia; the committee considered document 301 on 16 June (see also CO 1022/200, no 3).]

1. *Malaya*

It was noted in sub-para. (c) of FE(0)(53) 5th Meeting that any political study of this sort would be subject to military considerations which might well be paramount. This is clearly so in the case of Malaya, but only if Siam should go bad, ceasing to be a protective barrier for Malaya and bringing the threat of external Communist aggression right down to the Malayan frontier. So long as Siam remains secure from Communism and prepared to cooperate with the free world the potential dangers now being assessed are unlikely to materialise in full force.

The military consequences in Malaya of further deterioration of the situation in Indo-China have already been considered at length by the Chiefs of Staff. From the political point of view Sir G. Templer has recently described public morale in Malaya as greatly improved but still brittle. The tonic effect on the Malayan Communists of major Viet Minh successes in Indo-China would combine dangerously with the depressing effect which such successes would have on those in Malaya who now give active support to the Government.

On the one hand, the Communists would be encouraged not only to renew with fresh vigour their campaign of violence but also to intensify their efforts to subvert the mass of the people and especially to penetrate and corrupt the trade unions. On the other hand, the concomitant decay in public morale would weaken the capacity of the people to resist these attacks and in particular would tend once more to set in motion among the Chinese the vicious spiral of collaboration with the Communists leading to Communist successes, increased collaboration and so on. The situation would deteriorate still further and more rapidly if, as might well happen, the economic life of the country were again seriously disrupted, with an accompaniment of unemployment, unrest among organised labour and enforced general retrenchment in social services and other fields. Above all, any substantial cut in the supply of rice from Siam, upon which the people of Malaya so largely depend to sustain life, would have a disastrous effect upon the great mass of Malays and Chinese alike, with results too obvious to require statement.

These damaging developments in the Federation would almost certainly be accompanied by dislocation of the Government's plans for political advance. Since the pressure of the Emergency began to fall off last year there have been many indications that Malaya was entering a period of increased political activity. The Federation Government are devoting particular attention to progressive political development and a committee representing all the substantial interests of the country has been set up to consider constitutional advance. In Singapore also the tempo of political development is quickening, and further measures of constitutional advance are under consideration. In both a fresh attempt is about to be made to draw them together in closer political association. It is likely that in both territories the next year or two will be a formative period of great political importance. H.M.G.'s policy is to help the territories towards self-government but the small size and political division of Malaya, the racial problems arising from its plural society and its importance from the defence point of view will make the transfer of power a very delicate process. In the circumstances of Malaya H.M.G.'s policy will stand a much greater chance of success if external political influences are contained within the narrowest possible limits. If those influences are not sufficiently contained, and a threat from the north develops with a real force, with the possible consequences already described—a disaffected Chinese and a distressed Malay community—it is hardly conceivable that sound political progress can be maintained, and the alternative is likely to be a retrogressive rather than a static situation. At the very least the Government's policy of "Malayanisation" would become much more difficult of achievement: at the worst an open breach might develop between the majority of the Chinese community on the one hand and the Malays, Indians and Europeans, with a minority of the Chinese, on the other. . . .

302   T 220/284, f 23   **30 July 1953**

[Financial difficulties]: letter from Mr Lyttelton to Mr Butler seeking an assurance of UK assistance to Malaya

[Despite improvements in internal security, the costs of the emergency did not diminish. Indeed, during a Cabinet discussion of public expenditure on 28 July, Lyttelton informed his colleagues that 'Malaya faced a serious budget deficit, which might well cost the Exchequer about £18 millions' (CAB 128/26/2, CC 46(53)4). In addition to seeking a UK contribution to emergency operations, the federal government had drawn up a loan programme for various capital works, and the Treasury agreed in principle to Malaya's raising a loan of about £6 million in London in 1954 (CO 1022/275, nos 85, 89 and 91).]

I enclose a statement[1] which Sir Donald MacGillivray, the Deputy High Commissioner for the Federation of Malaya, who is over here at present, has prepared about the financial position of the Federation. You will see (paragraph 8) that the prospects for 1954 are extremely serious: even if every cent of the country's realisable surplus balances is committed revenue still seems likely to fall short of expenditure by over 80 million Malayan dollars—or about £10 million.

There are three main reasons for this. First, although Malaya has succeeded in containing the Communist terrorists and getting on top of the emergency, the battle is still far from won and it will be necessary for some time to come to maintain the effort in the shooting war at a level not far below that of to-day. Second, ultimate success in defeating the terrorists depends as much upon social and economic development as upon police and military operations. Particularly now that there has been solid improvement in the situation, and life has become much more normal, morale in Malaya—which is good but still unreliable, and upon which in the last analysis everything depends—will not be maintained if such development is greatly retarded. There is thus little room for economy in expenditure, although the Federation Government are pursuing it by all means within their power. On the other hand, the recent marked fall in the prices of rubber and tin—the sources of nearly all the country's wealth—means that next year revenue will be very greatly reduced.

Our two Departments have already begun discussions of this grave situation and will be pursuing them further urgently and in detail. But it is already clear that, if

---

[1] Not printed.

Malaya is not to lose much of the ground gained in the last two years, Her Majesty's Government will next year have to make good in material terms the pledges of financial support which have more than once been given to the Federation Government. You will remember, for example, that in 1950 our predecessors said:—

". . . His Majesty's Government, as they always have been, are willing to give Malaya all the assistance that may be shewn to be necessary both for the effective prosecution of the anti-bandit campaign and to enable her to go ahead with her plans of social and economic development. It is His Majesty's Government's desire that the heavy burden that Malaya is continuing to bear in the common effort against Communist banditry should not be allowed to impede, for financial reasons this very necessary development programme."[2]

Again, last year, although the statement was never used in public, we told the Federation Government:—

". . . Her Majesty's Government are commited to giving whatever assistance may be necessary and will never let the Federation down. . . . It is Her Majesty's Government's view that the Federation Government can plan for the defence and development of the country in the confidence that Her Majesty's Government will not permit the burden of emergency expenditure to retard these plans. . . . In considering any help that may be required later Her Majesty's Government would, of course, have to take into account the extent to which the Federation had shewn "self-help" by e.g., increasing taxation and raising local loans."

Until our two Departments have completed their examination of the problem it will not be possible to determine the exact amount of aid which Malaya will require in 1954 but it will almost certainly be substantial.

The Executive Council and the Finance Committee of the Federation will begin to consider the 1954 Budget next month and it will be introduced into the Legislative Council in November. What the Federation Government now ask is that the High Commissioner should be free to tell his Executive Council and Finance Committee next month that, in accordance with their pledges, Her Majesty's Government have undertaken to come to the aid of Malaya next year. It will not at that stage be necessary to mention a figure, although one will be required when the Budget is presented to the Legislative Council in November.

I very much hope that you will be able to agree that the High Commissioner may be authorised to convey such an assurance to his Executive Council and Finance Committee next month. The exact figure and the form which the assistance should take would be worked out between our two Departments, in consultation with the Federation Government, in time for November.[3]

---

[2] J Griffiths, written answer to A J Champion, *H of C Debs*, vol 482, col 219, 15 Dec 1950.

[3] On 5 Aug Butler gave this assurance. He informed Lyttelton that, although 'it will clearly take some time before we can decide the exact amount and form of the financial assistance which we can give Malaya next year . . ., meanwhile I must admit that the situation as presented in the Memorandum [by MacGillivray] leaves no reasonable doubt that we shall, in fact, have to give Malaya something'. Inter-departmental discussions over figures continued, see part III of this volume, 305 and 306.

303   CO 1022/58, no 8   28 Aug 1953

['White area' in Malacca]: inward savingram no 1480/53 from Sir G
Templer to Mr Lyttelton on a proposed relaxation of emergency
regulations in part of the Settlement

In my proposal telegram No. 880 of August 26th, I explained my decision to declare a part of MALACCA a WHITE AREA on 3rd September 1953. You may wish to have further details of this project.

2. There is no doubt that by strictest possible control of food supplies and restrictions on movement of food, vehicles and individuals in certain areas and at certain times, we have imposed a great strain on the CTs.[1] There is ample information from intelligence sources that in areas where food denial operations have been carried out properly CTs have suffered severely. It is a very potent weapon.

3. It has however long been my feeling that it would give a great fillip to morale if I could raise some of these irksome restrictions on the liberty of the individual in areas where, in the opinion of the local authorities, it could safely be done. Such an area I call a WHITE area. A scheme of this sort might have considerable results. Apart from its repercussions on public opinion outside Malaya, it might well have a great effect for good on the local population here, encouraging those people in areas where restrictions are still, of necessity, imposed, to co-operate more freely with Government to remove the CTs so that they also could reap the benefits of greater freedom. Quite apart from these aspects it is, I consider, essential that we should in any case keep ERs[2] constantly under review.

4. The Resident Commissioner Malacca recently proposed that an area of that settlement should be declared WHITE. The area includes Malacca itself and contains over 50% of the population of the Settlement. After investigation I have agreed to the proposal.

5. Within the area all curfews are lifted. No food controls will be imposed. For example people will be able to take out mid-day meals to their work, a necessary restriction in the past and one which has caused hardship to the manual labourer. No one will be searched for food at village gates. Restrictions on shopkeepers will be lifted.

6. From a legal point of view this is achieved by gazetting a new amendment to ER. 17EA, which is the only regulation affected, giving Resident Commissioners and Mentri[s] Besar in any State/Settlement power to suspend the operation in a specified area, of certain provisions and orders now in force under that regulation. Power is reserved to re-impose restrictions at once if the need arises.

7. Though parts of this ER will be suspended there will be no other relaxations. No dispersal of new villages or regrouped labour lines will be allowed. No Emergency Regulations will be cancelled or repealed. There will be proper security checks on all roads leading out of the area. There will be no easing of Security Force vigilance.

8. This is an experiment with a slight element of risk that some food may leak out or some CTs may filter in. It is a risk I accept. Its success will lie in the co-operation of the people themselves who will be under no illusions that I shall reimpose all

---

[1] Communist terrorists.   [2] Emergency regulations.

restrictions if they fail me. The project does not mean the end of the emergency in Malacca but it will be a big step forward. I hope that from time to time other parts of Malaya will be able to follow its good example. If this happens we shall have dealt the CTs a shrewd blow.[3]

---

[3] On receipt of this telegram the same day, A M MacKintosh minuted: 'I am sure that this risk is well worth taking. Coming fairly soon after the abolition of Regulation 17D (for mass detention) it should help still further to rebut the charges of a military regime in Malaya & of personal ruthlessness in General Templer which are so often levelled out of ignorance or malice'. On 3 Sept Templer visited Malacca and declared 221 square miles to be a 'white area'. By the time he left Malaya in mid-1954, 'white areas' had been extended to include over 1,300,000 people living along much of west-coast Malaya.

Index of Main Subjects and Persons: Parts I–III

This is a consolidated index for all three parts of the volume. It is not a comprehensive index, but a simplified and straightforward index to document numbers, together with page references to the Introduction in part I, the latter being given at the beginning of the entry in lower case roman numerals. The index is designed to be used in conjunction with the summary lists of the preliminary pages to each part of the volume. A preceding asterisk indicates inclusion in the Biographical Notes at the end of Part III. Where necessary (eg particularly in long documents), and if possible, paragraph or section numbers are given inside round brackets. In the case of a British official or minister (such as Lennox-Boyd, Malcolm MacDonald and Templer), who appears prominently in the volume, the index indicates the first and last documents of his period of office. Further references to his contribution can be identified from the summary lists.

The following abbreviations are used:

A – appendix or annex (thus 257 A I = first appendix to document 257)
E – enclosure
N – editor's link note (before main text of document)
n – footnote.

Documents are divided between the three parts of the volume as follows:

nos 1–138 part I
nos 139–303 part II
nos 304–467 part III.

Abdoolcader, Sir Husein Hasanally 460 (8)
Abdul Aziz, Sultan of Perak (*see also* Malay rulers) 57
Abdul Aziz bin Haji Abdul Majid 392 N, 410
* Abdul Aziz bin Ishak lxxiii, 237 n 2, 360 (4), 368, 370, 414
Abdul Hamid, Mr Justice (*see also* Reid Commission) lxxvii–lxxviii, 401 n 1, 429, 438 n 4, 439
Abdul Kadir Samsuddin 392 N, 410 N
Abdul Rahman, Yam Tuan of Negri Sembilan (*see also* Malay rulers, Yang di- Pertuan Agong) 57, 367
Abdul Rahman bin Mohd Yasin, Dato 72 n 1, 99 N
* Abdul Rahman Putra Al-Haj, Tunku
  leader of UMNO 244, 271, 279, 296, 297
  leader of Alliance lxxi, lxxii–lxxxi, 295
  member of Executive Council 269 (2), 304
  Alliance delegation to London (1954) 313–321
  Alliance boycott (1954) 322, 323, 325–328, 330–334

federal elections (1955) 350 N, 354 (1), 359–362
chief minister lxxv–lxxxi, 360
  meetings with Lennox-Boyd (1955) 365–370
  Baling talks with MCP li, lxxvi–lxxvii, 371, 373–382, 385, 386, 391
  constitutional conference (Jan–Feb 1956) lxxvii, 392–406
  defence talks lxxviii, 407, 410, 414, 417, 462
  Reid Commission 426, 427, 429, 446
  London talks (Dec 1956–Jan 1957) 441
  constitutional conference (May 1957) 450
  good relations with Britain 405 (2), 450 n 2
  appointment of governors of Penang and Malacca 459, 460
  achievement of independence lxxix–lxxxi, 467
  post-independence outlook for 454
Abdul Rashid Mahiden 371 N, 391
* Abdul Razak bin Hussein, Dato
  UMNO 279
  Alliance delegation to London (1954) 318

federal elections, plans for 328
minister for education (1955) 360 (4), 364 n 3, 415
meetings with Lennox-Boyd (1955) 368, 370
constitutional conference (Jan–Feb 1956) 392 N
defence talks 410
Reid Commission 427, 429
London talks (May 1957) 450
* Abdul Wahab bin Toh Muda Abdul Aziz, Haji (Dato Panglima Bukit Gantang)
UMNO lix, 90
Onn 182 n 8, 295
National Conference 297, 298 (1)
Malay rights 287 (4)
Executive Council 304 (6)
Alliance boycott 330 (13)
constitutional conference (Jan–Feb 1956) 392 N
London talks (May 1957) 450
Abdullah bin Mohamed 173 n 3
Abell, Sir A 267 n 1
aborigines 199 n 5, 271 (25)
Abu Bakar, Sultan of Pahang (see also Malay rulers) 57
Abu Bakar, Tunku of Johore 57
Adams, Sir T 96 n 1, 99 N
Addison, Lord 58 n 3, 69 N, 70, 110
Adkins, G C S 170 A
Africa, Cambridge summer school on local government 167 (5)
Ahmad bin Haji Abdullah, Haji 279 (18)
* Ahmad Boestamam lxxv, 94 (32), 116, 415 (8)
Alam Shah, Sultan of Selangor (see also Malay rulers) 53 N, 57, 60, 96 n 1 , 165 n 1, 235 N, 325 n 3, 333 (4)
Alexander, A V 185
Alexander, Lord 251 n 1, 259 n 2
Ali, Raja of Trengganu 53 N, 57
All Malayan Council of Joint Action (see Pan Malayan Council of Joint Action)
Allen, A M 398
Allen, W D 335, 343 n 6, 347, 398
Alliance (see also UMNO, MCA and MIC)
formation of Alliance lxxi, 269 (2), 271 (24), 304 n 1
leadership 295, 296
constitutional 'blue print' lxxii, 297, 298 (1)
delegation to London 313–321
boycott (1954) li, lxxiii, 322, 323, 325, 327, 328, 330–333
agreement on elections 334
commitment to independence 362
electoral victory (1955) 359–362
delegation to London conference (Jan–Feb 1956) 392, 395 (see also constitutional conference)
defence negotiations 407, 408, 410
education policy 415

Reid Commission 426, 427, 429
post-independence outlook for 454
Allison, J A 148 N
Alport, C J M 467 N
Amery, L 9, 24
amnesty (see also Baling talks)
MCP's first peace offer (May–June 1955) 350–353
Alliance electoral commitment 350 N, 362 (2), 365 (9), 366, 368 (2), 370 (32)
run-up to Baling talks 371, 373–382, 385, 386
summary of Baling talks 391
Ang Bin Hoey Society 130 (2)
Anglo-Malayan defence agreement (see also defence)
ANZAM 339, 343, 348, 400, 432, 441, 462
API (Angkatan Pemuda Insaf) 94 (32), 116, 160 n 1, 162
Archer, G 49 n 2
Arden-Clarke, Sir C xxxvi, 1, 189 N, 267 n 4
Armstrong, E A 58 n 3, 95 N
Ascoli, F D 251
Ashley Clarke, H 3, 4, 5, 24, 243
Associated Chinese Chambers of Commerce 131–134, 330
Association of British Malaya 149, 251
Atlantic Charter (1941) 8
* Attlee, C R xxxviii, xliv, xlvi, lxviii, 342 (6)
deputy prime minister 9, 24, 25, 31
prime minister (1945–1950) 40 n 2, 58 n 3, 80, 93, 120 n 3, 155, 160 n 3, 185, 198 n 2, 235 N, 268 N
prime minister (1950–1951) 206, 207, 209, 210, 227 n 2, 230, 232, 233, 234, 238
Australia (see also defence, ANZAM, SEATO) 339, 340, 376, 380, 394 N, 398, 413, 437, 462
Awbery, S S xlvii, lxxxii n 23, 153 n 2, 318 n 1

Badlishah, Sultan of Kedah (see also Malay rulers) 53 N, 57, 64, 96 (3)
Bahaman bin Samsuddin 360 (5)
Balan, R G 162
Baling talks (Dec 1956) (see also amnesty) xlvi, li, lii, lxxvi
lead up to 371, 373–382, 385, 386
summary of 391
Bandung conference 350
banishment & repatriation (see also emergency regulations) 129, 130, 147, 149, 150, 169, 219 (11), 221, 257 A XI
Barclay, R E 335 n 3
Barlow, T B 63
Barnes, L 227 (25)
Bartlett, V 309 n 8
Battershill, Sir W 11
Baxter, R L 309, 330 n 4

BBC xxi, 173 n 3, 309, 421 (7), 463
Bedale, H (report) lxxxii n 23, 280 n 3, 290 (1)
Bell, E P 142 N
Benham, F C C 211 (4), 214, 275
Bennett, J C 149
* Bennett, (Sir) J C Sterndale 58
Bennett, J S xxxix
Bevin, E lxvi, 40 n 2, 81, 118, 160 N, 198 n 3, 211 N
Bingham, R P 117 n 2
Black, E R 282 n 2
Black, Sir R 371 (1)
Blacking, J 309 (2)
Blythe, W L 140, 258 (6), 260 (9)
Boestamam (see Ahmad Boestamam)
Borneo (including North Borneo and Sarawak; see also closer association) 8, 12, 15, 227 (11), 267, 286, 346 (12)
Bose, R B 129 n 2
Bose, S C 129 n 2
Boucher, Major-General C H 188 E, 199
Bourdillon, H T xlii, xlix
    Malayan Union policy 48 N, 52, 55, 59, 64, 73, 75, 85, 91
    federal negotiations 99, 101, 106, 107, 115, 136, 138
    regional co-ordination 120, 141
    labour unrest in Malaya 122, 129
    Indonesian influences 137
    rural development 273
    financial difficulties of Malays 305
Bourne, (Sir) G 259, 308 n 3, 341, 371 (1), 376, 377, 386
Bovenschen, Sir F 18 N, 40 n 6
Bower, General R H 422
Bowyer, E B 194
Boyd, R 273 n 3
Boyd-Carpenter, J A 306
Braddell, R 99 N, 105 E, 205
Bradley, E N 149
Braithwaite, F J St G 410
Brazier, J A 117, 230
Bridges, Sir E 58 n 3, 120
* Briggs, Sir H (see also Briggs plan) xliv, lxviii, 206, 207, 220, 222, 230 N, 232, 233, 235, 239, 242, 248, 249 (12), 251, 252
Briggs plan xliv, lxviii, lxx, 216, 219, 220 (5), 226, 232–234, 236, 251, 252
British advisers (see also constitutional conference (1956), Malay rulers) lii, lxxv, 331, 365 (7), 367 (10), 369, 370 (24), 388, 435
British aims and interests
    in Malaya 10, 145, 167, 174, 177, 181, 183–185, 227 (18), 230, 268, 270, 337, 343, 375, 454
    in SE Asia 196, 198, 293, 336, 343
British Association of Straits Merchants 149, 251

British Defence Co-ordinating Committee (Far East) (see also commissioner-general, regional policy) 158, 175 N, 216, 231, 252, 339, 363, 402, 437, 454 N, 464
British Insurance Association 149 N
British Military Administration xlv, li, lii, lvii–lix, 43–81 passim
    establishment 44, 45
    transition to civil government 62, 70
Brittain, Sir H 306, 364 n 2
broadcasts (see also BBC)
    Lyttelton (Dec 1951) 257 A II
    Macmillan (Aug 1957) 463
Brockway, F xlvii, 318 n 1
Brodie, T V A 446 N, 450
* Brook, Sir N 346 n 2, 348, 440, 458, 467 N
Brooke-Popham, Sir H 1 n 2
Broome, R N 43 N, 159 n 4
Brownjohn, General N C D 222 n 3
* Burhanuddin Al-Helmy, Dr lxxv, 90 n 3, 454
Burma liv, lvii, lxiii, lxxxi, 38, 39, 177, 193, 258 (4)
Burt-Andrews, C B E 410 N
business interests in Malaya lviii, lxv, lxvii, 63, 149, 150, 183, 184, 186, 251, 343 n 4
Bustamente, A 1 (7), 173 N
Butler, R A 302, 305, 306, 364 n 2

Cabinet
    policymaking xlv–xlvi
    Malayan Union policy 20–22, 24, 25, 31, 36, 48, 50, 56 N, 69, 76
    War Cabinet Committee on Malaya & Borneo (1944–1945) 20–22, 24, 25, 31
    Cabinet Colonial Affairs Committee 109, 110
    declaration of emergency lxvi, 153, 158–161
    review of emergency operations by Labour
        Cabinet & Defence Committee lxviii, lxix, 180, 219, 221, 226, 227, 232–234
    Cabinet Malaya Committee (1950–1951) lxviii, lxix, 209, 210, 215, 216, 220, 222
    review of emergency operations by Conservative government (1951–1952) 252, 253, 257, 266
    Cabinet Committee on Malaya (1951–1952) 263, 266
    Cabinet Colonial Policy Committee (1955–1957) 372 n 1, 380, 382 n 6, 394, 448, 449
    Cabinet Policy Review Committee (1956) 421
    constitutional developments (1955–1957) lxxvi, 356–358, 372, 394, 400, 403–406, 436 n 1, 448, 449
    Baling talks (1955) 379, 386
Caccia, Sir H 250 N
Cahill, M L 389
* Caine, Sir S xli, 16 N, 19, 32, 34, 35, 141, 282, 396 (6)

Calcutta conference (Feb 1948)   lxiii
Calder, J   57, 267 (6)
Canberra bombers   462 n 4
Carbonell W L R   389 n 5
Carey, R B   269 (3), 304 (5)
Carnell, F G   272, 309
Carr-Saunders, Sir A   170 n 4
Carstairs, C Y   309
Cary, M   398 n 3
Casey, R G   376 (1), 431, 432
Central Africa   184, 217 (3–4), 458
Ceylon   138 n 2, 407 n 3
Chadwick, G W St J   431, 450
Chaplin, A G T   194
Chapman, F S   43 N, 57
Cheeseman, H R   lxii, 110 n 3
Cheeseman consultative committee   lx, lxii, 110 n
    3, 111, 121 N, 123 (1–7)
Chen Tian   371 N, 385 n 6, 391
Chiang Kai-shek   lvi
Chilver R C   431
* Chin Peng (see also Baling talks, emergency,
    MCP)   xlvi, lii, lxiii
    wartime resistance   43 N
    MCP's first peace offer (May–June 1955)
        350–353
    Baling talks   li, lxxvi-lxxvii, 371, 373–382, 385,
        386, 391, 395 (2)
    post-independence outlook for   454
Chin Swee Onn   295 (2), 297
China, People's Republic of
    British recognition of   lxviii, 192 N, 197, 199,
        202
    British policy towards   202, 213, 336
    propaganda from   190, 195 (1), 342
China Democratic League   168 E
Chinese, in Malaya
    British assessments of   139, 163, 168–172, 178,
        227 (16–17), 245, 247, 252, 272, 342
    British attempts to enlist support of (see also
        MCA formation of)   163, 171, 172, 227 (5)
    British policy towards   191, 204
Chinese consuls   199, 205, 213, 342 (9)
Chinese protectorate   140, 170 A (6), 172 n 1
Chinese schools (see also education policy)   lxxiv,
    345, 415
Chinese secretariat (Department of Chinese
    Affairs)   191, 195 (1), 252 (3)
Cho Yew Fai   409 (8), 411 (1)
Chou En-lai   336 (9), 350 N
Christian, I D   148 N
Chung Shing Jit Pao   168 n 2
Churchill, Major-General T B L   410
* Churchill, (Sir) W, prime minister
    (1951–1955)   xliv, lxix, 248, 252 n 1, 256, 257
    N, 259, 260, 262, 263, 268 N, 308, 348 N
citizenship (see also Malayan Union, constitutional

conference (Jan–Feb 1956), Reid commission)
    Malayan Union   lv, lix, 29 n 2, 66 (7), 74, 75,
        77, 80
    federal negotiations (1946–1948)   lxiii,
        100–107, 123 (30–34), 128
    demands and developments (1948–1955)
        lxviii, lxx, 203, 205, 212, 227 (12), 280, 297
    independence constitution   lxxvii, lxxviii, 409,
        411, 412, 448 (14–18), 450 (4), 451–453
Clauson, Sir G   194, 251
Clementi, Sir C   liii, lviii, 19 n 2, 73 n 1
Clifford, Sir H   liii
closer association of Malaya and Singapore   lxviii,
    lxxii, lxxiv, lxxx, 19, 98, 112, 115 (8), 121, 141,
    143, 218 (27–29), 267, 276, 286, 288, 292, 293,
    300, 324, 344, 346, 348
Clough, A H   200, 229
Codner, M   285 n 1
Cohen, A   141 N & n 3
cold war (see also communism)   lxv-lxviii, 311,
    339, 340
collective punishment   lxxi, 285
Collier, A J   305 n 6
Colombo conference   201 N, 211, 225 n 4
Colombo plan   274, 421, 440
Colombo powers   336
Colonial Development Corporation   208, 211
Colonial Development and Welfare funds   208,
    211, 440, 441 (11), 456 (9)
colonial policymaking   xxxviii–l
commissioner-general, SE Asia (see also M J
    MacDonald, R Scott, regional policy)
    conferences   143, 197, 198, 202, 218, 249 n 2,
        284, 311, 454 N
    role of   243, 266, 335, 338, 348
Commonwealth
    role in SE Asia (see also Australia, New
        Zealand)   196, 211
    Malayan membership   lxxvii, lxxix, 346 (9–11),
        444, 445, 447, 454, 457, 458, 467
Commonwealth Parliamentary Association   276
    (3), 467 N
communalism (see also Communities Liaison
    Committee)   94, 192, 195, 227 (6–9), 337 (8)
communism (see also cold war, emergency,
    MCP)   lxv–lxvii, 189 (3), 227 (10), 284, 339, 340
Communities Liaison Committee   lxviii, 171, 182,
    195 (4–5), 204, 205, 218 (17–18)
Conservative Party's Far Eastern Sub-
    Committee   451, 452
Constituency Delineation Commission   310 (7),
    318 n 3
constitutional commission (see Reid commission)
constitutional conference (Jan–Feb 1956)   l, lii,
    lxxvi–lxxvii, lxxx
    preparations for   382 n 6, 384, 389, 390,
        392–401

proceedings and conclusions 402–406
constitutional conference (May 1957) 1
    proceedings 449, 450
    amendments to proposals 453
constitutional development, pace of lxviii, lxxvi–
    lxxvii, lxxx, 218 (1–16), 263 n 2, 268 n 1, 277,
    283, 293 (16), 299, 356, 357, 368 (3), 378, 381,
    382 n 6, 384 (9)
Copleston, E R 38 n 2
Corfield, F D lxiv, lxxxiii n 43
Corry, W C S 261 (7), 264 (6), 265
Council of Joint Action (see Pan-Malayan Council
    of Joint Action)
counter-insurgency (see also Briggs plan,
    emergency, internal security, police,
    Templer) lxvii–lxxii, 180, 188, 189, 199, 220,
    226, 227, 337 (5), 341
    psychological warfare 350 (21)
Cranborne, Lord (Lord Salisbury from 1947) (see
    Salisbury, Lord)
Creasy, Sir George 233
Creasy, Sir Gerald xlix
* Creech Jones, A xlviii, lviii, lxii, lxv, 258 (2)
    Malayan Union 48 N, 55, 76 n 1, 80–135
        passim
    outbreak of emergency 144–155 passim
    developments under Gurney 156–204 passim
    independence celebrations 467 N
Creswell, M J 243 N
Cripps, Sir S 58 n 3, 161, 194 n 2, 198 n 3, 221,
    223, 224 N
Crombie, J I C 175, 200
Crookshank, H F C 380
Crown jurisdiction in Malay states 142 (see also
    Malay rulers)
Cruikshank, J A C 364 n 2
Cumarasami, M N 360 (3)
Cunningham, Sir A 157 (3)
Curtin, J 161 n 6
Cyprus 375 (11)

Dahari Ali 90 n 3
Daily Mail 183, 184
Daily Telegraph 173 (17)
Daily Worker xlvi
Dale, W L 456 n 6
Dalley, J D 86 n 2, 137 N
Dalley, F W lxxxii n 23, 153 (10), 218 (10), 227
    (26)
Dalton, H J N 50
Dato Panglima Bukit Gantang (see Abdul Wahab
    bin Toh Muda Abdul Aziz)
David, E 261 (7), 292 (10)
Davis, J L H 43 N, 46, 159 n 4, 204 n 2
Day, E V G 64
de Castries, General lxxiii

de Lattre de Tassigny, General lxix, 235, 258 (4)
de Silva, M W H 457
defence (see also internal security, regional
    security, Thai border)
    defence implications of constitutional
        development 346 (6–8), 356 (4), 363, 366,
        375, 383, 394 (8), 398
    Anglo-Malayan defence agreement lxxvii–
        lxxviii, lxxx, 402, 407, 408, 410, 414, 417, 431,
        432, 441, 462
    post-independence outlook 454
* del Tufo, (Sir) M xlvii, 245 N, 246, 247, 258
    (6), 260 (6), 264 (6)
Dempsey, Sir M 53, 59
* Dening, (Sir) M xlv, 39, 51, 54, 58, 71 N, 81, 95
    n 1, 119, 120, 243 N
deportation (see banishment)
detention and detainees 147, 169, 220 (7), 222,
    233, 257 A XI, 279 n 3, 391 (27–31)
Devasar, K L 360 (3)
Diefenbaker, J 457
Dien Bien Phu lxxiii, 324 N, 342 (6)
district officers 291
documents, selection of xxxi–xxxviii
Doherty, A H 149
Donner, Squadron Leader 110 n 3
Dow, Sir H 323 n 2
Drake, A E 305, 306, 347, 355 N
Driberg, T xlvii
Duckwith, F V 304 (7)
Duff Cooper, A xlviii, 11 (6), 39, 40, 41
Dulles, J F 324 N
Duncan (Sir) H 48 N, 55 N

Eady, Sir W 32 n 1, 120
East Africa 141, 183, 205, 217 (3–4), 323 (2)
    High Commission 141 (5), 300
    troops 233, 234, 238 (3)
East India Company lii
Eastern Exchange Banks Association 149, 251
Eber, J 115 n 2, 309
economic and financial policies for Malaya (see also
    business interests)
    wartime planning for postwar
        reconstruction 19, 32–35, 37, 38
    economic adviser 49
    diversification 145 (2)
    rice 145, 208
    rural development and Malays lxvii, lxxi, 145
        (3), 173, 273–275, 278, 282, 289
    development policies 167, 208, 219, 227
        (20–27), 273, 274, 275, 282, 337 (15)
    Colonial Development & Welfare funds 173,
        208, 211, 440, 441 (11), 456 (9)
    financing the emergency lxvii, lxviii, lxxi, 175,
        200, 219 (16–17), 221, 223–225, 227–229,

302, 305, 306, 341 (7), 440 (5), 441 (11)
tin   xliii, lxxiv, 194, 208, 223 (5), 225, 251
Malaya and the sterling area   lxxiv, lxxx, 201 N,
   214, 393 (9), 396, 454
rubber   lxxiv, 208, 223 (5), 225, 251, 305, 306
Colonial Development Corporation   208, 211
taxation in Malaya   223, 257 A XIII, 263 (3),
   266 (11), 393 (4)
land bank   273, 278
World Bank assistance   274, 275, 282, 396 (8)
financial relationship between Britain &
   Federation   356 (4)
financial aspects of constitutional
   development   390, 393, 394 (15–16), 396,
   400, 403, 405, 406
central bank   393 (9)
post-colonial financial settlement   lxxvii-
   lxxviii, 441, 446, 454, 456 (9)
economic and financial policies for SE Asia (see
   also Colombo plan)   196, 198, 201, 211, 274 E,
   421, 440
* Eden, (Sir) A   xliv, lxxvi, 4 N, 9, 182, 183
   foreign secretary (1951–1955)   249, 256, 301
   N, 324 N, 335, 338–340, 343, 345 n 3
   prime minister (1955–1957)   348, 351, 353,
   355 N, 374, 375, 378 (1), 379–381, 394 N, 421
   N, 425, 444
Edmonds, E R   309
Edmunds, Colonel W R   194
education policy   lxxi, 203, 208 (12–13), 227 (25),
   257 (71–75), 289 (3), 347, 355, 364, 415
   Chinese schools   345
   National Schools   345, 347, 355, 364, 370 (33)
   Razak report   364 n 3, 415 (9)
Ee Yew Kim   179
Egmont Hake, H B   149, 251
elections in Britain
   (1945)   36 N, 40 n 2
   (1950)   lxviii, 206 N
   (1951)   lxix, 243 N, 248 N
elections in Malaya
   plans for   lxxi, 115 (8), 167, 270, 280, 283, 290,
   299, 304, 356
   municipal   lxxi, 212, 269 (2), 280, 335 N
   state   270, 280, 312, 325 (2), 335 N, 365 (8)
   federal elections committee   lxxii–lxxiii, 286 n
   2, 294, 295 N, 298, 307, 310, 313 N, 332 n 11
   federal elections committee & Alliance
   demands   313–323, 325–328, 330–334
   federal elections results (1955)   359–362
Elibank, Lord   xlvii, lviii, 80 N
Eliot, Sir W   232
Emanuel, A   214
emergency (see counter-insurgency, MCP)   lxiii-
   lxxxi
   declaration   li, lxiii–lxvii, 148, 149
   review of operations   158, 159, 180, 190, 206,

207, 209, 210, 222, 226, 230, 232–234, 238,
   239, 242, 257, 343
   military reinforcements   159 (5–7), 161, 175,
   180, 252
   proscription of MCP   160
   regulations   169, 188 n 6, 190, 216 (17), 220
   (7), 247, 257, 303, 386 (5)
   financial costs   lxvii, lxviii, lxxi, 175, 200, 219
   (17), 221, 223–225, 227–229, 302, 305, 306,
   341 (7), 440 (5), 441 (11)
   insurance cover   189 (16)
   Cabinet Malaya Committee (1950–1951)   209,
   210, 220
   'white areas'   303
   post-independence commitments   413, 422,
   437, 454
Empson, C   118 n 2
Emrys-Evans, P V   24
Evatt, H V   119 (3)
Executive Council (see also member system)   237,
   304, 360, 368, 370

Facer, H H   149, 269 (3)
Federation of Malaya (1948) (see also citizenship,
   constitutional development, elections)
   Anglo-Malay negotiations (1946)   lx–lxiii,
   99–110
   consultative process (1947) (see also Cheeseman
   consultative committee)   111, 112 n 3
   final constitutional proposals   123, 124, 126–
   128, 131–134
   agreement (1948)   136, 138, 142, 329 n 2, 332 (4)
   secretariat   xlvii
   state powers   164, 173 n 2, 174, 227 (4), 257 A
   III, 265, 337 (10)
   Federal War Council   216 (8), 222, 232, 233,
   257, 257 A III, 265, 266, 269
   armed forces   lxxi, 281
Fenn, Dr W P (see Fenn-Wu report)
Fenn-Wu report   227 n 4, 345 (12)
Ferguson, J F   199 n 8
'ferret force'   159 (3)
fforde, A F B   38
Fijian troops   233
financial problems and policies (see economic and
   financial policies)
Fletcher, W   xlvii, lxv, 184
Force 136   lv, 43 N, 46, 47, 341 (9)
Foreign Jurisdiction Acts   13 n 4, 47 n 4
Foster, J   80 n 2
Foster-Sutton, S W   235 n 3
France, A W   194
Fraser, H   254 N, 261, 264, 265
Fressanges, Sir F   363

Gaitskell, H T N   224, 225, 228, 229
Gammans, L D   xlvii, lviii, lxv, 64 N, 73 n 1, 90 n 2
Gann, A S   251, 270, 280, 283, 290
* Gater, Sir G   xliii, 17, 40, 42, 48 N, 49, 55, 59,
    60, 63, 68, 70, 85, 105
General Labour Union (see labour relations)
Geneva Conference (1954)   lxxiii–lxxiv, 324 N,
    335 N, 342 (6)
* Gent, (Sir) E Gent   xxxv, xlvii
    CO official (1942–1946)   xlii, xliii, liii, 3–7, 9,
      11, 15, 17, 19, 24, 41, 48 N, 55
    governor, Malayan Union (1946–1948)   lix–lxii,
      82–136 passim
    high commissioner, Federation (1948)   xlviii,
      xlix, li, lxiii–lxvii, 138, 143, 144, 148, 149,
      164
    recall & death   li, lxv–lxvii, 144, 151, 152, 154,
      155
Gilbert, Sir B   200 n 3
Gilchrist, A G   343 n 6
Gimson, Sir F   98, 141, 143, 149 N, 151 (7–8),
    163, 170, 199, 218, 260 (8), 267, 276 (5)
Gloucester, Duke & Duchess   465, 466, 467 N
Godsall W D   99 N, 278
Gold Coast (Ghana)   xxxvi, xlix, l, lxxvii, lxxix, 189
    N, 205, 330 (6), 389 n 4
    public services   419
    Commonwealth membership   444, 445, 458
    independence   455, 456, 458, 463
Gordon-Walker, P   22
governor-general (see also M J MacDonald,
    regional policy)
    conferences   98, 111, 112, 117
Gracey, General D D   lvii, 118 (46)
Grantham, Sir A   151
Gray, D   304 (2), 314, 327, 333 N
Gray, S A   149
* Gray, W N   xl, 153 (15), 178, 188 E, 190 n 7 & n
    8, 203, 251 n 2, 258 (6), 260 (7)
Greenwood, A   76 n 1
Griffin, R Allen   216 n 1
* Griffiths, J   258 (2), 302 n 2, 318 n 1, 320, 328
    secretary of state for colonies   lxix, 206–246
      passim
    visit to Malaya (1950)   xliii, xlix, lxviii, 218,
      219, 221
Grigg, Sir J   20, 24
Grimond, J   285
Guillemard, Sir L   liii
* Gurney, Sir H   xxxv, xxxvi, xl, xliii, 258 (3), 260
    (5)
    appointment   151, 152, 154, 156, 157, 165, 166
    high commissioner   lxvii–lxx, 168–246 passim
    offers resignation   xlviii, lxix, 235, 236
    assassination   xlv, xlix, li, lxix–lxx, 246, 249
      (12)
Gurney, Lady   246

Hailey, Lord   1 n 5, 13
* Hall, G H   lviii, lx, 48, 50, 55, 56, 58 n 3, 67, 69,
    76, 82, 83, 86–89, 91–93, 96, 97, 100, 102–104
Hall, H P   423 n 1
Hall-Patch, Sir E   282 n 2
Hamid, Mr Justice A (see Abdul Hamid, Mr Justice)
Hamilton, A P   251
Hammerskjold, D   342 (6)
Hamzah, Tengku Syed   53 N, 57
Hamzah bin Abdullah, Dato   57, 99 N, 344 n 3
Han Suyin   309 (5)
Harding, Sir J   lxix, 199, 220 (1), 233, 234, 250,
    259 N
Harris, Sir A   259 N
Hart, G V   450
hartal   lxii, 131 N, 162
Harvey, J A   57
Hashim Ghani   205
Hay, M C   57, 59
Haynes, A S   73 n 1
Head, A (later Lord Head)   xliv, 339, 340, 343
Headly, D   57
Heah Joo Seng   295 (2)
Helsby, Sir L   120
Henderson, K J   423 n 1, 439, 443
Hennings, J   xxxiv, 431, 462 n 4
Hertogh riots   232, 258 (6), 260 (9–10)
Hicks, E C   309
* Higham, J D   xlii, xlix, 162 N
    Gurney's period   176, 182, 183, 232, 233, 237,
      240, 241 n 2, 244
    Lyttelton's visit   254, 255
    Templer's period   267, 270, 272, 274–277, 280,
      282, 283, 288, 292, 296
high commissioner's veto powers   365 (3), 390 (3),
    395 (3)
Himsworth, E   329 n 3
HMS Alert   lxxiii, lxxv, 333
Hodgkinson, J D   269 (2)
* Hogan, M J P   lxxii, 246, 283, 292, 298 n 6, 299,
    300, 313, 333 N, 368, 370
Holt, H E   457
* Home, Lord   348 N, 394 N, 403 n 3, 449, 455,
    457, 458 n 8, 463
* Hone, (Sir) R   xlv, lv, lvii, 16, 23, 68, 74, 77, 91,
    98, 99 N, 143, 267
Hong Kong   liii, 2, 11, 183, 195, 206, 207, 230 N,
    248, 258 (5), 375 (9)
Howitt, C R   344 n 3
Hull, Cordell   8 (2)
Humphrey, A H P   360 (4), 370
Hunt R C C   398, 458
Hussein Onn   240, 244 n 1
Hutton, N K   450, 456

Ibrahim, Sultan of Johore (see also Malay

rulers) xliii, lviii, lix, lxxv, 54, 57, 59, 90 n 1, 120 n 2, 135 (4), 203 n 4, 331 N, 388 n 1, 394 (5), 435
Ibrahim, Sultan of Kelantan (*see also* Malay rulers) 53 N, 57
Ibrahim bin Ismail 43 N
Incorporated Society of Planters 149, 251
independence
  prospects for independence movements 139, 140
  date 384 (9), 390, 394 (6), 395 (2), 397, 399, 404 n 2
  definition xxxix, 397
  constitution 451–453
  legislation for 453 n 1, 456, 458 n 8
  celebrations lxxvii, lxxix, 455, 463, 467
  post-independence outlook lxxx, 454
Independence of Malaya Party (*see also* Onn bin Jaafar) lxix, lxxi, 240, 241, 244, 295, 310 (4)
India (*see also* Nehru) lxvi, 193, 196
Indian Independence League 129 n 2
Indian National Army 129 n 2
Indian New Democratic Youth League 160 n 1
Indo-China lvi, lvii, lxiii, lxix, lxxiii, 118 (43–46), 196, 230 N, 232, 239 (2), 258 (4), 301, 308 N, 311, 324 N, 335
Indonesia lvi, lvii, lxi, lxiii, 92 (9), 94 (32), 115 (6), 118 (35–42), 137, 196, 205, 227 (11), 283, 286 n 2, 382 n 5
Institute of Pacific Relations, conference (1942) 3, 8, 12 N
intelligence services & reports xxxix, 271, 279
  Malayan Union lx–lxi, 72, 79, 86 (3), 90, 94
  Indonesian influences 137 N
  communist insurgency lxv, 162, 189
  reorganisation lxx–lxxi, 257 A IX
  Baling talks 387
internal security (*see also* emergency, counter-insurgency, police) lxxv–lxxvii, lxxx, 281, 365 (4)
  lawlessness 146, 147, 159
  restoration of law & order 175, 178, 180, 186, 188, 189
  Alliance demands for control (*see also* constitutional conference, Jan–Feb 1956) 356 (4), 366, 370 (19), 389, 390, 394 (9–14)
  British role after independence 413, 422, 437, 461, 464–466
International Bank for Reconstruction and Development (*see* World Bank)
* Ishak bin Haji Mohamed 279 n 3
Ismail, Sultan of Trengganu (*see* Malay rulers)
* Ismail bin Dato Abdul Rahman, Dr Dato lxxii, lxxxiv n 53, 72 n 1
  member for trade, mines & communications (1953) 304

acting president of UMNO (1954) 317 (5)
  Alliance boycott (1954) 321, 322, 330, 332–334
  minister for natural resources (1955) 360
  meetings with Lennox-Boyd 368, 370
  views on talks with Chin Peng 382 (4)
  Alliance delegation to London conference (1956) 392 N
  minister of commerce & industry 415 (8)
Ismail bin Yahya, Tunku 450

Jackson, I C 450
Jackson, R L 199 n 8
Jamaica, economic development 274, 275, 278, 282
Japanese period in Malaya
  conquest li, liii–liv
  British lessons from Japanese conquest 1, 11
  Japanese surrender lvi–lvii, 42 n 2, 54
  Malay rulers' activities during 57
  aftermath 81 (158–170), 94 N
  memories of 177, 247
Jeffries, (Sir) C 2
Jenkin, Sir W 199 n 7, 249 (12)
Jennings, Sir I (*see also* Reid Commission) lxxvii, 401 n 1, 423 n 2, 427, 439
Jerrom, T S 251, 270, 277, 280, 289–291, 300, 307, 309, 312
John, Sir C 464
Johnson, W C 199
Johnston, Sir A 306
* Johnston, J B xlii, 324
  Malayanisation 416, 419, 420
  Reid Commission 438, 442, 443
  Commonwealth membership 444, 446
  constitutional talks (1957) 450
  future of Penang & Malacca 459
  Chiefs of Staff Committee 464
Johore, 1895 constitution 59 n 3, 72 n 1
Jones, A C (*see* Creech Jones, A)
Judicial Committee of the Privy Council lxxvii, 436, 448 (13), 449, 450 (3), 453
jurisdiction, British (*see* Malay rulers)

Kamaralzaman bin Raja Mansur, Raja 57, 99 N
Kang, Y C 295 (2), 297
Keightley, Sir C 250
Kemp, A S H 370
Kenya (*see* Corfield, East Africa)
Keynes, Lord 32, 34, 35, 37
Khoo Teik Eee 176 n 2
Kiddle, H D 149, 251
* Killearn, Lord xlviii, 58 n 3, 71, 95, 118–120
Kilmuir, Lord (Sir D Maxwell Fyfe to 1954) 257, 449, 467

Kirkness, D J   146 n 2
Kirkpatrick, Sir I   324 n 3, 336
Korean war   lxviii, lxxi, 223 (5), 230 N, 232, 239 (2), 311, 376 n 4
Kotelawala, Sir J   376 (6)

Labour Party (Malaya)   361, 362, 454 N
labour policy & industrial relations   lxiv, lxvi, 117, 122, 125, 129, 153, 162, 227 (26–27)
Lai Tek   lxiv, 43 N
Laird, E O   410 N, 423 n 1, 439, 450, 453
Laithwaite, Sir G   xxxix, 24
Lam Swee   162 n 2
Lang, H G   431
Langworthy, H B   57, 129 (12), 153 n 5
Larmour, E N   410 N
Lau Pak Khuan   187, 409 (8), 411, 412
Law, R   4 n 2, 7
lawlessness   lxv–lxvi, 129, 130, 146–150, 153, 162, 163, 168, 170
Lawson, J J   45
Lawson, N   442 n 4, 450
* Lee, Colonel H S   lxxii, lxxxiv n 53, 270 (3), 325 n 3
   British Military Administration   65
   formation of MCA   179, 187
   criticised by Onn   297
   Alliance constitutional 'blue-print' (1953)   297
   member for railways & ports   304
   Alliance boycott (1954)   321, 322, 330, 332–334
   MCP's first peace offer (May–June 1954)   350 (2)
   minister of transport (1955)   360
   meetings with Lennox-Boyd (1955)   368, 370
   amnesty talks   377 (4)
   delegate to London constitutional conference   392 N
   tensions within MCA (1956)   409, 411, 412
   Anglo-Malayan defence talks   410
Lee Kong Chian   131 n 1, 133, 134
Lee Meng   xlvi
Lee Tiang Keng   332 n 7
Legislative Council (see also elections, member system)   lxviii, lxxii–lxxv, 237, 270, 361, 362
Leisching, Sir P   445, 447
* Lennox-Boyd, A   xxxvi, xliv, l, 251
   appointed secretary of state for colonies   335 N
   secretary of state for colonies   338–467 passim
   visits Malaya (1955)   xliii, xlix, lxxv, 356 N, 359, 365–370, 372
Leong Chee Cheong   409 (8)
* Leong Yew Koh   269 (2), 321, 322, 350 n 3, 360, 368, 370, 460
Leung Cheung Ling   176 n 2
Liew Yit Fun   162 n 3

Light, F   193 n 2
Lim Bo Seng   43 N
Lim Cheong Eu   460
Lim Lean Geok   409 (8), 411 (1)
Lim Yew Hock   446 n 1
Lim Yit Fun   162 n 3
Linehan, W   99 N, 102, N, 139
Linggajati agreement (1946)   137 n 1
Lintott, H J B   445, 447
Listowel, Lord   141, 235 N
Lloyd, J Selwyn   348 N, 380, 394 N, 421 N, 457
* Lloyd, (Sir) T   xlii, xliii
   Gent's period in Malaya   101, 108, 132, 141
   Gurney's period   163, 168, 170, 174, 177, 181, 184, 217, 235, 236
   Templer's period   250, 276, 277, 286, 292, 294, 299, 300, 307, 324
   MacGillivray's period   348 N
local government   167, 174, 193, 204, 280
Lockhart, Sir R   xlviii, 248, 249, 256, 264 (6), 269 (2)
Loewen, (Sir) C   363, 376 (4), 422
Longden, G   451, 452
Louw, E H   457, 458
Lugard, Lord   140 (5)
* Lyttelton, O   39 n 3
   secretary of state for colonies   xxxv, xxxviii, xliv, xlvii, l, lxix–lxxiii, 128 n 3, 165 N, 248–334 passim
   visit to Malaya (Dec 1951)   xliii, xlv, xlix, 245 N, 248, 252–257
Lyttelton report (Dec 1951)   257
   itinerary & sources of information   A   I
   text of broadcast in Singapore, 11 Dec   A   II
   federal & state councils etc   A   III
   armoured vehicles for police   A   IV
   arms, clothing & equipment for police   A   V
   earth-shifting equipment   A   VI
   chemical defoliation of roadside jungle   A   VII
   language teaching   A   VIII
   intelligence services etc   A   IX
   British officers, other ranks & Malay Regiment   A   X
   detention & repatriation   A   XI
   manpower & national service   A   XII
   tax evasion   A   XIII
   financial devolution   A   XIV
   extension of service beyond retirement age   A   XV

MacArthur, General D   81 n 2
McDonald, L   184
* MacDonald, M J   xxxiv, xxxv, xlviii, xlix, l
   governor-general   lx–lxiii, 87 n 2, 91–137 passim

commissioner-general (under Labour
government) 141–234 passim
commissioner-general (under Conservative
government) 250–349 passim
MacDonald, T 376 (1), 457
MacDougall, D M 4 n 1, 6
McFadzean, F S 57
* MacGillivray, (Sir) D xxxv, xlvii, xlix, l
deputy high commissioner lxxii, 272–325
passim
high commissioner xliv, lxxiii–lxxxi, 308, 327–
467 passim
Machtig, Sir E 40 n 6
McIntyre, L R 431
McKell, Sir W (see also Reid Commission) lxxvii,
401 n 1, 429, 439
MacKenzie, C 43 N, 47
MacKenzie, H E 280 n 4
McKerron, P A B xxvi, lvii, 16 n 1, 98, 143 n 3
* MacKintosh, A M xxxiv, xlii, 277 n 3, 303 n 3
with Lyttelton in Malaya 254, 255
constitutional development 290, 299, 300
regional policy 324
with Lennox-Boyd in Malaya 367 N, 368, 370
amnesty 371 (1), 378 (6)
defence negotiations 383
constitutional conference (Jan–Feb 1956) 390,
392–394, 398, 399
McLean, Sir K 233
Macleod, W N 295 (6)
* MacMichael, Sir H xlix, lviii–lx, 48, 50, 52 n 7,
55, 58 n 3, 59, 60, 64, 66–68, 109 (1–2), 313,
428 n 1
MacMichael treaties xxxii, lviii–lx, 50, 59, 60, 64,
85, 91 n 2, 93, 96, 97, 136 N, 142
* Macmillan, M H
minister 39 n 3, 257 N, 348 N, 403 n 3, 406,
421 N
prime minister xliv, lxxxi, 455, 457, 458, 462,
463, 465–467
McNeice, T P F 170 A
* Macpherson, Sir J xliii, 152, 165
Mahmud bin Mat, Dato 279 N, 280 n 6
Mahyiddeen, Tengku 57 n 16
Majlis 72 N, 344 (9)
Makins, A C 149
Malacca
'white area' lxxi, 303
British jurisdiction & constitutional
change 404, 425, 430, 438, 451
appointment of Malayan governor lxxvii, 448
(12), 449, 453, 459, 460
Malan, Dr D F lxxix
Malay deputy high commissioner 173 n 1
Malay Mail 344 (9)
Malay Nationalist Party 90, 105, 115 (6), 139, 162
Malay Regiment 159 (3), 223 (12), 229, 234, 238,

239, 252, 257 AX, 263, 266 (9–10), 281
Malay rulers
sovereignty lii, lviii, lix, 13, 91, 142, 329
wartime gifts to Britain 33 n 3
British Military Administration 53
interviews with Willan 57
MacMichael mission (see also MacMichael
treaties) 59, 60, 64, 96
boycott of Gent's installation 82, 83
constitutional negotiations (1946) 86–89, 91
Federation of Malaya 136, 337 (10)
attitude to Gurney 165
relations with Onn 173 n 1, 182, 203, 205
emergency 233, 247
Malayan Civil Service 287
elections 294, 310, 313, 322, 325, 328
relations with Alliance (1954) 330–334
Lennox-Boyd's visit to Malaya 359, 367–369
withdrawal of British advisers 388, 435
Reid commission 401, 428–430, 438, 448
independence constitution 449, 453, 456
Yang di-Pertuan Agong 449, 453, 455, 459
Malayan Association 149
Malayan Chamber of Mines 251
Malayan Chinese Association (see also
Alliance) lxxii, 272, 297
formation (1949) lxvii, 171, 176, 179, 195 (1)
emergency 188, 245, 252 A II
member system 304
citizenship 409, 411, 412
post-independence outlook for 454
Malayan Civil Service (see also public service)
Chinese-speaking officers 204, 257 A VIII
terms of employment 257 (76–83) & A X
reform of 287
Malayan Communist Party lvii, lxi, 245, 341, 342
post-war aims 51
labour unrest 117
outbreak of emergency & proscription lxiii–
lxvii, 153, 158, 159, 160, 162
Present day situation and duties (1949) lxvi,
160 n 2, 215
directive (1951) lxx, 342 (8)
'entryism' lxxi, lxxiv, lxxvi, 284, 301, 311, 342
peace offer (May–June 1955) lxxiv, 350–353
amnesty talks (Baling) lxxv–lxxvii, lxxx, 371,
373–382, 385, 386, 391
military retreat 341, 422
support 342
schools 345
recognition of 391
post-independence outlook for 454
Malayan Indian Congress (see also Alliance) lxxi,
115 (6), 139, 298, 454
Malayan Party 451, 452
Malayan Peoples' Anti-British Army (see also
Malayan Races' Liberation Army) 148 N

Malayan Peoples' Anti-Japanese Army   lv, lvii, 43 N, 46, 47, 94 N, 350 (12)

Malayan Peoples' Anti-Japanese Army Ex-Servicemen's Association   160 n 1

Malayan Planning Unit   liv, 16 N

Malayan Races' Liberation Army   215, 216, 245, 350, 352

Malayan Security Service (see also intelligence)   162

Malayan students in Britain   309

Malayan Union (see also MacMichael treaties)
wartime planning   liv–lv, 1–42 passim
Cabinet discussions & approval   lv, 20–22, 24, 25, 31, 36, 48, 50, 56 N, 69, 76
publicity for   23, 29–31, 36, 47, 51, 52, 56
implementation   lix–lx, 43–81 passim
citizenship   lv, lix, lxiii, 66 (7), 74, 75, 77, 80, 100–107, 123 (30–34), 128
reactions to   li, lix–lx, 66, 72–76, 79, 82–85, 88, 90
concessions to Malay opposition   lx–lxi, 80, 86, 87, 89, 91–93, 96, 97, 99, 101

Malcolm, A R   149

Malik, B (see also Reid Commission)   lxxvii, 401 n 1, 427, 429, 439

Malik Feroze Khan Noon   457

Mallaby, Brigadier A W S   57 n 1

Manchester Guardian   241 (5), 309 (5)

Manila Treaty (1954) (see also SEATO)   lxxxiv n 58, 335 N, 340, 343

Mann, C   149

Mansergh, E C   57 n 1

Mao Zedong   195 n 1

Marchwood, Lord   xlvii, lviii, 80 N

Markham, Sir H   40 n 6

Marshall, D   358 n 3
amnesty talks (Baling)   lxxvi, 371, 372 n 2, 374–376, 379, 381, 386, 391

Marshall, P H R   450, 454 N

* Martin, (Sir) J   xxxv, xlii, xliii
constitutional developments in Templer's period   323, 327–332
and commissioner-general   324, 335
education policy   347
amnesty talks (Baling)   385
constitutional conference (Jan–Feb 1956)   lxxvi, 392 N, 399
independence arrangements   413, 428, 450, 459

Maude, Sir J   85 n 5, 91 (3)

Maxwell, Sir A   199 n 8, 203

Maxwell, Sir G   lviii, 73 n 1, 289, n 2

Maxwell Fyfe, Sir D (Lord Kilmuir from 1954) (see Lord Kilmuir)

Mead, J D   269 (3)

Meiklereid, E W   118 (46)

Melville, E   xlii, 422, 431, 441 n 1, 450, 459

member system   xlvii, lxviii, lxxi, lxxii
Gurney's period   205, 212, 217, 218 (19–26), 227 (14), 235, 237
Templer's period   294, 304

Menon, V K K   457

Menzies, Sir R   457, 458

Meredith Jenkins, Sir E   149

Merthyr, Lord   318 (4)

MI5   272 n 2

Miller, H   xxxvi, 149 n 3, 385 n 2

Milverton, Lord   151, 154, 156, 157, 165

Min Yuen   216, 227 (10), 238, 239, 245

Mitchell, Sir P   183 n 6

Mohamed Khir Johari   427, 429

Mohamed Noh bin Omar, Haji   279 (22)

Mohamed Salleh bin Abdul Karim, Kiyai   94

Mohamed Sheriff, Haji   57, 64, 99 N

Mohamed Sopiee bin Sheikh Ibrahim   279 (25)

Mohammed Hatta   205 n 5

Mokhtaruddin Lasso   90 n 3

Molotov, V M   324 N

Monckton, Sir W   394 N, 408, 421 N

* Monson, W B L   12, 18, 24 n 1

Monteath, Sir D   40 n 6

Montgomery, Lord   lxx, 161, 257 N, 258, 260

Moran, Lord   262 N

Moreton, J O   463 n 3

Morgan, W S   79

Morris, O H   122, 141, 149, 168 N, 171 N, 199

Morrison, H   58 n 3, 233

Mosley, Sir O   146 n 3

* Mountbatten, Lord (see also South East Asia Command)   xxiv, xlviii, l, lv, 41, 42, 58
Malayan Union planning   23, 26–30
British Military Administration   44, 45, 53, 67, 71
possible regional supremo (1950)   230

Mudie report   393 n 4

multi-racialism (see also communalism, Communities Liaison Committee)   lxix, lxx, lxxi, lxxv, lxxvi, lxxx

Munster, Lord   332 (11)

Murdock, A M   410

Murphy, C H W   410

Murray, J Dalton   243

Musa-Eddin, Tengku   53 N, 57, 96 n 1

* Mustapha Albakri, Haji   410, 417 (15), 450

Nanda, G   376 (9)

Nanyang Siang Pao   65 n 2, 411 (5)

Narayanan, P P   295 (4)

Nathan, Lord   95 n 1

National Association of Perak   361

National Conference   lxxi, lxxii, 295, 298

National Congress   295 N, 297, 298

National Convention   lxxii, 298 n 6

national movements   139, 140, 196, 227
national service (Malayan)   257 A XI
nationality (*see also* citizenship, Reid
   Commission)   lxxvii, lxxviii, 203, 356 (4), 409,
   411, 412
NATO   408, 410, 417 (17)
Nehru, J   336 (9), 342 (6), 454 (20), 457
New Democratic Youth League   160 n 1
New Statesman   lxxi, 280
New Zealand (*see also* ANZAM, defence agreement,
   SEATO)   339, 340, 376, 380, 394 N, 398, 413,
   437, 462
* Newboult, (Sir) A
   British Military Administration   xlvii, 59, 64,
      66, 68, 73, 74
   Malayan Union   98, 99 N, 105 E
   Federation of Malaya   143, 154, 155, 157, 163–
      165, 203
Newsam, R W   389 n 3, 450
Newton, R   274
Ng Ek Teong   427, 429
Nicoll, (Sir) J   276, 292, 300
Nigeria & public services   416, 419, 420
* Nik Ahmed Kamil bin Nik Mahmood, Dato   57,
   99 N, 279 N, 295, 304 (5), 392 N
Nkrumah, Dr K   189 N, 455, 457
Noel-Baker, P   40 n 2, 161
North Borneo (*see also* Borneo, closer
   association)   12, 14, 17, 18, 20, 25, 48
Nye, Sir A   151, 154, 243

Observer   241 (3)
O'Connor, K K   55 n 3, 99 N, 129 (12), 136
Ogmore, Lord (*see* D R Rees-Williams)
Oliver, Sir W   464
Ong Chong Keng, Dr   168, 191 (4)
* Ong Yoke Lin   360, 368, 370, 382 (4), 450
* Onn bin Jaafar, Dato (Sir)   xxxvii, xliii, xlviii,
   lix, lxii, lxxii, lxxix, 193, 218, 267 (2), 270 (2 &
   3), 274, 276, 279, 325 n 3
   opposition to Malayan Union   72 N, 83, 85, 96,
      97, 99 N, 114
   leadership of UMNO   90, 113, 174, 195 (2), 203,
      240, 241
   communalism   94 N
   relations with Gent   114, 135, 144, 164
   visits London (1948 & 1952)   lxvii, 144, 173,
      174, 277
   temperament   164, 173, 182
   Communities Liaison Committee   171, 195 (4)
   relations with Malay rulers   135 n 1, 173 n 1,
      182, 203, 205
   criticisms of Federation of Malaya   173, 182
   member system   205, 212, 237, 294, 304
   IMP   lxix, lxxi, 240, 241, 244
   resigns from UMNO   244

pace of constitutional advance   277 (1)
National Conference & National
   Convention   295, 297
   Party Negara   lxxi, lxxiii, lxxiv–lxxv, 298 n 5
   elections   299, 325 n 3, 330 (6 & 13), 333
   criticises H S Lee   297
   Reid Commission   439 (4), 446 (3 & 5)
Oon Beng Hong   272, 360 (3)
Ormerod, R C   431
Ormsby-Gore, W D   449
Ormsby-Gore, W G A (visit to Malaya, 1928)   xliii,
   13 n 5
Osman bin Talib   460

Pakenham, Lord   95 n 1
Palestine   lxxx–lxxxi, 152, 153 n 5, 154 (4), 159
   (3), 165, 189 (12), 235
Palmer, (Sir) S   149, 182 n 4, 251
Pan-Malayan Council of Joint Action   lxii, 111,
   113 N, 139, 162, 187
Pan-Malayan Federation of Chinese
   Associations   451, 452
Pan-Malayan Federation of Trades Unions (*see*
   labour policy)
Pan-Malayan Islamic Party   lxxv, 361, 362, 454
   (10)
Pan-Malayan Labour Party   279 n 10, 295 (4)
Pan-Malayan Malay Congress   lviii, lix, 72, 78, 82
   N, 84, 85
Parker, Sir H   lxxviii, 407, 408, 410, 414, 417
parliamentary debates, questions & statements on
   Malaya   xxxviii, xlvi–xlvii, 293
   Malayan Union   xlvii, lviii, 55 n 6, 59 n 1, 64 N,
      70, 75 n 2, 80, 109 n 5, 110 n 3
   outbreak of emergency   lxv, 147 n 1, 160 n 3
   Attlee's statements (1949 & 1950)   xxxviii, xlvi,
      xlviii, 185, 218 (8), 227 n 2, 268 N
   Griffiths & Strachey (July 1950)   221 n 3, 225
      (5)
   Griffiths on elections (Nov & Dec 1950)   270 n
      4, 302
   Lyttelton   254, 277, 328 n 1, 332 (11)
   Templer's methods   lxxi
   independence legislation   453 n 1, 456 N
parliamentary papers on Malaya   xxxviii, lviii, lxii,
   13 n 5, 16 n 2, 69, 75 n 3, 92 n 4, 121 N, 128 n 4,
   405 n 2
Party Negara   lxxi, lxxiv–lxxv, 298 n 5, 322 (11),
   325 (1), 328 (2), 332, 333
   federal elections (1955)   361, 362
Party Ra'ayat   454 N & (10)
* Paskin, (Sir) J   xlii, xlix
   Malayan Union   48 N, 63, 85
   correspondence with Gurney   173, 179, 187,
      190, 192, 203, 205
   emergency (1951)   233, 251, 254 N

constitutional developments (1951–1953) 243,
267, 272, 283, 286, 288, 290, 292, 296, 299,
300, 307
Paton, E W 149
Pearkes, G R 457
Pearson, L 376 (1)
Peck, A D 398
Penang lii
secession movement 172, 182, 183, 235 n 2,
237
municipal elections lxxi
British jurisdiction 193, 404, 425, 430, 438,
451
appointment of Malayan governor lxxvii, 448
(12), 449, 453, 459, 460
Percival, General A liii
Perham, M 1 (14–17)
Perth, Lord 450, 452, 453 n 1, 467 N
PETA 160 n 1, 162
Pethick-Lawrence, Lord 58 n 3
Pickering, W A (see also Chinese
protectorate) 140 (4)
Plowden, Sir E N 201 N
police lxi, lxvi, lxvii
outbreak of emergency 149, 153 (15), 158, 159
(3 & 4)
counter-insurgency (1949–1951) 175, 188,
189, 199, 216, 219, 221, 222, 223 (12), 233,
238, 239, 242, 247
police mission (1949–1950) 199 n 8, 203
reorganisation (1952) 252, 257 A IV & V, 266 (8)
conduct of emergency (1955) 341
Malayan control of 389, 390, 394 (9–14), 395,
400, 405 A (II)
population 153 (2), 249 n 5, 257 (7)
Portal, Lord 259
Potsdam Conference (1945) lvi, 29 n 3
Powell, Lt-Commander C 149, 251
Powell, Sir R 383, 398, 402, 414
* Poynton, Sir H 194, 214, 218, 251, 364
Privy Council (see Judicial Committee of Privy
Council)
Proctor, W T 318 n 1, 328, 332 (11)
Profumo, J D 450, 462, 465
public service
Malayanisation lxxi, lxxiv, 287, 344, 362, 365
(6), 370 (25), 389, 390, 394 (17–20), 418–420
Malayanisation committee 354, 416
public service commission lxxvii, 416
* Purcell, V W W S xxxvi, lxxi, 65, 195 (3), 272,
279 (21), 309
PUTERA (see also Pan-Malayan Council of Joint
Action) 113 N, 162
Pyke, C J 49 n 2, 105

Raja Uda (see Uda bin Raja Muhammad, Raja)

Rajagopal, M P 344 (1)
Ramanathan, K 427, 429
Ramli bin Haji Tahir 279 (24)
Ramsden, C O I 465, 466
Reading, Lord 253, 284 N, 338 n 1, 376, 380,
421 N, 440
*Rees-Williams, D R (Lord Ogmore from 1950)
xliii, lxvi, lxxiii
visit to Malaya (1946) 90 n 2
parliamentary under-secretary 145, 149, 174,
183, 192 N, 193, 195, 204 n 1
supports Alliance on federal elections
(1954) 315, 316, 318 N, 320, 328, 332 (11),
333 n 2
regional policy
co-ordination of British interests (see also closer
association) xlv, xlviii, lxix, lxxx, 39, 41, 42,
58, 71, 95, 118–120, 230, 232, 243, 258, 260,
266, 324, 335, 338, 346, 348
defence (see also defence, ANZAM,
SEATO) lxxiv, lxxviii, 284, 311, 339, 340,
348, 421
economic policy 201, 421, 440
general policy 196, 198, 336
rehabilitation (1945) 61
* Reid, Lord lii, lxxvii, 401 n 1, 404, 423, 424,
427–430, 438, 439, 443, 448, 453
Reid Commission lxxv, lxxvii–lxxviii, lxxx
Alliance demand constitutional
commission 322 (7), 325, 329, 356, 365 (2),
368, 369, 370 (6), 384 (7–9), 389, 390
London constitutional conference (1956) 392,
394, 395, 400
appointment & terms of references 401, 404
proceedings 423, 424, 426–430, 436, 438, 439
report 442, 443, 446, 448, 449, 453
Anglo-Malayan working party (1957) 446, 448
(11)
London constitutional conference (1957) 449,
450
Rendel, Sir G 298 n 7
Rendel Commission 313
Renville agreement (1948) 137 n 1
Reuter 254
rice (see also economic and financial policies,
Killearn) 145, 208
Ritchie, Sir N 159 n 6
*Roberts-Wray, (Sir) K 91 n 5, 142 N, 283, 397,
450, 456
Robertson, Sir B 259 N
Rogers, P 85 n 6
Rolleston, W L 11
Ross, J M 450
Rothery, G W 190 n 3
Rowan, T L 93
Rowe, H P 450
rubber (see also business interests, economic and

financial policies) lxxiv, 208, 223 (5), 225, 251, 305, 306
Rubber Growers' Association 63, 149, 251
Rubber Trade Association of London 149, 251
Rural & Industrial Development Authority (*see also* economic & financial policies) 212 (17), 219 (16), 240, 273, 289 (3)
Rushford, A R 397 n 1
Russell, H S 149

Sabben-Clare, E E 138 n 3
Sabine, N J B 1
*Salisbury, Lord (Lord Cranborne to 1947) xl, liv, 3, 4 N, 6, 7, 9, 10, 70, 257 N, 266, 380, 421 N
*Sambanthan, V T 360, 368, 370, 427, 429, 450
Sanders, Sir A 233
Sanders, E xlvi
Sanders, J 304 (2)
Sandys, D 462 n 4
Sarawak (*see also* Borneo) 12, 14, 17, 18, 21, 25, 48
*Sardon bin Haji Jubir lxxiii, 113 (6), 279, 317 (4), 325 (2), 360, 368, 370, 415 (8)
Sargent, Sir O 40–42, 58 n 3, 120
Savory, R C 149
Scarborough Report 172 n 1
*Scott, (Sir) R xxxv, xliv, xlv, xlviii, lxxiv, lxxviii
  with Lord Killearn 118 n 1
  Foreign Office 232, 233, 243, 249, 301 N
  commissioner-general 348 N, 363, 371 (1), 374–376, 407, 410, 414, 432, 462 n 4
Scott-Moncrieff, Sir A 363
SEATO (South-East Asia Treaty Organisation) (*see also* regional policy) lxxiv, lxxviii, lxxxiv n 58, 335 N, 338 n 2, 339, 340, 342 (5 & 11), 343, 348, 375 (4), 400, 410, 417 n 4, 431, 432, 441, 454 N & (19), 462
Seel, G F xlii, 120, 141, 146, 149
Selwyn, P 396 n 2
Senu bin Abdul Rahman 113 (6 & 7), 427, 429
Shamsuddin bin Nain 450
Shanahan, F 348 n 2, 408 (4), 410
Shawcross, Sir H 142
Shearn, E D 149, 251
Shelley, G 295 (2)
Sheriff, Haji Mohamed (*see* Mohamed Sheriff, Haji)
Shields, J 57
Shinwell, E xliv, xlv, lxviii, 185, 206, 209, 210, 222, 226, 232, 233, 238
Silcock, Professor T H 195 (3)
Simonds, Lord 401 n 1
Singapore (*see also* closer association, Malayan Union, regional policy)
  fall (1942) li, 1, 11
  constitution (1948) 112, 131 (9)
  Lennox-Boyd's visit (1955) 372

security 363, 375, 383, 446 n 2
Singapore Standard 309 (5), 330 (12), 332 (12), 382 (10), 411, 414 (5)
Sjharir, S 137 n 2
Slessor, Sir J 232
Slim, Sir W lv, 23 N, 53 n 1, 199, 204, 232, 253, 258, 259 N & n 2
Smith, T E 272 n 4, 361 (15)
Smith, Trafford xxxix
Smithers, P 451 n 2
Snelling, A W 458, 464
social policy (*see also* education policy) 208, 221, 223, 227 (20)
Somervell, Sir D 24
Somerville, D A 57, 435 (7)
Sorensen, R W 318 n 1
Soskice, Sir F 142
South Africa, Commonwealth membership lxxix, 444, 445, 447, 457, 458
South East Asia Command (SEAC) (*see also* Mountbatten) lv–lvii, 31 N, 39–47, 58, 81, 95
special commissioner (*see* Lord Killearn, regional policy)
Spectator 189 (6)
Speed, Sir E 70
*Spencer, O A 273–275, 278, 282, 370, 396
Spens, I 251
squatters (*see also* emergency, Briggs plan) lxvii, 169, 190, 195 (1), 204, 212 (17), 216, 233, 234
Stalin, J 213 (7), 258 (4)
*Stanley, O xxxviii, lxv, 20–22, 24, 26–30, 36
Staples, D J 246
Steel, H 450, 456 n 3
Stent, P J H 139 N
sterling area (*see* economic & financial policies)
Sterndale Bennett, (Sir) J (*see* Bennett, (Sir) J C Sterndale)
Stewart, D 149
Stockwell, Sir H 308 n 3
*Strachey, E J St L xlv, lxviii–lxix, 215, 220–222, 226, 230
Straits Times xxxvi, lxxiii, 1, 149 n 8, 322 (2), 330 (4), 334 N, 344 (9), 359 (3), 411
Strang, Sir W 243 n 2
Street, Sir A 40 n 6
Strijdom, J G lxxix, 444, 445, 447, 458
Suez crisis (1956) lxxviii, 421 N, 431 N, 432 n 2, 433, 434, 467 N
Suhrawardy, H S 457
*Suleiman bin Dato Abdul Rahman, Dato 72 n 1, 360, 368, 370, 415 (8)
Sullivan, W J 149
Sully, L T G 410 N
Sungei Siput killings lxiii–lxv, lxx, 148 N, 149 n 3, 169 (3)
Surridge, B J 278 n 4
Sweet-Escott, B A C 43, 46

Swettenham, Sir F   lviii, 63 n 2, 73 n 1
Swinton, Lord   257 N
Syed Putra, Raja of Perlis (see also Malay
    rulers)   57

Tan, C C   240, 267 n 2, 276 (6)
*Tan Cheng Lock (Dato Sir Cheng-lock
    Tan)   131, 330 (13), 331 N
    Pan-Malayan Council of Joint Action   113 N
    protests against Gent's recall   155, 157 (4)
    Malayan Chinese Association   176 n 2, 179, 187
    Communities Liaison Committee   195 (4)
    counter-insurgency   203, 247
    citizenship & nationality   205
    Independence of Malaya Party   lxix, 240
    Alliance   lxxi, 295 (7), 296
    federal elections   313–317, 318 N
    Baling talks   lxxvi, 371 N, 391
    Malayan governors of Penang & Malacca   459,
        460
Tan Chin Tuan   267
Tan Kah Kee   195 n 3
*Tan Siew Sin   178, 297, 350 n 3, 409 (3), 411,
    460
*Tan Tong Hye (T H Tan)   309 n 7, 317, 318, 392
    N
Tanjong Malim   lxxi, 285
taxation in Malaya   223, 257 A XIII, 263 (3), 266
    (11), 393 (4)
Tedder, Lord   161, 243 n 3
*Templer, Sir G   xxxv, xxxix, xlvii, xlviii, xlix, l,
    341, 356 n 2
    appointment   xliii, xliv, xlv, lxix–lxx, 259–264
    directive   xliv, 268
    high commissioner   lxix–lxxiii, 269–325
        passim
    departure   325 n 3
Templer, Lady   325 n 3
Thailand   lvi, 301 N
    Thai border   159 n 5, 180, 230 N, 231, 249 (3),
        311 (6), 324 N, 386 n 6
Thio Chan Bee   143 n 2
Thivy, J   111 n 2, 115 (6), 178
Thomas, A R   418
Thomas, C J   370, 393 (1)
Thomas, I B   115
Thompson, R C K   159 n 4
Thondar Padai   129, 162
Thorneycroft, P   403 n 3
*Thuraisingham, Dato E E C   270 (2), 277, 295,
    297
The Times (London)   1, 195 (3), 254, 309 (5), 330
    (12)
tin (see also economic & financial policies,
    business interests)   xliii, lxxiv, 194, 208, 223
    (5), 225, 251

Too Joon Hing   360 (5), 385 n 6, 391 N
Tory, G W   454 N, 462 n 4, 467 N
trade unions (see also labour policy)   117, 122,
    125
Trevelyan, H   336 (10)
Treble, G D   269 (3)
Truman, President   230 N, 259 n 2
Tunku Abdul Rahman (see Abdul Rahman Putra
    Al-Haj, Tunku)
Turnbull, Sir R   324 n 6
Twining, Sir E   267 n 4
Twistleton-Wykeham-Fiennes, J S W   456 n 5

U Nu   336 (9), 342 (6), 454 (20)
*Uda bin Raja Muhammad, Raja   57, 269 (2), 279
    N, 359 (4), 459, 460
United Malays National Organisation (UMNO) (see
    also Alliance)   lix, lx, lxii
    inauguration   85 n 3, 89 (2), 90
    Dato Onn's leadership   90, 113, 174, 195 (2),
        203, 240, 241, 244
    general assemblies   113, 203 n 3, 244, 271,
        279, 304 (1), 330 (6)
    membership   190 n 5, 240, 244 N
    Tunku Abdul Rahman's leadership   244, 271,
        279, 296, 297
    Alliance   lxxi, 295
    member system   304
    federal elections committee   310
    federal elections results   lxxv, 360–362
    citizenship   409, 411, 412
    Reid report   446
    post-independence outlook for   454
United Planters Association   129, 149, 350
United States of America
    anti-imperialism   4–9
    economic aid for SE Asia   106, 211, 216
    policy in SE Asia   249 (3), 336
University of Malaya   170 n 4
Urquhart, Major-General R W   220 (1)
Utusan Melayu   237 n 2, 330 (11), 332 (12),
    350 n 3

Van Lare, W B   330 n 4
Van Mook, Dr H J   3
Vietminh   lxxiii, 339
Vile, R J   278

Waight, L   38 n 3
Walker, A   148 N
Wallace, H A   8 (2)
Wan Idris, Dato   392 N
Wan (Wong) Shee Fun   330 (3)
Ward, J M D   463

Warta Masharakat 344 (9)
Warta Negara 344 (9)
*Watherston, (Sir) D xlvii
  Anglo-Malay working committee (1946) 99 N
  re-organisation of government (1952) 261 (7)
  MCP's first peace offer (1955) 350
  Lennox-Boyd's visit to Malaya (1955) 368, 370
  constitutional talks (Jan–Feb 1956) 384
  reports tension over citizenship &
    nationality 409, 411, 412
  Malayanisation 416, 418–420
  Reid Commission 428, 439, 446
Watson, G M 396 n 4
Watson, N D 183
Watt, Sir A 348 n 1, 408 (4)
Watt, I B 307 n 1, 444
Way, R G K 464
Webb, Sir C 431
Webb, G W 170 A
Welensky, Sir R 458 n 5
Welles, Sumner 8
Wheare, Professor K C 283 n 1
'white areas' lii, lxxi, 303, 341 (2)
*Willan, (Sir) H lvii, lviii, 16 N, 43 N, 57, 68 n 3
Williams, A 99 N
Williams, J B 145, 146, 149, 163 N
Wilson, Sir S 16 n 2
Wilson Smith, Sir H 49
Wiltshire, A E 260 n 6
Wiltshire, E H T 24 n 1
Winnifrith, A J D 33, 37, 38

Winstedt, Sir R 64 N, 73 n 1
Wisdom, G E C 296
World Bank 37 n 3, 274, 275, 282, 396 (8)
Wright, M 118 n 3
Wu Tek-yao, Dr (*see* Fenn-Wu Report)
Wurtzburg, C E 149
Wyatt, W 254 n 1
Wylie, I C 385 n 6

Yaacob, Tunku 64, 304 (7)
Yang di-Pertuan Agong (*see also* Malay rulers, Reid
  Commission report) 449, 453, 455, 459
Yong Pung How 427, 429
Yong Shook Lin 176 n 2, 179, 295 (2), 297
Yong, S M 360 (3)
Young, Colonel A lxx, lxxxiii n 50
Young, A S 33 n 2
Younger, K 210, 213, 232
Yusoff bin Ishak 237 n 2
Yussuf, Sultan of Perak (*see* Malay rulers)
Yusuf, C M 279 (23)

Zain binti Suleiman, Hajah 279 (19)
Zainal Abidin bin Ahmad (Za'ba) 72 N
Zainal Abidin bin Haji Abas 203
Zhdanov doctrine lxiii
'Zipper' operation lv, lvii, 51
Zulkifli Ownie 90 n 3
Zulueta, P de 463

Malaya

The British Documents on
the End of Empire Project
gratefully acknowledges
the generous assistance of
the Leverhulme Trust.